THE QUEST FOR CONTEXT
AND MEANING

BIBLICAL
INTERPRETATION
SERIES

VOLUME 28

THE QUEST FOR CONTEXT AND MEANING

Studies in Biblical Intertextuality
in Honor of James A. Sanders

EDITED BY

CRAIG A. EVANS

AND

SHEMARYAHU TALMON

BRILL
LEIDEN · NEW YORK · KÖLN
1997

This book is printed on acid-free paper.

ISSN   0928-0731
ISBN   90 04 10835 1

CONTENTS

PART THREE
TEXT AND CANON

PART FOUR
THE FIRST TESTAMENT IN THE SECOND

PREFACE

The present volume, written, assembled, and edited in honor of James A. Sanders, appropriately appears in the year commemorating the fiftieth anniversary of the discovery of the first of the caves containing the celebrated "Dead Sea Scrolls." This year Professor Sanders, a pioneer of Scrolls research, celebrates his seventieth birthday. The contributors to this volume are among his many pupils, colleagues, and friends. We all salute him and wish him well.

The volume is organized around topics that have been of special interest to Professor Sanders. These include the text, canon, and intertextuality of the Bible, the Dead Sea Scrolls, and early Jewish and Rabbinic interpretation. A thread that runs throughout Professor Sanders' long, productive career has been his interest in the way sacred tradition, oral and written, is called upon and interpreted in the light of new situations in the life of believing communities. This thread runs throughout the essays contained in this volume.

The editors are grateful to Professor Rolf Rendtorff, Professor R. Alan Culpepper, and Dr. David E. Orton for accepting this collection of studies for publication in Brill's Biblical Interpretation Series. The editors also wish to thank Mrs. Sharon Sawatzky for her assistance in the preparation of the final draft of the manuscript, Mrs. Ginny Evans for preparing the indexes, and Mr. Ted Goshulak, reference librarian for the Marion Alloway Library of Trinity Western University, for his assistance in locating hard to find bibliographical data.

Craig A. Evans   July, 1997
Trinity Western University
Langley, British Columbia

Shemaryahu Talmon
Hebrew University
Jerusalem

ABBREVIATIONS

AB	Anchor Bible (Commentary)
ABD	D. N. Freedman (ed.), *Anchor Bible Dictionary*
ABRL	Anchor Bible Reference Library
AfO	*Archiv für Orientforschung*
AGJU	Arbeiten zur Geschichte des antiken Judentums und des Urchristentums
AnBib	Analecta biblica
ANQ	*Andover Newton Quarterly*
ANRW	W. Haase and E. Temporini (eds.), *Aufstieg und Niedergang der römischen Welt*
ArBib	The Aramaic Bible
ASTI	*Annual of the Swedish Theological Institute*
ATD	Das Alte Testament Deutsch
BA	*Biblical Archaeologist*
BAG	W. Bauer, W. F. Arndt, and F. W. Gingrich, *A Greek-English Lexicon of the New Testament* (1957)
BARev	*Biblical Archaeology Review*
BASOR	*Bulletin of the American Schools of Oriental Research*
BDB	F. Brown, S. R. Driver, and C. A. Briggs, *Hebrew and English Lexicon of the Old Testament*
BETL	Bibliotheca ephemeridum theologicarum lovaniensium
Bib	*Biblica*
BO	*Bibliotheca orientalis*
BibRev	*Bible Review*
BibSem	The Biblical Seminar
BIOSCS	*Bulletin of the International Organization for Septuagint and Cognate Studies*
BJS	Brown Judaic Studies
BTB	*Biblical Theology Bulletin*
BZAW	Beihefte zur *Zeitschrift für die alttestamentliche Wissenschaft*
BZNW	Beihefte zur *Zeitschrift für die neutestamentliche Wissenschaft*
CBQ	*Catholic Biblical Quarterly*
CBQMS	Catholical Biblical Quarterly Monograph Series
ConBNT	Coniectanea biblica, New Testament
CRINT	Compendia rerum iudaicarum ad novum testamentum
CSCO	Corpus scriptorum christianorum orientalium
DJD	Discoveries in the Judaean Desert
DSD	*Dead Sea Discoveries*
Ébib	Études bibliques
EncJud	C. Roth and G. Wigoder (eds.), *Encyclopaedia Judaica*
EvQ	*Evangelical Quarterly*
ExpTim	*Expository Times*

FB	Forschung zur Bibel
FOTL	Forms of Old Testament Literature
GCS	Griechischen christlichen Schriftsteller
GNB	Good News Bible
GNS	Good News Studies
HAR	*Hebrew Annual Review*
HAT	Handbuch zum Alten Testament
HBT	*Horizons in Biblical Theology*
HDR	Harvard Dissertations in Religion
HNTC	Harper New Testament Commentary
HSM	Harvard Semitic Monographs
HSS	Harvard Semitic Studies
HTKNT	Herders theologischer Kommentar zum Neuen Testament
HTR	*Harvard Theological Review*
HTS	Harvard Theological Studies
HUCA	*Hebrew Union College Annual*
ICC	International Critical Commentary
IDB	G. A Buttrick (ed.), *The Interpreter's Dictionary of the Bible* (1962)
IEJ	*Israel Exploration Journal*
Int	*Interpretation*
IOS	*Israel Oriental Society*
JANESCU	*Journal of the Ancient Near Eastern Society of Columbia University*
JAOS	*Journal of the American Oriental Society*
JBL	*Journal of Biblical Literature*
JBR	*Journal of Bible and Religion*
JJS	*Journal of Jewish Studies*
JNES	*Journal of Near Eastern Studies*
JPS	Jewish Publication Society (translation of the Bible)
JQR	*Jewish Quarterly Review*
JR	*Journal of Religion*
JSJ	*Journal for the Study of Judaism in the Persian, Hellenistic and Roman Period*
JSNT	*Journal for the Study of the New Testament*
JSNTSup	*Journal for the Study of the New Testament*, Supplement Series
JSOT	*Journal for the Study of the Old Testament*
JSOTSup	*Journal for the Study of the Old Testament*, Supplement Series
JSP	*Journal for the Study of the Pseudepigrapha*
JSPSup	*Journal for the Study of the Pseudepigrapha*, Supplement Series
JSS	*Journal of Semitic Studies*
KAI	H. Donner and W. Rollig, *Kanaanäische und aramäische Inschriften*
LCL	Loeb Classical Library
LD	Lectio divina
Leš	*Lešonénu*
McCQ	*McCormick Quarterly*
NAWG	Nachrichten von der kön. Gesellschaft der Wissenschaft zu Göttingen, Phil.-Hist. Klasse
NEB	New English Bible

Neot	*Neotestamentica*
NIGTC	New International Greek Testament Commentary
NITC	New International Theological Commentary
NIV	New International Version
NJB	New Jerusalem Bible
NovT	*Novum Testamentum*
NovTSup	*Novum Tetamentum*, Supplements
NRSV	New Revised Standard Version
NTC	The New Testament in Context
NTS	*New Testament Studies*
NTTS	New Testament Tools and Studies
OBO	Orbis biblicus et orientalis
Or	*Orientalia*
OTL	Old Testament Library
OTS	*Oudtestamentische Studiën* (journal)
OTS	Oudtestamentische Studiën (monograph series)
PAM	Palestine Archaeological Museum (in reference to the accession numbers of the photographs of the Dead Sea Scrolls)
PCB	M. Black and H. H. Rowley (eds.), *Peake's Commentary on the Bible*
RB	*Revue biblique*
REB	Revised English Bible
RestQ	*Restoration Quarterly*
RevQ	*Revue de Qumran*
RGG	*Religion in Geschichte und Gegenwart*
RivBSup	*Rivista biblica*, Supplements
RelSRev	*Religious Studies Review*
RSV	Revised Standard Version
SBLABS	Society of Biblical Literature Archaeology and Biblical Studies
SBLDS	Society of Biblical Literature Dissertation Series
SBLEJL	Society of Biblical Literature Early Judaism and Its Literature
SBLMS	Society of Biblical Literature Monograph Series
SBLRBS	Society of Biblical Literature Resources for Biblical Study
SBLSBS	Society of Biblical Literature Sources for Biblical Study
SBLSCS	Society of Biblical Literature Septuagint and Cognate Studies
SBLSP	Society of Biblical Literature Seminar Papers
SBLTT	Society of Biblical Literature Texts and Translations
SBS	Stuttgarter Bibelstudien
SBT	Studies in Biblical Theology
SC	Sources chrétiennes
SJLA	Studies in Judaism in Late Antiquity
SJT	*Scottish Journal of Theology*
SNTSMS	Society for New Testament Studies Monograph Series
SNTU	Studien zum Neuen Testament und seiner Umwelt
SOTSMS	Society for Old Testament Study Monograph Series
SPB	Studia postbiblica
SSEJC	Studies in Scripture in Early Judaism and Christianity
SSN	Studia semitica neerlandica

ST	*Studia theologica*
STDJ	Studies on the Texts of the Desert of Judah
StOr	Studia orientalia
TBei	*Theologische Beiträge*
TDNT	G. Kittel and G. Friedrich (eds.), *Theological Dictionary of the New Testament*
TJT	*Toronto Journal of Theology*
TS	*Theological Studies*
TSAJ	Texte und Studien zum antiken Judentum
TSJTSA	Theological Studies of the Jewish Theological Seminary of America
TTS	Trierer theologische Studien
TU	Texte und Untersuchungen
TWAT	G. J. Botterweck, H. Ringgren, and H.-J. Fabry (eds.), *Theologisches Wörterbuch zum Alten Testament*
TWNT	G. Kittel and G. Friedrich (eds.), *Theologisches Wörterbuch zum Neuen Testament*
TZ	*Theologische Zeitschrift*
UBS	United Bible Society
USQR	*Union Seminary Quarterly Review*
VT	*Vetus Testamentum*
VTSup	*Vetus Testamentum*, Supplements
WBC	Word Biblical Commentary
WMANT	Wissenschaftliche Monographien zum Alten und Neuen Testament
WUNT	Wissenschaftliche Untersuchungen zum Neuen Testament
YJS	Yale Judaica Series
ZAW	*Zeitschrift für die alttestamentliche Wissenschaft*
ZDMG	*Zeitschrift der deutschen morgenländischen Gesellschaft*
ZKT	*Zeitschrift für katholische Theologie*
ZNW	*Zeitschrift für die neutestamentliche Wissenschaft*
ZRGG	*Zeitschrift für Religions- und Geistesgeschichte*

CONTRIBUTORS

Lewis M. Barth
Hebrew Union College – Jewish Institute of Religion
Los Angeles, California

James H. Charlesworth
Princeton Theological Seminary
Princeton, New Jersey

Bruce Chilton
Bard College
Annandale-on-Hudson, New York

John J. Collins
University of Chicago
Chicago, Illinois

Johann Cook
University of Stellenbosch
Stellenbosch, South Africa

Robert Davidson
The University of Glasgow
Glasgow, Scotland

W. D. Davies
Duke University
Durham, North Carolina

Paul E. Dinter
Cortlandt Manor, New York

Elliot N. Dorff
University of Judaism
Los Angeles, California

Craig A. Evans
Trinity Western University
Langley, British Columbia

Louis H. Feldman
Yeshiva University
New York, New York

Michael Fishbane
University of Chicago
Chicago, Illinois

Peter W. Flint
Trinity Western University
Langley, British Columbia

Reginald H. Fuller
Virginia Theological Seminary
Alexandria, Virginia

Lester L. Grabbe
The University of Hull
Hull, England

Rolf P. Knierim
School of Theology
Claremont, California

Eugene E. Lemcio
Seattle Pacific University
Seattle, Washington

J. Louis Martyn
Union Theological Seminary in New York
New York, New York

Lee Martin McDonald
First Baptist Church
Alhambra, California

Jacob Milgrom
University of California at Berkeley
Berkeley, California

Kenneth E. Pomykala
Calvin College
Grand Rapids, Michigan

Rolf Rendtorff
University of Heidelberg
Heidelberg, Germany

Alexander Rofé
The Hebrew University of Jerusalem
Jerusalem, Israel

Lawrence Schiffman
New York University
New York, New York

Michael A. Signer
University of Notre Dame
Notre Dame, Indiana

Frank Anthony Spina
Seattle Pacific University
Seattle, Washington

Shemaryahu Talmon
The Hebrew University of Jerusalem
Jerusalem, Israel

Emanuel Tov
The Hebrew University of Jerusalem
Jerusalem, Israel

Eugene Ulrich
University of Notre Dame
Notre Dame, Indiana

Adam S. van der Woude
Qumran Instituut
Groningen, The Netherlands

James C. VanderKam
University of Notre Dame
Notre Dame, Indiana

Robert W. Wall
Seattle Pacific University
Seattle, Washington

Ziony Zevit
University of Judaism
Los Angeles, California

CURRICULUM VITAE OF JAMES A. SANDERS

Background and Education
Born 28 November 1927 in Memphis TN
B.A., magna cum laude, Vanderbilt University, 1948
Fulbright Grant, 1950–51
Visiting graduate student, La Faculté libre de théologie protestante de Paris and
    L'École des hautes études de l'Université de Paris, 1950–51
B.D., with distinction, Vanderbilt Divinity School, 1951
Married 30 June 1951 to Dora Geil Cargille
Lefkowitz and Rabinowitz Fellowships, 1951–53
Rockefeller Grants, 1953–54
Ordained by the Presbytery of Cincinnati OH, for teaching ministry, 1955
Ph.D., Hebrew Union College, 1955

Honorary Degrees
Litt.D., Acadia University, 1973
S.T.D., University of Glasgow, 1975
D.H.L., Coe College, 1988
D.H.L., Hebrew Union College, 1988
D.H.L., Hastings College, 1996

Professional Posts
Colgate Rochester Divinity School, 1954–65 (from Instructor to Full Professor)
Auburn Professor of Biblical Studies, Union Theological Seminary at New York,
    1965–77
Professor of Intertestamental and Biblical Studies, School of Theology at Clare-
    mont, and Professor of Religion, Claremont Graduate School, 1977–97
Alexander Robertson Lecturer, Glasgow University, 1990–91
Visiting Professor of Old Testament, Union Theological Seminary, New York
    City, 1997-98

Professional Activities and Honors
Phi Sigma Iota, 1946
Phi Beta Kappa, 1948
Guggenheim Fellow, 1961–62
Ancient Manuscripts Committee, American Schools of Oriental Research, 1962–
    present
Associate in Council, Society of Biblical Literature, 1963–66
Associate Trustee, American Schools of Oriental Research, 1963–66
President, Alumni Association, American Schools of Oriental Research, 1964
Associate Editor, Hebrew Old Testament Text Project of the United Bible Societies,
    1969–present

Advisory Board, *Journal for the Study of Judaism*, 1970–present
Editorial Board, *Journal of Biblical Literature*, 1970–76
Founding Trustee, Albright Institute of Archaeological Research, 1970–75
Guggenheim Fellow, 1972–73
Fellow, Ecumenical Institute for Advanced Theological Study, 1972
Advisory Council, *Interpretation*, 1973–78
Theta Chi Beta, 1974
Trustee, American Schools of Oriental Research, 1975–77
Research Council, Institute for Antiquity and Christianity, Claremont CA, 1977–present
President, Society of Biblical Literature, 1977–78
National Council of Churches Task Force to study revisions in the Revised Standard Version of the Bible, 1979–80
Revised Standard Version Bible Committee, 1981–present
Lilly Endowment Grant, 1981
Fellow, Ecumenical Institute for Advanced Theological Study, 1985
Resident Scholar, Villa Serbelloni, Bellagio, Italy, Rockefeller Foundation, 1985
Rockefeller Grant, 1985
Editorial Board, *Biblical Theology Bulletin*, 1985–present
Co–Chair, with Craig A. Evans, Scripture in Early Judaism and Christianity Section, Society of Biblical Literature, 1989–96
Honored with Festschrift: *A Gift of God in Due Season: Essays on Scripture and Community in Honor of James A. Sanders*, edited by Richard D. Weis and David M. Carr (JSOTSup 225; Sheffield: Sheffield Academic Press, 1996).

Selected Lectures and Visiting Professorships
Annual Professor, American Schools of Oriental Research, Albright Institute, 1961–62
Cunningham Lecturer, Austin College, 1968
Visiting Professor, Rochester Center for Theological Studies, 1970
Ayer Lecturer, Rochester Center for Theological Studies, 1971
Fellow of the Institute for Theological Studies, Tantur, Jerusalem, 1972-73
Shaffer Lecturer, Yale University, 1972
Visiting Professor, summer session, Princeton Theological Seminary, 1972
Address at Sheloshim Memorial Service for Abraham Joshua Heschel, 1973
Convocation Lecturer, Acadia University, 1973
Willis Fisher Lecturer, School of Theology at Claremont, 1973
Theta Chi Beta Lecturer, Syracuse University, 1974
Visiting Professor, summer session, Princeton Theological Seminary, 1974
I. W. Anderson Lecturer, Presbyterian College, 1975
Fondren Lecturer, Southern Methodist University, 1975
Visiting Professor, Princeton Theological Seminary, 1975
Currie Lecturer, Austin Presbyterian Seminary, 1976
R. J. Wig Lecturer, Pasadena Presbyterian Church, 1976, 1977, 1978, 1979
Visiting Professor, summer session, Princeton Theological Seminary, 1976
Crozer Lecturer and Ayer Lecturer, Rochester Center for Theological Studies, 1979

Ernest Cadman Colwell Lecturer, School of Theology at Claremont, 1979
McFadin Lecturer, Texas Christian University, 1979
William Conrad Lecturer, Lancaster Theological Seminary, 1979
Gordon Frazee Lecturer, Linfield College, 1981
J. W. Stiles Lecturer, Memphis Theological Seminary, 1981
John Leith Lecturer, First Presbyterian Church, Auburn AL, 1981
Oreon E. Scott Lecturer, Phillips University, 1981
Troisieme cycle lecturer, L'Université de Fribourg Suisse, 1981 (in French)
Zion Bible Lecturer, Principia College, 1981
Visiting Lecturer, University of Notre Dame, 1982
Gordon Frazee Lecturer, Linfield College, 1984
President's Lecturer, Garrett Evangelical Theological Seminary, 1984
Fellow at the Institute for Theological Studies, Tantur, Jerusalem, 1985-86
Visiting Professor, summer session, Pacific School of Religion, 1985
Research Scholar, Rockefeller Study Center at Bellagio, Italy, 1985
Visiting Professor, summer session, Columbia Theological Seminary, 1986
Currie Lecturer, Austin Presbyterian Seminary, 1987
Visiting Professor, summer session, Vancouver School of Theology, 1987
William H. Brownlee Lecturer, Institute for Antiquity and Christianity, 1987
Invited lecturer at the Oriental Institute of the University of Chicago, 1987
Alumni/ae Lecturer, Columbia Presbyterian Seminary, 1988
Britt Lecturer, First United Methodist Church, Honolulu HI, 1988
The Gray Lectures, Duke University, 1988
The Sizemore Lectuers, Midwestern Baptist Theological Seminary, 1988
Weinstein–Rosenthal Lectures, University of Richmond, 1988
Hebrew Union College commencement address, 1988
Carol Anne Cook Lectures, Redondo Beach United Methodist Church, 1989
Georgetown University bicentenary lecture, 1989
Knippa Interfaith Lecturer, Tulsa OK, 1989
Philadelphia Lutheran Seminary lecture, 1989
Seton Hall Univerity guest lecturer, 1989
University of Notre Dame conference lecture, 1989
University of Stellenbosch guest lecturer, 1989
Visiting Professor, summer session, Vancouver School of Theology, 1989
The Wells Sermons, Texas Christian University, 1989
Sprinkle Lectures, Atlantic Christian College, 1990
Visiting Lecturer, L'Université de Fribourg en Suisse, 1990
Biblical Archaeological Society lectures, Washington DC, 1991–92
Address at *Sheloshim* Memorial Service for Rabbi Prof. Jakob Josef Petuchowski
    in Temple Israel, Roslyn Heights NY, 1991
American Bible Society's 175th anniversary celebration address, 1991
Gustafson Lectures, United Theological Seminary, 1991
Fifth Annual Morrow-McCombs Memorial Lecture, California State University at
    San Bernardino, 1992
Pasadena Methodist Foundation annual lecture, 1992

Pittsburgh Presbyterian Theological Seminary annual archaeology lecture, 1992
Second Annual Lily Rosman Lecture, Skirball Museum, Hebrew Union College in
    Los Angeles CA, 1992
American Schools of Oriental Research Lecturer, Baltimore MD, 1993
Peter Craigie Memorial Lecturer, University of Calgary, 1993
Samuel Iwry Annual Lecturer, Johns Hopkins University, 1993
University of Arizona convocation lecture, 1993
Willamette University annual lectureship in religion, 1993
Biblical Archaeological Society lectures, San Diego CA, 1994
Colgate Rochester Divinity School lecture on the Dead Sea Scrolls, 1994
Biblical Archaeological Society lectures, Phoenix AZ, 1995, 1997
Address on Edmond Wilson at the Mercantile Library, New York City, 1995
Invited lecturer at the University of Michigan, 1995
Invited lecturer at Universität Heidelberg, 1995
Visiting lecturer, Creighton University, 1995
Invited lecturer at the International Conference on the Dead Sea Scrolls at Brigham
    Young University, 1996
Third Annual Womack Lectures, Methodist College, 1996
Guest Lecturer, Dead Sea Scrolls Institute, Trinity Western University, 1997
Session chair at the International Conference on the Dead Sea Scrolls at Hebrew
    University, Jerusalem, 1997
Invited lecturer at the World Congress of Jewish Studies, Hebrew University, Jeru-
    salem, 1997

BIBLIOGRAPHY OF JAMES A. SANDERS

1955

1. *Suffering as Divine Discipline in the Old Testament and Post-Biblical Judaism*. Special Issue of *Colgate Rochester Divinity School Bulletin* 28 (Rochester: Colgate Rochester Divinity School, 1955).

2. Review of E. A. Leslie, *Jeremiah*, in *Colgate Rochester Divinity School Bulletin* 27 (March 1955) 6.

3. Review of William Neil, *The Rediscovery of the Bible*, in *Colgate Rochester Divinity School Bulletin* 28 (October 1955) B.

4. Review of B. D. Napier, *From Faith to Faith, Essays on Old Testament Literature*, in *Colgate Rochester Divinity School Bulletin* 28 (December 1955) B.

1956

5. "Thy God Reigneth," *Motive* 16 (February 1956) 28-31.

6. Review of G. A. Buttrick (ed.), *The Interpreter's Bible*. Vol. 5: *Ecclesiastes, Song of Songs, Isaiah, Jeremiah*, in *JBR* 24 (1956) 200-202.

7. Review of E. G. Kraeling, *The Old Testament Since the Reformation*, in *Colgate Rochester Divinity School Bulletin* 28 (June 1956) B.

8. Review of E. W. Heaton, *Everyday Life in Old Testament Times*, in *Colgate Rochester Divinity School Bulletin* 29 (December 1956) B.

1957

9. "Facts," *Colgate Rochester Divinity School Bulletin* 29 (1957) 30-33.

10. Review of B. H. Kelly and D. G. Miller (eds.), *Tools for Bible Study*, in *Colgate Rochester Divinity School Bulletin* 29 (March 1957) B.

11. Review of J. A. Bewer, *The Prophets*, in *Colgate Rochester Divinity School Bulletin* 29 (March 1957) B.

12. Review of H. H. Rowley, *Prophecy and Religion*, in *Colgate Rochester Divinity School Bulletin* 29 (March 1957) B.

1958

13. "It is Finished," *Colgate Rochester Divinity School Bulletin* 30 (1958) 70-74.

14. Review of S. Blank, *Prophetic Faith in Isaiah*, in *JBL* 77 (1958) 379.

15. Review of J. K. S. Reid, *The Authority of Scripture*, in *Colgate Rochester Divinity School Bulletin* 30 (March 1958) B.

16. Review of M. Noth, *The History of Israel*, in *Colgate Rochester Divinity School Bulletin* 30 (June 1958) B.

17. Review of E. Jacob, *Theology of the Old Testament*, in *Colgate Rochester Divinity School Bulletin* 31 (October 1958) B.

18. Review of L. Köhler, *Old Testament Theology*, in *Colgate Rochester Divinity School Bulletin* 31 (December 1958) B.

1959

19. "Habakkuk in Qumran, Paul and the Old Testament," *JR* 39 (1959) 232-44.

20. "It is Finished," *The Pulpit* 30 (1959) 81-83.

21. Review of W. Holladay, *The Root Sûbh in the Old Testament*, in *JBL* 78 (1959) 262.

22. Review of C. C. McCown, *Man, Morals and History: A Study of the Historical Process*, in *Colgate Rochester Divinity School Bulletin* 31 (March 1959) B.

23. Review of N. K. Gottwald, *A Light to the Nations*, in *Colgate Rochester Divinity School Bulletin* 32 (December 1959) B.

1960

24. Review of F. F. Bruce, *Biblical Exegesis in the Qumran Texts*, in *JBL* 79 (1960) 193.

25. Review of T. Reik, *Mystery on the Mount*, in *JBL* 79 (1960) 394.

26. Review of K. Schubert, *The Dead Sea Community; Its Origin and Teachings*, in *Colgate Rochester Divinity School Bulletin* 32 (May 1960) B.

27. Review of H. H. Guthrie, *God and History in the Old Testament*, in *Colgate Rochester Divinity School Bulletin* 33 (December 1960) B.

1961

28. *The Old Testament in the Cross* (New York: Harper & Brothers, 1961).

29. "The Grace of God in the Prophets," *Foundations* 4 (July 1961) 262-65.

30. Review of *Esaïe*. Vol. 1: *Connaître la Bible*, in *JBL* 80 (1961) 202.

31. Review of C. Kuhl, *The Prophets of Israel*, in *JBL* 80 (1961) 198.

32. Review of C. Kuhl, *The Old Testament: Its Origins and Composition*, in *Colgate Rochester Divinity School Bulletin* 34 (October 1961) B.

1962

33. "The Scroll of Psalms (11QPss) from Cave 11: A Preliminary Report," *BASOR* 165 (February 1962) 11-15.

34. "The Grace of God in the Prophets (Part III)," *Foundations* 5 (January 1962) 74-77.

35. "Dispersion," "Enemy," "Exile," and some twenty other entries, *Interpreter's*

Dictionary of the Bible (New York: Abingdon, 1962).

1963

36. "Psalm 151 in 11QPss," *ZAW* 75 (1963) 73-86.

37. "God is God," *Foundations* 6 (1963) 343-61.

38. "They Belong Together," *Colgate Rochester Divinity School Bulletin* 35 (June 1963) 12-15.

39. Review of A. Weiser, *The Psalms: A Commentary*, in *JBL* 82 (1963) 127.

1964

40. "Two Non-Canonical Psalms in 11QPsª," *ZAW* (1964) 57-75.

41. "Responsum," *ZAW* 76 (1964) 200.

42. "To Tell the Truth," *Christian Century* 81 (10 June 1964) 763-66.

43. "The Sound of the Trumpet," *Colgate Rochester Divinity School Bulletin* 36 (1964) 90-97.

44. Review of *Men of God: Studies in Old Testament History and Prophecy*, in *Colgate Rochester Divinity School Bulletin* 36 (May 1964) B.

45. Review of E. C. Rust, *Salvation History: A Bible Interpretation*, in *Foundations* 7 (January 1964) 89-90.

46. Review of W. F. Albright, *History, Archaeology and Christian Humanism*, in *Colgate Rochester Divinity School Bulletin* 36 (May 1964) B.

1965

47. *The Psalms Scroll of Qumrân Cave 11 (11QPsª)* (DJD 4; Oxford: Clarendon, 1965).

48. "Pre-Masoretic Psalter Texts," *CBQ* 27 (1965) 114-23.

49. "The Banquet of the Dispossessed," *USQR* 20 (1965) 355-63.

50. "Ναζωραῖος in Matt. 2:23," *JBL* 84 (1965) 169-72.

51. Review of A. Richardson, *History, Sacred and Profane*, in *JBR* 33 (1965) 176-77.

52. Review of D. S. Russell, *The Method and Message of Jewish Apocalyptic*, in *Colgate Rochester Divinity School Bulletin* 37 (March 1965) 3.

1966

53. "The Vitality of the Old Testament: Three Theses," *USQR* 21 (1966) 161-84.

54. "Variorum in 11QPsª," *HTR* 59 (1966) 83-94.

55. "Promise and Providence," *USQR* 21 (1966) 295-303.

56. "The Psalter at the Time of Christ," *The Bible Today* 22 (1966) 1462-69.

57. "The Old Testament and the Death of God," *Pulpit Digest* 46 (January 1966) 9-16.

58. Review of O. Eissfeldt, *The Old Testament: An Introduction*, in *USQR* 21 (1966) 347.

59. Review of M. Noth, *The Old Testament World*, in *USQR* 21 (1966) 476-78.

60. Review of M. Dahood, *Psalms I (1–50)*, in *USQR* 21 (1966) 478-81.

1967

61. *The Dead Sea Psalms Scroll* (Ithaca: Cornell University, 1967).

62. Contributor to *Scrolls from the Wilderness of the Dead Sea* (Jerusalem: American Schools of Oriental Research, 1967).

63. "Biblical Faith and the Death of God Movement," in J. L. Ice and J. J. Carey (eds.), *The Death of God Debate* (Philadelphia: Westminster, 1967) 122-32.

64. "To Tell the Truth," in C. W. Christian and G. R. Wittig (eds.), *Radical Theology: Phase Two* (Philadelphia: Lippincott, 1967) 71-80.

65. "Palestinian Manuscripts 1947–67," *JBL* 86 (1967) 431-40.

66. "Urbis et Orbis: Jerusalem Today," *Christian Century* 84 (1967) 967-70.

67. "Ten Commandments in Marriage," with Mrs. Sanders, *Faith at Work* 80 (1967) 18.

68. Review of J. Haspecker, *Gottesfurcht bei Jesus Sirach*, in *JBL* 86 (1967) 480-81.

69. Review of J. Barr, *Old and New in Interpretation*, in *USQR* 22 (1967) 147-50.

70. Review of G. von Rad, *Deuteronomy: A Commentary*, in *USQR* 22 (1967) 269-72.

1968

71. "Cave 11 Surprises and the Question of Canon," *McCQ* 21 (1968) 284-98.

72. *The New History: Joseph, Our Brother* (essay published as a pamphlet by the American Baptist Convention, 1968).

73. "The Sovereign God," in E. K. Garber and J. M. Crossett (eds.), *Liberal and Conservative* (Glenview: Scott, Foresman, 1968) 75-82.

74. "Museum Exhibit Tells the Masada Story," *Christian Century* 85 (1968) 89-90.

75. "Teaching and Learning. The Old Testament at Union," *The Tower* (Fall 1968) 3-5.

76. Review of N. Glueck, *Ḥesed in the Bible*, in *Central Conference of American Rabbis Journal* 15 (January 1968) 96.

77. Review of W. Eichrodt, *Theology of the Old Testament*, Vol. 2, in *USQR* 23 (1968) 201-203.

78. Review of T. C. Vriezen, *The Religion of Ancient Israel*, in *USQR* 23 (1968) 407.

1969

79. "Cave 11 Surprises and the Question of Canon," in D. N. Freedman and J. C. Greenfield (eds.), *New Directions in Biblical Archaeology* (New York: Doubleday, 1969) 101-16.

80. "Dissenting Deities and Philippians 2:1-11," *JBL* 88 (1969) 279-90.

81. "Outside the Camp," *USQR* 24 (1969) 239-46.

82. "The Best One-Volume Commentary": Review of the *Jerome Biblical Commentary*, in *Int* 23 (1969) 468-73.

83. Review of M. Gaster, *The Exempla of the Rabbis*, with prolegomenon by W. Braude, in *USQR* 24 (1969) 442-43.

84. Review of C. D. Ginsburg, *Jacob Ben Chayyim Ibn Adonijah's Introduction to the Rabbinic Bible* and *The Massoreth Ha-Massoreth of Elias Levita*, with prolegomenon by N. Snaith, in *USQR* 24 (1969) 446-47.

1970

85. Editor, *Near Eastern Archaeology in the Twentieth Century: Essays in Honor of Nelson Glueck* (Garden City: Doubleday, 1970).

86. "This is for a Celebration: Foreword," in J. A. Sanders (ed.), *Near Eastern Archaeology in the Twentieth Century: Essays in Honor of Nelson Glueck* (Garden City: Doubleday, 1970).

87. "In the Same Night," *USQR* 25 (1970) 333-41.

88. Translation of "2 Kings" for *New American Bible* (Paterson: St. Anthony Guild, 1970).

89. "Models of God's Government": Review of G. E. Wright, *The Old Testament and Theology*, in *Int* 24 (1970) 359-68.

90. "The New English Bible: A Comparison," *Christian Century* 87 (1970) 326-28.

91. "Mirror for Identity," *Thesis Theological Cassettes* 1 no. 10 (1970).

92. Review of E. G. Wright, *The Old Testament and Theology*, in *USQR* 25 (1970) 392-94.

1971

93. "The Sirach 51 Acrostic," in A. Caquot and M. Philonenko (eds.), *Mélanges Dupont-Sommer* (Paris: Librairie D'Amérique et D'Orient Adrien-Maisonneuve, 1971) 429-38.

94. "Cave 11 Surprises and the Question of Canon," in D. N. Freedman and J. C. Greenfield (eds.), *New Directions in Biblical Archaeology* (New York: Doubleday, 1971) 113-30. [paperback edition]

95. "Introduction" to R. Le Déaut, "A Propos a Definition of Midrash," *Int* 25 (1971) 259-61.

96. "What Happened at Nazareth?" *Thesis Theological Cassettes* 2 no. 10 (1971).

97. "Text Criticism and the NJV Torah": Review of H. Orlinsky, in *JAAR* 39 (1971) 193-97.

98. Review of J. R. Rosenbloom, *The Dead Sea Isaiah Scroll*, in *USQR* 26 (1971) 195-97.

99. Review of B. Childs, *Biblical Theology in Crisis*, in *USQR* 26 (1971) 299-304.

100. Review of R. H. Hiers, *The Kingdom of God in the Synoptic Tradition*, in *TS* 32 (1971) 303-304.

1972

101. *Torah and Canon* (Philadelphia: Fortress, 1972; 10th printing, 1995).

102. *Scrolls from Qumran Cave 1*, from photographs of J. C. Trever, with D. N. Freedman and F. M. Cross (Jerusalem: Albright Institute of Archaeological Research and The Shrine of the Book, 1972).

103. "Cave 11 Surprises and the Question of Canon," in R. Weis and I. Tov (eds.), *Nosah ha-miqra' be-qumran* (Jerusalem: Hebrew University, 1972) 104-13.

104. "Jeremiah and the Future of Theological Scholarship," *ANQ* 13 (1972) 113-45.

105. Review of H. P. Routtenberg, *Amos of Tekoa*, in *Jewish Social Studies* 33 (1972) 319-20.

1973

106. With D. Barthélemy et al., *Preliminary and Interim Report on the Pentateuch*, Vol. 1 (London: United Bible Society, 1973).

107. "Palestinian Manuscripts 1947-72," *JJS* 24 (1973) 74-83.

108. "An Apostle to the Gentiles," *Conservative Judaism* 28 (1973) 61-3.

109. "The Dead Sea Scrolls—A Quarter Century of Study," *BA* 36 (1973) 109-48.

110. "Invitation to the Dispossessed," *Thesis Theological Cassettes*, 4 no. 6 (July 1973).

1974

111. *Scrolls from Qumran Cave 1*, from photographs of J. C. Trever, with D. N. Freedman and F. M. Cross (Jerusalem: Albright Institute of Archaeological Research and The Shrine of the Book, 1974). [reprint of no. 102]

112. "Cave 11 Surprises and the Question of Canon," in Sid Z. Leiman (ed.), *The Canon and Masorah of the Hebrew Bible*, ed. by (New York: Ktav, 1974) 37-51. [reprint of no. 79]

113. "The Qumran Psalms Scroll (11QPs^a) Reviewed," in M. Black and W. Smalley (eds.), *On Language, Culture and Religion in Honor of Eugene Nida* (The Hague: Mouton, 1974) 79-99.

114. "The Ethic of Election in Luke's Great Banquet Parable," in J. L. Crenshaw

and J. T. Willis (eds.), *Essays in Old Testament Ethics (J. Philip Hyatt, In Memoriam)* (New York: Ktav, 1974) 245-71.

115. "The Old Testament in 11Q Melchizedek," *JANESCU* 5 (1973) 373-82.

116. "Reopening Old Questions about Scripture": Review of J. Barr, *The Bible in the Modern World*, in *Int* 28 (1974) 321-30.

117. "Mysterium Salutis," in J. V. Allman (ed.), *Year-Book 1972/73* (Jerusalem: Ecumenical Institute, 1974) 103-27.

118. *Epistle to the Hebrews: A Brief Comment*, cassette (Alba House, 1974).

1975

119. *Identité de la Bible* (Paris: Cerf, 1975). [translation of no. 101]

120. "From Isaiah 61 to Luke 4," in J. Neusner (ed.), *Christianity, Judaism and Other Greco-Roman Cults: Studies for Morton Smith at Sixty*, Part I (SJLA 12; Leiden: Brill, 1975) 75-106.

121. "Palestinian Manuscripts 1947–72," in F. M. Cross and S. Talmon (eds.), *Qumran and the History of the Biblical Text* (Cambridge: Harvard University, 1975) 401-13.

122. "Torah and Christ," *Int* 29 (1975) 372-90.

123. Review of H. M. Shires, *Finding the Old Testament in the New*, in *USQR* 30 (1975) 241-46.

1976

124. With D. Barthélemy et al., *Preliminary and Interim Report on the Historical Books*, Vol. 2 (Stuttgart: United Bible Society, 1976).

125. "Adaptable for Life: The Nature and Function of Canon," in F. M. Cross, W. E. Lemke, and P. D. Miller, Jr. (eds.), *Magnalia Dei: The Mighty Acts of God. Essays on the Bible and Archaeology in Memory of G. E. Wright* (New York: Doubleday, 1976) 531-60.

126. "The Integrity of God," *Concern* (December 1976) 9-10.

127. "Hermeneutics" and "Torah," in *The Interpreter's Dictionary of the Bible. Supplement* (Nashville: Abingdon, 1976) 402-407, 909-11.

128. Review with S. Skiles, of R. N. Longenecker, *Biblical Exegesis in the Apostolic Period*, in *Int* 30 (1976) 212-13.

129. Review of J. A. Fitzmyer, *The Dead Sea Scrolls: Major Publications and Tools for Study*, in *RelSRev* 2 (1976) 29.

130. Review of F. M. Cross and S. Talmon, *Qumran and the History of the Biblical Text*, in *RelSRev* 2 (1976) 29.

131. Review of B. Childs, *Book of Exodus*, in *JBL* 95 (1976) 286-90.

1977

132. With D. Barthélemy et al., *Preliminary and Interim Report on the Hebrew Old*

Testament Text Project, Vol. 3: *The Poetic Books* (Stuttgart: United Bible Societies, 1977).

133. Translation of "Psalm 151," in B. M. Metzger (ed.), *The Oxford Annotated Apocrypha of the Old Testament: Expanded Edition Containing the Third and Fourth Books of the Maccabees and Psalm 151* (New York: Oxford University Press, 1977) 330-31.

134. "Hermeneutics of True and False Prophecy" in G. W. Coats and B. O. Long (eds.), *Canon and Authority: Essays in Old Testament Religion and Authority* (W. Zimmerli Festschrift; Philadelphia: Fortress, 1977) 21-41.

135. "Torah and Paul," in W. A. Meeks (ed.), *God's Christ and His People* (Nils Dahl Festschrift; Oslo: Universitetsforlaget, 1977) 132-40.

136. "Biblical Criticism and the Bible as Canon," *USQR* 32 (1977) 157-65.

137. "The Promise is for All," *Concern* (June 1977) whole issue.

138. Review of J. Bowman, *The Samaritan Problem*, in *RelSRev* 3 (1977) 60.

139. Review of S. Z. Leimann, *The Canonization of Hebrew Scripture*, in *JBL* 96 (1977) 590-91.

140. Review of L. M. Russell, *The Liberating Word*, in *USQR* 32 (1977) 186-88.

1978

141. "Comparative Wisdom: L'Oeuvre Terrien," in J. G. Gammie, W. A. Brueggemann, W. L. Humphreys, J. M. Ward (eds.), *Israelite Wisdom: Theological and Literary Essays in Honor of Samuel Terrien* (Missoula: Scholars Press, 1978) 3-14.

142. With W. Lowndes Lipscomb, "Wisdom at Qumran," in J. G. Gammie, W. A. Brueggemann, W. L. Humphreys, J. M. Ward (eds.), *Israelite Wisdom: Theological and Literary Essays in Honor of Samuel Terrien* (Missoula Scholars Press, 1978) 277-285.

143. "The Gospels and the Canonical Process: A Response to Lou H. Silberman," in W. O. Walker, Jr. (ed.), *The Relationship Among the Gospels: An Interdisciplinary Dialogue* (San Antonio: Trinity University Press, 1978) 219-36.

144. "Isaiah 55:1-9," *Int* 32 (1978) 291-95.

145. Review of J. T. Milik, *The Books of Enoch: Aramaic Fragments of Qumrân Cave 4*, in *JBL* 97 (1978) 446-47.

146. Review of R. E. Brown, *The Birth of the Messiah: A Commentary on the Infancy Narratives in Matthew and Luke*, in *USQR* 33 (1978) 193-96.

147. Review of J. Blankinsopp, *Prophecy and Canon: A Contribution to the Study of Jewish Origins*, in *CBQ* 40 (1978) 598-600.

148. Review of E.-M. Laperrousaz, *Qumrân: L'Establissement essénien des bords de la Mer Morte: histoire et archéologie du site*, in *BASOR* 231 (1978) 79-80.

1979

149. *God Has a Story Too: Sermons in Context* (Philadelphia: Fortress, 1979).

150. With D. Barthélemy et al., *Preliminary and Interim Report on the Hebrew Old Testament Text Project*, Vol. 4: *The Prophetic Books I* (Stuttgart: United Bible Societies, 1979).

151. "Text and Canon: Concepts and Method," *JBL* 98 (1979) 5-29. [Presidential address delivered 19 November 1978 at the annual meeting]

152. Review of *Biblia Hebraica Stuttgartensia*, in *JBL* 98 (1979) 417-19.

1980

153. With D. Barthélemy et al., *Preliminary and Interim Report on the Hebrew Old Testament Text Project*, Vol. 5: *The Prophetic Books II* (Stuttgart: United Bible Societies, 1980).

154. "Canonical Context and Canonical Criticism," *HBT* 2 (1980) 173-97.

1981

155. "Text and Canon: Old Testament and New," in P. Casetti et al. (eds.), *Mélanges Dominique Barthélemy: Etudes bibliques* (OBO 38; Fribourg: Editions Universitaires, 1981) 373-94.

156. "Response" (to E. Lemcio's "The Gospels and Canonical Criticism"), *BTB* 11 (1981) 122-24.

157. "The Bible as Canon," *The Christian Century* 98 (2 December 1981) 1250-55.

158. *Luke—The Theological Historian.* A series of seven, thirty-minute videotapes studying the Gospel of Luke and the Acts of the Apostles. United Methodist Communications (Nashville, 1981).

1982

159. With D. Barthélemy et al., *Critique textuelle de l'Ancien Testament*, Vol. 1 (OBO 50.1; Fribourg: Presses Universitaires, 1982).

160. "The Conversion of Paul," in *A Living Witness to Oikodome: Essays in Honor of Ronald E. Osborn* (Impact 9; Claremont: Disciples Seminary Foundation, 1982) 71-93.

161. "Isaiah in Luke," *Int* 36 (1982) 144-55.

162. *True and False Prophecy.* A series of six, thirty-minute videotapes studying the great Old Testament prophets in their historical setting. United Methodist Communications (Nashville, 1982).

1983

163. "Canon and Calendar: An Alternative Lectionary Proposal," in D. T. Hessel (ed.), *Social Themes of the Christian Year: A Commentary on the Lectionary* (Philadelphia: Geneva, 1983) 257-63.

164. Review of B. P. Kittel, *The Hymns of Qumran: Translation and Commentary*, in *JBL* 102 (1983) 330-32.

1984

165. *Canon and Community: A Guide to Canonical Criticism* (Philadelphia: Fortress, 1984). [the Fondren (1975) and Currie (1976) Lectures]

166. *Torah and Canon* in Japanese, translated by Dr. Yoji Sato (Tokyo: Kyo-Bun-Kwan, 1984).

167. "Canonical Criticism: An Introduction," in O. Wermelinger, et al. (eds.), *Le Canon de l'Ancien Testament: sa formation et son histoire* (Geneve: Labor et Fides, 1984) 341-62.

168. "Presenting the Issue," *BTB* 14.3 (1984) 82-83.

169. Review of W. Brueggemann, *The Creative Word: Canon as a Model for Biblical Education*, in *JBL* 103 (1984) 435-36.

170. Review of M. Goshen-Gottstein, *The Book of Isaiah. Volume Two: Chapters 22–44*, in *JBL* 103 (1984) 448-49.

171. Review of P. R. Davies, *The Damascus Covenant*, in *JAOS* 104 (1984) 773-74.

1985

172. "Canonical Hermeneutics in the Light of Biblical, Literary and Historical Criticism," *Proceedings of the Catholic Theological Society of America* 40 (1985) 54-63.

173. "A Multivalent Text: Psalm 151:3-4 Revisited," *Biblical and Other Studies in Honor of Sheldon H. Blank: HAR* 8 (1985) 167-84.

174. *The Bible as Canon*. A series of six, thirty-minute videotapes explaining and demonstrating Canonical Criticism for lay audiences. Distributed by EcuFilm/UMCom, Nashville, TN.

175. *Biblical Reflections*. Four thirty-minute videotapes containing four Lenten sermons. Distributed by EcuFilm/UMCom, Nashville, TN.

176. Review of L. H. Schiffman, *Sectarian Laws in the Dead Sea Scrolls: Courts, Testimony and the Penal Code*, in *JAOS* 105 (1985) 146-47.

177. Review of B. Z. Wacholder, *Dawn of Qumran*, in *JAOS* 105 (1985) 147-48.

178. Review of J. Barr, *Holy Scripture: Canon, Authority, Criticism*, in *JBL* 104 (1985) 501-502.

1986

179. With D. Barthélemy et al., *Critique textuelle de l'Ancien Testament*, Vol. 2 (OBO 50.2; Fribourg: Editions Universitaires, 1986).

180. "The Bible and the Believing Communities" in Donald G. Miller (ed.), *The Hermeneutical Quest. Essays in Honor of James Luther Mays on His Sixty-Fifth Birthday* (Allison Park: Pickwith Publications, 1986) 145-57.

1987

181. *From Sacred Story to Sacred Text: Canon as Paradigm* (Philadelphia: Fortress, 1987).

182. "A New Testament Hermeneutic Fabric: Psalm 118 in the Entrance Narrative," in C. A. Evans and W. F. Stinespring (eds.), *Early Jewish and Christian Exegesis: Studies in Memory of William Hugh Brownlee* (Homage 10; Atlanta: Scholars Press, 1987) 177-90.

183. "Isaiah in Luke," in J. L. Mays and P. J. Achtemeier (eds.), *Interpreting the Prophets* (Philadelphia: Fortress, 1987) 75-85. [reprint of no. 161]

184. "First Testament and Second," *BTB* 17 (1987) 47-49.

185. "Extravagant Love," *New Blackfriars* 68 (June 1987) 278-84.

186. "The Bible and the Believing Community," *Biblical Literacy Today* 1 (summer 1987) 4-6.

187. "The Challenge of Fundamentalism: One God and World Peace," *Impact* 19 (1987) 12-30.

188. Review of M. Fishbane, *Biblical Interpretation in Ancient Israel*, in *CBQ* 49 (1987) 302-305.

189. Review of R. Beckwith, *The Old Testament Canon of the New Testament Church*, in *TToday* 44 (1987) 131-34.

190. Review of G. H. Wilson, *The Editing of the Hebrew Psalter*, in *JBL* 106 (1987) 321.

1988

191. "Fundamentalism and the Church: Theological Crisis for Mainline Protestants," *BTB* 18.2 (1988) 43-49.

192. "The Strangeness of the Bible," *USQR* 42 (1988) 33-37.

193. "Annunciations," *Scripture in Church* 18 (1988) 115-20.

194. "The Mainline Churches and Theology," *Religion: Journal of the Kansas School of Religion* 25.3 (1988) 1-5.

1989

195. "Deuteronomy," in B.W. Anderson (ed.), *The Books of the Bible*, Vol. 1: *The Old Testament/The Hebrew Bible* (New York: Scribner's, 1989) 89-102.

196. Response to E. N. Dorff in J. Hick and E. Meltzer (eds.), *Three Faiths—One God* (London: Macmillan, 1989) 30-34.

197. "Sanders Bible Ministry Project," a set of six exegetic discussions of various biblical passages video-taped and distributed by *SpiritQuest* of Claremont.

198. Review of R. C. Tannehill's *The Narrative Unity of Luke-Acts*, Vol. 1, in *Pacific Theological Review* 22 (1989) 79-81.

199. Review of J. W. Groves' *Actualization and Interpretation in the Old Testament*, in *CBQ* 51 (1989) 329-31.

1990

200. Contributor to *New Revised Standard Version* of the Bible; member of translation committee of North American scholars, for the National Council of Churches.

201. "'Nor do I . . .': A Canonical Reading of the Challenge to Jesus in John 8," in B. R. Gaventa and R. T. Fortna (eds.), *The Conversation Continues: Studies in Paul and John in Honor of J. Louis Martyn* (Nashville: Abingdon, 1990) 337-47.

202. "Hebrew Bible and Old Testament: Textual Criticism in Service of Biblical Studies," in R. Brooks and J. J. Collins (eds.), *Hebrew Bible or Old Testament? Studying the Bible in Judaism and Christianity* (Notre Dame: University of Notre Dame Press, 1990) 41-68.

203. "Extravagant Love," *Scripture in Church* 20 (1990) 97-103.

1991

204. Introductions and annotations to: Baruch; The Letter of Jeremiah; The "Additions" (Prayer of Azariah, Song of the Three Young Men, Susanna, Bel and the Dragon) to the Greek Book of Daniel; The Prayer of Manasseh; Psalm 151, in B. M. Metzger and R. Murphy (eds.), *The New Oxford Annotated Bible with the Apocrypha: An Ecumenical Study Bible for the NRSV* (Oxford: Oxford University Press, 1991).

205. "Stability and Fluidity in Text and Canon," in G. Norton and S. Pisano (eds.), *Tradition of the Text: Studies offered to Dominique Barthélemy in Celebration of his 70th Birthday* (OBO 109; Fribourg: Presses Universitaires, 1991) 203-17.

206. "Understanding the Development of the Biblical Text," in H. Shanks (ed.), *The Dead Sea Scrolls After Forty Years* (Washington: Biblical Archaeological Society, 1991) 57-73.

207. "The Integrity of Biblical Pluralism," in J. Sitterson and J. Rosenblatt (eds.), *Not in Heaven . . .* (Bloomington: Indiana University Press, 1991) 154-69.

208. "Canon as Shape and Function," in J. Reumann (ed.), *The Promise and Practice of Biblical Theology* (Minneapolis, Fortress 1991) 87-97.

209. "Scripture, Canon of the," in A. Atiya (ed.), *The Coptic Encyclopedia* (New York: Macmillan, 1991) 2108-12.

210. "Dead Sea Scrolls Access: A New Reality," *The Folio: The Newsletter of the Ancient Biblical Manuscript Center for Preservation and Research* 11.3 (Fall 1991) 1-4.

211. Review of P. D. Miller, *Deuteronomy* in *TToday* 48 (1991) 366-70.

212. Review of M. Fishbane, *The Garments of Torah: Essays in Biblical Hermeneutics*, in *TToday* 47 (1991) 433-35.

1992

213. *From Sacred Story to Sacred Text* (Minneapolis: Fortress, 1992). [repr. of no. 181; paperback]

214. With D. Barthélemy, *Critique textuelle de l'Ancien Testament* (OBO 50.3; Fribourg: Editions Universitaires, 1992).

215. "Communities and Canon" in the *Oxford Study Bible Based on the Revised English Bible* (Oxford: Oxford University Press, 1992) 91-100.

216. "The Dead Sea Scrolls and Biblical Studies," in M. Fishbane, E. Tov, and W. Fields (eds.), *Sha'arei Talmon: Studies in the Bible, Qumran, and the Ancient Near East Presented to Shemaryahu Talmon* (Winona Lake: Eisenbrauns, 1992) 323-36.

217. "Canon," *ABD* 1.837-52.

218. "Sins, Debts and Jubilee Release," in R. P. Carroll (ed.), *Text as Pretext: Essays in Honour of Robert Davidson* (JSOTSup 138; Sheffield Academic Press, 1992) 273-81.

219. "Qumran Update: What Can Happen in a Year?" in *BA* 55 (March 1992) 37-42.

220. Preface to R. W. Wall and E. E. Lemcio, *The New Testament as Canon: A reader in Canonical Criticism* (Sheffield: JSOT Press, 1992) 7-11.

221. Review of M. J. Mulder (ed.), *Mikra*, in *JAOS* 111 (1992) 2.

1993

222. *Luke and Scripture: The Function of Sacred Tradition in Luke-Acts*, with C. A. Evans (Minneapolis: Fortress Press, 1993).

223. Editor, with C. A. Evans, *Paul and the Scriptures of Israel* (JSNTSup 83; SSEJC 1; Sheffield: JSOT Press, 1993).

224. "Paul and Theological History," in C. A. Evans and J. A. Sanders, *Paul and the Scriptures of Israel* (JSNTSup 83; SSEJC 1; Sheffield: JSOT Press, 1993) 52-57.

225. "Habakkuk in Qumran, Paul and the Old Testament," in C. A. Evans and J. A. Sanders, *Paul and the Scriptures of Israel* (JSNTSup 83; SSEJC 1; Sheffield: JSOT Press, 1993) 98-117. [revision of no. 19 above]

226. "Psalm 154 Revisited," in G. Braulik, W. Gross, S. McEvenue (eds.), *Biblische Theologie und gesellschaftlicher Wandel: Für Norbert Lohfink, SJ* (Freiburg: Herder, 1993) 296-306.

227. Introductions and Annotations for "Prayer of Manasseh" and "Psalm 151," in W. A. Meeks (ed.), *The Harper Collins Study Bible* (New York: HarperCollins, 1993) 1746-48, 1749-51.

228. "Introduction: Why the Pseudepigrapha?" in J. H. Charlesworth and C. A. Evans (eds.), *The Pseudepigrapha and Early Biblical Interpretation* (JSPSup 14; SSEJC 2; Sheffield: JSOT Press, 1993) 13-19.

229. "Masorah" and "Masoretic Text," in *The Oxford Companion to the Bible* (New York: Oxford University Press, 1993) 500-501.

230. "Response" to paper by J. A. Fitzmyer in H. C. Kee (ed.), *The Bible in the Twenty-First Century* (New York: American Bible Society, 1993) 26-29.

231. "Foreword," in C. A. Evans and D. A. Hagner (eds.), *Anti-Semitism and Early Christianity: Issues of Polemic and Faith* (Minneapolis: Fortress, 1993) ix-xvii.

1994

232. "Ναζωραῖος in Matthew 2:23," in C. A. Evans and W. R. Stegner (eds.), *The Gospels and the Scriptures of Israel* (JSNTSup 104; SSEJC 3; Sheffield: JSOT Press, 1994) 116-28. [revision of no. 50 above]

1995

233. "Hermeneutics" in W. Willamon and R. Laetcher (eds.), *A Concise Encyclopedia of Preaching* (Louisville: Westminster/John Knox Press, 1995) 175-82.

234. "Scripture as Canon for Post-Modern Times," *BTB* 25 (1995) 56-63.

235. "Hermeneutics of Text Criticism," *Textus: Studies of the Hebrew University Bible Project* 18 (1995) 1-26.

236. "From Manuscripts to Translations," *The Folio* 13.2 (fall 1995) 1-2.

237. Review of O. Betz and R. Riesner, *Jesus, Qumran and the Vatican*, in *Int* 49 (1995) 300-302; repr. in *The Folio* 13.2 (fall 1995).

1997

238. "The Task of Text Criticism," in H. T. C. Sun and K. Eades (eds.), *Problems in Biblical Theology: Essays in Honor of Rolf Knierim* (Grand Rapids: Eerdmans, 1997) 315-27.

Forthcoming

239. Editor, with C. A. Evans, *Early Christian Interpretation of the Scriptures of Israel: Investigations and Proposals* (JSNTSup; SSEJC 5; Sheffield: Sheffield Academic Press).

240. Translations, introductions and annotations to Psalms 151, 154, 155, Sirach 51:13ff, Plea for Deliverance, Hymn to the Creator, Apostrophe to Zion, Eschatological Hymn, Apostrophe to Judah, David's Compositions in 11QPsᵃ, and the apotropaic prayers in 11QPsAp, in J. H. Charlesworth (ed.), *Princeton Theological Seminary Dead Sea Scrolls Project* (Tübingen: Mohr [Siebeck]; Louisville: Westminster/John Knox Press).

241. "Identity and Dialogue" for the second Lou Silberman Festschrift, edited by William Dever, University of Arizona.

242. "Intertextuality and Dialogue" for a volume on interfaith dialogue edited by J. H. Charlesworth for the American Interfaith Institute, Philadelphia.

243. "Scripture as Canon in Post-Modern Terms," in J. Gorak (ed.), *Reflections on the Cultural Revolution: Canons and Disciplinary Change* (Garland Press).

244. "Hermeneutics of Translation," forthcoming in *The Next Step: Removing Anti-Semitism from the Church* (Philadelphia: Interfaith Institute, 1995).

245. "The Impact of the Dead Sea Scrolls on Biblical Studies," in D. Parry and E. Ulrich (eds.), *Technological Innovations, New Texts, and New and Reformulated Issues* (STDJ; Leiden: Brill).

246. "The Exile and Canon Formation," forthcoming in J. M. Scott (ed.), *Exile: Old Testament, Jewish and Christian Conceptions* (JSJSup; Leiden: Brill).

247. "Intertextuality and Canon," forthcoming in S. L. Cook and S. C. Winter (eds.), *On the Way to Nineveh: Studies in Honor of George M. Landes* (American Schools of Oriental Research publications).

248. "Setting the Canon of the Tanak," in A. J. Hauser and D. F. Watson (eds.), *History of Biblical Interpretation* (4 vols., Grand Rapids: Eerdmans).

249. "Dead Sea Scrolls," in A. Hastings (ed.), *Oxford Companion to Christian Thought* (Oxford University Press).

250. "The Oldest Complete Hebrew Bible in the World," an article on Codex Leningradensis for Sheffield Press.

251. With Astrid Beck an article on Codex Leningradensis for *Bible Review*.

In Preparation

252. Editor, with C. A. Evans, *The Formation and Early Interpretation of the Scriptures of Israel* (JSNTSup; SSEJC 6; Sheffield: Sheffield Academic Press).

253. "Scripture at the Time of Christ," for a symposium at Florida Southern College 6–8 February 1997, to be published later.

254. *The Impact of the Dead Sea Scrolls on Biblical Study.*

255. *How Luke Read Scripture.*

256. *The Canonical Process.*

PART ONE

THE FIRST TESTAMENT

THE "FACE OF GOD"
ESAU IN CANONICAL CONTEXT

Frank Anthony Spina

INTRODUCTION

Almost without exception, scholars have regarded the biblical depiction of Esau, Jacob's older twin and the eponymous ancestor of Edom, as uniformly negative. Cresson typifies this outlook: " . . . it is scarcely hyperbolic to say that never a kind word is spoken about Edom in the Old Testament."[1] This holds for Esau as well.[2] At first, such an assessment seems indisputable. After all, Yahweh selected the younger Jacob over the elder Esau to carry forward the ancestral promise of land and progeny (Gen 28:13-15; 35:9-12; cf. 25:23). For his part, Esau foolishly traded his birthright for a single meal (Gen 25:29-34) and grieved his parents by marrying outside the family (Gen 26:34-35; cf. 24:1-67). Further, Esau/Edom refused Israel safe passage to Canaan (Num 20:14, 18, 20-21), an action that presaged a long period of enmity between the two countries (e.g. 1 Sam 14:47; 2 Sam 8:14; 1 Kgs 11:14-16; 2 Kgs 8:20-22; 14:7, 10; 1 Chr 18:11-13; 2 Chr 21:8-10; 25:19-20). In the prophetic corpus, Edom is excoriated so relentlessly that Stinespring posits a "Damn-Edom theology."[3] Finally, the epitome of Esau/Edom's negative

---

[1]   Bruce C. Cresson, "The Condemnation of Edom in Postexilic Judaism," in James M. Efird (ed.), *The Use of the Old Testament in the New and Other Essays: Studies in Honor of William Franklin Stinespring* (Durham: Duke University Press, 1972) 125.

[2]   Of the texts treating Edom or Esau, Roger Syrén (*The Forsaken First-Born: A Study of a Recurrent Motif in the Patriarchal Narratives* [JSOTSup 133; Sheffield: JSOT Press, 1993] 114-15) classifies all of them as "negative," excepting Deut 2:4-6; 23:7-8 (= "positive") and Num 21:4; 33:37; 34:3; Josh 15:1; 1 Kgs 9:26; 2 Kgs 3:9; Jer 40:11; Dan 11:41 (= "neutral").

[3]   See Cresson, "Condemnation," 125. Bert Dicou (*Edom, Israel's Brother and Antagonist: The Role of Edom in Biblical Prophecy and Story* [JSOTSup 169; Sheffield: Sheffield Academic Press, 1994] 26) argues that Edom assumes the position of "representative" of the foreign nations that deserve divine denunciation and judgment. The relevant prophetic passages are: Isa 11:14; 34:5-6; 63:1; Jer

image in TANAK is expressed in Yahweh's statement: " . . . I have loved (וָאֹהַב) Jacob but I have hated (שָׂנֵאתִי) Esau" (Mal 1:2 [RSV]).

Granted, Esau is occasionally cast in a slightly more positive light. Realizing the consternation his Hittite wives caused his parents, he married Abraham's grandaughter (Gen 28:6-9). Also, though he had vowed to kill Jacob for taking his birthright and blessing, he never avenged the wrong (Gen 27:41; 33:1-17). Once, Esau/Edom made common cause with Israel and Judah against Moab (2 Kgs 3:8-9, 12, 20, 26). And, there is an admonition that Edomites are not to be abhorred or denied access to the temple (Deut 23:8-9 [Eng. 23:7-8]). Notwithstanding, scholars have either regarded these references as negligible or less clearly positive than they appear on the surface.[4] The fact remains that for most interpreters the Bible presents Esau/ Edom in consistently and unambiguously pejorative terms.

Generally, this dark representation has been attributed to socio-political realities. Extreme political antagonism between Israel and Edom gave rise to hostile texts, whereas periods when more amicable relationships obtained provided the impetus for more innocuous texts.[5] The narratives that concentrate on Esau and Jacob as individuals locate the aetiology for later political strife in the original personal struggles of the eponymous ancestors.[6] However, as scholars have increasingly approached the texts from literary perspectives, they postulate less correlation with actual historical events.[7] Fraternal conflict is instead to be seen as a literary motif.[8]

9:24-25 (Eng. 9:25-26); 25:21; 49:7-22; Ezek 25:12-14; 32:29; 35:1-15; 36:1-7; Joel 4:19 (Eng. 3:19); Amos 1:6, 9, 11-12; 9:12; Obadiah; Mal 1:2-4. See also Pss 60:10-11 (Eng. 60:8-9); 83:7 (Eng. 83:6); 108:10-11 (Eng. 108:9-10); 137:7; Lam 4:21-22.

[4]   E.g. see Benno Jacob, *Genesis* (Berlin: Schocken, 1934) 645-46; Fredrick C. Holmgren, "Holding Your Own Against God! Genesis 32:22-32 (In the Context of Genesis 31–33)," *Int* 44 (1990) 12-14.

[5]   This outlook is basically taken by the scholars who have contributed the set of essays found in Diana Vikander Edelman (ed.), *You Shall Not Abhor an Edomite For He is Your Brother: Edom and Seir in History and Tradition* (SBLABS 3; Atlanta: Scholars Press, 1995).

[6]   Thomas L. Thompson, "Conflict Themes in the Jacob Narratives," *Semeia* 15 (1979) 8.

[7]   Thompson, "Conflict Themes," 15.

[8]   See the contention by George W. Coats ("Strife without Reconciliation—A Narrative Theme in the Jacob Traditions," in R. Albertz, H.-P. Müller, Hans

My intention is to examine the portrayal of Esau from an intertextual, canonical vantage point. Rather than attempting to ascertain the ostensive socio-political realities "behind" the texts, I want to attend to the theological import of the treatment of Esau in its received canonical form. Exegetes have tended to neglect the theological dimension found in the Esau texts. Syrén, for example, avers that Esau has " . . . no apparent theological role to play."[9] To the contrary, I contend that the picture of Esau in TANAK resulted precisely from a theological rendering of the pertinent traditions. The task before us is to ascertain the theological points that are scored in the depiction of Esau's role in ancestral and other traditions when viewed from the standpoint of canonical intertextuality.

BIRTH AND BIRTHRIGHT

From the beginning, the relationship between Esau and Jacob is complex. This complexity is revealed at the outset in the irony reflected in the birth account. Though the twins' birth resulted from divine intervention, they were not destined to share the same future. Isaac had prayed in response to Rebekah's barrenness, whereupon God acceded to the request (Gen 25:21).[10] Nearing delivery, a distraught Rebekah learned from God that she was carrying twins and that the younger child and his descendants would be ascendant over the older child and his descendants (Gen 25:23). The irony is that Rebekah had sought (לִדְרֹשׁ) Yahweh in the first place due to distress brought about by the struggling going on in her womb (וַיִּתְרֹצֲצוּ; Gen 25:22).[11] This implies that the twins were engaged in

---

Walter Wolff, W. Zimmerli [eds.], *Werden und Wirken des Alten Testaments* [Claus Westermann Festschrift; Göttingen: Vandenhoeck & Ruprecht; Neukirchen-Vluyn: Neukirchener Verlag, 1980] 82-106) that "strife without reconciliation" is the theme of the primary stage of the Jacob traditions before the promise motif was secondarily added.

9   Syrén, *The Forsaken First-Born*, 73.

10   The Masoretic tradents note that the verb used in this instance (וַיֶּעְתַּר) is used elsewhere four times; in each case God is implored and immediately responds (Exod 8:26 [Eng. 8:30]; cf. vv. 24-25 [Eng. vv. 28-29]; 10:18; cf. v. 17; Judg 13:8).

11   Isaac's intercession (עתר) and Rebekah's seeking (דרש) divine help may have cultic associations. See Ronald S. Hendel, *The Epic of the Patriarch: The Jacob Cycle and the Narrative Traditions of Canaan and Israel* (HSM 42; Atlanta: Scholars Press, 1987) 39; J. P. Fokkelman, *Narrative Art in Genesis: Specimens*

a proleptic contest to emerge first so as to claim first-born privileges.[12] However, according to the divine prediction, it ended up being a disadvantage to be born first! Esau would have been better off had his brother, who was still vying for position up to the very last moment, won this initial contest (Gen 25:25-26). Yahweh had named no names; He had only said that the younger would be pre-eminent over the elder.

Once the twins are grown, Jacob is not depicted as necessarily morally superior to Esau. The text describes Esau as "a man who knows hunting—a man of the field" (אִישׁ יֹדֵעַ צַיִד אִישׁ שָׂדֶה; Gen 25:27). Some hold that this description is subtly unflattering, hinting that Esau is crude, uncultured, and instinctual.[13] The plausibility of this reading is supported by the statement that Isaac loved Esau because "game was in his [i.e. Isaac's] mouth" (כִּי־צַיִד בְּפִיו) — possibly an inelegant way of indicating Isaac's fondness for the food that Esau caught and prepared (Gen 25:28). Also, in the famous birthright account, Esau returned hungry from the field and blurted out, "let me cram my maw with this red stuff" (הַלְעִיטֵנִי נָא מִן־הָאָדֹם הָאָדֹם הַזֶּה), thereby exposing that he was the embodiment of "inarticulate appetite."[14] After the fateful negotiations over the birthright, a succession of verbs further betrays Esau's ill-mannered ways: " . . . he ate, drank, got up, and left" (וַיֹּאכַל וַיֵּשְׁתְּ וַיָּקָם וַיֵּלַךְ; Gen 25:34).[15] Thus, Warmoes refers to Esau as "le rude chasseur."[16] But if Esau lacks social graces, is he morally deficient as well?

A fifth consecutive verb answers that query: " . . . so Esau de-

---

of Stylistic and Structural Analysis (2nd ed., BibSem 12; Sheffield: JSOT Press, 1991) 88 n. 4.

12   Syrén, The Forsaken First-Born, 81; Fokkelman, Narrative Art, 88; M. Malul, "'AQEB 'Heel' and 'AQAB 'To Supplant' and the Concept of Succession in the Jacob-Esau Narratives," VT 46 (1996) 196.

13   E. A. Speiser, Genesis (AB 1; Garden City: Doubleday, 1964) 196; cf. Malul, "'AQEB 'Heel' and 'AQAB 'To Supplant'," 206-207.

14   The phrase is Robert Alter's (The Art of Biblical Narrative [New York: Basic Books, 1981] 44). He also suggests that לעט, which is found only once in TANAK, usually is used for the feeding of animals; BDB (p. 542) cites a meaning "to stuff cattle with food" in "late Hebrew."

15   Speiser (Genesis, 196) refers to the "drumbeat effect" of these five verbs. The fifth verb is "and he despised [his birthright]."

16   R. P. P. Warmoes, "Jacob ravit la bénédiction d'Isaac (Gen 27,6-40)," Assemblées du Seigneur 29 (1966) 23.

spised the birthright" (וַיִּבֶז עֵשָׂו אֶת־הַבְּכֹרָה; Gen 25:34).[17] Surely this
is moral failure. Though the narration confirms that he was truly
hungry (וְהוּא עָיֵף; Gen 25:29), Esau inexplicably thought that he was
at death's door (אָנֹכִי הוֹלֵךְ לָמוּת; Gen 25:32]). His hunger pangs
clouded his judgment, making the birthright worthless in his eyes. In
short, Esau lacked not only etiquette but virtue. Nothing but food
had any value, so he rashly ceded his legal rights and squandered his
future. Possessing no sense of restraint, proportion, or priority, Esau
had indeed "despised" his birthright, thus treating that precious item
as dispensible.

Nevertheless, as bad as Esau looks at this point, his brother Jacob
hardly dazzles by comparison. To be sure, he was as shrewd as Esau
was impetuous. Still, Jacob was far from commendable. In fact, the
narration fairly invites us to surmise that Jacob had been waiting for
an occasion when Esau might be susceptible to exploitation. Demanding the transfer of a birthright is not exactly a natural response to a
brother's request for food, manners or no manners. Clearly, Jacob
had an eye for the future, was up on legal procedures ("swear to me
today"), and had been on the lookout for an opportune moment.
Thus armed, Jacob thoroughly outwitted his careless brother. Without doubt, Jacob was superior in this exchange in the sense that he
ran circles around the foolhardy and intemperate Esau. Yet, he was
not *morally* superior. Jacob was more resolute than Esau, smarter,
more determined to secure the future, but he was no better at being
brotherly. If Esau was crass and stupid, Jacob was coldly extortion-
ate.[18] The judgment on Esau is explicit: "he despised his birthright."
At the same time, the reader is left with an implicit negative estima-
tion of Jacob. Fokkelmann infers from this text that, "Morally
speaking there are only losers."[19]

It needs to be kept in mind that the moral make-up of the twins
had already been adumbrated in their initial descriptions. Irony is

---

[17]   "Despised" is the RSV's translation; JPS renders the term "spurn." In Prov
19:16 בזה is opposite of שמר, "to regard, pay attention to, be careful about, guard"
etc. "Disregard" may be acceptable in the Genesis passage, though perhaps too
anemic. The contextual idea seems to be "wantonly disregard." Malul ("'AQEB
'Heel' and 'AQAB 'To Supplant'," 205-206) presents an elaborate argument that
בזה in this instance should be seen in the light of ancient Near Eastern legal
procedures having to do with relinquishing of property rights.

[18]   See Alter, *Art*, 45-46.

[19]   Fokkelman, *Narrative Art*, 97.

evident here, too. As already noted, Esau was identified in terms of his occupation—he was a hunter, a man of the field. What is said about Jacob, however, seems curious: he was תָּם and a tent dweller (יֹשֵׁב אֹהָלִים; Gen 25:27). The latter is straightforward; it contrasts to Esau's being a "man of the field."[20] But תָּם is the more interesting term. Translators have often rendered this word as indicative of an unassuming disposition.[21] Yet, other uses of תָּם connote moral innocence or integrity (e.g. Gen 6:9; 20:5-6; Job 1:8; 2:3). What reason may be adduced as to why תָּם does not imply moral excellence in this case also?[22] This is where irony may come into play again, since תָּם may be an antoymn to עָקַב, the root from which Jacob's name is derived.[23] That is, Jacob is simultaneously morally bankrupt and morally upright. He is a "supplanter," as both his name implies and his actions confirm, but he is also called to be a moral exemplar in his eventual role as the bearer of the divine ancestral promise. So far, Jacob the morally questionable man has over-whelmed Jacob the morally compelling man (cf. Gen 27:36); currently, עָקַב overshadows תָּם. For this to be reversed, profound changes will have to occur. Though Esau is far from תָּם himself, and will never be described as such, he may have more to do with Jacob's pending moral reversal than seems evident at this point.

---

20   If a cultural contrast between the "desert and the sown" was once indicated by this juxtaposition, it has been largely subordinated in the present literary context. See the discussion of Noth's understanding of the antithesis between the huntsman and the herdsman in J. R. Bartlett, "The Brotherhood of Edom," *JSOT* 4 (1977) 16. Malul's suggestion ("ʿAQEB 'Heel' and ʿAQAB 'To Supplant'," 206) that Esau became an "outlaw" dwelling in the steppes after losing his legal rights is not cogent in that Esau was already a "man of the field" before any dealings with Jacob.

21   RSV: "quiet"; JPS: "mild." See Hendel, *Epic*, 112 (= "mild"); cf. n. 35; Speiser, *Genesis*, 193 (= "retiring"); Warmoes, "Jacob ravit la bénédiction d'Isaac," 18 (= "homme tranquille"). These renderings seem inconsistent with the later characterization of Jacob whose reputation was that he had "striven with God and men and had prevailed" (Gen 32:29). Source critics have identified Gen 25:37-34 and Gen 32:22-32 as Yahwistic, so that these different characterizations—if one accepted that תָּם meant "mild" or the like—could not be explained by being imbedded in discrete sources. See M. Noth, *A History of Pentateuchal Traditions* (Englewood Cliffs: Prentice-Hall, 1972) 264-65. Fokkelman (*Narrative Art*, 91) translates "bent on one purpose," which has a moral connotation in the sense of "single-mindedness," but not necessarily in the sense of "upright."

22   See S. D. Walters, "Jacob Narrative," *ABD* 3.600; Alter, *Art*, 43.

23   Alter, *Art*, 43.

BLESSING AND FUTURE

Esau brackets the story in which his rightful blessing as the first-born is cynically taken away from him by means of the plot Rebekah hatched and Jacob executed (Gen 27:1-45). Poised to receive Isaac's blessing, Esau needed only to hunt game, prepare his father's favorite dish, and receive the coveted prize (Gen 27:1-4). One wonders at this juncture whether Esau's procuring the blessing will nullify the effects of having lost the birthright. At the very least, getting the blessing should even things out somewhat. But when the episode has concluded, Esau has lost both birthright and blessing.

Seen from one angle, this turn of events simply fulfills the future which God had predicted for the elder scion (Gen 25:23). Seen from another angle, Esau is actually the only sympathetic actor in the scene—the others are seriously flawed. Granted, Isaac did nothing immoral. Still, he appears incompetent, confused, and helpless. As for Rebekah, her actions were as dubious as they were brilliant and duplicitous.[24] Like Jacob in the birthright account, she appears to have been waiting for an opportunity to make a bold, decisive move (Gen 27:5). Without any hesitation or qualms, she apprised Jacob of her strategy and insisted on his complete cooperation (Gen 27:6-10), brushing aside any potential consequences of discovery (Gen 27:11-13). Because we never learn whether Rebekah's efforts to promote Jacob at Esau's expense were a function of her knowledge of the divine oracle or of blatant favoritism, or both (Gen 25:23, 28), her motives remain shrouded. Nonetheless, regardless of motive, her actions cannot be justified morally.

Jacob's behavior was likewise reprehensible. Initially protesting his mother's tactics, his sole concern was the possibility of being discovered (Gen 27:11-12). Once he agreed to go ahead with the ruse, he lied cooly and evidently without compunction when he stood

---

24 Christine Garside Allen ("On Me Be the Curse, My Son!" in M. Buss [ed.], *Encounter with the Text: Form and History in the Hebrew Bible* [SemSup 8; Philadelphia: Fortress; Missoula: Scholars Press, 1979] 163-71) argues that Rebekah should be viewed positively in this story in that she made it possible for God's will to be accomplished. She notes that Jewish exegetical sources are generally more positive about Rebekah than Christian ones. While it is true that God's will is made possible by Rebekah's actions, one need not construe those actions as necessarily positive or moral. This would not be the only time that a biblical character "meant it for evil while God meant it for good" (e.g. Gen 45:5-8; 50:20).

alone before his father. Remarkably, the first time Jacob, who will become one of Israel's patriarchal triumvirate, is asked his name he prevaricates: "I am Esau your firstborn" (Gen 27:19).[25] When pressed, he reaffirms the lie (Gen 27:24). Equally, the first time Jacob mentioned God, he was dishonest. Asked how he had caught game so quickly, Jacob responded, "Because Yahweh your God helped me out" (Gen 27:20).[26] Indeed, the only time Jacob told the truth in the entire pericope was when he reminded his mother that he was an אִישׁ חָלָק, a "smooth man," and therefore apt to be detected (Gen 27:11). There is a definite *double entendre* in this phrase, meaning literally that Jacob was not hirsute and metaphorically that he was "smooth," "slick," or "slippery" in the sense of being untrustworthy.[27] In addition to these instances of self-incrimination, Jacob's character is divulged by other voices. Isaac told Esau that "your brother came with guile and took your blessing" (בָּא אָחִיךָ בְּמִרְמָה וַיִּקַּח בִּרְכָתֶךָ; Gen 27:35). Esau's verdict was more damning: "Is he not well named Jacob, since he has supplanted me these two times: my birthright he took and now my blessing he took" (הֲכִי קָרָא שְׁמוֹ יַעֲקֹב וַיַּעְקְבֵנִי זֶה פַעֲמַיִם אֶת־בְּכֹרָתִי לָקָח וְהִנֵּה עַתָּה לָקַח בִּרְכָתִי; Gen 27:36).[28]

However, even though Jacob was complicitous in his mother's scheme and robbed Esau of something precious for a second time, he will nevertheless be privileged to carry forward the ancestral promise (see Gen 28:2-4, 13-15). The narrative never downplays Jacob's mendacity. Still, Jacob's moral failures do not disqualify him from fulfilling his divinely appointed destiny. At the same time, there is more to Esau's future than commonly perceived, both in terms of his

---

25   The next time Jacob offers his name, it serves as a confession (Gen 32:27). Note that he does not name himself explicitly when he encounters his mother's family (Gen 29:12). Walters ("Jacob," 605) suggests that Jacob's providing his name to the mysterious "man" with whom he wrestled functions as the confession which is missing from Jacob's prayer in Gen 32:9-12.

26   See Warmoes, "Jacob ravit la bénédiction d'Isaac," 22: "Pour se tirer d'embarras et rendre le mensonge plus efficace, il va jusqu'à faire appel à Yahvé lui-même!"

27   Compare verbal and nominal forms of חלק in Isa 30:10; Ezek 12:24; Ps 5:10 (Eng. 5:9); 12:3-5 (Eng. 12:2-4); Prov 2:16; 5:3; 7:5; 26:28; 28:23; 29:5; Dan 11:32; cf. Dicou, *Edom*, 603. Also see Walters, "Jacob Narrative," 603.

28   For the manner in which the Genesis narrator uses other voices as "displaced personae" for his own voice, see Michael Fishbane, *Biblical Interpretation in Ancient Israel* (Oxford: Clarendon, 1985) 377. Compare Gen 29:25-26.

personal fortunes and the difference he makes to Jacob's future and therefore to the ancestral promise. This may be seen preliminarily in a comparison of the two futures Isaac outlined for his sons.

There is no doubt that Jacob receives a primary blessing while Esau receives something secondary.[29] This is underscored in two ways. The first is by the way the language of blessing "surrounds" Jacob. Except for Isaac's preliminary arrangements (Gen 27:4), virtually every reference to blessing in the rest of the pericope is directed toward Jacob (Gen 27:19, 23, 25, 27, 30). This is the case even though Isaac *thinks* he is addressing Esau, but the reader knows that Jacob is the one actually being addressed. When Esau's return brings the deception to light, Isaac proceeds to confirm Jacob's blessing (Gen 27:33, 35). For Esau's part, he is relegated to repeating his father's bad news and begging for his own blessing, even if only one (Gen 27:31, 34, 36, 38). Even after this, Isaac does not "bless," he only "answers" (Gen 27:39). The second way the primacy of Jacob's blessing is highlighted is by the content. Jacob's future is without question to be preferred over Esau's.

However, though perhaps not a full-fledged blessing, the content of Isaac's pronouncement allows us to consider it much more positively than a curse.[30] In fact, regarding the issue of future prosperity, Esau fares virtually as well as Jacob. This has been obscured by translators and interpreters who have insisted on treating Isaac's two statements as antitheses.[31] But Isaac promises that both his sons will enjoy the benefits "of the dew of heaven" and "of the fat of the land" (Gen 27:27b-28, 39). In both instances, the מִן is partitive, rather than partitive in the first and privative in the second. Perhaps Jacob's blessing is to be seen as more fulsome than Esau's — given the fuller expression and concentration of vocabulary — but

---

29   Fokkelman argues that the "second blessing" (i.e. Esau's) shows that the story is equally concerned with Esau. *Narrative Art*, 100.

30   Boecker refers to what Esau receives from his father as a curse even though he grants the technical lanuage of curse is missing. See Hans Jochen Boecker, *1. Moses 25,12–37,1 Isaak und Jakob* (Zürcher Bibelkommentar; H. H. Schmid, ed.; Zürich: Theologischer Verlag, 1992) 50.

31   So RSV and NRSV (but see the footnote). See John R. Bartlett, "Edom in the Nonprophetical Corpus," in Edelman (ed.), *You Shall Not Abhor an Edomite*, 17; Dicou, *Edom*, 119; Fokkelman, *Narrative Art*, 101, 111; Syrén, *Forsaken*, 99; Claus Westermann, *Genesis 12-36* (Minneapolis: Augsburg, 1985) 27. Westermann rejects the interpretation, however, that the expression is "virtually a curse."

that does not negate the fact that both are promised economic
security.[32] This interpretation will be borne out later when Esau is
shown to have become wealthy in his own right (e.g. Gen 32:7 [Eng.
32:6]; 33:1, 9; 36:6-7).

It is the second part of the respective blessings that is truly anti-
podal. Jacob is promised service, deference, and lordship from
"peoples and nations" (לְאֻמִּים/עַמִּים) and his brother(s) (Gen 27:29).[33]
But Esau is destined to live by the sword (וְעַל־חַרְבְּךָ תִחְיֶה) and serve
his brother (וְאֶת־אָחִיךָ תַּעֲבֹד; Gen 27:40). At the same time, one day
Esau will break free and remove Jacob's yoke from his neck.[34]

By all means, Jacob got the better bargain. But the distinction is
not that Jacob is blessed and Esau is cursed—the distinction is that
the twins have received different kinds of blessings. Esau will never
attain Jacob's role and status, nor will he ever be the "child of promise" who bears Israel's glorious future (see Gen 28:3-4, 10-15; 35:9-
12). But there are indications that Esau's prospects for the future
were better than a wronged and rejected brother/son might have
expected.[35] There are glimmers of this before the narrative leaves
Esau in the background and concentrates exclusively on the fugitive
Jacob for the next twenty years. First, when it becomes necessary for
Jacob to flee (Gen 27:41–28:2), we are struck by the ironical fact
that Jacob the "child of promise" is forced to vacate (Gen 27:41–
28:5) the "land of promise" while Esau, without birthright or
primary blessing, gets to remain in the land. Second, the last thing
Esau did before dropping out of the story for a period was try to
make amends for the consternation his Hittite wives caused (Gen
26:34-35; 27:46). It is noteworthy that Esau took his next wife from
within the family as a direct response to the disappointment
registered by his parents (Gen 28:6-9).[36]

---

[32]   So JPS. See Walters, "Jacob Narrative," 601-602; I. Willi-Plein, "Genesis
27 als Rebekkageschichte: Zu einem historiographischen Kunstgriff der biblischen
Vätergeschichten," *TZ* 45 (1989) 320-22: "vom Fetten der Erde her wird dein
Wohnsitz sein und vom Tau des Himmels von oben."

[33]   On the last line of the blessing and its relationship to Gen 12:3 and Num
24:9b, see Westermann, *Genesis*, 441.

[34]   On taking תָּרִיד from רוד, see Fokkelman, *Narrative Art*, 112 n. 37.

[35]   Walters, "Jacob Narrative," 602.

[36]   See Syrén, *Forsaken Firstborn*, 121. Hendel notes (*Epic*, 148) that when
Esau marries Ishmael's daughter, he takes a "proper wife."

REUNION

Esau disappears into the background of the story for some twenty years while the spotlight is on Jacob's conflicted encounters with his uncle Laban (Gen 28:10-31:54). Once a peaceful separation has finally been negotiated, Jacob and his vast company leave Laban, at which point Esau once again appears on the horizon. The preparations for the difficult meeting with Esau become frantic when Jacob's messengers bring word that Esau "is coming to meet you and four-hundred men are with him" (וְגַם הֹלֵךְ לִקְרָאתְךָ וְאַרְבַּע־מֵאוֹת אִישׁ עִמּוֹ ; Gen 32:7 [Eng. 32:6]). Jacob's alarm (Gen 32:8 [Eng. 32:7]) is due to his surmise that the "men" with Esau are doubtless armed.[37] At this point in the drama there is every reason to side with Jacob and be leery of Esau's motives. Can there be any doubt that Esau, just as he threatened so long ago (Gen 27:41), is intent on avenging Jacob's heartless theft of the blessing? Of course, Esau had said—and Jacob had been informed of this—that he would not harm his brother while Isaac was alive, something that Jacob had either forgotten or chose to ignore, unless he now presumed that his father had died (Gen 27:41-45).

Every one of Jacob's actions as he braces for Esau's dreaded arrival are telling. In the first instance, Jacob instructed his messengers to locate Esau and let him know two things: (a) that Jacob was exceedingly wealthy, and (b) that Jacob was seeking an accommodation (וָאֶשְׁלְחָה לְהַגִּיד לַאדֹנִי לִמְצֹא־חֵן בְּעֵינֶיךָ ; Gen 32:5-6). Nothing whatsoever is said about offering an apology or expressing a desire for establishing a fraternal relationship.[38] Jacob's message is little more than a thinly disguised offer of a bribe.[39]

Secondly, Jacob moves to cut his losses by dividing his camp once he is convinced that Esau is about to attack (Gen 32:8-9). Retention of as much wealth as possible appears to be what motivates him at this point.

---

37 Of course, sometimes לִקְרַאת is used to indicate military confrontation. See Judg 7:24; 20:25, 31; 1 Sam 4:1; 1 Kgs 20:27, etc. Still, there is nothing explicit in the text to suggest that Esau's men are armed retainers.

38 One might speak of "re-establishing" a fraternal relationship, but strictly speaking Jacob and Esau never had one. They are never described as having a single amicable encounter. Walter Brueggemann (*Genesis* [Atlanta: John Knox, 1982] 262) comments on this passage, "There is no hint of remorse on his [i.e. Jacob's] part."

39 Coats ("Strife Without Reconciliation," 103) correctly sees that Jacob prepares the present "as a means for buying off the anger of his brother."

Thirdly, Jacob offers a quintessential "foxhole" prayer (Gen 32:10-13 [Eng. 32:9-12]). But it is not a prayer of confession, for it lacks any acknowledgement of wrongdoing.[40] Commendably, Jacob admits to being unworthy of the divine benefits extended to him, but this is not a confession per se.[41] His desperate petition for rescue from Esau is based entirely on an appeal to Yahweh's promises, not on any expression of remorse for the wrong he had perpetrated against his brother (cf. Gen 28:15).

Fourthly, Jacob's veiled offer of a bribe becomes overt. He arranged for a gift of animals to be presented to Esau—the number is staggering (Gen 32:15-16 [Eng. 32:14-15]). Any gift this lavish is a bribe all but impossible to refuse. The reader does not have to guess about Jacob's motives in preparing this unbelievably magnificent present. By means of interior dialogue, his purpose is laid bare: "For he thought, 'I will *cover his face* [i.e. appease him] with the present advancing before me; thus, afterwards when I see his face perhaps he will *lift up my face* [i.e. forgive or accept me]'" (כִּי־אָמַר אֲכַפְּרָה פָנָיו בַּמִּנְחָה הַהֹלֶכֶת לְפָנָי וְאַחֲרֵי־כֵן אֶרְאֶה פָנָיו אוּלַי יִשָּׂא פָנָי; Gen 32:21).[42]

Strictly speaking, Jacob's all-night wrestling encounter with the "man" (אִישׁ) is not parallel to the previous four prepatory moves in that Jacob did not initiate this action (Gen 32:23-33 [Eng. 32:22-32]). At the same time, this mysterious event is the culmination of Jacob's just concluded actions. For that matter, it is the culmination of Jacob's entire life up to this point, because the unnamed man symbolizes every person with whom Jacob ever struggled—Esau, Isaac, Laban. Still, the "man" at the beginning of the encounter is undoubtedly God at the end, as the ineffability of the divine name and Jacob's recognition of the divine face indicate. Thus, this strange episode blends Jacob's conflicts with people and God into a single event.[43] In any case, after this final episode it is at last time for Jacob to meet his estranged brother.

As the reunion scene of Genesis 32 unfolds, the prophecy that

---

40 Walters, "Jacob Narrative," 605. Fokkelman (*Narrative Art*, 204) regards the prayer as "impressive" and faithfully expressed.

41 The verb קָטֹנְתִּי suggests not only unworthiness, but alludes to Jacob's being the younger (קָטָן; see Gen 27:15, 42). See Brueggemann, *Genesis*, 264; Walters, "Jacob Narrative," 605.

42 Procksch notes (cited by Westermann, *Genesis 12-36*, 510) that כפר פנים always connotes guilt. Compare Prov 16:14.

43 Walters, "Jacob Narrative," 605.

Jacob was to be lord and master over his brother appears to be reversed, at least temporarily (vv. 5, 6, 19, 21 [Eng. 4, 5, 18, 20]).[44] This reversal is also indicated when Jacob bows low in anticipation of a reunion whose outcome he hopes will be benign, but fears may be deadly (see Gen 32:12, 21 [Eng. 32:11, 20]). Finally, the dramatic tension that had been building since Jacob knew that Esau was on his way is released. A succession of verbs having Esau as subject shows that the reunion will not only be peaceful, but perhaps conciliatory and constructive: "Esau ran to meet him, embraced him, fell on his neck, and kissed him" (וַיָּרָץ עֵשָׂו לִקְרָאתוֹ וַיְחַבְּקֵהוּ וַיִּפֹּל עַל־צַוָּארָו וַיִּשָּׁקֵהוּ; Gen 33:4).[45] A fifth successive verb, this time with a plural subject, puts an exclamation mark on this moving scene: "they wept" (וַיִּבְכּוּ; Gen 33:4). The last time Esau wept, it was alone, because of what Jacob had done to him (Gen 27:38).[46]

In the context of this stunning encounter a great deal is revealed about Esau. First, he completely forswore violence and revenge. His comported himself as a brother, not an enemy bent on getting even. No explanation for this change of heart is offered, but every indication in the text is that Esau was without question sincere.[47] Second, Esau had also become rich during Jacob's sojourn with Laban. This was first hinted at when Jacob's messengers mentioned that four hundred men were with Esau, for only a man of means could have so many at his disposal. More significantly, Esau's response to Jacob's

---

44 Fokkelman, *Narrative Art*, 200.

45 This succession of verbs serves to remind us of the succession in the birthright episode. See Hendel, *Epic*, 130. Note a similar succession in the scene where Laban meets Jacob for the first time, with the exception of falling on the neck (Gen 29:13). Boecker (*Mose*, 107) remarks on this reunion scene: "An keiner Stelle des Alten Testaments aber steht das alles, wie hier, beieinander, wird von einer so herzlichen und intensiven Begrüßung erzählt wie von dieser."

46 Jacob weeps one other time in the story—when he meets Rachel (Gen 29:11).

47 Jacob accepts that Esau is sincere, but sees this not as a function of moral character but on the mood swings attributable to a wild man who is given to rash anger or plentious compassion. However, Jacob (*Genesis*, 645-46) argues that the refusal of the gift is insincere. Holmgren ("Holding Your Own Against God!" 14) acknowledges that Christian readers of this narrative tend to sympathize with Esau and criticize Jacob. But this is moralistic in his view. For Holmgren, a Jewish perspective is more on the mark: " . . . Jacob is the sincere participant in this meeting, and Esau is the manipulative, crafty one who covers up his vengeful desires with insincere words and acts of love."

offer of the fabulous present calls attention to his impressive holdings, "I have plenty, my brother, keep what you have for yourself"
(יֶשׁ־לִי רָב אָחִי יְהִי לְךָ אֲשֶׁר־לָךְ; Gen 33:8-9).[48] Hearing about Esau's
wealth makes us recall that Isaac's pronouncement concerning his
elder son included prosperity (Gen 27:39). Later on, we discover
that Esau's wealth was the reason he had to move to Seir, since the
land could not support the wealth that both he and his brother had
accumulated.[49]

Third, and most importantly, Esau's actions in the reunion scene
underscored his extraordinary graciousness. Esau's refusing the
present which was really a bribe gave concrete expression to his
unconditional acceptance of Jacob. Esau did not so much as ask for
an apology. Jacob's reaction to Esau's refusal provides a fitting
commentary on their exchange: "No, please, if I have found favor in
your eyes (i.e. 'been regarded graciously by you'), then take my gift
from my hand, for truly seeing your face is the same as seeing God's
face, because you have treated me so favorably" (אַל־נָא אִם־נָא מָצָאתִי
חֵן בְּעֵינֶיךָ וְלָקַחְתָּ מִנְחָתִי מִיָּדִי כִּי עַל־כֵּן רָאִיתִי פָנֶיךָ כִּרְאֹת פְּנֵי אֱלֹהִים
וַתִּרְצֵנִי; Gen 33:10).[50] Jacob, the recepient of God's elective grace
and therefore the one destined to bear the ancestral promise into the
future, began to understand the nature of that grace by experiencing
the munificent generosity of Esau, whom God had bypassed, at least
in terms of the ancestral promise. It is telling that this was Jacob's
second encounter with the "face of God."[51] The first had been in the
wrestling match with the "man" who turned out mysteriously and
inexplicably to be God (Gen 32:23-33 [Eng. 32:22-32]). The second
was in the reunion with a brother from whom he rightfully expected
only animosity and aggression, but from whom he received

---

[48] W. G. Plaut ("Genesis," in *Torah: A Modern Commentary* [New York:
Union of American Hebrew Congregations, 1981] 219) plays down Esau's initial
refusal of the present by suggesting that it was an "old custom" to preface the
acceptance of a large gift by first politely refusing it. Equally, he sees no
significance in Jacob's saying that he saw the "face of God" in Esau, dismissing
this as "extreme flattery."

[49] See Gen 36:6-8. Note the similarity of the language with that used in the
separation of Abram and Lot (Gen 13:5-7).

[50] We are likely supposed to see a connection between Hebrew רצצ in Gen
25:22 and רצה; that is, the twins relationship began with "struggle" (רצצ), but
concluded with "favor" (רצה).

[51] See Walters, "Jacob Narrative," 605; Coats, "Reconciliation Without
Strife," 101 (see nn. 40-41).

abounding grace.

Though he had not been seeking a reward, in the end Esau gets a most surprising one. With only one exception, every reference to Jacob's present in chapters 32 and 33 uses the word מִנְחָה. But when Jacob gets to the point where he insists that Esau accept the present he has prepared, another word is employed. The reader is astounded to see that in the end Jacob offers nothing less than the *blessing* back to Esau: "Take now my blessing . . . " (קַח־נָא אֶת־בִּרְכָתִי; Gen 33:11)! In effect, the blessing which Jacob had stolen has now been symbolically returned.[52] To be sure, this will not alter God's elective plans for the twins, but it serves to relativize the crooked machinations whereby Jacob gained ascendancy over Esau and emphasizes that Esau's future is also a function of providence.

Ironically, Isaac had predicted that Esau would live by his sword and one day break Jacob's yoke from his neck.[53] But the repeat of the word "neck" in the reunion scene dramatically illustrates that Isaac's prophecy was reversed. Esau did not use the sword to remove Jacob's yoke. Instead, with a gesture that can only be described as accepting and reconciling, he fell on his brother's neck and by that action "freed" himself. Forgiveness, not the sword, had become Esau's preferred instrument in his dealings with his brother. It was completely appropriate that Jacob should view this gracious display as comparable to divine grace. In more ways than one, seeing Esau's face was tantamount to seeing the "face of God."

Standard scholarly efforts to interpret this scene as merely a retrojection of later friendly national relationships between Edom and Israel into the personal lives of the country's respective eponymous ancestors unfortunately blunt the poignant theological emphasis of this narrative. Likewise, the persistent efforts of interpreters to view

---

52 Fokkelman, *Narrative Art*, 234.

53 In other contexts, having the yoke on one's neck broken is a figure for liberation. See Bob Becking, "'I will break his yoke from off your neck': Remarks on Jeremiah xxx 4-11," in A. S. Van der Woude (ed.), *New Avenues in the Study of the Old Testament: A Collection of Old Testament Studies Published on the Occasion of the Fiftieth Anniversary of the Oudtestamentisch Werkgezelschap and the Retirement of Prof. M. J. Mudder* (OTS 25; Leiden: Brill, 1989) 63-76. Thompson ("Conflict Theme," 17) suggests that this text reflects a socio-political situation that has been retrojected into the Jacob-Esau ficitional tale. On the meaning of תְּרִיד in Gen 27:40 (cf. Jer 2:31; Ps 55:3 [Eng. 55:2]) see Fokkelman, *Narrative Art*, 112.

this particular pericope and the whole Jacob-Esau story in general against a socio-political background obscures the theological issues being addressed. For example, Crüsemann argues that the reconciliation between the twins means that the divine word predicting on-going national tension has not been fulfilled.[54] But in the context of the ancestral stories in Genesis, the divine word means primarily that Esau/Edom ("two *nations* are in your womb") will be subordinate to Jacob/ Israel *with respect to to the ancestral promises* and not necessarily with respect to ancient Near Eastern *Realpolitik*. The divine will is achieved by Jacob's becoming the child of promise and not by a fatalistic, inexorably determined political fate of the countries Israel and Edom.[55]

Of course, the reunion between the estranged brothers, though truly impressive, was not as complete as it might have been. Given that Laban and Jacob had made a mutual agreement (וְעַתָּה לְכָה נִכְרְתָה בְרִית אֲנִי וָאָתָּה) and had eaten a meal together (וַיֹּאכְלוּ) when they decided to settle their differences (Gen 31:44, 46), one should perhaps expect those same ingredients in the reconciliation between Esau and Jacob.[56] Be that as it may, there is no question that Jacob is reticent about accepting Esau's offer of assistance and, apparently, hospitality in Seir. Jacob implied that he and his company would join Esau there in a short while—allowing only for the slower pace required by nursing animals and small children—but in fact he made no effort to head toward Esau's home (Gen 33:12-17). It turns out that Jacob, for whatever reason, preferred buying land from Hamor to settling down with or near Esau (Gen 33:18-20; cf. 34:1-31). Granted, this move made good sense in light of the direction in which the larger narrative was going, but at this juncture there is no suggestion of nobility or awareness of ultimate providential purpose on Jacob's part. It is as though Jacob does not quite trust Esau to

---

[54]   Frank Crüsemann, "Dominion, Guilt, and Reconciliation: The Contribution of the Jacob Narrative in Genesis to Political Ethics," *Semeia* 66 (1994) 6.

[55]   Crüsemann's efforts ("Dominion," 75) to read this story in a general political context rather than the specific canonical context leads him to view the text finally as having to do with the ethical problem of nations exercising dominion over other nations. That this has been a problem over the course of human history cannot be denied. But that this is the problem brought to the forefront by the ancestral narratives in Genesis seems utterly contrived.

[56]   Walters, "Jacob Narrative," 605; Coats, "Strife Without Reconciliation," 103.

continue in the gracious mode already exhibited. The brothers come together only once more in the story, when they bury Isaac their father (Gen 35:27-29).

ESAU'S FUTURE

In its present placement, Genesis 36 is one of two genealogies that brackets the Jacob cycle. Since these genealogies feature sons outside of God's elective purposes for Israel's future, the structure as well as the content of the text underscores the fact that Jacob and Jacob alone is the bearer of the ancestral promise.[57] At the same time, Ishmael and Esau both are destined to have good futures in spite of the fact that they do not fit into God's plans for Israel.[58] In Esau's case, his claim on the future derived from his father's pronouncements after bestowing the primary blessing on Jacob (Gen 27:39-40). As we saw above, by the time of his reunion with Jacob, he had already become wealthy, thus fulfilling one feature of the paternal blessing.

Genesis 36 also emphasizes Esau's wealth. Indeed, this chapter gives as the reason for Esau's moving to Seir the fact that the land of Canaan was not able to accommodate his vast wealth and that of his brother (Gen 36:6-8).[59] To be sure, in terms of a linear narrative this detail contradicts the fact that Jacob was not wealthy until he returned after the sojourn with Laban. Jacob had even reminded God that when he left Canaan the first time he possessed nothing but his staff (Gen 32:11 [Eng. 32:10]). Since Esau was already wealthy and already resided in Seir at the time of the reunion, how could the separation have been due to the twins' respective holdings? There is no editorial attempt to remove this discrepancy by conflating the separate sources. Instead, the chronological problem raised by the textual structure is simply moved to the background, while the larger point that Esau's wealth was equal to Jacob's is highlighted. Thus, Isaac's prediction that Esau's future would be just as prosperous as

---

57   Walters, "Jacob Narrative," 599. For a comparison of Ishmael and Esau, see Dicou, *Edom*, 132-135.

58   With respect to Ishmael, see Gen 16:7-15; 21:13-21; 25:12-18. Ironically, Ishmaelites, descended from Abraham and the Egyptian Hagar, were the ones who sold Joseph to the Egyptians (Gen 16:1; 37:25-28).

59   As noted, the language is reminiscent of Gen 13:5-13, when Abram's and Lot's holdings were too great for the land to sustain. That situation also led to a parting of the ways, with Abram staying in the land of promise and Lot moving outside of it (Gen 13:9-13).

Jacob's is confirmed by an artistic narrative account (Gen 33:1, 9) and this more straightforward genealogical account (Gen 36:6-8).

But Esau's future included more than wealth. Esau also became a country: Edom. Three times in the chapter we encounter the explanatory gloss regarding Esau: הוּא אֱדוֹם (36:1, 8, 19). While I agree that these glosses are secondary, I submit that they are to be regarded as theologically and literarily interpretive.[60] These glosses make explicit what is only implicit in the birth story of the twins. There Esau is associated with אֱדוֹם and שֵׂעִיר in the puns involving his complexion and hirsuteness (שֵׂעָר/אַדְמוֹנִי; Gen 25:25; מִן־הָאָדם הָאָדם הַזֶּה; 25:30). Now, however, Esau's connection with Edom and Seir is manifest. In addition, Esau is referred to as the ancestor/father of Edom (vv. 9, 43). Whatever historical reasons there may have been for equating Esau and Edom, in the present textual set-up this equation now serves to underscore Esau's positive future.[61] This chapter celebrates Esau's posterity by providing an elaborate genealogy which extends Esau's descendants well into the future and by making clear that Esau the person eventually became Edom the nation (cf. Gen 25:23: לְאֻמִּים/גוֹיִם).

The text even makes the point that Edom had kings before Israel did (Gen 36:31; וְאֵלֶּה הַמְּלָכִים אֲשֶׁר מָלְכוּ בְּאֶרֶץ אֱדוֹם לִפְנֵי מְלָךְ־מֶלֶךְ לִבְנֵי יִשְׂרָאֵל; cf. 1 Chr 1:43). Ironically, although God had expressly promised that kings would issue from Jacob (Gen 35:11; see also 17:6 [Abram], 16 [Sarah]), Esau—who never received such a promise—had kings issue from him first. In spite of ambivalent attitudes toward kings and kingship in many biblical passages (e.g. 1 Samuel 8), kings are viewed as an overall positive in the ancestral texts (cf. Gen 49:10; Deut 17:14-20). Thus, Yahweh's statements that there would be kings in the ancestors' future can only be seen as an enrichment of the general promise. Consequently, Edom's having kings (Gen 36:31-39) prior to Israel means that Israel had to wait to enjoy some future benefits which Edom already experienced.

Moreover, according to Deuteronomy Esau's future nationhood and land holdings were an explicit function of God's provision. Israel was forbidden from taking any of Edom's territory, precisely because God had bequeathed the land (Deut 2:5, 12, 22). In fact,

---

60   See Fishbane, *Biblical Interpretation*, 46; Westermann, *Genesis*, 562.

61   For a historical approach see Ernst A. Knauf, "Alter und Herkunft der edomitischen Königsliste Gen 36,31-39," *ZAW* 97 (1985) 245-53.

there is a striking similarity of vocabulary when one compares Israel's providential fortunes to Edom's. Esau's/Edom's land is a "possession" which Yahweh "gave" (כִּי־יְרֻשָּׁה לְעֵשָׂו נָתַתִּי אֶת־הַר שֵׂעִיר; v. 5). Esau/Edom had its own "conquest" of the land, dispossessing and destroying the previous indigenous inhabitants (וּבְשֵׂעִיר יָשְׁבוּ הַחֹרִים לְפָנִים וּבְנֵי עֵשָׂו יִירָשׁוּם וַיַּשְׁמִידוּם מִפְּנֵיהֶם וַיֵּשְׁבוּ תַחְתָּם; v. 12). The parallel with Israel's and Edom's respective conquests is even made explicit: כַּאֲשֶׁר עָשָׂה יִשְׂרָאֵל לְאֶרֶץ יְרֻשָּׁתוֹ אֲשֶׁר־נָתַן יְהוָה לָהֶם (v. 12).[62] This comparison also obtains in Josh 24:4, where Joshua notes that Esau had received his country from God while Jacob and his children had had to postpone their takeover by diverting to Egypt.

To be sure, nothing could compensate Esau for missing out on being the bearer of the ancestral promise. Due to the inscrutable will of Yahweh, that role was reserved for Jacob. Nevertheless, Esau was blessed with an excellent future consisting of progeny, prosperity, land, statehood, and kings. His own gracious magnimity provided the impetus for reconciliation with the brother he had once despised and vowed to murder. By blood and deportment, he and those descended from him were to have a special relationship with Israel, through whom Yahweh was determined to bless the whole world (Gen 12:1-4). In the end, this relationship was codified in Torah: "You shall not abhor an Edomite, for he is your brother [לֹא־תְתַעֵב אֲדֹמִי כִּי אָחִיךָ הוּא]" (Deut 23:8).

CONCLUSION

If the above analysis is on the mark, it is incumbant upon us to reject simplistic interpretations of Jacob and Esau which view them as one-dimensional opposites. The nuances of the portrayal of the two brothers in Torah mitigate against seeing Jacob as elected, blessed, favored, and righteous while seeing Esau as rejected, cursed, disadvantaged, and unrighteous. There is no denying the strategic importance of Jacob's being chosen over his elder brother to fulfill the salvific role which Yahweh had in mind for the ancestors and their descendants (Gen 12:1-3). But acknowledging that should not obscure either the fact that Esau's future was enviable in many ways

---

62   Similar language occurs in Deut 2:21-22. Note that the descendants of Lot receive similar benefits, presumably by virtue of the relationship to Abram (Deut 2:9-11).

or that his deportment was ultimately commendable, exemplary, and, most importantly, utterly gracious.

In fact, leaving *Heilsgeschichte* aside for the moment, from some perspectives Esau's future was equal to if not superior to Jacob's. Esau acquired his wealth and children in Canaan, the land of promise, whereas Jacob acquired his wealth and children outside the land. Esau took ownership of his divinely promised national territory almost immediately whereas Jacob's descendants had to undergo a long period of foreign subjugation first (cf. Gen 15:13; 37–50; Exodus 1–12; Josh 24:4) And Esau/Edom could boast kings long before that was possible for Jacob/Israel.

Nevertheless, in spite of this positive slant Esau/Edom is vilified unmercifully in the prophetic materials. As noted, scholars have attempted to account for this phenomenon by correlating periods of extreme political hostility between Israel and Edom with the negative prophetic texts. But these efforts have been frustrated by two factors. One is that the historical record is insufficient to remove the necessity of speculation. For example, Botterweck is insistent that the harsh passage in Malachi (1:5)—where Yahweh loves Jacob and hates Esau—is related to actual historical events: "Edoms Untergang ist also Auswirkung des göttlichen Hasses und Fluches wegen Edoms Schuld und Vergehen gegen Israel." At the same time, he admits there is no way to determine to which events this might refer: "Auf welche konkreten politischen Ereignisse der Prophet hier anspielt, ist nicht auszumachen."[63]

The other factor is that nothing in the historical record seems adequate to explain Edom's attaining its "most hated nation" status. If it is true that Edom in the prophetic corpus has become the archetype of Israelite enemies, it is difficult to imagine what in the historical record justified that dubious assessment. One could understand Egypt, Assyria, or Babylon achieving this almost legendary reputation as the quintessential Israelite enemy, but what would explain a bit historical player like Edom filling that role? In my view, most explanations for this fact fall short.[64]

---

[63]   Botterweck, "Jakob habe ich lieb," 38. See the various historical reconstructions in Edelman (ed.), *You Shall Not Abhor an Edomite.*

[64]   See, for example, Beth Glazier-McDonald's assertion ("Edom in the Prophetical Corpus," in Edelman [ed.], *You Shall Not Abhor an Edomite*, 31) that Edom's transformation from *an* enemy to *the* enemy par excellence is a function of the Edomite move into southern Judah, which was seen as Yahweh's, and therefore

I have proposed that the canonical ordering of the Esau/Edom traditions have the effect of drawing primary attention to two issues. One is the fact that Esau is Jacob's brother.[65] The second is that theological perspectives are brought to the fore while historical considerations are relegated to the background.

On the matter of brotherhood, we have seen that Esau was at first presented in rather uncomplimentary terms in Genesis. Yet, in the end, in spite of his having to give way to Jacob as the divinely chosen bearer of the ancestral promise, Esau not only acted most admirably, but was by his twin's own admission sufficiently gracious to reflect the face of God (Gen 33:10). Esau behaved in a truly fraternal manner toward his brother despite what he had suffered at Jacob's hands. There was no reason that such a posture could not have characterized Edom's relationship toward Israel in perpetuity.

Esau's remarkable behavior may be instructively contrasted with the reaction of Cain to Yahweh's rejection of his offering and acceptance of Abel's (Gen 4:1-16). This also is a story in which one brother is disadvantaged through no particular fault of his own. Cain could have dealt with the situation appropriately had he only heeded Yahweh's admonition. But he sought to avenge his rejection and his brother's acceptance. The result was murder and judgment.[66] In stark contrast, Esau, who was perhaps even more disadvantaged,

---

Israel's, exclusive territory. While this inference may be possible or even reasonable to a degree, it still does not account for Edom's special status. Why should Edom elicit more hatred than any other country that usurped Israelite territory?

65   Bartlett rehearses the possibilities for why Edom came to be equated with Esau. He finally settles ("The Brotherhood of Edom," *JSOT* 4 [1977] 7) on the religious similarities between the two countries. He lists the "brotherhood" texts as Gen 25:19-34; 27:27-29, 39-40; 36:1, 8, 9, 19, 43; Num 20:14-21; Deut 2:4, 8; 23:7 (MT 23:8); Jer 49:7-11; Amos 1:11; Obad 10, 12; Mal 1:2-4.

66   I have argued elsewhere ("The 'Ground' for Cain's Rejection (Gen 4): *'adamah* in the Context of Gen 1–11," *ZAW* 104 [1992] 319-32) that Cain's rejection was a function of the cursed אֲדָמָה and therefore not related to anything he had done. Jewish exegetes have also linked Cain and Esau, although they have tended to see both as equally morally culpable in spite of the fact that Cain committed fratricide whereas Esau forgave and acted graciously toward his brother. See C. T. R. Hayward, "A Portrait of the Wicked Esau in the Targum of Codex Neofiti 1," in D. R. G. Beattie and M. J. McNamara (eds.), *The Aramaic Bible: Targums in their Historical Context* (JSOTSup 166; Sheffield: Sheffield Academic

eschewed the vengeance he had sworn to seek and instead responded
to the brother who had wronged him with forgiving acceptance. Cain
foreswore brotherhood, Esau embraced it. Arguably, Esau's embrace of Jacob after having been so egregiously treated makes Esau
the quintessential gracious brother in TANAK.

Consequently, when Edom departed from the exemplary brotherly
behavior of their eponymous ancestor, it was only natural for them
to be singled out for particular prophetic criticism. It is bad enough
to deal with an enemy who delights in one's misfortune; it is much
worse when that enemy is a brother who once displayed incompar-
able fraternal grace. Esau not only forgave Jacob, he also attempted
to establish a truly brotherly relationship with him (Genesis 33).
Unfortunately, Edom refused to follow in those impressive footsteps.
Thus, Edom's transition from Israel's brother to their archtypical
enemy naturally elicited excessive prophetic opprobrium.

Regardless of whether attitudes toward Edom originally had an
historical aetiology, and regardless of what events might have
prompted such negative feelings on Israel's part, the canonical shaping finally construes the matter theologically. Even Cresson, who
believes that the "damn Edom" syndrome in the prophetic corpus
began as a natural historical reaction, concludes that this reaction was
transformed into a concept of eschatological significance expressing
hope for and confidence in the destruction of the enemies of Israel as
the chosen people.[67] Simian sounds a similar note: "Die prophetisch-
en Worte über/gegen Edom beziehen sich nicht ausschliesslich und
nicht hauptsachlich auf eine historische Auseinandersetzung . . . Die
prophetischen Worte über/gegen Edom sind richtiger als ein Element
innerhalb einer Heilszusage an Jerusalem/ Juda/Israel oder innerhalb
einer Gerichtsankündigung gegen alle Völker zu bezeichnen."[68]

Theological nuances are no less evident in the depiction of Esau in
Genesis. At first his character is suspect, for he is rash, crude,
stupid, and short-sighted. As such, he is easily taken advantage of by
his duplicitous brother and scheming mother. It is hard to shake the

---

Press, 1994) 303-308.

[67]   See B. C. Cresson, "Israel and Edom: A Study of the Anti-Edom Bias in
Old Testament Religion," (dissertation, Duke University, 1963) 51, cited by Dicou,
Edom, 188.

[68]   H. Simian, *Die theologische Nachgeschichte der Prophetie Ezechiels: Form-
und traditionskritische Untersuchung zu Ez 6; 35; 36* (FB 14: Würzburg: Echter,
1974) 321.

feeling that Esau more or less *deserved* to be betrayed and shunted aside! But in the end Esau acted the way one would suppose the "chosen" ancestor should have acted, with acceptance, forgiveness, and graciousness. Jacob was called to be תָּם, but Esau first behaved as though he were תָּם. Had personal merit been a criterion for selection as bearer of the promise—which, of course, it was not[69]— Esau would have held his own vis à vis Jacob.[70] Be that as it may, Esau was destined only to be Jacob's brother, not the coveted bearer of the ancestral promise. Nevertheless, that circumstance did not prevent him from finally acting graciously toward Jacob, and in that action he allowed his chosen twin to glimpse God's face.

---

[69]   The Apostle Paul makes this point in Rom 9:10-13. See also Botterweck's contention ("Jakob habe ich lieb," 35) that the "love" (= choice) of Jacob and "hatred" (= rejection) of Esau was completely a function of Yahweh's will: "Diese zunächst paradox erscheinende Erklärung der göttlichen Liebe zu Jakob aus dem Haß gegen Esau betont zunächst die Unverdientheit und Ungeschuldetheit der Liebe Jawhes; sie gründet einzig under allein in der freien und souveränen Entscheidung Gottes. Liebe und Haß, Vorzug und Hintansetzung, Erwählung und Verwerfung sind Gottes Entscheidung, über die er keine Rechenschaft schuldet."

[70]   Jacob shines morally for the first time when he operates as a religious reformer in Genesis 35.

SAMUEL THE PROPHET
A LINK BETWEEN MOSES AND THE KINGS

Rolf Rendtorff

"In those days there was no king in Israel; everyone did what was right in his own eyes." The last sentence of the Book of Judges sums up what had happened in those dark days. The reader knows that "what was right in one's own eyes" could also mean what was "wrong in the eyes of the LORD," as expressed at the very beginning of that period (Judg 2:11). "No king" means no one who would tell the people how to do "what was right in the eyes of the LORD."

In Israel's story as told in the canonical books of the Hebrew Bible the time of the Judges was an intermediate period. Earlier Israel had been guided by Moses who had appeared on the scene at the moment when Israel became a people. Then Joshua continued to lead Israel as Moses' successor and in his name. He knew from Moses' torah what was "the right in the eyes of the LORD." The torah had been all the time his own guide, and at the end of his lifetime he had admonished Israel "to observe and do all that is written in the book of the torah of Moses" (Josh 23:6). But after the whole generation had died that had lived under the guidance of Joshua and of the torah "another generation grew up after them, who did not know the LORD or the work that he had done for Israel" (Judg 2:10; cf. Josh 24:31). Looking from the last sentence of the Book of Judges one might add: They did not know because there was no one to tell them and to guide them.

Then the Book of Samuel begins with the announcement of a particular birth that will be a special gift of God. Reading this in continuity with what has been told before, the reader would expect that now this bad intermediate time will be brought to an end and the impending birth will bring forth a new leader of the people.[1] When

---

[1]   See R. Rendtorff, "The Birth of the Deliverer: 'The Childhood of Samuel' Story in Its Literary Framework," in Rendtorff, *Canon and Theology: Overtures to an Old Testament Theology* (Minneapolis: Fortress, 1993) 135-45.

Hannah prays her psalm she speaks like a prophetess[2] about the king and the מָשִׁיחַ (1 Sam 2:10). But when the child is born and grown up he does not become a king but a prophet. Of course, the praying Hannah was not simply wrong. Yet the king could not come by himself but only by the mediatorship of someone else. If he shall be the מָשִׁיחַ, the anointed one, there must be someone to anoint him. Therefore, the first step to overcome the bad situation must be the birth of the one who will be entitled to anoint a king.

The first definition given about Samuel's office says that "all Israel recognized that Samuel was attested as a prophet of YHWH" (1 Sam 3:20). What makes him a prophet is the "word (or words) of YHWH" that Samuel received and that did not "fall to the ground" (v. 17, 20). But Samuel is "more than a prophet." He is depicted as the leader of the people who acts in different capacities and is generally accepted as the only authority. It is said that he "judged Israel all the time of his life" and that he executed this function in several places around the country (7:15-17). "To judge" obviously means to decide law cases; this is quite clear when Samuel later installs his two sons as judges and they "take bribe and pervert justice" (8:1-3). At that time this seems to be the only office with a nation-wide function and acceptance so that it gave Samuel a corresponding authority. It is also related that Samuel helps Israel when it is oppressed by the Philistines (7:2-14). Obviously he is the only one to whom the people could turn to ask for help. And he does help, but not by military means but by prayer and sacrifice (v. 5, 9).

Samuel's undisputed leading role becomes particularly obvious when the "elders of Israel" come to him and ask him to install a king to govern them "like all the nations" (8:4-5). This is a very ambiguous situation. Samuel is the accepted leader, but at the same moment he is the only one who would have the authority and the power to change the political structure of the nation into a form of government that is common to "all the nations" but had never existed in Israel.

Samuel enters in a discussion with God about whether to accept the request of the people or not (8:6-9). This is of particular importance because in the biblical tradition no one had this kind of immediate encounter with God since Moses. The parallelism between Samuel and Moses will be seen at other points as well (see below). God's

---

2   Cf. *b. Meg.* 14a.

answer is highly ambivalent. On the one hand he sharply criticizes the desire of the people to have a king, declaring: "they have not rejected you, but they have rejected me from being king over them" (v. 7). That shows that the king is not at all what God wants. On the other hand it also stresses that Samuel's leading position, as high as it is, is not independent but is given by God. To contest Samuel's leadership means to question God's own authority. Here the first time the word "king" appears in this context (except in Hannah's prayer). But it is God himself who claims this title.

On the other hand God tells Samuel to accept the people's request (vv. 7a, 9), and by that he opens a new chapter in Israel's history. Kingship is not according to God's original plans. It will be established with his explicit agreement, but it will remain under the condition formulated in Samuel's final admonition: "If" and "if not." If the people and its king will fear and serve and follow the LORD, the kingdom will be lasting; otherwise "the hand of the LORD will be against you and your king" (12:14-15). Obviously the king is not the one to tell the people what is "the right in the eyes of the LORD." He belongs on the side of the people and has to listen and to obey.

It would go beyond the scope of this paper to discuss the problems of the relationship of the two (or three) stories in 1 Samuel 9–11 that relate the beginning of Saul's kingship.[3] In our context the main point is that Samuel is always the acting figure. In chaps. 9–10 there happens what was to be expected from the "prophetic" words of Hannah: Samuel anoints Saul according to God's explicit advise (10:1).[4] In this context Samuel is introduced as "man of God" (9:6-10) and as "seer," with the latter term being explained as an older term for "prophet" (v. 9). Thus the prophet anoints the king, and this is the beginning of kingship in Israel. But also in the other stories in this framework Samuel is the acting one: in 10:17-27 as well as in 11:12-15.

The information we get from these texts is twofold. First, kingship came into being by prophetic activity. Without the prophet there

---

3   See F. Crüsemann, *Der Widerstand gegen das Königtum: Die antiköniglichen Texte des Alten Testamentes und der Kampf um den frühen israelitischen Staat* (WMANT 49; Neukirchen-Vluyn: Neukirchener, 1978) 54-84.

4   Here the word נָגִיד is used instead of "king." This problem cannot be discussed here. In the context it is obvious that Saul becomes king, see 10:16, 24; 11:15.

would be no king. Second, Samuel, the prophet who anointed the
first king, had been the leader of the people before that time. The
figure of Samuel is badly neglected in scholarly literature.[5] Usually
scholars complain that it would be difficult to define what office
Samuel had in historical reality. Was he a priest, a prophet, a judge,
a charismatic leader, or something else? It is true that the texts label
his office or his activities differently. But what unites the different
aspects is the great authority that is ascribed to Samuel in all his
functions. He is *the* leader of the people.

*   *   *

Let us stay here for a moment. The leading position unanimously
ascribed to Samuel by 1 Samuel 3–12 is very unusual in Israel's
history as reported in the Hebrew Bible. Samuel's position is
grounded in two factors: the office of a judge for all Israel, and his
individual divinely decreed legitimacy. The authority coming from
the first factor may not have been that unusual. We are not informed
about the authority that earlier persons enjoyed who are said to have
"judged Israel" (Judg 3:10; 10:2, 3; 12:7, 8-9, 11, 13-14; 15:20;
16:31). A number of them followed one upon the other, in particular
those mentioned in chaps. 10 and 12. Some of them held the office
for decades; but nothing is reported about their official activities and
their reputation.[6] Nevertheless, it might be possible to see Samuel in
continuity with those earlier office-holders.

But this is not the main aspect of Samuel's unusual authority. In 1
Sam 3:19-21 it is clearly said that "all Israel recognized that Samuel
was attested as a prophet of YHWH." How could the Israelites know
what a prophet is? They had no experience at all with prophets. But
the reader knows. Before Samuel there had been one great prophet:
Moses. He was the prophet *par excellence* (Num 12:6-8), and after
him there was no prophet like him (Deut 34:10). But there *are* prophets after him, and the first one is Samuel. He is "attested" (נֶאֱמָן) as
prophet. This sounds like an echo of the divine word about Moses

---

    5   In R. Albertz's two volume *Religionsgeschichte Israels in alttestamentlicher
Zeit* (Göttingen: Vandenhoeck & Ruprecht, 1992; ET: *A History of Israelite Religion
in the Old Testament Period* [2 vols., London: SCM, 1994]) the name of Samuel
does not appear in the index.

    6   This is mainly valid for the so-called "minor judges," while the "major
judges" are not depicted as holders of a specific "office."

that he is "entrusted [נֶאֱמָן] with all my house" (Num 12:7). Even more striking is the parallelism of Samuel and Moses insofar as since Moses no one had had such an immediate encounter with God as Samuel (1 Sam 3:1-18; 8:6-9; 9:15-17; 15:10-11, 16; 16:1-13). In particular when the Israelites demanded a king, there ensued a discussion between Samuel and God (8:6-9) similar to Moses' encounters with God.

The main and basic parallelism between Moses and Samuel is the fact that both actually were the leaders of the people at their time. Yet neither held a definable "office." Rather, they were guided by divine inspiration. This becomes particularly clear in the case of Samuel. We are able to study his position in relation and in contrast to the just established office of the king. The first observation is that kingship has no right of its own. It needs to be established and religiously legitimated by the prophet who acts in the name of God. But from the beginning human kingship contains an element of tension relative to the idea of the kingship of God. One of the main questions for a succesful future of kingship will be whether and how the king will perform his office in concordance with the divine will. This implies that, religiously speaking, the king can never be independent. The prophet will continue to supervise his activities, and draw consequences if necessary. From that point of view the story between Samuel and Saul seems to be exemplary. Saul never reached the required correspondence with the will of God, for whatever reasons. Therefore, ultimately his kingship failed. But the prophet is at hand to anoint a new person as king, again acting by divine advice.

Before tracing the history of prophecy and kingship in their development, let us look back from Samuel to Moses. He is the first leader of Israel. He demonstrates that actually only a person guided directly by God can be the leader of God's people. Even for him it was an extremely difficult task and more than once he felt it to be too heavy to carry (e.g. Exod 32:32; Num 11:14). But in his case there was no discrepancy between the immediate relation to God and the leading of the people. Compared to Samuel, Moses was, so to speak, prophet and king in one person. Therefore he was the ideal leader of Israel—an ideal that never again could be reached after him. And therefore he is called the first prophet who remains a model for all his successors. That Moses even as a prophet was Israel's leader is expressed by Hosea: "Through a prophet the LORD brought Israel up from Egypt, and through a prophet they were guided" (Hos 12:14).

At the beginning of his carreer Samuel also served in both functions: as prophet and as leader of the people. The parallelism to Moses is evident (cf. Jer 15:1; Ps 99:6). But then the political situation caused the people to request a king. This was a turning point in Israel's history. From now on prophecy and kingship are divided. But that means at the same time that from now on there was a permanent tension between kingship and religious leadership.

*   *   *

In the following history of Israel this tension is always present and in a number of cases it becomes virulent. To repeat, the story of Samuel and Saul is exemplary. But also in the following epoch again and again prophets appear, be it to confirm to a king God's consent with his activities and even to herald to him a divine promise, be it to speak against a king who violates God's will and commandments and to announce to him God's judgment and punishment. The appearance of prophets is not at all accidental, rather they are present at many, if not at almost every important or critical point in the history of kingship in Israel and Judah.

Let us look at some relevant examples. The epoch of David and Solomon is framed by a number of prophetic actions and words. At the beginning it is Samuel who anoints David as successor of Saul who failed (1 Sam 16:1-13). In a sense God himself erred when he appointed Saul who then showed himself to be the wrong person. Now David is bearing great expectations. They are later confirmed by Nathan who promises David the permanence of his dynasty (2 Samuel 7). But it is important to realize that Nathan is a different type of prophet compared with Samuel. The latter had great authority in respect to all Israel, including the king. Nathan however (together with Gad) is a kind of court prophet who belongs more or less to the royal household. This does not mean that he would not speak out against the king in the name of YHWH. But he is no longer a prophet like Samuel. His function is reduced to religiously accompanying and observing and, if necessary, criticizing the king's activities. Later, when Solomon at the end of his reign departs from YHWH's commandments, Ahija the Shilonite announces to Jeroboam that he will become king over ten of the twelve tribes of Israel (1

Kgs 11:29-39) and this announcement was realized after Solomon's death. Thus, the beginning, the divine confirmation, and the end of the epoch of the united kingdoms under David and Solomon are marked by the appearance of prophets who critically assess the activities and the religious behavior of the kings.

The appearance of Ahija shows again a change in the situation of the prophet. He meets Jeroboam "on the way" outside the city in a kind of conspiracy. From now on, prophets, usually living far from the royal court, are often in opposition to the kings. But nevertheless, in critical situations they are present. And a prophet's appearance in public has great impact on the king and/or on his opponents. Therefore one should not conceive of the prophets as outsiders that only appear occasionally but should see them in continuity with Samuel, the great initiator of prophecy in relationship to kingship.

The reign of Jeroboam is also framed by prophetic words. At the beginning there stands the announcement of Ahija that Jeroboam will be given kingship over the ten tribes. This was the founding word for the kingdom of "Israel." At the end of Jeroboam's reign it is again Ahija who prophesies the destruction of his dynasty because of his cultic sins (1 Kgs 14:10-11). Also the next usurper, Baasha, does not succeed and again there is a prophet, Jehu son of Hanani, who announces to him the end of his "house" like that of Jeroboam (16:1-4).

Then it is the dynasty of Omri and Ahab that particularly provokes prophetic reactions. It is important to realize that at that time there appear several prophets and nobody seems to be surprised that there *are* prophets. There are the main figures Elijah and Elisha; there is the Micaiah, one solitary prophet of YHWH, confronted by four hundred court prophets (1 Kings 22); various prophetic figures are called "prophet" (20:13, 22), "man of God" (v. 28), "one of the disciples of the prophets" (v. 35), and again "prophet" (v. 37, 38, 41), and "one of the prophets" (v. 41). There are also "disciples of the prophets" in the entourage of Elisha (2 Kings 2–9). It is not my intention here to analyze the relations among these different types of prophets or the problems of terminology. I just want to stress that the appearance of a prophet is not at all surprising, at least at that time. I want to add that it is against the text to say that Elijah was a loner, as is commonly assumed in scholarly literature. He himself deplores that he alone was left when the "prophets of the LORD" were killed (1 Kgs 18:22; 19:10). And in 2 Kings 2 he is shown in the context of the "disciples of the prophet" around Elisha who obviously know him very well. Of course, Elijah is a very peculiar personality, but he belongs nevertheless within the wider prophetic context.

What was particular about Elijah was his vehement fight against the cultic politics of Ahab (1 Kings 18). But even in this confrontation Elijah is in clear continuity with the earlier prophets, in particular with Ahija, who spoke out against the "sins of Jeroboam" (14:9, 16). Now Elijah is confronted with an even more dangerous development: the immense increase of Baal worship in Israel. It is again not my intention to enter here into the question of the role of Baal in the development of Israel's religion, of polytheism and monotheism and the like. The texts prove that in the time of Ahab there had emerged a quite special situation by the strong official promotion of the cult of Baal.

The stories are well-known. Elijah fights against Ahab's religious politics, and later Elisha announces the impending end of the dynasty of Omri and Ahab, again through one of the "disciples of the prophets" (2 Kings 9). Of Jehu it is said that he "eradicated the Baal from Israel" (10:28). The Books of Kings do not mention further prophetic activities against the kings of Israel in the following years. Yet we are informed of those activities in the books of Amos and Hosea. But pursuing this topic would go beyond the scope of the present essay.

*   *   *

My starting point was the figure of Samuel. I tried to take the two dominating aspects of his picture at face value, viz. that he is called a prophet, and that he is portrayed as the undisputed leader of the people: in the political arena, in the legal area, in military matters, and above all in the realm of cult and religion. The uniqueness of his portrayal turned the attention back to Moses. Everything that could be said about Samuel could be said about Moses as well, and even to a much higher degree. Moses was the leader of the people in every respect, and he was the first prophet. As a prophet he led Israel, as Hosea has expressed it (Hos 12:14).

But there is one fundamental difference. Moses is portrayed as the ideal leader who was active in the foundation period of Israel's history. At that time Israel did not face the problems it faced later when living in the midst of other nations. Samuel, however, was confronted with the political reality which caused the people to request a king "like all the nations." Now the question arose what will happen with the specific Israelite element in Samuel's leadership: the prophetic one. It is obvious that the king cannot take over this part. It also shows that it would have been wishful thinking to believe that the king could teach the people how to do "the right in the eyes of the LORD." On the contrary, the king had to be under the supervision and control of the prophet.

Samuel exercised that function during his lifetime. But it remained clear that even after his death kingship could not exist without prophecy. The biblical texts show that in every critical situation prophets appeared to take on that task. In addition to the emphasis on the relation between Samuel and Moses, it is my second main point, to highlight the continuity in the prophet's critical task to monitor the activities of the kings, especially from the religious point of view. In some cases this led to dramatic crises in the history of kingship in Israel when dynasties were established or brought down as a result of prophetic interventions.

When reading the biblical texts in their transmitted form and sequence, Moses stands at the beginning of a succession of prophets who in one way or another were involved in leading the people of Israel. Moses himself combined in his person the two functions of the prophet as the receiver of God's word and will and of the leader of the people in every respect. The same holds true for Samuel in the first part of his life. Later he had to hand over the leadership to a king, but he still kept the function and responsibility of the prophet. Also, in the history that followed, this separation continued. The king never could fulfill the task of the prophet. But Israel always needed prophecy as a supervision, critique and correction of a leadership that too often left the way that had been shown by Moses and Samuel. Kingship without prophecy never could exist.

*   *   *

Some final remarks. This synchronic reading of the biblical texts is not too far from what a diachronic reader would have to say, at least at several points. And indeed, something of what I have tried to explain in this paper has already been said by other scholars, if even

with different accents.[7] In particular the uniqueness of the figure of
Samuel stands out in all texts at all levels. But the question is whether
we should try to reconstruct the "original" office of Samuel and his
"real" activities or rather should endeavor to understand what the
texts in their given shape want to express. The same is true with the
ensuing history of kingship and prophecy: Should we be mainly
interested in the historical development of kingship and take the
prophets as marginal figures, or should we listen to the given text
which ascribes great importance to the prophets for the development
of Israel's history? Finally, with regard to Moses, we leave the field
of possible historical reconstruction, at least in any detail. But
reading the whole story of early Israel in its continuity it seems to be
evident that Moses is depicted as the ideal model of leadership in
Israel—a model which includes the two main elements of leadership
that later fell apart. Thus, at all times Israel could look back in order
to understand what real leadership of the people of God should be
and at least try to come as close as possible to that ideal. Therefore
prophecy always was needed:

> What made Israel Israel throughout her history was the presence, in all
> periods at all the crucial issues, of a thin line of peculiar people who stood over
> against the state and the populace and created the tension, which the very
> presence of God's word created to make the covenant people into something
> more than a normal, run-of-the-mill ancient Near Eastern manifestation of self-
> indulgent nationalism.[8]

---

7   See e.g. J. Blenkinsopp, *A History of Prophecy in Israel* (Philadelphia:
Westminster, 1983) 63-65.

8   J. A. Sanders, "Prophets and the State," in Sanders, *Torah and Canon*
(Philadelphia: Fortress Press, 1972) 61-62.

THE IMAGERY OF ISAIAH 40:6-8
IN TRADITION AND INTERPRETATION

Robert Davidson

6 A voice says, "Cry out!"
And I said, "What shall I cry?"
All people are grass,
their constancy is like the flower of the field.
7 The grass withers, the flower fades,
when the breath of the LORD blows upon it;
surely the people are grass.
8 The grass withers, the flower fades;
but the word of our God will stand forever.

Thus the NRSV translates Isa 40:6-8.[1] The passage, however, is not without its textual problems, particularly when we compare the Hebrew (MT and 1QIsaiah^a) and the LXX textual traditions. The LXX is significantly shorter with the omission of the whole of v. 7 or alternately v. 7b and v. 8a.

The LXX rendering of חסדו by δόξα ἀνθρώπου has spawned a variety of unnecessary suggested emendations of the Hebrew text. In the light of the number of Hebrew words which the translators of the LXX rendered as δόξα it is tempting to suggest that this was where they sought refuge when in doubt as to how to render a Hebrew word in certain contexts.[2] It is likewise open to argument whether in v. 6 the Hebrew textual tradition should be rendered "And I said" following the LXX and 1QIsaiah^a, or whether it should be rendered "one says," third person, as in the Targum (cf. NEB).

---

[1]   Unless otherwise indicated biblical quotations are taken from the NRSV, an acknowledgement that my copy of the NRSV was a gift from James A. Sanders, a member of the NRSV committee, the latest of many kindnesses and much stimulation received since we first met in 1965, in what was then Colgate Rochester Divinity School.

[2]   E. Hatch and H. A. Redpath (*A Concordance to the Septuagint and the Other Greek Versions of the Old Testament* [Oxford: Clarendon, 1897] 341-43) list twenty-five different Hebrew words rendered by δόξα.

These textual issues, however, do not impinge significantly upon the primary interest of this study, namely the value to be given to the imagery contained in certain key words, "all flesh" (כל בשׂר) and the related echoing use of "grass" (חציר) and "flower" (ציץ) which occur twice in the LXX, with "grass" occuring four times in the MT and "flower" three times.

No attempt is made here to explore or analyse the wide ranging use, physical and psychological, of the word "flesh" in the biblical tradition.[3] We are concerned with the way in which this cluster of images is used to refer to people in general or to certain categories of people and/or their ways of behavior.

OLD TESTAMENT INTERPRETATION

We begin with the Isaianic corpus itself. Broadly speaking there seem to be three different lines of interpretation.

(1) "All flesh" is interpreted in terms of the human race. This is how most modern translations render it in Isa 40:6—"all people" (NRSV), "all mankind" (NEB, GNB), "all men" (NIV), "all mortals" (REB), "All humanity" (NJB).

Isaiah 49:22-26, an oracle which depicts the nations as willing, or unwilling, spectators of the coming deliverance of God's people, climaxes in the words (v. 26):

> I will make your oppressors eat their own flesh,
> and they shall be drunk with their own blood as with wine.
> Then all flesh shall know
> that I am the LORD your Savior,
> and your Redeemer, the Mighty One of Jacob.

Echoing the phrase and playing upon it in v. 26a concerning the oppressors eating "their own flesh," "all flesh" in v. 26b means in context "all mankind" (REB), including the nations and the peoples previously mentioned in v. 22. The passage parallels in thought the claim in Isa 40:5 where the revelation of the glory of God is to be seen by "all flesh."

Isaiah 51:12-16, which adapts the oracle of salvation form, has many points of contact with Isaiah 40. There is the initial use of the *pi'el* of נחם to describe God's activity (40:1; 51:12); the description

---

3   See *inter alia* the entry on בשׂר by N. Bratsiosis, in G. T. Botterweck and H. Ringgren (eds.), *A Theological Dictionary of the Old Testament*, vol. 2 (Grand Rapids: Eerdmans, 1975) 317-31.

of the exiles as "my people" (40:1; 51:16) and the use of the "fear not" motif (40:9; cf. 51:12). After the emphatic self assertion of Yahweh, "I, I am he who comforts you" (51:12), the irrationality of fear is laid bare. Why should they be afraid of "a mere mortal" (אנוש) who must die, "a human being [בן אדם] who fades like the grass." Over against such basic human weakness and transience the prophet places Yahweh, "your Maker, who stretched out the heavens and founded the earth" (51:13).

Although the passage goes on to contextualise such mortal weakness in the person of "the oppressor" (המציק), the shift in thought is clearly from the general to the specific. It is anyone who belongs to the human race who is characterised as one "who fades like the grass" (51:12), or perhaps more accurately, "are but grass" (NIV: חציר ינתן)

If this passage focuses upon the weakness and transience of "all flesh," Isa 66:23 gives voice to the ultimate hope of the unity of all humanity, of Israelite and non-Israelite, when it declares:

> From new moon to new moon,
> and from sabbath to sabbath,
> all flesh shall come to worship before me,
> says the LORD.

(2) There is a much more specific use of "flesh" to refer to those who are clearly regarded as the enemies of God's purposes and are thus to be sharply distinguished from Israel the people of God. In a situation where the Jerusalem government was firmly committed to a policy of "real politik" and seeking help from the Egyptians to clothe its military nakedness, Isaiah attacks the folly of such moves (31:3):

> The Egyptians are human [אדם] and not God;
> their horses are flesh [בשר] and not spirit [רוח].

The same contrast between "flesh" and the רוח of Yahweh is central to Isa 40:6-8, whether we translate in v. 7 "the breath of the LORD," or as traditional translations tend to do, "the spirit of the LORD." In Isa 31:3 "flesh" clearly characterizes the military machine of Egypt, which far from being an agent of deliverance plays no part whatever in God's purposes and is doomed to fail and to perish.

There is evidence of a similar specific use of the "grass" imagery. In Isa 37:27 in the context of a series of oracles against the Assyrians, the blasphemy and arrogance of Assyria is to meet its nemesis, its fortified cities and their inhabitants are to be shorn of strength:

> They have become like plants of the field
> and like tender grass (or herbs),
> like grass on the housetops [חציר גגות]
> blighted before it is grown.

(3) A different referent for the "flower that fades" imagery is to be found in Isaiah 28. Twice in the context of a searing attack on the corruption and irresponsible conduct of those sarcastically described as "the drunkards of Ephraim" (28:1, 3) there is reference to the "fading flower [ציץ נבל; the same expression as in 40:7] of its glorious beauty" (28:1, 4), doomed to be plucked and to wither away. In this case the imagery specifically describes the frailty and the transience of the life of the community, or elements within that community, which ought to have known how to behave as the people of God but sadly took another course. The imagery in this case is directed inwards towards Israel and to certain aspects of Israel's life.

Thus within the Isaianic corpus there are broadly speaking three lines of the interpretation of the imagery which appears in Isaiah 40:6-8. The same three approaches are to be found more widely in the Hebrew Bible.

(1) Psalm 103:15 is the passage that has the closest links linguistically with Isa 40:6-8 and centers on the frailty and transience of the human race in general. In this passage, the focus is on אנוש, translated "mortals" in the NRSV:

> . . . their days are like grass [חציר];
> they flourish like a flower in a field [ציץ השׂדה];
> for the wind passes over it, and it is gone,
> and its place knows it no more.

Per contra the Psalmist stresses that it is the חֶסֶד of the LORD which is from everlasting to everlasting on those who fear him (v. 17). However we translate it, "steadfast love," or constancy as in 40:6, this is the sole lasting and unchangeable factor in the midst of the weakness and limitations of human existence.

Similarly Ps 90:5-6 draws attention to the inevitable death which awaits all members of the human race:

> You sweep them away; they are like a dream,
> like grass [חציר] that is renewed in the morning;
> in the morning it flourishes and is renewed;
> in the evening it fades and withers [נבל].

Job, giving voice to his pessimism (Job 14:1-2), speaks of:

> A mortal, born of woman [אדם ילוד אשה],
> few of days and full of trouble,
> comes up like a flower and withers,
> flees like a shadow and does not last.

All these passages use the imagery of "grass" and "flower" to make their point, but the use of "all flesh" with similar effect is well documented in many other passages. Jeremiah 32:27 seeks to challenge a superficial theology which insists that God would never allow his own people to be destroyed, by asserting that Yahweh is not merely the patron saint of Israel. All human power, all of history lie in his control: "See, I am the LORD, the God of all flesh; is anything too hard for me?"

It follows, therefore, that no part of the human race is exempt from the judgment of God. According to Jer 25:31 (cf. 45:5 and Zech 2:13, where the NRSV translates "all people"):

> The clamor will resound to the ends of the earth,
> for the LORD has an indictment against the nations;
> he is entering into judgment with all flesh,
> and the guilty he will put to the sword,
> says the LORD.

(2) There are several passages, however, notably in the Psalms, which use this imagery to point to those who are considered to be a threat to the people of God or to a faithful member of that community. In Ps 37:2 it is those described in v. 1 as "the wicked" and "wrongdoers" who are not to be envied:

> for they will soon fade away like the grass [חציר],
> and wither like the green herb.

The Psalmist in 56:4, affirming a robust and joyful trust in God which negates fear, defiantly asks, "What can flesh do to me?" Flesh, in this context, is his dismissive way of referring to those whom he has previously described in vv. 1 and 2 as "people" (אנוש), but more specifically as "foes" (לחם), "my enemies" (שוררי) and the many who "fight against me" (רבים לחמים לי).

Psalm 129 responds to those who have attacked Israel and who hate Zion by expressing the hope that they (vv. 5b-6)

> be put to shame and turned backward.
> Let them be like the grass on the housetops [חציר גגות]
> that withers before it grows up . . .

In all these passages a specific enemy—or enemies—is clearly in mind.

(3) Jeremiah 17:5 introduces an oracle which has links with the wisdom tradition and has been taken as a generalised wisdom saying[4]:

> Thus says the LORD:
> Cursed are those who trust in mere mortals [אדם]
> and make mere flesh [בשר] their strength,
> whose hearts turn away from the LORD.

There seems little reason not to give this a context within the experience of the prophet; in which case this is an attack upon those within Judah who demonstrate their alienation from God by seeking security elsewhere, probably in military and political alliances. It is this self confident arrogance which is dismissed as "flesh."

In Psalm 78, with its unfolding story of a people's rebellion and disobedience in response to God's continuing goodness and compassion, it is claimed that such divine compassion is rooted in the recognition that such people (Ps 78.39):

> ... were but flesh [בשר],
> a wind that passes and does not come again.

It is also likely that in the oracle against the Negeb, in Ezek 20:45-48, the "all flesh" (v. 48) who will see that it is the LORD who is responsible for the consuming fire are none other than the Jews inhabiting the southern regions of the land.

Thus both within the Isaianic corpus and in the Hebrew Bible as a whole there is evidence of three lines of approach to the understanding of the imagery which is used in Isa 40:6-8: (1) with reference to the human race as a whole; (2) with reference to specific enemies of the purposes of God for his people; (3) with reference to the people of God themselves and to certain of their attitudes or practices which can only lead to disaster.

THE VERSIONS

When we turn to the versions the issues raised by the shorter LXX text and 1QIsaiah[a] need not concern us in this context. The Targum,

---

4   See R. P. Carroll, *Jeremiah* (OTL; London: SCM; Philadelphia: Westminster, 1986) 362-64. For a different view, see R. Davidson, *Jeremiah*, vol. 1 (Daily Study Bible; Edinburgh: Saint Andrew Press; Philadelphia: Westminster, 1983) 144.

however, provides an interesting interpretation which reflects some of its overall theological concerns.[5] One of the key concerns of the Targum is to underline the rich benefits which come to the people of God because of the promises God made to Abraham. Since, however, such promises must be considered in the light of the people's history of rebellion, the future points to a coming time of judgment, often linked with the sanctuary, a time when the righteous will be rewarded and the wicked punished. For example, in the series of judgment oracles in Isa 24:13 the MT has an indefinite subject:

> For thus *it* shall be on the earth and among the nations,
> as when an olive tree is beaten,
> as at the gleaning when the harvest is ended.

This becomes in the Targum: "For thus shall the *righteous* be left solitary in the midst of the world among kingdoms, like the plucking of an olive tree, as the gleanings after the vintage."

In v. 16 the MT emphasizes the prophet's distress at the treachery which he sees around him:

> But I say, I pine away,
> I pine away. Woe is me!
> For the treacherous deal treacherously,
> the treacherous deal very treacherously.

This becomes in the Targum: "The prophet said, 'The mystery of the reward of the righteous has been shown unto me; the mystery of the punishment of the wicked has been revealed to me. Woe to the oppressors, for they shall be oppressed, and to the spoiling of the spoilers, for behold they shall be spoiled.'"

In the concluding verse of Isaiah 66 (v. 24) the phrase "all flesh" occurs twice in the MT. In the preceding verse (v. 23), as we have seen, it looks forward to the whole of humanity coming to share in the worship of Yahweh. In the last verse (v. 24), in the context of judgment against those who have rebelled against God, it is claimed that the fate of such people will be viewed with horror by "all flesh." The Targum retains "the sons of all flesh" in v. 23, but in v. 24 the concluding words become: "and the wicked shall be judged in Gehinnom until the righteous say concerning them, 'We have seen enough.'" Thus the second "all flesh" becomes more specific and in context is identified with the righteous as opposed to the wicked. A

---

5   Quotations for the Aramaic Targum follow J. F.Stenning, *The Targum of Isaiah* (Oxford: Clarendon, 1949) 74, 76, 222, 130 (in the order of quotation).

similar trend may be seen in the Targum version of Isa 53:2, 9.

We find the same shift from the general to the more specific in the two occurences of "all flesh" in Isaiah 40. In v. 5, in a salvation context where the glory of the LORD is to be revealed to "all flesh," the Targum renders to "the sons of all flesh." In vv. 6b-8, however, there is a decided shift to the more specific, this time to identify "all flesh" with the wicked. Thus the prophetic cry, in the Aramaic, becomes:

> All the wicked are as grass,
> and all their strength as the flower of the field.
> The grass withereth, its flower fadeth;
> for the wind from before the LORD hath blown upon it;
> therefore the wicked among the people are counted as grass.
> The wicked dieth, his thoughts (or, *plans*) perish;
> but the word of our God abideth for ever.

All the varied imagery of the passage has been given a consistent reinterpretation: "all flesh" in v. 6 becomes "all the wicked"; "the people" of v. 7 become "the wicked among the people"; the "grass" and the "flower" of v. 8 becomes "the wicked" and "his thoughts" (or "plans").

RABBINIC INTERPRETATION

The same tendency to target more precisely the meaning of the word flesh is to be found in the Midrash Rabbah.[6] The comment on Gen 21:1 quotes Isaiah 40: "The grass withereth, the flower fadeth: that means the grass of Abimelech withereth and his flower fadeth, but the word of our God shall stand for ever, hence 'and the LORD remembered Sarah, as he has said . . .'" (*Gen. Rab.* 53.3 [on Gen 21:1]).

It is likely that the "flower" that fadeth is a reference to Abimelech's wives and family, while the word of God that stands for ever is the promises made to Abraham and Sarah concerning the son they would have, promises which seemed to have been under threat because of Sarah's involvement with Abimelech.

The Midrash Rabbah on Numbers (*Num. Rab.* 16.3 [on Num 13:2]), commenting on the unwillingness of the people to go up to possess

---

[6]   Quotation from H. Freedman, "Genesis," in H. Freedman and M. Simon (eds.), *Midrash Rabbah* (10 vols., London: Soncino Press, 1939; 3rd ed., 1983) 1.463.

the land of Canaan, quotes Isa 40:6-8 in full, then continues:

> To what is this like? To the case of a king who has a friend with whom
> he makes a stipulation saying, "Come with me and I will give you a
> present." He went with him and died. Said the king to the friend's son:
> "Although your father is dead, I will not withdraw the promise of the
> present I made to him. You come and take it." So it is the case here. The
> king is the supreme King of Kings, the Holy One, blessed be He, and the
> friend is Abraham, as it says "the seed of Abraham my friend" [Isa 41:8].
> The Holy One, blessed be He, said to him, "Come with me, 'Get thee out
> of this country and from thy kindred and thy father's house' [Gen 12:1]."
> He stipulated with him that he would give him a present: as he says, "Arise,
> walk through the land" [Gen 13:17], and this is supported by the text "For
> all the land thou seest, to thee I will give it." The Holy One, blessed be He,
> said to Moses: "Although it is to the patriarchs that I made a promise to give
> this land, and they are dead, I will not retreat, but 'The word of our God
> shall stand for ever.'"[7]

Thus in the Midrash Rabbah on Genesis the imagery of "grass" and
"flower" is applied to Abimelech and his family who cannot thwart
the promises that God intends to fulfill in and through Abraham and
Sarah; while in the Midrash Rabbah on Numbers Isa 40:6-8 is
applied to the mortal frailty of Abraham and the patriarchs, long
dead, but to whom God made promises which are still alive, promises now confirmed to Moses.

NEW TESTAMENT INTERPRETATION

It seems clear[8] that there has been a similar shift in the use made
of Isa 40:6-8 in the New Testament, in Jas 1:9-11, where the passage,
though not specifically quoted, provides the writer with his imagery:

> Let the believer who is lowly boast in being raised up, and the rich in
> being brought low, because the rich will disappear like a flower in the field.
> For the sun rises with its scorching heat and withers the field; its flower
> falls, and its beauty perishes. It is the same way with the rich; in the midst
> of a busy life, they will wither away.

In the main this follows the thought pattern and the structure of Isa
40:6-8. It introduces a simile "like a flower in a field," followed by a
description of what ensues, it "falls and its beauty perishes." Where it

---

7   Quotation from J. J. Slotki, "Numbers," in Freedman and Simon (eds.),
Midrash Rabbah, 6.675-76.

8   Needlessly queried by M. Dibelius, *Der Brief des Jacobus* (Göttingen:
Vandenhoeck & Ruprecht, 1984).

differs from Isa 40:6-8 is that instead of ending with the prophetic contrast between what is inevitably transient and the enduring word of God, it returns to apply the simile, "So is it with the rich . . ."

It has been argued that what is doomed to disappear like a flower in a field is not the rich person, but his wealth, with the subject of the verb "disappear" taken to be "it" not "he." In this case the reference, as in Isa 40:6-8, would be to human life in general, the life of both rich and poor, "Both alike share in the shortness and uncertainty of life."[9] It seems more reasonable, however, to apply the simile to the rich alone. In the light of the tradition reflected in the Aramaic Targum, the not infrequent identification in the Hebrew Bible of the rich with the wicked or the oppressor, and the poor with the righteous, may have paved the way for James' use of the passage.[10] Whether the rich person referred to in James is to be identified with certain people within the Christian community or primarily with those outside that community in society in general, has been much discussed.[11] At times both may be intended (cf. Jas 2:2, 6; 5:1), but the main thrust seems to be concerned with sociological tensions within the emerging Christian community. Whatever view we take, the Isaiah passage is being used specifically, and in a condemnatory context, to refer to those who are regarded by the writer as constituting a threat to the continued well being of the people of God.

1 Peter 1:24 quotes Isa 40:6b-8, following with minor variations the LXX text, and maintaining the contrast which is central to the original. "All flesh" is here identified with what in the previous verse has been described as "perishable" seed, the human race in all its frailty—"its glory like the flower of the grass"—in contrast to the "imperishable seed," the new humanity called into being by the living and enduring word of God. A similar use of "all flesh" or "flesh" to refer to the human race in general is found elsewhere in the New Testament. In the great priestly prayer in John 17 Jesus claims to

---

[9]   C. L. Mitton, *The Epistle of James* (London: Marshall, Morgan & Scott; Grand Rapids: Eerdmans, 1961) 41.

[10]   Such an identification is found frequently in prophetic teaching (e.g. Amos 2:7; 6:1-7; Isa 3:15-16) and in the Psalms (e.g. Psalms 37 and 49) as well as in the wisdom tradition upon which James draws extensively (e.g. Prov 29:7).

[11]   In general, see G. Theissen, *The Social Setting of Pauline Christianity* (Philadelphia: Fortress, 1983); and more specifically the balanced discussion in P. U. Maynard Rico, *Poverty and Wealth in James* (New York: Orbis, 1987).

have received from his heavenly Father "authority over all flesh [NRSV: "all people"] to give eternal life to all whom you have given him" (John 17:2).

In the apocalyptic material in Matthew 24, it is stated concerning the period of suffering which is to come that ". . . if those days had not been cut short, no one [lit. "no flesh"] would be saved; but for the sake of the elect these days will be cut short" (Matt 24:22). In both of these Gospel passages "all flesh," referring to humanity in general, is placed in sharp contrast to those chosen to belong to the new humanity.

Thus in the New Testament we can find echoes of at least two out of the three lines of interpretation of Isa 40:6-8 vouched for in the Isaianic corpus and more widely in the Hebrew Bible.

INTERPRETATION IN THE PSEUDEPIGRAPHA

In the pseudepigraphic literature there are frequent references to passages from Isaiah, notably Isaiah 6, with its awesome heavenly retinue, the solemn trisagaion and the prophetic call, and Isaiah 11 with its messianic implications. There 2 Baruch, with concern for the fate of the Jewish people post-70 CE, declares (2 Bar. 82:3-8):

> For now we see the multitude of the happiness of the nations although they have acted wickedly: but they are like vapor . . . And we see the strength of their power, while they resist the Mighty One every hour, but they will be reckoned as spittle . . . . And we think about the beauty of their gracefulness while they go down in impurities; but like the grass which is withered they will fade away. And we ponder about the strength of their cruelty while they themselves do not think about the end; but they will be broken like the passing wave.[12]

The language of "vapor . . . spittle . . . grass withering and fading away . . . and passing wave," would be consistent with the influence of the Isaianic tradition: "Vapor" would link closely with the thought of Isa 40:15, though the word does not occur there, "spittle" with 50:6 and "waves" with 51:15. If such an Isaianic influence could be proven, then "grass" withering and fading would be an echo of Isa 40:7. Equally, however, much of this imagery could have been influenced by the book of Job.

---

12   Quotation from A. F. Klijn, "2 (Syriac Apocalypse of) Baruch," in J. H. Charlesworth (ed.), *The Old Testament Pseudepigrapha* (2 vols., London: Darton, Longman and Todd; New York: Doubleday, 1983-85) 1.649.

The only other possible reference seems to be in 2 Esdras in the Judgment on Asia (15:1–16:78), where we find the words "The glory of your manhood will wither like a blossom . . ." In the light of the variety of passages in the Hebrew Bible, however,which use this imagery, it would be difficult to argue for definite influence of Isa 40:7.

POST-NEW TESTAMENT CHRISTIAN INTERPRETATION

From the way in which certain main stream theologians in the early church react, it is evident that Isa 40:6-8 had considerable attraction for some gnostic thinkers and groups. Clement of Alexandria, for example, attacks those who use the passage to disparage the flesh and natural generation. He appeals to New Testament teaching to give the passage a wider reference (*Stromata* 4.26):

> For "the flower of the grass" and "walking after the flesh" and "being carnal" according to the apostle are those who are in their sins. The soul of man is confessedly the better part and the body the inferior. But neither is the soul good by nature, nor on the other hand is the body evil by nature . . . The constitution of man, therefore, which has its place among the senses was necessarily composed of things divine and not opposite-body and soul.[13]

Clement is therefore arguing that "flesh" is that sinful humanity which by definition we all share.

Tertullian in *De Resurrectione Carnis* 10 attacks those who wish to disparage the flesh. he points to texts which enoble it, including Isaiah 40: "All flesh is grass . . . well, but Isaiah was not content to say only this, but he also declares 'All flesh shall see the salvation of God'" (cf. Isa 40:5). He then goes on to argue in the light of Paul's teaching that "it is not the *substance* of the flesh, but its *actions* which are censured"[14] and that it is therefore illegitimate to use Isa 40:7 to deny that flesh can be part of the resurrection life.

It is clear that the contemporary theological dialogue is here setting the agenda. In both cases we are hearing a response to what is regarded as an unjustifiable use of Scripture, a response which takes the form of giving a different and what is regarded as a more legiti-

---

[13]   A. Roberts and J. Donaldson (eds.), *The Ante-Nicene Fathers*, vol. 2 (Edinburgh: T. & T. Clark, 1859; repr. Grand Rapids: Eerdmans, 1989) 439.

[14]   Roberts and Donaldson (ed.), *The Ante-Nicene Fathers*, vol. 3 (Edinburgh: T. & T. Clark, 1870; repr. Grand Rapids: Eerdmans, 1989) 233.

mate interpretation of the same text to which appeal has been made.

Cyprian uses Isa 40:6-8 in two different ways[15]:

(1) as a proof text to sustain the argument that "No one ought to be saddened by death since life brings suffering and danger, but death brings peace and assurance" (*Testimonia* 3.58). That is to say he uses Isa 40:6-8 to underline the uncertainty and frailty involved in all human existence, then adds to it a Christian gloss which springs from his belief in the life everlasting.

(2) In his address to virgins he warns them of the dangers of indulging in excessive external adornment: "You defile yourself," he says,"with the stain of carnal desire although you are a candidate for innocence and modesty. God says to Isaiah . . . [here he quotes Isa 40:6b-8]. It is not becoming for any Christian and especially not for a virgin to consider the glory and honour of the flesh. Rather she ought to seek only the word of God to embrace blessings which will endure for ever." In this case we see Cyprian using Isa 40:6b-8 as part of his pastoral concern, even if we think this pastoral concern is somewhat one sided.

The sixth century Roman senator Flavius Magnus Aurelius Cassiodorus, after his conversion circa 530 CE wrote an exposition on Psalms.[16] Commenting on Ps 91:8 he writes:

> You will only look with your eyes
> and see the punishment of the wicked.

He claims that the Church teaches "that sinners flourish for a brief period in the world, but at the judgment when they obtain a worthy recompense for their deeds she maintains that they swiftly perish. As the prophet Jeremiah says . . ."; at which point to quotes Isa 40:6! He adds the comment, "Holy Mother Church has instructed us how sinners perish like grass, and how the just flourish like the palm tree."

This clearly belongs to the line of interpretation which identifies "all flesh" with those who stand under the judgment of God, whether they are designated as "the wicked" (the Targum), "the rich" (James) or, as here, "sinners."

Let us now turn to the two dominant theological and biblical figures of the Reformation period. For Luther, not surprisingly,

---

15   M. A. Fahey, *Cyprian and the Bible: A Study in Third Century Exegesis* (Tübingen: Mohr [Siebeck], 1971).

16   P. G. Walsh, *Cassiodorus*, vol. 2 (New York: Paulist Press, 1991).

"flesh" tends to stand for anything which he considers to be a threat to his central doctrine of justification. In his commentary on Isaiah[17] he dismisses what he claims to be the view of Jerome concerning 40:6-8, namely that the spirit of the LORD (v. 7) indicates God's wrath poured out over flesh which is to be identified with the Jewish people. He argues that it is:

> The Holy Spirit and the Spirit of Christ who will "convict the world of sin" [John 16:8] and blow against the flower of the flesh . . .The Spirit blowing on the grass is nothing else than the Spirit convincing the world of sin, and thus through the ministry of the Word the Spirit condemns all verdure flower of the grass. Our little religious people do not want to put up with this and they think that by prohibiting the blowing they will be in true flower and stand fast on a golden foundation and a silver superstructure. This, then, is a passage concerning justification, that is, outside of the Spirit of God there is no justification. Jerome, Erasmus and the sects do not see that the whole glory of the flesh is being condemned. Therefore they live in celibacy and ceremonial works, and have not yet been in the abyss of sin.

Flesh, he goes on to insist, means "the whole man," as opposed to any attempt to equate it with his lower nature. It is called "people" in v. 7, he claims, because it indicates an establishment with worship and external government.

> This people is here called flesh and grass. Therefore flesh does not mean the lowest parts of man but the higher. For envy, heresy, etc. are the works and fruit not of the lower but of the higher, and they are sins.

Luther is here contextualizing the passage to use it against all forms of religion and religious activity which run contrary to his basic understanding of justification. He therefore, uncharacteristically at this point, stands outside any tradition of interpretation which would see in the passage an attack on the Jewish people or Jewish religion. He has firmly in his sight the inner Christian conflicts and debartes of his own day.

Calvin's approach is different.[18] He begins with a general comment on v. 6:

> David indeed compares this life to grass (Psalm 103.15) because it is fleeting and transitory; but the context shows that the prophet does not speak only of the outward man but includes the gifts of the mind of which

---

[17] H. C. Oswald (ed.), *Luther's Works*, vol.17 (St. Louis: Concordia, 1972) 17.

[18] Quotations from Calvin are taken from *Calvin's Commentaries* (Edinburgh: T. & T. Clark, 1845).

men are exceedingly proud, such as prudence, courage, acuteness, judgment, skill in the transaction of business, in which they think they excel other animals.

This is in line with his comments on Ps 32:4:

> For day and night your hand was heavy upon me;
> my strength was dried up as by the heat of summer.

All human strength fails, he claims, when God appears as Judge to humble them under his displeasure: "Thus is fulfilled the saying of Isaiah [cf. 40:7], 'the grass withereth, the flower fadeth, because the Spirit of the LORD bloweth upon it.'"

From such general comments he moves to a more specific comment on חֶסֶד, which he renders "grace":

> Some commentators refer this to the Assyrians, as if the prophet by exterminating their power and their wealth and industry and exertions, or rather by treating them as if they had no existence, freed the mind of the Jews from terror. They bring out the meaning in this manner, "If you are terrified at the strength of men, remember they are flesh which quickly gives way through its own weakness." But their error is shown by the context in which the prophet explicitly applies it to the Jews themselves.[19]

This is his understanding of the phrase "the people is grass," adding:

> that all might know that he was not speaking about foreigners, but of the people which gloried in the name of God; for the Jews might have thought that they were more excellent and held a higher rank than other men and that on this account they ought to be exempt from the common fate.

The contrast between Luther and Calvin here is interesting, because it is usually Luther who gleans from the text highly judgmental references to the Jews. In Ps 1:1, for example, the "advice of the wicked" is the designs of the Jews who afterwards crucified Christ, whereas for Calvin the reference is to ungodly men in general as opposed to the true servants of God. Luther's commentary on Psalms is liberally adorned with hostile, often sneering references to the Jews, always in a condemnatory context, while Calvin's historico-critical theological wrestling with the text closes the door on such comments. In this case, however, it is precisely Calvin's critical wrestling with the text which leads to his conviction that in context the people referred to as grass in v. 7 must be the Jewish people, while Luther can happily take refuge in a more allegorical spiritual

---

19   *Calvin's Commentaries*, 209-10.

approach which leads him into the ecclesiastical controversies of his day.

The history of Christian exegesis, therefore, up to and including the reformation period bears witness to the three lines of interpretation which we initially found in the Isaianic corpus and more widely in the Hebrew Bible, with Isa 40:6-8 being read in terms of human life as a whole (e.g. Cyprian), in terms of particular enemies, both ethical and spiritual (e.g. Luther) and in terms of the Jews as the people of God (e.g. Calvin).

The distinguished 18th century English biblical commentator and divine Matthew Henry witnesses to two of these strands.[20] Commenting on the words "all flesh is grass" in Isa 40:6, he argues that they mean:

(1) "The power of man when it does appear *against* deliverance is not to be feared . . . The insulting Babylonians, who promise themselves that the desolations of Jerusalem are to be perpetual, are but as grass when the Spirit of the LORD blows upon, makes nothing of, but blasts all its glory." Such power can never frustrate the Word of God.

(2) "The power of man when it would appear *for* deliverance is not to be trusted . . . When God is about to work salvation for his people he will take them off from depending upon creatures and looking for it from the hills and the mountains . . . for God will have no creature to be a rival with him for the hope and confidence of his people; and as it is his word alone that shall stand for ever, so in that word only must our faith stand. When we are brought to this, then, and not till then, are we fit for mercy."

More modern commentators still work on the whole within the same three fold parameters: (1) C. R. North[21] heads his section on Isa 40:6-8, "Creaturely Transience and Divine Permanence." The burden of the prophetic proclamation he asserts is "that all sentient life is as evanescent as the flower which fades. By contrast 'the word of God' will endure for ever." The חֶסֶד of which Isa 40:6 speaks is not the חֶסֶד of flowers, but the חֶסֶד of all flesh which in v. 7 "the gloss(?) interprets rightly enough of mankind." The "people" (הָעָם) is here taken to have the same sense as the word has in Isa 42:5 where, in a creation context, it is said that God "gives breath to the

---

[20]   M. Henry, *Commentary on the Bible*, vol. 5 (London: Nisbet, 1856) 233.

[21]   C. R. North, *The Second Isaiah* (Oxford: Clarendon, 1964) 77.

people" upon the earth, and that can hardly mean only to the people of Israel!

J. L. Mackenzie in the Anchor Bible,[22] though arguing that the glossator misunderstood and interpreted the "people" as referring to Israel, claims that minus the gloss vv. 6-7 represent

> a kind of sententious wisdom, which is typical of the wisdom literature. The voice gives "a wisdom riddle" to which the people discover the answer. It contrasts the wisdom of men with the power of Yahweh . . . Man is no more enduring than the grass; the only underlying reality is the experience of the word of Yahweh.

Page Kelly in the *Broadman Bible Commentary*[23] argues that the prophet's initial reaction to his call is one of despair. He states:

> The ground and cause of his reluctnce is his pessimistic view of man. In his eyes all flesh is as transient as grass, all its steadfastness (*chesed*) like the flower of the field (cf Hos.6.4). These metaphors underscore the concept of the frailty and the transience of human existence (cf Job 14:1-2; Ps 90:5-6; Luke 12:28).[24]

As we have seen, it is this first line of interpretation which is followed by most modern translations in their rendering of "all flesh."

(2) There are those who while they begin by nodding in the direction of a general statement about human frailty and transience, move quickly to identify such frailty and transience with identifiable enemies of the people of God. Thus Franz Delitzsch,[25] while stressing that "the imperishableness of the word has the perishableness of all flesh and beauty as its dark foil," immediately adds, "The tyrants of Israel are mortal; perishable the loveliness by which they impose and infatuate."

The *Speaker's Bible*[26] notes that the people addressed being in Babylon were "surrounded by the imposing fabric of a great Empire, crushed into silent submission by its power, awed, at times half

---

22   J. L. Mackenzie, *The Second Isaiah* (AB 20; Garden City: Doubleday, 1968) 18.

23   P. H. Kelly, "Isaiah," in C. J. Allen (ed.), *The Broadman Bible Commentary*, vol. 5 (Nashville: Broadman, 1971) 298.

24   See also G. A. F. Knight, *Servant Theology* (NITC; Grand Rapids: Eerdmann, 1984); J. F. A. Sawyer, *Isaiah II* (Daily Study Bible; Edinburgh: Saint Andrew Press; Philadelphia: Westminster, 1986) 45.

25   F. Delitzsch, *Isaiah* (vol. 2; London: Hodder and Stoughton, 1892) 139.

26   "The Book of Isaiah," in E. Hastings (ed.), *The Speaker's Bible* (Aberdeen: Speaker's Bible Office, 1935; repr. Grand Rapids: Baker, 1963) 12.

fascinated by its splendour. It was to men whose eyes were resting on this scene of magnificence and power that the solemn words were spoken 'all flesh is grass.'" Thus "all flesh" is here identified with the greatness that is Babylon, the threat to the continued existence of the people of God.

(3) There are those who identify "all flesh" as the people of God or some aspect of the life of that people. George Adam Smith in the *Expositor's Bible* comments:

> Everything human may perish; the day may be past of the great prophets, of the priests, of the King in his beauty who was the vice-regent of God. But the people have God's word; when all their leaders have fallen and every visible authority for God is taken away, this shall be their rally and confidence . . . Their political and religious institutions which had so often proved to be the initiative of a new movement or served as a bridge to carry the nation across disaster to a larger future were not in existence.[27]

Thus it is precisely the religious institutions which had been central to Israel's experience in the past which now come under the rubric of "flesh," human constructions which can no longer bear the burden of Israel's present needs or futuer hopes.

A variation of this is to be found in Claus Westermann's Isaiah commentary.[28] After characterising Isa 40:6-8 as a well defined literary form, common in the Psalms, a lament provoked by the evanescence of all things, he comments:

> If, however, the prophet's counter cry was due to a particular set of circumstances, how can he substantiate it by means of such general sentiments? The answer is that the exiles' greatest temptation . . . was precisely to be resigned to thinking of themselves as caught up in the general transience of all things, to believe that nothing could be done to halt the extinction of their national existence, and to say "just like countless other nations destroyed before our time, in our time and after our time, we are a nation that perishes: all flesh is grass."

He further argues that the addition, "surely the people is grass" is saying Amen to that, "one of the numerous examples of additions and glosses which constitute valuable witnesses as to what happens to the biblical text as it was read by or to the congregation of the faithful."

We have come full circle, back to where we began with the inter-textuality in the Hebrew Bible itself. There we found three main lines of approach to the interpretation of the imagery which occurs

---

27 G. A. Smith, *Isaiah* (London: Hodder and Stoughton, 1890) 83.
28 C. Westermann, *Isaiah 40–66* (OTL: Philadelphia: Westminster, 1969) 41.

in Isa 40:6-8. These three approaches have continued across the centuries because they have proved to be adaptable, able to provide a biblical context for understanding the particular political, sociological and theological circumstances of changing times.

LEVITICUS 26 AND EZEKIEL

Jacob Milgrom

All the commentators have noted the extraordinary correspondence between the language of Ezekiel and that of the Holiness source in general, and Leviticus 26 in particular. There is no consensus, however, with regard to the chronological relationship. Who borrowed from whom? Or did Ezekiel and the Holiness source borrow from a third source?[1] The issue, I submit, can be settled only by examining those passages where there is irrefutable evidence that one source has clearly altered the other. I shall devote this brief essay to Leviticus 26 where the parallels are abundant.

* * *

1. A glaring example of borrowing is found in Ezek 34:24-28. The parallels are set in italicized print (and will be throughout):

24 *וַאֲנִי יְהוָה אֶהְיֶה לָהֶם לֵאלֹהִים וְעַבְדִּי* דָוִד נָשִׂיא בְתוֹכָם אֲנִי יְהוָה דִּבַּרְתִּי
25 *וְכָרַתִּי לָהֶם בְּרִית שָׁלוֹם וְהִשְׁבַּתִּי חַיָּה־רָעָה מִן־הָאָרֶץ וְיָשְׁבוּ בַמִּדְבָּר לָבֶטַח וְיָשְׁנוּ*
בַיְּעָרִים 26 *וְנָתַתִּי אוֹתָם וּסְבִיבוֹת גִּבְעָתִי בְּרָכָה וְהוֹרַדְתִּי הַגֶּשֶׁם בְּעִתּוֹ גִּשְׁמֵי בְרָכָה יִהְיוּ*
27 *וְנָתַן עֵץ הַשָּׂדֶה אֶת־פִּרְיוֹ וְהָאָרֶץ תִּתֵּן יְבוּלָהּ וְהָיוּ עַל־אַדְמָתָם לָבֶטַח* וְיָדְעוּ כִּי־
כִּי־אֲנִי יְהוָה בְּשִׁבְרִי אֶת־מֹטוֹת עֻלָּם וְהִצַּלְתִּים מִיַּד הָעֹבְדִים בָּהֶם 28 וְלֹא־יִהְיוּ עוֹד
בַּז לַגּוֹיִם וְחַיַּת הָאָרֶץ לֹא תֹאכְלֵם *וְיָשְׁבוּ לָבֶטַח וְאֵין מַחֲרִיד*

24 I *YHWH will be their God*, and my servant David shall be a ruler among them—*I YHWH* have spoken. 25 And I will strike with them a covenant of *friendship. I will banish vicious beasts from* their *land, and they shall live secure* in the wasteland, they shall even sleep in the woodland. 26 I will make these and the environs of my hill (?) a blessing: I will send down *the rain in its season*, rains that bring blessing. 27 *The trees of the field shall yield their fruit and the land shall yield its produce.* And they (Israel) shall continue *secure on their own soil.* They shall know that *I am YHWH when I break the bars of their yoke* and rescue them from those *who enslave them.* 28 They shall no longer be spoil for the nations, and the beasts of the earth shall not devour them. *They shall dwell secure and untroubled.*

---

[1]   For a summary of older views, see M. Burrows, *The Literary Relations of Ezekiel* (Philadelphia: Jewish Publication Society, 1925) 28-30.

In general it can be seen that Ezekiel 34 has transformed the blessings of Leviticus 26 into the image of sheep.[2] We also observe that the blessings are now linked with the idealized Davidic king (the shepherd of vv. 23-24).[3] The details are even more revealing.

Verse 24 has selected from Lev 26:12aβ, 13aα (וְהָיִיתִי לָכֶם לֵאלֹהִים אֲנִי יְהוָה . . .) and added the reference to David the ruler as part of the divine ordinance. Verse 25a has reworked 26:6a, bα. שָׁלוֹם of the latter has been strengthened by the term בְּרִית ("covenant"), borrowed from Num 25:12. This has necessitated the change from וְנָתַתִּי ("grant") to וְכָרַתִּי ("strike"). In Leviticus 26 שָׁלוֹם is granted to the land; in Ezekiel 34 a covenant is struck "with them," that is, with the sheep, with Israel. In Leviticus the meaning is peace, that is, absence of violence; in Ezekiel a relationship with Israel is in view. For this reason I translate "friendship." The image of the sheep in Ezekiel 34 necessitates that they dwell (and sleep) securely not in the land (Lev 26:5b) but in the wasteland and woodland (Ezek 34:25b).

Verse 26a is, unfortunately, obscure. Verse 26b, on the other hand, is clearly an explication of Lev 26:4a: Ezekiel explains that "rain" (sing.) denotes "rains" (plural), and if they fall in their proper season "they bring blessing." The subject, however, has been switched from the people (v. 25) to the land. Paran points out that nowhere else but in Ezekiel do we find that the action of God or the skies bringing rain is described by the verb יָרַד (rather than נָתַן).[4]

Verse 27 is a combination of Lev 26:4b, 5bβ, and 13aγ-bα, and consists of two inversions (cp. v. 27aα with Lev 26:4b and v. 27bβγ with Lev 26:13aγ-bα) and a change from the past Egyptians enslavers, an expression found frequently in the Holiness source (e.g. Lev 25:38, 42, 55), to the present but unnamed enslavers. The subject has once again been altered from the land (v. 27a) to the people (v. 27b).

Finally, v. 28aβ, b inverts (and rephrases) Lev 26:6bα with 6aβ. Again the rephrasing is essential since the subject is no longer the land (Lev 26:6b) but the people. Thus, the mixed metaphors, changes of subject, stylistic inversions, and explanatory expansions make it

---

2   Already noted by D. Z. Hoffmann, *Die wichtigsten Instanzen gegen die Graf-Welhausenische Hypothese* (Jerusalem: Darom, 1928 [Hebrew and German orig., 1904]) 23.

3   See J. R. Porter, *Leviticus* (CBC; Cambridge: Cambridge University Press, 1976).

4   M. Paran, *Literary Features of the Priestly Code: Stylistic Patterns, Idioms and Structures* (Jerusalem: Magnes, 1989) 111 n. 66 (Hebrew).

amply clear that Ezekiel has reworked the blessings of Lev 26:3-13. Several other verses from the blessings of Leviticus are reworked by Ezekiel. Some of these are treated in the balance of this essay.

2. "Then you shall know I am YHWH, whose laws you did not follow and whose rules you did not obey, acting instead according to rules of the nations around you" (Ezek 11:12). This verse is modeled on Lev 26:3, 15, 43b (a favorite Ezekielian condemnation; cf. Ezek 5:6, 7; 11:20; 20:13, 16, 19, 21, 24), but what betrays the direction of the borrowing is the second half of the verse, which is an adaptation of Lev 18:3-4, changing the specific mention of Egyptians and the long defunct Canaanites to the unspecified but all-embracing nations surrounding Israel (cf. also Ezek 5:5-7).

3. Ezekiel uses the expression עָבַר/הֶעֱבִיר בָּאָרֶץ ("traverse/cause to traverse the land") in reference to the calamities of pestilence, bloodshed, wild beasts, and sword (Ezekiel 5:17; 14:15, 17). But in the latter case the context is revealing: אוֹ חֶרֶב אָבִיא עַל־הָאָרֶץ הַהִיא וְאָמַרְתִּי חֶרֶב תַּעֲבֹר בָּאָרֶץ וְהִכְרַתִּי מִמֶּנָּה אָדָם וּבְהֵמָה ("Or, if I were to bring a sword upon the land and decree, '*Let a sword traverse the land* so that I may cut off from it man and beast'"; Ezek 14:17). Only here do we find an inner quotation. The italicized words betray the source—it is Lev 26:6bβ. The rest of the divine decree, however, is a borrowing and reworking of the wild beast curse (Lev 26:22aβ) where, one must concede, the wording is more logical: One would expect predatory beasts and not the sword to cut down (הִכְרִית) domestic animals.

4. Ezekiel 36:9-11 is an expansion and reworking of Lev 26:9. Observe the following parallels (set in italicized print): . . . . וּפָנִיתִי אֲלֵיכֶם וְהִרְבֵּיתִי עֲלֵיכֶם אָדָם . . . וְהִרְבֵּיתִי עֲלֵיכֶם אָדָם וּבְהֵמָה וְרָבוּ וּפָרוּ ("*And I will turn to you* . . . and *multiply* upon you persons . . . *and multiply* upon you persons and livestock"). This is the only place in Ezekiel where God says וּפָנִיתִי ("I will turn to you"). The twice-cited verb וְהִרְבֵּיתִי ("I will multiply") also points to Lev 26:9 as the source. That the borrowing cannot have gone in the reverse direction, from Ezekiel to Leviticus, is evident not only by contrasting the tightness of the latter in contrast to the expansiveness of the former, but by comparing the contexts: Ezekiel is addressing the mountains and, as a result, he has to change Leviticus' direct object אֶתְכֶם to עֲלֵיכֶם ("upon you"). In other words, Ezekiel takes the natural promise of God to multiply Israel and turns it into the forced image of God performing Israel's multiplication on the mountains.

5. Ezekiel 37:26-27 is an expansion and reworking of Lev 26:9, 11a, 12, underscored by the italics: וְכָרַתִּי לָהֶם בְּרִית שָׁלוֹם בְּרִית עוֹלָם יִהְיֶה אוֹתָם וּנְתַתִּים וְהִרְבֵּיתִי אוֹתָם וְנָתַתִּי אֶת־מִקְדָּשִׁי בְּתוֹכָם לְעוֹלָם וְהָיָה מִשְׁכָּנִי עֲלֵיהֶם וְהָיִיתִי לָהֶם לֵאלֹהִים וְהֵמָּה יִהְיוּ־לִי לְעָם ("And I will make *a covenant* of friendship with them—it shall be an everlasting *covenant* with them—I will establish (?) them and *multiply them, and I will place* my sanctuary among them forever. *My presence* shall rest over them; *I will be their God* and they *shall be my people*"). Since Ezekiel is speaking of a new covenant, he alters וַהֲקִימֹתִי ("And I will maintain") in Lev 26:9b to וְכָרַתִּי ("And I will make, establish"), adding "it shall be an eternal covenant." It is followed by "and I will multiply them" (Lev 26:9a). This reversal of the two halves of Lev 26:9 is another indication of borrowing. The next sentence וְנָתַתִּי אֶת־מִקְדָּשִׁי בְּתוֹכָם לְעוֹלָם is a reworking of וְנָתַתִּי מִשְׁכָּנִי בְּתוֹכְכֶם (Lev 26:11a), first emphasizing the eternity of the new sanctuary, which is then followed by Leviticus' מִשְׁכָּנִי ("my presence") and its clarifying preposition עֲלֵיהֶם ("over them"). Strikingly, Ezekiel has passed over Lev 26:10 which is irrelevant, as has been pointed out, contextually belonging with v. 5, and put here only for the sake of the structure of vv. 3-12. Ezekiel also rejects v. 11b, which—because of its negativity—creates problems for the commentators, and is irrelevant to Ezekiel's purpose. Ezekiel follows with the adoption formula of Lev 26:12 and, in conclusion, repeats his mention of the new sanctuary, emphasizing its significance for Israel and the nations (Ezek 37:28).

6. Turning to the curses, we note first that in Lev 26:22 vicious beasts destroy livestock. Ezekiel, however, in one of his chapters, attributes a similar destruction of livestock (using the same verb הִכְרִית) to famine (14:13), sword (14:17), and pestilence (14:19). But surprisingly in the section dealing with vicious beasts (14:15), he omits mention of the livestock where it logically belongs (though he lists it in his summary, v. 21; cf. 25:13; 29:8; Baudissin, cited by Hoffmann[5]).

7. Ezekiel 4:16, הִנְנִי שֹׁבֵר מַטֵּה־לֶחֶם בִּירוּשָׁלַם וְאָכְלוּ־לֶחֶם בְּמִשְׁקָל ("I am going to break the staff of bread in Jerusalem, and they shall eat bread by weight [in anxiety, and drink water by measure, in honor]"), is almost a verbatim quotations of Lev 26:26, except for its application to Jerusalem and its expansion in the rest of the verse.

---

5   Hoffmann, *Die wichtigsten Instanzen*, 246 n. 6.

That Ezekiel is the borrower (and not the originator, as claimed by Levine[6]) is confirmed by two other citations of this quotation (Ezek 5:16; 14:13) where the metaphor "break the staff of bread" is accompanied by a gloss explaining that it refers to famine.

8. As recognized by Wellhausen,[7] Ezekiel replaces the older formula of vertical retribution with his doctrine of individual retribution and, therefore, is compelled in 24:23 (cf. also 4:17; 33:10) to omit בַּעֲוֹנֹת אֲבֹתָם ("because of the iniquities of their ancestors") from his citation of Lev 26:39.

9. Finally, Ezekiel borrows from Lev 26:29, וַאֲכַלְתֶּם בְּשַׂר בְּנֵיכֶם וּבְשַׂר בְּנֹתֵיכֶם תֹּאכֵלוּ ("You shall eat the flesh of your sons, and the flesh of your daughters you shall eat"), expanding it into a reciprocal curse in Ezek 5:10a: לָכֵן אָבוֹת יֹאכְלוּ בָנִים בְּתוֹכֵךְ וּבָנִים יֹאכְלוּ אֲבוֹתָם ("Therefore parents shall eat their children, and children shall eat their parents").

* * *

These nine examples of intertextuality (and there are others) indicate signs of borrowing, and they all point in one direction, from Leviticus 26 to Ezekiel. It is Ezekiel who exhibits expansions, omissions, and reformulations, all of which lead to the conclusion that Ezekiel is the borrower. That he probably had the entire text of Lev 26:3-39 (as is now preserved in the MT) before him is further supported by the host of other parallels between Ezekiel and Leviticus 26. For example, Lev 26:17aα (cf. 17:10; 20:3, 5, 6) and Ezek 14:8; 15:7; Lev 26:19a and Ezek 3:24; 30:6, 18; 33:28; Lev 26:25aα and Ezek 5:17; 6:3; 11:8; 14:17; 33:2; Lev 26:25aβ and Ezek 24:8; 25:12, 15; Lev 26:25bα and Ezek 5:17; 14:19, 21; 28:23; Lev 26:28a and Ezek 5:15b (חֵמָה for increased hostility); Lev 26:31a and Ezek 5:14; 6:6; 25:13; 29:10; 30:12; 35:4; Lev 26:32 and Ezek 30:12, 14; 26:16; Lev 26:33a and Ezek 5:2, 12; 12:14; Lev 26:38b and Ezek 36:13; Lev 26:40aγ and Ezek 14:13; 15:8; 17:20; 18:24; 20:27; 39:26; Lev 26:43bα and Ezek 13:10; 36:3; and Lev 26:45bα and Ezek 20:9, 14, 22 (note the inversion!).

---

6   B. A. Levine, *Leviticus* (Philadelphia: Jewish Publication Society, 1989) 281.

7   J. Welhausen, *Die Composition des Hexateuchs und die historischen Bücher des Alten Testaments* (4th ed., Berlin: de Gruyter, 1963 [1st ed., 1885]) 169.

Thus there can be no doubt that Ezekiel had Leviticus 26 before him, at least vv. 3-39 (minus vv. 33b-35) where evidence of borrowing by Ezekiel has been demonstrated. As for vv. 40-45, no conclusion can be drawn. Clearly, borrowing has taken place, but without the kind of evidence demonstrated by the nine examples given above, the direction of the borrowing cannot be determined.

PROPHETIC PREDICTION, POLITICAL PROGNOSTICATION, AND FIRM BELIEF

Reflections on Daniel 11:40–12:3

Adam S. van der Woude

In the "Writing of Truth" found in Daniel 11 and the first three verses of Daniel 12, the critical exegete can easily make a distinction between events which belong to the past or the own days of the author, and occurrences which the latter expected to happen but eventually did not materialize (respectively Dan 11:2-39 and 11:40-45; 12:1-3). The prophecy of Dan 11:2-39, written after the recorded facts had already taken place, may be looked upon by modern readers as some kind of swindle, inappropiate to serious literature, let alone to Holy Scripture.[1] This impression, however, seems to be unjustified. It does not take into consideration the genuine motive which prompted the author to avail himself of the literary genre of the *vaticinium ex eventu*: his conviction that all events on earth occur in accordance with a pre-established divine plan. The transition from past and contemporaneous events to future events which is strongly emphasized by modern commentators, apparently did not bother the author of Daniel 11. He did not draw a clear-cut line between past and contemporaneous events which already had been realized in accordance with God's *predestined* course of history, and the impending eschatological events predicted by the prophets, whose words were *inspired* by the same Lord.[2] His point of view reminds us of the convictions expressed in the Qumran

---

[1] For affinities with Near Eastern *vaticinia ex eventu*, see e.g. E. Osswald, "Zum Problem der *vaticinia ex eventu*," *ZAW* 75 (1963) 27-44, esp. 28-29; K. Müller, "Die Ansätze der Apokalyptik," in J. Maier and J. Schreiner (eds.), *Literatur und Religion des Frühjudentums* (Würzburg and Gütersloh: Echter Verlag, 1973) 31-42; W. G. Lambert, *The Background of Jewish Apocalyptic*, (London: Athlone, 1978); J. J. Collins, *Daniel with an Introduction to Apocalyptic Literature* (FOTL 20; Grand Rapids: Eerdmans, 1984) 99-100.

[2] Cf. E. Osswald, "Zum Problem der *vaticinia ex eventu*."

scrolls: "All the ages of God come at the right time, as He established for them in the mysteries of his prudence" (1QpHab 7:3-14); "God declared all what is going to happen to the final generation of his people by means of his prophets" (1QpHab 2:9-10).

Bearing these things in mind, it seems worth while to reconsider the motives and hermeneutical concepts that in all likelihood prompted the author to write the "non-historical" sections Dan 11:40-45 and 12:1-3, because these passages elicited a *Wirkungs-geschichte* which had a considerable impact on both Jewish and Christian apocalyptic thought.[3]

It is extremely doubtful that the text of Dan 11:40–12:3 sprung solely from the author's own imagination.[4] He apparently belonged to the מַשְׂכִּילִים, the thoughtful teachers of the Jewish people of his days, who according to Dan 11:33 presumably instructed the רַבִּים in the paths of righteousness and the mysteries of the eschaton. These teachers in all probability shared more or less identical ideas about the final fate of Antiochus IV Epiphanes and the redemption of the God-chosen. In any case, our author's predictions seem to be based on at least two "sources": contemporaneous political expectations and (in particular) the witness of the prophets, interpreted in the framework of his own religious persuasion.

In order to elucidate these matters, let us first try to reconstruct how the author understood the political situation of his day when he wrote vv. 40-45. The contents of these verses can be summarized as follows: The king of the South will confront the king of the North and the latter will come storming against the former with immense land and naval forces. In the course of this expedition he will

---

[3]   On the use of Daniel in Jewish and Christian apocalyptic, cf. G. K. Beale, *The Use of Daniel in Jewish Apocalyptic Literature and in the Revelation of St. John* (Lanham and New York: University Press of America, 1984). An early use of Dan 11:40-45 is found in the Scroll of the War of the Sons of Light against the Sons of Darkness (1QM) col. 1.

[4]   As suggested by L. F. Hartman and A. A. di Lella, *The Book of Daniel* (AB 23; Garden City: Doubleday, 1983) 303: "it is best to view these verses as the sacred author's imaginative expectation of what would happen in the final days of Antiochus' career." Other authors point to prophetic predictions as the motive of the author's expectation, so e.g. A. Bentzen, *Daniel* (HAT 19; Tübingen: Mohr [Siebeck], 1937) 51: "Der Untergang des Tyrannen ist wahrscheinlich als Erfüllung von Jes 10:28-34 gedacht und dementsprechend geweissagt worden (Driver)."

overrun the Land of Israel and tens of thousands[5] shall fall victims. Edom, Moab and the élite[6] of the Ammonites will, however, escape his hand[7] in contradistinction to Egypt, Lybia and Nubia, which will be subdued and plundered. Rumours from the east and the north will force the king to return. On his way back he will meet his fate in the Holy Land.

Pace Porphyry,[8] this description of Antiochus' expedition against Egypt cannot be reconciled with the actual events of the king's final years. It seems, however, to reflect expectations nurtured by the idea that Egypt would retaliate Antiochus' iterated invasion of the land of the Nile, further increased by suspicions raised by the festival which Antiochus IV arranged at Daphne in the spring of 166 BCE. According to Polybius (*Histories* 30.25-27) this festival consisted of games, gladiatorial shows, beastfights and banquets and was opened with a military parade in which more than 50,000 soldiers participated. The parade could easily convey the impression of a review of troops, preceding a planned military campaign of large proportions. Against whom it would be directed was an open question at the time but in view of the king's former abortive expeditions against Egypt it might evoke the impression that another campaign by the king against the land of the Nile was at hand. In any case, Rome was not easy on that score. Shortly after the games, Tiberius Gracchus and other legates arrived in Antioch as inspectors (Polybius, *Histories* 30.27). They were, however, welcomed by Antiochus in such an impressive and courteous way that they did not harbor any real suspicion about evil intentions of the king nor did they detect anything indicative of disaffection to what had happened to him in Egypt when he was forced by C. Popilius Laenas to leave the country of the

---

5   Reading רֻבּוֹת.

6   There does not seem to be a cogent reason for changing רֵאשִׁית into שְׁאֵרִית (the remnant).

7   The passage is obscure. Perhaps the said peoples will be saved from an attack by Antiochus because they had shown themselves as being pro-Seleucid or because they were the traditional enemies of Israel, cf. J. J. Collins, *Daniel* (Hermeneia; Minneapolis: Fortress, 1993) 389. In any case, according to 1QM 1 they aligned with Belial and the Sons of Darkness.

8   Porphyry claimed that Antiochus launched another (third) campaign against Egypt. His remark is noticeable in view of his assertion that the prophecy of Daniel 11 is in fact a *vaticinium ex eventu*. There is, however, no historical evidence that Antiochus invaded Egypt a third time.

Nile immediately. They even discredited those who said anything of the kind, in view of the exceedingly kind reception by Antiochus IV. Polybius adds, however, that the king's real feelings were quite the reverse of the impression he conveyed to his well treated guests.

What can be inferred from this is that at least a number of the king's contemporaries presumed that Antiochus had made provisions for a new campaign against Egypt in retaliation of the humilation he suffered in 168 BCE due to Roman intervention. Rumours about such an intended expedition must have been widespread in the Near East in those days (although the Roman embassy eventually tried to discredit them) and may easily have reached the author of the book of Daniel as well. He apparently took them seriously and concluded that Egypt once again would be overrun and plundered by Antiochus, as soon as it would provoke a third war of the Seleucid against the land of the Nile. Later on, he apparently heard of the sedition of Artaxias in Armenia and of bad news that reached Antiochus from Persia. In particular the words "rumours from the east and the north" in Dan 11:44 are too specific as to deny that reports concerning the international political situation influenced him when he composed the section Dan 11:40-45.

The rumours which came to the author's attention, at least partially concurred with what could be concluded from prophetic words, taken by him (in conformity with the hermeneutics of the covenanters of Qumran) as predictions of the eschatological era. The latter were without doubt looked upon by him as more decisive than his own prognostication of the future on the basis of political considerations. Because he equated "Assyria" in the prophetic books, in particular in the book of Isaiah, to "Syria," i.e. the Seleucid empire, he turned his attention primarily towards those prophetic texts in the Bible which were speaking about the future fate of "Assyria." In this connection, it is noteworthy that already Dan 11:2-39 sometimes links together historical facts and prophetic predictions. As outlined by H. L. Ginsberg,[9] what is told about the Kittite ships in Dan 11: 30 conveyed to the reader the impression that the events in question were the fulfillment of Balaam's oracle of Num. 24:24a, understood by the Danielic author to mean: "And the ships from Kittim shall afflict Assyria, which in turn shall afflict the

---

[9]   H. L. Ginsberg, "The Oldest Interpretation of the Suffering Servant," *VT* 3 (1953) 400-404.

Hebrews." The expression "he will overwhelm and pass over" (שָׁטַף
וְעָבָר) found in Dan 11:10 and 40, derives from Isa 8:8. The final
words of Dan 11:27 and 35 contain an allusion to Hab 2:3a. More
important, however, is the remark made in Dan 11:36b that
Antiochus IV "will prosper until the indignation (of God) is finished,
for that which is decreed will happen." These words refer to the
prophetic prediction of Isa 10:23, part of a section in which
"Assyria" is said to be the rod of God's anger and the staff of his
indignation (Isa 10:5), but in which also the promise is found that the
Lord's indignation will soon spend itself (Isa 10:25): then Assyria
(i.e. the Seleucid empire) will no longer be able to wield the rod
over the people of Israel, but instead the Lord will wield a rod over
Assyria. In conclusion, in the verses which the author of Daniel 11
devotes to past and present events, he already linked them together
with what the prophets had foretold. Conversely, he felt confident
that the prophetic predictions which were not yet fulfilled would
materialize at the earliest moment.

In the book of Isaiah the fall of Assyria is predicted in Isa 10:12-
14, 24-27, in 10:33-34, and especially in 14:24-27. In the latter text
it is stated that the Lord will break the "Assyrian" in God's own land
and that the Lord's plan to do so is prepared for the whole earth.
This passage not only suggests an invasion of the Holy Land, in the
words of the author of Daniel 11 the "magnificent country" (Dan
11:16, 41), but also of the whole earth outside the "Assyrian" (i.e.
Seleucid) empire, exemplified in the text of Daniel (11:42) by Egypt
and regions as distant as the land of the Libyans and Cushites. The
motif of the subjugation of the peoples by "Assyria" and the
plundering of their treasures taken up by the author in Dan 11:43, is
found in Isa 10:13-14, although the Danielic wording is different
from that used in the Isaian passage. That the "Assyrian," looked
upon as the eschatological enemy and assimilated to a mythic pattern,
would meet his fate in the Holy Land (Isa 14:25) received
confirmation from Ezekiel 38–39 where Gog is said to fall on the
mountains of Israel. These considerations unmistakably lead to the
conclusion that the picture drawn in Dan 11:40-45 is primarily
inspired by Holy Scripture, taken as "canonical literature" in the
sense of God-given prediction (cf. Dan 9:2).

The author's reliance on contemporaneous political expectations
and in particular on the witness of the prophets was of course embedded in the inherited religious persuasion of his own community,

shaped on the basis of ongoing biblical interpretation as well as political, religious and social experiences. The context of 11:40-45 attests to the views held by him and his co-religionists: that the *eschaton* was at hand, that therefore the contemporaneous events were not just another relatively insignificant part of history, that the oppressor of the present time was the "anti-christ" of the last days, that God's vindication of the pious would be realized in near future, that the Lord's promises and covenant did not apply to the whole of Israel, that he and his community belonged to the God-chosen, that the fate of this world was predestined by the world above, that the archangel Michael as God's representative and Israel's patron would soon interfere in history, that the pious would find their reward in the kingdom-to-come etc. All these convictions were the ingredients of a particular belief system which the author did not invent himself but which he had inherited from a community which had cherished them already for considerable time. Pseudepigraphical writings, especially I Enoch, and the Dead Sea scrolls help us in tracing the origin and development of this apocalyptic belief system, which (in view of the fact that the book of Daniel eventually was included in the canon) seems to have been rather widespread in Palestinian Jewish circles of the third and second centuries BCE.

The remarks made in the preceding paragragh are of course common knowledge but the matters to which they refer, explain the confidence with which the author of these Danielic passages drafted his picture of the final salvation. In view of his religious convictions, his political sensitivity and the eschatologization of prophecy, he could hardly have presented otherwise his ideas about the imminent future of his people. Nevertheless, decisive in this connection is not the form in which he presented his future hope but the latter itself, nurtured by the faith that inspired him and the prophetic predictions that were his lead. Therefore, he cannot have felt the transition of his (what we call) *vaticinium ex eventu* to the expected events as a major and decisive caesura. The fact that the book of Daniel was eventually canonized as Holy Scripture in spite of the soon ascertainable erroneous predictions of a third expedition by Antiochus IV against Egypt and his death in the Holy Land, proves that believers in early Judaism, because of their reliance on God's promises as worded by the prophets, could overcome historical experiences by reinterpreting Antiochus' final fate as referring to the fall of the eschatological enemy who would meet his end on the soil of Israel. Consequently, it does not come as a surprise that the Qumran covenanters applied the passage in question to the final fate of (the chief of) the Kittîm, the adversary of God's people in the last days who would be utterly defeated in the Holy Land.[10] Modern fundamentalists may find in this reinterpretation of Dan 11:40-45 some justification for their (faulty) assertion that these verses refer (also) to an "antichrist" yet to come, not (only) to Antiochus IV.

The section Dan 12:1-3[11] is equally dependent on prophetic predictions interpreted in the framework of the convictions held by the author and his community. In accordance with the idea that the destiny of mankind corresponds to the battle which is going on in heaven between the angelic rulers of the nations, the author felt obliged to mention Israel's patron angel Michael as the protagonist of the final redemption of God's people in his description of the unprecedented time of anguish which would befall Israel before its ultimate salvation. Apparently, the "time of anguish such as not has been from the beginning of the nation[12] to that time" is based on the prediction of the great Day of the Lord beyond all comparison of Jer 30:7 which would be "a time of anguish for Jacob" but from which "he yet be will saved." However, in accordance with the convictions of the author and his community, not the people of Israel as a whole would be delivered but only "those who are written in the book" (cf. Mal 3:13-18, esp. v. 16), the remnant of the holy ones who according to Isa 4:3 are recorded for life in Jerusalem. That the "book" indeed refers to the book of life is corroborated by the prayer of 4QDibHam[a] (4Q504) 6:12-14: "Free your people Isra[el from all] the countries, near and far, [to] where [You have scattered us], all who are recorded in the book of life."[13] This text may be older than the Danielic passage in question.[14] It does not only elucidate the latter

---

[10]   Cf. 1QM and in particular 4QWar Scroll[g] = 4Q285, frag. 5.

[11]   On this section see in particular G. W. E. Nickelsburg, Jr., *Resurrection, Immortality, and Eternal Life in Intertestamental Judaism* (HTS 36; Cambridge and London: Harvard University Press, 1972) 11-27.

[12]   Because of the dependence on Jer 30:7 גוי is best understood as referring to Israel, not to the nations in general.

[13]   See M. Baillet, *Qumrân grotte 4 III (4Q482–4Q520)* (DJD 7; Oxford: Clarendon, 1982) 148.

[14]   Baillet (*Qumrân grotte 4 III*, 137) dates 4Q504 to about 150 BCE. Since it obviously is a copy of an older manuscript, the contents must have been composed at least somewhat earlier. See also M. Baillet, "Un recueil liturgique de Qumran,

but in all likelihood also indicates that the author of the Book of
Truth availed himself of contemporaneous literature which was in
line with his own religious persuasion.

However one wants to interpret the text of Isa 26:19, it is beyond
question that Dan 12:2a echoes this passage and that the author of
Daniel understood it in terms of individual resurrection. Accordingly, the many (רַבִּים) seem to refer here to deceased of Israel, a
number of whom will be resurrected to everlasting life and the
others to eternal abhorrence (דְּרָאוֹן). The latter word is apparently
taken from Isa 66:24, where it is said that the righteous will gaze at
the dead bodies of those who rebelled against God, whose "worm
shall not die nor their fire be quenched" and who "shall be an abhorrence to all mankind."

So far, we have tried to point out that the author of Dan 11:40–
12:3 composed his picture of the last days primarily on the basis of
prophetic literature, taken by him as authoritative Scripture. We
have added, however, that he also shaped his message in the context
of his own belief system and historical experiences. Therefore, we
have to guard carefully against overstating the influence of prophetic
preaching, although it undoubtedly largely determined his argument.
In view of this, it is questionable whether Ginsberg's thesis that Dan
12:3 constitutes the oldest interpretation of the Suffering Servant of
Isaiah 53, is correct.[15] The text of Dan 12:3 deals with the glorification of the מַשְׂכִּלִים and the מַצְדִּיקֵי הָרַבִּים. Because of the *parallelismus membrorum* of the verse, the latter seem to be identical with

---

grotte 4: Les Paroles des luminaires," *RB* 68 (1961) 235-38.

15   Ginsberg, "The Oldest Interpretation of the Suffering Servant," 400-404.
His suggestion is followed by almost all commentators, cf. e.g. M. Delcor, *Le livre
de Daniel* (Sources Bibliques; Paris: Gabalda, 1971) 256; Hartman and A. A. di
Lella, *Daniel*, 274; A. Lacocque, *The Book of Daniel* (Atlanta: John Knox, 1979)
243 ("midrashic reuse"); Collins, *Daniel*, 393; see also M. Fishbane, *Biblical
Interpretation in Ancient Israel* (Oxford: Oxford University Press, 1985) 493; and
M. A. Knibb, "You Are Indeed Wiser Than Daniel": Reflections on the Character
of the Book of Daniel," in A. S. van der Woude (ed.), *The Book of Daniel in the
Light of New Findings* (BETL 106; Leuven: Peeters and Leuven University Press,
1993) 406. J. A. Montgomery (*The Book of Daniel* [ICC; Edinburgh: T. & T.
Clark, 1927] 472) noted already that "the present text of Is. 53:11 may be compared"; and A. Bentzen (*Daniel*, 52) stated that "der Ausdruck . . . stammt aus Jes
53:11." N. W. Porteous (*Das Danielbuch* [ATD 23; Göttingen: Vandenhoeck &
Ruprecht, 1962] 144) more cautiously remarks that Isa 53:11 "hier die Wortwahl
beeinflußt haben könnte."

the former. That the epithet מַשְׂכִּלִים is taken from Isa 52:13 must be doubted. This assumption can hardly be based on the latter text, where it is merely said that "my Servant יַשְׂכִּיל" (which, incidentally, means that "he will prosper," not that he will be a wise teacher). The use of the term מַשְׂכִּיל in the Qumran documents for a leading instructor in the community of the Dead Sea covenanters militates against connecting this designation with the Servant song of Isa 52:13–53:12.[16] The supposition that the term מַשְׂכִּלִים in Dan (11:33 and) 12:3 is taken from the fourth song of the Suffering Servant seems therefore to rest only on the inference that מַצְדִּיקֵי הָרַבִּים is derived from Isa 53:11bα. Ginsberg asserts that there can be no doubt about (what he calls) the plain fact that the author of Daniel 11–12 has simply identified the Servant of Isa 52:13–53:12 with the מַשְׂכִּלִים of his day, and the Many of the said passage with the Many of Dan 11:33, 34 etc.: "The Maskilim, like the Servant, justify the Many; and tho [sic] one sense of this phrase in Daniel may be that they instruct them and induce them to take the right path (Dan xi 33), some of the Maskilim do also suffer martyrdom and are resurrected, and it is only to these that the epithet of 'justifiers of the Many' certainly applies (Dan xii 3). And the ultimate glory of these martyrs (Dan xii 3) is so reminiscent of that of the Servant! Undoubtedly our author has identified the Many of Isa lii 13–liii 12 with the masses in the time of the Antiochan religious persecution, and the Servant with the minority of steadfast anti-hellenizers."[17] Ginsberg's assertion gives rise to at least two problems: (a) in contradistinction to Hellenistic Judaism and medieval Jewish sources, in early Palestinian Judaism the Servant of Isaiah 53 was (as far as we know) never interpreted as an collective entity[18] but as a (presumably messianic) individual[19]; (b) the מַשְׂכִּלִים of the book of Daniel are never described as martyrs whose martyrdom would be propitiatory. On the contrary, they are only presented as teachers of

---

[16] As far as I know, there is no indication that the מַשְׂכִּיל mentioned in the Dead Sea scrolls would have compared himself to the Suffering Servant of Isaiah 53.

[17] Ginsberg, "The Oldest Interpretation of the Suffering Servant," 402.

[18] Cf. J. Jeremias, "παῖς θεοῦ," TWNT 5.682-683 = TDNT 5.684-86. The collective interpretation of "Servant of the Lord" occurs for the first time in Hellenistic Judaism in the Wis 2:13. Whether this text refers to Isaiah 53 is a moot question.

[19] Cf. K. Koch, "Messias und Sündenvergebung in Jesaja 53-Targum," JSJ 3 (1972) 117-48.

the רַבִּים (Dan 11:33). In view of the evidence provided by the Qumran scrolls, the רַבִּים do not seem to be "the common people,"[20] but the community of those who adhered to the paternal laws. Because 11:35 speaks of some of the מַשְׂכִּלִים who "stumbled,"[21] it is likely that in 11:33-34 this community is the subject of "stumbling [נִכְשְׁלוּ] by sword and flame and captivity and plunder for some days," that it is this community which "will receive little help" and to whose ranks "many will join insincerely" (Dan 11:34). The niphʿal derivations of the verb כשׁל point to falling victims (cf. 11:41), not to martyrdom in the proper sense of the word,[22] let alone to justification of the רַבִּים by vicarious suffering. Apart from the fact that Dan 12:3 does not exactly reproduce Isa 53:11b (יַצְדִּיק . . . לָרַבִּים), the semantic meaning of the hiphʿil of צדק in Dan 12:3 does not coincide with that of Isa 53:11. In conformity with the meaning of מַשְׂכִּלִים and in view of the parallelismus membrorum, the expression מַצְדִּיקֵי הָרַבִּים rather suggests the idea of teachers and wise men who by their instruction lead the רַבִּים to righteousness (cf. for this meaning CD 20:18). Thus the hiphʿil participle of צדק in Dan 12:3 is used in a sense which comes very near to the hiphʿil of בין in Dan 11:33. Because there is no cogent reason to regard the terms רַבִּים (which already in other parts of the Old Testament is used as a designation of a mass of people) and מַשְׂכִּלִים as being taken from Isaiah 53 and a collective interpretation of this chapter is alien to early Palestinian Judaism, it is extremely doubtful that the Danielic writer of 12:3 formulated the words מַצְדִּיקֵי הָרַבִּים with Isa 53:11 in mind. In this case, his words seem to have sprung from his own inherited religious convictions. Finally, one can doubt whether Dan 12:3 points to celestial ascension (cf. *1 Enoch* 104:2-4).[23] It is much more likely that the future glory of the מַשְׂכִּלִים in the expected kingdom of God is compared to celestial glory.

---

20   So Collins, *Daniel*, 385.

21   Seemingly, 11:35 does not once again speak about the מַשְׂכִּלִים after a description of their sufferings in vv. 33-34. It is much more likely that 11:35 states that not only many of the community but even some of the מַשְׂכִּלִים "stumbled." Therefore, in 11:33 the subject of נִכְשְׁלוּ seems to be the רַבִּים.

22   As noticed by J.-C. Lebram, *Das Buch Daniel* (Zürcher Bibelkommentare; Zürich: Theologische Verlag, 1984) 132.

23   As suggested by J. J. Collins, "Apocalyptic Eschatology as the Transcendence of Death," *CBQ* 36 (1974) 33-35, on the basis of *1 Enoch* 104:3, 6; 39:5 and Matt 22:30. See the objections made by Hartman and A. A. di Lella, *Daniel*, 310.

Far from being a strange and odd piece of biblical literature, Dan 11:40–12:3 testifies in an impressive way to the firm belief of a representative of tempted men that the Lord would bring about the vindication and the glorification of the God-chosen in accordance with the Lord's prophetic promises and the author's own persuasion. That he erred in understanding the "signs of the times" cannot be denied and should not be gainsaid. But even so, his reliance on the words of the prophets and his allegiance to the inherited religious traditions in the face of terrifying political circumstances should at least come home to the modern reader of Dan 11:40–12:3 as a moving testimony of firm belief which was not based on sheer imagination but on what the author thought to be reliable predictions and authoritative data. Modern believers owe a debt of gratitude to him for having put into words the conviction that God eventually will vindicate those who endure to the end.

It is a great honor to have been invited to contribute to this *Festschrift* dedicated to a highly respected colleague and a dear friend who has made a major contribution to our understanding of the canonization process of the Hebrew Bible, the Dead Sea scrolls and problems of intertextuality. These lines are devoted to him in sincere admiration of his achievements and with best wishes for the years to come.

THE SIGNIFICATION OF שָׁלוֹם AND ITS SEMANTIC FIELD IN THE HEBREW BIBLE[1]

Shemaryahu Talmon

> "The subjective is always present
> even in the posing of questions:
> different questions, different facts,
> different connections, different inter-
> pretation."[2]

INTRODUCTION

The attempt to gauge the conceptual content of שָׁלוֹם is beset by several difficulties which inhere in the biblical literature:

The modern reader, trained to express his notions in a sequential, structured and systematic disposition, is perplexed by the almost total unavailability in the Hebrew Bible of any noticeable attempt to formulate comprehensively and methodically facets of human thought, which in the biblical period were current in the Israelite marketplace of ideas. Some incipient conceptualization comes indeed into view in diverse components of the biblical "canon,"[3] especially

---

[1]   I dedicate this essay (part of which was presented at the Annual Meeting of the Society of Biblical Literature in Chicago, 21 November 1994) to my friend Jim Sanders—scholar and colleague—at his turning septuagenarian: עוֹד יְנוּב בְּשֵׂיבָה (Ps 92:15).

[2]   J. Huizinga, "Historical Conceptualization," in F. Stern (ed.), *The Varieties of History* (2nd ed., London: Macmillan, 1970) 289-303.

[3]   I use the term "canon" for the sake of convenience, having explained my reservations in "Heiliges Schrifttum und kanonische Bücher aus jüdischer Sicht— Überlegungen zur Ausbildung der Grösse 'Die Schrift' im Judentum," in M. Klop-fenstein, U. Luz, S. Talmon, and E. Tov (eds.), *Mitte der Schrift? Ein jüdisch-christliches Gespräch: Texte des Berner Symposions vom 6.-12. Januar 1985* (Bern: Peter Lang, 1987) 45-80 = idem, *Israels Gedankenwelt in der Hebräischen Bibel* (Gesammelte Aufsätze Band 3; Information Judentum 13; Neukirchen-Vluyn: Neukirchener Verlag, 1995) 241-71.

in the books of the prophets, Psalms, and in wisdom writings.[4] But even in these components of the Hebrew Bible, conceptualization surfaces only sporadically.[5]

The conspicuous absence of conceptual systematization engenders the surmise that the apparent deficiency did not result from mere happenstance. Rather, it seems to be rooted in the intrinsic mode of thinking of the biblical literati, who deliberately refrained from abstractions, and preferred to encapsulate their speculative thought in factual accounts of "historical" events and situations. Only occasionally, the presentation transcends plain actuality. In such instances, biblical writers are wont to give expression to their evaluation of the recorded circumstances in stereotype summaries. These subscripts sometimes exhibit a negative assessment of the facts reported which contradicts the positive appreciation that shows in the main account, or vice versa. The feature is especially noticeable in the Book of Kings,[6] and in Chronicles.[7] Or else, a redactor/editor will insert into the consecutive register of historical exposés an interpretative excursus, which evinces an incipient endeavor to extract from the "historical events" their essential significance, so as to integrate the "facts" in a seminal framework of conceptualization.[8] However, even when viewed in toto, these incidental summary notations, interpretative appendixes and parenetic excursus cannot be construed as a Lehrgebäude, viz., a methodically worked-out system of any aspect of philosophy, history or theology.

---

[4]   The matter is well known, and needs not to be pursued here. The reader is referred, inter alia, to J. Pedersen's discussion of the ancient Israelites' world of thought: Israel, its Life and Culture (London: Oxford University Press; Copenhagen: Branner, vols. 1-2, 1926; vols. 3-4, 1940).

[5]   See, inter alia, W. A. Irwin, "The Hebrews," in H. and H. A. Frankfort, J. A. Wilson, T. Jacobsen, W. A. Irwin, The Intellectual Adventure of Ancient Man, An Essay on Speculative Thought in the Ancient Near East (Chicago: University of Chicago Press, 1946) 223-362.

[6]   E.g. in the antagonistic résumés of the reigns of kings of northern Israel: Baasha (1 Kgs 15:34–16:4 vs. 16:5-6); Omri (16:25-26 vs. 16:24, 27-28); Ahab (22:39 vs. the preceding block of accounts 20:1-34); Jehu (2 Kgs 10:31-33 vs. 10:34-36); Jehoahaz (13:8-9 vs. 13:2-7); Jehoash (13:10-11 vs. 13:12-25; 14:9-16); Jeroboam ben Joash (14:23-24 vs. 14:25-29); Menachem ben Gadi (15:16 vs. 15:18).

[7]   E.g. in the comparison of the Chronicler's account of Rehoboam's reign (2 Chr 11:5-12; 12:13) with the appended summary (12:14).

[8]   See e.g. 2 Kgs 17:7-23.

An accurate assessment of the degree to which the ancient Israelites conceptualized prominent facets in the world of ideas is further impeded by the diversity of sources, literary strands, genres etc., conjoined in the Hebrew Bible, which originated at different times in heterogenous strata of the Israelite society. Most components of the corpus are not internally dated, or else the credibility of dates recorded is put in doubt. Therefore, one cannot extract from them unequivocal information for tracing the progressive development in the biblical period of any concept under review.

The combination of pluriformity, chronological indetermination, and the only parenthetically offered non-systematic fractions of speculative thought, prescribes the approach by which an appraisement of the signification of שׁלום in the Bible can be attempted. The exegete is called upon, as it were, to emulate the ancient Israelites' way of thinking conceptually by association, rather than by systematization, and by conjoining disjunctive data, extracted from a diversity of texts.[9] By thus proceeding, one cannot expect to paint a full and detailed picture of the issue under review. Rather, the investigation is bound to produce an incomplete mosaic in which many pieces are missing, and some of the available ones do not fit in at all.[10]

These difficulties cause that scholars tend to analyze the use of the vocable שׁלום and to elucidate the speculative thought which it presumably encapsulates, in the compass of a specific component of the biblical literature—a literary stratum or a cluster of compositions ascribed to a particular "source," e.g. in writings affiliated with the "deuteronomistic school."[11] The legitimacy of these partial inquiries is beyond debate, and their indispensability evident. However, such limited studies cannot throw light on the

---

9   For a discussion of this issue in respect to other cultures in the Ancient Near East, see Frankfort et al., *The Intellectual Adventure* (in n. 5 above), and H. Frankfort (ed.), *Kingship and the Gods* (Chicago: The University of Chicago Press, 1948) esp. Frankfort's chapter, "The Hebrews," 337-46.

10   *Mutatis mutandis*, this characterization pertains also to rabbinic literature.

11   See, inter alia, G. Braulik, "Zur deuteronomistischen Konzeption von Freiheit und Frieden," in J. A. Emerton (ed.), *Congress Volume Salamanca 1983* (VTSup 36; Leiden: Brill, 1985) 29-39; F. M. Cross, "The Themes of the Book of Kings and the Structure of the Deuteronomistic History," in Cross, *Canaanite Myth and Hebrew Epic: Essays in the History of the Religion of Israel* (Cambridge: Harvard University Press, 1973) 274-289.

gamut of meanings of the term שׁלוֹם in the comprehensive biblical corpus, but can only clarify its employment in the specific component brought under scrutiny.

In the ensuing analysis of the connotation or connotations of שׁלוֹם, I propose to take a synoptic or holistic approach. I aim at bringing under review all occurrences of the term in the Hebrew Scriptures, or as many as possible, so as to gauge its intrinsic signification and the range of its applications in the entire corpus in its transmitted form. The synopsis reveals indeed noticeable variations in the uses of שׁלוֹם, but practically all can be integrated in a classificatory system.[12]

A comprehensive intertextual analysis of שׁלוֹם brings to light what may be described as an ongoing dialogue in the biblical writings which bridges chronological gaps and crosses the boundaries of "sources," irrespective of the presumed association of one or the other author with this or that school of thought. Idiomatic expressions, motifs and literary patterns woven around שׁלוֹם persisted in the biblical writers' vocabulary throughout the ages, and linked the diverse components of the corpus in an overarching wealth of shared figures of speech.[13] Therefore, as will yet be shown, an expression or a tale which centers on שׁלוֹם can often help in the interpretation of a "distant parallel" in a different textual

---

[12]   There remain the open questions whether the variegations can be traced to discrete "sources" or "schools of thought" (see above), and whether they evince synchronous variations or diachronous developments in the employment of the vocable שׁלוֹם. These issues require detailed in depth analyses which in the present context can be addressed only *en passant*.

[13]   On this matter see, inter alia, M. Fishbane, *Biblical Interpretation in Ancient Israel* (Oxford: Clarendon Press, 1985). I have discussed some such phenomena in "The Desert Motif in the Bible and in Qumran Literature," in A. Altmann (ed.), *Biblical Motifs: Origin and Transformations* (Cambridge: Harvard University Press, 1966) 31-63; repr. in Talmon, *Literary Studies in the Hebrew Bible, Form and Content* (Jerusalem: Magnes, 1992) 216-54; idem, "The Navel of the Earth and the Comparative Method," ibid., 50-75; idem, "Literary Motifs and Speculative Thought in the Hebrew Bible," *Hebrew University Studies in Literature and the Arts* 16 (1988) 150-68; idem, "The 'Topped Triad': A Biblical Literary Convention and the 'Ascending Numerical Pattern,' in R. J. Ratner, L. M. Barth, M. L. Gevirtz, B. Zuckerman (eds.), *Let Your Colleagues Praise You: Studies in Memory of Stanley Gevirtz*, Part II *Maarav* 8 (1992) 181-98; S. Talmon and W. W. Fields, "The Collocation משׁתין בקיר ועצור ועזוב and its Meaning," *ZAW* 101 (1989) 85-110.

framework, and sometimes even in the elucidation of a textual crux. Drawing upon a phrase in Job, early Jewish commentators defined this method of interpretation by יַגִּיד עָלָיו רֵעוֹ (36:33), and construed it to mean "one verse may help in ascertaining the meaning of another." From this basic exegetical principle were derived several of the 32 rules laid down by the Galilean sage Eliezer ben Yosei: "What is said in one place may also be applied in another similar context" (rule 19); "the meaning of an expression can be ascertained with the help of its employment in another passage" (rule 22); "some texts shed light on others" (rule 23) etc.[14]

The dividing lines between successive stages in an assumedly diachronical development of the signification of שָׁלוֹם may at times become blurred: A late text will occasionally preserve a pristine connotation of שָׁלוֹם, whereas in a presumedly early text the employment of the term may have been contaminated by subsequent modifications.[15] Last but not least, the originally precise connotation of an idiomatic expression, even of a technical term, may dissipate in the course of time. Widespread employment of such a vocable has often a levelling impact on its initially exact signification, so much so that it can become part of a run-of-the-mill collocation.[16] Such a neutralizing process is especially prone to affect "reach me down" terms, like שָׁלוֹם, which adapt easily to a broad range of circumstances.

Our investigation revolves in part on traditions which are presented as records of "historical realities." Therefore, before going into *medias res*, the obvious must be emphasized: I am not concerned with assessing the factuality or non-factuality of biblical reports in which שָׁלוֹם is prominently employed, but solely with the exegetical endeavor of assessing the authors' understanding of the signification of the term.

---

14   For an illustration of this exegetical method, see, inter alia, my "Emendations of Biblical Texts on the Basis of Ugaritic Parallels," in S. Japhet (ed.), *Studies in Bible* (Scripta Hierosolymitana 31; Jerusalem: Magnes, 1986) 279–300.

15   As a result, the dating of texts brought under scrutiny will necessarily affect conclusions concerning the changing or developing signification of שָׁלוֹם. For example, the question whether Zech 9:10 evinces a late stage in the use of שָׁלוֹם and Zech 6:13; 8:10 an earlier one, will be differently answered by scholars who predate or postdate Zechariah 9–12 to 1–8.

16   However, also the opposite development may occur. In the course of time, a general vocable can become invested with a very specific meaning.

PHENOMENA

A. Occurrences of שלום[17]

The noun שָׁלוֹם is attested 238 times in the Hebrew Bible.[18] שָׁלוֹם occurs mostly in the absolute (209), predominantly in the naked absolute (116); five times with the definite article;[19] six times with conjunctive וֹ; twice with both the definitie article and conjunctive וֹ. The term is used 35 times with the preposition בְּ, 30 times with לְ, and once with מִ. There are 13 occurrences of שלום in the stative construct, and ten with a personal pronoun. Three occurrences in the plural are contextually doubtful (Jer 13:19; Ps 55:21; 69:23), and the connection of the phrase שְׁלֻמֵי אֱמוּנֵי יִשְׂרָאֵל (2 Sam 20:19) with שלום is considered uncertain.

Several personal, probably theophoric names contain the noun שְׁלוּמִי,[21] שֶׁל(וּ)מוֹת,[20] שְׁלוֹמִית, שְׁלוֹמִיאֵל, שַׁלְמוֹן, שְׁלֶמְיָה, שַׁלּוּם, שָׁלוֹם: et sim., foremost the names of David's sons, אַבְשָׁלוֹם and שְׁלֹמֹה (see below).[22] The city name יְרוּשָׁלֵ(י)ם, whose pre-Israelite form *uru-šilimma* means "city" or "foundation" dedicated to the ancient Semitic deity *šulmānitu*, was later reinterpreted as "City of Peace."

The *pa'al* of denominative שלם connotes personal prosperity or safety (Job 9:4 and 22:21). The *pi'el* שִׁלֵּם can signify "to protect" or

---

[17] See now F. J. Stendebach's discussion of שלום *šālôm* with an ample apparatus of pertinent literature in *TWAT* 8 (1994) 12-46, which came to my attention only after the completion of this paper.

[18] Figures are given here according to A. Even-Shoshan, *A New Concordance of the Bible* (Jerusalem: Kiryath Sefer, 1981). Slight differences in comparison with listings in other handbooks, concordances and dictionaries, arise from the fact that in some instances the etymological relation of a vocable with שלום is uncertain (see below). However, these discrepancies do not affect the results of the ensuing analysis.

[19] הַשָּׁלוֹם in 2 Kgs 9:22b should be vocalized הֲשָׁלוֹם, as a question, like in the first half of the verse. Cp. 9:17, 18.

[20] This nominative proper is found on seals, and as the name of the son of Sanballat, governor of Samaria, in the Elephantine Papyri.

[21] The name was discovered at Hazor, inscribed on a jar from the 7th or 6th century BCE.

[22] Cp. the Assyrian royal names: *šalim-aḫum*, *šulmānu-ašarēdu* (M. H. Pope, "Šaḫr and Šalim," *WbMyth* 1.307), and the divine names, *šulmān*, *šulamānitu* (W. F. Albright, "The Syro-Mesopotamian God Šulmân Ešmûn and Related Figures," *AfO* 7 [1931-32] 164-69). Theophoric names which contain the divine epithet *šalim/salim* turn up in Mari texts (see J. J. Stamm, "Hebräische Ersatznamen," *OBO* 30 [1980] 59-79).

"give peace" (as in Job 8:6).[23] The *hiph'il* serves seven times as a technical term which defines the cessation of hostilities and the establishment of "peace," mostly in the wake of warfare (Deut 20:12; Josh 10:1,4; 11:19; 2 Sam 10:19 = 1 Chr 19:19; Prov. 16:7 et al.; see below).

In the phrase וַיָּבֹא יַעֲקֹב שָׁלֵם עִיר שְׁכֶם (Gen 33:18), adverbial שָׁלֵם means "safely";[24] and in the statement הָאֲנָשִׁים הָאֵלֶּה שְׁלֵמִים הֵם אִתָּנוּ (34:21) "friendly" or "peaceful." It is debatable whether the expressions הִגְלָת יְהוּדָה כֻּלָּה הָגְלָת שְׁלוֹמִים (Amos 1:6, 9) and גָּלוּת שְׁלֵמָה (Jer 13:19) signify "total deportation" or "exilation in times of peace" (cp. 1 Kgs 2:5: בְּשָׁלֹם דְּמֵי־מִלְחָמָה בְּשָׁלֹם; Job 15:21: בַּשָּׁלוֹם שׁוֹדֵד יְבוֹאֶנּוּ).[25]

B. Etymology of שָׁלוֹם

The vocable שָׁלוֹם is usually derived from the stem שׁלם, found in several Semitic languages in a variety of forms and applications,[26] and as a loanword also in Egyptian *šrm*. In many instances, the term conveys the positive notion of "wholeness," as does Ugaritic *šlm* I. The denominative adjective שָׁלֵם means "complete, unharmed" et sim. In reference to the individual, "wholeness" spells physical and spiritual wellbeing. On the collective level, it indicates harmonious interpersonal and inter-group relations. In Pedersen's words: "A community . . . is characterized by the harmony arising in that the whole of the community is penetrated by the blessing. This harmony the Israelite calls *shalōm*, the word which is usually rendered by peace. Its fundamental meaning is totality; it means the untrammelled free growth of the soul. But this in its turn means the same as the harmonious community. There is totality in a community, when there is harmony."[27]

---

23   וַאֲשַׁלֵּם נִחֻמִים לוֹ וְלַאֲבֵלָיו (Isa 57:18) may be rendered somewhat freely: "I will give peace and (or: of) consolation, him and all who mourned for him."

24   Cp. וְשַׁבְתִּי בְשָׁלוֹם אֶל־בֵּית אָבִי in Jacob's vow to build a house of God in Bethel (Gen 28:21).

25   For a more detailed analysis of the use of שָׁלֵם *šālēm*, see now K. J. Illman's entry in *TWAT* 8.93-101.

26   See G. Bergsträsser, *Einführung in die semitischen Sprachen: Sprachproben und grammatische Skizzen* (2nd ed., Darmstadt: Wissenschaftliche Buchgesellschaft, 1977) 189; ET: *Introduction to the Semitic Languages: Specimens and Grammatical Sketches* (Winona Lake: Eisenbrauns, 1983).

27   Pedersen, *Israel*, 2.263. Cp. G. von Rad, *Theologie des Alten Testaments*,

C. Translations of שָׁלוֹם

The renditions of שָׁלוֹם (Aram. שְׁלָם, Syr. ܫܠܡܐ) in non-semitic target languages—εἰρήνη and *pax* in the ancient Greek[28] and Latin versions, and the routine translations into modern languages—peace, paix, paz, pace, Frieden etc., are but approximations which do not accurately reflect the intrinsic signification of the Hebrew term nor its connotative range.[29] In this case, as in reference to other fundamental biblical terms, such as בְּרִית,[30] the adage holds true: *tradutore traditore*. Therefore, in the ensuing discussion, I prefer to use predominantly the Hebrew term שָׁלוֹם.

D. The Range of Connotations of שָׁלוֹם[31]

At this juncture I propose a classification of the uses of שָׁלוֹם in rough outline. The system will be refined in the analysis of the distribution of the noun and the vocabulary connected with it in diverse components of the biblical corpus, leading to some conclusions concerning its intrinsic signification.

(1) שָׁלוֹם connotes a state of personal "well-being," "comfort," "prosperity," "safety," "ease," *sans souci*, often seen as a proverbial reward for the godfearing (Ps 35:27), but denied to the sinner (Ps 38:4). The righteous can lie down at night without worry, בְּשָׁלוֹם, fully assured that in the morning he will wake up hale and hearty,

---

vol. 1 (München: Kaiser, 1957) 136: "שלום bezeichnet nämlich die Unversehrtheit, die Ganzheit eines Gemeinschaftsverhältnisses, also einen Zustand harmonischen Gleichgewichtes, der Ausgewogenheit aller Ansprüche und Bedürfnisse zwischen zwei Partnern."

28   In the LXX, εἰρήνη serves exclusively as a translation of שלום. In some instances the Hebrew term is translated σωτήριον (Gen 41:16), σωτηρία (Gen 26:31; 28:21), ὑγιαίνεν (Gen 29:6; 37:14; Josh 10:21) etc.

29   See, inter alia, von Rad, *Theologie*, 1.136: "Das von einem Bundesschluss garantierte Verhältnis wird gern durch das Wort שלום bezeichnet (Gen 26,30 ff.; I Kön 5,26; Jes 54,10; Hi 5,23), für das wiederum unser Wort Friede nur als eine unzureichende Entsprechung dienen kann."

30   To quote again von Rad, *Theologie*, 1.135: "'Bund' ist nur eine behelfsmässige Wiedergabe des hebräischen Wortes ברית."

31   The diverse significations of שלום will be illustrated in each instance by a selection of examples. The roster can be easily amplified. No hard and fast boundaries divide the sub-categories in the classification suggested. A given text can often be subsumed under more than one heading. There are also border cases which appear to evince a deliberate *double entendre*.

לָבֶטַח (Ps 4:9).[32] "Abundant prosperity (is given) to those who love your torah, they incur no adversity [שָׁלוֹם רָב לְאֹהֲבֵי תוֹרָתֶךָ וְאֵין־לָמוֹ מִכְשׁוֹל]" (Ps 119:165);[33] "for long life and years (in plenty) and prosperity will they (God's commandments) bring you [כִּי אֹרֶךְ יָמִים וּשְׁנוֹת חַיִּים וְשָׁלוֹם יוֹסִיפוּ לָךְ]" (Prov 3:2); "the humble shall possess the land and thrive on great prosperity [וַעֲנָוִים יִירְשׁוּ־אָרֶץ וְהִתְעַנְּגוּ עַל־רֹב שָׁלוֹם]" (Ps 37:11); "You will know that all is well with your household, look around your home and find nothing amiss [וְיָדַעְתָּ כִּי־שָׁלוֹם אָהֳלֶךָ וּפָקַדְתָּ נָוְךָ וְלֹא תֶחֱטָא]" (Job 5:24).[34] Also nature is in accord with the righteous: "for you have a covenant with the stones of the field, and are at one with the beasts of the field [כִּי עִם־אַבְנֵי הַשָּׂדֶה בְרִיתֶךָ וְחַיַּת הַשָּׂדֶה הָשְׁלְמָה־לָךְ]"[35] (Job 5:23; cp. Hos 2:20).[36] In contrast, "the wicked will have no comfort [... אֵין שָׁלוֹם לָרְשָׁעִים]" (Isa 48:22; 57:21, cp. Jer 6:14; 8:11; Ezek 13:10,16).

The term signifies a situation free of danger or harm. God allays Gideon's fear that he will die after having seen an angel face to face: "Greetings (or: you are safe), be not afraid, you shall not die [שָׁלוֹם לְךָ אַל־תִּירָא לֹא תָמוּת]" (Judg 6:22-23). To commemorate the vision in which God had greeted him with שׁלום, Gideon built an altar which he named יהוה שׁלום (6:24), like Abraham had named יהוה יִרְאֶה the place where by divine intervention, אֱלֹהִים יִרְאֶה־לּוֹ הַשֶּׂה (Gen 22:8), he had seen the ram, וַיִּרָא וְהִנֵּה־אַיִל, which he sacrificed instead of his son (22:13).[37] The comparison suggests that the phrase יהוה שׁלום in the Gideon tradition cannot be construed as an epithet of YHWH who is thereby presented, as it were, as the "God of Peace." Similarly, the heavenly messengers encourage Daniel not to be afraid: אַל־תִּירָא דָנִיֵּאל ... אַל־תִּירָא אִישׁ־חֲמֻדוֹת שָׁלוֹם לָךְ (Dan 10:12, 19). And Jonathan assures David: "I swear to

---

32   For the equation שׁלום = בטה/בטחון, see discussion below.

33   Note the antithesis שׁלום – מכשׁול.

34   חטא contrasts שָׁלוֹם/שָׁלֵם.

35   Denominative hophʿal.

36   Cp. complaints about the undeserved comfort of evildoers: "I see that the wicked prosper [שְׁלוֹם רְשָׁעִים אֶרְאֶה]" (Ps 73:3); "their homes are safe of danger [בָּתֵּיהֶם שָׁלוֹם מִפָּחַד]" (Job 21:7-9, cp. Deut 29:18; Jer 23:17), with פהד serving as an antonym of שׁלום.

37   The Hagar-Ishmael tradition (Gen 21:14-19) exhibits similar features. The angel comforts Hagar, "do not be afraid [אַל־תִּירְאִי]," and assures her that Ishmael will be saved (Gen 21:17-18). There is no mention of שׁלום in the context, also in the conferment of a commemorative name on the place of the vision (16:13).

God, you are safe, do not be afraid [כִּי־שָׁלוֹם לְךָ וְאֵין דָּבָר חַי־יהוה]"
(1 Sam 20:21; cp. 2 Sam 19:31).[38]

(2) שָׁלוֹם pertains to interpersonal relations, e.g. in an inquiry
concerning someone's intentions. When the elders of Bethlehem
apprehensively question Samuel: שָׁלוֹם בּוֹאֶךָ(ה),[39] he replies: שָׁלוֹם,
and reassures them by adding, "I have come to sacrifice to YHWH"
(1 Sam 16:4-5). Equally, when Adonijah approaches Bathsheba, "she
asks: 'Do you come as a friend?' 'As a friend,' he answered [וַתֹּאמֶר
הֲשָׁלוֹם בֹּאֶךָ וַיֹּאמֶר שָׁלוֹם]" (1 Kgs 2:13). The short dialogue between
Gehazi and Naaman in the Elisha tradition may be similarly understood: "When Naaman saw him running after him . . . he asked
הֲשָׁלוֹם, and Gehazi replied שָׁלוֹם" (2 Kgs 5:21-22). In the episode of
Jehu's encounter with Jehoram and Jezebel, greetings with שלום turn
up five times with somewhat different nuances of meaning:
"Welcome" (2 Kgs 9:19), "How are things?" (9:17, 18a, 22a, 31),
triggering three times Jehu's brusque reply מַה־לְּךָ וּלְשָׁלוֹם: "what is
shalom to you?" or more bluntly, "get lost" (9:18b, 19b, 22b).[40]

The idiom שָׁאַל לְשָׁלוֹם, and similar phrases such as שָׁלוֹם לְךָ (Judg
19:20), serve as formulaic expressions of greeting in situations in
which the people involved do not harbor any suspicion. At his
father's bidding (1 Sam 17:18), David went to Saul's camp to inquire
about the wellbeing of his brothers. Coming there, he greeted or
asked them, "how are you?" [וַיִּשְׁאַל לְאֶחָיו לְשָׁלוֹם] (1 Sam 17:22; cp.
Judg 18:15; 1 Sam 10:4; 25:35; 30:21; 2 Sam 8:10 = 1 Chr 18:10;
Esth 9:30; 10:3).[41] I suggest that apocopated versions of שאל לְשָׁלוֹם
as of the *hapax legomenon* פקד לשלום in the *niphᶜal* turn up in
David's conversation with Jonathan concerning Saul's intentions: "If
your father should enquire about me (or: my whereabouts), tell him,
'David took leave from me' [אִם־פָּקֹד יִפְקְדֵנִי אָבִיךָ וְאָמַרְתָּ נִשְׁאֹל

---

[38]   The implied meaning of וְאֵין דָּבָר is evidently "nothing to fear." My translation aims at highlighting the essential meaning of the Hebrew texts rather than at a
literal rendition.

[39]   The text should be thus amended with the versions and many mss of the MT.

[40]   W. Eisenbeis (*Die Wurzel שלום im Alten Testament* [BZAW 113; Berlin:
Töpelmann, 1969] 104) defines as "slang" the use of שלום in the question of Jehu's
fellow-officers who ask him for the reason of his secret meeting with Elisha's
emissary: הֲשָׁלוֹם מַדּוּעַ בָּא־הַמְשֻׁגָּע הַזֶּה אֵלֶיךָ (2 Kgs 9:11).

[41]   The sense of וַיִּשְׁאַל לְאֶחָיו/לָהֶם לְשָׁלוֹם is perfectly caught in the somewhat free
Greek rendition of the same phrase in Gen 43:27 by πῶς ἔχετε.

"[נִשְׁאַל מִמֶּנִּי דָוִד] (1 Sam 20:6).[42]

In contrast, if someone does not greet another with שָׁלוֹם, or does not care for that person's שָׁלוֹם, the omission discloses animosity. The psalmist complains: "For a long time I dwelled among men who hated concord. Whenever I spoke in amity, they were for discord [אֲנִי־שָׁלוֹם וְכִי אֲדַבֵּר הֵמָּה לַמִּלְחָמָה]" (Ps 120:6-7). Even worse are those "who speak civilly to their neighbors with malice in their hearts [דֹּבְרֵי שָׁלוֹם עִם־רֵעֵיהֶם וְרָעָה בִּלְבָבָם]" (Ps 28:3), and the apparently trustworthy, but actually treacherous friend: אִישׁ שְׁלוֹמִי אֲשֶׁר־בָּטַחְתִּי בוֹ . . . הִגְדִּיל עָלַי עָקֵב (Ps 41:10), who is on the watch for a false step (cp. Jer 20:10: כֹּל אֱנוֹשׁ שְׁלוֹמִי שֹׁמְרֵי צַלְעִי; and Jer 38:22 = Obad 7).

In the post-exilic period, the returners from the exile were instructed to deny שָׁלוֹם to the local population of the land, the עַמֵּי הָאֲרָצוֹת: "never seek their welfare [שְׁלֹמָם] or prosperity" (Ezra 9:12; cp. Gen 37:4-5),[43] as Israel had been commanded after the Exodus to shun the Ammonites and Moabites: (וְ)לֹא־תִדְרֹשׁ(וּ) שְׁלֹמָם וְטֹבָתָם (Deut 23:7).[44] The Jerusalemites accuse Jeremiah that "he is not pursuing the people's welfare [אֵינֶנּוּ דֹרֵשׁ לְשָׁלוֹם לָעָם הַזֶּה],[45] but their ruin [רָעָה]" (Jer 38:4). The accusation echoes Jeremiah's controversy with priests and prophets in Jerusalem who mislead the people, assuring them "all is well [שָׁלוֹם שָׁלוֹם]," whereas he foresees impending ruin and desolation: וְאֵין שָׁלוֹם (Jer 6:14; 8:11).[46] The recurrence of וְאֵין שָׁלוֹם in Ezekiel's argument against the false prophets who in his days proclaimed שָׁלוֹם שָׁלוֹם, not necessarily in a context of "war and peace" (Ezek 13:10, 16), highlights the formulaic character of these phrases, which are seemingly used as slogans or catch-words.

Similarly, שָׁלוֹם occurs in a stereotype idiom of leave taking.[47] Eli

---

42   To be understood as: אִם־פָּקֹד יִפְקְדֵנִי אָבִיךָ [אֶת שְׁלוֹמִי] וְאָמַרְתָּ נִשְׁאַל [שָׁלוֹם] מִמֶּנִּי. Later in the tale, the vocables יָפְקֹד . . . וְנִפְקַדְתָּ (1 Sam 20:18) connote absence.

43   In these contexts, מִלְחָמָה and רָע(ה) are antonyms of שָׁלוֹם and טוֹב(ה), as in 1 Sam 29:7; Jer 23:17; 29:11; 33:9; Ps 34:15; etc. See below.

44   See below.

45   Contrast Jer 29:7: "seek the welfare of the city [וְדִרְשׁוּ אֶת־שְׁלוֹם הָעִיר], to which I have exiled you . . . because when she prospers, also you will fare well [כִּי בִשְׁלוֹמָהּ יִהְיֶה לָכֶם שָׁלוֹם]."

46   The question whether or not the similarly worded passages Jer 6:12-15 and 8:10-12 are both original does not need to occupy us here.

47   Occasionally, לֵךְ/לְכִי/לְכוּ לְשָׁלוֹם and שְׁאַל לְשָׁלוֹם complement each other, as

tells Hannah to return home without worrying, לְכִי לְשָׁלוֹם, and assures her that God will grant (LXX: + her) her request (1 Sam 1:17; cp. Gen 44:17; Exod 4:18; 1 Sam 20:13, 42; 29:7; 2 Sam 3:21-23; 15:9, 27; 2 Kgs 4:23; 5:19). Micah's priest sends the Danite spies on their way, wishing them godspeed: לְכוּ לְשָׁלוֹם נֹכַח יהוה דַּרְכְּכֶם אֲשֶׁר תֵּלְכוּ־בָהּ (Judg 18:6). As in other instances, the mention of God is stereotypical, and does not evince the speaker's intention to invest the greeting with a distinctive theological content (cp. Ruth 2:4). This conclusion is suggested by the occurrence of the phrase with or without an invocation of the deity in one and the same context. Jonathan promises that he would warn David and urge him to leave in haste, if he should find out that his father Saul plans to harm him: וְשִׁלַּחְתִּיךָ וְהָלַכְתָּ לְשָׁלוֹם (1 Sam 20:13) and וַיֹּאמֶר יְהוֹנָתָן לְדָוִד לֵךְ לְשָׁלוֹם (20:42). But when he explains the agreed upon sign which signals David to flee, the parallel phrase reads: "the Lord is sending you away [כִּי שִׁלַּחֲךָ יהוה]" (20:22).

When used by a speaker (A) who asks a dialogue partner (B) for information concerning a not present person or object (C), שָׁאַל לְשָׁלוֹם takes on the sense of an enquiry about the wellbeing of that person or object. The idiom turns up three times in David's request of Uriah to give him news concerning Joab and the troops that beleaguer Rabbat Ammon, and how the campaign was going: וַיִּשְׁאַל דָּוִד לִשְׁלוֹם יוֹאָב וְלִשְׁלוֹם הָעָם וְלִשְׁלוֹם הַמִּלְחָמָה (2 Sam 11:7); and four times when the prophet Elisha dispatches his servant Gehazi to obtain information about the situation of the woman and her family: "Hurry to her, and ask her 'Are you well, is your husband well, is the boy well?' She answered: '(All is/are) well' [רוּץ־נָא לִקְרָאתָהּ וֶאֱמָר־לָהּ הֲשָׁלוֹם לָךְ הֲשָׁלוֹם לְאִישֵׁךְ הֲשָׁלוֹם לַיָּלֶד: וַתֹּאמֶר שָׁלוֹם]" (2 Kgs 4:26; cp. 1 Kgs 2:13; 2 Kgs 5:21-22).[48]

The formula שָׁאַל לְשָׁלוֹם has sometimes the sense of politely "wish someone well." David instructs his men whom he sent to Nabal the Carmelite: "Go to Nabal, greet him in my name, and say (to him) ... 'may all be well with you, may all be well with your household, and may all be well with all that is yours' [וּבָאתֶם אֶל־נָבָל וּשְׁאֶלְתֶּם־לוֹ

---

in Exod 4:18/18:7; Judg 18:6/18:15.

[48]   Cp. the reply of Ahaziah's confrères to Jehu's question, וַנֵּרֶד לִשְׁלוֹם בְּנֵי־הַמֶּלֶךְ וּבְנֵי הַגְּבִירָה, which means: "We are on our way to enquire about the well-being of the king's and the queen's family" (2 Kgs 10:13). Due to haplography, לִשְׁאֹל was omitted before לִשְׁלוֹם.

"[בִשְׁמִי לְשָׁלוֹם וַאֲמַרְתֶּם . . . אַתָּה שָׁלוֹם וּבֵיתְךָ שָׁלוֹם וְכֹל אֲשֶׁר־לְךָ שָׁלוֹם
(1 Sam 25:5-6).[49] This connotation becomes especially noticeable in
the combination of שְׁאַל לְשָׁלוֹם with בֵרַךְ, e.g. in the message which
the king of Hamath conveys to David: "Toʿi sent his son Joram to
King David to greet him and wish him well [וַיִּשְׁלַח תֹּעִי אֶת־יוֹרָם־בְּנוֹ
אֶל־הַמֶּלֶךְ־דָּוִד לִשְׁאָל־לוֹ לְשָׁלוֹם וּלְבָרֲכוֹ]" (2 Sam 8:10 = 1 Chr
18:10).[50] A somewhat different thrust has the Psalmist's quest: "Pray
for the wellbeing of Jerusalem [שַׁאֲלוּ שְׁלוֹם יְרוּשָׁלָם]" (Ps 122:6), in
contrast to Jeremiah's rhetorical question concerning (the inhabitants
of) the city: "who will go out of his way to wish you well [מִי יָסוּר
לִשְׁאָל לְשָׁלֹם לָךְ]?" (Jer 15:5).

The same sense is conferred by עָנָה שָׁלוֹם (see below), and הִשְׁמִיעַ
שָׁלוֹם, as in the prophet's words of comfort: "(How lovely on the
mountains are the feet of the herald) who proclaims wellbeing (NEB:
prosperity), brings good (tidings), announces deliverance [מַשְׁמִיעַ
הִנֵּה מַבְשֵּׂר טוֹב מַשְׁמִיעַ יְשׁוּעָה שָׁלוֹם]" (Isa 52:7), echoed in Nah 2:1 [הִנֵּה
עַל־הֶהָרִים רַגְלֵי מְבַשֵּׂר מַשְׁמִיעַ שָׁלוֹם]. The phrase finds an extra-
biblical application in the Lachish ostraca: ישמע יהוה את אדני שמעת
שלם (nos. 2-4; restored in nos. 5, 9, 10, 21), or שמעת טוב (no. 8),[51]
next to the parallel epistolary formula of greeting: ירא יהוה את אדני
את העת הזה שלם (no. 6).[52] Shortened Aramaic versions of the
epistolary formula of greeting are preserved in the messages of
Nebuchadnezzar and Darius to "all peoples and nations of every
language living in the whole world: 'May your prosperity increase'
[שְׁלָמְכוֹן יִשְׂגֵּא]" (Dan 3:31 [4:1]; 6:26); and in the introits of letters,
which officials in the province of "Abar Nahara" sent to the Persian
kings Artachshasta and Darius respectively: שְׁלָם (Ezra 4:17) and
שְׁלָמָא כֹלָּא (5:7).

(3) שָׁלוֹם pertaining to intra-group and inter-group relations. The
cessation of internal discord or of war with an external enemy, for
whatever length of time, is often termed שָׁלוֹם. In most cases, the
suspension of hostilities is imposed by a superior on a subordinate
party, and results in a situation which does not produce active co-

---

49   Cp. the similar formula in a letter from Taanach: *ilānu lišʾalū šulumka šulum
bītika mārīka*; cp. S. E. Loewenstamm, "Ugaritic Formulas of Greeting," *BASOR*
194 (1969) 52-55.

50   NEB: "and congratulate him."

51   Also here טוב serves as a synonym of שָׁלוֹם.

52   *KAI* 1.192-97, 2.189-98.

operation of equals (see below).

A termination of internal fighting is signalled in the "Concubine of Gibeah" episode when "the whole community sent (word) to the Benjaminites at the Rock of Rimmon proclaiming שָׁלוֹם" (Judg 21:13), after their tribe had been almost totally wiped out (21:3). To ensure the continued existence of Benjamin, the tribal alliance supplied the survivors with 400 wives from the town of Jabesh Gilead whose male population had been put to the sword (21:5-12), and also permitted them to abduct an additional contingent of Shilonite maidens (21:19-23). However, these measures merely effected a situation of suspended belligerence, not a true reconciliation of the other tribes with Benjamin, as can be deduced from the opposition of certain factions, בְּנֵי בְלִיַּעַל, to Saul's election as king over Israel.[53]

The tale of the Gibeonites illustrates a similar use of שלום in reference to a potential external enemy. The Gibeonites approached Joshua, asking for a compact, כָּרְתוּ־לָנוּ בְרִית (Josh 9:6) and declaring their readiness to become Israel's "vassals": עֲבָדֵיכֶם אֲנַחְנוּ (9:11). Joshua and the chiefs of Israel granted them a suzerain-treaty, וַיַּעַשׂ לָהֶם יְהוֹשֻׁעַ שָׁלוֹם (9:15), which is later referred to by a denominative verb of שלום in the hiph'il: גִבְעוֹן (הִשְׁלִימוּ יֹשְׁבֵי) הִשְׁלִימָה אֶת־(יְהוֹשֻׁעַ וְאֶת־בְּנֵי) יִשְׂרָאֵל (10:1, 4). When it subsequently transpired that the Gibeonites had acted under false pretenses, they were demoted to the status of minor cult personnel (9:16-27),[54] viz. were made עֲבָדִים in the sense of "slaves."[55]

A state of non-belligerence between non-Israelite collectives, evidently based on a suzerain–vassal treaty, can also be defined by שלום. For example, "there was שָׁלוֹם between Jabin king of Hazor and the clan of Heber the Kenite" (Judg 4:17). But this שָׁלוֹם did not prevent Heber's wife Jael from cunningly killing Sisera, the fugitive commander of Jabin's army (4:18-22; 5:24-27), although a breach of peace is considered a sinful deed.[56]

In a different category fall the intermittent spells of suspended

---

53   See 1 Sam 10:20-27.

54   It is of no consequence for the ascertainment of the signification of שלום whether the pericope 9:16-27 is a self-contained unit or not.

55   Different connotations attach to the term עבד in 9:8, 11, 24 and in 9:23 (cp. 1 Kgs 9:21-22), as in the use of נער in the account of Samuel's youth (1 Sam 1:21–3:21).

56   See Pedersen, Israel, 1-2.418.

warfare in the period of the settlement, whenever a "judge" achieved a decisive victory over the one or the other enemy in a single campaign. However, the sources do not report that these sporadic successes led to the establishment of a treaty of whatever kind. It would appear that for this reason, the term שָׁלוֹם is not used in the concise notations in which such spells of tranquility between wars are recorded. Rather, they are identified by the formulaic statement "the land was at rest [וַתִּשְׁקֹט הָאָרֶץ]," for "forty years" in the wake of the victorious battles fought by Othniel (Judg 3:11), Barak-Deborah (5:31) and Gideon (8:28), and for "eighty years" after Ehud had vanquished the Moabites (3:30).[57] The same pertains to the application of the formula in several reports in other biblical historiographies. In the days of Asa, king of Judah, "the land was at rest for ten years." The Chronicler explicates "during those years there was no war with him for YHWH had given him security [וְאֵין־עִמּוֹ מִלְחָמָה בַּשָּׁנִים הָאֵלֶּה כִּי־הֵנִיחַ יהוה לוֹ]" (2 Chr 13:23-14:5; cp. further Josh 11:23; 14:15; 2 Chr 20:30).

E. Synonyms of שָׁלוֹם and Explanatory Expressions

A satisfactory understanding of the intrinsic connotation of שָׁלוֹם cannot be achieved by an etymological analysis alone. The identification of the root of a word does not yet disclose its inherent meaning in a given corpus of literature. As said, the signification and the scope of meanings of שָׁלוֹם can be more reliably ascertained by reviewing the use of the term intertextually and synoptically in the entire gamut of the biblical writings. In this process, the whole range of vocables and explanatory expressions must be brought under consideration which fall in the semantic field of שָׁלוֹם by collating synonyms and coterminous idioms from a variety of passages. The investigation demonstrates that also those synonyms and coterminous expressions mostly connotate "well-being," "friendship/goodwill" in general, while antonyms signify "need/exigency," "dislike/hate." The infrequently attested signification "peace" in contrast to "war," may indeed be a secondary development.[58] A few texts from various

---

57   That is to say, for one or two generations.

58   In a lengthy discussion of "peace," Pedersen (*Israel*, 1-2.263-377) widens the signification of שָׁלוֹם beyond defensible limits, actually identifying the term with בְּרִית, "covenant." Von Rad (*Theologie*, 1.135-36) offers a similar approximation of בְּרִית and שָׁלוֹם.

biblical books will suffice to bear out this proposition.

The psalmist implores God to proclaim שָׁלוֹם for his loyal people: שָׁלוֹם אֶל־עַמּוֹ וְאֶל־חֲסִידָיו.[59] In his prayer he enumerates the qualities of שָׁלוֹם: divine deliverance, יֵשַׁע, so that glory may dwell in our land, לִשְׁכֹּן כָּבוֹד בְּאַרְצֵנוּ;[60] true fidelity, צֶדֶק וְשָׁלוֹם/חֶסֶד־וֶאֱמֶת, on earth and in heaven; prosperity, הַטּוֹב,[61] and a rich yield of the fields, וְאַרְצֵנוּ תִּתֵּן יְבוּלָהּ (Ps 85:9-14). The nouns אמת, חסד, כבוד,[62] הטוב, הארץ יבול, and the verb שכן,[63] are constitutive components of the vocabulary of שָׁלוֹם, shared by many biblical writers.

The author of Isa 32:15-18 adduces some of the above vocables, like צדק(ה) and שכן, and introduces additional expressions to highlight the promise of security and serenity which divinely granted שלום holds out for Israel: "justice and righteousness shall dwell in the desert [וְשָׁכַן בַּמִּדְבָּר מִשְׁפָּט וּצְדָקָה בַּכַּרְמֶל תֵּשֵׁב],"[64] and produce "tranquility and safety lasting for ever [הַשְׁקֵט וָבֶטַח עַד־עוֹלָם], then my people shall live in a haven of serenity, in secure dwellings, in rest and ease [וְיָשַׁב עַמִּי בִּנְוֵה שָׁלוֹם וּבְמִשְׁכְּנוֹת מִבְטַחִים וּבִמְנוּחֹת שַׁאֲנַנּוֹת]" (Isa 32:16-18).

Most prevalent is the conjunction of שלום with vocables connoting safety or security, pertaining either to personal "ease/welfare" or signifying "peace" in the political arena: בטח(ה)/בטחון (Lev 26:5-6; Isa 26:3; Jer 12:5; Ezek 34:24-27; Ps 41:10); שקט (2 Chr 14:4-5; 20:30; 23:21);[65] שלוה (combined with טוב in Ps 122:6-9) and מנוחה (Deut 3:20; 12:9-10; Josh 1:15; 2 Sam 7:11; 1 Kgs 8:56).[66] A dimension of peace and safety attaches to these vocables in idioms which

---

59   Possibly a hendiadys.

60   More instances of hendiadys.

61   For שלום = טוב(ה); cp. inter alia, Deut. 23:7 = Ezra 9:12 (see above); Isa 52:7; Jer. 14:19; 33:11; Ps 122:8-9; further 1 Sam 20:7.

62   אמת is recurrently conjoined with שלום in what appears to be another hendiadys, mostly in the A/B sequence שלום ו(אמת) (inter alia, in 2 Kgs 20:19 = Isa 39:8; Jer 14:13; 33:6; Esth 9:30), but also in the inverted B/A order והאמת והשלום (Zech 8:19). Cp. the parallel conjunction of שלום with משפט (Zech 8:16) and/or מישרים/ מישור (Mal 2:6), in which מישור equals צדק (Ps 45:7-8). מישור is used in an apparent double entendre in Jer 48:20-21: כִּי שֻׁדַּד מוֹאָב וּמִשְׁפָּט בָּא אֶל־אֶרֶץ הַמִּישֹׁר.

63   Cp. 2 Sam 7:10 = 1 Chr 17:9 et al.

64   The מדבר is the proverbial abode of outlaws and evil men, such as the mighty and mean Nabal who lived at Carmel in the wilderness of Maon (1 Sam 25:1-39); see Talmon, "The Desert Motif in the Bible and in Qumran Literature," 31-63.

65   Especially in the stereotype idiom: וַתִּשְׁקֹ(ו)ט הָאָרֶץ (see discussion above).

66   This is the sense of וְאַנְחֵהוּ in Isa 57:18; cp. Deut 25:19 et al. See n. 68 below.

are preponderantly employed in visions of the "national ideal" (see below), and in which they indeed signify "peace" in antithesis to "war" (e.g. Deut 12:9-10; Zech 14:11), even when שָׁלוֹם is not mentioned in the context (Zech 14:1-15).

A deficiency of שָׁלוֹם connotating "wholeness," in the private or the public domain, is expressed in negative terms and metaphors derived from the stems אֹרֶךְ and רפא, which belong in the semantic field of "health": "Why did you smite us, and there is no remedy for us, we hoped for שָׁלוֹם, and there is nothing good,[67] [מַדּוּעַ הִכִּיתָנוּ וְאֵין לָנוּ מַרְפֵּא קַוֵּה לְשָׁלוֹם וְאֵין טוֹב וּלְעֵת מַרְפֵּא וְהִנֵּה בְעָתָה]" (Jer 14:19). The deficiency is redressed when God has mercy with the repentant sinner, gives him relief and restores him to health: "דְּרָכָיו רָאִיתִי וְאֶרְפָּאֵהוּ וְאַנְחֵהוּ וַאֲשַׁלֵּם נִחֻמִים לוֹ . . . שָׁלוֹם שָׁלוֹם לָרָחוֹק וְלַקָּרוֹב, says YHWH, (so) I cured him [וּרְפָאתִיו]" (Isa 57:18-19).[68] Unlike the priests and false prophets who "lightly heal the wounds of the people [וַיְרַפְּאוּ אֶת־שֶׁבֶר עַמִּי עַל־נְקַלָּה],[69] proclaiming שָׁלוֹם שָׁלוֹם while there is no שָׁלוֹם" (Jer 6:14; 8:11; cp. Ezek 13:10, 16; Mic 3:5), God brings true healing and peace to Jerusalem and those who dwell in her: הִנְנִי מַעֲלֶה־לָּהּ אֲרֻכָה וּמַרְפֵּא וּרְפָאתִים וְגִלֵּיתִי לָהֶם עֲתֶרֶת שָׁלוֹם וֶאֱמֶת (Jer 33:6); "Come, let us return to YHWH; for he has torn us and will heal us, he has struck us and he will bind up our wounds [לְכוּ וְנָשׁוּבָה אֶל־יְהוָה כִּי הוּא טָרָף וְיִרְפָּאֵנוּ יַךְ וְיַחְבְּשֵׁנוּ]" (Hos 6:1; cp. Mal 3:20).[70]

F. The Distribution of שָׁלוֹם in Biblical Literature

The term שָׁלוֹם turns up in all books, sources and literary strata of the Bible. The widespread employment invites speculations about the reasons for its rare presence in specific components of the biblical literature and its total absence from major sections. An analysis of the factors which presumably caused such apparent anomalies may

---

67   טוב equals שָׁלוֹם. See discussion above.

68   The denominative verb וְאַנְחֵהוּ is derived from מנוחה, quietude/serenity, and וַאֲשַׁלֵּם from שָׁלוֹם (see above).

69   שֶׁבֶר is an antithesis of שָׁלוֹם, both in the sense of "wholeness" and "peace." Cp. Isa 15:5; 51:19; 60:18; Jer 4:20; 10:19; 14:17; 30:12; 50:22; Nah 3:19; Zeph 1:10; Lam 2:11-13; 3:47-48; etc.

70   The antonyms and antinomous idioms of שָׁלוֹם, such as inter alia, חרב, מלחמה, אין שלום, השקט לא יוכל, פחד, רע(ה), חטא, שבר, מכשול, ריב(ה), require an in depth discussion which cannot be attempted in this paper. Isa 59:7-9 provides a typical example.

hold out promise for a more accurate definition of the intrinsic meaning or meanings of שלום.

The use of the term in the Pentateuch is a case in point:

(1) Twenty-three occurrences of שלום in the Pentateuch amount to no more than ca. 10 per cent of the 237 mentions of the term in biblical literature, although the five books of the Torah make up approximately 25 per cent of the text of the Hebrew Bible, with the Former and Latter Prophets, and the Paralipomena constituting ca. 75 per cent.[71]

No less conspicuous is the fact that שלום is not found even once in Genesis 1–11, that is to say, in the block of traditions which pertain to what may be termed the "constitutive age of humanity." Then all the "firsts" were established, which humans encounter as individuals and in the various concretizations of societal life: cosmic phenomena, discrete categories of species, birth and death, sibling rivalry, cardinal professions, differentiation of languages and peoples, etc. "Facts" and "events" set in the constitutive age are considered prototypical or aetiological, and are viewed as foreshadowing or determining anthropological and social phenomena experienced in historical reality. But they themselves are not subject to the circumstances and factors which actually governed the individual's and the nation's life. And exactly this existential actuality is the frame of reference of שלום. Therefore, the term could not be applied in Genesis 1–11, viz. in texts which pertain exclusively to pre-historical phenomena of the primordial constitutive age.

The remaining part of Genesis (12–50) is only marginally concerned with the realities of peoplehood. Israel's history as a sovereign nation-state lies altogether beyond the horizon of this section, rich in genealogies and genealogical tales, such as Esau's and Jacob's family-trees (Genesis 36; 46:5-27) and the Judah–Tamar episode (Genesis 38). These pericopes bear comparison with the lineage lists and short genealogical narratives in 1 Chronicles 1–8. The Genesis traditions are without doubt retrospectively colored by events which in later history determined the internal constitution of the Israelite society and its external relations with other ethnic-political entities in the area. For example, the "Joseph and his brothers" cycle evidently foreshadows the primacy of the house of Joseph in the era of the monarchy. And the tension which marks the

---

[71]   Irrespective of whether words are counted or pages in a printed edition.

Jacob–Esau traditions projects the hatred and never ending hostilities which marked the relations between the nation-states Israel and Edom in biblical and post-biblical times.[72]

But in order to preserve the "family-ambiance" of the traditions collected in Genesis 12–50, שָׁלוֹם is used there only, presumably with deliberation, in reference to (a) individuals and (b) interpersonal relations:

(a) God promises Abraham: "you shall join your fathers in peace, and be buried in a good old age [וְאַתָּה תָּבוֹא אֶל־אֲבֹתֶיךָ בְּשָׁלוֹם תִּקָּבֵר בְּשֵׂיבָה טוֹבָה]" (Gen 15:15; cp. 2 Kgs 22:20; Isa 57:1-2, 19; Jer 34:5);[73] and the fugitive Jacob hopes to return hale and hearty [בְשָׁלוֹם], to his father's house (Gen 28:21; cp. 44:17; Isa 55:12).

(b) שָׁאַל לְשָׁלוֹם serves as a formulaic phrase in enquiries about someone's well-being, or in expressions of polite concern for the addressee's or a third person's welfare:[74] Jacob questioned the shepherds in Haran about Laban: "'Is he well?' And they answered, 'Yes, he is well' [הֲשָׁלוֹם לוֹ וַיֹּאמְרוּ שָׁלוֹם]" (Gen 29:6). Sending out Joseph to bring news about his other sons who tended their flocks near Shechem, he twice uses שָׁלוֹם: "Go and see whether all is well with brothers and the sheep [לֶךְ־נָא רְאֵה אֶת־שְׁלוֹם אַחֶיךָ וְאֶת־שְׁלוֹם הַצֹּאן]" (Gen 37:14).[75] Likewise, after Joseph had greeted his brothers who came to Egypt [וַיִּשְׁאַל לָהֶם לְשָׁלוֹם], he asked them: "Is your old father well [הֲשָׁלוֹם אֲבִיכֶם הַזָּקֵן]?" And they replied: "Your servant, our father is well [שָׁלוֹם לְעַבְדְּךָ לְאָבִינוּ]" (Gen 43:27-28; cp. 2 Sam 18:32; 2 Kgs 5:21; Esth 2:11). Joseph signals peaceful intentions by assuring his apprehensive brothers [שָׁלוֹם לָכֶם אַל־תִּירָאוּ] (Gen 43:23; cp. Judg 6:23; Dan 10:19). He professes a courtier's concern for the king of Egypt by addressing him with the stereotype greeting formula "may God take care of Pharaoh's welfare [אֱלֹהִים יַעֲנֶה אֶת־שְׁלוֹם פַּרְעֹה] (Gen 41:16), which does not seem to have an intrinsic

---

72 The mutual animosity permeates the several collections of "oracles against the nations," which spill over with harsh accusations levelled against Edom and anti-Edom proclamations (Amos 1:11-12; cp. v. 9; Joel 4:19; Ezek 25:12-14). Typical examples are Obadiah's prophecy (cp. Jer 49:7-22), Malachi's bitter anti-Edom oracle (Mal 1:1-5), and the cursing of Edom in the essentially anti-Babylon psalm (Ps 137:7). The identification of Edom with Babylon caused that in some rabbinic writings Edom becomes a cover name for Rome and also for Christianity.

73 Cp. further Gen 37:34 and contrast 1 Kgs 2:6; 2 Chr 34:28.

74 Like in the instances adduced above.

75 Cp. 2 Sam 11:7.

religious connotation.[76]

In contrast, as already said, the refusal to greet someone with שלום spells enmity.[77] Joseph's brothers hated him so much that they would not give him the time of the day: לֹא יָכְלוּ דַּבְּרוֹ לְשָׁלֹם (37:4; cp. Ps 35:20). But eventually, Joseph was reconciled with them (45:1-15), as he deserved: "When the Lord is pleased with a man and his ways, he reconciles even his enemies with him [בִּרְצוֹת יהוה דַּרְכֵי־אִישׁ גַּם־אוֹיְבָיו יַשְׁלִם אִתּוֹ]" (Prov 16:7).

(c) The border line between inter-personal and inter-(ethnic) group relations becomes blurred in the report of Isaac's and Abimelech's vow not to let differences over grazing rights interfere with their mutual שלום intentions (Gen 26:29, 31). In a similar situation, Abraham strives to prevent further clashes between his shepherds and Lot's so as to maintain friendly relations with him (Gen 13:5-7). Since a close kinsman is involved, his amicable intentions are not defined by שָׁלֹם, but rather by the negation of its antonym מריבה/ריב: "Let there be no quarrel between you and me [אַל־נָא תְהִי מְרִיבָה בֵּינִי וּבֵינֶיךָ]" (13:7-8).

(2) Similar observations pertain to occurrences of שלום in the Book of Exodus, in narratives which revolve around Moses the Israelite and Jethro the Midianite. שלום serves once in a formula of greeting: "Moses went out to meet his father-in-law, bowed low to him, and kissed him, and they greeted each other [וַיֵּצֵא מֹשֶׁה לִקְרַאת חֹתְנוֹ וַיִּשְׁתַּחוּ וַיִּשַּׁק־לוֹ וַיִּשְׁאֲלוּ אִישׁ־לְרֵעֵהוּ לְשָׁלוֹם]" (Exod 18:7; cp. Judg 18:15; 19:20; 2 Sam 18:28; 1 Chr 12:19); and once in a situation of leave-taking: "Jethro said to Moses, 'Farewell' [לֵךְ לְשָׁלוֹם]" (4:18). In the third instance, the clause [הָעָם הַזֶּה עַל־מְקֹמוֹ יָבֹא בְשָׁלוֹם] can be rendered somewhat freely: "This (whole) people will reach its destination unharmed (or: will live in harmony)" (Exod 18:23).[78] The events reported, in which Moses and Jethro act amicably as private persons, fall in the category of "interpersonal relations."

---

[76]   Cp. parallel Babylonian epistolary formulas, such as *šulumka mahar Šamaš ū Marduk lū dari*: "your well-being may be always before Samas and Marduk" (E. Salonen, *Die Gruss und Höflichkeitsformeln in babylonisch-assyrischen Briefen* [StOr 38; Helsinki: Finnish Oriental Society, 1967]; idem, "Gruss," RLA 3.668-70), or *ilānu šulumka šulum bītika lišʾal*: "may the deity attend to your wellbeing and the well-being of your house" (Loewenstamm, "Ugaritic Formulas," 52-55).

[77]   See discussion above.

[78]   The same idea seems to be implied in Ahitophel's advice to Absalom: כָּל־הָעָם יִהְיֶה שָׁלוֹם (2 Sam 17:3).

They precede the later inimical encounters of Israel and Midian as ethnic entities or nation-states in history (Num 25:6-18; 31:1-53; Judg 6:1-8:12).[79]

(3) The one mention of שׁלוֹם in Leviticus occurs in a wistful portrayal of Israel's future situation in the land (Lev 26:3-12), which proleptically reflects the lofty visionary image of the biblical authors' national ideal:[80] "If you conform to my statutes, if you observe my commandments and carry them out . . . I will give you rain at the proper time, the land shall yield its produce and the trees of the countryside their fruit . . . you shall eat your fill and live secure [לָבֶטַח] in your land. I will give peace in the land,[81] and you shall lie down to sleep with no one to terrify you. I will rid your land of dangerous beasts [חַיָּה רָעָה],[82] and it shall not be ravaged by war. You shall put your enemies to flight and . . . your enemies shall fall by the sword before you" (Lev 26:3-8). Attention centers on natural phenomena, which determine the individual's welfare, and the societal weal generally: ample and well-timed rains in the appropriate seasons, abundant crops and a surplus of agricultural produce to be enjoyed in security (לָבֶטַח) by all Israel, a happy family life and population increase (Lev 26:4-6a, 9-10), in a country freed of dangerous beasts (26:6b; cp. Ezek 34:25-27).[83] The two-part notation of good fortune and economic success, frames inclusio-fashion a passage which relates to Israel's triumph over its enemies and to the

---

79　See below.

80　The wishful nature of this passage is put in relief by the Deuteronomist's realistic statement that Israel has not yet achieved that aspired state of safety and serenity: כִּי לֹא־בָאתֶם עַד־עָתָּה אֶל־הַמְּנוּחָה וְאֶל־הַנַּחֲלָה (Deut 12:9-10). See below.

81　Cp. Deut 28:1-14. For an Assyrian parallel of this phrase, see A. Oded, "'And I Will Give Peace in the Land' (Lev. 26:6)—An Assyrian Perspective," in S. Aḥituv and B. A. Levine (eds.), *Eretz Israel 24: A. Malamat Volume* (Jerusalem: Israel Exploration Society, 1993) 148-157 (Hebrew).

82　The inclusion of inanimate (rain, crops, etc.) and animate nature seems to derive from prophetic literature. There, it constitutes a prominent component of the prophets' vision of a pacified universe freed from all tension, rivalry and warfare (e.g. Isa 11:6-10; Hos 2:20-25; see below), which finds a parallel in Mesopotamian and Egyptian portrayals of "the world at creation." See H. Gross, *Die Idee des ewigen und allgemeinen Weltfriedens im Alten Orient und im Alten Testament* (TTS 7; Trier: Paulinus, 1956); H. H. Schmid, *šalôm 'Frieden' im Alten Orient und im Alten Testament* (SBS 51; Stuttgart: Katholisches Bibelwerk, 1971).

83　חיה רעה occurs five times in priestly traditions (Lev 26:6; Ezek 5:17; 14:15, 21; 34:25), and twice in Gen 37:20, 33.

cessation of war (26:6b-8), a *conditio sine qua non* for the establishment of peace in the political arena.[84] The pericope is enveloped by references to God's covenant with his people (Lev 26:3, 11-12), which give it a theological-credal outlook.[85]

The absence of any allusion to tangible facts of statehood and political sovereignty prompts the conclusion that like the scenario of the primordial "constitutive age" in Genesis 1–11, the visionary model presented in Leviticus relates to an uncharted future era which lies beyond the historical reality to which, as said, שָׁלוֹם intrinsically pertains.

(4) An evident theological dimension attaches to the two mentions of שָׁלוֹם in the Book of Numbers. One occurs in the closing line of the public blessing, in which the priests pray for divine protection of every individual in the Israelite community:[86] "May the Lord turn his face (benevolence) upon you and grant you prosperity [יִשָּׂא יהוה פָּנָיו אֵלֶיךָ וְיָשֵׂם לְךָ שָׁלוֹם]" (Num 6:26; cp. v. 25).[87] שָׁלוֹם occurs again in a self-contained pericope of a manifest sacral character (Num 25:10-15).[88] Phinehas the priest had distinguished himself by

---

84 See below.

85 H. H. Schrey's understanding of the intrinsic signification of שָׁלוֹם as "Ganzheit, Wohlsein, Heil, Teilhabe der Gemeinschaft am Segen als Vorbedingung gedeihlichen Wachstums im Bund Jh-v mit Israel" (*RGG* 2 [1958] 1133) fits admirably the employment of the term in the above passage.

86 The text of this priestly blessing is partly preserved on an inscribed silver amulet from the second half of the 7th century BCE, discovered in a burial cave near St. Andrew's church in Jerusalem. See G. Barkai, "The Priestly Blessing on a Silver Strip from Ketef Hinnom in Jerusalem," *Kathedra* 52 (1989) 176-85 (Hebrew); A. Yardeni, "Remarks on the Priestly Blessing on Two Ancient Amulets from Jerusalem," *VT* 41 (1991) 178-85.

87 The translation of וְיָשֵׂם לְךָ שָׁלוֹם by "give/grant you peace" (NEB), which seems to imply an understanding of the phrase as "life without war," attaches an unwarranted "political" dimension to the priestly blessing (6:22-26).

88 The Massoretes identified Num 25:10-15 as a separate text-unit by enclosing these verses between two *parashah* dividers (פ). I propose that it was secondarily spliced into the split account of Israel's encounter with the Midianites. The first part of that report opens in 25:6 and ends in the middle of 25:19 with a *pisqāh beʾemṣāʿ pāsûq*. After a lengthy insert (26:1–30:17), the main narrative thread is picked up again in 31:1 and spun out to the end of the chapter (31:54). For a discussion of the *pisqāh beʾemṣāʿ pāsûq*, see S. Talmon, "Pisqāh Beʾemṣāʿ Pāsûq and 11QPsᵃ," *Textus* 5 (1966) 11-21; repr. in Talmon, *The World of Qumran From Within* (Jerusalem: Magnes, 1989) 264-72.

killing an Israelite chief and his Midianite consort for their shared
sin in the Baal Peor incident. As a reward, God bestowed upon him
and his descendants the priesthood as an everlasting covenant: הִנְנִי
נֹתֵן לוֹ אֶת־בְּרִיתִי שָׁלוֹם וְהָיְתָה לּוֹ וּלְזַרְעוֹ אַחֲרָיו בְּרִית כְּהֻנַּת עוֹלָם
(25:12-13).[89]

Against the background of the use of שָׁלוֹם in Numbers in contexts
of a personal-sacral character, attention must be given to the conspicuous absence of the term from traditions concerning "mundane"
affairs, first and foremost from the conciliatory messages which
Moses sent to the kings of Edom and the Amorites requesting safe
passage through their territories, and promising to refrain from any
infringement of the addressees' possessions and interests. The
Israelites' profoundly "peaceful" intentions are repeatedly stressed,
but the term שָׁלוֹם is not brought into play:[90] "Moses sent envoys to
the king of Edom (the Amorite king Sihon) . . . 'Grant us passsage
through your country. We will not trespass on field or vineyard nor
drink from your wells. We will travel by the king's highway; we
will not turn off to right or left until we have crossed your territory
. . . if we and our flocks drink your water, we will pay you for it'"
(Num 20:17, 19; 21:22).

(5) One of the four occurrences of שָׁלוֹם in Deuteronomy con-
forms to the category "personal well-being" in a theological or
credal setting. It relates to a person who worships foreign gods, and
nevertheless believes that he will escape punishment: "All will be
well with me [וְהִתְבָּרֵךְ בִּלְבָבוֹ . . . שָׁלוֹם יִהְיֶה־לִּי]" (Deut 29:18; cp.
Jer 23:17). Another pertains to "group relations," again in a theological rather than in a historical-political context, namely to the already
mentioned prohibition of ever admitting an Ammonite or a Moabite
into the congregation of Israel: . . . לֹא־יָבֹא עַמּוֹנִי וּמוֹאָבִי בִּקְהַל יהוה
לֹא־תִדְרֹשׁ שְׁלֹמָם וְטֹבָתָם כָּל־יָמֶיךָ לְעוֹלָם (Deut 23:4-7 = Ezra 9:12;
cp. Gen 37:4).

An entirely different situation obtains in respect to the remaining
two mentions, in which שָׁלוֹם decidedly connotes "peace" in the political sphere in contrast to "war." In distinction from the introduction
of the message which Moses sent to the Amorites in Num 21:22, in
which, as pointed out, שָׁלוֹם does not occur, the term figures promi-

---

[89] NEB: "covenant of security of tenure." The passage is echoed in Mal 2:4-5:
שְׁלַחְתִּי אֲלֵיכֶם אֵת הַמִּצְוָה הַזֹּאת לִהְיוֹת בְּרִיתִי אֶת־לֵוִי . . . בְּרִיתִי הָיְתָה אִתּוֹ הַחַיִּים וְהַשָּׁלוֹם.

[90] In distinction from the parallel account in Deut 2:26. See below.

nently in the otherwise identically worded text of his communication
to Sihon in Deut 2:26-28: אֶל־סִיחוֹן מֶלֶךְ חֶשְׁבּוֹן . . . וָאֶשְׁלַח מַלְאָכִים
דִּבְרֵי שָׁלוֹם לֵאמֹר אֶעְבְּרָה בְאַרְצֶךָ בַּדֶּרֶךְ בַּדֶּרֶךְ אֵלֵךְ לֹא אָסוּר יָמִין
וּשְׂמֹאל אֹכֶל בַּכֶּסֶף תַּשְׁבִּרֵנִי וְאָכַלְתִּי וּמַיִם בַּכֶּסֶף תִּתֶּן־לִי וְשָׁתִיתִי. Both
versions report that Sihon rejected the "peaceful" overtures, and
attacked Israel. In the ensuing battle the Israelites vanquished his
troops and "captured all his cities" (Num 21:23-26; Deut 2:32-36). I
suggest that the mention of a peace offer, דִּבְרֵי שָׁלוֹם in Deut 2:26,
was triggered by the reference to the Israelites' seizure of Sihon's
cities, so as to make sure that the steps taken in the war against the
Amorites conform with the injunction in the Deuteronomic "war
code": "When you advance on a city to attack it, make an offer of
peace. If the city accepts the offer of שָׁלוֹם and opens its gates to you,
then all the people in it shall be put to forced labor and shall serve
you. If it does not make peace with you but offers battle, you shall
besiege it and YHWH your God will deliver it into your hands [כִּי־תִקְרַב
אֶל־עִיר לְהִלָּחֵם עָלֶיהָ וְקָרָאתָ אֵלֶיהָ לְשָׁלוֹם וְהָיָה אִם־שָׁלוֹם תַּעַנְךָ וּפָתְחָה
לָךְ וְהָיָה כָּל־הָעָם הַנִּמְצָא־בָהּ יִהְיוּ לְךָ לָמַס וַעֲבָדוּךְ וְאִם־לֹא תַשְׁלִים
עִמָּךְ וְעָשְׂתָה עִמְּךָ מִלְחָמָה וְצַרְתָּ עָלֶיהָ וּנְתָנָהּ יְהוָה אֱלֹהֶיךָ בְּיָדֶךָ]" (Deut
20:10-13a). The "war code" is not recorded in the book of Numbers.
Therefore, its author did not feel constrained to present Moses as
acting in accord with the above injunction by formally offering
Sihon שלום before attacking and capturing his cities.

The introduction of שלום in the Deuteronomy version of the Sihon
episode, makes the more conspicuous the absence of the term from
the "catalogue" of prospective blessings which a faithful Israel will
enjoy in the land (Deut 28:1-14),[91] whereas the parallel roster in Lev
26:4-13 contains the only occurrence of שלום in that book (26:6). I
shall yet propose an explanation of this seemingly surprising
"omission" in my discussion of the biblical vision of a future era of a
"world at peace" or "cosmic peace."

I propose that the above texts do not necessarily reveal the
Deuteronomist's linguistic idiosyncracy or a particular conception of
שלום entertained by the "deuteronomistic school."[92] Rather, it

---

[91] According to von Rad, *Theologie*, 1.228, this is the most prominent biblical
illustration of *Heilsmaterialismus*.

[92] See Braulik ("Konzeption," 29) who speaks of a system of statements
found exclusively in the deuteronomistic historiography and in the Chronist's
Geschichtswerk which depends on it.

accords with the conditions of Israel's existence as a nation among nations in the Land of Canaan foreshadowed in Deuteronomy, which differed fundamentally from the situations mirrored in the tetra-teuchal traditions. That later historical stage is reflected in the biblical historiographies and books which pertain to the period of the settlement and the age of the monarchy. For this reason, the merely incipient employment in Deuteronomy of שָׁלוֹם as connoting "peace" in the political sphere will come into full view in the Former and Later Prophets, and in the Paralipomena, especially in Chronicles, which contain nine out of ten occurrences of the term in the Hebrew Bible.[93] The numbers of occurrences of שָׁלוֹם and vocables from its semantic field differ indeed from one book and one text unit to another. One may also perceive nuances of emphasis on this or that connotative aspect of the term, relative to the general subject matter of the specific literary unit and the context in which it is employed. But these variations do not evince divergences in the understanding of שָׁלוֹם which would warrant a separate treatment of its employment in discrete components of the Prophets or the Paralipomena.

G. שָׁלוֹם Signifying "Peace"

Historical experience made biblical thinkers realize that שָׁלוֹם, viz. the aspired situation of safety and tranquility in the political arena, presupposes a preceding stage of turmoil and war.[94] Their acquies-cence in the interrelation of peace and war, considered deplorable but inevitable, finds an expression not only in reports of the early days of the monarchy, as Westermann maintains,[95] but emerges in a wide gamut of scriptural texts, irrespective of the period to which they relate. It is succinctly captured in the pithy wisdom adage: "For everything its season . . . a time to kill and a time to heal, a time to love and a time to hate, a time for war and a time for peace [עֵת מִלְחָמָה וְעֵת שָׁלוֹם]" (Qoh 3:8).[96] This viewpoint was evidently shared

---

93   See discussion above.

94   See, inter alia, P. D. Hanson, "War and Peace in the Hebrew Bible," *Int* 30 (1984) 341-62; idem, "War, Peace and Justice in Early Israel," *BibRev* 3 (1987) 32-45.

95   C. Westermann, "Der Frieden im Alten Testament," *TBei* 55 (1974) 215.

96   Like some Ancient Near Eastern documents, the Bible speaks of an annual season, or annual seasons, in which kings went customarily to war: עֵת צֵאת הַמְּלָכִים (2 Sam 11:1-2 = 1 Chr 20:1-2); viz. before or after the rainfalls, and were actually expected to do so. This expectation caused that an Assyrian king will sometimes

by some Ancient Near Eastern thinkers, e.g. by the author of the Epic of Tukulti Ninurta I: "Peace will not be established without war, and harmony will not be accomplished without strife."[97] This proverbial saying is seemingly echoed in the realistic-pessimistic Latin aphorism: *Si vis pacem para bellum*.

Not all instances of "peace" are of one cloth. Sociologists distinguish between "negative peace," viz. a state of non-belligerence between ethnic or national entities forced by a superior on an inferior party, or by the victor on the vanquished, and "positive peace" founded on the mutual consent of equal partners, that is to say an *entente cordiale* towards the pursuit of shared goals. In a discussion of the biblical concept of שלום in relation to history, I prefer to use the terms "imposed peace" and "contractual peace."

Most mentions in the Bible of "peace" in the political arena fall in the category of "imposed peace." This is illustrated by the peace to which Egypt or a Mesopotamian power recurrently subjected the northern or the southern kingdom respectively, or which Israel variously imposed on neighboring states. An instructive case is the vassal treaty which Sanherib's envoy Rabshakeh offers Hezekiah of Judah, as a condition for averting an Assyrian attack on Jerusalem: "Enter into an agreement (evidently, of submission) with my master, the king of Assyria [הִתְעָרֶב נָא אֶת־אֲדֹנִי אֶת־מֶלֶךְ אַשּׁוּר]" (2 Kgs 18:23; Isa 36:8). However, when "quoting" Rabshakeh's proposal, the writer does not refer to it as an offer of שלום but rather introduces the synonym ברכה: עֲשׂוּ־אִתִּי בְרָכָה וּצְאוּ אֵלַי (2 Kgs 18:31; Isa 36:16).[98] Further examples are the already mentioned שלום-relations between Israel and the Gibeonites, as between Jabin of Hazor and the

---

report in his annals that he campaigned at the appropriate times of the year, although it can be proven that he had stayed happily at home.

[97]   Col. III, 15-16: *uliššakan salīmu bālu mithusi* [. . .] *ul ibbašši tūbtu bālu sītnunima* [. . .], Cited after Oded (see n. 81 above) 150. Note the synonymity of *salīmu* and *tūbtu* in contrast to *mithusi* and *sītnunima*, which parallels the antonimity of שלום = טוב and מלחמה = רע(ה). See discussion above.

[98]   The equivalence of שלום and ברכה is highlighted by the promise of general "welfare" which the proposed pact holds in store for the Judeans (2 Kgs 18:31-32; Isa 37:16-17), described in terms which echo the biblical visions of a future era of peace (see below). Cp. the use of ברכה in Abigail's declaration of submission to David (1 Sam 25:27), so as to keep him from attacking her husband Nabal who had callously rejected David's peace offer (25:6-10).

Kenites.[99] and the intermittent suspension of hostilities between Israel and various Canaanite states in the days of the "Judges."[100]

In the period of the monarchy such a tenuous peace was established in the wake of David's victory over the coalition headed by Hadadezer, king of Aram, who had come to the assistance of the Ammonites in their war with Israel. The author of Kings reports that "for three years[101] there was no war between Aram and Israel" (1 Kgs 22:1). But "in the third year[102] [וַיְהִי בַּשָּׁנָה הַשְּׁלִישִׁית]" (22:2), hostilities broke out (22:4). In the summary of the battle report the denominative verb הִשְׁלִים rather than the noun שָׁלוֹם is employed:[103] "The Arameans fled before Israel . . . When all the vassal kings of Hadadezer saw that they had been put to flight before Israel, they made (sued for) peace and submitted to Israel [וַיָּנָס אֲרָם מִפְּנֵי יִשְׂרָאֵל . . . וַיִּרְאוּ כָל־הַמְּלָכִים עַבְדֵי הֲדַדְעֶזֶר כִּי נִגְּפוּ לִפְנֵי יִשְׂרָאֵל וַיַּשְׁלִמוּ אֶת־יִשְׂרָאֵל וַיַּעַבְדוּם]" (2 Sam 10:18-19; cp. the slightly different version in 1 Chr 19:19).

The text presents a rather interesting picture: Having utterly routed Hadadezer (2 Sam 10:16-18), David imposed a vassal treaty on the minor coalition partners—Aram Beth-Rehob, Aram Zobah, the king of Maacah, and (the men of) Tob (2 Sam 10:6-8), who had lost the support of their champion. But he could not subject the evidently much more powerful Hadadezer to such a treaty. The resulting situation helps in explaining the somewhat baffling notation "there was peace between Israel and the Amorites [וַיְהִי שָׁלוֹם בֵּין יִשְׂרָאֵל וּבֵין הָאֱמֹרִי]" (1 Sam 7:14b), which is glaringly out of context in a report of Israel's decisive victory over the Philistines (1 Sam 7:5-14a). The comparison suggests that just as the defeat of Hadadezer forced his allies to submit to a vassal treaty with the victorious David, the latter's defeat of the mighty Philistines equally compelled the Amorites to submit to an "imposed שָׁלוֹם" with Israel.

---

99   See above.

100   See discussion above.

101   A stereotype figure. Cp. e.g. three years of siege (2 Kgs 17:5; 18:10), of the occupation of a country (2 Kgs 24:1), or of exile (2 Sam 13:38). See Talmon, "'Topped Triad': A Biblical Literary Convention," 181-99.

102   Meaning most probably "after" the third, viz. in the fourth year. The 3 + 1 pattern is another biblical motif. See Talmon, "'Topped Triad': A Biblical Literary Convention," 184-90.

103   See discussion above, p. 81; and cp. 1 Kgs 22:45: וַיַּשְׁלֵם יְהוֹשָׁפָט עִם־מֶלֶךְ יִשְׂרָאֵל.

In distinction, the alliance between Israel and Tyre is seemingly a singular case of "contractual peace," based on a covenant treaty as a means for promoting a gainful state of affairs for both partners (1 Kgs 5:15-25): "There was שָׁלוֹם between Hiram and Solomon and they established a בְּרִית" (5:26).[104]

H. The Biblical Conception of Positive שׁלום

We can now bring under consideration the biblical conception of "positive peace." The foregoing comprehensive investigation has shown that the term שׁלום relates preponderantly to a variety of events and situations in the private and the public domain, and that only in a comparatively small number of occurrences recorded in the Bible, the term connotes "peace" between peoples or nations in the political arena in "historical reality."

It is my thesis that the reality-oriented thrust which inheres in שׁלום also informs the biblical writers' visions of a fervently aspired future era of unlimited "positive peace." This "national ideal" finds expression in a model of three concentric circles in which the term שׁלום and its semantic field are pivotal: Israel at peace internally; externally, among all nations in a "world at peace"; and at peace in a "pacified universe." I am fully aware of the supreme credal content of these visions. Nevertheless, I intend to highlight the "restorative" underpinning of their "utopian" make-up, that is to say, the basic historical realism which shows in them,[105] and the persuasive "factuality" of their formulations.[106] In the world of biblical Israel, like in other ancient cultures, the spheres of the sacred and the secular are

---

104 Von Rad, *Theologie*, 1.136 defines such conditions as follows: "Das von einem Bundeschluss garantierte Verhältnis wird gern durch das Wort שׁלום bezeichnet (Gen 26[30] ff.; 1 Kön 5[26]; Jes 54[10]; Hi 5[23]) für das wiederum unser Wort Friede nur als eine unzureichende Entsprechung gelten kann. שׁלום bezeichnet nämlich die Unversehrtheit, die Ganzheit eines Gemeinschaftsverhältnisses, also einen Zustand."

105 The claim of Eisenbeis (*Die Wurzel שׁלום*, 156) that most mentions of שׁלום evince a theological meaning is unfounded.

106 Scholars who wish to make the biblical visions of a future world the kingpin of a modern peace-ideology fail to take note of the restorative, realism-oriented thrust of these visions. See, e.g. J. Kegler, "Prophetisches Reden von Zukünftigem," in H. Merklein and E. Zenger (eds.), *Eschatologie und Friedenshandeln: Exegetische Beiträge zur Frage christlicher Friedensverantwortung* (SBS 101; Stuttgart: Katholisches Bibelwerk, 1981) 15-58. A more balanced view is presented by U. Luz, "Die Bedeutung der biblischen Zeugnisse für kirchliches Friedenshandeln," in Merklein and Zenger (eds.), *Eschatologie*, 195-214.

one. The distinction between *civis dei* and *civis terrae* which will emerge in medieval times, lies far beyond their conceptual horizon.

The biblical authors' acquiescence in the correlation of war and peace in the human world is reflected in their acceptance of contrastive anthropomorphic characteristics attributed to Israel's God. On the one hand, YHWH is recurrently portrayed as "a hero who leads in battle [אִישׁ מִלְחָמָה]" (MT Exod 15:3) or גבור מלחמה (SP). The synonymous terms אִישׁ and גבור were evidently combined in Isa 42:13: יהוה כַּגִּבּוֹר יֵצֵא כְּאִישׁ מִלְחָמוֹת (cp. Judg 4:14; 1 Sam 8:20; 2 Sam 5:24 = 1 Chr 14:15; Ps 68:8),[107] YHWH who annihilates foes and enemies: לְהַשְׁבִּית אוֹיֵב וּמִתְנַקֵּם (Ps 8:3 et sim.). Again, "The Lord is a mighty warrior, a champion in war [יהוה עִזּוּז וְגִבּוֹר יהוה גִּבּוֹר מִלְחָמָה]" (Ps 24:8). On the other hand, YHWH is praised for ending wars and abolishing warfare: "He terminates wars (from end) to end of the earth, he snaps the bow and breaks the spear, burns (war) wagons (NEB: shields) in the fire [מַשְׁבִּית מִלְחָמוֹת עַד־קְצֵה הָאָרֶץ קֶשֶׁת יְשַׁבֵּר וְקִצֵּץ חֲנִית עֲגָלוֹת יִשְׂרֹף בָּאֵשׁ]"[108] (Ps 46:10; cp. Hos 1:5; Zech 9:10; et al.).[109] In conjunction, these attributes evince divine omnipotence: "Fearsome authority rests with him who (also) establishes peace in heaven [הַמְשֵׁל וָפַחַד עִמּוֹ עֹשֶׂה שָׁלוֹם בִּמְרוֹמָיו]" (Job 25:2),[110] from the days of Creation: "I am God, there is no other; I bring forth the light and create darkness, fashion peace, and create adversity [עֹשֶׂה שָׁלוֹם וּבוֹרֵא רָע]" (Isa 45:7). רָע equalling מִלְחָמָה, serves here, as in other texts and also in Ancient Near Eastern writings, as an antonym of שָׁלוֹם and טוֹב.[111]

In history, the Janus-head-duality of war and peace found its most

---

[107] The common verb יצא, serves at times as a technical military term, e.g. in the idiom בְּעֵת צֵאת הַמְּלָכִים, "the season when kings take the field" (2 Sam 11:1 = 1 Chr 20:1; see n. 96 above), especially in conjunction with the equally common verb בוא (e.g. Num 27:17; 1 Kgs 20:39; 1 Chr 14:8; 2 Chr 1:10; 20:17; 28:9). All the tribes of Israel submitted to David's rule, because he had (already) been the commander of the army in Saul's days, (ה)מוֹצִיא וְהַמֵּבִי(א) אֶת־יִשְׂרָאֵל, possibly a formal title (2 Sam 5:2 = 1 Chr 11:2). In view of this usage, I suggest to translate the phrase וְלַיּוֹצֵא וְלַבָּא אֵין־שָׁלוֹם מִן־הַצָּר (Zech 8:10), "The man at arms (i.e. the army) never had respite from (the pursuit of) the enemy."

[108] שבת and שבר are coterminous in this context (cp. Ezek 30:10).

[109] LXX introduces this notion also in Exod 15:3 by translating יהוה/אִישׁ מִלְחָמָה גִבּוֹר, κύριος συντρίβων πολέμους.

[110] For the antithesis of שלום and פחד equalling מלחמה, see n. 36 above.

[111] See, inter alia, A. Malamat, "Origins of Statecraft," *BA Reader* 3 (1970) 163; M. Fox, "Tôb as Covenant Terminology," *BASOR* 209 (1973) 41-42.

persuasive realization in the era of the "united monarchy": The successful military commander David personifies the image of the divine warrior on the earthly plane. In contrast, Solomon, the inexperienced youngster (וְאָנֹכִי נַעַר קָטֹן)[112] who professes that he never saw war in his life (לֹא אֵדַע צֵאת וָבֹא; 1 Kgs 3:7),[113] is presented aphoristically as the "man of peace": אִישׁ שָׁלוֹם. He embodies on earth the attribute of God who establishes שׁלום in the upper spheres.[114] The Chronicler evidently considered Solomon's admitted lack of experience in warfare a deficiency which needed to be remedied. In his version of Solomon's night-vision, the young king implores God: "Give me now wisdom and knowledge that I may lead this people (in battle), because who else could govern this great people of yours [עַתָּה חָכְמָה וּמַדָּע תֶּן־לִי וְאֵצְאָה לִפְנֵי הָעָם־הַזֶּה וְאָבוֹאָה כִּי־מִי יִשְׁפֹּט אֶת־עַמְּךָ הַזֶּה הַגָּדוֹל]?" (2 Chr 1:10).[115]

Biblical literati conceived of the idealized combined reigns of David and Solomon as the prototype on which they modeled their visionary image of a future era in which Israel will again enjoy שׁלום, untold success and prosperity. Their depictions of the shining future age reflect the glorious *Vorzeit* of the days of the united monarchy, and not an "Edenic *Urzeit*."[116] An instructive example is the

---

[112] In this context, נַעַר קָטָן/קָטֹן may actually connotate "crown prince" (see 1 Kgs 11:17); cp. 1 Chr 22:5: וַיֹּאמֶר דָּוִיד שְׁלֹמֹה בְנִי נַעַר וָרָךְ.

[113] For this technical connotation of צֵאת וָבֹא, see nn. 96 and 107 above.

[114] It is of interest to note that Moses and Aaron are sometimes similarly characterized in rabbinic literature. The midrash (*Exod. Rab.* 5.10 [on Exod 4:27]; *Tanh. Exod.* §28 [on 4:47]; et al.) interprets the phrase וַיִּפְגְּשֵׁהוּ .... וַיִּשַּׁק־לֹו in the episode of Aaron's meeting with Moses (Exod 4:27), in the light of Ps 85:11: חֶסֶד־וֶאֱמֶת נִפְגָּשׁוּ צֶדֶק וְשָׁלוֹם נָשָׁקוּ. Moses represents severity and strict abidance by the law. To him the verse applies: צִדְקַת יהוה עָשָׂה זֶה מֹשֶׁה (Deut 33:21). Aaron is viewed as the proverbial pursuer of peace: שָׁלוֹם זֶה אַהֲרֹן (Mal 2:4-6; Ps 34:15). But at the same time, the brothers complement each other and speak with one voice: שְׁנֵיהֶם יָצְאוּ בְּקוֹל אֶחָד (*Midr. Sam.* 9:1).

[115] The wording echoes the people's demand of Samuel to give them a king: "We want a king over us . . . to govern us [וּשְׁפָטָנוּ], to lead us out to war [וְיָצָא לְפָנֵינוּ] and fight our battles [וְנִלְחַם אֶת־מִלְחֲמֹתֵנוּ]" (1 Sam 8:20; cp. 8:5-6). See also nn. 96 and 107 above.

[116] See e.g. von Rad, *Theologie*, 1.180 (in reference to Isaiah 11): "Der dritte Teil (v. 6-8) spricht in Übereinstimmung mit traditionellen Vorstellungen vom paradiesischen Frieden, der mit der Regierung dieses Gesalbten sogar den Bereich der Natur ordnen und entspannen wird." Y. Kaufmann justifiedly rejects the Eden-theory, which appears to derive from Vergil's *Aeneid*.

Chronicler's panegyric of the Solomonic era of peace which capped David's turbulent reign. He significantly employs there next to שָׁלוֹם the interpretative synonyms מְנוּחה and שֶׁקט which fall in its wider semantic field:[117]

"You (David, said the Lord) have shed much blood in my sight and waged great wars; for this reason you shall not build a house in honour of my name. But you will have a son [הִנֵּה־בֵן נוֹלָד לָךְ], who shall be a man of serenity [אִישׁ מְנוּחָה]; I will give him rest [וַהֲנִחוֹתִי לוֹ] from all his enemies around; his name shall be [שְׁלֹמֹה; viz. 'man of peace'] and I will grant peace and tranquility [שָׁלוֹם וָשֶׁקֶט] to Israel in his days . . . he shall be my son and I will be a father to him [וְהוּא יִהְיֶה־לִּי לְבֵן וַאֲנִי־לוֹ לְאָב], and I will establish the throne of his sovereignty [כִּסֵּא מַלְכוּתוֹ] over Israel for ever [עַל־יִשְׂרָאֵל עַד־עוֹלָם"] (1 Chr 22:8-10).[118] Never before Solomon's days nor after did Israel experience such peace and safety: "For till now you have not attained the serenity [מְנוּחָה] in the patrimony [נַחֲלָה], which YHWH your God is giving you. But when you cross the Jordan, and settle in the land . . . he will grant you tranquility [וְהֵנִיחַ לָכֶם] from all your enemies around, and you will live in security [וִישַׁבְתֶּם־בֶּטַח]" (Deut 12:9-10).[119] The promise was only realized when God destroyed all of David's enemies, established his people (in the land) to dwell in it, [וְשָׁכַן], without ever being disturbed again, and never again to be oppressed as before (2 Sam 7:9-10).[120]

The effect of the Chronicler's praise of the Solomonic era is enhanced by the conjunction of his "prospective" appraisal with the "retrospective" summary of Solomon's reign, which the author of Kings offers. In Solomon's days came to fruit all promises which God had given to his people, from the days of the patriarchs to the establishment of the monarchy:

---

[117] See discussion above.

[118] The passage has no exact analogy in the parallel traditions in 2 Samuel 7 and 1 Kgs 3:6-9; 8:15-26. Note, though, that after the execution of Joab at the hands of Benaiahu, in revenge of the murders of Amasa and Abner, the author of the Book of Kings puts in Solomon's mouth a plea for everlasting peace: "May David and his descendants, his house and his throne, enjoy perpetual peace from YHWH [וּלְדָוִד וּלְזַרְעוֹ וּלְבֵיתוֹ וּלְכִסְאוֹ יִהְיֶה שָׁלוֹם עַד־עוֹלָם מֵעִם יהוה"] (1 Kgs 2:33).

[119] מְנוּחָה and יָשַׁב בֶּטַח are prominent functions of שָׁלוֹם (see discussion above and below).

[120] לְעַנּוֹתוֹ (וְלֹא־יֹסִיפוּ בְנֵי־עַוְלָה) echoes the tradition of Israel's serfdom in Egypt (cp. Exod 1:11, 12).

"The people of Judah and Israel were countless as the sands of the sea (shore); they ate and drank and were joyful. Solomon ruled over all the kingdoms from the river Euphrates to Philistia and as far as the frontier of Egypt; they paid tribute and were subject to him [וְעֹבְדִים אֶת־שְׁלֹמֹה] all his life . . . For he held sway over all (the lands) beyond the river (Euphrates) [רֹדֶה בְּכָל־עֵבֶר הַנָּהָר], from Tiphsah to Gaza, over all the kings of עֵבֶר הַנָּהָר, and he had שָׁלוֹם all around him . . . Judah and Israel lived securely [לָבֶטַח], everyone under his own vine and fig-tree, from Dan to Beersheba, all through Solomon's days" (1 Kgs 5:1-5; LXX: 4:20-25; 2 Chr 9:26).

The hyperbolical description of the grandeur of the Davidic-Solomonic commonwealth, once experienced in actual history, becomes the supreme expression of the biblical authors' historical aspirations. This vocabulary is their literary stock in trade and not, as said, the phraseology of the Garden of Eden tradition, neither in the Genesis (Genesis 2–3) nor the Ezekiel (Ezek 28:11-19) version. They injected that vocabulary retrospectively into the wordings of the conditional divine promise, outlined in various records pertaining to Israel's pre-Canaanite history in which the ideal course of Israel's progress in the Land is proleptically charted, e.g. in Lev 26:3-12 and Deut 12:9-10.[121] They projected that verbal picture into their visionary depictions of a radiant era of "peace." The divinely determined turning point in time (not the End of Time), termed קֵץ, יוֹם יהוה et sim., is expected to be realized within the frame of history, not in meta-history. However, not in the lifetime of the present generation, but always in "days to come" (אחרית הימים), the days of the next or next but one generation.[122] The deferment of its realization into a situation not yet experienced in reality, allows for the interweaving of an eschatological "utopian" strand into its basically "restorative" composition:[123] Biblical Israel's hope is the memory of an embellished historical past translated into the future.

The envisaged restoration of the *pax salomonica* in "the days to come" is probably the most important aspect of the conception of

---

[121] See discussion above.

[122] For this interpretation of the pregnant terms, see S. Talmon, "Eschatology and History in Biblical Thought," in Talmon, *Literary Studies in the Hebrew Bible, Form and Content*, 165-77.

[123] See S. Talmon, "Types of Messianic Expectations at the Turn of the Era," in Talmon, *King, Cult and Calendar in Ancient Israel* (Jerusalem: Magnes, 1986) 202-24.

"peace" in biblical literature. It needs to be prefaced by the following observations:

The progressive expansion of the semantic field of שָׁלוֹם outlined above, and the concurrent enrichment of the pertinent vocabulary, enabled biblical authors to describe that blissful future era of "peace" by having recourse to synonyms and explanatory phraseology of שָׁלוֹם, without necessarily employing the term itself.

In the context of the envisaged restoration of the *pax salomonica*, the biblical idea of שָׁלוֹם links up with two differently accentuated portrayals of the future with which it tends to become fused. A close analysis of the relevant texts suggests that on the one hand, we can still discern a vision which centers on an "Anointed" who will arise and ring in the eon of eternal peace, and on the other hand there is a "Diffuse-Redemption-Hope," which does not revolve on any central figure.[124] In consequence, the range of texts which should be brought under scrutiny in an analysis of the concept of שָׁלוֹם widens beyond what can be achieved in the present context.[125] Therefore, I shall necessarily restrict myself to the consideration of only a few illustrative examples.

As said, the notion of the future era of "peace" can be presented in a model of three ever-widening concentric circles: (1) Israel at peace; (2) the world at peace; and (3) cosmic peace.[126]

(1) Attention centers on the portrayal of Israel internally at peace, enjoying prosperity and well-being, ruled by a Davidic scion, and not threatened by external enemies, as in the era of the united monarchy, first and foremost in Solomon's days.

Fathers and sons will be reconciled when the prophet Elijah arises to announce the new era: וְהֵשִׁיב לֵב־אָבוֹת עַל־בָּנִים וְלֵב בָּנִים עַל־אֲבוֹתָם (Mal 3:23-24). Judah and Ephraim will be reunited and again become one "Israel" (Mic 5:2 et al.). Peaceful relations and concord shall prevail among the leaders of the community, the royal scion of

---

124 See S. Talmon, "Biblical Visions of the Future Ideal Age," in Talmon, *King, Cult*, 140-64.

125 The issue is brought under discussion in a series of articles by U. Luz, J. Kegler, F. Lampe, P. Hoffmann, in *Eschatologie und Friedenshandeln: Exegetische Beiträge zur Frage christlicher Friedensverantwortung* (SBS; Stuttgart: Katholisches Bibelwerk, 1981).

126 See L. Perlitt, "Israel und die Völker," in G. Liedke (ed.), *Frieden – Bibel – Kirche: Studien zur Friedensforschung* (Stuttgart: Klett; München: Kösel, 1972) 17-64.

David's line and the highpriest, וַעֲצַת שָׁלוֹם תִּהְיֶה בֵּין שְׁנֵיהֶם (Zech 6:13), involving the whole people, וּמִשְׁפַּט שָׁלוֹם שִׁפְטוּ בְּשַׁעֲרֵיכֶם (Zech 8:16). Then "in this place will I grant prosperity [וּבַמָּקוֹם הַזֶּה אֶתֵּן שָׁלוֹם]" (Hag 2:9). "Each one shall dwell under his own vine, and under his own fig-tree, unafraid [וְיָשְׁבוּ אִישׁ תַּחַת גַּפְנוֹ וְתַחַת תְּאֵנָתוֹ וְאֵין מַחֲרִיד]" (Mic 4:4-5), as in Solomon's days.[127]

The conception of the era of the united monarchy as the idealized *Vorzeit* shows most clearly in visions of a future ruler who shall arise for Israel, such as are ascribed to Isaiah and Micah of the first generation of "missionary" prophets. Through the use of the history-laden term שלום the authors of these pronouncements foresee the reconstitution in an appreciably near future of the *pax salomonica*, in which culminated the era of the united monarchy:

"For a boy was born for us, a son given to us [כִּי־יֶלֶד יֻלַּד־לָנוּ בֵּן נִתַּן־לָנוּ], the (symbol of) dominion will be on his shoulder [וַתְּהִי הַמִּשְׂרָה עַל־שִׁכְמוֹ], his name shall be [וַיִּקְרָא שְׁמוֹ][128] 'wonderful advisor,'[129] 'divine warrior,'[130] 'eternal father' [אֲבִי־עַד],[131] 'prince of peace' [שַׂר־שָׁלוֹם].[132] He shall enlarge the dominion, and (make) boundless the peace [וּלְשָׁלוֹם אֵין־קֵץ],[133] (bestowed) on David's throne and in his kingdom . . . with justice and righteous power [בְּמִשְׁפָּט וּבִצְדָקָה],[134] for now and evermore [מֵעַתָּה וְעַד־עוֹלָם]" (Isa 9:5-6; cp. 1 Kgs 2:33; 1 Chr 22:9-10).

"Then a shoot shall grow from the stock of Jesse, and a branch shall sprout from his roots.[135] The spirit of YHWH shall rest upon him, a spirit of wisdom and understanding . . . counsel and valor

---

[127] The short Micah passage is an almost verbal reprise of 1 Kgs 5:5. It remains an open question whether the vision applies exclusively to Israelites or also to members of other nations.

[128] Read possibly וְיִקְרָא שְׁמוֹ.

[129] The epithet fits the "wise" Solomon perfectly.

[130] An epithet of David.

[131] Possibly an allusion to the divine promise concerning Solomon: הוּא יִהְיֶה־לִּי לְבֵן וַאֲנִי־לוֹ לְאָב (1 Chr 22:10).

[132] A word play on the name of שְׁלֹמֹה, the prototypical אִישׁ מְנוּחָה, in whose days Israel lived in שָׁלוֹם וָשֶׁקֶט (1 Chr 22:9-10), and who had שָׁלוֹם all around him (1 Kgs 5:4).

[133] Cp. 1 Kgs 5:1, 4.

[134] צדק, and similarly (מ)שׁפט, often connote the power to dispense justice. This is one more distinctive trait which the author of Kings ascribes to Solomon (1 Kgs 3:4-15, 16-28; 5:9-14; 10:1-13).

[135] Cp. Zech 3:8; 6:12.

[גְּבוּרָה], of knowledge and awe of YHWH . . . He shall not judge by what he sees nor decide by what he hears. He shall strike the ruthless with the scourge of his mouth, and with the breath (word) of his mouth he shall slay the wicked . . . On that day (the sprout out of) the root of Jesse shall be set up as a signal to the peoples, the nations shall rally to it, and its (place) of rest (serenity) [מְנֻחָתוֹ], will be glory" (Isa 11:1-5, 10).

The essence of these oracles and the similar vocabulary leave little doubt that the wording hearks back to Isaiah's pronouncement that the unidentified pregnant עַלְמָה in Hezekiah's entourage, correctly understood by many commentators as "the queen," will bear a son [הִנֵּה הָעַלְמָה הָרָה וְיֹלֶדֶת בֵּן], who shall be given the comforting name "Immanuel." In the days of that son, viz. of the future king, the present danger will be averted from Judah (Isa 7:14-20), and the people will enjoy serenity and prosperity (7:21-25; cp. 60:16-18).[136]

The faculties attributed to the future ruler in whose reign Israel will enjoy מְנֻחָה and כָּבוֹד again prove that the prophet patterned his image after that of the wise, just and peace-loving Solomon. The ascription of valor, גְּבוּרָה (Isa 11:2), to the self-confessed inexperienced youngster who never saw war in his life, וְאָנֹכִי נַעַר קָטֹן לֹא אֵדַע צֵאת וָבֹא (1 Kgs 3:7),[137] is seemingly out of place. But it is possibly intended to invest the "shoot" also with David's most characteristic quality, and to thus bestow upon his future reign the past glory of the united monarchy.

The major motifs employed in the above texts surface in Micah's announcement of the rise of a future ruler of David's line: "You, Bethlehem Ephratah . . . out of you shall come forth a ruler over Israel [מוֹשֵׁל בְּיִשְׂרָאֵל],[138] one whose roots are far back in the past, in

---

136 When in such a prophecy vocables are employed which have a less explicit chronological implication than הָרָה, בֵּן, יֶלֶד, and the term שָׁלֵם is absent, the omission possibly signals the recognition that a larger hiatus than that of one generation separates the historical present from the hoped for era of restoration.

137 Cp. 1 Chr 22:5: וַיֹּאמֶר דָּוִיד שְׁלֹמֹה בְנִי נַעַר וָרָךְ.

138 מוֹשֵׁל parallels מֶלֶךְ (Ps 105:20). It is a royal attribute of God, king of the universe (Ps 59:14; 66:7; 103:19; Job 25:2; 1 Chr 29:12), which also recurrently designates rulers of the Davidic dynasty (Jer 22:30 = 33:26; Zech 6:13; 2 Chr 7:18), first and foremost Solomon (1 Kgs 5:1; 2 Chr 9:26). But the term also refers to foreign kings (Daniel 11 passim; et al.). In the psalm which bears the superscription "David's last words" (2 Sam 23:1-7), the singer applies the term twice to himself: "the Rock of Israel spoke of me: 'Just ruler of mankind, ruler in the fear of

days gone by. (The Lord) will appoint him,[139] when she who is in labor gives birth . . . and (the best of)[140] his brothers will rejoin Israel. He will rise up and lead (them) [וְעָמַד וְרָעָה],[141] in the strength of YHWH, in the majesty of the name of YHWH his God, and they will live (in safety),[142] for now (his power) shall reach to the end of the world. And this shall be peace [וְהָיָה זֶה שָׁלוֹם] (5:1-4).[143]

The basic concept which permeates the above passages, appears to be captured in the partly identical and partly similar phraseology of the opening and the closing lines of the famous oracle in Zechariah: "Rejoice, rejoice, daughter of Zion, shout aloud, daughter of Jerusalem, for your king is coming to you, a righteous savior, [צַדִּיק וְנוֹשָׁע],[144] humble, but riding on an ass, on a foal of a she-ass[145] . . .

God' [מוֹשֵׁל בָּאָדָם צַדִּיק מוֹשֵׁל יִרְאַת אֱלֹהִים]" (23:3). It is plausible that the author of David's autobiographical psalm, preserved in 11QPsª 28 = Psalm 151A (see J. A. Sanders, *The Psalms Scroll of Qumran Cave 11 (11QPsª)* [DJD 4; Oxford: Clarendon, 1965] 49, 54-60) took his clue from here, when he has David relate: "my father appointed me . . . ruler over his kids [וַיְשִׂימֵנִי רוֹעֶה לְצֹאנוֹ]" (line 3); and then God "appointed me leader of his people and ruler over the sons of his covenant [וַיְשִׂימֵנִי נָגִיד לְעַמּוֹ וּמוֹשֵׁל בִּבְנֵי בְרִיתוֹ]" (line 12). שִׂים parallels נָתַן. Both verbs interchange with הִמְלִיךְ in the sense of to appoint a king or ruler, as in the tale of Saul's election (1 Sam 8:5, 6, 22; 10:19; 12:1; cp. Deut 17:14-15) et al.

[139] For the technical connotation "appoint as king" of the common verb נָתַן, cp. 1 Sam 8:6 and 12:13 with 8:5, 22; 12:12-14. Read יִתְּנוּ for MT's יִתְּנֵם. I assume that נו was misread ם (cp. e.g. 2 Kgs 22:4 and 22:5), while the נ was still retained. Textual variants involving a final ם which resulted from a misread ligature of נו were collated by R. Weiss, "On Ligatures in the Hebrew Bible," *JBL* 82 (1963) 188-94. A fair number of similar "mistakes" can be added to the ones listed there.

[140] For this understanding of יֶתֶר, cp. e.g Gen 49:3; Num 31:32 and Jer 27:19.

[141] The shepherd motif is recurrently applied to David and his line (see e.g. 2 Sam 5:2; 7:7 = 1 Chr 17:6; Ps 78:71).

[142] This is the contextually implied connotation of יָשַׁב (see above).

[143] The NEB felicitous rendition of the somewhat opaque phrase: "and he (lit. 'this one') shall be a man of peace," points to the title שַׂר־שָׁלוֹם (Isa 9:5) and to Solomon's epithet אִישׁ מְנוּחָה (1 Chr 22:9). Cp. further אִישׁ שָׁלוֹם (Ps 37:37).

[144] The apparent passive participle נוֹשָׁע has in fact the active connotation "savior." It was correctly rendered in the LXX: δίκαιος καὶ σώζων αὐτός. Possibly due to a *lapsus calami* involving an interchange of מ with נ, an original מוֹשִׁ(י)עַ became נוֹשָׁע.

[145] Riding on one of these animals is a sign of distinction and rank: חֲמוֹר (Gen 22:3; Josh 15:18 = Judg 1:14; 1 Sam 25:20, 23, 42; 2 Sam 17:23; 1 Kgs 2:40; 13:13, 23, 27). חֲמוֹר parallels סוּס (2 Kgs 7:10; Prov 26:3); אָתוֹן (Num 22:21-33; Judg 5:10; 1 Sam 9-10; 2 Kgs 4:22-24); עַיִר (Judg 10:4; 12:14).

he will announce peace to the nations." In this oracle, the vision of a future era of peace is significantly enhanced by God's promise to protect the king's achievements and keep the land safe of enemies:[146] "He shall banish chariots from Ephraim and war-horses from Jerusalem, the warrior's bow shall be banished" (9:9-11a), thus guaranteeing that the king's rule shall indeed extend "from sea to sea,[147] and from the River to the ends of the earth" (Zech 9:9-10). The depiction of the future ruler as צַדִּיק וְנוֹשָׁע, whose realm shall expand from the river (Euphrates) to the end of the world, [מִנָּהָר עַד־אַפְסֵי־אָרֶץ][148] who will proclaim שׁלום to the nations, is again an embellished reflection of Solomon's rule "from the Euphrates to the borders of Egypt [מִן־הַנָּהָר אֶרֶץ פְּלִשְׁתִּים וְעַד גְּבוּל מִצְרָיִם]" (1 Kgs 5:1, 4; cp. and Ps 72:8) including the land of the Philistines.

The biblical authors' admiration of the *pax salomonica* finds its supreme expression in Psalm 72,[149] in which the singer extols the greatness of a king who is the son of a king: אֱלֹהִים מִשְׁפָּטֶיךָ לְמֶלֶךְ תֵּן וְצִדְקָתְךָ לְבֶן־מֶלֶךְ (72:1). He evidently refers to Solomon, the first son who inherited the throne in dynastic succession.[150] In this panegyric, the phrases שָׁלוֹם לָעָם (72:3) and רֹב שָׁלוֹם (72:7) figure prominently. It may be viewed as a *summa summarum* of all praiseworthy characteristics which biblical authors ascribe to David and Solomon, the total of all achievements which they saw realized in the era of the united monarchy—success, fame and safety in the political arena (72:8-11,17); law and justice, צדק and מׁשׁפט (72:1-4, 12-14); prosperity all around (72:6,15-16).[151] The song reads like a collocation of vocables, idioms and explanatory expressions which fall in the semantic field of שׁלום and characterize the *pax salomonica*.

(2) In most texts quoted so far, the envisaged era of peace is geographically and conceptually limited. It pertains basically to Israel, a people isolated from others: "a people that dwells alone, that

---

146 Cp. Ps 29:11: "YHWH will give strength to his people, YHWH will bless his people with peace"; 147:12-14 et al.

147 In historical terms, מִיָּם עַד־יָם would have meant from the Mediterranean to the Dead Sea.

148 Cp. Mic 5:3: עַתָּה יִגְדַּל עַד־אַפְסֵי־אָרֶץ.

149 This psalm closes the second part of the Book of Psalms, כָּלּוּ תְפִלּוֹת דָּוִד בֶּן־יִשָׁי (72:20), which tradition divides into five compendia (another Pentateuch). The first two contain most of the songs ascribed to David.

150 Saul's intention to establish a dynasty was foiled by David.

151 Cp. Isa 32:1-8, 15-20.

has not made itself one with the nations [עָם לְבָדָד יִשְׁכֹּן וּבַגּוֹיִם
לֹא יִתְחַשָּׁב]" (Num 23:9), "living in security, by themselves, in a land
of corn and wine [וַיִּשְׁכֹּן יִשְׂרָאֵל בֶּטַח בָּדָד עֵין יַעֲקֹב אֶל־אֶרֶץ דָּגָן
וְתִירוֹשׁ]" (Deut 33:28; Zech 14:10-11). But the repeated mentions of
שלום לגוים reveal a progressive expansion, culminating in the vision
of universal peace which embraces "all (or) many [רַבִּים] peoples"
(Isa 2:2-3; Mic 4:1-2).[152] Israel remains center stage, but is now
perceived as "a nation among nations." In the "days to come [בְּאַחֲרִית
הַיָּמִים]," (the) nations will stream to Jerusalem from where divine
instruction issues, to be taught the ways of the God of Jacob, and
walk in his paths. YHWH is presented as the supreme judge. All
nations, near and far (מֵרָחֹק), will abide by his arbitration, so that
"nation shall not lift (anymore) sword against nation, nor ever again
train for war." Destructive weaponry shall become obsolete, and
shall be turned into productive tools, ploughshares and pruning
knives, symbols of abundant harvests and of prosperity (Isa 4:3-4;
Mic 4:2-3). The conjunction of war and peace, traditionally considered a constant and inevitable phenomenon of history, will be
categorically disjoined in the future eon:[153] Warfare as such will
cease to exist in a world of unlimited peace. But, *nota bene*, the
history-laden term שלום is never used in either one of these texts.

In a concluding line of the Isaiah version, which concomitantly
links this passage with the ensuing pericope, Israel is accorded a
special position in respect to other nations also in the age to come:
"O house of Jacob, come, let us walk in the light of YHWH [בֵּית יַעֲקֹב
לְכוּ וְנֵלְכָה בְּאוֹר יהוה]" (Isa 2:5). In Micah this verse is missing. But
its sense is even more forcefully expressed in a parallel summary
line: "All peoples shall walk each in the name of his god, but we shall
walk in the name of YHWH our God for ever and ever" (Mic 4:5).
The individuality and intrinsic separateness of nations, established by
the Creator in the primordial "constitutive eon,"[154] and acted out in
history, is reaffirmed and projected into the glorious future age. The
resulting "restorative" thrust, presumably intended to impress the

---

[152] The Micah text reads עַמִּים, the Isaiah version כָּל־הַגּוֹיִם. רַבִּים can mean
"many" or "great."

[153] In Zech 14:16, the "going up" of the nations to Jerusalem is yet presented as
an annual pilgrimage of only "the remnant of all peoples, כָּל־הַנּוֹתָר מִכָּל־הַגּוֹיִם הַבָּאִים
עַל־יְרוּשָׁלַם," who had survived the preceding war of cataclysmic dimensions (14:1-
14).

[154] See above.

stamp of reality on the "utopian" vision, which conjures up the memory of Solomon's days, is further underscored by the introduction of a central שלום motif, "each one shall dwell under his own vine, under his own fig-tree undisturbed" (Mic 4:4). But in difference from the days of the "historical" *pax salomonica*, when welfare and security had been granted to Israel alone: וַיֵּשֶׁב יְהוּדָה וְיִשְׂרָאֵל לָבֶטַח אִישׁ תַּחַת גַּפְנוֹ וְתַחַת תְּאֵנָתוֹ מִדָּן וְעַד־בְּאֵר שָׁבַע (1 Kgs 5:5), the envisaged future serenity and prosperity is seen as enfolding "all peoples."

The recurrent use of the terms (כל) העמים and (כל) הגוים, which by definition imply divisiveness, rather than the employment of more inclusive designations, like (כל) בני אדם or (כל) בני איש, prompts the suggestion that the apparent "universality" of the above texts encompasses in fact only the peoples and states in an area which lay within the ancient Israelites' intellectual grasp, viz. the nations of the Ancient Near East. In literary terms, the peoples involved are identified in the clusters of "Oracles Against the Nations," incorporated in the books of the three "great prophets": Isaiah (13:1-19:23; 20:3-24:23), Jeremiah (46:1-51:58),[155] Ezekiel (25:1-32:32), and in some of the "Twelve," foremost in Amos 1:2–2:3 (cp. Joel 4:1-17 et al.).

The envisaged abolition of war will make room for the constitution of a *commmunitas communitatum* in which these nations will be united, their separate individualities unimpaired, "each one walking in the ways of its god" (Mic 4:5). As said, Israel is accorded a special place in this blue-print. "The world," viz. the community of small nations, will be led by an imperial triad, constituted of Israel, Egypt and Assyria: "When that day comes Israel shall be a triad with Egypt and Assyria, a blessing [בְּרָכָה] amidst the world" (Isa 19:24). Also in this instance, בְּרָכָה substitutes for שָׁלוֹם. Accordingly, I would render the phrase בַּיּוֹם הַהוּא יִהְיֶה יִשְׂרָאֵל שְׁלִישִׁיָּה לְמִצְרַיִם וּלְאַשּׁוּר בְּרָכָה בְּקֶרֶב הָאָרֶץ, "on that day the triad Israel, Egypt and Assyria[156] will be (a beacon or a guarantor of) peace in the world." The statement again reflects the *pax salomonica*, the only period in history in which the Bible presents Israel as being on an equal footing with Egypt, when "Solomon allied himself to Pharaoh, king of Egypt, by

---

155 In the LXX, the cluster comes after the notation: "all that is written in this book, all that Jeremiah has prophesied against these peoples" (25:13). MT has there a mere summary of oracles (25:15-31) which possibly serves as a *custos*.

156 In the context, Assyria stands for a symbolical, not a historical value.

marrying his daughter," and bringing her "to the City of David" (1 Kgs 3:1; 9:24).

(3) The biblical concept of שׁלום also entails hope for cosmic peace. The apex of biblical Israel's hope for peace is reached in prophetic visions which transcend the horizon of human experience. The added dimension comes into full view in the prophecies of Second (or Third) Isaiah. Jerusalem and Israel remain centerstage, with everyone enjoying a good life in safety, as in Solomon's time: "People shall build houses and live to inhabit them, plant vineyards and eat their fruit ... They shall not toil in vain or raise children for misfortune" (Isa 65:21-23).[157] The "reconstituted creation" will pale anything humanity had ever known before (65:17). No one will die before his life has run its full course (65:20). "Weeping and cries for help shall never again be heard" (65:19). Even the animal world will exist without tension and discord: "Wolf and lamb shall feed together, lion shall eat straw like cattle, and the snake shall eat dust" (65:25; cp. Gen 3:14).

This last line reads like a concise summary of the more elaborate depiction of peace in the animal world in Isa 11:6-9: "Wolf shall live with sheep, leopard lie down with a kid; calf and (full grown) lion shall graze[158] together, and a little child shall lead them; cow and bear shall forage together, (together) their young shall lie down; lion shall eat straw like cattle; an infant shall play over the hole of a snake, and a toddler[159] put his hand into a viper's nest."

Also in these visions of cosmic peace, the crucial term is never employed, nor any characteristic phrase and motif which fall in its semantic field, just as this vocabulary is missing in Genesis 1–11. This absence confers upon the visions of cosmic peace a mythical-eschatological aura. We seem to have come full circle: Like the constitutive primordial eon, also the visionary future age cannot be described in שׁלום terminology whose true *Sitz im Leben* is the reality of this world, the reality of situations experienced in history.

But, says Martin Buber, "'Eschatological' hope—in Israel, the 'historical people par excellence' (Tillich), but not in Israel alone—is first always historical hope, it becomes eschatological only through growing historical disillusionment. In this process faith seizes upon

---

157 Cp. Hos 2:20-25.

158 Read יִמְרְאוּ, instead of the MT's וּמְרִיא. 1QIsaᵃ reads ומרי.

159 Literally: a weaned child (גָּמוּל).

the future as the unconditioned turning point of history, then as the unconditioned overcoming of history. From this point of vantage it can be explained that the eschatologization of those actual-historical ideas includes their mythicization . . . Myth is the spontaneous and legitimate language of expecting, as of remembering, faith. But it is not its substance . . . The genuine eschatological life of faith is in the great labour-pains of historical experience—born from the genuine historical life of faith."[160]

In the above vision of "cosmic peace" in Isa 11:6-9, two factors still provide the expected linkage with history: The pericope is wedged in between two oracles pertaining to the "shoot," the future king from the house of Jesse (Isa 11:1-5, 10-16). Hereby, the memory of David is invoked. And the proverb-like quality of the description brings to the reader's mind the presentation of the just, peace-loving and wise Solomon as the author of three thousand proverbs: "He discoursed of trees . . . of beasts and birds, of reptiles and fishes" (1 Kgs 5:13-14). In the last count, the restorative national ideal, the future reconstitution of an Israelite polity patterned after the united monarchy and the *pax salomonica*, inspired also the biblical authors' utopian-mythic visions of an ideal future age.[161]

---

160 M. Buber, "Introduction," in Buber, *Kingship of God* (London: George Allen & Unwin, 1967).

161 I wish to express thanks to my assistant, Jonathan Ben-Dov, for his help in the preparation of the final version of this essay.

ON BIBLICAL THEOLOGY*

Rolf P. Knierim

I

In the so-called Western civilization and in the parts of those civilizations that are influenced by or in dialogue with it, the Bible is today read for three main reasons: for its contribution to our knowledge of ancient history, for being part of the body of classical world literature, and for its role in the Jewish and Christian religions.

It is important that the Bible is not only read for religious reasons. As a source for historical knowledge and as a document of world literature, it represents a significant contribution to the total body of human knowledge and already for this reason belongs not only to the Jewish and Christian communities but to the total human race.

However, the Bible is essentially a religious book. Even where it informs us about history, literature, and much more, its information functions for the religious purposes of its writers. Without these purposes, the biblical books would not have been written.

The fact of its religious purposes does not mean that the Bible belongs to only those communities who produced it. The Bible is not esoteric literature for esoteric religious sects. It is also the religious contribution of its respective communities to all societies and cultures and to all human beings. In this contribution, the biblically based communities have expressed their understanding of reality as the basis for the way of life for all and therefore also for themselves. This understanding is religious, and because its religiosity focuses on God, it is essentially *theo*logical. And the Jewish and Christian

---

*   Dedicated to Professor James A. Sanders, my colleague in Claremont since 1977, on the occasion of his seventieth birthday with the best wishes for a long and healthy life.

This paper was originally read at the Methodist Seminary in Seoul Korea, on May 17, 1994, and at the Tokyo United Theological Seminary (TUTS) in Japan, on May 27, 1994. It is published in Japanese in the TUTS Annual, and its English version is by agreement published here in dedication to James Sanders.

communities read their respective Bibles today because they are the original sources for the theological shape of their religions.

II

Jewish and Christian communities do not have the same Bible. Whereas the Jewish community has the Hebrew Bible, the TANAK, followed by Mishnah, Talmud, and Midrash—but not the Christian New Testament, the Christian community has one Bible of two parts, the Christian New Testament and also the Jewish Bible as its Old Testament.**

A. The origin of the Christian Bible of two Testaments dates back to the second century when the church decided, against Marcion, to continue to recognize the Jewish Bible as a part of its total Bible rather than reject it as the document of an evil religion. The rejection of Marcion was justified because the Jewish Scriptures had already in the original Christian writings been recognized as Holy Scriptures inspired by the same God who had ultimately revealed himself in Jesus Christ.

Nevertheless, the juxtaposition of the two Testaments in the Christian Bible generated a problem with which the church has had to live throughout its history, and which in my opinion is not sufficiently diagnosed let alone answered to this day. It is the problem of how the two Testaments are related. We have no consensus on what each Testament means for the other, especially on whether or not the two Testaments are mutually open to each other.

B. In the tradition of Christian theology, the relationship of the two Testaments has scarcely ever been one of mutually equal openness. From the earliest Christian writings of the first century on, it was the Christian theology of the ultimate revelation of God in Jesus Christ which determined the validity of everything else. The principles for theological validity were controlled by Christology, and this Christology also predetermined the sense in which the Jewish Bible could still have a function for humanity from the perspective of the Christian faith.

**   I speak here in general terms. The respective canons of early Jewish and Christian communities differed. Besides the obvious examples, such as many of the writings that make up the Old Testament Apocrypha (or deutero-canonical books), there were various books that enjoyed canonical status in some communities for certain periods of time (and in some cases still do in eastern churches).

The original and basic paradigms for this function are contained in the New Testament:

(1) The Old Testament is prophecy, whereas the Christian faith teaches the fulfillment of this prophecy—so especially in Matthew.

(2) Moses gave the law, but "grace and truth came through Jesus Christ"—so in John (1:17). It is the truth of the living water and bread, of light rather than darkness, and of resurrection as eternal life rather than eternal death.

(3) According to Luke, "the law and the prophets were until John [the Baptist]; since then the gospel of the kingdom of God is preached" (16:16), and—so in Acts—the Holy Spirit is poured out.

(4) For Paul, the gospel and life in the Spirit reveal that every way of life, religious or not, including the way revealed by God to Israel, is the way under the law rather than the liberty of existence. It is under judgment because it is not reconciled through God's work in Jesus Christ. The original creation under the law belongs to the past because the new creation has come.

(5) According to the Letter to the Hebrews, Israel's believing community only foreshadows the final believing community of those by now once and for all times atoned by Christ's sacrifice.

The decisive ground for these definitions is the Christian belief in the ultimacy of God's revelation in Jesus Christ. In view of this ultimacy, everything said in the Old Testament is at best penultimate. Prophecy is surpassed and replaced by fulfillment; Moses' law by grace and truth; the time of law and the prophets by the time of the gospel; existence as sinner by liberation from death, sin and law; the old by the new believing community; and *in toto* the old by the new creation.

The Christian belief in the ultimacy of God's revelation in Jesus Christ is, of course, based on the affirmation of the resurrection of the crucified Jesus by God from the dead. Unlike other resurrections, the resurrection of Jesus by God was understood as the decisive watershed mark in the history of the universe, as the replacement of the validity of the first creation by the breaking-in of the new creation into the still existing yet soon ending old creation. It is the root for the affirmation that Jesus is, ultimately the Messiah, the only Son of the living God, the only Logos who was with God before creation, and the *kyrios*, the only LORD over heaven and earth. Hence, the eschatological event happened. The new creation has arrived, exists, and will therefore soon be fully revealed in the second coming of Christ. This second coming may be delayed, but it is nevertheless always close and the disciples must therefore always be prepared for it. The temporal eschatology of the second coming of Christ was not an incidental, discardable shell. It was essential for the Christologically based world view of the early Christians. Since the new creation is only present in signs but has not yet subsumed the old creation, the completion of the replacement of the old by the new creation had to be expected.

Only in the gospel of John does the temporal eschatology step back in favor of the ultimacy of life in Christ in terms of eternal life in both life and death.

From this Christian theology of religion, the theology of the Jewish Bible has from the earliest Christian writings on appeared to be at best preliminary, preparatory, penultimate, relative, an example for how not, or no longer, to believe, and at worst irrelevant, negligible, or to be rejected. The relationship between these writings and the Old Testament was not one of mutually equal openness, an openness in which the Old Testament and these writings could jointly determine the scope of the religious understanding of reality. This relationship was unilaterally predetermined by Christians and their Christian agenda.

This situation was reinforced by the canonization of the early Christian writings in the New Testament. Ever since this canonization, the relationship between the two Testaments has not only meant that the Christian Bible consists of two Testaments. It has especially meant that the judgment of the New over the Old Testament, and with it the judgment of Christians over Israel, has canonic authority and is a canonic requirement.

This understanding was basic for the churches of the Protestant Reformation, for the Protestant orthodoxy, for the periods of Rationalism and the Enlightenment, for the religious concepts of romanticism and idealism and the religio-historical school, and for virtually all New and Old Testament theologies in the twentieth century from Karl Barth to Walther Eichrodt, Rudolf Bultmann, Gerhard von Rad, Walther Zimmerli, Claus Westermann, Brevard Childs, and many more.

C. Despite varying emphases, all Christian interpreters of the Old or the New Testament reflect the essential position which Johann Philipp Gabler presented in his 1787 inaugural lecture "About the just discrimination of biblical and dogmatic theology and the correctly governing boundaries of each," in which he program-matically declared that biblical theology is a discipline independent of dogmatics.

Gabler's demand for the liberation of biblical theology from its subservience to dogmatic theology was not new. This demand rested on the Protestant principle that the Bible is the basis and criterion for the doctrine of the church rather than dependent on or intertwined with this doctrine. This principle had to be clearly restored in his own time. Also, he succeeded, in my analysis, in demonstrating that the criteria for biblical theology are found within the Bible, without dogmatics, even as the criteria for dogmatics are the same as those found in the Bible, just as they should be as long as dogmatics claims to rest on the Bible.

However, Gabler's concept for the biblical theology of both Testaments is decisively derived from those passages and concepts in the New Testament that most clearly express the criterion for the theological evaluation of all other passages in the New as well as especially in the Old Testament. Those passages and concepts contain the one doctrine which is the most important doctrine in the entire Bible. This one doctrine belongs, first of all, to those doctrines in the entire Bible that are not restricted to passing times but are valid for all places and times. And of those it is the one doctrine which is most decisive and therefore the most specifically Christian, namely, the doctrine of our eternal salvation. Only this doctrine represents the true foundation of the Christian religion.

This doctrine is only found in the New Testament. Compared to it, other doctrines or opinions found even in the New Testament are relative or irrelevant, whereas the Old Testament does not have this doctrine at all. The Old Testament as a whole is, therefore, not only less important than this fundamental Christian doctrine; it is also less important than the New Testament as a whole because even the time-restricted opinions in the New Testament evolved from their Christian foundation, which is nowhere the case in the Old Testament. Not even truly universal doctrines (which are for all places and times) found in the Old Testament—e.g. the doctrines of creation, the fall, the ten commandments, and monotheism—represent truly Christian doctrines let alone the pure Christian doctrine of our salvation. The Old Testament as a whole is, however preparatory and divinely inspired, inferior, old, not as important as the newer and better Testament.

It has sometimes been said that Gabler did not develop a program for a separate Old Testament theology—as if he might have done so had he wanted it. In fact, he quite clearly outlined the method for an Old Testament theology. More important is that he saw no reason for two separate theologies, one of the Old and another of the New Testament. It was programmatic that he spoke of two Testamentally distinct theologies within one united biblical theology. For him, biblical theology had to include the total Christian Bible, with only one decisive distinction: While the Old Testament is not Christian but for Christians, the New Testament is not only Christian but also by Christians. In whatever way the Old Testament must be understood as divinely inspired and written by sacred writers, it can, precisely by being juxtaposed to and compared with the New Testament, only simultaneously reveal two things: its own inferiority and the superiority of the New Testament.

Contrary to a long held opinion, Gabler did not propose that biblical theology be worked out as the history of the biblical religion. He proposed the precise definition and comparison of all biblical doctrines including those within the New Testament, even those written by Paul in his very same letters. The comparison of these doctrines shows their relative and decisive differences, and above all the one pure doctrine of the Christian religion which is the criterion for the critical evaluation of all other theologies in the total Bible. His biblical theology is a method by which the biblical doctrine of the pure Christian religion can be worked out, a purpose which can only be clearly fulfilled if all doctrines of the Christian Bible are included and compared. This clarification had in his time become extremely necessary. To prove the result of this goal, a biblical theology was necessary rather than two separate theologies of the two Testaments as we have had them for a long time.

Nevertheless, the theological difference between the two Testaments remained fundamental for Gabler, and remains so to this day, notwithstanding aspects common to both such as word of God, inspiration, monotheism, history, canonicity, authority, and so on. This basic difference is the reason why the separation of the theologies of the two Testaments has been stronger than a united biblical theology and why biblical theology is and has never been anything but in crisis.

When considering a biblical theology, we must realize that in view of their basic difference, the search for a theological unity of the two

Testaments is futile. For whatever reason a biblical theology is required, it can only be based on the recognition of the fundamentally different theological concepts of the two Testaments rather than on what both have in common despite that difference. A biblical theology must at its outset interpret this difference.

III

In order to confront the issue of biblical theology, more is then necessary than the two thousand year old reading of the Old Testament from the New Testament and from the perspective of its specifically Christological theology. Attention is necessary to the difference between the Bible's doctrine of the kingdom of God, its *theo*logy proper, and the New Testament's focus on Christology. The difference between *theo*logy and *Christo*logy is clearly attested also in the New Testament, where the reign of Jesus Christ is never regarded as having replaced the reign of God.

A. The New Testament's perspective is decisively determined by its eschatologically based Christology, and the pneumatology and ecclesiology resulting from this Christology. The eschatological reality of the new creation has begun with Christ; and the church is the new, eschatological humanity on earth. The lifestyle of the church is guided by the Holy Spirit, and marked by the eschatological sign of the sacraments of baptism and the Eucharist, by being crucified with Christ, by agape in this world, all based on faith in and hope for the new world. The church's members are assured of eternal salvation, in death as well as already in all hardships of this earthly life.

But as much as these eschatological signs are already experienced, the full realization of the new creation has not yet happened in the sense that the old creation no longer exists. The expectation of this full realization in the second coming of Christ is therefore both intrinsic to the eschatological Christology of the new creation and the indispensable condition for the existence of Christians in this old world. Except for the gospel of John, the entire extant New Testament makes it clear that Christians await, for very decisive reasons, Christ's second coming, because they already belong to the new creation while they still have to endure the old one. Their ethos is totally determined by this expectation and their preparation for the second coming. It is for this reason neither controlled by nor even interested in the structures of this ongoing old and especially sinful world. Even for the gospel of John, in which the expectation of the second coming is at best peripheral, the separation of the disciples from the structures of this old world is fundamental.

To be sure, the Jesus of the gospels, as retrospectively understood decades after his resurrection, did good works of various sorts and also challenged the religious authorities. And the Christian disciples did and were called to do the same in their non-Christian environment. They even developed strategies of communal, including economic, life within the Christian congregations and among the congregations of the wider church, as in the case of their support— not for the city of but—for the church in Jerusalem.

However, neither Jesus nor the early churches were involved in the structures which are constitutive for the affairs of this ongoing world. They did not intend to establish the kingdom of God let alone the reign of Christ in it. The policies of the Roman empire were for them of no concern, such as its subjection of other countries by military force, its tax system, its social stratification and economic organization. The field of public law, embodied in the historically famous Roman Law, a field central in all ancient societies, is not challenged by the criteria of God's or Christ's reign. Indeed, Christians have to observe it as it is—as God given. Thus, the slaves had to remain slaves, and women had no place in public life, not even a place in the church equal to that of men. Also absent in the New Testament is, except for the discipline of ancient rhetoric, the entire breadth of the state of science in the Roman empire, and so on.

It is very clear that the early Christian movement was focusing on the salvation of the individuals from the world, on joining them to the new humanity which prepares for the arrival of the new world in the second coming of Christ, rather than on the transformation of the structures of the indefinitely ongoing old world through God's constant presence and involvement everywhere in these structures. The old world had to be left aside and behind. This theological position was not incidental but programmatic. It was the logical consequence from the eschatologically based Christology and ecclesiology.

B. In the meantime, Jesus Christ has not come again in two thousand years, and it is undeniable that the temporal eschatological expectation of the early Christians was not only not fulfilled, it was also—next to John's theology of eschatological ultimacy—the reason for their neglect of God's presence in this indefinitely ongoing world with all its sinfulness. And while many essential doctrines of the New Testament—especially those of justification by grace, of ultimate salvation and freedom in life and death, of agape and life guided by the Holy Spirit—represent unsurpassable truth quite independently of the temporal eschatology, it is obvious that the eschatologically determined and restricted early Christian world view has amounted to a significant limitation of the vision of the presence and involvement of God in the totality of this world in all places and at all times. Instead of saying that God will always come because God is always and everywhere present, one said that God is present because, and where, and in the sense that, God comes. The vision of the reign of God, and of Jesus Christ as well, has been deprived of its true universality. And the New Testament's legacy consists not only of its unsurpassable advantages but also of the deprivation of the vision of God's presence and involvement in the totality of reality by neglecting this presence and involvement in God's indefinitely ongoing old and imperfect world.

At any rate, the delay of the parousia for two thousand years means that its expectation was an insufficient ground for the world view of the early Christians, and is even more insufficient for us today. When Christ comes again, or whether or not he ever comes again, is at best a question of relative validity, and a shaky foundation for biblical theology and human faith in the reign of God and Jesus Christ. Indeed, this theology and faith stand in the way of the much more urgent reason for the human openness to God's radical call to conversion, today rather than tomorrow, because God is present today and an answer tomorrow means that today will forever be lost.

C. By contrast, where the New Testament has its deficiency, the Old Testament enters the stage with full legitimacy. For its most part by far, it focuses on what the New Testament ignores: on the presence and involvement of God in this world in both space and time, in its cosmic order as well as in the order of this earth, in the midst of sinful human history and in imperfect human existence. Heaven and earth may "wear out like a garment" and "pass away" (Ps 102:26), but they are the original creation which continues to be upheld by the deity despite the sinful human history.

In the primeval history of the Pentateuch, the deity is seen as constantly at work in preventing humanity from total self-destruction. The election of Israel from the patriarchs on and throughout the Pentateuch is a history of God's people in the midst of the ongoing human history in this indefinitely ongoing world, with its focus on the realities of this world: on land, food, population growth, social and political liberation, international relations, the organization of public justice, law and ethos, and on the cult, especially for the constant opportunity for the liberation from the always re-occurring destructive influences of guilt.

The deuteronomistic and Chronicler's history works, as well as the prophets and many psalms, focus on Israel's existence in this world, its socio-political structure and international relations, all involving the deity's critical presence. Other psalms and the books of Proverbs, Ecclesiastes, and Job focus on the basic kinds of human experience lived by all human beings. The issue of war and peace is addressed everywhere, and the international state of scientific knowledge and practice has directly influenced many texts.

Compared to this overwhelming focus—throughout a thousand years—on the realities of this ongoing world, including the many prophetic announcements of Israel's restoration after the judgment, the texts about the otherworldly new creation, as in Trito-Isaiah and Daniel, are minimal. Those few texts in particular have not replaced the vast majority of texts which focus on the realities in this ongoing old and imperfect world and on God's presence and involvement in it. The assumption that the history of Israel's religion developed over the centuries from an inner-worldly to an apocalyptic-eschatological world view represents at best a very one-sided, and lastly a false construct of that development. The composition of the tripartite Hebrew Bible in the late postexilic period proves Israel's overwhelming preoccupation with the affairs of this indefinitely ongoing world, both in that period and beyond it.

D. It has always been pointed out that the Old Testament's focus on this world, when compared to the New Testament's focus, reveals its theological deficiency because Israel's election in the Old Testament is considered in terms of a political system; in terms of hierocracy rather than theocracy; of ethnic nationality; a particular land and the oppression, expulsion and even extinction of the original inhabitants of that land and of their culture—none of which belongs to the ideal doctrine of the *ekklesia*. One has said that the Old Testament speaks of liberation only socially and politically rather than in terms of ultimacy, and of forgiveness of sins only from case to case rather than once and for all.

Some of these arguments are valid, others are one-sided. It is true that the concept of God's elected people in terms of national and territorial identity is invalid when compared to the concept of a people internationally and at all places on earth. It is especially true that Israel's election is in the Old Testament very often—not always—depicted preferentially and at the expense of humanity rather than as a model for God's presence in humanity equally. In these respects, the Christian doctrine—though often not the history of Christianity!—is better than the particularistic notion of Israel's election.

However, it is also true that Israel's participation in all affairs of humanity testifies to a presence of God in this ongoing world which has no parallel in the New Testament, and which is as important today as it was for Israel and would have been for the early Christians. After all, the Christian expectation of the impending end of the world through the coming of the kingdom remains not only unfulfilled to this day; it was wrong in its own time and was the main reason for their unjustifiable neglect of God's presence in the totality of this ongoing world, its human history, and the earthly existence of all humans.

Through Christ, the humans are assured of forgiveness ultimately. Nevertheless, this forgiveness must still be reappropriated from case to case, from day to day. Israel must be forgiven from case to case, but it can always be assured of God's unshakable loyalty and willingness to forgive. The difference between the two concepts is relative. These and other comparisons show that each Testament has advantages as well as disadvantages; that each complements as well as it corrects the other; and that it is one-sided and unjustifiable if we only read the Old Testament from the vantage point of the New Testament and not also the New Testament from the vantage point of the Old Testament.

Fundamentally, the two Testaments differ in that the Old Testament focuses on God's presence in the totality of this ongoing creation, whereas the New Testament focuses on the new creation. Within these respective foci, each Testament has, when compared to the other, theological advantages but also disadvantages. The difference between the Testaments, in their mutual critical complementarity, is not a weakness but a strength. It amounts to the strength of a biblical theology. The New Testament, with its focus on the ultimate meaning of the reign of God, says unsurpassable things. The Old Testament, with its focus on the reality of this world, makes sure that God is not absent from its imperfection. This aspect is especially relevant for us. Just as our world has lasted indefinitely, so it may continue to last—unless we humans destroy it ourselves, a possibility which neither Testament ever thought possible.

What I am saying amounts to a program for a biblical theology of the Christian Bible in which the two Testaments are mutually and equally open for each other. Such a theology must rest on a vision of the total reality rather than of one of its aspects at the expense of the other. It must include the aspect of ultimacy in the world's penultimacy, but also the aspect of the world's penultimacy itself. God is not only the God of the new but also the God of the original creation; not only the God from afar but also the God who is near; or God is not the God of the whole world. When one considers the whole world as the realm of God's presence, penultimately and ultimately, in terms of the world's imperfection and its realistic utopia, it is especially the Old Testament in the Christian tradition which must be upgraded to a status equal to that of the New Testament. Whenever the new world comes and whether or not it will ever come as originally expected, the Old Testament says that God's salvation is at work in this ongoing world, with nothing in it excepted, everywhere, at all times, and for everyone, as long as this world lasts.***

*** I am indebted to Mrs. Brenda Hahn and Ms. Mignon R. Jacobs for editorial assistance during the evolution of this paper.

PART TWO

THE DEAD SEA SCROLLS

THE SCRIBES OF THE TEXTS
FOUND IN THE JUDEAN DESERT

Emanuel Tov

IDENTITY, NATURE AND STATUS

Copyists, Scribes, and Soferim. In the study of the scribal practices reflected in the documents found in the Judean Desert, attention must be given also to the scribes and their background. This interest leads us to examine various issues relating to these scribes, namely, their identity, adherence to tradition, place in society, systems of copying, etc. According to our modern concepts and terminology, this investigation relates to copyists of the texts, but when using the term "copyist," we probably think more of the conditions of writing in the Middle Ages than of antiquity. Although the three terms "copyist," "scribe," and its Hebrew equivalent, *sofer*, are more or less equivalent, they denote persons who were involved in similar, yet different and sometimes very different activities. All three types of persons were involved in scribal activity, but the nature of that activity differed in each instance.

The term "copyist" stresses the technical nature of the scribe's work and is based on the assumption that the essence of scribal activity is to transmit as precisely as possible the content of the copyist's text. The assumption underlying the description is based on the realia of the scribes of the Middle Ages who worked within so-called scriptoria. One wonders whether scribes of this type existed at all in antiquity, and if so, in the area covered by this study it would be mainly in the group of tradents of the MT.

The majority of the persons involved in antiquity in the transmission of the biblical text, as well as of other texts, took more liberties in the course of that procedure than copyists. As explained below in greater detail, many scribes actually took an active part in the shaping of the final form of the text, and therefore the general term "scribe" is more appropriate than copyist for the persons involved in the transmission of compositions, since it covers all aspects of scribal activity, and could easily include creative aspects of that activity. At the same time, viewed from another angle, the use of the term "scribe" may create confusion, especially when used in the plural. For the scribes known from rabbinic texts, *soferim*, were scribes of a special type who had a very specific role in the production and perpetuation of the biblical text as well as of other texts in the religious realm. Moreover, the *soferim,* especially as known from rabbinic sources and the synoptic gospels (γραμματεῖς), had a special place in society and they appear in the New Testament as a unified group. Since only some of the texts found in the Judean Desert were produced locally, and probably most had been imported from elsewhere, it is very likely that some *tefillin* and biblical texts found in the Judean Desert had been written by these *soferim.* Because of this reason the *soferim* must be included in our analysis.

Scribes and Soferim in Ancient Israel. Because of its complicated technical nature, the trade of a scribe must be considered a profession, rather than an occasional activity, although the Bible also mentions occasional writing.[1] Unnamed as well as identified scribes are mentioned several times in the Bible. Qiryat Sefer (e.g. Josh 15:15), the earlier name of Debir, literally "the city of the book" (the site where an archive was kept?) may have been the site where many such scribes lived. The explanation of that name as an archive is supported by the LXX translation πόλις (τῶν) γραμμάτων, for example, in Josh 15:15. On the other hand, the transliteration of the LXX in Judg 1:11 Καριασσωφαρ (MSS Bdfsz; other MSS similarly) reflects an understanding of the name as "the city of the *sofer.*" It is not impossible that 1 Chr 2:55 ("the families of *soferim* who lived at Jabez") refers to family-like guilds of scribes. As for individual scribes, 1 Chr 24:6 mentions a Shemayah son of Netanel, הסופר מן הלוי (a scribe from the tribe of Levi), one of the royal scribes known from the Bible. The best known scribe in the Bible is Ezra, named סופר מהיר (a skilled scribe) in Ezra 7:6 and, like Shemayah, deriving from a priestly family (his direct lineage from Aaron is specified in Ezra 7:1-4). From ancient times onwards the connection between the function of the scribe and various aspects of the public

---

1   For an analysis of the evidence, see M. Fishbane, *Biblical Interpretation in Ancient Israel* (Oxford: Oxford Univesity Press, 1985); A. Demsky, "Writing in Ancient Israel and Early Judaism, Part One: The Biblical Period," in M. J. Mulder (ed.), *Mikra* (CRINT 2.1; Assen: Van Gorcum; Philadelphia: Fortress, 1988) 2-20; idem, "Scribe," *EncJud* 14.1041-1043; A. J. Saldarini, "Scribes," *ABD* 5.1011-16.

administration is evident. Likewise, in the period to which the texts from the Judean Desert pertain, some scribes functioned as secretaries of towns.

In this period, scribes occupied themselves with all aspects of scribal activity, that is, the copying of existing documents and literary compositions, as well as the writing of documentary texts (such as found in Murabbaʿat and Naḥal Ḥever) and the creative composing of new literary works. In addition, scribes were involved in various aspects of administrative activity. The use of the word *sofer* for an author in 11QPsᵃ col. xxvii is rather unique. In that scroll David is mentioned as a *sofer*, in the sense of "author" rather than "scribe" since the text focuses on his compositions and not on his copying of texts.

From rabbinic sources we obtain a one-sided picture, since they mainly record the activity of scribes in the religious realm, namely, the copying of religious documents: scripture, especially Torah scrolls, *tefillin*, and marriage and divorce documents (for the latter, cf. *m. Giṭ.* 7:1 [גט] אמרו לסופר וכתב). These activities did not involve any creative writing which lay beyond the interest of rabbinic sources. Therefore one should not equate the scribes (*soferim*) mentioned in the Talmud with all the scribes who were active in the period covered by rabbinic literature

Because of the manifold activities of the scribes and their intimate knowledge of the compositions copied by them and the topics on which they wrote, the connection between scribes and wisdom is stressed in several sources, especially in religious literature. A scribe for whom that connection is described in great detail is the one depicted by Ben Sira in the early second century BCE in 38:24–39:11.[2] His wisdom is described in 38:24 as σοφία γραμματέως = חכמת סופר. That scribe, one might say, the ideal scribe, is portrayed as an expert in all areas of knowledge and administration. His wisdom is divinely inspired, since his main source of knowledge is the "law of the Most High" which helps him "to seek out the wisdom of the ancients" and to "be concerned with prophecies" and "proverbs" (39:1). That scribe is not only a scholar and teacher, but also an

---

2   Cf. H. Stadelman, *Ben Sira als Schriftgelehrter* (WUNT 2.6; Tübingen: Mohr [Siebeck], 1980) esp. 216-46; D. J. Harrington, "The Wisdom of the Scribe according to Ben Sira," in G. W. E. Nickelsburg and J. J. Collins (eds.), *Ideal Figures in Ancient Judaism—Profiles and Paradigms* (SBLSCS 12; Chico: Scholars Press, 1980) 181-88.

administrator of the highest level (39:4; 38:32-33). Ben Sira himself
was probably a scribe of that type. Also Enoch was such a scribe (see
1 Enoch 92:1). At the same time, one should carefully distinguish
between the realm of the scribe, which usually is that of a technician,
and that of the wise men or intellectuals, as pointed out by
Bickerman.[3]

Beyond this general background information on scribes in
Palestine, in the period under discussion very few specific details are
known about the scribes who actually copied the documents found in
the Judean Desert, especially since in most cases we do not know
where these documents were written. For one thing, the scribes did
not record their names in the texts themselves since the custom of
writing colophons had not yet been formed in Hebrew and Aramaic
manuscripts.[4] The only information available about the many aspects
of scribal activity is therefore culled from the texts themselves.[5]
These texts allow us to form an opinion on the collaboration between
individual scribes, their approach to the texts from which they
copied, including the degree of precision of individual scribes, the
materials used, writing practices, including the use of scribal marks
and correction procedures, handwriting, mistakes and correction
procedures, scripts, characteristic scribal features of certain types of
documents, the influence of Aramaic on their writing in Hebrew,
etc.[6]

---

3   E. Bickerman, *The Jews in the Greek Age* (Cambridge: Harvard University
Press, 1988) 161-76 ("Scribes and Sages") esp. 163.

4   An isolated word אמר, possibly indicating the remains of such a colophon,
was written three lines below the end of Isaiah in the last column of 1QIsa[a].

5   More extensive information on scribes and book production is available for
a later period covered by the documents from the Cairo Genizah. See especially N.
Alony, "The Book and Book Production in Palestine in the Middle Ages," *Shalem*
4 (1984) 1-25 (Hebrew). Alony writes, among other things, about the learning of
writing skills, about scripts, writing materials, the number of lines in manuscripts,
the places of writing, the time needed for writing a Torah scroll (one year), and the
prices paid.

6   If many of the Qumran scrolls were indeed written *in situ*, it may be considered unusual that no reference is made in the texts to any writing activity by the
members of that community, other than for administrative purposes. However, an
argument of this type referring to the mentioning of writing activities is not relevant
to the present description, and besides, it may be contradicted by the lack of reference in the scrolls to other activities of the Qumranites, such as their specific types
of manual work, including the recently revealed date industry. The Qumran texts

We do not know of any official qualifications required of or restrictions placed on persons who wrote or could write literary texts, including religious texts. The only restriction known is the one recorded in rabbinic texts stating that religious writings (Torah, *tefillin*, and *mezuzot*) written by a heretic (מין), pagan (עובד כוכבים), informer (against his fellow-Jews to the Roman authorities; מסור), Samaritan (כותי), converted Jew (ישראל מומר), slave, woman, and minor were not acceptable (thus the various opinions in *b. Giṭ.* 45b; cf. *b. Menaḥ.* 42b and *Sof.* 1.13).

Information on Scribes in Rabbinic Sources. Scattered information about the writing of Scripture, *tefillin, mezuzot,* and marriage and divorce documents, as well as about scribes and *soferim* themselves, is found in the Talmud. In that literature instructions for writing pertain to specific issues, but more frequently they are grouped in compilations dealing with various matters, such as *b. Menaḥ.* 29b–32b; *b. Meg. passim; b. Šabb.* 103a–105a; and *y. Meg.* 1.71d–72a. Another significant block of traditions was laid down in a more organized fashion in *Massekhet Soferim.*[7] Although this tractate is post-Talmudic (ninth century), it is based on *Massekhet Sefer Torah*[8] as well as on several early sources, and thus preserves earlier traditions which go back to the Talmud and Talmudic period. The rabbinic instructions pertain to such matters as writing materials, skins and the preparation of leather, scribes, measurements of sheets, columns, lines, and margins, correction of errors, the writing of

---

mention the administrative registering of the members of the Qumran community, sometimes by the *mebaqqer* (e.g. 1QS 5:23; 6:22; and 4QS[d] frag. 3, 2:3; CD 13:12), who also wrote down the sins committed in his private notebook (CD 9:18). 4Q477Rebukes Reported by the Overseer probably contains such personal remarks about certain individuals of the Qumran community. In the Qumran texts the *sofer* is mentioned a few times. In 11QPs[a] col. XXVII David is mentioned as a *sofer*, in the sense of 'author' rather than 'scribe.' Second, in the Aramaic fragments of *1 Enoch*, Enoch is named ספר פרשא, 'a distinguished scribe' (4QEnGiants[b] 2:14). Finally, the fragmentary narrative 4QNarrative B (4Q461) frag. 2 includes the word *soferim* without any context. Writing was also an essential part of the warfare in the War Scroll which records in detail the inscriptions inscribed on the standards and engraved on the trumpets and shields to be used in the future war. Writing is mentioned also in 4QJub[a] 4:6 (*Jub.* 1:27) and 4QMMT[e] frags. 14-17 ii 2.

   7   M. Higger, *Mskt swprym wnlww ʿlyh mdrš, mskt swprym b'* (New York: Bloch, 1937; repr. Jerusalem: Makor, 1970).

   8   M. Higger, *Seven Minor Treatises: Sefer Torah; Mezuzah; Tefillin; Ẓiẓith; ʿAbadim; Kutim; Gerim* (New York: Bloch, 1930).

divine names, and the storage and reading of books.⁹ The information contained in these sources is very valuable for our survey, as
long as it is remembered that the rabbinic descriptions and prescriptions refer mainly to the writing of religious texts, at a later period,
and to circles which only partially overlapped with the circles which
produced the texts found in the Judean Desert. In other words, it can
probably be said with reasonable certainty that only the biblical texts
of Masoretic character and some *tefillin* and *mezuzot* derived from
the same circles as described in the Talmudic literature, though in
reference to an earlier period.

Scribes are known from rabbinic sources by various appelations,
especially with reference to the writing of scripture and religious
documents:

1. The most frequent term was סופר (*sofer*). This term refers to a
person who was basically independent, but who sometimes worked
exclusively for a certain Rabbi (e.g. Yohanan the *sofer* [almost
secretary] of Rabban Gamliel mentioned in *y. Sanh.* 1.18d; *b Sanh.*
11b) or for the affairs of a city (סופר מתא, the scribe of the city; see
b. B. Bat. 21a).

2. כותב (copyist), with the connotation of calligrapher.

3. לבלר, a loanword from Greek (λιβελλάριος), itself a loanword
from Latin *libellarius*. According to Blau, *Studien,* 183 the *sofer* and
libellarius refer to two distinct groups, while according to Kraus,
Talmudische Archäologie, 3.169, the two words denote the same
persons, although the loanword may have carried a somewhat more
formal connotation.

4. נוטרין (*notarii*), or notary. It stands to reason that literary texts
were copied from written *Vorlagen*. There is thus no reason to
assume that scribes who knew their biblical texts well wrote them
from memory. Indeed, according to the prescriptions in the rabbinic
literature, scribes were forbidden to copy scripture without a text in
front of them, even if they knew the whole Bible by heart, out of
reverence to the text and in order to secure precision in copying (*b.
Meg.* 18b and parallels).

The prescriptions of the rabbis with regard to the copying of

---

⁹ The relevant discussions in rabbinic literature were analyzed at length in the
valuable monographs by L. Blau, *Studien zum althebräischen Buchwesen und zur
biblischen Literatur- und Textgeschichte* (Strassburg: Trübner, 1902); S. Krauss,
Talmudische Archäologie (3 vols., Leipzig: Fock, 1912) 3.131-98. See further S.
Lieberman, *Hellenism in Jewish Palestine* (TSJTSA 18; New York: JTSA, 1962).

sacred texts were not followed by all scribes in Israel. In light of this situation, it is not impossible that some scribes wrote from dictation[10] or that mass production (dictating to several scribes at the same time) took place, but there is no evidence supporting this view. Phonetic variation as evidenced in many Qumran texts does not necessarily prove that they were written by dictation, since any scribe copying from a document could make phonetic mistakes or change the orthography, consciously or not.[11]

Scribal activity in respect to scripture and *tefillin* was considered so important by the rabbis that scribes of such texts were not supposed to interrupt their work for the duty of prayer (*y. Šabb.* 1.3b; *y. Ber.* 1.3b; *y. Bikk.* 3.65c)—let alone for less significant tasks.

In the rabbinic literature there are some references to scribes who produced multiple copies. Thus according to *b. B. Bat.* 14a Rab Huna wrote seventy Torah scrolls and Rabbi Ami 400 scrolls.

Soferim. The word *soferim* is used in rabbinic literature with two different meanings, one could say, with either a lower case or an upper case letter. The *soferim* were individual copyists, as portrayed in the tractate bearing that name. But they were also known as a more or less organized group of scribes, *soferim* (henceforth referred to with a lower case letter as *soferim*) with authoritative legal capacities. Scholars do not agree on the nature of these *soferim* who carried out legal functions, but only some aspects of this discussion pertain to the present analysis. According to some scholars these *soferim* functioned as the central persons of a certain era and at a later stage also constituted a political power.[12]

---

[10]   Thus with regard to 1QIsa[a]: M. Burrows, "Orthography, Morphology, and Syntax of the St. Mark's Manuscript," *JBL* 68 (1949) 195-211, esp. 196; H. M. Orlinsky, "Studies in the St. Mark's Isaiah Manuscript," *JBL* 69 (1950) 149-66, esp. 165.

[11]   Thus already E. Hammershaimb reacting to the theories regarding 1QIsa[a]: "On the Method Applied in the Copying of Manuscripts in Qumran," *VT* 9 (1959) 415-18.

[12]   Note the remarks of Ginsburg in his description of the development of the Masorah: "The labours of the Massorites may be regarded as a later development and continuation of the earlier work which was carried on by the Sopherim (סופרים, γραμματεῖς) = the doctors and authorised interpreters of the Law soon after the return of the Jews from the Babylonish captivity (comp. Ezra VII 6; Neh. VIII 1 &c.)." See C. D. Ginsburg, *Introduction to the Massoretico-Critical Edition of the Hebrew Bible* (London: Longmans, Green, 1897; repr. New York: Ktav, 1966) chap. 11; the quotation is from p. 287. At a different level, E. Schürer (*A History*

In rabbinic writings, from the Mishna onwards, these *soferim* are mentioned as authoritative scribes and teachers to whom a number of teachings and *halakhot* are ascribed. As a result the *soferim* are considered to have been influential figures in ancient Israel from the time of Ezra until the second century CE, both in rabbinic tradition and in modern scholarship. Among other things, they are mentioned in the New Testament and Josephus as γραμματεῖς and as ἱερογραμματεῖς (Matt 2:4; Josephus, *J.W.* 6.5.3 §292). This term shows that these persons dealt mainly with religious writings, and were possibly of priestly descent (indeed, most of the *soferim* whose genealogy is known were priests). The term *soferim* refers to the combined activities of the copying of texts, especially of scripture and other sacred documents, and an intimate knowledge of these documents. It is often difficult to decide which nuance of the term is intended. This difficulty probably reflects the fact that most *soferim* were skilled in both aspects of their profession.

Various aspects of the *soferim* mentioned in the rabbinic literature are of direct relevance to the present analysis. They were actively involved in the transmission of Hebrew scripture, and while on the one hand they had a purely passive task in connection with the preservation of the biblical text, on the other hand they occasionally changed that text. That is, if the rabbinic traditions are trustworthy, the *soferim* made corrections in the text. Even if these traditions are incorrect, the very assumption that the *soferim* made these corrections was thus tolerated. It should be admitted that the presumed precision of the *soferim* in the transmission of scripture cannot be

---

of the Jewish People in the Time of Jesus Christ, Second Division, I [Edinburgh: T. & T. Clark, 1891] 306-79) devoted 75 pages to what he called "Scribism." The view that there was a "period of the *soferim*" was suggested for the first time in scholarship by R. Nachman Krochmal in his book *Moreh Nevukhe Ha-zeman* (edited posthumously by L. Zunz and published in 1851; quoted by Urbach, below). Against this view wrote, among others, E. E. Urbach, "The Derasha as a Basis of the Halakha and the Problem of the Soferim," *Tarbiz* 27 (1958) 166-182. For a summary on the views expressed on the *soferim* and for much bibliography, see H. Mantel, "The *Soferim*," in M. Avi-Yonah and Z. Baras (eds.), *Society and Religion in the Second Temple Period* (Jerusalem and Tel Aviv: Jewish Historical Publications, 1983) 35-38 (Hebrew). Among these studies, see especially M. H. Segal, "The Promulgation of the Authoritative Text of the Hebrew Bible," *JBL* 72 (1953) 35-48; M. Greenberg, "The Stabilization of the Text of the Hebrew Bible, Reviewed in the Light of the Biblical Materials from the Judean Desert," *JAOS* 76 (1956) 157-67.

tallied with the changes inserted by them. This argument militates possibly against the assumption of the trustworthiness of the tradition about the changes in the text introduced by the *soferim*. The most pervasive group of changes made by the *soferim* is that of the so-called *tiqqunê hasoferim*, the "corrections of the scribes" (*Sifre Num.* §84 [on Num 10:35]; *Mek.* to Exod 15:7 [*Širata* §6]; *Midrash Tanḥuma* to Exod 15:7 [*Bešallaḥ* §16]). These corrections involve a number of changes in the MT (8 to 18 according to the different traditions), mainly of euphemistic nature. Other changes ascribed to the *soferim* are five "omissions of the *soferim*," referring to the omission of the *waw* conjunctive. *B. Ned.* 37b also mentions the *Miqraʾ soferim,* "the reading of the *soferim*," relating to three words. The examples are not explained, but they may indicate the beginning of vocalization, instituted by the *soferim*.[13]

LEARNING THE SCRIBAL SKILLS

Little is known about the training of scribes in the biblical and postbiblical period. Possibly the aforementioned family-like guilds of scribes (1 Chr 2:55) underwent some training. Information about the learning process of scribes comes from other cultures in the ancient Near East,[14] but it is unclear to what extent parallels may be drawn to ancient Israelite practices.

The documents found in the Judean Desert reflect different levels of scribal skills, visible not only in the degree of the carefulness of the handwriting and the transmission, but also in the knowledge of and adherence to certain scribal conventions. Most non-documentary texts were written by skilled hands, while letters were often written in irregular scripts. The difference between the different levels of scribal skill is reflected inter alia in the well-written contracts from Naḥal Ḥever and Wadi Murabbaʿat as compared with their irregular-

---

13   At a different level, rabbinic literature mentions several *halakhot*, especially on matters of purity, which are described as דברי סופרים, *dibrê soferim*. These *dibrê soferim* refer only to *halakhot* that had been determined in previous generations, and which at the time of the Mishna had already become authoritative (e.g. *m. Kelim* 13:7; *m. Tohor.* 4:7; *m. Tebul Yom* 4:6).

14   B. Landsberger, "Scribal Concepts of Education," in C. H. Kraeling and R. M. Adams (eds.), *City Invincible* (Chicago: University of Chicago Press, 1960) 94-102; W. Hallo, "New Viewpoints on Cuneiform Literature," *IEJ* 12 (1962) 13-26, esp. 22-25; R. J. Williams, "Scribal Training in Ancient Egypt," *JAOS* 92 (1972) 214-21.

ly written signatures.[15]

Some scribes, certainly some of the scribes of the Qumran documents, copied sacred as well as nonsacred documents, while others,
especially in temple circles, specialized in the writing of sacred texts.
Those specializing in sacred texts copied biblical texts as well as
tefillin, mezuzot, marriage and divorce documents. Some scribes
were independent, while others worked mainly for specific Rabbis,
for a city, or the Sanhedrin.

Scribes were introduced into their trade in the course of a training
period, in which they learned writing itself and the various scribal
procedures connected with it (such as writing meticulously below
ruled lines and in columns; the content division of the composition;
how to treat the divine names; how to correct mistakes, etc.). Furthermore, scribes had to master various technical skills relating to
the features of the material on which they wrote, the use of writing
implements, and the preparation of ink.

The abecedaries found in Qumran,[16] Murabba'at,[17] and at many
additional sites dating to the period of the First and Second Temple[18]
probably witness to such a learning process with regard to writing
skills. It was claimed by Lemaire, with reference to Israel in the
First Temple period that these abecedaries point to the existence of
scribal schools, and this argument may be valid also with regard to
Qumran.[19]

---

[15]   See, among others, Mur 42 (a letter written by the administrators of Beth
Mashiko to Yeshua' ben Galgula) in DJD 2 (Oxford: Clarendon, 1961).

[16]   For a good photograph of the Qumran ostracon containing an abecedary
(PAM 40.405), see R. de Vaux, "Fouilles du Khirbet Qumrân," *RB* 61 (1954) pl.
Xa, and J. Allegro, *The People of the Dead Sea Scrolls* (London: Routledge &
Kegan Paul, 1959) 183. This ostracon is displayed in the Shrine of the Book in the
Israel Museum. Two additional abecedaries, described as deriving from the first
century BCE, are displayed in the Israel Museum as "Qumran?"

[17]   Some abecedaries were written on parchment (Mur 10B, 11), while others
were inscribed on sherds (Mur 73, 78-80), all published in DJD 2.

[18]   See E. Puech, "Abécédaire et liste alphabétique de noms hébreux du début
des IIe S.A.D.," *RB* 87 (1980) 118-26; A. Lemaire, *Les écoles et la formation de la
Bible dans l'ancien Israël* (OBO 39; Göttingen: Vandenhoeck & Ruprecht, 1981) 7-
32; M. Haran, "On the Diffusion of Literacy and Schools in Ancient Israel," in J.
A. Emerton (ed.), *Congress Volume: Jerusalem 1986* (VTSup 40; Leiden: Brill,
1988) 81-95.

[19]   Lemaire, *Les écoles,* 7-33. However, the strongest positive evidence for the
existence of a Qumran scribal school is internal, referring to scribal traits common

Such a learning process is possibly reflected in 4QExercitium Calami A and B (4Q423, 4Q360) and 4QExercitium Calami C (4Q341) containing a list of names and other words (also elsewhere lists of names served as scribal exercises). This text contains among other things a sequence of names starting with the letter mem and a series of words, mainly proper names, in alphabetical order, from *bet* to *zayin*. 4QExercitium Calami A (4Q234) contains words written in three different directions. Some of the Qumran documents, admittedly written badly, were considered by some scholars to have been written by apprentice scribes. Thus Milik considered 4QEn[a] to be a "school-exercise copied by a young scribe from the master's dictation."[20] Skehan considered 4Q236 (4QPs89) to be a "practice page from memory"[21] and Milik considered 4QDanSus (?) ar to have been written by an apprentice scribe.[22] We cautiously suggest that 4QGen[f] also constitutes such an exercise, as this fragment was written on a single sheet with no signs of sewing on the right side. It contains Gen 48:1-11 and was written with an unskilled hand. Exercise tablets are also known from the cuneiform literature. Hallo noted that "two small tablets from Assur . . . show extracts, not just from two or three compositions, but from ten different series, all of them identifiable as standard books in the neo-Assyrian stream of tradition."[23] Since the compositions are excerpted in exactly the same order in both tablets, Hallo considered them exercise tablets.

Other aspects of the training process of members of the Qumran community, especially the study of the Law and of the rites of the community were described by Lemaire on the basis of descriptions by Josephus and in the Qumran Rules.[24]

---

to certain documents.

[20]   J. T. Milik, *The Books of Enoch, Aramaic Fragments of Qumrân Cave 4* (Oxford: Clarendon, 1976) 141.

[21]   P. W. Skehan, "Gleanings from Psalm Texts from Qumran," in A. Caquot and M. Delcor (eds.), *Mélanges bibliques et orientaux en l'honneur de M. Henri Cazelles* (Alter Orient und Altes Testament 212; Neukirchen–Vluyn: Neukirchener Verlag, 1981) 439-52.

[22]   J. T. Milik, "Daniel et Susanne à Qumrân?" in M. Carrez et al. (eds.), *De la Tôrah au Messie* (Paris: Desclée, 1981) 337-59, esp. 355.

[23]   W. Hallo, "New Viewpoints on Cuneiform Literature," *IEJ* 12 (1962) 13-26; the quote is from pp. 22-23.

[24]   A. Lemaire, "L'enseignement essénien et l'école de Qumrân," in A. Caquot et al. (eds.), *Hellenica et Judaica: Hommage à Valentin Nikiprowetzky* (Leuven: Peeters and Leuven University Press, 1986) 191-203.

LOCAL PRODUCTION OF TEXTS IN QUMRAN AND MASADA?

If it can be proven that locus 30 in Qumran served as a room in which documents were written (a scriptorium in the medieval terminology),[25] the assumption of a Qumran scribal school would receive further support. But the relevance of the evidence pointing to the existence of such a scriptorium is questionable.[26] Beyond the

---

[25]   Thus the majority opinion of scholars ever since the description by R. de Vaux, *L'archéologie et les manuscrits de la Mer Morte* (London: Oxford University Press, 1961) 23-26; idem, *Archaeology and the Dead Sea Scrolls* (The Schweich Lectures of the British Academy; London: Oxford Univesity Press, 1973) 29-33; see also recently R. Reich, "A Note on the Function of Room 30 (the 'Scriptorium') at Khirbet Qumran," *JJS* 46 (1995) 157-60.

[26]   In this room archeologists found a five-meter long table, small tables, and several inkwells (cf. PAM 42.865), which were either situated in this room or on a second floor which according to some scholars was situated above this room. See J.-B. Humbert and A. Chambon, *Fouilles de Khirbet Qumrân et de Aïn Feshkha*, vol 1 (Novum Testamentum et Orbis Antiquus, Series Archaeologica 1; Göttingen: Vandenhoeck & Ruprecht, 1994), plates 114-20. However, doubts have been raised with regard to this identification. Several scholars have claimed that the height of the table, 40 cm, was too low for writing; see B. M. Metzger, "The Furniture of the Scriptorium at Qumran," *RevQ* 1 (1958) 509-15; K. G. Pedley, "The Library at Qumran," *RevQ* 2 (1959) 21-41, esp. 35; K. W. Clark, "The Posture of the Ancient Scribe," *BA* 26 (1963) 63-72. This claim was also made by A. Lemaire, "L'enseignement essénien," 199, who suggested that this room was the center of the intellectual life of the members of the community. The most detailed disagreement with the assumption of a scriptorium is provided by N. Golb. According to Golb the fact that no remnants of scrolls were found in the room also proves that it was not used for the purpose of writing: "The Problem of Origin and Identification of the Dead Sea Scrolls," *Proceedings of the American Philosophical Society* 124 (1980) 1-24; "Who Hid the Dead Sea Scrolls?" *BA* 48 (1985) 68-82; "Khirbet Qumran and the Manuscripts of the Judaean Wilderness—Observations on the Logic of Their Investigation," *JNES* 49 (1990) 103-14; *Who Wrote the Dead Sea Scrolls—The Search for the Secret of Qumran* (New York: Scribner's, 1994). Before Golb similar doubts, though in less detail, had been voiced by H. E. del Medico, *L'énigme des manuscrits de la Mer Morte* (Paris: Plon, 1957); K. H. Rengstorf, *Hirbet Qumrân und die Bibliothek vom Toten Meer* (Studia Delitzschiana 5; Stuttgart: Kohlhammer, 1960). The theory of Golb was refuted in detail by F. García Martínez and A. S. van der Woude, "A 'Groningen' Hypothesis of Qumran Origins and Early History," *RevQ* 14 (1990) 521-41, but the doubts about the relevance of the artifacts found in locus 30 remain. For a more recent analysis, see M. O. Wise, *Thunder in Gemini, and Other Essays on the History, Language and Literature of Second Temple Palestine* (JSPSup 15; Sheffield: Sheffield Academic Press, 1994) esp. 120.

archeological relevance of locus 30, on the basis of the contents of the scrolls most scholars now believe that some, many, or all of the documents found in Qumran had been copied locally.

Stegemann holds a maximalistic view on this issue, assuming that most Qumran scrolls were written on the spot. According to him,[27] one of the main occupations of the Qumran community was the preparation of parchment and leather for writing and the mass-production of written texts. These texts were offered for sale by the Qumran community to the outside world, and Stegemann pinpoints the places in the community buildings in which the scrolls were manufactured, stored, and offered for sale. Golb (see n. 26), expressing a minimalistic view, claimed that none of the Qumran documents was written locally (Golb does not express himself with regard to the other documents from the Judean Desert).

Accordingly there is no consensus about the locality or localities of the copying of the Qumran documents, but since most scholars believe that at least some, if not many of the texts from Qumran were written locally, it remains correct to refer to the texts found in Qumran as the Qumran corpus, as long as the necessary reservations are kept in mind. A similar type of reasoning applies to the texts found at the other sites in the Judean Desert, although few scholars have claimed that texts were actually written at Masada, at Murabbaꜥat, or Naḥal Ḥever.

As a result of this analysis, the scribes of the texts found in the Judean Desert remain as anonymous today as they were two generations ago. But while a generation ago the corpus of the Qumran documents as well as their scribes were automatically identified with the Qumran community, this claim is not made today, although undoubtedly some of the texts were copied by that community. By the same token, the documents found in Masada should not be identified with the people who occupied that site. These documents, too, reflect the work of scribes from all of Israel, possibly including some local scribes. This pertains also to the letters found in Naḥal Ḥever and Wadi Murabbaꜥat.

CHARACTERISTIC FEATURES OF INDIVIDUAL SCRIBES

Because of the lack of external information on the scribes who

---

27   H. Stegemann, *Die Essener, Qumran, Johannes der Taufer und Jesus: Ein Sachbuch* (4th ed., Freiburg im Breisgau: Herder, 1994) 77-82.

copied or wrote the documents found in the Judean Desert, our sole
source of information about them is the scribal activity reflected in
the documents themselves. Whether a scribal copy under discussion
is a copy of an earlier document or an autograph, the scribal practices reflected in it do provide information which is relevant to the
study of these scribal practices. However, in the analysis of these
practices it is often difficult to distinguish between the personal input
of the scribes and elements transmitted to them or the scribal
tradition in general. Thus the division into sense units and the
specific layout of poetic units embedded in the Qumran texts derives
probably from the first copies of these compositions, although in the
transmission of these elements there was room for the scribes'
personal touch. The more scribes adhered to the scribal practices
embedded in the texts from which they were copying, the less their
texts reflected their personality. Since we do not know the *Vorlagen*
of the Qumran manuscripts, it is obviously difficult to distinguish
between the scribe's input and the impact of tradition. In another
case, the exact number of lines per column and the existence of guide
dots probably were determined by the size of the scroll as it left the
hands of the scroll manufacturer, although scribes could probably
choose between scrolls of different sizes. In the case of small size
scrolls, such as the copies of the Five Scrolls, it was probably not the
individual scribe who decided that short compositions were to be
written on scrolls of limited dimensions. Rather custom dictated the
choice of small scrolls for short compositions. On the other hand,
such matters as the neatness of the handwriting, the care taken in the
copying, adherence to the left margin and the ruled lines, and correction procedures, were very much exponents of the individuality of
the scribes.

Within this analysis, the following elements in texts thus reflect to
some extent the personal input of the scribes:

1. Approach towards the Base Text. Scribes approached their
Vorlagen in different ways representing different levels of freedom.
Their personality is reflected both in the approach and in the details
themselves which were inserted or changed in the manuscripts.
Scholars have been discussed these details at some length for the
biblical manuscripts, and they are beginning to be analyzed for the
nonbiblical texts.

2. Handwriting and Copying. The size of the letters in the
handwriting of the different scribes differs greatly. Petite and even

minuscule letters were used in *tefillin*, while several documents were written in large characters. Note, for example, fragments written in a regular size, next to fragments written in a smaller handwriting (2QJub[a,b] and 2QapDavid) on plate XV of DJD 3 (Oxford, 1962). On plate xxvi in the same volume one finds next to fragments written in regular handwriting the smaller handwriting of 6QApoc ar and the larger handwriting of 6QPriestProph. When two or more scribes wrote segments of the same manuscript, such differences are sometimes very clearly visible. Thus, scribe B of 1QH[a], who started in col. xi, line 22, used much larger characters than scribe A.

At the ends of lines, letters were sometimes crowded in order to adhere as much as possible to the column structure or in order to be able to write the words within the borders of the existing piece of leather. When towards the end of the line or the piece of leather the scribe realized that the available space did not enable him to write a long word before the (sometimes imaginary) vertical left line of the column, he could either leave the space uninscribed, or attempt to crowd the letters into the available space. In rare cases one or more letters of the uncompleted word were written above or beneath it. See the ends of the words of 4Q236 (4QPs89) as described by Skehan (see n. 21). This was also standard procedure in the writing of the *tefillin*, see 4QPhyl A, B, G-I, J-K, L-N, S.

Also, in documents written in the same style there were occasional differences in the size of letters, but these were probably not meant to convey a specific message such as putting emphasis on certain letters. There are numerous examples of such differences, for instance the much larger second *kaph* in כול וכול in 1QS 11:11 and מות compared with the context in 4QRP[e] frag. 3, line 4. Similar large letters in the MT, which were probably originally unintentional, have become part and parcel of the transmission of the text: for example, Gen 30:42; ובהעטיף; Num 27:5; משפטן; Deut 29:27; וישלכם.[28] On the other hand, the top part of a very large *lamed* in

---

28   At the same time, other large letters in the MT do convey a certain message. Large or uppercase letters were indicated in most manuscripts and many editions in order to emphasize certain details. In this way the first letter of a book (Genesis [בראשית], Proverbs, Canticles, Chronicles) or section (סוף, Qoh 12:13), the middle letter in the Torah (גחון, Lev 11:42), and the middle verse in the Torah (והתגלח, Lev 13:33) were emphasized. Cf. *b. Qidd.* 30a: "The ancients were called *soferim* because they counted every letter in the Torah. They said that the *waw* in גחון (Lev 11:42) is the middle consonant in the Torah, דרש דרש (Lev 10:16) the middle

4QM[a] (4Q491) frag. 11, col. i, next to lines 19-22, served a very specific purpose, which is not clear, however.

3. *Errors.* Scribes approached their *Vorlagen* differently. By the same token, they also displayed different degrees of precision. These errors reflected in the texts from the Judean Desert do not differ from errors found in any other text of that period. Some scribes erred more than others in specific types of errors, such as haplography. Thus scribe B of 1QIsa[a] erroneously omitted several relatively long sections which were added subsequently in that scroll (e.g. 28:18; 30:11; 32:14).

As for interchanges of consonants, in the period covered by the texts from the Judean Desert, the closest similarity between any two letters exists between *yod* and *waw*, so that the largest number of mistakes is made with these letters. Indeed, in several scrolls, such as in 11QPs[a], there is hardly a distinction between these two letters; furthermore, in that scroll ligatures of *ʿayin/waw*, *ʿayin/zayin*, and *ʿayin/yod* are not distinguishable (incidentally, all three combinations resemble a *sin/šin*). In other scrolls, a combination *ʿayin/pe* would be very similar.

Interchanges of consonants are often mentioned in the rabbinic literature, for example, in *Sifre Deut.* §36 (on Deut 6:9): "If one has written an *ʿayin* instead of an *ʾaleph*, an *ʾaleph* instead of an *ʿayin*, a *kaph* instead of a *bet*, a *bet* instead of a *kaph*, a *ṣadi* instead of a *gimel*, a *gimel* instead of a *ṣadi*, a *resh* instead of a *daleth*, a *daleth* instead of a *resh*, a *ḥeth* instead of a *he*, a *he* instead of a *ḥeth*, a *yod* instead of a *waw*, a *waw* instead of a *yod*, a *nun* instead of a *zayin*, a *zayin* instead of a *nun*, a *pe* instead of a *ṭet*, a *ṭet* instead of a pe . . . a

---

word, and והתגלח (Lev 13:33) the middle verse." Cf. F. I. Andersen and A. D. Forbes, "What *Did* the Scribes Count?" in D. N. Freedman et al. (eds.), *Studies in Hebrew and Aramaic Orthography* (Winona Lake: Eisenbrauns, 1992) 297–318.

The Masorah, *b. Qidd.* 66b, and *Sof.* 9.1-7 also indicated a few imperfectly written letters, such as Num 25:12 (שלום), written with a "broken *waw*," that is, a *waw* with a crack in the middle. There are countless such letters in the Qumran texts and these do not reflect any special message. Broken letters (אותיות . . . מקורעות) are also mentioned in *b. Meg.* 18b.

At least some of the special letters (for lists, see Elias Levita, *Massoreth Ha-Massoreth* [Venice, 1538] 230-33, in the edition of C. D. Ginsburg [London: Longmans, Green, 1867]) were already written in this way in ancient texts and were mentioned in the Talmud. Thus in *b. Menaḥ.* 29b בה״בראם ("when they <the heaven and earth> were created," Gen 2:4) was exegetically explained as representing two words, בה, "with the letter *he*," and בראם, "He created them."

samekh instead of a *mem*, a *mem* instead of a *samekh* . . . such parchments should be hidden [and are invalid]."

4. *Correction Procedures and the Degree of Scribal Intervention.* The procedures used in correcting mistakes and the frequency of such intervention reflected to a great extent the personal preferences of scribes.

5. *Sense Divisions.* There is room for a personal approach in the indication or non-indication of sense divisions, the choice between open and closed sections, as well as the decision whether or not to indent the beginning of a new section. At the same time, it is almost impossible for us to decide which elements reflect the personal input of scribes and which reflect traditions passed on to them. That there were different scribal approaches in this regard is shown by the differences between the various manuscripts of the same biblical book. Thus some texts, such as 4QSam^c, indicated content breaks only infrequently, if at all.

6. *Special Layout of Poetical Units.* In the texts from the Judean Desert a special arrangement for the writing of poetical units is known exclusively for biblical texts (including Ben Sira!). This special layout is evidenced for two poems in the Pentateuch (Exodus 15; Deuteronomy 32) and for the books of Psalms (esp. Psalm 119), Job, Proverbs, and Lamentations. Twenty-four texts were written completely or partially in a special layout, while other scrolls of the same biblical books were written without any stichometric arrangement (e.g. 1QPs^{b,c}, 4QPs^{a,e,j,k,q}). In the light of these different ways of presenting the biblical texts in the Qumran scrolls it is relevant to examine the background of these different texts. However, it is hard to know whether the use or non-use of a special layout follows a pattern, and to what extent the choice was up to the personal preference of the scribe.

7. *Scribal Markings.* The texts from the Judean Desert, especially from Qumran, contain various scribal markings, some of which recur in several texts. These markings indicate the content division of the text, scribal intervention, mainly for the correction of errors, line-fillers, and other types of notes. The very use of scribal markings was somehow connected to the background of the texts, since they occur especially in texts written in the Qumran scribal practice, especially in 1QIsa^a and 1QS-1QSa-1QSb (the latter three compositions were written by the same scribe who also inserted some corrections in 1QIsa^a), 4Q502-511, 4QpIsa^c, and 4QCant^b.

8. Final and Nonfinal Letters. It was left to the individual scribes as to whether or not and to what extent final letters were used at the ends of words. Most scribes used final letters.

9. Adherence to Ruled Lines and Marginal Guide Lines. Most manuscripts were ruled with dry ruling. Most scribes adhered to these ruled lines under which they hung the letters, while a very few wrote on the lines or disregarded the dry rulings altogether, writing through the lines. Virtually all scribes adhered to the right vertical ruling, indicating the beginning of the column, but only the more precise scribes adhered to the vertical lines at the left margin (see above on the cramming of letters).

THE IDENTIFICATION OF SCRIBAL HANDS AND ITS IMPLICATIONS

With the aid of paleographical analysis different scribal hands can be identified within the same documents, although scholars often disagree on key issues. Thus, the assumption that in 1QIsa[a] a second scribe started his work at the beginning of col. xxviii (= Isaiah 33) at the beginning of a new sheet was accepted by several scholars, while Martin maintained that the two segments of that scroll were written by the same scribe.[29] However, the assumption of the bipartition of the scroll[30] seems to be defensible not only on the level of paleography, but also on other levels. The second scribe adopted a fuller orthography than the first,[31] he corrected more gutturals than scribe A,[32] he used specific scribal marks, and he left out more sections than the first scribe—these sections were subsequently filled in by a different hand, in small letters, between the lines and in the margin: col. xxxii, line 14 (= Isa 38:21), xxxiii, line 7 (= Isa 40:7)

---

[29]   M. Martin, *The Scribal Character of the Dead Sea Scrolls* I-II (Bibliothèque du Muséon 44,45; Louvain: Publications Universitaires, 1958) 65-73. Thus also E. Y. Kutscher, *The Language and Linguistic Background of the Isaiah Scroll (1 Q Is[a])* (STDJ 6; Leiden: Brill, 1974) 564-66; J Cook, "Orthographical Peculiarities in the Dead Sea Biblical Scrolls," *RevQ* 14 (1989) 293-305, esp. 303-304.

[30]   Thus M. Noth, "Eine Bemerkung zur Jesajarolle vom Toten Meer," *VT* 1 (1951) 224-26; C. Kuhl, "Schreibereigentümlichkeiten: Bemerkungen zur Jesajarolle (DSIa)," *VT* 2 (1952) 307-33, esp. 332-33.

[31]   Note, for example, the preponderance of the shorter form of the second person singular masculine suffix in the first part of the scroll as against the longer form in the second part.

[32]   R. L. Giese, "Further Evidence for the Bisection of 1QIs[a]," *Textus* 14 (1988) 61-70.

and xxxiii, line 14 (= Isa 40:14).

Likewise, the three fragments ascribed to different scrolls by Tov, now named 4QJer[b], 4QJer[d] and 4QJer[e] and ascribed to different scrolls by Tov were previously considered to belong to the same scroll (named 4QJer[b]).[33]

Several large scrolls were written by more than one scribe. Even such a small scroll as 4QApPsalm and Prayer (4Q448) was written by two different hands (one scribe wrote cols. A and another one cols. B and C). Changes of hand in the middle of the text are clearly visible in several documents, but the background of these changes is often not readily understandable. Thus towards the end of 1QpHab, scribe B started his work in the middle of col. xii, line 13, copying only the end of that column and the four lines of the next column, until the end of the composition. The first scribe of 1QH[a] probably copied the text from col. i to the middle of col. xi, line 22. From that point scribe B took over for a very short stretch of text (lines 23-26), while scribe C copied col. xi 27-35 and col. xii. Regardless of the correctness of these details, it is clear that the beginning of the column was written by a different scribe than the end. The letters at the end are larger, different, and less regular. It is difficult to understand these unusual changes of hand, but several scenarios can be devised. In the aforementioned case of 1QIsa[a] three lines were left empty at the end of the last column written by scribe A, col. xxvii. This space at the end of the column *may* indicate that the two scribes of this long scroll worked concurrently.[34] The first scribe of 11QT[a] wrote only cols. i-v, while the second one wrote the remainder (cols. vi-lxvi).[35] The change of hands between scribe A of

---

33   See E. Tov, "The Jeremiah Scrolls from Qumran," *RevQ* 14 (1989) 189-206.

34   For a discussion of the two scribal hands of Isaiah, see W. H. Brownlee, "The Literary Significance of the Bisection of Isaiah in the Ancient Scroll of Isaiah from Qumran," *Proceedings of the 25th Congress of Orientalists*, vol. 1 (Moscow: Tzolatel'sto Vostochnoi Literary, 1962-63) 431-37; K. H. Richards, "A Note on the Bisection of Isaiah," *RevQ* 5 (1965) 257-58; R. L. Giese, "Further Evidence for the Bisection of 1QIs[a]," *Textus* 14 (1988) 61-70; J. Cook, "The Dichotomy of 1QIsa[a]," in Z. J. Kapera (ed.), *Intertestamental Essays in Honour of Józef Tadeusz Milik*, Part I (Qumranica Mogilanensia 6; Kraków: Enigma, 1992) 7-24.

35   Y. Yadin (*The Temple Scroll*, vol. 1 [Jerusalem: The Israel Exploration Society, 1983] 11-12) believes that when the scroll was worn, the first columns were replaced with new ones.

4QJub[a] (4Q216) and scribe B is clearly visible in frag. 12 of that manuscript which constitutes the dividing line between the sections written by the two scribes. This fragment consists of the last column of a sheet written by scribe A and the first column of a sheet written by scribe B, stitched together with a thread. According to J. VanderKam and J. T. Milik, who published this text in DJD 13, the beginning of the scroll written by scribe A contains a repair sheet, but it seems equally possible that the scroll was written by two different scribes. Whether in all these cases the change of hands indicates a collaboration of some kind between scribes is difficult to tell. An alternative solution would be that the second hand reflects a corrective passage or a repair sheet (see the aforementioned suggestion for 4QJub[a]). The situation becomes even more complicated when the hand of a scribe B or C is also recognized in the corrections of the work of a scribe A. For example, according to Martin, scribe C of 1QH[a] corrected the work of scribe A, while scribe B corrected that of both scribes A and C. Patterns of this type in the large scrolls from cave 1 were identified especially by Martin in his detailed work on these texts.[36] As for Greek manuscripts, scribe B of 8ḤevXIIgr started in the middle of Zechariah. Differences between the two hands in material, letters, and scribal practices were described in DJD 8 (Oxford, 1990) 13.

It is difficult to identify scribal hands by an analysis of handwriting and other scribal features, partly because of the formal character of several texts, but if this uncertainty is taken into consideration, the following is of interest. For our understanding of the nature of the Qumran scrolls it is relevant to note that among the Qumran manuscripts very few individual scribes can be identified who copied more than one manuscript. It stands to reason that several of the manuscripts known to us were written by the same scribe, but we are not able to easily detect such links, partly because of the fragmentary status of the evidence and partly because of the often formal character of the handwriting. Further research may lead to some identifications. In the meantime, some examples are mentioned in the literature, all referring to texts written in the Qumran scribal practice:

(a) One individual apparently copied 1QS, 1QSa, 1QSb, and 4QSam[c], and his hand is also visible in several corrections in

---

[36]   See Martin, *Scribal Character*, 63.

1QIsaa.[37] According to Allegro, that same scribe, or more precisely, the scribe who copied 1QS, also copied 4Q175.[38]

(b) Martin tentatively identified the final hand of 1QS with hand B of 1QpHab.[39]

(c) According to van der Ploeg, one scribe copied both 11QTb and 1QpHab.[40]

(d) According to J. Davila in DJD 12 (Oxford, 1994) 57, 4QGenf and 4QGeng were probably written by the same scribe.

(e) Strugnell ascribed 4QTQahat ar (4Q542) to the same hand as 4QSamc.[41]

If indeed most scrolls were written by different scribes, certain conclusions may be drawn. Since most scribes were professionals, apparently only a very small proportion of the scrolls written by these scribes are known to us.

BACKGROUND OF THE SCRIBAL TRADITIONS

The scribal practices embedded in the documents found in the Judean Desert reflect the writing of the period under review. But at the same time they also continue writing styles of earlier periods when scribal practices developed for literary and documentary texts on papyrus and parchment as well as for inscriptions on various types of material. Several details which the scribal traditions of the documents from the Judean Desert have in common with Aramaic documents of the fifth century BCE lead us to believe that many

---

37   E. Ulrich, "4QSamc: A Fragmentary Manuscript of 2 Samuel 14–15 from the Scribe of the *Serek Hayyahad* (1QS)," *BASOR* 235 (1979) 1-25.

38   J. M. Allegro, *Qumrân Cave 4,I (4Q158–4Q186)* (DJD 5; Oxford: Clarendon, 1968) 58.

39   Martin, *Scribal Character*, 2.710.

40   J. P. M. van der Ploeg, "Les manuscrits de la grotte XI de Qumrân," *RevQ* 12 (1985-87) 9; "Une *halakha* inédite de Qumran," in M. Delcor (ed.), *Qumrân: sa piété, sa théologie et son milieu* (BETL 46; Leuven: Leuven University Press, 1978) 107-13. In this publication van der Ploeg remarks on the identity of the scribe of the two documents, but he does not identify the cave 11 document as 11QTb.

41   See G. Bonani, M. Broshi, I. Carmi, S. Ivy, J. Strugnell, and W. Wölfli, "Radio-carbon Dating of the Dead Sea Scrolls," *Atiqot* 20 (1991) 27-32, esp. 28. G. Doudna ("Callibrated Radiocarbon Dates from Tucson and Zurich on Dead Sea Texts and Linen" [paper delivered to the SBL conference, Philadelphia 1995] 6) disagrees, referring to both Carbon-14 tests and paleographical considerations.

documents from the Judean Desert continue earlier traditions of writing in the square script. To a lesser degree scribes were influenced by scribal traditions of the Alexandrian Hellenistic tradition. The background of several scribal practices is still unclear. In particular it is not known whether certain scribal practices had come into being at an earlier stage of the writing of Hebrew in square characters, or were influenced by contemporary customs in neighboring countries.

NON-JEWS IN THE DEAD SEA SCROLLS

Lawrence H. Schiffman

The corpus known generally as the Dead Sea Scrolls contains a wide variety of texts composed in the latter part of the Second Temple period, mostly from the second century BCE through the first century CE. Attempts to refute this dating can easily be discounted in light of archaeological, palaeographic and textual data, and now by the recently completed carbon-14 dating.[1] It was in this period that the Dead Sea sect gathered at Qumran the library of some 800 scrolls (most of which are preserved in fragmentary condition) which we know of as the Dead Sea Scrolls.[2]

This library consisted of a variety of compositions: At the core are a group of documents which describe the beliefs, history and law of a sectarian group, identified with the Essenes by most modern scholars. This group also gathered biblical scrolls, only a minority of which were actually copied by members of the sect. In addition, apocryphal compositions, some previously known and most new to us, were also included, and it is certain that most of these texts preexisted the Qumran sect. Apparently, some texts were also included that represented the teachings of allied or similar groups which, like the Qumran sect, flourished ca. 150 BCE–70 CE.

We can be virtually certain about the origins of the sect. The still hotly contested 4QMiqsat Ma'aseh Ha-Torah proves beyond a doubt that the sect came into being when a group of Sadducean priests refused to accept the new order of things in the Temple in the aftermath of the Maccabean revolt. At that time, the Hasmoneans, making common cause with the Pharisees, took over the control of the Temple and introduced Pharisaic practices, many of which were later enshrined in the Mishnaic texts. This group of pious Sadducees,

---

[1] See G. Bonani, M. Broshi, I. Carmi, S. Ivy, J. Strugnell, W. Wölfli, "Radiocarbon Dating of the Dead Sea Scrolls," 'Atiqot 20 (1991) 27-32.

[2] See L. H. Schiffman, "The Significance of the Scrolls," *BR* 6.5 (1990) 18-27, 52 for a survey of recent developments in the study of the Qumran scrolls.

under the direction of the teacher of righteousness, developed into the Dead Sea sect as we know it from the sectarian compositions.[3]

A study such as this must define itself more precisely within the literature of the Dead Sea Scrolls. We will concentrate on the sectarian corpus—those documents which were authored by the sect and which testify to its particular approach.[4] We will want to know, in particular, how the sect which gathered the scrolls in the Qumran collection looked at their non-Jewish neighbors.

Most Jews throughout the ages defined themselves over and against non-Jewish majorities. More often than not these majorities were hostile to the Jews and helped in the erection of the very barriers which the Jews employed to define themselves. In the case of the Qumran sect, the sect defined itself primarily over and against other Jews. It took a particularly dim view—indeed an intolerant one—of the Pharisees and Sadducees, and clearly had little use for the approaches to Judaism of the Hasmoneans and, to say the least, of the Hellenized Jews. Yet here we will be concerned not with the sect's attitudes to its fellow Jews, but rather with their outlook on the nations which surrounded them and the pagans who populated the land of Israel in the Greco-Roman period.

In passing, it needs to be stressed that the scrolls contain no references to Christianity, a movement which began as a Jewish sect and then developed into a separate religious group. This is because the sectarian documents were authored before the career of Jesus and John the Baptist who are in no way mentioned or alluded to in the scrolls—all falacious claims to the contrary not withstanding.[5] This is the case even though the sectarian settlement at Qumran continued to be occupied until 68 CE and even though some of the manuscripts may have been copied in the first century CE.

We will see that there are numerous references to non-Jews in the scrolls, both published and unpublished. Quite prominent are texts dealing with the halakhic status of non-Jews, regarding Sabbath law,

---

[3]   L. H. Schiffman, "The New Halakhic Letter (4QMMT) and the origins of the Dead Sea Sect," *BA* 53 (1990) 64-73.

[4]   We have also omitted *Jubilees, 1 Enoch*, Genesis Apocryphon, and *T. Levi* which are pre-sectarian works.

[5]   See most recently, G. Vermes, "The Oxford Forum for Qumran Research: Seminar on the Rule of War from cave 4 (4Q285)," *JJS* 43 (1992) 85-90, excerpted in "The 'Pierced Messiah' Text—An Interpretation Evaporates," *BARev* 18.4 (1992) 80-82.

purity regulations, and commerce. Other passages deal with the application of the biblical laws banning idolatrous practices. Another major theme is the role of the gentiles in the expected eschatological battle in which they are to be defeated by the sectarians. In this case, the "nations" play a central role in the unfolding of God's plan of history. A number of texts we shall examine, basing themselves on biblical precedent, refer to the demonstration of God's might in the presence of the nations. Others speak of the chosen people. Attention will also be given to the status of proselytes in the Qumran texts. In what follows, each of these aspects will be discussed in the hope that the general picture which we sketch will help in writing the overall history of the relations of Jews and non-Jews.

NON-JEWS IN THE SECTARIAN LAW OF THE ZADOKITE FRAGMENTS

While the Qumran corpus contains no specific information about what constitutes Jewish identity and, hence, how to define a non-Jew, it does give us quite a number of laws relating to non-Jews.[6] At the outset, we should turn to a series of laws regarding gentiles in the Zadokite Fragments (Damascus Document) which directly address this issue.[7] While the Zadokite Fragments legislates for members of the sect who lived throughout the Land of Israel, it is clear that the legal sections of this document were also in force for members of the sect at the Qumran center.[8]

The regulations of this text begin by indicating that it is forbidden to "shed the blood of anyone from among the non-Jews for the sake of wealth and profit" (CD 12:6-7).[9] Our text makes no reference to

---

6   It seems most likely that there was already a consensus on the definitions of a Jew and, for that reason, we encounter no argument on this question. See L. H. Schiffman, *Who was a Jew? Rabbinic and Halakhic Perspectives on the Jewish Christian Schism* (New York: Ktav, 1985) 1-39.

7   For a detailed study of these laws, see L. H. Schiffman, "Legislation Concerning Relations with Non-Jews in the *Zadokite Fragments* and in Tannaitic Literature," *RevQ* 11 (1983) 379-89.

8   While this text was first uncovered in medieval manuscripts in the Cairo Genizah, some ten manuscripts from the Qumran caves have recently appeared in preliminary publication. There is no question, therefore, that this text reflects the law and ideology of the Qumran sect.

9   The beginning of this law is preserved in 4QD^c 3 i 21. See B. Z. Wacholder and M. G. Abegg, Jr., *A Preliminary Edition of the Unpublished Dead Sea Scrolls: The Hebrew and Aramaic Texts from Cave Four* (Fascicle 1; Washington: Biblical

any penalty. Schechter is probably correct in noting that killing for self-defense would have been permitted.[10] We see this law as having a particular purpose. It was a polemic against the Hasmonean rulers intended to prohibit the undertaking of campaigns designed only to add territory to their country or to accumulate spoils of war.[11] A similar view is expressed in the Habakkuk Pesher which condemns "the last priests of Jerusalem who gather wealth and property from the spoil of the nations" (9:4-6).

In accord with this same purpose, the text goes on to prohibit carrying off the property of non-Jews "so that they not blaspheme, except if it be done in accord with the decision of the Community of Israel" (CD 12:7-8). This is certainly a prohibition on robbing non-Jews, in this context prohibiting military action to take their property. Most interesting is the explanation given: lest they blaspheme God. This idea is the same as the tannaitic ruling (t. B. Qam. 10.15) that stealing from non-Jews is prohibited because it leads to profanation of God's name. Such actions reflect badly on the Jewish people and, hence, on their God. Finally, this prescription also makes clear that war could only be undertaken with the permission of the council. Under such conditions, the war could be considered just and certainly not undertaken solely in order to plunder the enemy.[12]

The series of laws then turns to the prohibition of selling pure (kosher) animals and fowl to non-Jews lest they sacrifice them (CD 12:8-9). Such laws also existed in tannaitic tradition and were intended to make certain that Jews did not support, even indirectly, idolatrous worship, a matter to which we will return below.[13]

Also prohibited here are the sale to non-Jews of the produce "from his threshing floor and from his winepress" (CD 12:9-10). This law prohibits the sale of the produce directly from these installations, i.e. before it is tithed. Sale to non-Jews does not exempt Jewish produce from tithing.[14]

The final law in this series prohibits selling male or female

---

Archaeological Society, 1991) 26.

[10] S. Schechter, *Documents of Jewish Sectaries* (New York: Ktav, 1970) 82 n. 13.

[11] Schiffman, "Legislation," 380-82.

[12] Schiffman, "Legislation," 382-85.

[13] Schiffman, "Legislation," 385-87.

[14] Schiffman, "Legislation," 387-88.

servants to non-Jews "since they (the servants) have entered into the covenant of Abraham" (CD 12:10-11). This law clearly concerns those servants who, like the tannaitic classification עבד כנעני, literally "Canaanite slave," have begun a process of conversion to Judaism.[15] The same regulation exists in tannaitic law where such slaves automatically gained their freedom if sold to non-Jews (M. Gittin 4:6). This law was intended to prevent such slaves from being rendered unable to fulfill the commandments which they had undertaken.[16] In this context, we should note that 4QOrdinances prohibits a Jew from being a servant to a non-Jew (4Q 159 2-4 2).[17]

In the area of Jewish/non-Jewish relations, the Zadokite Fragments presents a sort of summary of what later Rabbinic tradition would enshrine in the Mishnah tractate ʿAboda Zara. From the point of view of the laws of the sect, we can conclude that in this area, their laws are simply a reflection of those followed by a number of Jewish groups, including the Pharisees, the forerunners of the tannaim (the Mishnaic Rabbis). The sectarians, like other non-Hellenized Jews of the Second Temple era, eschewed the killing or robbing of gentiles, as was to be expected, but also in accord with the sectarian understanding of the Torah's legislation, they made sure to avoid supporting or encouraging idolatrous worship in any way.

Another area of law in the Zadokite Fragments where non-Jews are discussed is that of the Sabbath.[18] The text, again exactly like tannaitic law, prohibits the sending of non-Jews to do labor prohibited on the Sabbath on behalf of Jews (CD 11:2). The non-Jew would then become an agent of the Jew who would be violating the Sabbath law indirectly.[19] Indeed, a similar prohibition exists regarding male and female servants (CD 11:12). This law certainly refers to the "Canaanite slaves" in the process of conversion.[20]

A strange prescription, most likely with no parallel in tannaitic law but perhaps parallel to some later Karaite views, prohibits spending the Sabbath "[in] a place close to the gentiles" (CD 11:14-

---

15   See Schiffman, *Who Was a Jew?*, 36-37.

16   Schiffman, "Legislation," p. 388.

17   See my edition, translation, and commentary to this text in the collection to be edited by J. Charlesworth.

18   For detailed discussion of Qumran Sabbath law, see L. H. Schiffman, *The Halakhah at Qumran* (Leiden: Brill, 1975) 84-131.

19   Schiffman, *Halakhah*, 104-6.

20   Schiffman, *Halakhah*, 120-21.

15). This law is most probably aimed to ensure ritual purity on the Sabbath, a matter important in sectarian circles. On the other hand, if it is to indicate that a technical residency for carrying or traveling on the Sabbath may not be made in partnership with non-Jews (*b.* *ʿErub.* 62a), as they do not have Sabbath obligations in Jewish law, it would accord fully with later Rabbinic tradition.[21]

Here we see that although non-Jews are not obligated to observe the Jewish Sabbath, it is forbidden for Jews to employ them to do prohibited labor, whether they be free or "Canaanite slaves." Again we observe that the sect's views on this topic are sufficiently close to those of the Pharisaic-Rabbinic tradition as to suggest that these were the views of many observant Jews in this period. A passing reference in CD 14:15 (also in 4QD[b] 18 iii 8) recognizes the need to redeem captives who may be "captured by a foreign nation." Priests captured by non-Jews were, in the view of.the sect, rendered unfit for priestly service.[22]

A fragmentary law preserved in three Qumran manuscripts of the Zadokite Fragments seems to outlaw the bringing (perhaps to the Temple or to the sectarian communal meals) of meat slaughtered by non-Jews. Further, metals—gold, silver, brass, tin, and lead—which have been used by non-Jews to make an idol were prohibited in the same manner.[23]

It was considered permitted, in line with Deut 15:3, to take interest from non-Jews, but not from Jews, according to 1QWords of Moses (iii 6).[24] The Zadokite Fragments similarly castigates anyone who takes interest from a fellow Jew.[25]

Extremely important, especially in light of the material to be cited below from the Temple Scroll, is an enigmatic passage which provides that, "Any man who shall dedicate (or destroy) any man according to the laws of the nations (בחוקי הגוים) is to be put to death" (CD 9:1).[26] This passage, certainly based on Lev 27:29 and

---

21   Schiffman, *Halakhah*, 123-4.

22   4QD[b] 6 ii 4-6; 4QD[d] 4 iii 8; Wacholder and Abegg, *A Preliminary Edition*, 10, 30.

23   4QD[c] 1 ii 8-9; 4QD[e] 7 20-21; 4QD[f] 19 3-4; Wacholder and Abegg, *A Preliminary Edition*, 24, 38, 51.

24   D. Barthélemy and J. T. Milik, *Qumran Cave I* (DJD 1; Oxford: Clarendon Press, 1955) 94-95.

25   D[d] 6:10-11; Wacholder and Abegg, *A Preliminary Edition*, 31.

26   That this passage is textually reliable is shown from comparison with 4QD[b]

Gen 9:6, has been debated by scholars, and a number of views have been put forth. It is most probable that we deal here with a law stating that one who has recourse to non-Jewish courts to accuse a fellow Jew of a crime is himself to be put to death (in the view of the sect) because he has informed against his fellow Jew.[27] Clearly, informing was a problem at this time, as we know also from somewhat later Rabbinic texts,[28] and strong measures to prevent it were necessary.

Informing also is prohibited in a passage which is in agreement with what we will see in the Temple Scroll. The Zadokite Fragments,[29] in a passage preserved only in a Qumran copy (4QD[e] 9 ii 12-15) which appears to be a list of offenses, includes "the person who reveals the secret of his people to the nations, or one who curses o[r speaks] slanderously" regarding the sect's leaders[30] or "leads [his people astray]."

PROHIBITIONS OF IDOLATRY

We have already seen that the Zadokite Fragments deals with the need to avoid supporting idolatrous practices in any way. 1QWords of Moses places into the mouth of Moses the assertion that Jews would go astray after the abominations of the nations (i 6-8, partly restored).[31] The issue of idolatry is dealt with in the Temple Scroll in its recapitulation of the biblical legislation on this topic. The Temple Scroll and its connection to the life of the Qumran sect are themselves a matter of controversy. Our view is that the scroll was edited in Hasmonean times by someone belonging to the sect or a related group, and that it includes Sadducean sources which the

---

(Wacholder and Abegg, *A Preliminary Edition*, 17) and 4Q[e] 10 iii 16 (Wacholder and Abegg, *A Preliminary Edition*, 43). Further, it is written immediately after a *vacat* (paragraph marker), indicating that no preceding text provides a fuller context for understanding this law.

27   The opposite view, namely that Jews are to be handed over to the non-Jewish authorities for execution (C. Rabin, *The Zadokite Documents* [Oxford: Clarendon Press, 1954] 44), is impossible in light of comparison with the Temple Scroll and all other systems of Jewish law.

28   Cf. Schiffman, *Who Was a Jew?*, 46-47.

29   Wacholder and Abegg, *A Preliminary Edition*, 41.

30   Or perhaps its prophets, cf. CD 5:21–6:1 and Wacholder and Abegg, *A Preliminary Edition*, 49 (משיחי הקודש).

31   DJD 1.92.

founders of the sect brought with them when they left the Temple service after the Hasmonean revolt. It is for this reason that the scroll has many important parallels with the laws of 4QMiqsat Maʿaseh Ha-Torah.[32] The Temple Scroll assembles biblical laws and then, by a combination of exegesis, modification, and addition, sets forth its views on how Jewish ritual, law and society should be structured in the Hasmonean period.[33] It takes up the biblical laws of idolatry as part of the Deuteronomic paraphrase, the section at the end of the scroll which was composed to round out the sources the author had in front of him and to give the impression that the scroll was a complete Torah.[34]

Indeed, in the introduction to the scroll the author, basing himself on Exod 34:10-17, incorporates the obligation to destroy idolatrous cult objects and to avoid idolatrous worship (11QT 2:6-12). His extensive treatment begins with the prohibition of idolatrous practice (11QT 51:19–52:3). This passage is based on Deut 16:21-22 (cf. Lev 26:1) and outlaws sacrificing throughout the land, the planting of Asherot, and the erecting of cultic pillars and figured stones. This law, however, adds nothing to biblical law, except as regards its formulation.

The scroll next paraphrases the law of the idolatrous prophet of Deut 13:2-6 (11QT 54:8-18). Although there are minor variations in the textual traditions behind this passage, as well as a few changes to eliminate ambiguities, the text simply repeats the biblical law requiring the death penalty for a "prophet" who advocates worship of other gods. Similar is the manner in which the scroll reviews the law of the enticer to idolatry of Deut 13:7-12 (11QT 54:19–55:1). In accord with Deuteronomy such a person is to be put to death. No significant innovations in the laws involved are introduced by the scroll.

More significant variants appear in the paraphrase of the law of the idolatrous city of Deut 13:13-19 (11QT 55:2-14). The biblical

---

[32] L. H. Schiffman, "*Miqsat Maʿaseh Ha-Torah* and the *Temple Scroll*," *RevQ* 14 (1990) 435-57.

[33] That it is not a messianic text is clear from an explicit statement in 11QT 29:1-10.

[34] See L. H. Schiffman, "Laws Concerning Idolatry in the Temple Scroll," to appear in H. N. Richardson Memorial Volume to be published by Eisenbrauns. Philological commentary is available in Y. Yadin, *The Temple Scroll* (2 vols., Jerusalem: Israel Exploration Society, 1983) 2.244-49.

legislation requires that a city which has gone astray and worshipped idols is to be totally destroyed, its inhabitants killed, and its spoils burned. The scroll introduces a number of requirements: All the inhabitants must have worshipped idols for the city to be entirely destroyed, as opposed to the notion that only the majority must have transgressed as known from tannaitic *halakhah* (*m. Sanh.* 4:1). That all the inhabitants are to be killed in the view of the scroll contrasts with the tannaitic view that the children are to be spared (*t. Sanh.* 14:3). The Temple Scroll mandates that all the animals are to be destroyed in contrast to the tannaitic interpretation according to which those dedicated for certain sacrificial offerings are to be spared (*t. Sanh.* 14.5; *Sifre Deut.* §94 [on Deut 13:16]).[35]

The final law on idolatry in the Temple Scroll is the law of the idolatrous individual in Deut 12:2-7 (11QT 55:15-56:04). While some ambiguities are eliminated, the text is essentially a recapitulation of the Deuteronomic prescription that an idolater be put to death if he can be convicted of his transgression in court under the applicable rules of testimony.

In all these laws we have seen that the text simply adhered to the biblical prohibitions with little addition or modification. In the case of the changes made in the law of the idolatrous city it is possible that they resulted from the Hasmonean attempts to eradicate idolatry from the country which led at times to the destruction, without the necessary investigation and trial, of entire cities.[36] Our author may have wanted to clarify that Hellenistic Jews, no matter how extreme, could not be destroyed in this manner if, as he argued, the entire city had not participated in idolatrous worship.

What emerges is that the author/redactor of the Temple Scroll had little if anything to add to the Torah's legislation on idolatry. Further, he says nothing about non-Jews who worship idols except that their cultic objects and cult places are to be destroyed. Following Deuteronomy, he is almost entirely concerned with eliminating idolatrous worship from amongst the Jews, an agenda which fit both

---

35   Cf. L. H. Schiffman, "The Septuagint and the Temple Scroll: Shared 'Halakhic Variants,'" in G.J. Brooke and B. Lindars (eds.), *Septuagint, Scrolls and Cognate Writings* (Atlanta: Scholars Press, 1992) 283-84.

36   On the destruction or Judaization of pagan cities by the Hasmoneans, see E. Schürer, *The History of the Jewish People in the Age of Jesus Christ*, vol. 1 (ed. G. Vermes, F. Millar, with P. Vermes, M. Black; Edinburgh: T. & T. Clark, 1973) 191-92, 207, 228.

the author of Deuteronomy and the author/redactor of our scroll.

OTHER LAWS IN THE TEMPLE SCROLL

At the beginning of the preserved portion of the Temple Scroll (11QT 2:1-15), in the same context as the requirement to destroy pagan cult objects, we find a recapitulation of the biblical prohibition on making covenants with the nations of Canaan who are to be destroyed (Exod 34:10-16). Both the Bible and our scroll state explicitly that this restri tion is intended to prevent intermarriage with these nations. This passage adheres so closely to the biblical source that we cannot tell from it if the prohibition of intermarriage was widened to include all nations, as took place already in the biblical period (1 Kgs 11:1-2; Ezra 9:1-2; Neh 10:31). But from elsewhere in the scroll it seems that all marriage between Jews and gentiles was prohibited (11QT 57:15-17).

The scroll no doubt would have prohibited non-Jews from entering the Temple since even proselytes were restricted from entering into the middle court until the fourth generation (11QT 39:5-7). Indeed, non-Jews as well as proselytes are excluded from the sanctuary, apparently in the end of days, of 4QFlorilegium (4Q174 1-2 i 4).[37]

In connection with the impurity of the dead we learn that the nations bury their dead everywhere, but Israel, in the view of the scroll, is to bury in specially set out cemeteries, one for each four cities (11QT 48:11-14). The purpose of this regulation is to maintain the ritual purity of the Land of Israel. While the phraseology of this legislation has roots in biblical language,[38] the contents here are unique to the scroll.[39] This law is to be compared with the scroll's condemnation of the fact that the nations offer sacrifice and erect cult places everywhere (11QT 15:19-21). The unstated (or perhaps unpreserved) implication is that Israel is to perform sacrificial worship only at its central Temple complex in Jerusalem.

---

[37]   See L. H. Schiffman, "Exclusion from the Sanctuary and the City of the Sanctuary in the Temple Scroll," *HAR* 9 (1985) 303-305 and the bibliography cited there.

[38]   Yadin, *The Temple Scroll*, 2.209.

[39]   See L. H. Schiffman, "The Impurity of the Dead in the Temple Scroll," in L. H. Schiffman (ed.), *Archaeology and History in the Dead Sea Scrolls* (Sheffield: JSOT Press, 1990) 137-38.

The abominations of the "nations" are listed as well: passing children through fire as part of Molekh worship, divination, augury and sorcery of different types, and necromancy.[40] Israel is told that because of these abominations the Canaanite nations have been expelled[41] from the land (11QT 60:16-61:02). But this passage is no more than a verbatim quotation of Deut 18:9-14 with minor textual variation.

The nations appear several times in the Law of the King, a separate source which the author/redactor of the scroll incorporated into his scroll.[42] Although Israel is to have a king "like all the (other) nations," that king must be Jewish (11QT 56:13-15), an exact echo of Deut 17:14-15.[43] He may only marry a Jewish woman (11QT 57:15-16).[44] Lest he be kidnapped by "the nations" or "a foreign nation," he must be protected by a guard of 12,000 chosen men (11QT 57:5-11). This was a central concern if we can judge from the repetition within the passage, undoubtedly intended for emphasis.

The scroll also expects that foreign nations will attack the Land of Israel to take booty, and specifies the necessary defensive military action (11QT 58:3-10).[45] Indeed, such action is conceived as a fundamental duty of the king. After the conclusion of the Law of the King there is again a recapitulation of the Deuteronomic laws of war according to which it is obligatory to kill all the Canaanites lest Israel learn from their abominable ways (11QT 62:11-16). Yet again we deal with a text of Deut 20:15-18,[46] rather than with independent Second Temple period material.

Two final examples from the Temple Scroll concern those to be

---

40   Cf. the prohibition of אוב and ידעוני alluded to in CD 12:2-3; 4QD^e 9 i 10; Wacholder and Abegg, *A Preliminary Edition*, 40.

41   The text uses the present tense, reflecting the language of the Bible. But in the context of the Temple Scroll the message is certainly that of the recounting of past events.

42   L. H. Schiffman, "The King, his Guard, and the Royal Council in the *Temple Scroll*," *PAAJR* 54 (1987) 237-59.

43   The prohibition on returning the people to Egypt is here interpreted to refer to making war (11QT 56:16).

44   Cf. the requirement that the high priest marry a "virgin from his people" (NJPS "kin") in Lev 21:14.

45   Cf. L. H. Schiffman, "The Laws of War in the Temple Scroll," *RQ* 13 (1988) 302-304.

46   Schiffman, "Laws of War," 304.

punished by "hanging."[47] The first prescribes that one who informs against his people or delivers them to "a foreign nation" shall be executed, apparently by crucifixion (11QT 64:6-9). The second is a law regarding one subject to the death penalty who flees "to the midst of the nations" and curses his people, the Israelites. He is to be put to death, apparently by crucifixion as well (11QT 64:9-13). Like the Targumim and the Rabbis, the Temple Scroll saw informing to the non-Jews as a particularly heinous crime, and, indeed, it has always been taken this way in Jewish tradition. This law is based on an exegesis of Lev 19:16, "Do not go about slandering your people." The prohibition of execration of the Jewish people and the punishment of this offense by "hanging," most probably crucifixion, is based on an interpretation of Deut 21:22-23.[48]

In general, most of the mentions of the non-Jews ("the nations") in the Temple Scroll are in material taken almost verbatim from Scripture. Particularly significant are those passages which the author created on his own. In this respect we saw the need to reject non-Jewish burial practices to ensure the purity of the land, the requirement that the king marry only a Jewish bride, fear of enemy attack by the non-Jews, fear that the king might be kidnapped, and the problem of informers and execrators against the Jewish people. In these areas, the concerns of the author/redactor or his sources, writing in the Second Temple period, can be observed. Indeed, intermarriage, treason, and the complex web of Hasmonean vs. pagan military activity were major concerns in this period.

NON-JEWS IN 4QMIQSAT MAᶜASEH HA-TORAH

4QMiqsat Maᶜaseh Ha-Torah (4QMMT), known as the "halakhic letter," is a foundation document for the Qumran sect. It specifies the reasons for the schism in which a group of Sadducean priests left the Temple service after the Hasmoneans took over the Temple ca. 152 and began to conduct the rituals in accord with Pharisaic views.[49] This document contains two laws (of a total of twenty-two) relating to non-Jews.

The founders of the sect write to their erstwhile priestly colleagues in Jerusalem and criticize them for accepting grain offerings

---

47   See Yadin, *The Temple Scroll*, 1.373-79.
48   Yadin, *The Temple Scroll*, 2.291.
49   See above, n. 3.

(*terumah*) from the produce of non-Jews. In their view, such produce is not to enter the Temple lest it defile the offerings collected from Jews. In fact, say the sectarians, it is forbidden to eat of such produce. No such law is known from the Pharisaic-Rabbinic tradition. They also oppose accepting sacrificial offerings (*zebaḥ*) from non-Jews which was the practice in the Temple.

These two cultic matters were certainly among those important to the founders of the sect. The ritually exclusivistic view of the authors fits well with the eschatological views which the sect developed. They expected the nations ultimately to disappear from the face of the earth. The alternative approach of the Pharisaic-Rabbinic tradition envisioned the nations as coming to Jerusalem to recognize God's sovereignty and participate in the worship the Lord.

NON-JEWS IN SECTARIAN TEACHING

The long admonition at the beginning of the Zadokite Fragments (pp. 1-9 and 19-20 in the Genizah version) is almost entirely directed to intra-Jewish issues, especially to the sect's self-image and polemic with the Pharisees.[50] The only time that non-Jews appear is in a *pesher*-like exegesis of Deut 32:33 which mentions the "kings of the peoples," their evil ways, and the "king of Greece" (i.e. Rome) who will take vengeance, most probably on the other kings (CD 8:9-12 = 19:21-25). This passage certainly looks like a reflection of the affairs of the Hasmonean period in which the Romans were slowly gobbling up the various local kings of the Mediterranean Basin and the Near East. The very same assumption is made in the Habakkuk Pesher (3:2-13, 3:17-4:9).[51]

A strange passage appears as part of a ritual for expelling miscreants from the sect in the Zadokite Fragments, preserved only in the Qumran manuscripts (4QD^b 18 v 5-14).[52] There we read that God created the various peoples of the earth "and You led them astray in confusion, and with no path, but You chose our forefathers . . ." (lines 10-11). We will encounter the chosen people motif in other texts as well. But here we are told that God caused the other nations

---

[50] See L. H. Schiffman, "New Light on the Pharisees, Insights from the Dead Sea Scrolls," *BR* 8.3 (1992) 30-33, 54.

[51] This text specifically identifies the Romans as worshipping idols (4QpHab 12:10–13:4).

[52] Wacholder and Abegg, *A Preliminary Edition*, 21.

to go astray. In other words, they were predestined to go astray, a view which fits well with the sect's predestinarian outlook and with the extreme ethical dualism in which they believed.[53]

The punishment of the Jews for their transgressions is to take place in the presence of the nations according to the Hosea Pesher (4QpHos[a] ii 12-13). The same text lists as a primary transgression the scheduling of feasts "according to the appointed times of the nations" (lines 15-16), a reference to following the wrong calendar. This is most probably a reference to the sect's adoption of a calendar based on solar months and solar years which it believed to be the correct calendar, as opposed to the calendar of lunar months adjusted to solar years which was followed by most of the Jewish community.[54]

THE DESTRUCTION OF THE "NATIONS"

The Dead Sea sect expected that the end of days would soon dawn. Their apocalyptic, messianic tendencies led them to develop a body of literature outlining the eschatological battle which would usher in the final age. From the study of the manuscripts of the Scroll of the War of the Sons of Light against the Sons of Darkness from caves 1 and 4 it is clear that varying recensions of these texts existed. This view is further supported by the existence of other related texts on this topic (including that which has been incorrectly and irresponsibly interpreted as describing the execution of a messiah[55]). In fact, it is most likely that the War Scroll as a whole was assembled from preexistent sources by a redactor. We can state with certainty that the War Scroll was in existence before the Roman conquest of 63 BCE.

A very schematized view of the battles which will take place is presented in the War Scroll (1QM). The "sons of light" are the sectarians who are to emerge victorious in the end of days. The nations

---

53   J. Licht, "An Analysis of the Treatise of the Two Spirits in DSD," in C. Rabin and Y. Yadin (eds.), *Aspects of the Dead Sea Scrolls* (Scripta Hierosolymitana 4; Jerusalem: Magnes Press, 1958) 88-100.

54   See S. Talmon, "The Calendar Reckoning of the Sect from the Judaean Desert," *Aspects of the Dead Sea Scrolls*, 162-99, which must be corected in light of recent evidence that the prayer texts preserved by the sect presumed lunar months, and that the solar and lunar systems were coordinated in some sectarian texts.

55   See n. 5 above.

are grouped with the "sons of darkness," including also those Jews who do not indicate by their behavior that they are predestined to be among the "sons of light." They are also assigned to the lot of Belial. The place of exile of the sect before this battle is termed "the desert of the peoples [עמים]". No remnant of these evil nations is to survive in the end of days (1QM 1:1-7; 14:5; 4QM^a 8–9 3; cf. 4QpHab 4:3-5).

In the author's scheme the peoples are designated by names from the table of nations in Genesis 10 (cf. 1QM 2:10-14). Most prominent of these are Assyria (Seleucid Syria) and the Kittim (Rome), the destruction of which is high on the author's agenda (1QM 1:4-6; 2:9-12; 11:11; 4QM^a 11 ii). The battles are assumed to take place in "all the lands of the nations" (1QM 2:7; cf. 11:12-13). Indeed, as one of their banners testified, the sect expected the "Annihilation by God of all nations of vanity" (1QM 4:12).[56] The final battle would exact retribution on these nations for their wickedness (1QM 6:6; cf. 9:8-9) and they would all be killed (1QM 19:10-11).

The text echoes the chosen people motif of the Bible (Deut 7:6, 14:2; 1 Chr 17:21) when it declares, "who is like unto Your people Israel which You have chosen for Yourself from all the nations of the lands, a people of those holy through the covenant" (1QM 10:9-10; 4QM^e 1). The passage continues to describe this chosenness as indicated by Israel's willingness to receive revelation and its openness to probe the depths of God's commands (lines 10-11). This passage, like other poetic and liturgical sections of the scroll, probably predated its final authorship. Further on, the sectarians themselves are designated "the chosen ones of the holy nation" (12:1).

One particular poem included twice in the scroll seems to be at variance with the assumption of the complete document that all the nations are to be destroyed in the end of days (1QM 12:9-15; 19:2-8; also in 4QM^b 1 2-8). Addressed primarily to God Who is asked to crush the nations, His adversaries, the poem turns to the city of Jerusalem and calls on it to "Open your gates forever, so that there will be brought in to you the wealth of the nations, and their kings shall serve you . . . and rule over the king[dom of the Kittim]." Certainly, this passage, based almost entirely on Isa 60:10-14, expects the na-

---

56 Trans. in Y. Yadin (ed.), *The Scroll of the War of the Sons of Light against the Sons of Darkness* (Oxford: University Press, 1962) 277. (War Scroll translations below are mine.)

tions, including the Romans, to survive into the messianic era when they will be subservient to Israel. That the nations will continue to exist but under the rule of the Davidic Messiah is expected in the Isaiah Pesher (4QpIsa^a 7 25).

This idea may also lie behind the expression, "to subdue the nations" in the messianic Rule of the Congregation (1QS^a 1:21), although this may also be a reference to their destruction. The same idea has been restored in the Rule of Benedictions (1QS^b 3:18).[57] This approach may be in evidence again in the same text where we are told in a blessing for the Prince of the Congregation that "be[fore you will bow all peoples, and all the nat]ions will serve you" (1QS^b 5:28-29).[58]

Certainly, however, the dominant theme of the War Scroll is that the nations are predestined to be destroyed in the great war which will usher in the end of days. The sectarians, aided by angelic forces, will defeat and kill all the non-Jews, and even those Jews who do not join the group will be destroyed. In the end of days, the world will be populated only by the members of the sect.

ISRAEL AND THE NATIONS IN LITURGICAL TEXTS

A "Lamentation" asks God "not to give our inheritance to strangers nor our property (or possessions) to foreigners" (5Q501 1). This text betokens an understanding of the coming conquest and destruction by Rome.

The chosen people motif appears again in a fragmentary prayer, most probably for the festival of Passover, in which God is praised "[W]ho cho[se] us from among [the] nations" (4Q503 vii frags. 24–25 4).[59] The same is asserted in the non-canonical Psalms (4Q381 76–77 15).[60]

4QDivre Ha-Me᾽orot (Words of the Luminaries) is a propitionary type prayer very much like the Rabbinic *tahanun* ("supplication") prayers. (By the way, it shows that such prayers already existed

---

[57]   Milik, DJD 1.124.

[58]   As restored by J. Licht, *Megillat Ha-Serakhim* (Jerusalem: Mosad Bialik, 1965) 289.

[59]   M. Baillet, *Qumran Grotte 4, III (4Q482-4Q520)* (DJD 7; Oxford: Clarendon, 1982) 111.

[60]   E. M. Schuller, *Non-Canonical Psalms from Qumran: a Pseudipigraphic Collection* (HSS 28; Atlanta: Scholars Press, 1986) 215.

before the destruction of the Second Temple.) It appeals to God to remember "Your wonders which You did before [לעיני] the nations" (4Q504 1–2 ii 12), appealing to the miracles of biblical times which had demonstrated God's power to the nations. A similar appeal is made to the fact "that (God) took us out (of Egypt) before all the nations" (4Q504 1–2 v 10). Yet the very same nations are regarded as "[no]thing before You" (4Q504 1–2 iii 3). God has created the Jewish people, made them His children, and called them "My son, My first born" before the nations (lines 4-6).

The chosen people motif is also prominent in this text: "You have loved Israel more than the (other) peoples" (4Q504 1–2 iv 4-5).[61] As a result, "all the nations saw Your glory in that You were sanctified among Your people Israel" (lines 8-9).[62]

This motif also occurs in 4Q Prayers for Festivals (4Q508 4 2). In one prayer we hear that "You chose a people . . . You set them aside for Yourself as holy (or for sanctity) from all the peoples" by vouchsafing to them visions of the divine and revelation of God's word (1Q34bis ii 5-7 = 4Q509 97–98 7-10).

PROSELYTES IN THE DEAD SEA SCROLLS

Despite the sect's notions of predestination and their view that the nations, the non-Jews, would be destroyed in the end of days, it recognized the institution of proselytism, or religious conversion to Judaism, which apparently existed by this time. Proselytes appear in the Zadokite Fragments (CD 14:3-6) in lists of the classes which made up the sect—priests, Levites, Israelites and proselytes. During the sectarian occupation of Qumran, sectarian officials maintained actual written documents which the sect used for the purposes of its mustering ceremony.[63] The Zadokite Fragments expects that the proselyte may be in need of economic help (6:21).

The sectarians saw the proselytes as constituting a class within

---

61 Cf. 4Q504 5 ii 1-2 and the parallels in 4Q505 124 6 and 4Q506 124 1-2.

62 A similar idea occurs in 4QVision of Samuel where it states, "that all the peoples of Your lands will know [. . .] many [will] understand that your people is [. . . ho]ly that you sanctified (4Q160 3–4 ii 5-7). Cf. he alternate restoration of this column in J. Strugnell, "Notes en marge du volume V des 'Discoveries in the Judaean Desert of Jordan,'" *RevQ* 7 (1970) 180-82.

63 Schiffman, *Halakhah at Qumran*, 66-67.

their society of a status different than that of full Israelites. In this respect, they agreed with an approach known to have been held by a minority of tannaim (*t. Qidd.* 5.1). Accordingly, as mentioned already above, the Temple Scroll expected that proselytes would be permitted to enter the Temple only in the fourth generation. The author of 4QFlorilegium wanted converts to be excluded from his messianic sanctuary.

We have seen that in the Qumran documents, slaves who had entered the status which the tannaim called "the Canaanite slave" were considered involved in a conversion process and, hence, might not be sold to non-Jews. Therefore, there can be no question that there were converts and conversion in the world view of the sect and probably actually in its ranks.

CONCLUSION

Although there is a certain animosity to other Jews who did not follow their laws, the distinction between Jews and non-Jews is never blurred in the Dead Sea Scrolls, and the sect's Jewish opponents are never accused of non-Jewish status. The material studied here presents a paradox. On the one hand, we have encountered non-Jews in what may be considered the classic position assigned to them by the Jewish legal system. They are not obligated to observe the laws of, for example, the Sabbath, or other Jewish commandments, yet they are forbidden to worship idols or to blaspheme God. Hence, our texts go out of their way to set forth the laws pertaining to idolaters and idolatry. Some of these laws deal, in reality, with the problems of the impact of pagan religious behavior on Jews. Nonetheless, non-Jews, even if idolaters, are to be protected from depredation and pillage from Jewish armies intended solely on enriching Jewish rulers or their subjects.

On the other hand, we find in some of the sectarian documents an eschatological view which, for the most part, expects that in the end of days the non-Jews, along with Jews who do not accept (or who are predestined not to accept) the way of the sect, will all be destroyed. For the Qumran sect, the eschaton was not to be the universal experience which was expected by the prophet Isaiah; it was to be theirs and theirs alone.

Ultimately, Judaism accepted many aspects of the common Jewish law of the Second Temple period as well as Pharisaic teachings, and these served as the basis for tannaitic *halakhah*. Many aspects of the Qumran legal tradition share the same presuppositions and rulings that we find in the Pharisaic-Rabbinic tradition. Yet at the same time, the Pharisaic-Rabbinic world view accorded much more fully with the words of the prophets of Israel, who saw the coming of the nations to the worship of God, under the leadership of Israel and at its holy mountain, as the true fulfillment of the ideals and aspirations of the messianic future.

THE "11QPsᵃ–PSALTER" IN THE DEAD SEA SCROLLS, INCLUDING THE PRELIMINARY EDITION OF 4QPsᵉ

Peter W. Flint

With his publication of 11QPsᵃ and in several articles, James Sanders achieved two milestones in twentieth-century Psalms scholarship: making available the most important of all the Psalms scrolls, and articulating its significance for our understanding of the Book of Psalms itself. This essay does not explore the issues that arise from study of 11QPsᵃ and the other Psalms scrolls, which I have addressed elsewhere,[1] but considers whether further copies of the "11QPsᵃ–Psalter"[2] are to be found among the Dead Sea Scrolls. After introducing 11QPsᵃ and the other Psalms Scrolls, I will identify further copies of this Psalter among the Scrolls, present the preliminary edition of 4QPsᵉ, and conclude with a few observations and a select bibliography. Because much of my own research since 1992 has focused on the Psalms Scrolls,[3] it is both an honour and a pleasure to participate in a *Festschrift* for the scholar whose work has defined the agenda for this area of study.

1. 11QPsᵃ AND THE "11QPsᵃ–PSALTER"

In 1965 James Sanders published the critical edition of 11QPsᵃ, the largest of all the Psalms scrolls,[4] and two years later a companion volume with a more general audience in view.[5] Often termed the

---

[1] Including "Psalms Scrolls from the Judaean Desert: Relationships and Textual Affilations," 31-52; "Methods for Determining Relationships," 197-209 + 210-11 "Of Psalms and Psalters," 65-83; and *Dead Sea Psalms Scrolls,* 135-236 (see Bibliography).

[2] For this term, see after Table 1 below.

[3] Culminating in *The Dead Sea Psalms Scrolls and the Book of Psalms,* which appeared in 1997.

[4] *The Psalms Scroll of Qumrân Cave 11 (11QPsᵃ)* (DJD 4; Oxford: Clarendon Press, 1965).

[5] *The Dead Sea Psalms Scroll* (Ithaca: Cornell University Press, 1967).

"Cornell Edition," the later work omits most of the technical data
and footnotes found in the *editio princeps*, and presents the Hebrew
text with a facing English translation. 11QPs^a is relatively well-
preserved; although some compositions are missing from the
beginning (frags. a–e), in the 29 joined columns every piece is at
least partly preserved with the sole exception of Ps 120 in col. II.
The end of the manuscript is clearly indicated by te final, blank
column. A total of 49 or 50 compositions are represented in 11QPs^a,
depending on whether the Catena in col. XVI is viewed as a separate
piece or as a pendant to Ps 136 which precedes it. The full listing is
given in Table 1 (on the next page).

In a series of articles commencing in 1966,[6] Sanders arrived at
several conclusions that challenge traditional views on the text and
canonization of the Book of Psalms. One of these is that 11QPs^a is
part of the "Qumran Psalter," an earlier form of the Hebrew Psalter
prior to its finalization and viewed by the community at Qumran as a
true Davidic Psalter. According to Sanders, the Qumran Psalter was
regarded by those who used it as "canonical" (since it incorporated
Psalms 1–89, which had been finalized), yet also as "open" (able to
admit additional contents or arrangements, since Psalms 90 onwards
were still fluid). He added that the process of stabilization was
arrested when the founders of the Qumran community left
Jerusalem, at a time when Psalms 1–89 had reached finalization. The
gathering of Psalms 90 and beyond then developed independently in
two directions, resuling in two collections which had Psalms 1–89 in
common but differed from Psalms 90 onwards. Sanders termed these
collections the "Qumran Psalter," of which almost all the second half
is represented by 11QPs^a, and the Psalter found in the Received Text
whose second half comprises Psalms 90–150.

For our purposes only two points are relevant. First, Sanders
understood the "Qumran Psalter" as being larger than the arrangement found in 11QPs^a, with the full collection also containing Psalms
1–89. On the analogy of the "MT–150 Psalter" he maintained that
this Psalter contained both Psalms 1–89 and the pieces that are found
in 11QPs^a. Second, the terminology used for this Psalter requires
careful definition. I have argued elsewhere that the collection was
not necessarily composed at Qumran, but is representative of a more

---

[6]   For example, "Variorum in the Psalms Scroll (11QPs^a)," 83-94; "Cave 11
Surprises," 1-15; "Qumran Psalms Scroll Reviewed," 79-99.

TABLE 1: THE CONTENTS OF 11QPs^a BY COMPOSITION*

Frags. a–e	Psalm 101	Col. XVI	→Catena	
	→102	Cols. XVI–XVII	→145	
	→103	Cols. XVII–XVIII	[+ subscript]	
	109		→154	
	118	Cols. XVIII–XIX	+ Plea for Deliverance	
	→104	Col. XIX–XX	→139	
	→147	Cols. XX–XXI	→137	
Frag. e–Col. I	→105		→138	
Cols. I–II	→146	Cols. XXI–XXII	→Sirach 51	
	→148		→Apostrophe to Zion	
	[+ 120]		→Psalm 93	
Col. III	→121	Col. XXII–XXIII	→141	
	→122		→133	
	→123	Cols. XXIII–XXIV	→144	
Cols. III–IV	→124		→155	
	→125	Col. XXIV–XXV	→142	
	→126		→143	
	→127	Col. XXV–XXVI	→149	
Cols. IV–V	→128		→150	
	→129		→Hymn to the Creator	
	→130	Col. XXVI–XXVII	→David's Last Words	
Cols. V–VI	→131		→David's Compositions	
	→132		→Psalm 140	
Cols. VI–XIV	→119	Col. XXVII–XXVIII	→134	
Cols. XIV–XV	→135		→151A	
Cols. XV–XVI	→136		→151B[end of scroll]	

*An arrow → indicates that a passage is continuous with the one listed before it. The plus sign + indicates that a passage follows the one before it, even though some text is no longer extant.

widespread form of Judaism for which the solar calender was authoritative.[7] The term "11QPs^a–Psalter" is thus to be preferred, since it is more neutral by referring to the arrangement found in the largest Psalms scroll without reaching conclusions as to its provenance. In the pages that follow, no attempt will be made to determine the provenance of the 11QPs^a–Psalter, but the evidence to be introduced will make it possible to determine whether this collection originally contained material from Psalms 1–89.

---

7   Flint, *Dead Sea Psalms Scrolls,* 199-201.

2. PSALMS SCROLLS FROM THE JUDAEAN DESERT

The Dead Sea Scrolls comprise almost 900 manuscripts written in Hebrew, Aramaic, and Greek.[8] Over 200 of these are classified as "biblical scrolls," since they contain material found in the canonical Hebrew Bible,[9] and constitute our earliest witnesses to the text of Scripture. Of all the books or works that have been identified, whether Biblical or otherwise, the Psalter is represented by the highest number of manuscripts: thirty-six from Qumran and three from other locations (see Table 2 on the following page).

When considered together, these manuscripts reveal several interesting features that are relevant for our understanding of the Psalms in the scrolls. For example, at least fifteen "apocryphal" Psalms or compositions are distributed among five Psalms manuscripts.[10] Seven of these pieces were previously familiar to scholars,[11] while the other nine were unknown prior to the discovery of the Dead Sea Scrolls.[12] A second observation is that twelve manuscripts contain major variations in comparison with the MT–150 Psalter. Differences in the *order* of Psalms alone appear in seven scrolls from Cave 4,[13] while variations in *content* (i.e. the inclusion of

---

[8]   Hartmut Stegemann previously indicated that "about 814 scrolls .... came to the museums" from Qumran ("Methods for the Reconstruction of Scrolls from Scattered Fragments," in Lawrence H. Schiffman [ed.], *Archaeology and History in the Dead Sea Scrolls. The New York University Conference in Memory of Yigael Yadin* [JSPSup 8; JSOT/ASOR Monographs 2; Sheffield: JSOT Press, 1990] 189-220, esp. 190, 208-209 n. 12). However, Stegemann has since pointed out that some manuscripts were listed together under a single Q number in certain editions, and now estimates the total number as closer to 900 (*Die Essener, Qumran, Johannes der Täufer und Jesus* [4th ed., Freiburg: Herder, 1994] 115). Martin Abegg (personal communication) arrives at a figure of 864 manuscripts for the Qumran material, which confirms Stegemann's higher estimate

[9]   Eugene Ulrich (Chief Editor of the Cave 4 Biblical Scrolls) suggests (personal communication) a number of "just on 200," while James VanderKam (*The Dead Sea Scrolls Today* [Grand Rapids: Eerdmans; London: SPCK, 1994] 30-31) estimates the number at 202 biblical scrolls, with 19 more found at other sites in the Judaean desert.

[10]   4QPs[f], 4Q522, 11QPs[a], 11QPs[b], 11QPsAp[a].

[11]   Psalms 151A, 151B, 154, 155, the Catena (most likely forming a single Psalm with 136), David's Last Words (= 2 Sam 23:1-7), and Sirach 51:13-30.

[12]   Apostrophe to Judah, Apostrophe to Zion, David's Compositions, Eschatological Hymn, Hymn to the Creator, Plea for Deliverance, Songs Against Demons.

[13]   4QPs[a], 4QPs[b], 4QPs[d], 4QPs[e], 4QPs[k], 4QPs[n], and 4QPs[q].

compositions not found in the MT) occur in two from Cave 4 and another from Cave 11.[14] Differences in both *order* and *content* are present in two manuscripts from Cave 11.[15] But we must return to the focal point of this article: are additional exemplars of the "11QPs^a–Psalter"[16] are to be found among the other thirty-eight Psalms scrolls? While most are too fragmentary for any form decision to be made, at least two more copies may be identified.

TABLE 2: THE PSALMS SCROLLS

(1) 1Q10. 1QPs^a	(14) 4Q91. 4QPs^j	(27) 4Q236. 4QPs89
(2) 1Q11. 1QPs^b	(15) 4Q92. 4QPs^k	(28) 4Q522. Place Names
(3) 1Q12. 1QPs^c	(16) 4Q93. 4QPs^l	(29) 5Q5. 5QPs
(4) 2Q14. 2QPs	(17) 4Q94. 4QPs^m	(30) pap6Q5. pap6QPs
(5) 3Q2. 3QPs	(18) 4Q95. 4QPs^n	(31) 8Q2. 8QPs
(6) 4Q83. 4QPs^a	(19) 4Q96. 4QPs^o	(32) 11Q5. 11QPs^a
(7) 4Q84. 4QPs^b	(20) 4Q97. 4QPs^p	(33) 11Q6. 11QPs^b
(8) 4Q85. 4QPs^c	(21) 4Q98. 4QPs^q	(34) 11Q7. 11QPs^c
(9) 4Q86. 4QPs^d	(22) 4Q98a. 4QPs^r	(35) 11Q8. 11QPs^d
(10) 4Q87. 4QPs^e	(23) 4Q98b. 4QPs^s	(36) 11Q11. 11QPsAp^a
(11) 4Q88. 4QPs^f	(24) 4Q98c. 4QPs^t	(37) 5/6Hev-Se4 Ps
(12) 4Q89. 4QPs^g	(25) 4Q98d. 4QPs^u	(38) MasPs^a (M1039–160)
(13) 4Q90. 4QPs^h	(26) 4Q98e. 4QPs^v(?)	(39) MasPs^b (M1103–1742)

---

3. ANOTHER COPY OF THE 11QPs^a–PSALTER FROM CAVE 11

Written in Herodian script, 11QPs^b survives in only ten fragments and dates from the first half of the first century CE.[17] The lines are written in a prose format, and the orthography may be described as expanded. In 1967, J. van der Ploeg convincingly demonstrated that this manuscript represents the Psalter found in 11QPs^a, since both share several distinctive features in contrast to the Masoretic Psalter.[18] Further fragments belonging to 11QPs^b were recently

---

[14] 4QPs^f, 4Q522, and 11QPsAp^a.

[15] 11QPs^a and 11QPs^b.

[16] For this term, see section 1 above.

[17] Van der Ploeg, "Un Manuscrit de Psaumes," 408; García Martínez and Tigchelaar, "Preliminary Edition," 75.

[18] See van der Ploeg, "Fragments d'un manuscrit," 408-12 + pl. XVIII.

identified by editors F. García Martínez and E. Tigchelaar.[19] In addition to reinforcing the relationship between 11QPs[b] and the 11QPs[a]–Psalter, these new pieces shows that this Psalter actually contains material prior to Psalm 90, as James Sanders originally proposed. Specific features that make 11QPs[b] highly significant in the present context are as follows: the inclusion of Ps 77:18–78:1; the sequence 141→133→144;[20] and portions of the Catena, the Plea for Deliverance, and the Apostrophe to Zion. The full collation of relevant variants is as follows:[21]

Catena (f. 3, lines 1–2)	Catena of Ps 118 11QPs[b] 11QPs[a]] > 𝕸 𝕲
118:15 (f. 3, line 1)	pr. v 1 [catena] 11QPs[b] and 11QPs[a]] pr. v 14 𝕸 𝕲 [Ps 117]
Plea (fs. 4–5, lines 3–16)	Plea for Deliverance 11QPs[b] 11QPs[a]] > 𝕸 𝕲
Ap. Zion (f. 6, lines 1–2)	Apostrophe to Zion 11QPs[b] 4QPs[f] 11QPs[a]] > 𝕸 𝕲
133:1 (fs. 7–10, line 2)	pr. Ps 141 11QPs[b] 11QPs[a]] pr. Ps 132 𝕸 𝕲 [131]
133:2 (fs. 7–10, line 4)	פי מדיו 11QPs[b] 11QPs[a]] פי מדותיו 𝕸; sing. 𝕲
133:3[fin] (fs. 7–10, line 5)	[עד עו]לם שלום עלן ישראל] 11QPs[b] 11QPs[a] (cf. 125:5 and 128:6)] עד העולם 𝕸 𝕲 (cf. Ken on 122:9)
144:1 (fs. 7–10, line 6)	pr. Ps 133 11QPs[b] 11QPs[a]] pr. Ps 143 𝕸 𝕲 [142]
144:1 (fs. 7–10, line 6)	[ברוך יהוה צו]רי 11QPs[b](vid.) 11QPs[a] 𝕸 [mss](Ken)] pr. לדוד 𝕸 𝕲 (+ πρὸς τὸν Γολιαδ)
144:1 (fs. 7–10, line 6)	[המלמ]ד] 11QPs[b] 11QPs[a corr] 𝕸 𝕲 (ὁ διδάσκων)] המלד 11QPs[a]*(error?)

4. A COPY OF THE 11QPs[a]–PSALTER FROM CAVE 4

My own research on the Psalms scrolls shows that Cave 4 contained at least one copy of the 11QPs[a]–Psalter in the form of 4QPs[e], which is dated on palaeographic grounds to the mid-first century CE.[22] The fragmentary condition of this manuscript requires a detailed explanation concerning its relationship to 11QPs[a], which will be followed by the preliminary edition. I then offer some concluding

---

[19] In addition to the material identified by van der Ploeg, the editors now include Pss 77:18–78:1; (?)109:3-4; 119:163-165; and the Apostrophe to Zion, vv 4-5. I am grateful to Prof. García Martínez and Dr Tigchelaar for making a draft of their edition available to me in advance of its publication in the DJD series.

[20] See cols. XVI, XIX, and XXIII of 11QPs[a]. For the siglum → see TABLE 1.

[21] The MS contains a few additional variants that are not included here.

[22] Cf. P. Flint, "Psalms Scrolls from the Judaean Desert," 40-44; *Dead Sea Psalms Scrolls*, 160-64.

comments on how this manuscript contributes to our understanding of the 11QPs^a–Psalter.

Four pieces of evidence unite to show that 4QPs^e shares with 11QPs^a the distinctive sequence of Pss 118→104→[147]→105→146, together with individual variants (cf. the RECONSTRUCTION on the next page).[23] (a) In both 4QPs^e and 11QPs^a Ps 104:1 is preceded by Ps 118. The four lines found in frag. 9 of 4QPs^e read as follows:

13   [ליהוה כי]טֺוֺב כי לֺעו]ולם חסדו]

14   [^{1} לדויד בר]כֺי נפשי אֺת יהוה יֺהֺ]וה אלוהינו גדלתה מואדה הוד והדר לבשתה ^{2}עוטה]

15   [אור כשלמֺ]ֺה נוטה שמים כי]ריעה ^{3}המקרה במים עליותיו השם עבים רכובו]

16   [המהלך על]כנפי רוחֺ] ^{4}עושה מלאכיו רוחות משרתיו אש לוהטת ^{5}יסד אֺרֺץ]

Had this manuscript conformed to the Masoretic ordering of material when it was fully extant, the words in line 11 that precede Psalm 104:1 require an explanation, since ברכי נפשי את יהוה forms the ending of Psalm 103. One possibility is that the refrain הודו ליהוה כי טוב כי לעולם חסדו belongs to Ps 103, but is simply not found in the Masoretic version. This is on the analogy of frag. e iii of 11QPs^a, where Ps 105:1 is preceded by the identical refrain at the end of Ps 147 (הודו ל𝔃𝔀𝔃𝔃 כי טוב כי [לעולם חסדו])., which is lacking in 𝔐. But there is a more plausible explanation: that line 11 is from the end of a completely different Psalm that precedes 104. The Masoretic Psalter yields only five instances of the phrase in question, of which four are at the beginning of specific Psalms (106:1; 107:1; 118:1; 136:1).[24] Only once is this refrain found at the *end* of a Psalm, namely 118:29, which precedes Ps 104 in 11QPs^a! The most likely explanation is that the four lines in 4QPs^e contain the end of Psalm 118 followed by the beginning of Psalm 104, which marks the first distinctive feature shared by 4QPs^e and 11QPs^a.

(b) This scroll supports the arrangement of Pss 104→147→105 in 11QPs^a as opposed to the MT. In 4QPs^e Ps 105 could not have followed immediately after 104, because the extant column tops and spacing require an additional piece of approximately 16 lines between 104 and 105. The only known (ancient) instance of a composition occurring between these two Psalms is found in 11QPs^a, where Ps 147 falls between 104 and 105.

---

[23] The four reconstructed columns are based on frags. 9–19 of 4QPs^e and incorporate the expanded orthography that is characteristic of this MS, as well as several variant readings found in 11QPs^a. The width of columns in this scroll is not consistent; compare I and IV (wider) with II and III (narrower).

[24] In 106:1 the refrain is preceded by הללויה.

RECONSTRUCTION OF 4QPSALMS^{e} (COLS I–IV)

Col. I: Psalms 118:[8-28 +] 29→104:1-3 [+ 4-19]

[top margin]

לחסות ביהוה מבטוח באדם [9]טוב לחסות ביהוה מבטוח בנדיבים טוב לבטוב
ביהוה מבטוח באלף עם [10]כול גויים סבבוני בשם יהוה כי אמילם [11]סבוני
גם סבבוני בשם יהוה כי אמילם [12]סבוני כדבורים דועכו כאש קוצים בשם
יהוה כי אמילם[13]דחוה דחיתני לנפול ויהוה עזרני [14]עזי וזמרת יה ויהי לי
לישועה [15]קול רנה וישועה באהלי צדיקים ימין יהוה עושה חיל [16]ימין יהוה
רומימה ימין יהוה עושה חיל [17]לוא אמות כי אחיה ואספר מעשי יה [18]יסור
יסרני יה ולמות לוא נתנני [19]פתחו לי שערי צדק אבוא בם אודה יה [20]זה השער
ליהוה צדיקים יבואו בו [21]אודכה כי עניתני ותהי לי לישועה [22]אבן מאסו
הבונים היתה לרואש פנה [23]מאית יהוה היתה זואת היא נפלאת בעינינו [24]זה
היום עשה יהוה נגילה ונשמחה בו [25]אנא יהוה הושיעה נא אנא יהוה הצליחה
נא [26]ברוכה הבא בשם יהוה ברכנוכם מבית יהוה [27]אל יהוה ויאר לנו אסורי
חג בעבותים עד קרנות המזבח [28]אלי אתה ואודכה אלוהי ארוממכה [29]הודה
[ליהוה כי]טׄוׄב כי לׄע[ולם חסדו]
[**104:1**לדויד בר]כׄי נפשי את יהוה יהׄ[וה אלוהינו גדלתה מואדה הוד והדר לבשתה [2]עוטה]
[אור כשלמ]הׄ נוטה שמים כי[ריעה [3]המקרה במים עליותיו השם עבים רכובו]
[המהלך על]כנפי רוח[[4]עושה מלאכיו רוחות משרתיו אש לוהטת [5]יסד ארץ]
על מכוניה בל תמוט עולם ועד [6]תהום כלבוש כסיתו על הרים יעמדו מים [7]מן
גערתכה ינוסון מן קול רעמכה יחפיזון [8]יעלו הרים ירדו בקעות אל מקום זה
יסדתה להם [9]גבול שמתה בל יעבורון בל ישובון לכסות הארץ [10]המשלח מעינים
בנחלים בין הרים יהלכון [11]ישקו כול חיתו שדי ישברו פראים צמאם [12]עליהם
עוף השמים ישכון מבין עפאים יתנו קול [13]משקה הרים מעליותיו מפרי מעשיכה
תשבע הארץ [14]מצמיח חציר לבהמה ועשב לעבודת האדם להוציא לחם מן
הארץ [15]ויין ישמח לבב אנוש להצהיל פנים משמן ולחם לבב אנוש יסעד [16]ישבעו
עצי יהוה ארזי לבנון אשר נטע [17]אשר שם צפרים יקננו חסידה ברושים ביתה
[18]הרים הגבוהים ליעלים סלעים מחסה לשפנים [19]עשה ירח למועדים שמש ידע

[bottom margin]

Col. II: Psalms 104:[19 +] 20-22 [+ 23-35 + 147:1-16]

top margin

[מבואו [20]תשת חושך ויהי ליל]ה בו תרמוׄש כול חית[ו]
[יער [21]הכפירים שואגים לטרף]ולבקש מאׄ[ל]אׄכׄל[ם [22]תזרח]
[השמש ויאספון ואל מעונ]ותׄמׄ[ ]יר[בצון [23]יצא אדם לפעלו]
ולעבודתו עד ערב [24]מה רבו מעשיכה יהוה כולם בחוכמה
עשיתה מלאה הארץ קנינכה [25]הים גדול ורחב ידים שמה
רמש הרבה ואין למספר חיות קטנות עם גדולות [26]שם אניות
יהלכון לויתן זה יצרתה לשחק בו [27]כולם אליכה ישברון לתת
להם אוכלם בעתו [28]תתן להם וילקטון תפתח ידכה ישבעון
טוב [29]תסתיר פניכה יבהלון תוסף רוחכה ויגועון ואל עפרם
ישובון [30]תשלח רוחכה ויבראון ותחדש פני אדמה [31]ויהי כבוד
יהוה לעולם ישמח יהוה במעשיו [32]המביט אל הארץ ותרעד
יגע בהרים ויעשנו [33]אשירה ליהוה בחיי אזמרה לאלוהי
בעודי [34]יערב עליו שיחי אנוכי אשמח ביהוה [35]כאשר יתמו
חוטאים מארץ ורשעים עוד אינם ברכי נפשי את יהוה הללויה
147:1הללויה כי טוב זמרה אלוהינו כי נעים נאוה תהלה [2]בונה
ירושלים יהוה נדחי ישראל יכנס [3]הרופא לשבורי לב ומחבש
לעצבותם [4]מונה מספר לכוכבים לכולם שמות יקרא [5]גדול
אדונינו ורב כוח לתבונתו אין מספר [6]מעודד ענוים יהוה
משפיל רשעים עדי ארץ [7]ענו ליהוה בתודה זמרו לאלוהינו
בכנור [8]המכסה שמים בעבים המכין לארץ מטר המצמיח הרים
חציר [9]נותן לבהמה לחמה לבני עורב אשר יקראו [10]לוא
בגבורת הסוס יחפץ לוא בשוקי האיש ירצה [11]רוצה יהוה את
יראיו את המיחלים לחסדו [12]שבחי ירושלים את יהוה הללי
אלוהיך ציון [13]כי חזק בריחי שעריך ברך בניך בקרבך
[14]השם גבולך שלום חלב חטים ישביעך [15]השולח אמרתו
ארץ עד מהרה ירוץ דברו [16]הנותן שלג כצמר כפור כאפר

[bottom margin]

Col. III: Pss [147:16-20 +] 105:1-3 [+ 4-22 +] 23-25 [+ 26-35]

[top margin]

Col. IV: Psalms 105:36-45→146:1 [+ 2-10 + 148:1-14]

top margin

[bottom margin]

Reconstruction[25] also indicates that 147 fits exactly in the required space in 4QPs^e. Despite the fragmentary state of the manuscript, the most logical conclusion is that 4QPs^e originally shared this sequence with 11QPs^a.

(c) The piece following Psalm 105 could be either 146 (as in 11QPs^a) or 106 (as in the MT–150 Psalter). Ps 105 is followed in 4QPs^e by just two extant words, הללו יה. In terms of the Masoretic arrangement, this would be the opening *halleluyah* of 106. But this configuration also supports the arrangement of 11QPs^a, where Ps 105 is followed by 146 with its opening *halleluyah*. Since 4QPs^e already deviates from the Masoretic order at two important places where it suggests the arrangement of 11QPs^a, it is very reasonable to identify הללו יה as the opening of Ps 146 rather than Ps 106.

(d) Individual variants indicate that 4QPs^e agrees with 11QPs^a rather than 𝔐. The three previous pieces of evidence involve macro-variants, or the arrangement of entire Psalms common to both 11QPs^a and 4QPs^e; these indicate that the sequence of Psalms 118→104[→147]→105→146 is very likely for 4QPs^e. Additional confirmation is obtained via a fourth piece of evidence: a series of individual variants, which further affirms the affinity of 4QPs^e with 11QPs^a. The relevant variants divide into three groups:

4QPs^e = 11QPs^a against 𝔐

104:1 (f. 9, line 2)	לדויד 4QPs^e(reconstructed) 11QPs^a] > 4QPs^d 𝔐
105:37 (fs. 14–19, line 1)	[ויוצא א[ת עמ]ו 4QPs^e 11QPs^a(ת עמ[ו])); cf. v 43] ויציאם 𝔐𝔊
125:4 (f. 26 i, line 4)	בלב 4QPs^e 11QPs^a 𝔊(τῇ καρδίᾳ)] בלבותם 𝔐
125:5 (f. 26 i, line 4)	עקלק' 4QPs^e* 11QPs^a] pr. והמטים 4QPs^e corr 𝔐𝔊
126:2 (f. 26 i, line 7)	בגויים 4QPs^e 11QPs^a] בגוים 𝔐 [ORTH]

4QPs^e = 𝔐 against 11QPs^a

125:5 (f. 26 i, line 4)	את פועלי 4QPs^e 𝔐(את פעלי) 𝔊(μετὰ τῶν ἐργαζ-ομένων)] את כול פועלי 11QPs^a
126:1 (f. 26 i, line 7)	כחלמים 4QPs^e 𝔐] כחלומים 11QPs^a [ORTH or VAR?]

4QPs^e corrected towards a text like 𝔐

125:5 (f. 26 i, line 4)	עקלק' 4QPs^e* 11QPs^a] pr. והמטים 4QPs^e corr 𝔐𝔊
125:5 (f. 26 i, line 4)	עקלקולים 4QPs^e*] עַקַלְקַלּוֹתָיִם(?) 4QPs^e corr; עקלקלותם 11QPs^a; עֲקַלְקַלּוֹתָם 𝔐𝔊(> suff.); cf. Jdg 5:6 [עֲקַלְקַלּוֹת])

---

[25] Reconstruction supposes columns of *ca*. 25-26 lines in length (cf. frags. 2 and 26) and varying from *c*. 35 (usually) to 44 letters (frags. 14–19) in width.

126:1 (f. 26 i, line 5)	בשוב 4QPs^e*] pr. שיר המעלות 4QPs^e corr 11QPs^a 𝔐 𝔊
126:2 (f. 26 i, line 7)	הגדיל 4QPs^e*] + יהוה 4QPs^e corr 11QPs^a 𝔐 𝔊
130:1 (f. 26 ii, lines 2–3)	ממ[עמקים] 4QPs^e*] pr. שיר המעלות 4QPs^e corr(vid.) (עול[) 11QPs^a 𝔐 𝔊

When these three groups of individual variants are weighed together, several results emerge. (a) It is evident from the first group that 4QPs^e frequently agrees with 11QPs^a against the Masoretic Text. (b) The second group shows that 4QPs^e clearly agrees with the MT–150 Psalter against 11QPs^a only once, with the omission of כול in 125:5.[26] (c) The third group indicates that the original reading of 4QPs^e has been systematically corrected towards another text. Although the last three cases could be viewed as corrections towards a text like 𝔐 or a text like 11QPs^a, the first two suggest that 4QPs^e has in fact been corrected towards the proto-Masoretic Text.[27] This suggests that all five corrections may be regarded as towards a text like 𝔐 rather than a text like 11QPs^a.

The four pieces of evidence that were presented above indicate that 4QPs^e most likely contained the same arrangement of material that is found in 11QPs^a. If this evaluation is correct, 4QPs^e is an important manuscript because it provides the first concrete evidence that an exemplar of the 11QPs^a–Psalter was stored in Cave 4. But it should not be regarded as an identical copy of 11QPs^a, although the palaeographical dating is about the same (mid-1st century CE). The corrections made in 4QPs^e suggest that it is most likely an earlier exemplar of the edition found in 11QPs^a, but has undergone subsequent correction towards a textual form similar to the one preserved in 𝔐.

5. THE PRELIMINARY EDITION OF 4QPs^e

(See Bibliography and Plates I–II)[28]

Contents and Physical Description

THE TWENTY-SIX surviving fragments preserve parts of twenty Psalms, ranging from Ps 76 to 146(?), but not always in the order of the

---

[26] כחלמים in 126:1 may be regarded as an orthographic variant.

[27] With the insertion of והמטים, and correction from עקלקולים* to a form (עקלקולתים) that seems as close as possible to 𝔐 (עֲקַלְקַלּוֹתָם).

[28] For the more detailed critical edition, see P. W. Skehan, E. Ulrich and P. W. Flint) "The Cave 4 Psalms Scrolls" (DJD 16, forthcoming).

received text. This is the only manuscript among the scrolls from the Judaean desert to preserve material from Psalms 76 and 120, although the latter piece was originally part of 11QPsᵃ as well.

TABLE 3: CONTENTS OF 4QPsᵉ

Fragment(s)	Preserved Contents
1	76:10-12; 77:1
2	78:6-7
2	78:31-33
3	81:2-3
4	86:10-11
5	88:1-5
6	89:44-48
8	89:50-53
9	118:29(?); 104:1-3
10, 11	104:20-22
12, 16 i	105:1-3
13	105:23-25
14–16 ii, 17–19	105:36-45; 146:1(?)
20	109:1(?)
21	109:8(?)
22	109:13
23	114:5(?)
24	115:15–116:3
25	120:6-7
26 i	125:2–126:5
26 ii	129:8–130:6

The leather is moderately thin and the original colour was tan with honey tones. The skin has been well-prepared on the writing (hair) side, but is somewhat coarse on the verso. The manuscript is now in a poor state of preservation, consisting mainly of small pieces. Some fragments are noticeably creased (9, 14, 24), and several have become considerably dark and brittle (10, 11, 15, 16). Much of the damage is due to moisture, although a worm-hole may be present in frag. 26. The largest extant fragment is 26, which is actually made up of several joined pieces, and measures 5.7 cm vertically, 10.1 cm horizontally, and 10.3 cm diagonally. Dry-point rulings are extremely difficult to detect, but frag. 26 ii seems to contain both a vertical line and several horizontal ones. There are no visible signs of stitching on the leather. Top margins are preserved on frags. 10 and 14; right margins on frags. 2 ii, 16 ii, 26 ii; and left margins on frags. 2i, 7?, 8, 16i, 26i. To judge from frags. 2 (Ps 78:6-33) and 26 (125:2–130:6), the complete columns must have contained 25-26 lines. The number of letter-spaces is usually *c.* 35-37 letters, but extends to *c.* 44 letters (see frags. 14–19, as well as the RECONSTRUCTION earlier in this article).

Palaeography and Orthography

The script is late Herodian (mid-1st century CE), which makes 4QPs^e roughly contemporaneous with 4QPs^c, 4QPs^g, 4QPs^j, 4QPs^q, 4QPs^s, 4QPs^t, 11QPs^a and 11QPsAp^a with respect to the date of copying. *Keraiai* are regularly found with *ʾalep* and *nun*, and final *mem* is elongated. The orthography is expanded, with generous use of *waw* and *yod* as vowel letters (but contrast כחלמים in 126:1 with כחלמים 𝔐; כחלומים 11QPs^a).

TABLE 4: ORTHOGRAPHY

Frag., line	Psalm	4QPs^e	11QPs^a	𝔐
1 2	76:11	חימות		חֵמֹת
1 3	76:12	יבילו		יוֹבִילוּ
3 2	81:3	תֹוף		תֹף
8 1	89:50	א[דֹ]וני		אֲדֹנָי
8 2	89:51	אדוני		אֲדֹנָי
10 1	104:20	תרמושׂ		תִּרְמֹשׂ
24 2	115:17	לוא		לֹא
26 i 6	126:1	כחלמים	כחלומים	כְּחֹלְמִים
26 i 7	126:2	בֿגוייֿם	בגויים	בַגּוֹיִם
26 i 8	126:4	שבה		שׁוּבָה

Format and Textual Character

This manuscript was written in prose format and contains several corrections in the form of changes and additions. The fact that all of these are on frag. 26 raises several intriguing questions. For example, why does the corrector seem to concentrate only on one section of the document? Was he particularly concerned with the Psalms of Ascent, several of which are represented in this fragment? Alternatively, could the concentration of corrections on this one piece imply that it represents an entirely separate manuscript that was written in the same hand? It is beyond the scope of the present article to answer these important and complex questions.

TABLE 5: CORRECTIONS IN 4QPs^e

Fr., line	Psalm	4QPs^c*	4QPs^ecorr	11QPs^a	𝔐
26 i 3	125:3	ידם	ידים	——	ידיהם
26 i 4	125:5	עקלק׳	pr. והמטים	עקלק׳	pr. והמטים
26 i 4	125:5	עקלקולים	(?)עקלקולחים	עקלקולות	עֲקַלְקַלּוֹתָם
26 i 5	126:1	בשוב	pr. שיר המעלות	pr. שיר המעלות	pr. שיר המעלות
26 i 7	126:2	הגדיל	יהוה +	יהוה +	יהוה +
26 ii 2–3	130:1	pr. [ממ]עמקים	(?)עול[ות] pr.	pr. שיר המעלות	pr. שיר המעלות

The preserved pieces of 4QPs^e share several significant readings with 11QPs^a. The most striking of these is the sequence of Psalms 118?-104-147-105, which is in contrast to the received text and to 4QPs^d (106?-147-104); details of this arrangement have been given in the first part of this article.[29] Other readings are more specific; for example, בלב in 125:4, which is found in 4QPs^e and 11QPs^a and supported by the Septuagint 𝕲 (τῇ καρδίᾳ); compare בלבותם found in 𝔐. Such evidence leads to the conclusion that 4QPs^e and 11QPs^a are in fact copies of the same Psalter (but not identical copies).[30]

Mus. Inv. 263   PAM 43.028

Misc. 40.618, 41.283, 41.287, 42.027, 42.029, 42.718, 42.719

Frag. 1   Psalms 76:10-12; 77:1

[אלוהים ל]הושיע[כול עני ארץ סרה ¹¹	1
[שא]רית חימות[תחגר ¹²	2
[אלוהיכם כול ס]ביביו יבילו [שי למורא ¹³	3
[נורא למלכי ארץ] vacat	4
[⁷⁷:¹למנצח על ידיתון]לאסו[ף מזמור	5

L. 5 (77:1) The positioning of the fragment can be calculated because since in this MS most new Psalms start at or near the right margin (cf. frags. 12 [Ps 105], 16 ii [Ps 146], 26 ii [Ps 130]). However, one of the Psalms of Ascent commences in the middle of a line (cf. frag. 26 i [Ps 126]).

---

[29] See section 4 above ("A Copy of the 11QPs^a–Psalter from Cave 4").

[30] See Flint, *Dead Sea Psalms Scrolls,* 160-64.

Frag. 2, col. i   Psalm 78:6-7

⁶למען ידעו דור אח]רון	]	1
⁷וישימו באלהים כ]סלם	]	2

The left margin is preserved for this column.

Frag. 2, col. ii   Psalm 78:31-33

³²משמנ̊יהם ובחורי ישראל הכריע	1
³³ולוא ה]אמינו בנפלאותיו	2
³⁴בבהל]ה	3

The right margin is preserved for this column.

L. 1 (78:31). משמנ̊יהם. Microscopic examination reveals traces of *nun*, although it is not visible on the photograph.

VARIANT

78:31 (f. 2 ii, line 1)   4QPs^e משמנ̊יהם [𝔐𝔊 במשמניהם

Frag. 3   Psalm 81:2-3

[⁸¹:¹]למנצח על הגתית לאסף ²ה]רנינו [לאלהים עוזנו הריעו]	1
[לאלהי יעקוב ³שאו זמרה ותנו]ת̊ו̊ף [כנור נעים עם נבל]	2

The blank leather on the left side does not indicate a left margin, since this manuscript often features gaps between words.

L. 1 (81:1). Psalm 81 began at or near the right margin.

Frag. 4   Psalm 86:10-11

¹¹אתה אלהים לבד]ך̊	1
¹²]ליר̊]אה שמך	2

Frag. 5   Psalm 88:1-5

משכיל]ל̊היםן האזר]חי	1
בליל]ה̊ נגדכה ³תבוא̊ לפניך	2
⁴כי שב]עה ברעות]	3
עם יור]ד̊י בור]ה̊]ייתי כגבר	4

Frags. 6, 7   Psalm 89:44-48

[אף תשיב צור חרבו ולא הקימותו]‎ ⁴⁵ל‌ֿמלחמה ה‌ֿ[שבת]   1

[מטהרו וכסאו לארץ מגרתה ⁴⁶הקצ]‌ֿרתה ימ‌ֿי עלומ[יו]   2

[העטית עליו בושה סלה ⁴⁷עד מה יהוה תסתו]ֿ‌ר לנצח   3

[תבער כמו־אש חמתך ⁴⁸זכר אני מה חלד על מה שו]א‌ֿ   4

The blank leather on the left sides of lines 3 and 4 indicates a probable left margin.

L. 1 (89:44) למלחמה. The top arm of *lamed* 1° is no longer extant due to the surface damage of the leather. For similar occurrences of the rather straight lower leg of letter, see *lamed* 2° in the same word and that in לבה[ך] (frag. 4 1).

VARIANTS

89:44 (f. 6, line 1)   למלחמה 4QPsᵉ] במלחמה 𝔐𝔊

Frag. 8   Psalm 89:50-53

[שאול סלה ⁵⁰איה חסדיך הראשונים א]ֿ‌דוני   1

[נשבעת לדויד באמונתך ⁵¹זכו]ֿ‌ר אדוני חרפת   2

[עבדיך שאתי בחיקי כול רבים עמים ⁵²]אשר חרפו   3

[אויביך יהוה אשר חרפו עקבות מ]שֿ‌יחכה ⁵³ברו‌ֿ[ך]   4

The left margin is preserved for this column.

L. 3-4 (89:51-53) The text found in is *c.* 6 letters too long for line 3 and *c.* 4 letters too long for line 4 in this format.

Frag. 9   Psalm 118:29(?) + 104:1-3

[ליהוה כי]טֿ‌וב כי ל‌ֿ[ע]ו[לם חסדו]   13

[¹⁰⁴:¹]לדויד בר]ֿ‌כי נפשי את יהוה י‌ֿ[ה]ו‌ֿה אלהי גדלת מאד הוד והדר לבשת]   14

[²עוטה אור כשלמ]ֿ‌ה נוטה שמים כי]ֿ‌ריעה ³המקרה במים עליותיו השם עבים]   15

[רכובו המהלך על]כנפי רוח] ⁴עושה מלאכיו רוחות משרתיו אש   16

The alignment of this fragment is possible because Ps 104 began at or near the right margin.

L. 2 (104:1) בר]ֿ‌כי. The left bottom tip of *kap* is barely visible on the photograph but confirmed by microscopic examination of the leather.

VARIANT

104:1 (f. 9, line 2)   pr. Ps 118 4QPs^e(?) 11QPs^a] pr. Ps 147 4QPs^d; pr. Ps 103 𝔐𝔊 [102]

104:2 (f. 9, line 3)   [כשלמ]ה נוטה שמים כי]ריעה] 4QPs^e 4QPs^dcorr 11QPs^a 𝔐𝔊] כשלמה 4QPs^d*

Frags. 10, 11   Psalm 104:20-22

top margin

ויהי ליל]ה בו תרמוש כול חיתו]ו יער   1

לטרף]ולבקש מא]ל א]כלם 22   2

[ירֹ]בצון   [∘∘]   23   3

The top margin is preserved for this column

Frags. 12, 16 col. i   Psalm 105:1-3

[הוד ליהוה קראו ב]שמו הוד]יעו בעמים עלילותי 2שירו לו זמר]ו   1

[לו שחו בכול נפלאו]תיו 3התה]ללו בשם קדשו ישמח]לב   2

One letter from the left margin of this column is extant.

VARIANTS

105:1 (fs. 12, 16 i, line 1)   pr. Ps 147 4QPs^e[reconstr.] 11QPs^a] pr. Ps 104 𝔐𝔊 [103]

Frag. 13   Psalm 105:23-25

[מצרים י]עקב   1

[מצריו 25ה]פך   2

Frags. 14–16 col. ii, 17–19   Ps 105:36-45 + 146:1(?)

top margin

[36וי]ך כל בכור בארצ]ם 37ראשית לכ]ל אונם ויוצא עמ]ו בכסף וזהב]   1

[ואי]ן בשבטי]ו] כושל 38שמחו מ]צרי]ם בצאתם כי נפל פח]דם עליהם]   2

[39פרש]ענן למסך ואש להאיר [לי]לה 40שא]ל ו]י]בא שלו ולחם]   3

[ש]מים י]שביעם 41פתח צור ויזובו [מים]הלכו בציות נ]הר 42כי [זכר את]   4

דבר קוד[שו]את[אברהם עבדו ⁴³ויוצא ע[מו בש[שון ברנה]   5

את בחיר[יו ⁴⁴ויתן להם א[רצות ג]וים ועמל לאמים יירשו ⁴⁵בעבור]   6

ישמר[ו חקיו ותורתיו י[נצרו]ו הללו יה]   7

הלליה[¹⁴⁶:¹   8

The top and right margins are preserved for this column.

VARIANTS

105:1 (fs. 12, 16 i, line 1)	pr. Ps 147 4QPsᵉ[reconstr.] 11QPsᵃ **]** pr. Ps 104 𝔐𝔊[103]
105:37 (fs. 14–19, line 1)	ויוצא א[ת עמו 4QPsᵉ 11QPsᵃ(ויוצא א[ת עמו]); cf. v 43 **]** 𝔐𝔊 ויציאם
105:38 (fs. 14–19, line 2)	שמחו 4QPsᵉ **]** 𝔐𝔊 שמח
146:1 (fs. 14–19, line 8)	pr. Ps 105 4QPsᵉ(?) 11QPsᵃ **]** pr. Ps 145 𝔐𝔊[144]

Frag. 20   Psalm 109:1(?)

]∘∘[1

[למנצח לד[ו]ד מזמו]ר   2

Frag. 21   Psalm 109:8(?)

פקדתו] יקח[אחר   1

Frag. 22   Psalm 109:13

¹³יהי אחרי[תו להכרית[1

]∘[2

Frag. 23   Psalm 114:5(?)

⁵מה לך הים כי]תנוס [הירדן   1

Frag. 24   Psalms 115:15–116:3

[¹⁵ברוכים אתם ליהוה]ע[שה שמים [וארץ ¹⁶השמים]   1

[שמים ליהוה והארץ נתן לבנ[י אדם ¹⁷לוא מתים יהל[לו יה ולא]   2

[כל ירדי דומה ¹⁸ואנחנו נברך יה מ[עתה ועד עולם הל[לו יה]   3

4   [116:1]אהבתי כי ישמע יהוה את קולי]תחנוני 2כי הטה א[זנו לי ובימי]

5   [אקרא 3אפפוני חבלי מות ומצרי שא]ול מצאוני צרה ו[יגון אמצא]

VARIANTS

115:17 (f. 24, line 2)   𝔐 לא המתים] 4QPse 𝔊mss(οὐχὶ νεκροί) לוא מתים
𝔊(οὐχ οἱ νεκροί)

Frag. 25   Psalm 120:6-7

1   ]∘[

2   6ר]בת שכנה לנפ[שי

3   ]∘∘ל[

L. 2 (120:6) לנפ[שי The dark spot on the photo to the left of the base of *pe* is
due to leather damage, not ink.

VARIANTS

120:6 (f. 25, line 2)   𝔊 לה >; 𝔐 לה נפשי] 4QPse לנפ[שי

Frag. 26, col. i   Psalms 125:2–126:5

1   [סביב לה ויהוה לע]מו סביב מעתה ועד ע]ולם 3[כי לו]א

2   [ינוח ש]בט הרשע על גורל הצדיקים למען ל]א[

3   [ישלחו]הצדיקים בעולתה יד ם 4היטיבה יהו]ה לטו[בים
                   5והמטים ת

4   [ולישר]ים בלב עקלקלים יוליכם יהוה את פועלי
                   126:1שיר המעלות

5   [האון ש]ל]ו[ם על ישראל   בשוב יה]וה]את שבות

6   [ציון היינו]כחלמים 2אז ימלא שחוק פינו ול]שו[נ]ו רנה
                        יהוה

7   [אז יאמרו]בגויים הגדיל לעשות עם אלה 3הגדיל

8   [יהוה לעשות עמנו]היינו שמחים 4שבה יהוה]א[ת

9   [שבותנו כאפיקים]בנגב 5הזורעים בד]מ[ה]ברנה]

10   ]∘∘[

The left margin is preserved for this column.

VARIANTS

125:2 (f. 26 i, line 1)   𝔐𝔊 tr. סביב לעמו] 4QPse [לע]מו סביב

125:3 (f. 26 i, line 3)   ידם 4QPs^e*] ידים 4QPs^e corr (= יְדֵים or יָדֵים [?], cf. 125:5); ידיהם 𝔐𝔊

125:4 (f. 26 i, line 4)   בלב 4QPs^e 11QPs^a 𝔊(τῇ καρδίᾳ)] בלבותם 𝔐

125:5 (f. 26 i, line 4)   עקלקל׳ 4QPs^e* 11QPs^a] pr. והמטים 4QPs^e corr 𝔐𝔊

125:5 (f. 26 i, line 4)   עקלקולים 4QPs^e*] עקלקולֹהֵים 4QPs^e corr (?); עֲקַלְקַלוֹתָם 11QPs^a; עקלקלות 𝔐𝔊(> suffix [εἰς τὰς στραγγαλιάς]); cf. Judges 5:6 [עֲקַלְקַלּוֹת])

125:5 (f. 26 i, line 4)   את פועלי 4QPs^e 𝔐(את פֹעֲלֵי)𝔊(μετὰ τῶν ἐργαζομένων)] את כול פועלי 11QPs^a

126:1 (f. 26 i, line 5)   בשוב 4QPs^e*] pr. שיר המעלות 4QPs^e corr 11QPs^a 𝔐𝔊

126:1 (f. 26 i, line 5)   שיבת 4QPs^e 𝔐^mss𝔊(αἰχμαλωσίαν)] שבות (√ שבה) 4QPs^e 𝔐^ms(√ שבה) שבית 𝔐;(√ ישב or √ שוב)

126:2 (f. 26 i, line 7)   הגדיל 4QPs^e*] + יהוה 4QPs^e corr 11QPs^a 𝔐𝔊

Frag. 26, col. ii   Psalms 129:8–130:6

[אמר]ו העברים ברכת יהוה אליכם ברכנו אתכם בשם]   1

יהו̇ה   2
           ^130:1 [עול]ות]
ממ[עמקים קראתיך יהוה ^2 אדני שמעה בקולי תהיינה אזניך]   3

קש[ו]בות לקול תחנוני ^3 אם עונות תשמר יה אדני מי]   4

יע[מד ^4 כי עמך הסליחה למען תורא ^5 קויתי יהוה]   5

[קותה נפשי ולדברו הוחלתי ^6 נפשי לאדני]   6

כש[ו]מרים לבקר שמרים לבקר ^7 יחל ישראל   [7

                [   ]°   8

The right margin is preserved for this column.

L. 3 (130:7) [עול]ות]. The corrector or supplemntor may have inserted שיר and המ at the end of the previous line (so as to produce the heading שיר המעולות), but this is problematic in view of the new Psalm beginning on line 3.

L. 8 (130:7)]°. This letter may be the *yod* of יהוה or the *kap* of כי which follows.

VARIANTS

130:1 (f. 26 ii, lines 2–3)   [ממ[עמקים 4QPs^e*] pr. שיר המעלות 4QPs^e corr (vid.) עול) 11QPs^a 𝔐𝔊 (|]

130:6 (f. 26 ii, line 7)   [כש[ו]מרים 4QPs^e] שמרים 𝔐; = מש)ו(מרים 𝔊 (or מאשמרת, cf. BHS^app)

6. SOME BRIEF CONCLUSIONS

How do the two additional copies of the "11QPs^a–Psalter" that have been identified (11QPs^b and 4QPs^e) advance our understanding of this collection? First, the presence of Ps 77:18–78:1 in 11QPs^b shows that the 11QPs^a–Psalter does contains material prior to Psalm 90, as James Sanders originally proposed. This observation is stongly reinforced by 4QPs^e, which preserves Psalms 76:10-12; 77:1; 78:6-7, 31-33; 81:2-3; 86:10-11; 88:1-5; and 89:44-48, 50-53.

Second, 4QPs^e contributes further towards our understanding of the 11QPs^a–Psalter by incorporating material that is missing from 11QPs^a. The presence of words or verses from Psalms 114–116 and 120 (frags. 23-25) suggests that these Psalms were originally part of 11QPs^a, with the first three between frags. d and e and Ps 120 in the missing part of col. II (cf. Table 1). It is beyond the scope of the present article to offer a full reconstruction of 11QPs^a, which I have published elsewhere,[31] but the evidence provided by 4QPs^e and 11QPs^b have proved most helpful in arriving at the following outline for the entire manuscript when it was copied.[32]

TABLE 6: STRUCTURAL OUTLINE OF 11QPs^a

Mainly Davidic Pieces (5)	101→102→103→109→[110]
Passover Hallel (6)	[113]→114→115→116→[117]→118
הללויה / הודו Psalms (5)	104→147→105→146→148
Psalms of Ascent (13)	120→121→122→123→124→125→126→127 →128→129→130→131→132
Wisdom Psalm (1)	119
Hymns of Praise (3)	135→136(with Catena)→145(with subscript)
Deliverance/Supplication (4)	154→Plea for Deliverance→139→137
Praise or Wisdom (4)	138→Sirach 51→Apostrophe to Zion→ 93
Mostly Supplication (6)	141→133→144→155→142→143
Liturgical Grouping (4)	149→150→Hymn to Creator→David's Last Words
Mainly Davidic Pieces (5)	David's Comp→Ps 140→134→151A→151B

---

[31] Flint, *Dead Sea Psalms Scrolls,* 172-201, esp. 189-98.

[32] Flint, *Dead Sea Psalms Scrolls,* 190, 192. This arrangement indicates that for 4QPs^e frags. 20–24 (which contain remnants of Psalms 109 and 114–116) should be placed between frags. 8 and 9. This has not been done for the preliminary edition in this article, but will probably be adopted for the critical edition in the DJD series.

While the earlier part of this Psalter is not found in 11QPs[a],[33] we shall presently see that both 4QPs[e] and 11QPs[b] preserve material from Psalms 1–89 and the arrangement evident in 11QPs[a]. According to Patrick Skehan,[34] the 11QPs[a]–Psalter is represented in only two manuscripts from Cave 11, namely 11QPs[a] and 11QPs[b]. This Chapter will demonstrate that at least one more exemplar was also stored in Cave 4 in the form of 4QPs[e].

---

[33]   And probably never was; cf. section 3 above ("The Original Contents of 11QPs[a]").

[34]   "Qumran and Old Testament Criticism," 165-67.

7. SELECT BIBLIOGRAPHY

Editions of the Psalms Scrolls Discussed:

García Martínez, F. and E. J. C. Tigchelaar. "Psalms Manuscripts from Qumran Cave 11: A Preliminary Edition," in F. García Martínez and É. Puech (eds.), *Hommage à Józef T. Milik, RevQ* 65-68 (1996) 73–107.

García Martínez, F., E. J. C. Tigchelaar and A. S. van der Woude. "Four Psalms Scrolls from Cave 11." [DJD 23; Oxford: Clarendon Press, forthcoming]

Ploeg, J. P. M. van der. "Fragments d'un manuscrit de Psaumes de Qumran (11QPs^b)," *RB* 74 (1967) 408–12 + pl. XVIII.

Sanders, J. A. *The Psalms Scroll of Qumrân Cave 11* [11QPs^a] (DJD 4; Oxford: Clarendon Press, 1965).

——. *The Dead Sea Psalms Scroll* (Ithaca: Cornell University Press, 1967).

Skehan, P. W., E. Ulrich, and P. W. Flint. "The Cave 4 Psalms Scrolls." [DJD 16; Oxford: Clarendon Press, forthcoming]

Reference Works and Secondary Literature:

Fitzmyer, J. A. *The Dead Sea Scrolls. Major Publications and Tools for Study* (rev. ed., SBLRBS 20; Atlanta: Scholars Press, 1990).

Flint, Peter W. "The Psalters at Qumran and the Book of Psalms." Ph. D. Dissertation, University of Notre Dame, USA (1993).

——. "The Psalms Scrolls from the Judaean Desert: Relationships and Textual Affilations," in George J. Brooke (ed.), *New Qumran Texts & Studies. Proceedings of the First Meeting of the International Organization for Qumran Studies, Paris 1992* (STDJ 15; Leiden: Brill, 1994) 31–52.

——. "Methods for Determining Relationships Among the Dead Sea Psalms Scrolls," in M. O. Wise et al (eds.), *Methods of Investigation of the Dead Sea Scrolls and the Khirbet Qumran Site: Present Realities and Future Prospects* (Annals of the New York Academy of Sciences 722; New York: New York Academy of Sciences, 1994) 197–209 + 210–211 (discussion).

——. "Of Psalms and Psalters: James Sanders' Investigation of the Psalms Scrolls," in Richard D. Weis and David M. Carr (eds.), *A Gift of God in Due Season: Essays on Scripture and Community in Honor of James A. Sanders* (JSOTSup 225; Sheffield Academic Press, 1996) 65–83.

——. *The Dead Sea Psalms Scrolls and the Book of Psalms* (STDJ 17; Leiden: Brill, 1997).

Ploeg, J. P. M. van der. "L'Édition des Manuscrits de la Grotte XI de Qumrân par l'Académie Royale des Sciences des Pays-Bas," in P. W. Pestman (ed.), *Acta Orientalia Neerlandica: Proceedings of the Congress of the Dutch Oriental Society, Held in Leiden on the Occasion of Its 50th Anniversary, 8th–9th May 1970* (Leiden: Brill, 1972) 43–45.

——. "Les manuscrits de la Grotte XI de Qumrân," *RevQ* 45 (1985) 3–15.

Reed, S. A., revised by M. J. Lundberg with the collaboration of M. J. Phelps. *The Dead Sea Scrolls Catalogue: Documents, Photographs and Museum Inventory Numbers* (SBLRBS 32; Atlanta: Scholars Press, 1994).

Sanders, J. A. "Pre-Masoretic Psalter Texts," *CBQ* 27 (1965) 114–23, esp. 116.

——. "Variorum in the Psalms Scroll (11QPsᵃ)," *HTR* 59 (1966) 83–94.

——. "The Ancient Versions of the Old Testament," in *PCB* (1967) 81–85.

——. "Cave 11 Surprises and the Question of Canon," *McCQ* 21 (1968) 1–15. Reprinted in D. N. Freedman, and J. C. Greenfield (eds.), *New Directions in Biblical Archaeology* (Garden City, NY: Doubleday, 1969) 101–116; and in Sid Z. Leiman, *The Canon and Masorah of the Hebrew Bible. An Introductory Reader* (New York: Ktav, 1974) 37–51.

——. "The Qumran Psalms Scroll (11QPsᵃ) Reviewed," in M. Black and W. A. Smalley (eds.), *On Language, Culture, and Religion: In Honor of Eugene A. Nida* (The Hague and Paris: Mouton, 1974) 79–99.

——. "Psalm 154 Revisited," in G. Braulik, W. Gross, and S. McEvenue (eds.), *Biblische Theologie und gesellschaftlicher Wandel. Für Norbert Lohfink S.J.* (Freiburg: Herder, 1993) 296–306.

Skehan, P. W. "Littérature de Qumran—A. Textes bibliques," *Supplément au Dictionnaire de la Bible* (1978) 9/10.805–22, esp. 813–17.

——. "Qumran and Old Testament Criticism," in M. Delcor (ed.), *Qumrân. Sa piété, sa théologie et son milieu* (BETL 46; Paris: Éditions Duculot; Leuven: Leuven University Press, 1978) 163–82.

Ulrich, E. "The Bible in the Making: The Scriptures at Qumran," in E. Ulrich and J. VanderKam (eds.), *The Community of the Renewed Covenant: The Notre Dame Symposium on the Dead Sea Scrolls* (Notre Dame: University of Notre Dame Press, 1994), 77–93.

——. "Multiple Literary Editions: Reflections toward a Theory of the History of the Biblical Text," in D. Parry and S. Ricks (eds.), *Current Research and Technological Developments on the Dead Sea Scrolls: Conference on the Texts from the Judean Desert, Jerusalem, 30 April 1995* (STDJ 20; Leiden: Brill) 78–105 + pls. I–II.

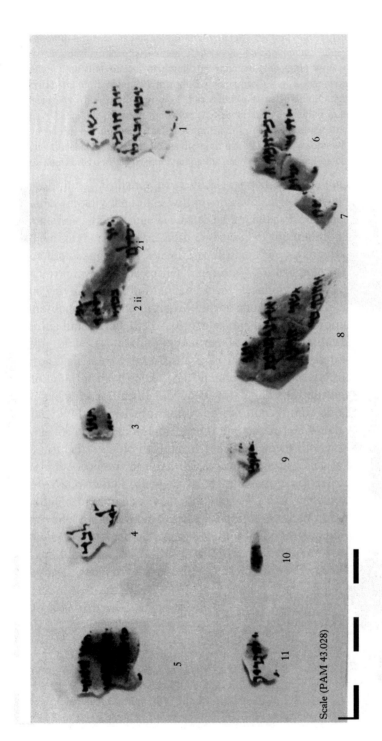

Scale (PAM 43.028)

Plate 1: 4QPs[e]

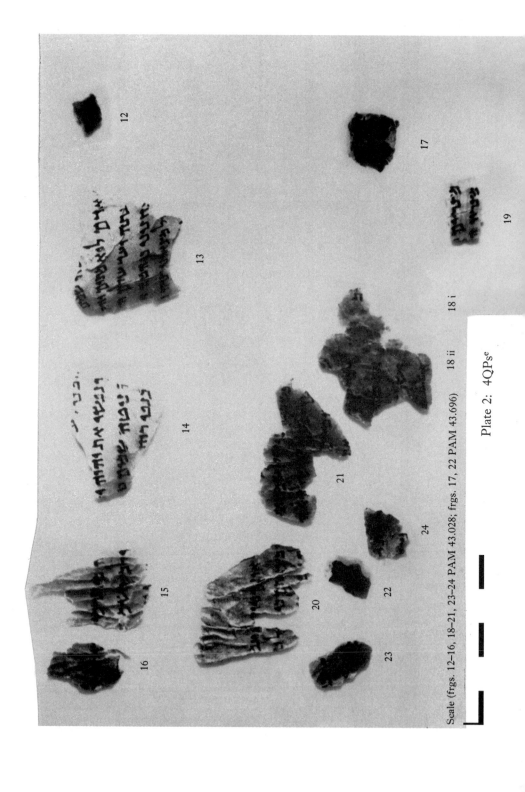

Scale (frgs. 12–16, 18–21, 23–24 PAM 43.028; frgs. 17, 22 PAM 43.696)   18 ii   18 i

Plate 2: 4QPs^e

26 ii   26 i

25

Scale (PAM 43.028)

Plate 3: 4QPs^e

INTERTEXTUALITY:
ISAIAH 40:3 AND THE SEREK HA-YAḤAD

James H. Charlesworth

In the Rule of the Community Isa 40:3 is introduced without citing the biblical source; but the origin of the citation is certain and the well-known scriptural formula כאשר כתוב, "as it is written," is used (1QS 8:14).[1] The formula clarifies that "the Men of the Community" (אנשי היחד [1QS 8:16]) are shaped by their interpretation and devotion to כתוב, what is written; that is, sacred Scripture. In the Rule of the Community we are confronted with both the People of the Book and what they have left us, the Book of the People,[2] which signifies the unity and organic development of what we unwisely have separated into canonical (1QIsaᵃ) and noncanonical (1QS) works. The Qumranites hid in Cave 1 both of these scrolls (1QIsaᵃ and 1QS) so that the Roman army, approaching from the north, could not destroy them. These leather manuscripts contained what the Qumranites believed to be God's Word—and God's Word directed to them at the End of Time.

The purpose of this chapter is to approach the Qumranites' world in light of what may be learned from intertextuality. As is well known,[3] this methodology was developed from J. Kristeva's

---

1   For texts and translations of, with introductions to, of all copies of the Rule of the Community, see J. H. Charlesworth, with F. M. Cross, J. Milgrom, E. Qimron, L. H. Schiffman, L. T. Stuckenbruck, and R. E. Whitaker, *Rule of the Community and Related Documents* (Princeton Theological Seminary Dead Sea Scrolls Project 1; Tübingen: Mohr [Siebeck]; Louisville: Westminster John Knox, 1994). For concorded materials, see J. H. Charlesworth et al., *Graphic Concordance to the Dead Sea Scrolls* (Tübingen: Mohr [Siebeck]; Louisville: Westminster/John Knox Press, 1991).

2   I am indebted to my colleague Shemaryahu Talmon for discussions on "the People of the Book" and "the Book of the People." The terms are interdependent; one without the other can be misleading.

3   See the discussion by R. P. Carroll, "Intertextuality and the Book of Jeremiah: Animadversions on Text and Theory," in J. C. Exum and D. J. A. Clines (eds.), *The New Literary Criticism and the Hebrew Bible* (Valley Forge:

"intertextualité," which resulted from her study of the Russian literary critic M. Bakhtin.[4] It seems to me singularly appropriate to dedicate my reflections to a mentor and friend for over thirty years. James A. Sanders was "from the beginning" of my career a faithful friend who had lived empathetically in the Qumran scriptorium (if only intermittently and imaginatively). Our perceptions of the biblical world were partially shaped (intertextually) as we studied the poetry and hymns of the Qumranites. He edited the Qumran Psalms Scroll; I edited the *Odes of Solomon*,[5] which is the earliest Christian hymnbook and may have been composed by an Essene who became a Christian.[6] He and I contributed jointly "More Psalms of David" to the *Old Testament Pseudepigrapha*.[7] And he was the first who mentioned "intertextuality" to me. As I think and write this chapter, I will frequently relive many precious moments shared here in America and in Israel with him. May he find some joy in my reflections and the intertextual dimension of our lives. We have both stressed that texts obtain life and vitality because of their connections with other texts with which they share a particular world of meaning, but also that each text has its own integrity which must not be lost through any form of comparison.[8]

Trinity Press International, 1994) 55-78; esp. see pp. 56-58. Also, see the notes that follow.

[4]   J. Kristeva, "Bakhtine, le mot, le dialogue et le roman," *Critique* 33 (1967) 438-65.

[5]   J. H. Charlesworth, *The Odes of Solomon* (Oxford: Oxford University Press, 1973; repr. SBLTT 13: Pseudepigrapha Series 7; Missoula: Scholars Press, 1978); idem, "Odes of Solomon," in Charlesworth (ed.), *The Old Testament Pseudepigrapha* (2 vols., ABRL 13-14; New York: Doubleday, 1983-85) 2.725-71.

[6]   See esp. J. Carmignac, "Un qumrânien converti au christianisme: l'auteur des Odes de Salomon," in H. Bardtke (ed.), *Qumran-Probleme* (Deutsche Akademie der Wissenschaften zu Berlin 42; Berlin: Akademie-Verlag, 1963) 75-108; J. H. Charlesworth, "Les Odes de Salomon et les manuscrits de la mer morte," *RB* 77 (1970) 522-49; J. A. Emerton, "The Odes of Solomon," in H. F. D. Sparks (ed.), *The Apocryphal Old Testament* (Oxford: Clarendon, 1984) 683-731.

[7]   J. H. Charlesworth and J. A. Sanders, "More Psalms of David," in Charlesworth (ed.), *The Old Testament Pseudepigrapha*, 2.609-24.

[8]   I imagine that in that sense we would both disagree with C. Grivel ("Thèses préparatoires sur les intertextes," in R. Lachmann (ed.), *Dialogizität* [Munich: Fink, 1982] 237-48, here p. 240) that "Il n'est de texte que d'intertexte."

INTRODUCTION
DEFINING INTETEXTUALITY

It is obvious that scholars a generation or so younger than Professor Sanders and I have made "intertextuality" vogue. At the same
time it is equally evident that competing and confusing definitions of
intertextuality are being employed. As H. F. Plett states, "Currently,
'intertextuality' is a fashionable term, but almost everybody who uses
it understands it somewhat differently."[9] Biblical scholars may be
divided into three groups: the "progressives," those, like the semio-
ticians, who are preoccupied with this methodology; the "traditional-
ists," those like the analytically and biblically trained translation
specialists, who find it is consonant with other methods of historical
criticism; and the "anti-intertextualists," those who are against
intertextuality because they consider it a confused methodology or
because they find it a too faddish name for what they have been
doing for decades.[10] If such characterizations are apposite, then I
certainly belong mostly in the second and partly in the third group,
in the sense that intertextuality helps refine and focus a methodology
that I have been using since the sixties.[11] A methodology quite similar
to intertextuality can be found, albeit *in nuce*, in such seminal works
as J. Barr's *The Semantics of Biblical Language*,[12] J. Licht's *Story-*

---

[9]   H. F. Plett, "Intertextualities," in Plett (ed.), *Intertextuality* (New York: de
Gruyter, 1991) 3-29; see the bibliography on pp. 27-29.

[10]   In these reflections I am indebted to H. F. Plett's comments in his
Intertextuality, 3-5.

[11]   J. Clayton and E. Rothstein offer the opinion, that "the new and voguish
'intertextuality' has served as a generational marker for younger critics who end up
doing very much what their elders do with influence and its partners, like 'context',
'allusion', and 'tradition'." This judgment is true only to a certain extent. Intertextuality may provide a more coherent methodology that opens up new vistas and
perceptions of the orginative force and creativity, as well as the literary world, of a
text. But that is what I shall attempt to demonstrate in this chapter. See Clayton and
Rothstein, "Figures in the Corpus: Theories of Influence and Intertextuality," in
Clayton and Rothstein (eds.), *Influence and Intertextuality in Literary History*
(Madison: University of Wisconsin Press, 1991) 3-36; see esp. 3.

[12]   J. Barr, *The Semantics of Biblical Language* (London: SCM; Philadelphia:
Trinity Press International, 1983, 1991 [orig. 1961]). Certainly on target and what
may be called an understanding of intertextuality that predates the method is Barr's
call for "a reinterpretation of the New Testament in terms of its setting in the
Hebraic mind, rather than in terms of its Hellenic affinities . . ." (p. 6).

telling in the Bible,[13] and G. Schille's *Frühchristliche Hymnen*.[14]

What is new about the method called intertextuality? In contrast to the older methodologies, such as *Redaktionsgeschichte* and Source Criticism, by which we study the influences of sources and editors on a text in focus, intertextuality enables us to understand a text as a complex network both within itself and then without in relation to other texts which are not only pretexts to it but intertexts to many others.[15] The intertext comes alive because of a world of literature with which it is almost inexhaustibly connected.[16] Thus, in contrast to earlier methodologies which examined the relation between a text and its sources, intertextuality helps us study the function and impact of a text or texts in a focal text.[17]

I do contend that our task as biblical exegetes is to focus on a particular text, without losing perspective of the social and literary context; thus we can understand the putative author and so comprehend his (or her) meaning, by careful, judicious, and where possible perspicacious use of historical, philological, and other methods such as sociology. We must avoid myopic focus on methodology in the concerted effort "to place textual and intertextual concerns within a comprehensive theoretical framework."[18] We must also see what is

---

[13]   J. Licht, *Storytelling in the Bible* (Jerusalem: Magnes Press, 1978; 2nd ed., 1986). Licht, *inter alia*, intends to show "that repetitions and repetitive situations can be used to produce various mimetic effects in the narrative convention of the Hebrew Bible" (p. 79). This method is not far removed from intertextuality.

[14]   G. Schille, *Früchristliche Hymnen* (Berlin: Evangelische Verlagsanstalt, 1965).

[15]   See esp. W. S. Vorster, "Intertextuality and Redaktionsgeschichte," in S. Draisma (ed.), *Intertextuality in Biblical Writings: Essays in Honour of Bas Van Iersel* (Kampen: Kok, 1989) 15-26.

[16]   As P. D. Miscall ("Isaiah, New Heavens, New Earth, New Book," in D. N. Fewell [ed.], *Reading Between Texts: Intertextuality and the Hebrew Bible* [Louisville: Westminster/John Knox Press, 1992] 41-56, here p. 43) states "anything 'written' is a text"; hence intertextuality can be defined so broadly as to include even "indirect allusions to common words and even letters to dependence on language itself" (p. 44). That is why I am convinced that intertextuality must be used conservatively and with carefully defined criteria.

[17]   See the comments by D. E. Aune, "Intertextuality and the Genre of the Apocalypse," in E. H. Lovering (ed.), *Society of Biblical Literature 1991 Seminar Papers* (SBLSP 30; Atlanta: Scholars Press, 1991) 142-60.

[18]   The quotation is from G. A. Phillips, "Sign/Text/Différance: The Contribution of Intertextual Theory to Biblical Criticism," in H. F. Plett (ed.), *Intertextuality* (Research in Text Theory/Untersuchungen zur Texttheorie 15; New

before us, a particular text, and not simply understand it as a mirror image of another text or family of texts. Its own unique voice must be heard, even if intertextuality helps us hear it within a chorus of supporting voices.

Yet, at this point we face a danger and without due caution improperly claim, with G. A. Phillips, that in addition to our well-tested historical-critical methodologies we also must add "a certain theoretical sophistication, a thinking systemically, a modeling structurally."[19] Let me be clear that I agree that we must observe "a certain theoretical sophistication," but surely M. Merleau-Ponty in his *Phenomenology of Perception* and M. Polanyi in his *Personal Knowledge* have demonstrated the distortionistic nature of any "system" and of any abstracted and modeled structure that is prior to careful observation.[20] In my work as a biblical exegete, that means that I must think coherently but never at the expense of shaping the text.[21] The latter, moreover, must neither become invisible to me as I only look at ostensible backgrounds nor be created *de novo* by a focus that sees it as unique and without any life-giving context. Any knowledge is certainly personal, but if it is to be something more than a pseudo-sophisticated attempt at "objectivity," then there must be an epistemological theory that can rightly be defended as sophisticated. Hence, I contend, we cannot talk about a system or synthesis that shapes the biblical and parabiblical texts; but we can—and should—contemplate a biblical universe of similitudes, metaphors, and symbols that show how unified these documents are especially when compared to other religious literatures, such as the texts of Buddhism or Hinduism.[22]

For me then, intertextuality cannot be a complex system of abstract terms that have not come to me from the text; the latter must

---

York: de Gruyter, 1991) 78-97; the quotation is on p. 79. I draw attention to his helpful bibliography on pp. 95-97.

19   Phillips, "Sign/Text/Différance," 79.

20   M. Merleau-Ponty, *Phenomenology of Perception* (International Library of Philosophy and Scientific Method; London: Routledge & Kegan Paul; New York: Humanities Press, 1962); and M. Polanyi, *Personal Knowledge: Towards a Post-Critical Philosophy* (New York: Harper & Row, 1964 [orig. 1958]).

21   As W. Weren shows (*Intertextualiteit en Bijbel* [Kampen: Kok, 1993] 18) in a chart, intertextuality encompasses many factors, including text and pretext, author and reader, context and language paradigms.

22   See esp. the reflections by J. Delorme, "Intertextualities about Mark," in Draisma (ed.), *Intertextuality in Biblical Writings*, 35-42.

govern my reflections. That is what is so attractive about intertextuality; the text is found alive within the critical term "inter*text*uality".
I shall thus look at one text, the Rule of the Community (1QS),
which has within it another text, Isa 40:3. After examining how this
text is cited, I shall subsequently seek to discern what words from
"this text within a text" are found elsewhere in 1QS, especially in
contiguous columns. In so doing intertextuality will help me comprehend better how and in what ways a portion of a text in another
context provides new life and fresh meanings to another earlier,
sacred text. Thus, in a very special sense, my present research leads
me to agree with R. P. Carroll that virtually "Every text makes its
readers aware of other texts. It insists on an intertextual reading."[23]

Thus, I shall add intertextuality to the other methods I have been
employing for decades,[24] but I use this new literary method in a
narrow sense. It has certainly helped me appreciate the literary
qualities of biblical and parabiblical texts. For the present work I
shall look only at the text of Isa 40:3 as it is quoted—that is, embedded—in the Rule of the Community; hence I shall not be forced to
speculate on so-called "presupposed texts," or be preoccupied with a
search for the meaning and borders of orality and tradition.

I shall seek subsequently to hear echoes of this excerpted text in
the Qumran scroll. I define "echoes" very strictly,[25] as words in the
quotation that appear either just prior to or just after the line in
which the quotation appears.[26] In so doing I shall ground the concept
of echo intertextually,[27] and avoid the criticisms of others who hear

---

23   Carroll in *The New Literary Criticism and the Hebrew Bible*, 58. Of course,
by "every" I do not mean "all"; I am thinking of the way that the Qumranites
expanded earlier texts deemed sacred and thus gave life to them and to new literary
creativity.

24   As M. A. Powell (*What is Narrative Criticism?* [Minneapolis: Fortress,
1990] 1) states: "The field of biblical criticism knows no methodology that
circumvents the act of reading or hearing the text."

25   See also J. Hollander, *The Figure of Echo: A Mode of Allusion in Milton
and After* (Berkeley: University of California Press, 1981); and R. B. Hays,
Echoes of Scripture in the Letters of Paul (New Haven and London: Yale
University Press, 1989) esp. 14-21.

26   Intertextuality helps me understand the form, scope, and purpose of a finely
chiseled literary unit, like 1QS 8:1–9:26. Intertextuality thus performs a service to
exegesis similar to that provided by rhetoric. See B. L. Mack, *Rhetoric and the
New Testament* (Mineapolis: Fortress, 1990) esp. 21.

27   My colleague A. K. M. Adam ("The Sign of Jonah: A Fish-eye View,"

echoes when there may be none.[28] Perhaps then I shall avoid the major criticisms of intertextuality; that is, the elusive criteria used to establish what is an intertext and what has influenced it.[29]

Before proceeding further, I must add my own voice to those who have warned about dangers in the misuse of intertextuality.[30] For example, Kristeva claims that "tout texte est absorption et transformation d'un autre texte."[31] This appears to be nonsense for two reasons. First, it breaks the "all fallacy"; that is, seldom may one use the word "tout" without misrepresenting that which one is examining and seeking to comprehend. Second, Kristeva's saying creates an abstract world divorced from phenomenal reality; that is, it reduces

---

Semeia 51 [1990] 177-91) has argued (against S. Fish) that the "text, while possibly existing as an objective set of data, cannot function in interpretation to authorize or rule out given readings apart from the set of interests and presuppositions which interpreters bring to their endeavors" (p. 181). I am convinced that by focusing on a portion of a pre-text in an intertext and the contiguous echoes of the quotation, intertextuality pulls us away from our own subjective exegesis to the form, function, and possible intended meaning of an author, compiler, and perhaps community. This methodology enables us through intertextuality to overcome most of the problems Fish and Adam have disclosed.

28   See esp. J. C. Beker, "Echoes and Intertextuality: On the Role of Scripture in Paul's Theology," in C. A. Evans and J. A. Sanders (eds.), *Paul and the Scriptures of Israel* (JSNTSup 83; SSEJC 1; Sheffield: Sheffield Academic Press, 1993) 64-69. Also, see the response by R. B. Hays on pp. 70-96. Beker rightly urges us to seek constraints for our use of "echoes" so that those which are thunderous are not confused with those that are subliminal. We must not confuse an echo in a text with autogenerative echoes. Biblical scholars may hear echoes that they bring to the text from their years of hearing texts; that would cause a text to be misread.

29   T. N. D. Mettinger ("Intertextuality: Allusion and Vertical Context Systems in Some Job Passages," in H. A. Mckay and D. J. A. Clines [eds.], *Of Prophets' Visions and the Wisdom of Sages: Essays in Honour of R. Norman Whybray on his Seventieth Birthday* [JSOTSup 162; Sheffield: Sheffield Academic Press, 1993] 262) rightly points out that the "main problem in all discussions of intertextuality is how to find criteria for establishing just what constitutes an intertext behind a certain text."

30   Exceedingly important are the studies similar to, but not influenced by intertextuality, especially the following two volumes: M. Fishbane, *Biblical Interpretation in Ancient Israel* (Oxford: Clarendon Press, 1985); M. J. Mulder and H. Sysling (eds.), *Mikra* (CRINT 2.1; Assen and Maastricht: Van Gorcum; Philadelphia: Fortress, 1988).

31   J. Kristeva, Σημειωτική: *Recherches pour une sémanalyse* (Paris: Editions du Seuil, 1969) 146, 255.

all texts to an imagined norm that may well be false to the author we
are eager to understand. For example, if I write in Hebrew on a
napkin in Jerusalem that I would like the bill (using the appropriate
word חשבון for bill),[32] that does not mean I intend to refer to the
Rule of the Community in which חשבון appears, nor am I thinking in
any way about that document. For someone to point to my decades of
work on this text and then to cite 6:20, "And he shall register it into
the account (בחשבון) with his hand," would certainly be to misunder-
stand me. In no way does the napkin text indicate that the Qumranic
document was a pretext for me intertextually. To claim that every
text absorbs and transforms another text—as so many who write
about intertextuality claim—undermines the ability to perceive the
difference between text and pretext and the important insights that
may be possible through intertextuality. I use intertextuality as one
aspect of historical criticism, and certainly not as the post-struc-
turalists do.

A text must be seen first and foremost as a distinct (if not
necessarily unique) text, with its own integrity. It may have no
written pretext, even though words found in it appear elsewhere. We
must not undermine the method of intertextuality by being blind to
the fact that when a text is seen to be shaped by a pretext that is an
important discovery, even if the pretext—as in Mark—may not be
quoted but merely help shape the narrative.[33] This observation opens
up new vistas for perception and reflection.[34]

Thus, there are real dangers if intertextuality is not carefully
defined and used conservatively. We must not *prima facie* assume
that because there is a biblical corpus in which texts characteristically

---

[32] Of course, I would usually speak the words (*anî roṣê et ha-ḥešbon*); but for
the sake of the present point the reader is to imagine me writing down the words,
which is conceivable in some circumstances in Jerusalem (especially near Jaffa
Street) when a waiter may be too elusive.

[33] See the comments by W. S. Vorster, "The Protevangelium of James and
Intertextuality," in *Text and Testimony*, 262-75, esp. 264.

[34] Also see the reflections by P. Tschuggnall, "'Das Wort ist Kein Ding': Eine
theologische Einübung in den literaturwissenschaftlichen Begriff der Intertextual-
ität," *ZKT* 116 (1994) 160-78. In the present chapter I hope to show how 1QS
gives new meaning to Isa 40:3a and leaves behind its "original" intentionality.
Thus, important is Tschuggnall's comment that a "Text, der zu einem Moment einer
intertextuellen Bewegung wird, kann in seinem neuen Sitz der Sinn und die
Bedeutung, die ihm im ursprünglichen Kontext zugekommen waren, verlieren und
im neuen Text 'aufgehoben' sein" (p. 163).

quote and echo others that intertextuality is a valid heuristic and hermeneutical methodology. This unexamined assumption or claim may be an invitation to read all biblical and parabiblical texts only in light of all other biblical and parabiblical texts. Such would surely be an "invitation to chaos."[35] Intertextuality must not become a substitute for older faithful methods, but an additional method in biblical historical criticism; and it must be employed using criteria and data provided only by the text before our eyes. Otherwise we are in danger of hearing our own echoes and not those we claim to find in a text. Hearing our own voice may be acceptable to some literary critics, but it is certainly not to historical-critical specialists.

By employing intertextuality so loosely, we might be attempting to communicate, but we would be contributing to the end of communication, as T. Eagleton and K. Nielsen have warned.[36] Surely, the Dead Sea Scrolls have awakened us to hard data and made us sensitive to the fact that often in this century biblical experts have been too preoccupied with concepts far removed from their phenomenological world. Any form of Husserlian eidetic abstraction should be recognized as intolerable.

These provisos help explain why the present work is only prolegomenous to an intertextual study of the Rule of the Community and of other Qumran sectarian scrolls.[37] In the following work I am

---

35   The words are those of J. Neusner (*Canon and Connection: Intertextuality in Judaism* [Studies in Judaism; London and New York: University Press of America, 1987] xiii), who attempts to demonstrate that the rabbinic "documents scarcely connect at all. Intertextuality constitutes a social construction, a theological conviction, not a literary dimension of the canon at hand, not an operative category for hermeneutics." I agree with Neusner that we must attend to the "inner integrity of logic and syntax" of a particular text, and refrain from reading a text from "the gross anachronism represented by the view that the way things came out all together at the end imposes its meaning and character upon the way things started out, one by one" (pp. 147-48). But, focusing through intertextuality on a quotation and its echoes in 1QS helps us understand the meaning of that intertext and the continuing vitality and new meanings of the pretext, Isaiah.

36   T. Eagleton, *Literary Theory: An Introduction* (Minneapolis and London: University of Minnesota Press, 1993 [orig. 1983]); K. Nielsen, "Intertextuality and Biblical Scholarship," *Scandinavian Journal of the Old Testament* 2 (1990) 89-95.

37   For a definition of "sectarian," see C. A. Newsom, "'Sectually Explicit' Literature from Qumran," in W. H. Propp et al. (eds.), *The Hebrew Bible and its Interpreters* (Winona Lake: Eisenbrauns, 1990) 167-87; also, see the studies cited by her on pp. 185-87.

seeking to express my reflections on how the text of the Rule of the
Community evolved out of the life of the *Moreh haṣ-Ṣedek,* the
Righteous Teacher and founder of the Community (יחד), and out of
the life of the Qumranites. Intertextuality gives us controls for
imagining how they held in their hands the sacred words of God
given to Isaiah (1QSa), and more importantly how such echoes
reverberated in their memory and daily life. The originating *raison
d'être* from a living text in their own language, Hebrew, provided
not only self-definition but also purpose and vision for the future or
Endtime.[38] It is in that sense I comprehend the meaning of Kristeva's
words that usually a "text is constructed as a mosaic of quotations";
that most texts absorb and transform others, and that the "notion of
intertextuality replaces that of intersubjectivity, and poetic language
is read as at least double."[39] It does not follow, as she contends, that
all texts are intertexts, even if all intertexts are texts.[40] I shall intend
in this chapter to demonstrate that the Rule of the Community
obtains its present form and meaning because it is an intertext in a
special way.[41]

1QS 8 AND ISAIAH 40:3

During a symposium on the Dead Sea Scrolls at the New York
Academy of Sciences, a scholar now specializing in these ancient
Jewish compositions criticized me publicly for my interpretation of
1QS 8. I had argued that the Qumranites went into the wilderness,
having been exiled from the Temple cult in Jerusalem, and later
found self-understanding in their interpretation of Isa 40:3, "A voice
calls, in the wilderness prepare the Way of Yahweh."[42] I am

---

38   The Hebrew אחרית המים does not necessarily mean the end of all time but
the next stage in history. See S. Talmon, *The World of Qumran from Within:
Collected Essays* (Jerusalem: Magnes; Leiden: Brill, 1989) 38-49; idem, "קץ,"
TWAT 7.84-92.

39   J. Kristeva, "Word, Dialogue and Novel," in T. Moi (ed.), *The Kristeva
Reader* (Oxford: Blackwell, 1986) 37. I am indebted to R. P. Carroll for this
quotation. Kristeva actually referred to "any text"; but, as I have already made clear,
that is not accurate and is close to being guilty of committing the "all" fallacy.

40   See the insights shared by Plett in his *Intertextuality,* 5.

41   I am also convinced that the Rule of the Community is virtually an intertext
for the *whole* Qumranic corpus.

42   It is conceivable that this consciousness began before the exodus from
Jerusalem. The beautiful Isaiah Scroll has a *lacuna* just before Isa 40:3, thus

persuaded that they understood the passage to mean that the Voice called them into the wilderness; they rejected the popular interpretation apparently regnant then and now that perceived Isaiah's message to denote the following: "A voice was calling in the wilderness." They heard the Voice in Jerusalem; She called them into the wilderness.[43]

The scholar who wanted to correct me, Norman Golb, claimed that 1QS 8:15 proved that the Qumranites interpreted Isa 40:3 to denote not that they were to go into the wilderness, but that they were to be devoted to "the study of Torah" (מדרש התורה). He was emphatic, having no doubt that the Qumranites were "using the words of Isaiah in a metaphorical way, to espouse the doctrine of study of the Torah."[44]

A study of the Rule of the Community, using intertextuality indicates to me, without any doubt, that Isa 40:3 meant to the Qumranites that they had been *literally "called" into the wilderness to prepare the Way of the Lord*. There, *in the wilderness, they studied Torah*, since God had revealed all the mysteries of the prophets to one and only one teacher, their *Moreh haṣ-Ṣedek* (as we know assuredly from 1QpHab 7).[45]

THE QUOTATION

By a quotation I mean that a segment of a pretext is found within a later text, and becomes an organic part of it, receiving new life and meaning even though it is clearly circumscribed (and might be removed without disrupting the grammar in the document).[46] A

---

signifying the importance of the verse. R. E. Brown (*The Birth of the Messiah* [Garden City: Doubleday, 1977] 284 n. 66) also concludes that the Qumranites "used" Isa 40:3 "as a self-interpretation (1QS viii 13-16)."

43   For studies on the hypostatic Voice, see J. H. Charlesworth, "The Jewish Roots of Christology: The Discovery of the Hypostatic Voice," *SJT* 13 (1985) 19-41; E. E. Urbach, *The Sages: Their Concepts and Beliefs* (2 vols., Jerusalem: Magnes, 1975-79) esp. 1.37-79.

44   N. Golb's comments on p. 282 in M. O. Wise et al. (eds.), *Methods of Investigation of the Dead Sea Scrolls and the Khirbet Qumran Site: Present Realities and Future Prospects* (Annals of the New York Academy of Sciences 722; New York: The New York Academy of Sciences, 1994).

45   1QpHab 7:4-5 explains that "God made known all the mysteries of the words of his servants, the prophets," to the Righteous Teacher.

46   To remove it, however, would be to kill the text; and that is what I mean by it being an organic part of 1QS.

portion of a text, Isa 40:3, appears in the Rule of the Community. The pretext is thus Second Isaiah (chaps. 40–55) which is sandwiched between First Isaiah (chaps. 1–39) and Third Isaiah (chaps. 56–66), but—of course—the Qumranites considered all of the book of Isaiah to be the work of the eighth-century Judean prophet, Isaiah, the son of Amoz, who lived in Jerusalem (as had the authors and compilers of the early sections of 1QS).[47] Obviously in our terminology, Second Isaiah intertextually echoes First Isaiah, and Third Isaiah echoes both of them. For example, Second Isaiah's מסלה and דרך echo Isa 35:8, "A highway (מסלול) shall be there, and it shall be called the Holy Way (ודרך הקדש) . . . it shall be for God's people . . ." (NRSV).

The portion quoted in the Rule of the Community from Second Isaiah is a self-contained unit: except for "a Voice is calling";[48] the intertext contains all of 40:3, "In the wilderness prepare the way of the Lord, make level in the desert a highway for our God" (1QS 8:14). The intertext is not all of the Rule of the Community; it is only the so-called Manifesto (8:1-16a and 9:3–10:8a) and its expansion (8:16b-19 and 8:20–9:2). As J. Murphy-O'Connor and J. Pouilly have shown at least in broad strokes,[49] the Rule of the Community is neither an illogical amalgam of fragments (pace H. E. del Medico) nor a logically developed writing (pace P. Guilbert). Instead, this quintessential Qumranic document reflects the history of

---

[47] Non-specialists have asked if the large scroll of Isaiah from Cave I shows any indication of separation between chaps. 39 and 40 and between 55 and 56; that is, is there any textual evidence for a significant division between the three sections of Isaiah. After examining the Kodansha photographs of 1QIsa[a], I can report that there is a very small *lacuna* before 40:1 (but it is not as large as the one before 39:5), and another small *lacuna* before 56:1 (plus a variant at the beginning of the verse—an additional כיא). Hence, these divisions are only indicative of a new unit of thought, not the beginning of a new writing. It is imperative to note, moreover, that there is a large *lacuna* before the key verse, 40:3, which is very near the beginning of the unit called "Second Isaiah." See the color photographs published by Kodansha: M. Sekine (ed.), *The Dead Sea Scrolls* (Tokyo: Kodansha, 1979).

[48] Perhaps the omission of קול קורא is another indication that they understood Isa 40:3 to contain a break in thought between "A voice is calling" and "in the wilderness . . . ." I am indebted to B. A. Strawn and J. B. Awwad for discussions on the omission of "A Voice calling" in the intertext.

[49] J. Murphy-O'Connor, "La genése littéraire de la Règle de la Communauté," *RB* 76 (1969) 528-49; J. Pouilly, *La règle de la Communauté de Qumrân: Son évolution littériare* (Cahiers de la RB 17; Paris: Gabalda, 1976).

development of the Qumran Community; that is, it—or, more specifically the recension knows as 1QS—evolves by a process in which additions are made to a primitive core, which is the precise section we shall be examining (8:1–10:8a)—the section called "Rules for the Holy Congregation."[50]

This phenomenon, the quotation of Isa 40:3 in 1QS 8, will be analyzed by means of the intertextual grammar of quotation:[51]

(1) *The text with the quotation (T1)*. The intertext is the Rule of the Community (1QS). It is in this Qumran document, at 8:14, that a portion of the text of Isaiah appears:

כאשר כתוב במדבר פנו דרך °°°° ישרו בערבה מסלה לאלוהינו

The entire line in 1QS is given for convenience. Here we find an example of a pretext, Isaiah, being deliberately reproduced in a receptor text. And the latter is clearly one of the most important of the Qumran sectarian documents, because it is both a depository of Qumran's essential teaching (and liturgy) and significantly influenced subsequent compositions at Qumran.

Pars pro toto. The author did not quote this section of Isaiah to remind the reader (or hearer) of the full book, even though the book would be in the mind (and perhaps memory) of the reader. The portion of the pre-text quoted was to serve a specific function: to explain to the reader, living in the wilderness to the northwest of the foul-smelling Dead Sea, just why he was living there. He and all the Sons of Light were living at Qumran "to prepare the Way of Yahweh." Time was elevated by this group of Jews and given unusual significance, as in some other Jewish groups, like those who composed the *Books of Enoch*. At the Endtime they were preparing "the Way."

The quotation served also to indicate that Isaiah was one of the major documents revered as sacred by the Qumranites. Two copies of it were safely deposited in Cave 1, which is certainly a cave in which scrolls were hidden from the Roman army; that is, it was not a main depository, like Caves 4a, 4b, and 8, or a cave in which Qumranites probably lived, as Cave 11.

(2) *The pre-text (T2)*. The source text is Isaiah, which antedates the target text by numerous centuries. Its importance is obvious not only by an examination of 1QSa and 1QSb, but also by the fact that Isaiah, unlike any other biblical book, left at least two Pesharim

---

50 Charlesworth in *Rule of the Community and Related Documents*, 1.

51 I am indebted here to Plett in his *Intertextuality*, 8–27.

(Isaiah Pesher 1–2 [4Q161–165]) and an "Isaianic Fragment" (4Q285).[52] Most importantly, the quotation is precisely like the section of the pre-text, as we see from 1QIsaᵃ (Col. 33):[53]

vacat קול קורא במדבר פנו דרך יהוה ישרו בערבה מסלה לאלוהינו

The text is identical with that in the Massoretic Text in the BHS, except for the plene writing. The tetragrammaton is written in the square script and without dots or paleohebrew characters. For us now, it is important to stress that the text is quoted precisely as the Qumranites knew it according to the document they owned, and placed in the same cave (probably as the most authoritative of their documents). The author of 1QS 8 did not copy קול קורא perhaps because he intended to stress the first word, במדבר. That is, he intended to explain not only why they were there (שם), but also what was their one focused function of being במדבר: to prepare the Way. He also did not need to quote "a Voice is calling" because he—and the Community to which he belonged—had heard the Voice and acted out the injunction. Perhaps, Second Isaiah was also chosen because in it "Isaiah" had not only described the *coming of Yahweh*, but also depicted heavenly voices speaking wisdom to those on earth.[54]

Marker. The one who created this section of 1QS indicated the beginning and end of the quotation. He could not use quotation marks or italics because they had not yet been invented. Yet, he needed to clarify the seams in his composition.

Our search for answers needs to be informed of the historical and philological context of his time; that is prior to circa 100–75 BCE, when he copied what we call 1QS (according to paleographical analysis). That is, he was living when final forms of some consonants were being accepted as norms, and when these Jews were developing

---

52   There is, of course, in addition the biblical scrolls from Cave 4.

53   According to the Kodansha photographs.

54   See the comments on Second Isaiah by J. L. McKenzie in *Second Isaiah* (AB 20; Garden City: Doubleday, 1968) esp. 16-17. The concept of a heavenly council would have been appealing to the Righteous Teacher and his followers, and that dimension of Second Isaiah is certainly clear. See R. N. Whybray, *The Heavenly Counsellor in Isaiah xl 13-14* (SOTSMS 1; Cambridge: Cambridge University Press, 1971); and F. M. Cross, "The Council of Yahweh in Second Isaiah," *JNES* 12 (1953) 274-77. For the concept in the Ancient Near East, see E. T. Muller, *The Divine Council in Canaanite and Early Hebrew Literature* (HSM 24; Chico: Scholars Press, 1980).

an analogous linguistic phenomenon for indicating morphological units of thought: the separation of words and groups of words by empty spaces and even by full uninscribed lines (*vacat*).

The author (or copyist), moreover, employs explicit intratextual markers to indicate the beginning of the quotation. First, he begins a new line, and it seems he planned this format two lines previously.[55] Second, he employs a preformative formula, "as it is written," (כתוב כאשר). This formula does not specify the source directly; it would have been memorized by all those who had passed over into the Community, and I am convinced it would have been part of their two-years of study and examination as novices (perhaps as בני שחר).[56]

The author (or copyist) also employs explicit intratextual markers to denote the ending of the quotation. First, he again begins a new line and makes the previous line (8:14) one of the shortest in this column. Second, he returns from the fragment of the pretext (C_2) to the intertext (C_1) by utilizing a postformative term (היאה) that indicates how he intended the quotation to be understood, "This (alludes to) . . ." (1QS 8:15). It is at this point that one might understand Professor Golb's interpretation. Line 15 means: "This (alludes to) the study of Torah" (היאה מדרש התורה). But, his interpretation is not valid, in my judgment, when one sees the ways the author has led up to the quotation in 8:12-13, which leads us to consider the prelude to the quotation.

Prelude. The author knows that he is about to quote from Isaiah, and he is leading up to it. He prepares his readers for the meaning that he wants them to obtain from the quotation. He writes, "When these become the Community in Israel they shall separate themselves from the session of the men of deceit in order to depart into the wilderness to prepare there the Way of the Lord . . ." (8:12b-13). The Sons of Light are to "separate themselves from the men of deceit" (יבדלו מתוך מושב הנשי[57] העול). This passage clearly means that they are to leave where they have been living; and most of them surely had been living in or near Jerusalem. Where are they to go? They are "to depart *into the wilderness*" (ללכת למדבר). In the

---

55 See the color photographs in Sekine (ed.), *The Dead Sea Scrolls.*

56 See 4Q298 1–2 i 1. I am grateful to S. Pfann for long discussions on this text and the function of the Maskilim at Qumran.

57 The ה like the א can at Qumran represent the soft pronunciation; for the correct reading (אנשי) see 4QS MS D.

prelude we have a clear echo of the quotation from Isaiah; that is, as
we shall see, the pre-text has supplied the noun "wilderness." The
prelude continues, specifying what they are to do in the wilderness:
"to prepare the Way of the Lord" (לפנות שם את דרכ הואהא). This
clearly echos the pre-text, as we shall see; in fact the text literally
means "to prepare there (that is in the wilderness) the Way of the
Lord."

As we have seen, in 1QS 8:14 in the direct quotation from Isa 40:3
four dots were used to signify the tetragrammaton, דרך °°°°. We
have also seen that in 1QS 8:13, the preceding line, a rare form of
the third person masculine pronoun is employed, דרכ הואהא. Is the
kaph in final position, but in initial or medial form, the result of the
Qumranites consciousness of the ineffableness of the tetragrammaton? That is, although the final kaph is sometimes not employed in
this section of 1QS, does the medial kaph here help the reader to pay
attention to the following form? While we must be cognizant of the
indiscriminate and usually meaningless use of medial forms in final
position,[58] the answer may be "yes"; דרכ הואהא was used to warn
the reader against pronouncing the name of the Lord, and to vocalize
"Adonai," the perpetual qere for YHWH. In any case, the tetragram-
matic הואה does, albeit infrequently, serve in the Qumran Scrolls as
a substitute for the tetragrammaton. Thus, orthography also assists us
in catching the echo of a text used intertextually, not only "in another
text" but surely also in the living oral tradition of a community in
which every discourse resounded with the Hebrew of Scripture
glossed.[59]

Quantity. The quotation forms a morphological and syntactic unit.
It is a whole verse. All of Isa 40:3 was quoted, except for קול קורא;
perhaps signifying that the concept of a verse is not only ancient but
also a primordial concept. The author quotes both parts of the
parallelismus membrorum; but he is interested primarily in the first

---

[58] See N. H. Tur-Sinai, הלשון והספר, אמרום, מנצפ"ך צופים (Jerusalem: Bialik,
1948) 1.10-31; and H. Yalon, מנצפ"ך לפי מקורות חז"ל—*Studies in the Dead Sea
Scrolls: Philological Essays* (Jerusalem: Shrine of the Book, 1967) 12-14.

[59] As D. Boyarin (*Intertextuality and the Reading of Midrash* [Indiana Studies
in Biblical Literature; Bloomington: Indiana University Press, 1990]) has shown,
the midrashim present us with radical examples of intertextuality; they help us
perceive the Bible as a self-glossing text. See the review of Boyarin by A. Samely,
"Justifying Midrash: On an 'Intertextual' Interpretation of Rabbinic Interpretation,"
JSS 39 (1994) 19-32.

stichos, "in the wilderness prepare the Way of Yahweh." Each of the nouns מדבר and דרך, as we shall see, shaped the development of Qumran theology.

When the author quoted this portion of Isaiah (i.e. 40:3), he made one impressive shift. He did not write יהוה. Instead, he wrote four dots to denote the ineffableness of God's name. A severe punishment, unknown because of a lacuna in 1QS 6:27 and unparalleled in the related 4Q fragments of the Rule of the Community, was meted out to those who pronounced God's ineffable name. Perhaps this rule reflected the practice, according to the Mishnah,[60] that the high priest alone could pronounce the name, יהוה, and then only in the Temple during the high moment on the Day of Atonement. If the Righteous Teacher had once served as high priest during the Yom Kippur services in the Temple,[61] then he would have remembered the rare opportunities in which he had spoken God's name before the assembled worshipers. Was he not congnizant of the only time the pronunciation of the tetragrammaton was permitted?

Quality. As we have seen, the quotation remains intact as a unit, except for "A Voice is calling." The Hebrew was not changed and no words were transposed. Both in the pretext and the intertext the words in focus (the quotation) are singled out as unusually important—in the pretext by a *lacuna* and in the target text with the well-known formula, "as it is written."

Distribution. In the target text the quotation appears in column eight, out of an eleven column work. Thus, it does not appear at the beginning or at the end of this scroll. Yet, this criterion in intertextuality is not helpful in the present case, because 1QS is composite. Nevertheless, we cannot conclude that it is an editorial introduction or conclusion. Most likely this section of 1QS antedates the composition known as the Rule of the Community.

Frequency. 1QS is not a collage of quotations. It is dissimilar from Testimonies (4Q175) which is a list of quotations. The fact that 1QS contains only three quotations from the Hebrew Bible indicates the strong force of the isolated quotation. It contained an idea that helped

---

60 See esp. *m. Yoma* 3:8 and 6:2.

61 H. Stegemann has argued for decades that the Righteous Teacher had served as high priest during the *intersacerdotum* of 159–152 BCE when Jonathan took over the duties of the high priest. For Stegemann's most recent argument, see "Das Hohepriesteramt des Lehrers der Gerechtigkeit," in his *Das Essener, Qumran, Johannes der Taüfer und Jesus* (Freiburg: Herder, 1993) 205-206.

shape the self-understanding of the Community. This becomes especially clear when we observe that this section of the Rule of the Community is commonly judged to be the oldest portion.[62]

The marker of the quotation from Isa 40:3, כאשר כתוב, appears eleven times in the sectarian Dead Sea Scrolls.[63] It appears in three documents only once.[64] In four documents it appears two times.[65] Most importantly one of these is the Rule of the Community (see 8:14 and 5:17). Which text is quoted? It is none other than Isaiah. The Qumranite is exhorted not to have any dealings with those who are impure (כול אנשי העול), "as it is written: 'Have nothing to do with the man whose breath is in his nostrils, for wherein can he be accounted?'" The pretext is Isa 2:22.

Thus Isa 40:3 and 2:22 are quoted in the documents collected together into the Rule of the Community. The third quotation is also found in column five, and it is preceded by the marker כיא כן כתוב, "for thus it is written." Then the author cites Exod 23:7. The low frequency of quotations from the Hebrew Bible signals that Isaiah, especially 40:3, was an exceedingly important text for the Qumranites.

Interference. The literary context of the receptor text, C_1, cannot be the same as the literary context of the pre-text, C_2. It is clear, however, that the section from the pretext does not disrupt the flow of the author's thought. In fact it was tacitly in his mind, as echoes (as we shall see), before it was explicitly quoted.

Echoes. Echoes of the quotation precede and follow it. They frame it. That this text was memorized by the "Men of the Community," the Sons of Light, seems to follow from the fact that the author can echo it even before he cites it. That is, he did not need to look up the quotation. It flowed from his life. The quotation mentions "in the wilderness" (במדבר). For the Qumran exegete, this is the most important word in the quotation from the pre-text. It is intertextually echoed prior to the quotation with the noun "into the wilderness" (למדבר).[66] The Qumranites thus defend their life-style and obtain

---

62   I am also persuaded that 1QS 3:13–4:14 is very old, and may well have been composed by the Righteous Teacher, perhaps in a final form at Qumran.

63   According to Charlesworth, *Graphic Concordance*, 299.

64   4Q 178 3 1:2; 4QCat[a] 10 + 1:1; CD 7:19.

65   11QMelch 1 + 2:9; 11QMelch 1 + 2:23; 4QFlor 1 + 1:2; 4QFlor 1 + 1:12; 4QpIsa[c] 6 + 2:18; 4QpIsa[c] 47 1:2; and esp. 1QS 5:17 and 8:14.

66   Most likely למדבר is a later form of Hebrew; earlier one might have

self-understanding from Scripture. They have gone למדבר because
God told them—through Isaiah, through the Voice, and through the
Righteous Teacher—to be במדבר.[67] The deeply symbolic meaning of
"wilderness" appears throughout the Bible and parabiblical texts; it
was clearly known by heart by many who lived at Qumran and studied
the Rule of the Community, as it was by the early followers of Jesus.[68]

The most important intertextual echo from the Isaianic quotation is
the pervasive use of דרך in the sectarian documents. As הדרך it
became a *terminus technicus* to denote the members of the community. They thought of themselves as "the perfect ones of the Way"
(תמימי דרך [1QH 1:36]). As the "perfect of the Way" they will cause
to vanish "all the wicked nations" (1QM 14:7). Moreover, this
technical term is intertextually echoed only a few lines before the
quotation in the intertext: "When these are established in the principles of the Community for two years *among the perfect of the Way*
they shall be set apart (as) holy in the midst of the Council of the
men of the Community" (1QS 8:10-11 [my emphasis]). In fact, this
phrase "the perfect of the Way" frames the quotation in the target
text; it appears not only in 8:10 but also in 8:18: "his works have
become purified from all deceit by walking with those *perfect of the
Way*." Intertextuality also helps elevate the preoccupation with purity
and the need for purification in the Community; that is, by walking
(another *terminus technicus*) "with those perfect of the Way" the one
who strays can be purified. Then, the phrase reappears in 8:21: "all
who enter into the Council of Holiness of those who walk with the
perfect of the Way as he commanded . . . ." Here we hear a double
echo of the quotation; the Way (בתמים דרכ)[69] is repeated and the
exhortation seems now elevated to a commandment (כאשר צוה): "go
into the wilderness."

---

expected אל מדבר, as in Exod 15:22.

67   4QS MS E has המדבר. Does this suggest that the Qumranties thought of "the
wilderness"? Does the fact that 4QS MS E dates from 50 to 25 BCE, according to F.
M. Cross (in Charlesworth (ed.), *Rule of the Community and Related Documents*,
57), suggest a deliberate change from "to the wilderness" to "the wilderness"?
Perhaps, but I doubt it; and as with many variants, I see no major historical or
theological significance in it.

68   See esp. U. Mauser, *Christ in the Wilderness: The Wilderness Theme in the
Second Gospel and its Basis in the Biblical Tradition* (SBT 39; Naperville:
Allenson, 1963).

69   Note the *kaph* in final position but in initial or medial form.

The quotation from Isa 40:3 is heard again in an echo that reverberates from the column which completes the rules and introduces the culminating hymn. In 9:19 we hear these words, "That is the time . . ." (עת היאה).[70] These words come with authoritative force. The person who speaks them has, as it were, become the קול קורא heard by the prophet Isaiah. The speaker is thus a prophetic person, and it is no wonder that experts have suggested he may be the *Moreh haṣ-Ṣedek*.[71]

The rhetoric is also clear: it is the time to do what? Here is the full sentence: "That is the time to prepare the way to the wilderness" (פנות הדרך למדבר).[72] These words are intertextual; they echo Isa 40:3. After echoing Isaiah, the author continues by prophesying that at that time "the chosen ones of *the Way*" (9:17-18)—another echo of Isa 40:3—will be instructed in all "that is found" (or revealed), and that "the norms of the *way* of the Master" (הדרך למשכיל)[73] will be clear. Then the compiler, surely different from the author of 1QS 8:1-9:26,[74] appends a hymn of praise to God; thus an echo of Isa 40:3 is heard before the concluding hymn of the Rule of the Community.

---

[70]   The erasure at the beginning of this clause is not represented; see Charlesworth (ed.), *Rule of the Community and Related Documents*, 40.

[71]   A. R. C. Leaney (*The Rule of Qumran and its Meaning* [The New Testament Library; London: SCM, 1966] 231) opined that the "writer speaks with authority," and continues: "No phrase in the whole of the *Rule* reads more like a manifesto nor gives so unmistakable an impression of being written by the actual founder of the community."

[72]   Note again the initial or medial *kaph* in final position. I am convinced the best explanation for this orthography is that such passages were copied from ancient manuscripts, from the first decade of the Community's existence, perhaps before they went "into the wilderness." At that time, surely sometime in the middle of the second century BCE, the *kaph* had not established itself as a consonant that took on another shape in final position. I have seen what appear to be a final *taw* and a final *aleph*; but these final forms never became part of Qumran orthography. I am convinced that final forms developed when the script was continuous, *scriptio continua*, and served to demarcate the end of a word (sentence or thought). Why did not all Hebrew consonants develop final forms? Most likely, some creative thinker perceived that separating words was a better solution than developing final forms for all consonants.

[73]   Again note the initial or medial *kaph* in final position.

[74]   As Leaney (*The Rule of Qumran*, 227) stated, this section of 1QS was "an originally independent early document." J. Murphy-O'Connor proved that hypothesis.

In a copy of the Rule of the Community found in Cave 4 there is a startling confirmation of the exegesis presented here.[75] According to MS E the Qumranites have gone into the wilderness to prepare *the way of truth*: "[When] these in Israel shall separate themselves from the session of the men of [deceit] in order to depart (into) the wilderness [to prepare ther]e the way of truth [את דרך האמת] as it is written, ["In the wild]erness pre[pare the way of the Lord, make le]vel in the desert a highway for our God" (4QS MS E 1 iii 3-5).[76] The Qumranites have separated from other Jews. They have departed especially from Jerusalem. They have gone into the wilderness, and there they are preparing the way of truth. As Talmon has demonstrated, the "wilderness" motif in biblical theology basically denoted the place for punishment and "a necessary transitory stage in the restoration of Israel to its ideal mode of life."[77] The latter aptly pertains to the Qumranites.

Type of Quotation. The quotation of Isaiah in the Rule of the Community is of a specific type, according to the categories in intertextuality. It is not an erudite quotation, since it is not meant to add validity to a scientific work. It is not an ornamental quotation, since it does not serve to decorate a text. It is not a poetic quotation, even though it is poetry (*parallelismus membrorum*), because it has a practical force: first to exhort going into the wilderness, and then to explain why the Qumranites are living in the wilderness. Thus, the quotation is an *authoritative quotation*. That means it specifies an obligation, is attached to a social institution (the Community which was hierarchically structured), is ritualistic, and underscores not only legal (the rules) but sacred tasks, especially those articulated by and for priests. The authoritative quotation amplifies the authority accorded to the sacred text of Isaiah. Intertextually the Rule of the Community receives authority from the pretext to which it gives

---

75   The exegesis developed in the present article represents the consensus among scholars. It was articulated long ago by Leaney (*The Rule of Qumran and its Meaning*, 221), who stated repeatedly that "the sect fulfilled both metaphorically and *literally* Isa. 40.3 . . ." (my emphasis).

76   Because of the limitations imposed by the present chapter, and also by the importance given to Isa 40:3a, the remainder of the verse will not be examined intertextually; hence, the following words will need further research: ישרו בערבה מסלה לאלוהינו.

77   S. Talmon, *Literary Studies in the Hebrew Bible: Form and Content* (Jerusalem: Magnes; Leiden: Brill, 1993) 223.

authority; both intertext and pretext speak to each other and receive mutual support. Biblical and parabiblical texts create a biblical world with characters and authors whose mimesis of the Creator supplies values and truth for all those who live within it or wish to cross over into it.

Critics who wish to stress that the one who authored this section of the Rule of the Community interpreted Isa 40:3 only metaphorically may miss how often such texts in antiquity were taken only literally.[78] In the Thanksgiving Hymns the Righteous Teacher literally interpreted Scripture so that the biblical metaphor of "planting" was taken to denote his followers (1QH 8).[79] A metaphorical meaning in a pretext is taken literally in a target text in the following selections: Job 38:3 (LXX), which is a metaphor for girding up your loins like a man, reappears in the *Testament of Job* 47 to denote "girdles" (χορδάς); Num 24:17 (LXX), which refers to a star (ἄστρον) from Jacob, is taken by Matthew to signify a star seen by magi (Matt 2:2); and—of course—Origen tragically interpreted Matt 19:12 literally and was even, amazingly, bothered by a literal interpretation of Rom 2:28-29 when that text is so clearly symbolic. According to the *Mekilta* Rabbi Yehoshua often rendered the biblical text literally; for example, he understood the "water" mentioned in Exod 15:22 to mean drinking water, while other Rabbis took the reference metaphorically to denote the words of Torah (*Mek.* on Exod 15:22 [*Vayasaʾ* §1]).[80]

INTERTEXTUALITY, THE BIBLE, AND PARABIBLICAL WORKS AS TEXTUAL GLOSSES

We have seen that intertextuality is the attempt to appreciate the meaning of a text by focusing on the text (or texts) within it; that is, quoted in it or echoed in it. Understanding that a gloss is a written

---

[78]   See A. Hilhorst, "Biblical Metaphors Taken Literally," in T. Baarda et al. (eds.), *Text and Testimony: Essays on New Testament and Apocryphal Literature in Honour of A.F.J. Klijn* (Kampen: Kok, 1988) 123-31.

[79]   See J. H. Charlesworth, "An Allegorical and Autobiographical Poem by the *Moreh haṣ-Ṣedek* (1QH 8:4-11)," in M. Fishbane, et al. (eds.), *"Shaʿarei Talmon": Studies in the Bible, Qumran, and the Ancient Near East Presented to Shemaryahu Talmon* (Winona Lake: Eisenbrauns, 1992) 295-307.

[80]   See D. Boyarin, "Inner Biblical Ambiguity, Intertextuality and the Dialectic of Midrash: The Waters of Marah," *Prooftexts* 10 (1990) 29-48, see esp. 35.

addition tied to a word or words; that is, it is an explanation of something unusual in a writing, let us speculate finally on the sevenfold importance of intertextuality:

(1) The criteria and control come out of the text (exegesis); that is, within the text we discover another text which receives freshness for itself and provides life to another, new and somewhat original, text.

(2) The world of the Bible includes all parabiblical and apocryphal compositions, and this phenomenon is important when we imagine Jews reading aloud, thinking, speaking, and writing in the same language, Hebrew (or in Aramaic which is also surely a sacred tongue for them).

(3) All biblical books and those related to them are important; that is, the Bible does not lose but gains by the perception of those compositions that surround and support its importance.

(4) The Bible and the parabiblical literature represent a documentary family of relationships that are glosses on each other; and these works certainly include at least the Dead Sea Scrolls, the Old Testament Apocrypha, and the Old Testament Pseudepigrapha, as well as—of course—the so-called canonical Hebrew Scriptures.

(5) The Bible is self-glossing; for example, using intertextuality one may perceive how Second Isaiah explains First Isaiah and itself, while at the same time providing for the intertextual completion in Third Isaiah (and, of course, the latter duplicates the intertextual process within the entire canonical Isaiah).

(6) Intertextuality clarifies some unity in, or illustrates the unified world of, the Bible and its family of texts.

(7) We are shown the task is to indwell the whole without preconceived normative judgments that such works as the Rule of the Community, the Prayer of Manasseh, the *Odes of Solomon*, and 4 Ezra are inferior because they are not in a putatively closed canon. For the historian of the first century BCE, there is no closed canon, at least not in the sense used by many church historians in the fifth century CE.

Intertextuality helps us comprehend that the Qumranites lived in a biblical world in which divine speech created meaning. Since Hebrew was alive not only in the sacred books but in the daily lives and thoughts—especially memory—of all the members of the יחד, speech created a unified world. Thus, an institution was formed,[81] and

---

[81] With Merleau-Ponty (*Phenomenology of Perception*, 184) I wish to stress

barriers were broken down. The heavens were not separated from the earth; rather, the יחד became the *axis mundi* in which angels could be experienced as present not only in the future final war (War Scroll) but in liturgical services (e.g. the Thanksgiving Hymns). The Men of the Community experienced their space literally as an ante-chamber of heaven, and the heavenly worship observed (Angelic Liturgy) was present on earth. The human who was a full member of the יחד is often indistinguishable from an angel; he was one of the קדושים (1QS 11:8 *et passim* at Qumran) and perhaps קדוש קדושים (4Q381 76) or קדושי קדושים (4Q400 1 i 2)—especially if he was designated by the phrase קדושי קדוש קדושים (4Q400 1 ii 6); thus, in translating we can never be certain if one of those so named or an אלים ("a divine being") is a heavenly being or a human. Indeed, it seems evident that for some of the Qumranites the יחד was the מקדש התורה (see 4QS MS E 1 iii 1).

Likewise, the neat (far too neat) bifurcation of time into future and present often collapses, so that the Qumranite could experience and live out the future Endtime in the present. Thus, intertextuality brings home the phenomenological truth that "it is within a world already spoken and speaking that we think."[82] And, even more is the axiom appropriate for the Qumranites who claimed to experience the presence of the *numina* and felt and thought in divine speech, Hebrew. That means, for them to think and to speak is to quote Scripture. For the Qumranites to say "hello" or to ask for water was to live intertextually with the Bible.[83]

Summary. The present study of the Rule of the Community has helped us to perceive more clearly that the ancient core of this document is an intertext with Isa 40:3 as the excerpted portion of the pretext. Only 40:3a was singularly and phenomenologically impor-tant to the Qumranites; and the very first word in the quotation, במדבר, is the main reason the pretext was excerpted. The pretext provided the Qumranites with the explanation for their main ques-tions of *who* they were, *where* they were, *why* they were in that

---

that we "live in a world where speech is an *institution*."

[82]   Merleau-Ponty, *Phenomenology of Perception*, 184.

[83]   Talmon (*The World of Qumran from Within*, 32) rightly stresses this fact: "Many יחד compositions are manifestly couched in an archaizing style and wording which reveal their authors as epigones who intentionally infused biblical linguistic coinage into their vernacular Mishnaic Hebrew."

place, and *what* they were called to do.[84] The Qumranites were those
who were called into the wilderness to prepare the Way of Yahweh.
They were the chosen ones of the Way (לבחירי דרך [9:17-18]);[85]
they were the perfect of the Way (8:10, 18, 21; 9:5, etc.). The
pretext also provided the explanation of where they were; they were
in the wilderness precisely because they were the only ones who
heard the Voice. Since they heard the Voice there was no reason to
quote from Second Isaiah קול קורא. What were they in the wilderness to do? Their answer is pellucidly clear, especially now thanks to
intertextuality. They were in the wilderness to prepare the Way of
Yahweh through worship (thus the Rule of the Community ends with
a hymn of praise) and study:[86] It was *in the wilderness*—not in the
Holy City, the center of the earth[87]—that they were to study Torah
(מדרש התורה).[88]

Finally, note how the echoes of the quotation in 1QS 8:14 cluster
around this line. First, note that "wilderness" appears only in three
places in the Rule of the Community, and always in the quotation or

---

[84]   A similar conclusion has been reached by G. J. Brooke, "Isaiah 40:3 and
the Wilderness Community," in G. J. Brooke and F. García Martínez (eds.), *New
Qumran Texts and Studies* (STDJ 15; Leiden: Brill, 1994) 132: "The community
which redacted and passed on these texts had a literal and actual experience in the
wilderness before which and during which the way was prepared metaphorically
through the study of the law."

[85]   I here follow the reading of 4QS MS D; 1QS has the odd לביחרי דרכ (with
initial or medial *kaph* in final position).

[86]   The other categories—especially ritualistic lustrations and other purifica-
tions, leading a perfect life, and devotion to God—are either other ways of understanding their concept of worship and Torah study or dependent upon them. Of
course, study was seen as an aspect of worship, but this Qumran attitude needs to
be adequately explored as B. T. Viviano (*Study as Worship: Aboth and the New
Testament* [SJLA 26; Leiden: Brill, 1978]) did with Rabbinics.

[87]   The Qumranites were very fond of *Jubilees*, and they may have struggled
with the concept of "in the wilderness" in light of the claim in *Jubilees* that
Jerusalem was the center of the earth (*Jub.* 8:19). Before the discovery of the Dead
Sea Scrolls *Jubilees* was often read in light of Rabbinics; now we know that we
must read it in light of the full library at Qumran, and one of the first experts to see
this importance was M. Teztuz in his *Les idées religieuses du livre des Jubilés*
(Geneva: E. Droz, 1960).

[88]   Professor Golb rightly perceived that the Qumranites were to study Torah,
but he missed the Qumranite emphasis that they have gone למדבר precisely because
the pretext enabled them to hear the Voice that called them into the wilderness to
study Torah.

in echoes contiguous with it:

8:13	ללכת למדבר
8:14	the excerpted pretext
9:19-20	היאה עת פנות הדרך למדבר

Second, observe the occurrences of the verb פנה in the Rule of the Community:

8:13	לפנות שם
8:14	the excerpted pretext
9:19	עת פנות

Finally, the concept of the Way is so intertextually linked with the excerpted text, and echoes it so distinctly that I am convinced that the Qumranites obtained their self-understanding primarily from their pneumatic and eschatological understanding of the pretext, especially 40:3a. Note how דרך appears in the section 8:1–10:8, especially as echoes after the excerpted pretext in the Rule of the Community:

8:10	בתמים דרך
8:13	דרכ הואהא
8:14	the excerpted pretext
8:18	להלכ בתמים דרכ
8:21	ההולכים בתמים דרכ
8:25	אמ תתם דרכו
9:2	לתמים דרכו
9:5	ותמים דרכ
9:9	בתמים דרכם
9:9	וללכת בתמים דרכ
9:17-18	לביחרי דרכ
9:19	עת פנות הדרכ למדבר
9:20	ולוא הסר דרכו
9:21	הדרכ למשכיל

I am amazed how often דרך is written with an initial or medial *kaph* in final position (i.e. דרכ);[89] perhaps this orthography is another indication of the antiquity of this portion of 1QS, thus reflecting the early struggles of living in the wilderness rather than in the opulent surroundings of the Temple. Intertextuality helps us see, then, the Righteous Teacher living out the meaning of a scroll (1QIsaᵃ) which

---

[89] We have also observed the use of medial מ where we normally expect to find final ם.

he may well have carried into the wilderness with him. That is, intertextuality shows us that when a text like Isa 40:3 is read, memorized, and interpreted pneumatically—as was surely the case with the Righteous Teacher and some of his followers—another text is also simultaneously being read: the experience of the passionate reader.[90] We can well imagine the little band of priests winding slowly out of the Temple and the Holy City to find meaning and promise in the wilderness; sometime in that process they lived out the conviction that they had heard the Voice calling them to prepare במדבר the Way of Yahweh. They understood their task because of the intertextuality of text; that is, they were some of the first of the faithful ones to live with total conviction (even passionate obsession) the Tanak as both *sefer hayyim* and as *ha-sefer šehakol bo*.[91]

CONCLUSION

The preceding study does not intend to exhaust the intertextual use of Isa 40:3 in the Qumran Community or in the Rule of the Community.[92] The research, thanks to the insights obtained through the methodology of intertextuality, confirms my thesis that this verse is the most important of all the prophetic words of Scripture for the development of the Qumranites conceptual universe and their own self-understanding.

Using intertextuality we have concluded that the Rule of the Community indicates that Isa 40:3a meant to the Qumranites that they had been "called" into the wilderness to prepare the Way of the Lord. Indeed, just before the formula in 8:14, כאשר כתוב, are these words in 8:12-13 that lead up to, and echo from the memory of, a text about to be cited but already memorized, and virtually daily chanted in Qumran services or in private devotion (or repeated quietly during chores): "When these become the Community in Israel they shall separate themselves from the session of the men of deceit

---

90   See the comments by J. W. Voelz in "Multiple Signs and Double Texts: Elements of Intertextuality," in Draisma (ed.), *Intertexuality in Biblical Writings*, 27-34, esp. see p. 32.

91   As J. A. Sanders states, the Book of Life (*sefer hayyim*) was eventually understood to be "the Book with Everything in It" (*ha-sefer shehakol bo*). See Sanders, *From Sacred Story to Sacred Text* (Philadelphia: Fortress, 1987; repr. 1992) esp. 182.

92   See also my comments in "The Rule of the Community, Isa 40:3, and Qumran Theology," in Wise et al. (eds.), *Methods of Investigation*, 279-81.

in order to depart into the wilderness to prepare there the Way of
the Lord [ללכת למדבר לפנות שם את דרכ הואהא]." There, שם, in
the wilderness they are to study Torah and purify themselves in
every way so that the Way will be prepared for the coming of the
Lord or his messenger.

Studying the Rule of the Community helps us see how Jews lived
with a living text, the Hebrew Scriptures. It is certainly clear that
these documents did not belong to a concluded process or a closed
canon.[93] The pretext came alive in the intertext, and as they echoed
back and forth a multiplicity of meanings gave hope to those
banished במדבר, but in reality lived on the highway of God, for
God.[94] Thus, the Qumranites found in the Bible, as a believing
Community, the mirror for their identity intertextually.[95]

---

[93]   See the reflections on the Revelation by S. Moyise, "Intertextuality and the
Book of Revelation," *ExpTim* 104 (1993) 195-98, esp. p. 197.

[94]   I use the verb "banished" intentionally. I am convinced that the Qumranites
were thrown out of or forced out of the Temple, as 1 Maccabees intimates. The
letter (4QMMT) contains the rationalizations of the Qumranites.

[95]   As J. A. Sanders (*Torah and Canon* [Philadelphia: Fortress, 1972] xvi)
clarifies, "The believing community abuses the Bible whenever it seeks in it models
for its morality but reads it with validity when it finds in the Bible mirrors for its
identity." Of course, the Qumranites did not "abuse" the Bible.

A HERALD OF GOOD TIDINGS
ISAIAH 61:1-3 AND ITS ACTUALIZATION
IN THE DEAD SEA SCROLLS

John J. Collins

Isaiah 61:1-3 is a passage that lends itself to the study of "comparative midrash." In the New Testament, it is given exceptional prominence as the text for Jesus' inaugural sermon in the Gospel of Luke.[1] It may also underlie the first three beatitudes of the Sermon on the Mount.[2] In addition to its treatment in Targum and Midrash, it is also featured in a number of texts from Qumran. James Sanders has studied the various readings of the text in an important article, first published more than two decades ago, and more recently revised.[3] Recently, however, another important text that draws on this passage has come to light among the Scrolls.[4] It is appropriate to ask whether this new text throws any light on the developing tradition, and whether it in turn is clarified when it is viewed in the context of the history of interpretation.

ISAIAH 61

The prophetic text itself is usually assigned to Trito-Isaiah (Isaiah 56-66), but it is universally admitted to be very close to, if not indis-

---

[1]   Cf. Theodoret of Cyr, *Commentaire sur Isaïe III* (SC 315; Paris: Cerf, 1984) 264-65: "It is not necessary that we give a detailed argumentation of the meaning of this prophecy, because the Master himself has made it clear to us."

[2]   D. Flusser, "Blessed are the Poor in Spirit . . ." *IEJ* 10 (1960) 1-13; repr. in Flusser, *Judaism and the Origins of Christianity* (Jerusalem: Magnes, 1988) 102-14.

[3]   J. A. Sanders, "From Isaiah 61 to Luke 4," in J. Neusner (ed.), *Christianity, Judaism and Other Greco-Roman Cults: Studies for Morton Smith at Sixty* (SJLA 12; Leiden: Brill, 1975) 75-106; revised in C. A. Evans and J. A. Sanders, *Luke and Scripture* (Minneapolis: Fortress, 1993) 46-69.

[4]   E. Puech, "Une Apocalypse Messianique (4Q521)," *RevQ* 15 (1992) 475-519.

tinguishable from, Deutero-Isaiah (Isaiah 40–55). The relevant verses
are translated as follows in the NRSV:

1   רוּחַ אֲדֹנָי יְהוִה עָלָי
    יַעַן מָשַׁח יְהוָה אֹתִי
    לְבַשֵּׂר עֲנָוִים שְׁלָחַנִי
    לַחֲבֹשׁ לְנִשְׁבְּרֵי־לֵב
    לִקְרֹא לִשְׁבוּיִם דְּרוֹר
    וְלַאֲסוּרִים פְּקַח־קוֹחַ
2   לִקְרֹא שְׁנַת־רָצוֹן לַיהוָה
    וְיוֹם נָקָם לֵאלֹהֵינוּ
    לְנַחֵם כָּל־אֲבֵלִים
3   לָשׂוּם לַאֲבֵלֵי צִיּוֹן . . .

1   The Spirit of the Lord God is upon me,
    because the Lord has anointed me;
    He has sent me to bring good news to the oppressed,
    to bind up the brokenhearted,
    to proclaim liberty to the captives,
    and release to the prisoners;
2   to proclaim the year of the Lord's favor,
    and the day of vengeance of our God;
    t213rovide for those who mourn in Zion . . .

There are clear echoes here of the description of the servant of the
Lord in Isaiah 42, of whom it is said, "I have put my spirit upon
him" (42:1), and who is appointed "to open the eyes that are blind, to
bring out the prisoners from the dungeon, and from the prison those
who sit in darkness" (42:7).[5] Another passage in Isa 49:8-9 speaks of
a "time of favor" and "a day of salvation" in connection with the
release of prisoners. It is not surprising then that some scholars have
viewed Isaiah 61 as an interpretation, or actualization, of Deutero-
Isaiah, and specifically of the figure of the servant.[6]

Most scholars have also seen this passage in Isaiah 61 as the programmatic self-description of the prophet.[7] The speaker is already

---

[5]   Cf. C. Stuhlmueller, "Deutero-Isaiah and Trito-Isaiah," in R. E. Brown, J.
A. Fitzmyer, and R. E. Murphy (eds.), *The New Jerome Biblical Commentary*
(Englewood Cliffs: Prentice Hall, 1990) 346.

[6]   W. A. M. Beuken, "Servant and Herald of Good Tidings: Isaiah 61 as an
Interpretation of Isaiah 40–55," in J. Vermeylen (ed.), *The Book of Isaiah: Le livre
d'Isaïe* (BETL 81; Leuven: Peeters and Leuven University Press, 1989) 411-42; P.
D. Hanson, *The Dawn of Apocalyptic* (Philadelphia: Fortress, 1975) 65-68.

[7]   K. Elliger, "Der Prophet Tritojesaja," *ZAW* 49 (1931) 112-41; C. Wester-

identified as "the prophet" in the Targum, and this identification is also standard in the medieval Jewish commentators. A few scholars have objected that prophets were not anointed in ancient Israel, and inferred that the figure in question must be a High Priest.[8] But in fact the anointing of prophets is not unknown: Elijah is commanded to anoint Elisha as prophet in his place, although he is never actually said to do so. Anointing here may already be metaphorical, and mean simply "appoint."[9] In any case, the Dead Sea Scrolls refer to prophets as "anointed ones" on several occasions, and give no indication that this usage was novel.[10] Nothing that is said of the anointed figure here is distinctively priestly, and the priesthood is apparently extended to all the people of Judah in 61:6.[11]

The prophetic character of the speaker is supported by the fact that he is told to announce good news (בשׂר) to the oppressed and to proclaim liberty to the captives. Announcing good news was not a characteristic function of the pre-exilic prophets,[12] but the root appears seven times in Isaiah 40–66. "How beautiful on the mountains are the feet of the herald of good tidings! who announces peace, brings good news, announces salvation!" (52:7). In Isa 40:9, Zion and Jerusalem are the bringers of good tidings to the other cities of Judah. The מבשׂר is a messenger; the role is nicely illustrated in 2 Sam 18:19-27, where the root is used repeatedly of bringing tidings to King David of Absalom's death. (The messengers mistakenly think they are bringing good news, because "the Lord has delivered him from the power of his enemies"). Another prophetic reference is found in Nahum 2:1 ("Behold upon the mountains the feet of the

---

mann, *Isaiah 40–66* (Philadelphia: Westminster, 1969) 366. J. Vermeylen (*Du prophète Isaïe à l'apocalyptique* [ÉBib; Paris: Gabalda, 1978] 2.478-83) regards the passage as an expression of the hope of the community. Similarly, Hanson (*The Dawn of Apocalyptic*, 67) speaks of "the collective adaptation of Israel's prophetic heritage."

8   H. Cazelles, *Autour de l'Exode* (Paris: Gabalda, 1987) 292; P. Grelot, "Sur Isaïe LXI: La Première Consécration d'un Grand-Prêtre," *RB* 97 (1990) 414-31.

9   So already B. Duhm, *Das Buch Jesaja* (Göttingen: Vandenhoeck & Ruprecht, 1914) 424-25.

10   CD 2:12; 6:1; 1QM 11:7. Cf. Ps 105:15, where "anointed ones" and "prophets" are used in parallelism ("Do not touch my anointed ones; do my prophets no harm"). The reference in the Psalm, however, is to the patriarchs.

11   *Pace* Cazelles, *Autour de l'Exode*, 292; Grelot, "Sur Isaïe LXI," 421-22.

12   Duhm, *Jesaja*, 424-25.

herald of good tidings, the one who proclaims peace"). The prominence of this word in Deutero-Isaiah bespeaks the altered nature of
prophecy in the new circumstances of the post-exilic period. The
time for accusation and rebuke was past. The prophet was now called
to comfort the people. The Targum reads Isa 40:9 as "Get ye up on a
high mountain, ye prophets that bring good tidings to Zion."

In Isaiah 61, the comforting takes the form of a proclamation of
liberation. The Hebrew word דרור (Akkadian *anduraru*) refers to
the release of debt slaves. Jeremiah tells us that King Zedekiah proclaimed a דרור, "that all should set free their Hebrew slaves, male
and female, so that no one should hold another Judean in slavery"
(Jer 34:9).[13] The people obeyed at first, but then reneged. Jeremiah
reminds them of the Deuteronomic law that slaves should be set free
every seven years (Deut 15:1-18). The word is also found in Lev
25:10, which requires that a דרור be proclaimed in the jubilee year:
"You shall count off seven weeks of years, seven times seven years,
so that the period of seven weeks of years gives forty-nine years.
Then you shall have the trumpet sounded loud; on the tenth day of
the seventh month—on the day of atonement—you shall have the
trumpet sounded throughout all your land. And you shall hallow the
fiftieth year and you shall proclaim liberty throughout the land to all
its inhabitants. It shall be a jubilee for you; you shall return, every
one of you, to your property and every one of you to your family ..."
Whether this law was ever observed must be regarded as very doubtful.[14]

Walther Zimmerli argued that Isaiah 61 presupposed not only the
liberation of captives described in Deutero-Isaiah, but also the
legislation of Leviticus 25.[15] But Isaiah 61 makes no mention of the
jubilee, the Day of Atonement or anything that would point distinctively to Leviticus. The liberation envisaged here is the same as that
envisaged in Isaiah 42: the liberation of captives, which can also be
stated metaphorically as opening the eyes of the blind.[16] The refer-

---

13   W. L. Holladay, *Jeremiah 2* (Hermeneia; Minneapolis: Fortress, 1989) 238-
39.

14   R. de Vaux, *Ancient Israel* (New York: McGraw-Hill, 1965) 2.175-77.

15   W. Zimmerli, "Das 'Gnadenjahr des Herrn'," in A. Kuschke and E. Kutsch
(ed.), *Archäologie und Altes Testament* (Tübingen: Mohr [Siebeck], 1970) 321-32.

16   S. Paul, "Deutero-Isaiah and Cuneiform Royal Inscriptions," in W. W.
Hallo (ed.), *Essays in Memory of E. A. Speiser* (New Haven: American Oriental
Society, 1968) 182.

ence is to the return of the exiles from Babylon and the restoration
of the community in Judah. This is quite clear in the context; e.g. Isa
60:4 says that "your sons shall come from far away, and your
daughters shall be carried on their nurses arms." Isa 61:4 speaks of
rebuilding ancient ruins. The release of the Jewish exiles from
captivity is compared to the liberation of slaves.[17] One of the recur-
ring motifs in Deutero-Isaiah is that of the Lord as גאל, the kinsman
who redeems his people.[18] In the background, of course, is the
paradigm of the release of the people of Israel from slavery in
Egypt. The release from Babylon is conceived as a re-enactment of
the Exodus.[19] The דרור is ultimately granted by God. The prophet is
his herald who runs ahead to proclaim the good news. In Isaiah 61,
the news has two aspects, the year of the Lord's favor (the year of
release) and the day of God's vengeance on the enemies of his
people.

THE HERALD IN THE SCROLLS

While Leviticus 25 is not necessarily in view in Isaiah 61, it
provides the starting point for the eschatological midrash in
11QMelchizedek.[20] In accordance with the usual exegetical
assumptions of the Dead Sea Scrolls, the jubilee year is interpreted
with reference to "the end of days." Because of the common theme
of דרור, Isaiah 61 is brought into the exposition.[21] The jubilee is the
time when the captives will be released (Isa 61:1). The captives are
identified with the inheritance of Melchizedek, who is introduced
here as a heavenly figure (an אלהים). It is he who proclaims the
דרור to the captives. In contrast to Isaiah 61, the liberation is not
economic but relief from the burden of sin, an idea that may be

---

[17]   It is possible that the passage is also addressing a problem of debt-slavery in
the restored community. So Beuken, "Servant and Herald," 439.

[18]   C. Stuhlmueller, *Creative Redemption in Second Isaiah* (Rome: Biblical
Institute, 1970) 99-123.

[19]   Stuhlmueller, *Creative Redemption*, 66-94.

[20]   A. S. van der Woude, "Melchizedek als himmlische Erlösergestalt in den
neugefundenen eschatologischen Midraschim aus Qumran Höhle XI," *OTS* 14
(1965) 354-73. See P. J. Kobelski, *Melchizedek and Melchireša‘* (CBQMS 10;
Washington: Catholic Biblical Association, 1981) 3-23; E. Puech, "Notes sur le
manuscrit 11QMelkîsédeq," *RevQ* 12 (1987) 483-513.

[21]   M. Miller, "The Function of Isa 61:1-2 in 11QMelchizedek," *JBL* 88 (1969)
467-69.

suggested by the reference to the Day of Atonement in Lev 25:9. Melchizedek, of course, was known in the Hebrew Bible as a priest (Gen 14:18; Ps 110:4), and he retains his priestly role in the Epistle to the Hebrews, chapter 7, where he is said to resemble the Son of God and to remain a priest forever. According to 11QMelchizedek, the Day of Atonement marks the end of the tenth jubilee. This is identified with the "year of favor" of Isaiah 61:2, but it is now Melchizedek's year of favor (11QMelch ii 9) and it is he who will exact the vengeance of God (ii 13). This occasion is further identified with the "time of favor" and "day of salvation" of Isa 49:8, and Isa 52:7 is further applied to this day: "how beautiful on the mountains are the feet of the herald who proclaims peace . . ." The herald (מבשר), we are told, is "the anointed of the spirit" (משוח הרוח),[22] of whom Daniel spoke.[23] His task is to comfort those who mourn, as in Isa 61:2-3. The phrase משוח הרוח is obviously derived from Isaiah 61 ("The spirit of the Lord God is upon me, because the Lord has anointed me . . ."). This passage also underlies the designation of prophets as משיחי רוח קדשו in CD 2:12.

Since it is Melchizedek who proclaims the דרור in 11QMelch ii 6, some scholars have assumed that he is also the herald in ii 18-19.[24] Exegesis in the Scrolls is notoriously atomistic, however, and so this is not necessarily so. The herald is more easily identified as a prophetic precursor of Melchizedek, who proclaims that the day of judgment and the day of salvation is at hand.[25]

---

[22]   Van der Woude ("Melchizedek als himmlische Erlösergestalt," 366) originally read this phrase as המשיח הואה. Y. Yadin ("A Note on Melchizedek and Qumran," *IEJ* 19 [1965] 152-54) proposed משוח הרוח. This reading is supported by T. H. Lim ("11QMelch, Luke 4 and the Dying Messiah," *JJS* 43 [1992] 91) on the basis of a computer enhanced image. M. de Jonge and A. S. van der Woude ("11QMelchizedek and the New Testament," *NTS* 12 [1965-66] 306) adopted the reading משיח הרוח. See also J. A. Fitzmyer, "Further Light on Melchizedek from Qumran Cave 11," in Fitzmyer, *Essays on the Semitic Background of the New Testament* (London: Chapman, 1971; repr. SBLSBS 5; Missoula: Scholars Press, 1974) 265.

[23]   Most scholars assume that the reference is to the anointed prince (משיח נגיד) of Dan 9:25, but M. Wise (in M. Wise, M. Abegg and E. Cook, *The Dead Sea Scrolls: A New Translation* [San Francisco: HarperSanFrancisco, 1996] 457) takes the reference to Dan 9:26 ("an anointed one shall be cut off"). See the discussion by Lim, "11Qmelch," 90-92.

[24]   So Sanders, "From Isaiah 61 to Luke 4," 57.

[25]   So de Jonge and van der Woude, "11QMelchizedek and the New

11QMelchizedek has much in common with the dualism of the two spirits in such documents as the Community Rule, War Rule and Testament of Amram.[26] Melchizedek is identified with the archangel Michael in later midrashic texts,[27] and there is good reason to think that Michael and Melchizedek are identified with the Prince of Light in the sectarian scrolls.[28] The emphasis on the jubilee fits with priestly theology of the scrolls. Isaiah 61 becomes relevant because of the common theme of the דרור, which is understood as liberation from sin rather than from social oppression. The text emphases the day of judgment more than the nature of salvation. The herald is a relatively minor figure in this scenario, evidently less important than Melchizedek, but he is important nonetheless, as he fulfills a biblical prophecy and shows that the day of salvation is at hand.

An intriguing possibility is suggested by 1QH 23 (formerly 18), where the speaker claims to be inspired by God: "You have opened a spring in the mouth of your servant . . . whom you have supported with your power, to [be], according to your truth . . . herald of your goodness, to proclaim to the poor the abundance of your mercies" (v. 14). Here the speaker, who may plausibly be identified as the Teacher of Righteousness, seems to assume the role of the herald of Isaiah 61.[29] In this case, what is proclaimed to the poor is the knowledge of God's mysteries. The intriguing possibility is that the Teacher may have claimed to be the "anointed of the spirit" who is identified as the one who preaches good news in 11QMelchizedek.

In fact, several scholars have entertained the possibility that the Teacher filled the role of the eschatological prophet (1QS 9:11) or the "prophet like Moses" (Deut 18:15-18; 4Q175 5 ([Testimonia]).[30]

Testament," 307; F. García Martínez, "Messianische Erwartungen in den Qumranschriften," *Jahrbuch für Biblische Theologie* 8 (1993) 203.

26   See at length Kobelski, *Melchizedek and Melchireša*.

27   See W. Lueken, *Michael* (Göttingen: Vandenhoeck & Ruprecht, 1898) 31; de Jonge and van der Woude, "11QMelchizedek and the New Testament," 305.

28   Kobelski, *Melchizedek and Melchireša*, 36. See further E. Puech, *La Croyance des Esséniens en la Vie Future: Immortalité, Résurrection, Vie Éternelle?* (Paris: Gabalda, 1993) 554-58, who emphasizes the affinities of Melchizedek with the Danielic "one like a son of man."

29   Flusser, "Blessed are the Poor in Spirit," 10. The role of herald may also be implied in 1QpHab 7:3 (on Hab 2:2), where the phrase "so that the one who reads it may run" is applied to the Teacher.

30   Among others: N. Wieder, "'The Law Interpreter' of the Sect of the Dead

In the words of Geza Vermes: "If the messianic Prophet (or prophetic Messiah) was to teach the truth revealed on the eve of the establishment of the Kingdom, it would follow that his part was to all intents and purposes to be the same as that attributed by the Essenes to the Teacher of Righteousness. In consequence, it would not be unreasonable to suggest that at some point of the sect's history the coming of the Prophet was no longer expected; he was believed to have already appeared in the person of the Teacher of Righteousness."[31] But caution is in order here. There is no doubt that the Teacher anticipated some of the functions of the eschatological prophet, and probably also of the eschatological priest, but it does not follow that he was identified with either figure or thought to be a messiah. The slipperiness of the categories can be seen in CD 6:7-11: "the staff is the interpreter of the law, of whom Isaiah said: 'He produces a tool for his labor.' And the nobles of the people are those who have arrived to dig the well with the staves that the scepter decreed, to walk in them throughout the whole age of wickedness, and without which they will not obtain it, until there arises one who teaches righteousness at the end of days." In this passage, the "interpreter of the law" is most plausibly identified with the historical Teacher, who established the exegetical principles of the sect. The one who teaches righteousness at the end of days is the eschatological prophet, who is yet to come. In other texts, however, the "interpreter of the law" is a future, eschatological figure (e.g. in the Florilegium, 4Q174). It appears then that the historical Teacher and the future prophet had similar functions, but were nonetheless distinguished. Consequently, when the Teacher plays the role of the herald of Isaiah 61 in preaching good news to the poor, he is not necessarily claiming to be the eschatological prophet, only to be filling a similar role.[32]

Sea Scrolls: The Second Moses," *JJS* 4 (1953) 158-75; A. S. van der Woude, *Die messianischen Vorstellungen der Gemeinde von Qumran* (SSN 3; Assen: van Gorcum, 1957) 186; H. M. Teeple, *The Mosaic Eschatological Prophet* (SBLMS 10; Philadelphia: Society of Biblical Literature, 1957) 54; M. O. Wise, "The Temple Scroll and the Teacher of Righteousness," in Z. J. Kapera (ed.), *Mogilany 1989: Papers on the Dead Sea Scrolls* (Kraków: Enigma, 1991) 142.

[31]   G. Vermes, *The Dead Sea Scrolls: Qumran in Perspective* (Philadelphia: Fortress, 1981) 185-86.

[32]   See further J. J. Collins, *The Scepter and the Star: The Messiahs of the Dead Sea Scrolls and Other Ancient Literature* (ABRL 10; New York: Doubleday, 1995) 112-14; M. Knibb, "The Teacher of Righteousness—A Messianic Title?" in

Preaching good news to the poor is also an activity of the end-time in 4Q521 fragment 2 ii:

1	כי הש[מ]ים והארץ ישמעו למשיחו
2	וכל א[ש]ר בם לוא יסוג ממצות קדושים
3	התאמצו מבקשי אדני בעבדתו
4	הלוא בזאת תמצאו את אדני כל המיחלים בלבם
5	כי אדני חסידים יבקר וצדיקים בשם יקרא
6	ועל ענוים רוחו תרחף ואמונים יחליף בכחו
7	כי יכבד את חסידים על כסא מלכות עד
8	מתיר אסורים פוקח עורים זוקף כפ[ו]פים]
9	ול[ע]לם אדבק [במ][יחלים ובחסדו י]שלם(?)[
10	ופר[י] מעש[ה] טוֹב לאיש לוא יתאחר
11	ונכ<ב>דות שלוא היו יעשה אדני כאשר ד[בר]
12	כי ירפא חללים ומתים יחיה ענוים יבשר
13	ו[דלי]ם ישב[י]ע] נתושים ינהל ורעבים יעשר
14	ונב[ונים] וכלם כקד[ושים(?)
15	וא[

1. . . . heaven and earth will obey his messiah
2. [and all th]at is in them will not turn away from the commandments of holy ones.
3. You who seek the Lord, strengthen yourselves in his service.
4. Is it not in this that you will find the Lord, all who hope in their hearts?
5. For the Lord will seek out the pious and call the righteous by name,
6. and his spirit will hover over the poor and he will renew the faithful by might.
7. For he will glorify the pious on the throne of an eternal kingdom,
8. releasing captives, giving sight to the blind, and raising up those who are bo[wed down].
9. Forever I will cleave to [those who] hope, and in his kindness . . .
10. The fru[it of a] good [wor]k will not be delayed for anyone . . .
11. and the glorious things that have not taken place the Lord will do as he s[aid]
12. for he will heal the wounded, give life to the dead, and preach good news to the poor
13. and he will [sat]isfy the [weak] ones and lead those who have been cast out and enrich the hungry . . .

This text was dubbed a "messianic apocalypse" by its editor,[33] but its genre has been identified more persuasively as an eschatological psalm.[34] The psalm is a pastiche of phrases from various biblical sources, most prominently Ps 146:5b-8.[35] The psalm declares blessed those

5 . . . שִׂבְרוֹ עַל־יְהוָה אֱלֹהָיו
6 עֹשֶׂה שָׁמַיִם וָאָרֶץ
אֶת־הַיָּם וְאֶת־כָּל־אֲשֶׁר־בָּם
הַשֹּׁמֵר אֱמֶת לְעוֹלָם
7 . . . יְהוָה מַתִּיר אֲסוּרִים
8 יְהוָה פֹּקֵחַ עִוְרִים
יְהוָה זֹקֵף כְּפוּפִים . . .

5   . . . .whose hope is in the Lord their God,
6   who made heaven and earth,
    the sea, and all that is in them;
    who keeps faith forever
7   . . . the Lord sets prisoners free;
8   the Lord opens the eyes of the blind;
    the Lord lifts up those who were bowed down . . .

The liberation of captives brings to mind a string of passages in Second and Third Isaiah (Isa 35:5; 42:7; 61:1). A clearer allusion to Isaiah 61 concerns preaching good news to the poor in v. 12.

Precisely this latter allusion, however, gives rise to the most controversial problem in the interpretation of this text. Grammatically, God is the subject of the verbs in v. 12, but nowhere else is God the subject of the verb בשׂר in the Hebrew Bible.[36] The verb refers to the activity of a herald or messenger, and so it would scarcely make sense to speak of God performing it directly. Consequently, the suspicion arises that God is supposed to act through an agent here.

P. R. Davies and R. T. White (eds.), *A Tribute to Geza Vermes. Essays on Jewish and Christian Literature and History* (JSOTSup 100; Sheffield: JSOT Press, 1990) 51-65. G. Jeremias, *Der Lehrer der Gerechtigkeit* (Göttingen: Vandenhoeck & Ruprecht, 1963) 287.

[33]   Puech, "Une Apocalypse Messianique." Text is taken from p. 485.

[34]   K.-W. Niebuhr, "4Q521,2 II – Ein Eschatologischer Psalm," in Z. J. Kapera (ed.), *Mogilany 1995* (Kraków: Enigma, 1996); cf. *The Qumran Chronicle* 5 (1995) 93-96. I am grateful to Prof. Niebuhr for providing me with a typescript of this article prior to publication.

[35]   Both Puech and Niebuhr document the allusions.

[36]   See O. Schilling, "בשׂר בשׂורה," *TWAT* 1 (1973) 845-49.

Works performed through an agent would, of course, be nonetheless the works of God.

Coincidentally, the other controversial problem in this text concerns the identity of the anointed one in v. 1. There is no anointed one in Psalm 146. His introduction here seems as gratuitous as that of Melchizedek in 11QMelchizedek. It can scarcely be coincidence, however, that the one who preaches good news to the poor in Isaiah 61 is an anointed one.[37] If we suppose that the anointed one whom heaven and earth obey in v. 1 is the agent of the miraculous works of the Lord in v. 12, we can at once understand why the anointed one is introduced, and how the good news is supposed to be preached. On this hypothesis, 4Q521 fragment 2, column 2 is a tightly coherent composition.[38] The anointed one in question is a prophet, as in Isaiah 61.[39] More specifically, he is a prophet after the manner of Elijah, the prophet most frequently given an eschatological role in Jewish tradition.[40] Elijah's command of the heavens was legendary. According to Ben Sira, "by the word of the Lord he shut up the heavens and also three times brought down fire" (Sir 48:3). The "two olive trees" in Rev 11:4-6, who have authority to shut up the sky so that no rain may fall and to turn the waters into blood, are usually identified as Elijah and Moses. It is not difficult, then, to see how heaven and earth could be said to obey such a prophet. Moreover, the association with Elijah also explains the most striking innovation in v. 12: the raising of the dead. This element was not present in Isaiah 61, nor in

---

37   O. Betz and R. Riesner, *Jesus, Qumran und die Vatikan* (Freiburg: Herder, 1993) 114.

38   In contrast, R. Bergmeier ("Beobachtungen zu 4 Q 521f 2, II, 1-13," *ZDMG* 145 [1995] 43) finds no coherence between the first two lines and the rest of the fragment and concludes that line 2 marks the end of one psalm and line 3 the beginning of another. This rather desperate proposal ignores the string of allusions to Psalm 146 in lines 1-9.

39   The word משיח occurs in two other passages in 4Q521, but both are fragmentary. Fragment 9 line 3 says "you will abandon by the power of (your) messiah(s)." Fragment 8 line 9 has a clear plural: "and all her anointed ones." Puech ("Une Apocalypse Messianique," 509) suggests that the reference is to priests, but elsewhere in the Scrolls the plural "anointed ones" refers to prophets. See Collins, *The Scepter and the Star*, 118.

40   Collins, *The Scepter and the Star*, 120-21; idem, "The Works of the Messiah," *Dead Sea Discoveries* 1 (1994) 98-112. Niebuhr objects that Elijah is not explicitly said to be anointed, but he was expected as eschatological prophet, and the eschatological prophet is elsewhere called an anointed one.

any of the biblical texts that are alluded to here. It is, however, associated with Elijah, both in his historical career and in his eschatological role.[41]

Two kinds of objection have been brought against this interpretation. First, it is true that the grammatical subject of the verbs in v. 12 is the Lord. No agent is made explicit at this point.[42] Merely to insist on this point, however, is to fail to address the anomalous use of the verb יבשׂר. While it is true that the agent who preaches the good news is a minor figure in the eschatological drama, and certainly not the focal point of the text, it does not follow that no such agent is implied. If the presence of such an agent is not inferred, then neither the reference to the anointed one in v. 1 nor the verb יבשׂר in v. 12 can be satisfactorily explained.

The second objection is that the word משׁיחו in v. 1 is parallel to "holy ones" in v. 2, and can possibly, though not necessarily, be read as a plural. K.-W. Niebuhr has argued at length that both terms should be understood to refer to priests.[43] Priests are often said to be anointed in the Hebrew Bible. They are also often said to be holy. Nonetheless, Niebuhr is unable to cite a single case where either term is used substantively as a noun with clear reference to priests in the plural,[44] and neither can he adduce any parallel for the idea that heaven and earth should obey priests. In the vast majority of cases in Hebrew and Aramaic, holy ones are angels, and angels are never anointed.[45] There is no reason to assume that the parallelism in 4Q521 is synonymous. The two terms may refer to distinct agents through whom divine commands are transmitted. For the commandments of holy ones, compare Dan 4:14: "by decree of the watchers is the sentence; the decree is the utterance of holy ones." The parallel-

---

[41]   Puech has recognized another allusion to Elijah in 4Q521 2 iii, which cites Mal 3:24. See Puech, "Une Apocalypse Messianique," 496-97; Collins, *The Scepter and the Star*, 120.

[42]   So F. Neirynck, "Scriptural Quotations and Interrelationship of the Gospels," paper presented at the *Colloquium Biblicum Lovaniense* XLV (1996); Bergmeier, "Beobachtungen," 44.

[43]   Niebuhr, "4Q521, 2 II."

[44]   The singular משׁיח is used for the eschatological High Priest in the case of the "messiah of Aaron," but there is no corresponding plural usage.

[45]   See J. J. Collins, *Daniel* (Hermeneia; Minneapolis: Fortress, 1993) 313-18. Where the "holy ones" are not angels, as in Ps 34:10, they are the community of the faithful. See also García Martínez, "Messianische Erwartungen," 183.

ism suggests that the anointed one enjoys a status comparable to the holy ones, or angels. A close parallel to this idea is found in *Pss. Sol.* 17:43, where it is said of the royal, Davidic, messiah that "his words are as the words of holy ones in the midst of sanctified peoples."[46] The expression "holy ones" also occurs in conjunction with preaching good news in *Pss. Sol.* 11:1: "Sound in Zion the trumpet to summon the saints. Proclaim in Jerusalem the voice of him who brings good tidings . . ." In this case the saints or holy ones would seem to be the community of the faithful, but the role assigned to "him who brings good tidings" is noteworthy.

The possibility that the word מׁשיחו should be read as a plural can not be fully ruled out. Whereas the spirit of God rests on a singular anointed one in Isaiah 61, in 4Q521 2 ii, v. 6 it hovers over the poor. This verse raises the possibility that the anointed prophet of Isaiah 61 has been "democratized," and that his functions are taken over by the community of the poor. There is no parallel, however, for the use of "anointed ones" with reference to a whole community. Neither can a whole community be envisaged as the agent of God in v. 12. The singular reading in v. 1 remains more satisfactory.[47]

It seems likely, then, that 4Q521, like 11QMelchizedek, envisages a role for an anointed herald or מבשׁר. This figure is not the focus of either text, but he has a significant role nonetheless. In both cases, this role is inferred from the reading of Isaiah 61. The overall theology of the two texts is quite different. 11QMelchizedek reads Isaiah 61 in the context of Leviticus 25, and also introduces the mythological figure of Melchizedek, the biblical High Priest who is understood here as an avenging angel. Neither Melchizedek nor Levitical theology play any role in 4Q521. While the Dead Sea sect often cast itself in the role of the poor, this self-identification was by

---

46   Bergmeier, "Beobachtungen," 43, who also sees an analogy with the universal authority of the messiah in Psalm 2. S. P. Brock ("The Psalms of Solomon," in H. F. D. Sparks, *The Apocryphal Old Testament* [Oxford: Clarendon, 1984] 680) mistakenly translates "holy men." J. Duhaime ("Le Messie et les Saints dans un Fragment Apocalyptique de Qumrân," in R. Kuntzmann [ed.], *Ce Dieu qui Vient. Mélanges Offerts à Bernard Renaud* [LD 159; Paris: Cerf, 1995] 272) proposes tentatively to take the messiah in 4Q521 as a royal messiah, and sees a reference to the one like a son of man and the holy ones in Daniel 7.

47   So also García Martínez, "Messianische Erwartungen," 182-83, who points to the use of singular suffixes referring to God in v. 6.

no means peculiar to Qumran.[48] There is nothing in 4Q521 that
points clearly to a sectarian origin, and the motif of resurrection
rather suggests that the text did not originate in the same community
as the sectarian scrolls. The eschatological reading of Isaiah 61, with
its implications for the role of an eschatological propet, was not
peculiar to the Dead Sea sect, although it received distinctive treatment in 11QMelchizedek.

THE NEW TESTAMENT

Isaiah 61 was also read eschatologically in the New Testament.
Matt 11:2-5 = Luke 7:22, which derive from the Sayings Source, Q,
provide a much-discussed parallel to 4Q521.[49] Jesus responds to the
Baptist's question, "are you the one who is to come, or are we to
wait for another?" by pointing to his deeds: "the blind receive their
sight, the lame walk, the lepers are cleansed, the deaf hear, the dead
are raised, the poor have the good news preached to them."[50] The
parallel with 4Q521 is remarkable, insofar as both include the raising of the dead in addition to the preaching of good news and other
wonders. Matthew refers to the deeds of Jesus as "the works of the
messiah." While Jesus, characteristically, does not identify himself as
the one anointed with the spirit, the implication seems clear in both
Gospels.[51] Jesus is responding to a question about his identity, and he
concludes by declaring blessed anyone who is takes no offense at

---

[48]   See N. Lohfink, *Lobgesänge der Armen* (SBS 143; Stuttgart: Katholisches
Bibelwerk, 1990). In addition to several Hodayot from Qumran, Lohfink discusses
Psalms 140, 146, 147, 149.

[49]   See especially J. D. Tabor and M. O. Wise, "4Q521 'On Resurrection' and
the Synoptic Gospel Tradition: A Preliminary Study," *JSP* 10 (1992) 149-62; repr.
in J. H. Charlesworth (ed.), *Qumran Questions* (BibSem 36; Sheffield: Sheffield
Academic Press, 1995) 151-63. For studies that compare Jesus' saying to the
Greek, Hebrew, and Aramaic versions of Isaiah 61, see R. H. Gundry, *The Use of
the Old Testament in St. Matthew's Gospel* (NovTSup 18; Leiden: Brill, 1967) 79-
80; R. T. France, *Jesus and the Old Testament* (London: Tyndale, 1971) 252-54.

[50]   Σὺ εἶ ὁ ἐρχόμενος ἢ ἕτερον προσδοκῶμεν; καὶ ἀποκριθεὶς ὁ Ἰησοῦς εἶπεν
αὐτοῖς, Πορευθέντες ἀπαγγείλατε Ἰωάννῃ ἃ ἀκούετε καὶ βλέπετε· τυφλοὶ ἀνα-
βλέπουσιν καὶ χωλοὶ περιπατοῦσιν, λεπροὶ καθαρίζονται καὶ κωφοὶ ἀκούουσιν,
καὶ νεκροὶ ἐγείρονται καὶ πτωχοὶ εὐαγγελίζονται (Matt 11:2-5).

[51]   Cf. B. Chilton and C. A. Evans, "Jesus and Israel's Scriptures," in Chilton
and Evans (eds.), *Studying the Historical Jesus: Evaluations of the State of Current
Research* (NTTS 19; Leiden: Brill, 1994) 325.

him. The same identification is implied in Luke 4, although here again the focus is on the events of the eschatological time rather than on the person of the messenger. When he is rejected by the people of Nazareth, Jesus retorts that "no prophet is accepted in his hometown" (Luke 4:24), with the clear implication that he is a prophet. J. A. Fitzmyer comments: "In quoting Second Isaiah, Jesus is presented as consciously aware of the influence of the Spirit upon him" and suggests an allusion to the "anointing" with the Spirit at the baptism of Jesus.[52] Finally, the identification is made explicit in Acts 10:36-38: "You know the message he sent to the people of Israel, preaching peace by Jesus Christ . . . how God anointed Jesus of Nazareth with the Holy Spirit and with power; how he went about doing good and healing all who were oppressed by the devil, for God was with him."

Niebuhr has argued that in these passages "Jesus wird nicht mit einer vorgegebenen messianischen Gestalt identifiziert."[53] Instead, what were the works of the Lord in 4Q521 are now ascribed to Jesus, and historicized as already underway. But Isaiah 61, which provides the common thread in all the texts discussed here, spoke quite clearly of an anointed prophet through whom God's proclamation and consolation were accomplished. This text could certainly be appropriated in different ways and with different emphases, but it established a messianic *Gestalt* that is attested several times in the extant Jewish literature from the period around the turn of the era. This was not the only messianic *Gestalt* with which Jesus was identified in the New Testament. He would also be identified with the more exalted figures of the Davidic messiah and the Danielic "Son of Man." It is clear from the Gospels, however, that Jesus did not preach himself, but the coming kingdom. Insofar as Isaiah 61 and the texts that allude to it emphasize the eschatological liberation rather than the person of the messenger, they provide a paradigm of messi-

---

52   J. A. Fitzmyer, *The Gospel According to Luke I-IX* (AB 28; Garden City: Doubleday, 1981) 529. He goes on to argue that the anointing of Jesus here is not political or kingly, but prophetic or heraldic. Cf. Chilton and Evans, "Jesus and Israel's Scriptures," 325: "By quoting this Isaian passage and claiming its fulfillment in his own person and ministry, Jesus has implied some sort of messianic status."

53   K.-W. Niebuhr, "Der Freudenbote der Heilzeit. Ein Beispiel für die Rezeption frühjüdischer Endzeiterwartungen bei der Wahrnehmung Jesu," unpublished typescript, p. 6. Again, I wish to thank Professor Niebuhr for sharing this manuscript with me before its publication.

anic action that would seem to fit well the career of the historical Jesus as it is described in the Synoptics.[54] The Gospels differ from 4Q521 insofar as they claim that the wonderful deeds are already taking place,[55] but they do make use of a pre-existing, Jewish, messianic *Gestalt*. If the people of Nazareth were shocked and offended by Jesus' sermon, what offended them was not the concept of the herald or his message, but the idea that the son of a local carpenter could claim such a role in the unfolding drama of salvation.[56]

---

[54] Those who accept the authenticity of Jesus' allusion to Isaiah 61 include R. Bultmann, *The History of the Synoptic Tradition* (Oxford: Blackwell, 1972) 110; B. F. Meyer, *The Aims of Jesus* (London: SCM, 1979) 157; A. E. Harvey, *Jesus and the Constraints of History* (London: Duckworth, 1982) 140-53; D. C. Allison and W. D. Davies, *The Gospel According to Saint Matthew* (3 vols., ICC; Edinburgh: T. & T. Clark, 1988-97) 2.244-46; M. de Jonge, *Christology in Context: The Earliest Christian Response to Jesus* (Philadelphia: Westminster, 1988) 206; C. A. Evans, *Jesus and His Contemporaries: Comparative Studies* (AGJU 25; Leiden: Brill, 1995) 120-21, 128-29.

[55] In the case of 11QMelchizedek it is not so clear whether the activity of the מבשר is still in the future.

[56] Sanders ("From Isaiah 61 to Luke 4," 68-69) argues that the offence lay in the prophetic critique, which he finds absent at Qumran. It does not seem to me, however, that the citation from Isaiah is especially critical, or that the audience need have perceived it as such. It is essentially a proclamation of good news. The sharpest critique arises when the audience rejects Jesus and he implies that Gentiles may be more receptive.

THE *AQEDAH, JUBILEES,* AND PSEUDOJUBILEES

James C. VanderKam

INTRODUCTION

Several of the recently accessible cave 4 manuscripts make it more obvious than ever before that Genesis was a text of great importance for the Qumran community. Works such as *1 Enoch, Jubilees,* and the Genesis Apocryphon had made the point abundantly clear decades ago, but, with the addition of new texts from Qumran cave 4, it is that much more apparent. 4Q252 (4QCommentary on Genesis[a]) has garnered more attention than other newly available texts related to Genesis,[1] but the list of such works is considerably longer. Examples are: 4Q213-14 (Aramaic Levi[a-e]), 4Q215 (Testament of Naphtali), 4Q225-27 (PseudoJubilees[a-c]), 4Q253-54a (Commentary on Genesis[b-d]), 4Q369 (Prayer of Enosh), 4Q370 (Apocryphon on the Flood), 4Q422 (Paraphrase of Genesis and Exodus), and 4Q464 (Exposition on the Patriarchs).

One of the recently published texts—4Q225 (4QpseudoJubilees[a])—survives in just three fragments, but the second of them is sufficiently large to reveal that it is a valuable and even intriguing addition to the Qumran exegetical literature on Genesis.[2] Frag. 2, which consists of two nearly contiguous pieces, contains two relatively well preserved columns that deal with several episodes in the life of Abraham. The largest amount of space in the columns is devoted to the story about the near-sacrifice of Isaac. As we will see, the version of Genesis 22 in 4Q225 demonstrates that at least one Jewish expositor, writing perhaps in the first century BCE,[3] was taking exegetical steps that

---

[1] For a presentation and discussion of 4Q252 (with photographs) and references to other studies, see G. J. Brooke, "The Thematic Content of 4Q252," *JQR* 85 (1994) 33-59. Brooke's editions of 4Q252-54a have now been published in DJD 22.

[2] For 4Q225, see the edition in J. T. Milik and J. C. VanderKam, *Qumran Cave 4 VIII: Parabiblical Texts, Part I* (DJD 13; Oxford: Clarendon, 1994) 141-55. All readings and translations of 4Q225 are taken from this edition.

[3] The manuscript was copied in a Herodian hand dating from ca. 30 BCE—20

previously were known to us only from much later Jewish sources.

In the DJD edition of 4Q225, it, with 4Q226-27, is labelled "Pseudo-Jubilees." The designation comes from J. T. Milik, the original editor of these and the *Jubilees* manuscripts from cave 4. To the best of my knowledge, Milik has never explained in print exactly what he meant to convey by calling these texts "PseudoJubilees." In scholarly parlance, a text is called "Pseudo-X" if there has been a tradition of attributing it to X, even though modern critical scholars maintain that it comes from a different author. This is what is meant by calling one of the targums to the pentateuch "Pseudo-Jonathan": it was understood to have been written by the author of the standard targum to the prophets, although it was clearly not compiled by the same Jonathan. Or, to cite another familiar example, Pseudo-Philo's *Biblical Antiquities* is so named because it was wrongly attributed to Philo and transmitted with Latin translations of his works.

It is most unlikely that Milik had this meaning of "Pseudo-" in mind when he decided to call 4Q225-27 "PseudoJubilees": since the texts were unknown until they were found in cave 4, there was no tradition of attributing them to the writer of *Jubilees*. I suggested in the DJD edition of these texts that Milik opted for the category "PseudoJubilees" to convey the idea that ". . . the texts employ language that is familiar from and to some extent characteristic of *Jubilees*, but the documents themselves are not actual copies of *Jubilees*."[4] Milik is not alone among Qumran editors in assigning such a label to texts. A glance at the lists of manuscripts from Qumran reveals these other cases: 4Q243-45 (Pseudo-Daniel[a-c]), 4Q385[a], 387[a], 388[a], 389, 390 (Pseudo-Moses[a-e]), and 4Q385-88, 391 (Pseudo-Ezekiel[a-e]).[5] In these instances the prefixed "Pseudo-" indicates that the speaker is presented as the biblical character in question but that his words are not ones attributed to him in canonical Scripture. There is some justication for the label given to these texts, and this seems to be more in line, as suggested above, with what Milik may have meant when he called 4Q225-27 "Pseudo-Jubilees."

The purpose of this paper is to offer a comparative study of how Genesis 22 is treated in *Jubilees* and in 4Q225 and, as a by-product

---

CE. See Milik and VanderKam, *Qumran Cave 4*, 141.

[4]   Milik and VanderKam, *Qumran Cave 4*, 142.

[5]   See E. Tov with the collaboration of S. J. Pfann, *Companion Volume to the Dead Sea Scrolls Microfiche Edition* (2nd rev. ed., Leiden: Brill, 1995).

of this study, to weigh the utility of the label "PseudoJubilees." The *Aqedah*[6] is the only passage in 4Q225 that is sufficiently long to allow significant conclusions about its character and to permit comparison with other works. How are *Jubilees* and 4Q225 related, if at all, in this particular case? Is 4Q225 so close to *Jubilees* that it is imitating its author and thus may be entitled "PseudoJubilees," or is it rather a more independent attempt to understand a disturbing biblical passage?

GENESIS 22 IN *JUBILEES* AND 4Q225

A. The character of the two compositions. It is readily apparent that *Jubilees* and what remains of 4Q225 are writings of a different character.

1. *Jubilees*: *Jubilees* is noteworthy among the many representatives of the so-called "Rewritten Bible" for how closely it adheres to the biblical text. Naturally it expands the scriptural base in many places, and it abbreviates it in others; in innumerable instances, however, it quotes the Hebrew text of Genesis that was available to the author and follows its order.[7] As a result, the writer treats Genesis 22 in its scriptural setting, after relating the events of chap. 21 and before moving on to those of subsequent chapters. And, in the section where he treats Genesis 22, he alters the wording very little. His presentation of the *Aqedah*, when he is dealing specifically with the text of Genesis 22, is largely a repetition of the biblical version (see below for the details).

2. 4Q225: The same can hardly be said for 4Q225. It may be that

---

6   The term *Aqedah* is used here, not to imply that the texts under discussion have a fully developed theory of Isaac's atoning sacrifice, but simply to refer to the events of Genesis 22 and the interpretation of them in *Jubilees* and 4Q225. Also, the purpose here is not to present a tradition history of Genesis 22 in Jewish and Christian writings. For a discussion of the meaning of *Aqedah* and for much material from the ancient sources, see P. R. Davies and B. D. Chilton, "The Aqedah: A Revised Tradition History," *CBQ* 40 (1978) 514-46.

7   The book has, since its "rediscovery" in the nineteenth century, been used as a witness to the wording of a Hebrew text of Genesis. See, for example, A. Dillmann, "Beiträge aus dem Buch der Jubiläen zur Kritik des Pentateuch-Textes," *Sitzungsberichte der königlichen preussischen Akademie der Wissenschaften zu Berlin* 1 (1882) 323-40; J. C. VanderKam, *Textual and Historical Studies in the Book of Jubilees* (HSM 14; Missoula: Scholars Press, 1977) 214-85; idem, "Jubilees and Hebrew Texts of Genesis-Exodus," *Textus* 14 (1986) 71-85.

the extant fragments offer only a small fraction of what the original text contained. The close parallels between 4Q225 and 226 and the words that can be read on the fragments of the two manuscripts strongly suggest that both are copies of one work that included not only events in Genesis but also some in Exodus and other books (e.g. Joshua) as well.[8] Yet, in those few places where we can follow the author's way of handling Genesis over several lines, it is evident that he did not consistently reproduce the full biblical story. Rather, his procedure was to excerpt passages that centered about a topic. Or at least that is the case in the best preserved parts of 4Q225 (see below). Moreover, as we will notice, where he relates the story of the binding of Isaac, he uses some of the words of Genesis 22 but ultimately fashions a narrative of his own.

B. The introductions to the *Aqedah* in *Jubilees* and 4Q225.

1. *Jubilees*: Although the writer of *Jubilees* remains very close to the biblical text, he prefaces a paragraph to the Genesis 22 material. The paragraph is partly exegetical because it explicates Gen 22:1a (וַיְהִי אַחַר הַדְּבָרִים הָאֵלֶּה וְהָאֱלֹהִים נִסָּה אֶת־אַבְרָהָם), which is not repeated later in the retelling of the biblical story. In a larger measure, however, the introductory paragraph is a new composition.

> 17:15 During the seventh week, in the first year during the first month—on the twelfth of this month—in this jubilee [2003], there were voices in heaven regarding Abraham, that he was faithful in everything that we told him, (that) the Lord loved him, and (that) in every difficulty he was faithful. 17:16 Then Prince Mastema came and said before God: "Abraham does indeed love his son Isaac and finds him more pleasing than anyone else. Tell him to offer him as a sacrifice on an altar. Then you will see whether he performs this order and will know whether he is faithful in everything through which you test him." 17:17 Now the Lord was aware that Abraham was faithful in every difficulty which he had told him. For he had tested him through his land and the famine; he had tested him through the wealth of kings; he had tested him again through his wife when she was taken forcibly, and through circumcision; and he had tested him through Ishmael and his servant girl Hagar when he sent them away. 17:18 In everything through which he tested him he was found faithful. He himself did not

---

[8]   For 4Q226, see Milik and VanderKam, *Qumran Cave 4*, 157-69. 4Q225 2 ii 8-14 and 4Q226 7 offer the same text. 4Q226 refers to incidents such as the meeting of God and Moses at the bush (frag. 1), the time in the wilderness (frag. 3), and crossing the Jordan (frag. 6 lines 4, 6), while it names Joshua so]n of Nun (frag. 4 line 1). 4Q225 frag. 1 has God address Moses directly (line 6) and also speaks about the seashore—presumably that of the Reed Sea.

grow impatient, nor was he slow to act; for he was faithful and one who loved the Lord.[9]

Several features in the introduction show that it reflects the concerns of the author and thus may have come from his hand.

(a) The date. As it does for so many events, *Jubilees* dates the binding of Isaac and places it in the year of the world 2003 (= the first year in the seventh week of the forty-first jubilee). The fact that the prince of Mastemah approached God in this year implies that Isaac, who was born in 1988 (see *Jub.* 16:15 where the promise of his birth occurs in 1987, and 17:1 which places his weaning in 1989), was 15 years of age at the time of the *Aqedah* and thus responsible for his own actions.[10]

More significantly, the entire adventure began in the first month, on the twelfth day (1/12). The twelfth day of the first month is a Sunday in the Jubilean calendar; it is a prime day for beginning activities that will take some time, since the sabbath has just been completed and there would be six days available for carrying out needed labors. *Jub.* 18:3 = Gen 22:3, the next time indicator in the story, relates that Abraham rose early on the next morning and set out on his journey to Mt. Moriah. He reached his destination on the third day (*Jub.* 18:3 = Gen 22:4). There is no indication in *Jubilees* or Genesis that Abraham and his party spent a night at the mountain before proceeding with sacrificial preparations and with the near-sacrifice. The time indicators in the story make it seem as if this is the chronology of the week of the *Aqedah*:

1/12: Mastemah issues his challenge
1/13: Abraham and the others set out for Mt. Moriah
1/15: They arrive on the third day
1/16-18: The return trip, like the journey there, took three days.

If we accept this reconstruction,[11] it would fit the later notice in

---

9   The translation is from VanderKam, *The Book of Jubilees* (2 vols., CSCO 510-11, Scriptores Aethiopici 87-88; Leuven: Peeters, 1989) vol. 2.

10   Josephus (*Ant.* 1.13.2 §227) says that he was 25 years of age.

11   A. Jaubert, to whom we are indebted for impressive and suggestive studies of the *Jubilees*-Qumran calendar, proposed that Abraham began his journey on 1/13 and returned on 1/17 ("Le calendrier des Jubilés et les jours liturgiques de la semaine," *VT* 7 [1957] 252-53). She later modified her proposal so that she had Abraham begin the trip on 1/12 and return on 1/17 (*La notion d'alliance dans la Judaïsme aux abords de l'ère chrétienne* [Paris: Le Seuil, 1963] 90 n. 5). In so doing she agreed with J. van Goudoever, *Biblical Calendars* (2nd ed.; Leiden:

Jubilees that the journey and the events that took place in connection
with it lasted seven days and served as the historical foundation for
the seven-day festival of unleavened bread: "He used to celebrate this
festival joyfully for seven days during all the years. He named it the
festival of the Lord in accord with the seven days during which he
went and returned safely." (18:18) The binding of Isaac would then
have transpired on 1/15, which is the first day of unleavened bread
and, according to Lev 23:14, a day for a מקרא קדש.

Roger Le Déaut, who has provided extensive documentation for
the connections drawn in ancient sources between the *Aqedah* and
Passover, has included *Jubilees'* version of the *Aqedah* in his
survey.[12] His reconstruction of the chronology is largely the one
given above, although he has Abraham leave on the very day that
Mastemah approached the Lord. Nevertheless, he somehow could
still identify the third day of *Jub.* 18:3 = Gen 22:4 as 1/15. "Le
sacrifice d'Isaac coïncide donc exactement avec la célébration de la
Pâque aux dernières heures du 14 Nisan et aux premières heures du
15 (cf. 49,1). Isaac devait donc être sacrifié au temps même où plus
tard serait immolé l'agneau pascal: mais il fut délivré par la substitution du bélier providentiel."[13]

While Le Déaut has properly highlighted the lines that connect
Jubilees' rendition of the *Aqedah* with Passover dates and events, his
chronological conclusions should be corrected. If Abraham departed
on 1/12, the fifteenth would not be the third day. Moreover, if his
return occupied days 16-18, he would have ended his journey on the
sabbath—something that would be very surprising in *Jubilees*.

The author of *Jubilees* in fact connects the *Aqedah* and Passover
more tightly than Le Déaut has indicated. The writer was prevented
by biblical fact from having Abraham celebrate Passover, since the
festival is inextricably linked to a post-Abrahamic event. Although
he had to refrain from mentioning Passover in the patriarch's time,
he does nevertheless have Abraham, who celebrated the festivals of
Unleavened Bread (18:18-19), Weeks (6:19), and Tabernacles
(16:20-31), anticipate this holiday by placing the binding of Isaac on
the date of Passover.

Brill, 1961) 68.

[12]   R. Le Déaut, *La nuit pascale: Essai sur la signification de la Pâque juive à
partir du Targum d'Exode XII 42* (AnBib 22; Rome: Biblical Institute Press, 1963).
His section on *Jubilees* may be found on pp. 179-84.

[13]   Le Déaut, *La nuit pascale*, 179.

If we follow the writer's clues carefully and recognize that he viewed the evening as the beginning of the day,[14] his chronology works this way.

1/12 *Day 1*
>   evening/night: Mastemah challenges God to test Abraham, and God commands the patriarch to go to Mt. Moriah.
>   morning/afternoon: Abraham rises early and journeys toward the mountain.

1/13 *Day 2*
>   evening/night:
>   morning/afternoon: A day of travel

1/14 *Day 3*
>   evening/night:
>   morning/afternoon: Travel and arrival at the mountain; the binding of Isaac

The implication is that the *Aqedah* occurred late in the afternoon or even early in the evening at the end of 1/14—the very time for the Passover meal. We may assume that, since it would have been dark soon after Abraham offered the ram as a substitute for his son, he did not begin the return journey immediately but waited for the morning light.

1/15 *Day 4*
>   evening/night: Abraham and his party spent the night at the mountain.
>   morning/afternoon: A day of travel

1/16 *Day 5*
>   evening/night:
>   morning/afternoon: A day of travel

1/17 *Day 6*
>   evening/night:
>   morning/afternoon: Travel with arrival at Beersheba comfortably before the beginning of the sabbath, just as Abraham had reached the mountain on the third day and still had enough time to climb the mountain, prepare for the near-sacrifice of Isaac, offer the ram, and walk down the mountain again

1/18 *Sabbath*
>   evening:
>   morning/afternoon:

Understood in this fashion, it would be sensible for Abraham to celebrate a seven-day festival, recalling six days of the drama and the seventh day of joyful rest that marked its conclusion.

A small item in *Jubilees* offers another indication that the writer

---

14   See J. Baumgarten, "The Beginning of the Day in the Calendar of Jubilees," *JBL* 77 (1958) 355-60; repr. in his *Studies in Qumran Law* (SJLA 24; Leiden: Brill, 1977) 124-30.

associates *Aqedah* and Passover-Exodus. The title "Prince (of) Mastemah" occurs in only two contexts in *Jubilees*: the binding of Isaac (17:16; 18:9, 12), and the events leading up to the Exodus from Egypt (48:2, 9, 12, 15) when this nefarious character tried to kill Moses and spare the Egyptians. He assisted the Egyptian magicians but the power of God prevailed. "Despite all the signs and miracles, the prince of Mastema was not put to shame until he gained strength and cried out to the Egyptians to pursue you with all the Egyptian army—with their chariots, their horses—and with all the throng of the Egyptian people" (48:12). In the next verse the Angel of the Presence, who is narrating the book, mentions that he stood between Moses, the Egyptians, and the Israelites. This is the only time in *Jubilees* when putting the Prince of Mastemah to shame is noted, other than in the *Aqedah* story (18:12). Also, in 18:9 the angel stood between Abraham and the Prince of Mastema, as he does in 48:13 on behalf of Moses and Israel. There is, then, a series of verbal reminiscences between these two stories that involve the same angels and that center on divine deliverance from extreme danger.

These seven days are presented as the origin of the seven-day festival of Unleavened Bread, but they clearly do not coincide with the dates assigned in the pentateuchal codes to the first pilgrimage festival. Why does the author assign the episode to 1/12-18 rather than to 1/15-21 as in Leviticus 23 and Numbers 28?[15] A likely answer is that associating the sacrifice of Isaac with the later date of Passover was very important to him. Also, it implied that the days of joy for Abraham, after the aborted sacrifice, began on the fifteenth, the first day of this festival of happiness. As we might expect in *Jubilees*, the law to celebrate the festival joyfully for seven days was inscribed on the heavenly tablets (18:19).

(b) Testing Abraham. *Jubilees* transparently places Genesis 22 in a Job-like setting in order to create a larger context for the disturbing words of Gen 22:1-2: ". . . God tested Abraham . . . . Take your son

---

[15]   Baumgarten ("The Calendar of the Book of Jubilees and the Bible" in his *Studies in Qumran Law*, 103-104) thinks that the dates for Abraham's travel should be those of the festival of unleavened bread (1/15-21); and I agreed with this in my essay, "The Origin, Character, and Early History of the 364-Day Calendar: A Reassessment of Jaubert's Hypotheses," *CBQ* 41 (1979) 394. The book itself, however, does not provide any indication that the journey coincided with the precise calendrical dates of the festival; it says only that, as he had gone and returned in seven days, so he celebrated a seven-day holiday.

... and offer him ... as a burnt offering."[16] In this respect it follows the lead of the Chronicler by explaining a potentially offensive divine initiative as actually coming from a malevolent being (cf. 2 Sam 24:1, where the Lord incites David to take a census; in the parallel in 1 Chr 21:1 Satan does so). The offending element in Genesis was not the verb "tested" (נסה) with God as the subject; the Lord, our author informs us, had tested Abraham six times before. The problem was that the test in this instance involved the execution of Abraham's son. We recognize the influence of Job 1–2 not only from the title of the malicious individual who challenges God to try Abraham—the Prince (of) Mastemah, reflecting Job's השטן—but also from the nature of the conversation that takes place between him and God. Here we discover that Abraham's virtues were being reported in heaven: he was faithful, loved by the Lord, and successful in all trials. The sorts of virtues that Abraham is said to possess are not the very same but are similar to those the deity specifies for Job who is blameless, unique, fears God, and turns aside from evil (e.g. Job 1:8).[17]

M. Kister[18] has shown that the motif of these heavenly "voices," or rather "words,"[19] is an exegetical inference that the author drew from וַיְהִי אַחַר הַדְּבָרִים הָאֵלֶּה in Gen 22:1. The term "these words" has been taken literally; hence, speech must have preceded the events of Genesis 22. Kister draws attention in this context to *Gen. Rab.* 55.4 (on Gen 21:1) and *b. Sanh.* 89b, both of which evidence a similar reading of the passage. In *Genesis Rabbah* one finds three

---

16   All biblical quotations are from the NRSV.

17   S. Talmon has written to me that Job, in the biblical book, is modeled on the figure of Abraham. Hence, when *Jubilees* imports Joban themes into the *Aqedah*, the result is intertextuality in two stages.

18   "Observations on Aspects of Exegesis, Tradition, and Theology in Midrash, Pseudepigrapha, and Other Jewish Writings" in J. Reeves (ed.), *Tracing the Threads: Studies in the Vitality of Jewish Pseudepigrapha* (SBLEJL 6; Atlanta: Scholars Press, 1994) 7-15, 20.

19   The Ethiopic term in question is *qālāt* which means *vox* like its Hebrew cognate, but also *sonus, sermo, oratio, verba* (cf. A. Dillmann, *Lexicon Linguae Aethiopicae* [repr. Osnabrück: Biblio Verlag, 1970] cols. 450-51); however, in light of the Hebrew term that lies behind it, "words" would be a more literal rendering in the context. The Ethiopic version of Genesis translates Gen 22:1 somewhat freely: *wa-ᵓem-dexra zentu mawāᶜel* ("and after these days"; see J. O. Boyd, *The Octateuch in Ethiopic* [Bibliotheca Abessinica 3; Leiden: Brill; Princeton: Princeton University Library, 1909] 58).

proposals for the discussion that preceded the events of Genesis 22. The first is that Abraham himself had certain thoughts or hesitations: "He said, 'I rejoiced and I gave joy to everyone, but I did not set aside for the Holy One, blessed be he, an ox or a ram.' Said the Holy One, blessed be he, to him, 'It was because if you were told to sacrifice your son to me, you would not hold him back.'"[20] In the next lines the group that brings the objection consists of the ministering angels,[21] and God makes a similar rejoinder. The third party to mention Abraham's failure is the nations; they receive the same divine answer.[22] The discussion here is not the same as in *Jubilees*, but the issue certainly is: in the face of objections from different quarters (including Abraham himself) about Abraham's true loyalty, God himself knows that, if he demanded it of his friend, Abraham would not withhold his son. In other words, the purpose of the test was not to instruct God; he already knew the nature of Abraham. Others, however, needed to be shown. *B. Sanh.* 89b attests a parallel tradition,[23] but in it the one making the objection is Satan; hence it is a later witness to the very motif that we find in both *Jubilees* and 4Q225.

It should also be noted that the new introductory paragraph lists six trials that Abraham had endured; thus the command to kill Isaac was hardly the first. Instead it was the significant seventh in the divine pedagogy of Abraham.[24] That is, *Jubilees* takes up the virtues

---

[20]   The translation is from J. Neusner, *Genesis Rabbah: The Judaic Commentary to the Book of Genesis: A New American Translation* (3 vols., BJS 104-106; Atlanta: Scholars Press, 1985) 2.269.

[21]   Their presence here is interesting in light of what is said about the angels in 4Q225 (see below). The exegetical basis for introducing these angels into the Genesis 22 scene is also given: "In accord with the view of R. Eleazar, who has said, 'Any passage in which it is said, "And the Lord," refers to him and his court' . . . ." Neusner's rendering is confusing here; the text does not say "the Lord" but "God," as one would expect from Gen 22:1 (וְהָאֱלֹהִים).

[22]   The third section is absent from Neusner's translation.

[23]   R. H. Charles (*The Book of Jubilees or the Little Genesis* [London: A. & C. Black, 1902] 120-21) drew attention to this parallel.

[24]   The list in this paragraph certainly makes it seem as if the *Aqedah* is the seventh trial. The first six are: (1) leaving his homeland; (2) famine; (3) the wealth of kings; (4) the forcible removal of his wife; (5) circumcision; and (6) sending Ishmael and Hagar away. A later passage, *Jub.* 19:8, mentions a tenth test that Abraham endured (the death of Sarah and purchase of a burial plot for her). It does not, however, name what the eighth and ninth were.

of Abraham and spells them out in detail, especially by noting that God had subjected him to a number of trials, in all of which the patriarch proved himself faithful. This, too, is reminiscent of Job—a man who was tested to the utmost by God and who, interestingly enough, actually lost his sons in the trials that befell him. *Jub.* 17:17 introduces the section with "Now the Lord was aware . . . ." These words seem to be directed against the inference a reader might draw from Genesis 22: God's ignorance of the patriarch's character led him to test Abraham. After all, in Gen 22:12 we read the words of the angel who speaks for God: ". . . for *now I know* that you fear God, since you have not withheld your son, your only son, from me." Did God, speaking through his angel, not know this before Abraham almost executed his son? *Jubilees* provides the answer: of course he knew, but the Prince of Mastemah had issued a challenge, and *he* was the one who had to be educated. It is odd, in light of *Jub.* 17:17, that the author still reproduces Gen 22:12 (= *Jub.* 18:11; but see v. 9), although the verse in its Jubilean setting may entail only that the Angel of the Presence who is telling the story acquired this new piece of information.

2. 4Q225. The lines that precede the story of the *Aqedah* in 4Q225 2 i read thus:

1 [   ] [   ]t that per[son] will be cut off
2 [from among] his [peo]ple. [he sta]yed in Haran twenty [ye]ars.
3 [And A]braham [said] to God: "My Lord, I go on being childless and Eli[ezer]
4 is [the son of my household,] and he will be my heir."   *vacat*
5 [The Lo]rd [said] to A[b]raham: "Lift up (your eyes) and observe the stars, and see
6 [and count] the sand which is on the seashore and the dust of the earth, for if
7 these [can be num]bered and al[so] if not, your seed will be like this." And [Abraham] be[lieved]
8 [in] G[o]d, and righteousness was accounted to him. A son was born af[ter] this
9 [to Abraha]m, and he named him Isaac.

The initial lines of 4Q225 2 i contain a formula attested in legal contexts: "that person will be cut off from his people" (lines 1-2; cf. Lev 7:20, 21, etc.; Num 15:31). Since virtually all the remaining material in 4Q225 2 i-ii deals in some way with Abraham, it is logical to assume that these words also came from an Abrahamic context. The only passage in the Abraham cycle in which the phrase occurs is Gen 17:14: "Any uncircumcised male who is not circumcised in the flesh of his foreskin shall be cut off from his people; he has broken my covenant." How the writer tied this theme with the sections that follow is not clear.[25] Nor do we know who the person is who "sta]yed in Haran twenty [ye]ars" at the end of line 2. The only biblical character who remained in Haran for 20 years was Jacob (Gen 31:38, 41; *Jub.* 27:19; 29:5); Abram spent only 14 or 17 years there.[26]

There is no break in the text (that is, no blank space) before 4Q225 2 i 3 where the biblical base is unmistakably Genesis 15. The writer nearly quotes Gen 15:2-3 at this point: "And A]braham [said] to God: 'My Lord, I go on being childless and Eli[ezer] is [the son of my household,] and he will be my heir'." (lines 3-4) Only after these words are cited does the scribe leave a sizable blank space, presumably to mark a break of some sort in the text. The fragmentary condition of the previous lines makes it difficult to see how Gen 15:2-3 is related (if it is) to the expressions "that person will be cut off from among his people" and "he stayed in Haran twenty years". In fact, there seems to be more continuity with the material that follows the *vacat*. Just before the blank space the issue of a son for Abraham arises; in the sequel that son is born and is nearly killed. However, the fact that his life is spared at the last moment allows for the births of the individuals whom the author names in the genealogy near the end of the next column (col. ii); it thus provides the possibility that the divine promise of numerous progeny will be fulfilled. These lines—4Q225 2 ii 10-11—read: "God the Lord blessed Is[aac all the days of his life. He became the father of] Jacob, and Jacob became the father of Levi, [a third] genera[tion." In other words, for about two columns of 4Q225, the writer is concerned with Abraham's progeny, with the sacred line that arises from him and his son Isaac. The theme of offspring for Abraham provides the setting for the author's rendition of the *Aqedah* story.

---

25   In light of the connection that *Jubilees* draws between the *Aqedah* and the festival of Unleavened Bread, it is at least interesting that the "cutting off" formula occurs twice with regard to the same holiday (Exod 12:15, 19). It is, however, used in other contexts as well, so little should be made of this.

26   For the chronology of Abra(ha)m's life in Genesis and *Jubilees* and a discussion of the issues involved, see J. C. VanderKam, "Das chronologische Konzept des Jubiläenbuches," *ZAW* 107 (1995) 88-96.

Once he has cited Abra(ha)m's claim from Gen 15:2-3, our author moves swiftly to Gen 15:5-6 as the immediate divine reply to what Abraham has said: "The Lo]rd [said] to A[b]raham: 'Lift up (your eyes) and observe the stars, and see [and count] the sand which is on the seashore and the dust of the earth, for if these [can be num]bered, and al[so] if not, your seed will be like this.' And [Abraham] be[lieved in] G[o]d, and righteousness was accounted to him." (4Q225 2 i 5-8) God's response is followed immediately by the birth notice about Isaac which is drawn from Gen 21:2-3. The writer's thematic concern, then, with texts that have to do with a son for Abraham is evident throughout: Abraham feared that he would die childless; God reiterated his promise of an innumerable progeny—a promise Abraham accepted; and Isaac was born. Intervening biblical material such as the birth and eventual expulsion of Ishmael,[27] the covenantal origins of circumcision, and the Sodom-Gomorrah cycle had no place in this selective format.

While the larger part of the material that precedes the Genesis 22 events in 4Q225 does not resemble the setting for them in *Jubilees*, the sentence that comes immediately before the first words from Genesis 22 is indeed strongly reminiscent of *Jubilees* in that 4Q225, too, envisages the action as occurring within a Joban context: "Then the Prince of the Ma[s]temah [שׂר המ[שׂ]טמ[ה] came [to G]od, and he accused [וישׂטים] Abraham regarding Isaac." These words not only

---

27   C. Werman ("The Attitude Towards Gentiles in The Book of Jubilees and Qumran Literature Compared with the Early Tanaaic Halakha and Contemporary Pseudepigrapha" [unpublished Ph. D. dissertation, the Hebrew University, 1995 (Hebrew)]) has devoted an appendix to her chapter on Ishmael to 4Q225 (pp. 142-46). She argues that the author creates an analogy between Abraham and Jacob (hence the 20 years in Haran for Abraham) and points out that here Abraham proposes Eliezer as heir whereas in Genesis he fears he will be his heir. In our text, she thinks, there is a struggle between Isaac and another individual who is not named in the extant parts but is alluded to in col. ii 10 (לא יהיה אהב). In this respect it resembles the midrashim that create a tension between Ishmael and Isaac in the context of the *Akedah*. As the Jacob stories are meant to exclude Esau from being a candidate for the position of heir, so this story is meant to exclude Ishmael; perhaps the role of Eliezer here also serves to diminish Ishmael's status. It is possible that such concerns underlie parts of 4Q225, but there is no way of knowing for sure whether circumcision is under discussion at the beginning of col. i and the referent of the 20-year stay in Haran is also not specified. And, of course, Ishmael is never mentioned in the text, nor does the context of ii 10 indicate what point is being made.

reveal the Hebrew original behind *Jubilees'* several references to the Prince (of) the Mastemah but also show the verbal action that gave rise to his title. The verb שטם is used by Job to describe God's attacks on him in 16:9; 30:21; in both places, though, it is used in the *qal* conjugation, not in the *hiphʿil* as in our text.[28]

As we have seen, *Jubilees* relates the binding of Isaac directly to the events of Passover and Exodus by means of how it dates the events of Genesis 22. It does so also by using the title "Prince (of) Mastemah" which occurs only in the *Aqedah* story and in the Exodus account (*Jub.* 17:16; 18:9, 12; 48:2, 9, 12, 15).[29] It may be that 4Q225, too, relates these stories, although the connection is drawn somewhat differently. The principal evidence arises from 4Q225 frag. 1. The piece comes from the top of a column and is therefore not part of either cols. i or ii of frag. 2, since the tops of both are preserved. Milik placed it before frag. 2, but there is no convincing reason for locating it there rather than after frag. 2 where it seems more logically to belong. In this fragment there is a series of hints that it is dealing in a Jubilean way with several events that happened in the time of the Exodus from Egypt.

1. In frag. 1 line 6 there is a direct address to Moses: ואתה מושה בדברי עמ[כה *vacat* [; the same phenomenon occurs a number of times in *Jubilees*.[30]

2. Line 3 contains the words ויכא אותם ב; while they may be referring to a different context, they do remind one of the plague narrative. Note especially *Jub.* 48:5: "The Lord effected a great revenge against them on account of Israel. He struck them . . . ."

3. Line 5 reads: [.ת מצרים וימכור אותם אלוהים[31] Since the direct object is plural in form, it does not refer to Joseph, whom his brothers sold into Egypt. Possibly the text is pointing to the period of Egyptian slavery before the Exodus.

4. Line 8 could also be construed in an Exodus setting: ה עומד[ויקם הו]אה.[32] The extant letters recall *Jub.* 48:8-9a: "The Lord did

---

28   In Zech 3:1 the wording for the satan and what he does is described thus: והשטן עמד על ימינו לשטנו.

29   The noun *Mastemah* alone appears in *Jub.* 10:8, 11; 11:5, 11; 19:28.

30   *Jub.* 23:32; 30:11; 33:13, 18; 49:22; cf. also 2:24; 6:13, 20, 32; 15:28; 41:26; 49:15.

31   The verb וימכור is written above the word אותם.

32   In this context ויקם probably derives from נקם, since a verb of standing immediately precedes it. Also, it may be that the ה at the right edge is the last letter

everything for the sake of Israel and in accord with his covenant which he made with Abraham to take revenge on them just as they were enslaving them with force. The Prince of Mastema would stand up against you . . . ."

5. Line 10 includes the expression עֽ[ל שפת ה]ים which may allude to the Reed Sea at the time of the crossing. Cf. *Jub.* 49:23: "For you celebrated this festival hastily when you were leaving Egypt until the time you crossed the sea into the Wilderness of Sur, because you completed it on the seashore."[33]

These are only hints, but Exodus themes were also part of 4Q225. The ones that figure in frag. 1 stand in an unclear relationship to the *Aqedah* account in frag. 2 i-ii. The last words of frag. 2 ii, however, are also reminiscent of *Jubilees'* story about the Exodus events. After listing the genealogy of Abraham-Isaac-Jacob-Levi and apparently specifying the sum of how many years they lived—a time-span that would cover all the period in Canaan and reach to the Egyptian era—the author writes:

> "The Prince of the Mastemah was bound on [account of them. The angels of
> holiness   were]
> the Prince of the Ma[s]temah. Belial listened to [the Prince of the Mastemah
> (?)]."[34]

These lines may refer to the days (1/14-18; see *Jub.* 48:15) when, according to *Jubilees*, Mastemah was tied up so that he could not, as his name implies he would, accuse the Israelites. CD 5:18-19 says that Belial inspired Jannes and his brother, the Egyptian magicians, to oppose Moses and Aaron.[35]

Consequently, there is some justification for saying that 4Q225, like *Jubilees*, relates the *Aqedah* in several ways to the great events of the Exodus.

C. The story of the binding of Isaac in *Jubilees* and 4Q225.

1. *Jubilees*: *Jubilees'* retelling of Gen 22:1-19 is, as noted above,

---

of המשטמה.

[33] Though other explanations are clearly possible, the words מעוון הזנות in line 1 could reflect Ezekiel 23 in which the Egyptian sojourn is characterized as a time of fornication (verbal and noun forms related to the root זנה are frequent in vv. 3, 8, 19-21, 27).

[34] The words and letters found on 4Q225 2 ii 13-14 can be supplemented at this point by 2Q226 7 lines 6-7. For a study of the two texts, see Milik and VanderKam, *Qumran Cave 4*, 153-54.

[35] For further references, see Milik and VanderKam, *Qumran Cave 4*, 154.

very nearly the same as in the Bible. In fact, it is accurate to say that,
apart from several cases of abbreviating the somewhat repetitive text
of Genesis, *Jubilees* generally deviates from the MT only in a text-
critical sense; that is, its differences from the MT are attested in
ancient versions of the Bible and probably derive from a slightly
different Hebrew biblical text.[36] Moreover, *Jubilees* omits no section
or even any verse of Gen 22:1-19, and it always reflects the order of
Genesis. In other words, for all practical purposes, *Jub*. 18:1-17
equals Gen 22:1b-19. More specifically, *Jub*. 18:1-8 = Gen 22:1b-10,
and *Jub*. 18:10-17 = Gen 22:11-19. There is one verse, however, in
which *Jubilees* offers a text not found in Genesis. At *Jub*. 18:9 we
read (the Angel of the Presence who narrates the book is speaking):
"Then I stood in front of him and in front of the Prince of
Mastema.[37] The Lord said: 'Tell him not to let his hand go down on
the child and not to do anything to him because I know that he is one
who fears the Lord'." These words prepare for Gen 22:11-12 and at
the same time express some more widespread concerns in *Jubilees*:
the angel has direct contact with Abraham, and this angel intervenes
between Abraham and the Prince of Mastemah who is also at the
scene. The angelic narration continues in vv. 10-11 where, in
contrast to the third-person form of Gen 22:11-12, he speaks in the
first person. Moreover, in v. 12a the writer reports that "the prince
of Mastema was put to shame" (cf. 48:12). These are the only major
interventions by the writer, apart from a few cases such as the gloss
identifying Moriah with Zion (v. 13).[38]

Once the writer of *Jubilees* has finished the story, he draws the
chronological and liturgical points about the festival of Unleavened
Bread that were noted above (18:18-19) and then turns his attention
to the events of Genesis 23 (the death of Sarah). Thus, his fidelity to
the text of Scripture has dictated the place that the *Aqedah* occupies
in his book and, to a very large extent, the wording of the story. The

---

[36]   Some examples are: *Jub*. 18:2 = Gen 22:2: ידידך [= LXX τὸν ἀγαπητόν]
for MT's יחידך; *Jub*. 18:12 = Gen 22:13: אחר [= Samaritan Pentateuch, LXX,
etc.] for MT's peculiar אחר; *Jub*. 18:15 = Gen 22:17: ערי [? = Peshitta, LXX, etc.]
for MT's שער.

[37]   As noted above, this is one of the clear parallels between this chapter and
the events before the Exodus as related in *Jubilees*.

[38]   1 Chr 3:1 is the earliest source for this identification. Later, it also appears
in *Tg. Neof.* and *Frag. Tg.*Gen. 22:14; Josephus, *Ant*. 1.13.2 §226; and *Gen.
Rab*. 56.10 (on Gen 22:14).

writer, after his special introduction that centers around the words of Gen 22:1a, has modified the text only slightly in subjecting it to the contours and aims of his Scriptural survey.

2. 4Q225. 4Q225 quotes (with a few small changes) the biblical text at the beginning of the story about the binding of Isaac (2 i 10–ii 4a), but from 2 ii 4b-12 it is almost totally unlike Genesis 22 and the version of it in *Jubilees* 18. In the initial section, where his text closely parallels that of Genesis, the author of 4Q225 does, however, continue abbreviating Scripture and making other minor modifications in it (e.g. in word-order). A few examples will make these features clear.

Gen 22:1-2	ויאמר אליו אברהם ויאמר הנני ויאמר קח נא את בנך את יחידך אשר אהבת את יצחק
4Q225 2 i 10-12	ויאמר [א]לוהים [אל אבר]הם קח את בנכה את ישחק את יחיד[כה אשר אתה אהב]תה
Gen 22:2	ולך לך אל ארץ המוריה והעלהו שם לעלה על אחד ההרים אשר אמר אליך
4Q225 2 i 12-13	והעלהו לי לעולה על אחד ההרים הגבוה]ים [אשר אומר] לכה
Gen 22:3	וישכם אברהם בבקר ... ויקם וילך אל המקום אשר אמר לו האלהים
4Q225 2 i 13	ויק[ום וי]ל[ך] מן הבארות על ה[ר מוריה]

Thus, for instance, our writer omits God's calling Abraham by name and the patriarch's response. For him it was enough to report ויאמר [א]לוהים [אל אבר]הם. Genesis (and *Jubilees*) have what could be called a more impersonal formulation of the command to sacrifice: Abraham is told simply to sacrifice his son. 4Q225 adds a small word—לי— which serves to soften the horrifying command slightly: the holocaust is to be offered to God himself. Perhaps the point would have been obvious from Gen 22:2, but 4Q225 alone expresses it. The next sentence reflects in shorter form parts of Gen 22:3. It omits such details as the identity of the individuals and materials Abraham brought with him. The only really unexpected feature here is the specification of the place from which Abraham is said to have departed–מן הבארות. The wells are fitting for the area of Beersheba: its name, of course, contains the word for "well", and it was also a place around which were a number of wells (see Gen 21:22-34; 26:15-22, cf. v. 33). Genesis puts Abraham in Beersheba just before the events of chap. 22 (21:33), and he returns to it after the journey to Mt. Moriah (22:19).

After line 13 the text becomes very fragmentary, but the

preserved letters show that here too Abraham lifted his eyes as he
neared the mountain (= Gen 22:4). It is possible that in the first line
of col. ii the word "fire" appears: if so, it would agree with some
later sources that indicate how it was that Abraham recognized the
correct mountain, which had previously been identified only as the
one that God would point out to him (perhaps called "one of the high
mountains" in line 12).[39] Once the text can again be read with
confidence, it reflects the words of Genesis quite closely, but
Abraham's instructions to his young men are omitted (the young men
are never mentioned in 4Q225). There is space at the end of line 1
only for reference to something like Abraham's placing the wood on
Isaac.

Gen 22:7-8	ויאמר יצחק אל אברהם אביו ויאמר אבי ויאמר הנני בני ויאמר
	הנה האש והעצים ואיה השה לעלה ויאמר אברהם אלהים יראה
	לו השה לעלה בני
4Q225 2 ii 2-3	ויאמר ישחק אל אברהם [אביו הנה האש והעצים ואיה השה] לעלה
	ויאמר אברהם אל[

Again we see the abbreviating tendency of the Qumran text, but the
essentials of the biblical lines are reproduced. The last preserved
letters in line 3 could be construed as the first two letters of אלהים as
in Gen 22:8 (note לו, the last word of Gen 22:8, at the beginning of
line 4), but there would have been too much space for only the
words of Gen 22:8 in the lost section at the end line 3, and the first
words in line 4 show that something different is happening. In
Genesis, after Abraham says that God will provide a lamb, Isaac
lapses into silence; he says nothing more in the entire story.
However, in 4Q225 2 ii 4 we have an unmistakable introduction to
another statement by Isaac: אמר ישחק אל אביו כ]. At this point
4Q225 parts company with Genesis 22 and takes its place among the
later retellings of the story. These lines appear as follows in the DJD
edition:

[	לו אמר ישחק אל אביו כ]פות אותי יפה	4
	ו	
[	מלאכי קודש עומדימ בוכים על] המזבח	5
	את בניו מן הארץ ומלאכי המ[שטמה	6
[אם]	שמחים ואומרים עכשו יאבד ו[בכול זה ינסה שר המשטמה	7
	ימצא כחש ואם לא ימצא נאמן א[ברהם לאלוהים ויקרא]	8
[	אברהם אברהם ויאמר הנני ויאמר ע[תה ידעתי כי	9

---

[39]   See Milik and VanderKam, *Qumran Cave 4*, 151 for references to the
ancient sources.

10 לא יהיה אהב ויברך אל יהוה את יׄשֿ]חק כל ימי חיו ויוליד את]
11 יעקוב ויעקוב הוליד את לוי דׄוֿ]ר שלישי *vacat* ויהיו כול]
12 ימי אברהם וישחק ויעקוב ולוֿ]י שנה]

The new elements vis-à-vis Genesis (and *Jubilees*) in lines 4-8a are:

1. Isaac's final saying which is attested in lengthier forms in a number of later texts.[40]

2. The reference to the angels of holiness who were standing by, weeping as they saw what was unfolding. *Gen. Rab.* 56.5 (on Gen 22:9) offers a very close parallel: "Now at the moment at which our father, Abraham, stretched out his hand to take the knife to slaughter his son, the ministering angels wept."[41]

3. The angels of Mastemah were rejoicing at their apparent victory over the divine plan. ויקרא (Gen 22:11) probably came at the end of line 4Q225 2 ii 8b because the first words of line 9 are from v. 11: וַיִּקְרָא אֵלָיו מַלְאַךְ יְהוָה מִן־הַשָּׁמַיִם וַיֹּאמֶר אַבְרָהָם אַבְרָהָם וַיֹּאמֶר הִנֵּנִי. It appears that the remainder of line 9 and the beginning of line 10 contained God's declaration about Abraham's faithfulness. God's blessing is then described, and the genealogy of Abraham and Isaac is given, together with the total number of years that they and Jacob and Levi lived. A continuation of the same setting may be present in the last lines of col. ii (lines 13-14): there is reference to the Prince of Mastemah's being bound; Belial is also mentioned (see above).

CONCLUSIONS REGARDING PSEUDOJUBILEES

Where does this analysis leave us with regard to the questions with which we began? Are the treatments of the *Aqedah* in *Jubilees* and 4Q225 so strongly similar that we may conclude 4Q225 is imitating

---

40 See Milik and VanderKam, *Qumran Cave 4*, 151-52 for sources that attribute another statement to Isaac. Since they use the verb כפת and a *kaph* is the first and only preserved letter of his speech in line 4, it has been restored there in the edition. The sources that attest a speech here are *Tg. Ps.-J.* Gen 22:10; *Tg. Neof.* Gen 22:10; and *Gen. Rab.* 56.7 (on Gen 22:11). These texts supply a longer statement for Isaac than the available space in 4Q225 would permit, but it seems likely that the Qumran text had a shorter version expressing a similar idea. According to these sources, the younger and more vigorous Isaac was concerned that he would move and thus blemish his father's sacrifice. Hence he urged him to tie him well.

41 See Milik and VanderKam, *Qumran Cave 4*, 152 for a fuller discussion of parallels. *Jubilees* speaks of just one angel; yet in 18:14 that angel mentions his companions.

Jubilees? Is the category "PseudoJubilees," therefore, a fitting one for a text such as 4Q225 insofar as we know it?

The first point to notice is that there are indeed some important similarities between the basic stances of the two texts. *Jubilees* and 4Q225 are, to the best of our knowledge, the oldest texts that present the *Aqedah* in a setting drawn from the book of Job, and both make their indebtedness plain at the very beginning of the story. That is, both state, before following the progression of the drama, that the entire episode resulted from the devilish scheme of the Prince of Mastemah. Like Job's Satan, he came forward and challenged Abraham regarding his son Isaac. The facts that both texts use this setting and that both employ the same name for the accuser are significant points of agreement between them.

A second point of agreement is that both texts evidence connections between Genesis 22 and the events of the Exodus from Egypt. The point is clearer in *Jubilees*, but 4Q225 frag. 1 and the end of 4Q225 frag. 2 ii suggest that the writer saw some relation between the *Aqedah* and the sequence of events that constituted the Exodus.

A third similarity is that angels play a role in both accounts. In *Jubilees* the Angel of the Presence who tells the story is the only significant actor (apart from the Prince of Mastemah), but he does mention others in 18:14. 4Q225 is more explicit: it has groups of God's angels and Mastemah's angels surround the altar on which Isaac is bound. It also notes something of the reaction of each to the events that unfolded.

While there are such significant parallels between the two texts, there are also prominent differences.

First, *Jubilees* retells the biblical story with an interesting preface. It does not deviate from the scriptural account in the large-scale way in which 4Q225 does. That is, *Jubilees* does not share the selective approach that 4Q225 shows in connection with the biblical text; moreover, it does not provide an extra speech for Isaac, nor does it detail the presence and reactions of the good and evil angels. *Jubilees* also does not connect the story with the priestly genealogy from Abraham through Levi. However, *Jubilees* does date the action to specific days in the first month of the year, and in this way it brings the *Aqedah* and the Passover into close relationship with each other. 4Q225 supplies no dates. And, perhaps more importantly, the two works have a different narrative setting: in *Jubilees* an Angel of the Presence tells the story, but in 4Q225 there is a third-person narrator who is never identified.

There are more similarities and dissimilarities between *Jubilees* and 4Q225, but the fact is that *Jubilees* and 4Q225 appear to be markedly different kinds of compositions. For all we know, they could be two largely independent embodiments of exegetical traditions; or, if the author of 4Q225 knew *Jubilees*, he manifestly altered it in his retelling of Genesis 22. There appears to be no justification for classifying the cave 4 text as "PseudoJubilees" because it is not, as nearly as we can tell, pretending to be the work of this author, nor is there any indication that anyone thought it was. 4Q225 seems to be another, extra-Jubilean interpretation of Genesis passages, another more independent witness to the importance of Genesis at Qumran.

A SCRIPTURE PROFILE OF THE BOOK OF THE WATCHERS

Kenneth E. Pomykala

The literature presently included in the Hebrew Bible offered early Jewish authors a rich reservoir of traditions, images, and terms on which to draw in order to express their own ideas to their contemporaries. Further, it is evident that between the scriptural texts and the newly composed documents lies an imaginative labor of no small proportion. Through assorted processes of selection, juxtaposition, modification, and elaboration, early Jewish authors not only recalled the Scriptures, but recast them. Moreover, it goes without saying that embedded in the above mentioned processes are hermeneutical judgments on the part of the authors—judgments no doubt motivated and shaped by the historical-social context from which these documents emerged or were meant to address. Today, this point "goes without saying" in large measure because Jim Sanders has consistently reminded us throughout his scholarly career to attend to the hermeneutical judgments embedded in early Jewish— and early Christian—texts.[1] Thus, for Sanders, it is always a question of *how* the Scriptures were used; or put another way, what were the hermeneutics?

Accordingly, the following essay investigates how the Hebrew Scriptures were utilized in the Book of the Watchers (henceforth: BW), an early Jewish apocalypse preserved as *1 Enoch* 1–36.[2] To do

---

[1]   See esp. J. A. Sanders, "Adaptable for Life: The Nature and Function of Canon," in F. M. Cross, W. E. Lemke, and P. D. Miller Jr. (eds.), *Magnalia Dei: The Mighty Acts of God. Essays on the Bible and Archaeology in Memory of G. Ernest Wright* (Garden City: Doubelday, 1976) 531-60; idem, "Hermeneutics in True and False Prophecy," in G. W. Coats and Burke O. Long (eds.), *Canon and Authority: Essays in Old Testament Religion and Theology* (Philadelphia: Fortress, 1977) 21-41; idem, *Canon and Community* (Guides to Biblical Scholarship; Philadelphia: Fortress, 1984).

[2]   An earlier version of this paper was presented at the Scripture in Early Judaism and Christianity Section, at the Annual Meeting of the Society of Biblical Literature, Chicago, 1994, under the title "Epic Imagination in the Book of the

this, I will set forth what I will call a scripture profile of BW—that
is, a catalog of its use of materials from the Scriptures that reviews
both the texts which were invoked and the ways they were employed.
While this catalog will be reasonably comprehensive, it will not be
exhaustive. Little would be gained in an attempt to find every
potential allusion to texts in the Hebrew Bible, some of which in any
case would remain debatable. Nonetheless, it is hoped that what is
included will satisfactorily represent the ways in which Scripture was
appropriated in BW. Then, in light of this scripture profile, I will
make five observations relative to the interpretive strategies
uncovered and the implications of such strategies.

Finally, it should be noted that BW represents an interesting candidate for investigating the use of biblical traditions in Second Temple
literature. On the one hand, the composition of BW is dated to ca.
200 BCE, making it one of the earliest examples of Jewish biblical
interpretation outside the Bible.[3] As a result, it reflects the use of
Scripture at a time when the Hebrew canon was still emerging.
(Indeed, it must be acknowledged that the terms "biblical" and
"Scripture," as I have used them above, do not carry the same force
here with respect to BW as the later use of these terms might imply.)
On the other hand, BW never explicitly appeals to "Scripture" as a
basis for its authority; instead it claims to present heavenly revelations
(*1 Enoch* 1:2; 13:8; 14:1). Both of these factors raise the question of
the relationship between BW and the texts and traditions it cites—
texts and traditions that were later recognized as canonical. For now
that question must be left open, but I will return to this subject in my
concluding observation.

A SCRIPTURE PROFILE OF BW

For the present purpose, BW can be divided into three main sections: the Blessing of Enoch (chaps. 1–5); the Myth of the Watchers
(chaps. 6–11); and the Story of Enoch and the Watchers (chaps. 12–
36). For each section, I will examine the use of biblical materials.

The Blessing of Enoch (*1 Enoch* 1–5) begins by introducing Enoch
as a figure who, on the basis of a heavenly vision, speaks a word of
blessing for the righteous of a distant generation in the day of

---

Watchers."

[3]   See J. J. Collins, *The Apocalyptic Imagination* (New York: Crossroad,
1984) 36, for the date and literary integrity of BW.

distress (*1 Enoch* 1:1-3a). The words used to characterize Enoch's blessing paraphrase Deut 33:1 and Num 24:3-4, the Blessing of Moses and the Blessing of Baalam, respectively.[4] In addition, the assertion that Enoch's blessing pertains to a distant generation appears to be modeled on Baalam's claim in Num 24:14 that he would tell Balak about matters "in the latter days" (באחרית הימים).[5] Hence, these scriptural allusions serve to set Enoch within the tradition of the great biblical prophets who spoke for God—both Israelite and non-Israelite—and to ground his eschatological vision within that prophetic tradition.

A report of Enoch's vision of a theophany at Mount Sinai follows (*1 Enoch* 1:3b-9). It opens with the words:

> The Holy and Great One will come out from his dwelling, and the Eternal God will tread from there upon Mount Sinai, and he will appear with his hosts, and will appear in the strength of his power from heaven (*1 Enoch* 1:3b-4).[6]

God appears for the purpose of judgment. His coming inspires fear in everyone, even the angels, and occasions assorted geologic deformations. Language and imagery used to describe the theophany derive principally from Mic 1:3-4, but also reflect other prophetic passages such as Habakkuk 3, Zechariah 14, and Isa 26:21.[7] References to Mount Sinai as the geographical location of God's appearance and to the ten thousand holy ones who accompany God (*1 Enoch* 1:9) are based on Deut 33:2, from the Blessing of Moses. Noteworthy, however, is the difference between Deut 33:2 and *1 Enoch* 1:4. In the biblical text, Moses refers retrospectively to the theophany at Mount Sinai as the location where God gave Israel the Law. In BW, Mount Sinai is the place where God will appear for eschatological judgment and the destruction of the earth. Finally, the

---

4   L. Hartman, *Asking for a Meaning: A Study of 1 Enoch 1–5* (ConBNT 12; Lund: Gleerup, 1979) 22-23.

5   Cf. J. C. VanderKam, "Biblical Interpretation in 1 Enoch and Jubilees," in J. H. Charlesworth and C. A. Evans (eds.), *The Pseudepigrapha and Early Biblical Interpretation* (JSPSup 14; SSEJC 2; Sheffield: Sheffield Academic Press, 1993) 102.

6   Unless otherwise noted, English translations are from M. A. Knibb, *The Ethiopic Book of Enoch: A New Edition in Light of the Aramaic Dead Sea Fragments* (2 vols., Oxford: Clarendon Press, 1978).

7   Hartman, *Asking*, 23–24. See also, J. C. VanderKam, "The Theophany of Enoch i, 3b–7, 9," *VT* 23 (1973) 129-50.

blessing of the righteous in *1 Enoch* 1:8 draws upon the high-priestly benediction in Num 6:24-26.

In chaps. 2–5, the obedience of the natural order is contrasted with the disobedience of the ungodly. Lars Hartman has suggested that behind this comparison lies the Deuteronomic idea of calling heaven and earth as witnesses against Israel (Deut 4:26; 30:19; 31:28; Deut 32:1-3).[8] Some connection between this Deuteronomic notion and *1 Enoch* 2–5 seems clear, yet an important difference exist with regard to the function of heaven and earth in Deuteronomy and BW. Whereas in Deuteronomy Moses calls heaven and earth as witnesses that he has presented the alternatives of life and death to Israel based on their response to the Sinai Law or as witnesses to God's faithfulness over against Israel's apostasy, in BW heaven and earth represent both the witnesses and the standard of obedience. In other words, for those addressed in chaps. 2–5, the moral order is lodged not in the Sinai Law, but in the natural order. Here, heaven and the earth no longer witness to the Sinai Law as the moral standard; they themselves constitute the standard. Lastly, it should be noted that the curses and blessings in *1 Enoch* 5:4-9 are indebted to Deut 28:18-20 and Num 6:24-26, respectively.

To summarize the use of scriptural traditions in this first section of BW, it is evident that the Hebrew Bible provided the language, imagery, and motifs for the portrayal of Enoch, the theophany, and the indictment of the wicked. Nevertheless, some of the biblical elements, such as Mount Sinai and the cosmos as witness, undergo a distinct transformation when employed in BW.

The Myth of the Watchers (chaps. 6–11) is an elaboration of portions of Genesis 6–9, focused primarily on 6:1-13, a passage which begins with an account of the sons of God taking wives among the daughters of men. The technique employed by the author is commonly called "rewritten Bible."[9] A comparison of Gen 6:1-2, 4 and *1 Enoch* 6:1-2; 7:1-2 is instructive.

When men began to multiply on the face of the ground, and daughters were

---

8   Hartman, *Asking*, 28-30.

9   See D. Dimant, "Use and Interpretation of Mikra in the Apocrypha and Pseudepigrapha," in J. Mulder (ed.), *Mikra* (CRINT 2.1; Assen: Van Gorcum; Philadelphia: Fortress, 1988) 402-406; G. W. E. Nickelsburg, "The Bible Rewritten and Expanded," in M. E. Stone (ed.), *Jewish Writings of the Second Temple Period* (CRINT 2.2; Assen: Van Gorcum; Philadelphia: Fortress, 1984) 90-92.

born to them, the sons of God saw that the daughters of men were fair; and they took to wife such of them as they chose (Gen 6:1-2) . . . The Nephilim were on the earth in those days, and also afterward, when the sons of God came in to the daughters of men, and they bore children to them. These were the mighty men that were of old, the men of renown (Gen 6:4).

And it came to pass, when the sons of men had increased, that in those days there were born to them fair and beautiful daughters. And the angels, the sons of heaven, saw and desired them. And they said to one another: "Come, let us choose for ourselves wives from the children of men, and let us beget for ourselves children" (*1 Enoch* 6:1-2) . . . And they took wives for themselves, and everyone chose for himself one each. And they began to go in to them and were promiscuous with them. And they taught them charms and spells, and showed them the cutting of roots and trees. And they became pregnant and bore large giants, and their height was three thousand cubits (*1 Enoch* 7:1-2).

The author of BW has introduced a number of interpretive changes into the base text from Gen 6:1-4. First, the sons of God are identified with angels (or Watchers). Secondly, whereas Gen 6:1-4 is neutral with regard to the moral quality of the actions of the sons of God, BW inserts a strongly negative judgment against the deeds of the Watchers. This is achieved by attributing lustful motives and pro-miscuous activities to the Watchers (*1 Enoch* 6:2; 7:1a), by adding material that characterizes their act as a premeditated conspiracy to commit a great sin (*1 Enoch* 6:3-8), and by reciting the disastrous results of their deeds (*1 Enoch* 7:3-6; 8:2-4). Thirdly, according to BW, the sin of the Watchers not only involves sexual intercourse with the women, but the revelation of illicit knowledge (*1 Enoch* 7:1b; 8:1, 3).[10] Fourthly, BW interprets the reference to the Nephilim in Gen 6:4 in two ways. According to Gen 6:4, the Nephilim are simply on the earth when the sons of God produced offspring through the daughters of men and are identified only as mighty men of old, men of renown. In contrast, in BW the Nephilim *are* the offspring of the Watchers and women and are further identified as giants, whose ravenous appetites, we are told in the

---

10   As widely recognized, the tradition about the revelation of illicit knowledge, connected with the angelic leader Asael, is one of at least two strands of tradition concerning rebellion in heaven, the other being a story of angels taking human women for wives, associated with the leader Semihazah (cf. G. W. E. Nickelsburg, "Apocalyptic and Myth in 1 Enoch 6–11," *JBL* 96 [1977] 383-405; P. D. Hanson, "Rebellion in Heaven, Azazel and Euhemeristic Heroes in 1 Enoch 6–11," *JBL* 96 [1977] 195-233).

subsequent verses, wreak havoc and oppression upon the earth.[11]

In Genesis, the account of Noah and the flood follows the story of the marriage between the sons of God and the daughters of men. This account begins with several statements about the depth of human sin and corruption:

> The Lord saw that the wickedness of man was great in the earth, and that every imagination of the thoughts of his heart was only evil continually (Gen 6:5) . . . Now the earth was corrupt in God's sight, and the earth was filled with violence. And God saw the earth, and behold, it was corrupt; for all flesh had corrupted their way upon the earth (Gen 6:11-12).

BW appears to explicate these biblical verses when it describes the earthly corruption that resulted from humans acquiring the recondite arts wrongfully revealed to them by Asael and his cohorts: "And there was great impiety and much fornication, and they went astray, and all their ways became corrupt" (*1 Enoch* 8:2). Similarly, the violence and destruction perpetrated by the giants (*1 Enoch* 7:3-6; 9:9; cf. 9:1) fits well the portrait of the earth in Gen 6:11. Here again, however, BW has introduced a new element, for in the biblical account, no explicit connection exists between the events related in Gen 6:1-4 and the human corruption reported at the beginning of the flood story, whereas according to BW the corruption and violence upon the earth is a direct result of the deeds of the Watchers. Indeed, the Watchers' actions account for the origin of evil—at least widespread evil—on the earth. Behind this explicit linking of the sin of the Watchers to the earthly corruption prior to the flood is perhaps an implied justification for God's radical act of judgment against the earth in the form of a deluge; such a devastating punishment was necessary because of the supernatural character of the evil afflicting the earth.[12]

In BW, human beings not only participate in the evil unleashed, they are victims of it.[13] Therefore, they cry out to heaven (*1 Enoch* 7:6; 8:4; cf. 9:2-3,10), another new feature in BW relative to the

---

[11]   The LXX of Gen 6:4 also designates the Nephilim "giants," and identifies them with the offspring of the women.

[12]   Cf. J. C. VanderKam, *Enoch: A Man for All Generations* (Studies on Personalities of the Old Testament; Columbia: University of South Carolina Press, 1995) 35.

[13]   This two-fold role for humanity in BW appears to be the result of the two strands of tradition represented in the Myth of the Watchers: in the Asael tradition, humans participate in the evil; in the Semihazah tradition, they are victims of it.

biblical text.[14] Moreover, whereas according to Genesis it is God who sees the wickedness on the earth and resolves to bring judgment (Gen 6:5-7,11-13), in BW the angels Michael, Gabriel, Suriel, and Uriel perceive the corruption, hear the human outcry, and petition God to do something about it (*1 Enoch* 9:1-11). James VanderKam has noted how this feature of the story in BW stems from a distinctive reading of Gen 6:11a.[15] This verse is typically translated: "Now the earth was corrupt in God's sight" (לִפְנֵי הָאלֹהִים). But the author of BW consistently read הָאלֹהִים (with the definite article) as a reference to angels, not God.[16] So, for the author of BW, Gen 6:11a said, "Now the earth was corrupt in *the angel's* sight." Accordingly, this verse provided the basis for the elaboration found in *1 Enoch* 9:1-11.

God's response to the situation presented by the angels begins with instructions for an angel to tell the son of Lamech (Noah) to hide himself that he might be preserved from the coming Deluge. This of course is based on Gen 6:13-22, although the account is abbreviated in BW. Beyond this initial response, God instructs other angels to move against the evil Watchers and their giant offspring. Here it is important to note that in the description of the judgment against the Watchers the temporal setting shifts.[17] In *1 Enoch* 10:12, God instructs Michael to bind the Watchers for seventy generations until the consummation of their judgment. Then *1 Enoch* 10:13 begins with the phrase "in those days," making clear that what follows describes the final judgment upon the Watchers. In other words, the temporal frame of reference has moved ahead seventy generation, to the eschaton. Moreover, in addition to statements about the final destruction of the Watchers, this description of the eschaton speaks of the elimination of all evil, the emergence of the "plant of righteousness and truth," and paradisal conditions upon the earth (*1 Enoch* 10:16–11:2). Language and imagery used to describe this

---

14   It is possible that the author of BW read רעת in Gen 6:5a not as רָעַת ("wickedness"), but as רֵעַת, a construct pl. from רֵעַ, ("shoutings/cryings"). For רֵעַ, see Exod 32:17; but the construct pl. is unattested.

15   VanderKam, *Generations*, 36.

16   See below BW's interpretation of Gen 5:22–24; this reading of הָאלֹהִים may reflect a heightened sense of God's transcendence; God's contact with the earth must therefore be mediated by angels.

17   See L. Hartman, "An Early Example of Jewish Exegesis: 1 Enoch 10:16–11:2," *Neot* 17 (1983) 16-26; Nickelsburg, "Apocalyptic and Myth," 388; Hanson, "Rebellion in Heaven," 202.

scene come from Genesis 8–9 and the salvation oracles of the prophets.[18] With this, the Myth of the Watchers comes to a close.

It should be clear from the above survey that the Myth of the Watchers represents a radical rewriting of texts from Genesis 6–9. Through a number of interpretive moves, the author has transformed a story about the marriage between the sons of God and daughters of men, which in Genesis preceded the story about Noah and the flood, into an etiology for the presence of evil in the world, along with a theodicy based on the promise of eschatological rectification.

The final section of BW relates the story of Enoch and the Watchers, including an account of Enoch's dealings with the Watchers, his vision of ascent to the throne of God, and his reports of otherworldly journeys (*1 Enoch* 12–36). The opening lines of this section derive from Gen 5:22-24, but incorporate an important interpretive move. A comparison between the biblical text and BW is again illuminating:

> Enoch walked with God [האלהים] after the birth of Methusalah three hundred years (Gen 5:22) . . . Enoch walked with God [האלהים]; and he was not, for God [אלהים] took him (Gen 5:24).

> And before everything Enoch had been hidden, and none of the sons of men knew where he was hidden, or where he was, or what had happened. And all his doings were with the Holy Ones and with the Watchers in his days (*1 Enoch* 12:1-2).

It is clear that while the author of BW read אלהים (without the definite article) as a reference to God, he interpreted האלהים (with the definite article) as a reference to the angels or Watchers.[19] Hence, an expression in the biblical text no doubt used to affirm Enoch's righteousness ("walking with God") is transformed into an explanation for Enoch's whereabouts when he was not on earth: he was with the angels. The significance of this interpretive move can hardly be overestimated. It is the wellspring from which the entire Enoch tradition flows, whether as the basis for Enoch's role as revealer of heavenly mysteries, as in the Astronomical Book (*1*

---

[18] Hartman, "Jewish Exegesis," 22; Nickelsburg, "Rewritten," 90-91; see esp. Isa 65:20-25.

[19] VanderKam (*Growth*, 131) observes that although the wording in *1 Enoch* 12:1-2 is closer to Gen 5:24, the author associates Enoch's dealings with the Watchers with his first "walk" with the angels, mentioned in Gen 5:22.

Enoch 72–82), or for his association with angels mentioned in the Myth of the Watchers. The remainder of BW then recounts Enoch's interaction with the angels, both the fallen and the faithful.

Enoch is summoned by faithful angels to announce condemnation upon the fallen Watchers. Having done so, the fallen Watchers persuade Enoch to intercede on their behalf. A negative response to his intercession comes in the form of a dream-vision that includes Enoch's ascent to the throne of God and otherworldly journeys. The depiction of the ascent to the throne of God (*1 Enoch* 14:8-25) is indebted to Ezekiel 1, Isaiah 6, and 1 Kgs 22:19-23 for phrases and imagery.[20]

As for the otherworldly journeys, while much of Enoch's description of various earthly and celestial phenomena goes beyond anything in the Hebrew Scriptures, four references to biblical traditions are present. First, Enoch sees a mountain etched with hollow places where the souls of the dead are gathered as they await the day of their final judgment (*1 Enoch* 22:1-4). Enoch recounts:

> There I saw the spirit of a dead man making accusation, and his lamentation ascending up to heaven, and crying out unceasingly and making accusation. Then I asked Raphael the Watcher and Holy One who was with me and I said to him: This spirit making accusation, whose is it, that in this manner his lamentation is ascending and crying out unceasingly and making accusation to heaven. And he answered me and said to me, saying: This spirit is the one which came out of Abel whom Cain, his brother, killed. And he will complain about him until his offspring is destroyed from the face of the earth, and from amongst the offspring of men his offspring perishes (*1 Enoch* 22:5-7).[21]

Although based on Gen 4:10, this passage introduces new ideas vis-à-vis the biblical text. In Gen 4:10, the voice of Abel's blood cries from the ground. According to BW, however, it is Abel's spirit that cries out in complaint from the rock chamber. The substitution of spirit for blood is no doubt based on Gen 9:4, where the life or spirit (נֶפֶשׁ) of human beings is assumed to reside in their blood (cf. also

---

20   Cf. M. Himmelfarb, *Ascent to Heaven in Jewish and Christian Apocalypses* (New York: Oxford University Press, 1993) 14-20; VanderKam, "Biblical Interpretation," 108-109.

21   Translation of 22:5-6 is from J. T. Milik, *The Books of Enoch: Aramaic Fragments of Qumrân Cave 4* (Oxford: Clarendon Press, 1976) 229-30, based on the Qumran Aramaic fragments of *1 Enoch*. Translation of 22:7 is from Knibb, *Book of Enoch*.

Lev 17:11,14). Moreover, the spirit of Abel cries out unceasingly against Cain until his offspring is destroyed from the earth. Here BW attaches an eschatological dimension to Abel's complaint, so that he symbolizes the cries of righteous victims pleading for the destruction of their oppressors in the final judgment.

Secondly, Enoch arrives at a mountain in the northwest upon which the throne of God is set (*1 Enoch* 24:3).[22] Among the trees that surround the throne is an especially beautiful and fragrant tree, the Tree of Life, mentioned in Genesis 2–3 (*1 Enoch* 24:4–25:6).[23] Enoch inquires about the tree, and the angel Michael explains that no creature may touch it until the final judgment when it will be given to the righteous and humble that they might have life from its fruit (*1 Enoch* 25:4-5a). Further, the tree "will be planted in a holy place, by the house of the Lord," where the righteous will rejoice and draw from it long life on earth, free from suffering (*1 Enoch* 25:5b-6).[24] So, the Tree of Life that once stood in the middle of the Garden of Eden (Gen 2:9) has been removed to the mountain of God's throne in the time of Enoch, but will be replanted by the eschatological temple after the final judgment.[25] Moreover, according to Gen 3:22-24 God prevents Adam and Eve from approaching the Tree of Life after their sin, lest they eat of its fruit and live forever, while in BW the righteous are given its fruit at the end times for the purpose of long and blissful life. The eschatological situation will, therefore, reverse the effects of the first humans' sin, returning the righteous to paradaisal conditions, albeit by the temple of God, not in the Garden of Eden. Accordingly, just as Abel's complaint was linked to the

---

22   Cf. Ezekiel 27.

23   Exactly why the Tree of Life has been transplanted from Eden, which is in the east and mentioned later in Enoch's otherworldly tour (32:3-6), to the mountain throne of God in the northwest is not clear (See M. Black, *The Book of Enoch or I Enoch* [Leiden: Brill, 1985] 179, who suggests that the presence of conflicting ideas about the location of paradise is rooted in the author's use of both hellenistic and oriental traditions.).

24   The Ethiopic text locates this holy place in the north, but this is probably a result of a mistaken translation (cf. VanderKam, *Generations*, 57).

25   M. Himmelfarb ("The Temple and the Garden of Eden in Ezekiel, the Book of the Watchers, and the Wisdom of ben Sira," in J. Scott and P. Simpson-Housley [eds.], *Sacred Places and Profane Spaces: Essays in the Geographics of Judaism, Christianity, and Islam* [Contributions to the Study of Religion 30; Westport: Greenwood, 1991] 69) notes that the idea of transplanting Eden to the eschatological temple occurs in Ezekiel.

eschatological scene, the Tree of Life is likewise connected to the end times.

Thirdly, *1 Enoch* 26–27 describes Jerusalem and its environs, a description inspired in part by Ezek 47:1-2 and Zech 14:8. Specifically, Enoch's report locates Jerusalem in the middle of the earth and draws attention, on the one hand, to the fertility and well-watered character of the holy mountain (*1 Enoch* 26:1-2; 27:1a) and, on the other, to an accursed valley between the mountains (*1 Enoch* 26:3; 27:1-4). The angel Raphael explains that the valley is the place of punishment for the wicked:

> Here they will gather them together, and here will be their place of judgment. And in the last day there will be the spectacle of the righteous judgment upon them before the righteous for ever, for evermore; here the merciful will bless the Lord of Glory, the Eternal King (*1 Enoch* 27:2b-3).

The notion that the righteous will watch the judgment of the wicked probably comes from Isa 66:18-24.[26] Nevertheless, the key point, no longer unexpected, is that Jerusalem is evoked not to highlight its status as the political and spiritual center within Jewish history, but for its role in the eschatological scenario.

Finally, when Enoch's journey brings him to the extremities of the east, he arrives at the Garden of Righteousness, where he sees the tree of wisdom from which the first humans ate, resulting in their expulsion from the garden (*1 Enoch* 32:3-6). The place is plainly the Garden of Eden and the tree, the Tree of the Knowledge of Good and Evil (Genesis 2–3), although neither is so named. Yet the purpose of this reference is difficult to ascertain.[27] The tree is described as "the tree of wisdom from which they eat and know great wisdom." Here, the identity of those who eat from the tree could either be angels or the righteous; if the latter, then perhaps they will eat of the tree as part of their eschatological reward.[28] Yet none of this is stated, so the significance of this passage remains

---

26   See R. H. Charles, "Book of Enoch," in R. H. Charles (ed.), *Apocrypha and Pseudepigrapha of the Old Testament* (2 vols., Oxford: Clarendon Press, 1913) 2.205.

27   Himmelfarb ("The Temple and the Garden," 71) notes that mentioning the Garden of Eden as the place where the first humans sinned even creates a tension with the Myth of the Watchers, which also accounts for the presence of sin and evil in the world.

28   Himmelfarb, "The Temple and the Garden," 71.

unclear.

We can now sum up the scripture profile of BW by briefly cataloging the ways in which the Hebrew Scriptures are used.[29] First, BW uses the technique of "rewritten Bible" in the Myth of the Watchers (*1 Enoch* 6–11). In addition, allusion to elements found in other narrative traditions in the Hebrew Bible, though not numerous, are nonetheless present. Thus, reference to Mount Sinai, Noah and the flood, Cain and Abel, the Tree of Life, Jerusalem, the Garden of Eden, and of course Enoch himself find a place in BW. Thirdly, biblical language and imagery, often from prophetic literature, is drawn on to describe several scenes, including Enoch's prophetic status and blessing, the theophany at Mount Sinai, the heavenly temple and throne room, and various features reviewed in the otherworldly journeys. Finally, motifs such as the witness of heaven and earth against Israel and perhaps the spectacle of the punishment of the wicked in the presence of the righteous shape the author's conception divine judgment. And as evident from the preceding survey, each of these techniques reflects the interpretive activity of the author.

OBSERVATIONS ON THE SCRIPTURAL PROFILE OF BW

In light of the preceding scripture profile, I will now set forth five observations. First, the entire story line of BW depends on a certain set of interpretative moves imposed on two key biblical texts—Gen 5:22-24 and Gen 6:1-13. Most of these moves have already been noted in the analysis of individual sections of BW, but a summary of them here will indicate just how extensive was the interpretive intervention. In the Myth of the Watchers (*1 Enoch* 6–11), we find Gen 6:1-13 reconfigured as follows: the sons of God become the Watchers; a strongly negative evaluation of the Watchers' deed is introduced; the sin of the Watchers is expanded to include the revelation of illicit knowledge; the Nephilim become giants, identified as the offspring of the Watchers and the women; human corruption prior to the Flood is linked to the Watchers' sin; the human victims of violence and corruption cry out to heaven; and the angels of heaven, not God, perceive the earthly crisis. In addition, in the Story of Enoch and the Watchers (*1 Enoch* 12–36), Gen 5:22-24

---

[29] See Dimant, "Mikra," 379-419, for a discussion of the types of usage found in early Jewish texts.

is understood to reveal that Enoch walked with the angels when absent from the earth. Finally, one additional interpretive move must be mentioned, since it is fundamental to the entire work, though almost too obvious to be perceived by the reader. This was to bring together the interpreted versions of Gen 5:24 and Gen 6:1-13. In the Hebrew Bible, these two texts lack any inherent connection. Their association first occurred in the imagination of the author—or in an earlier tradition to which the author was heir, no doubt facilitated by the fact that as interpreted both texts refer to angels or Watchers, by the relative proximity of these texts in Genesis, and by the supposed similar time frame for Enoch and the descent of the Watchers.[30]

The net result of this rather complex recasting of scriptural traditions was a new tradition that offered an explanation for the origin of evil and hope for its elimination through eschatological rectification. Consequently, when the full extent of this recasting of Scripture is recognized, there is something illusory about referring to BW as an elaboration of biblical texts. It is not an elaboration, but a reconfiguration of Scripture. Though much of the language and some of the characters and narrative pieces of the base texts remain, the semantic intentions of the biblical passages are almost wholly eclipsed, overlaid with a new constellation of meanings.[31] Accordingly, while passages from Genesis provided the raw materials for the author, the meaning conveyed by the new literary construction has few points of contact with the meanings of the base texts.

Moreover, this reconfiguration of Scripture exerted a profound influence on later authors. The story line of BW is presumed, summarized, or adapted in mid-second century BCE Jewish works, such as the Apocalypse of Weeks (*1 Enoch* 93:1-10; 91:11-17), the Animal Apocalypse (*1 Enoch* 85–91), and *Jubilees* (chap. 4), as well as later Jewish and Christian works, including the Similitudes of

---

[30]   Genesis 6:1-4 indicates only that the events it describes occurred "when men began to multiply on the face of the ground, and daughters were born to them," and presumably before the flood. BW specifies the descent of the Watchers as happening "in the days of Jared," Enoch's father, suggested perhaps by the word-play between the name Jared and the Hebrew for "descend" (ירד).

[31]   Cf. J. H. le Roux, "The Use of Scripture in 1 Enoch 6–11," *Neot* 17 (1983) 36-37; G. W. E. Nickelsburg, "Scripture in *1 Enoch* and *1 Enoch* as Scripture," in T. Fornberg and D. Hellholm (eds.), *Texts and Contexts: Biblical Texts in their Textual and Situational Contexts, Essays in Honor of Lars Hartman* (Oslo: Scandinavian University Press, 1995) 335.

Enoch, *2 Enoch*, patristic writings, rabbinic texts, and medieval works.[32] A broader point to be observed here is that while the Hebrew Scriptures certainly shaped and influenced BW, it is no less true that BW shaped and influenced the understanding of the Hebrew Scriptures. In other words, the recasting of scriptural traditions found in this early Jewish apocalypse acted, so to speak, as an interpretive lens through which the biblical material would subsequently be viewed. Hence, once derived from the biblical base texts, BW acted back on those base texts. Consequently, by investigating the interpretive moves embedded in a document, one is uncovering the construction of an interpretive tradition that in the case of BW exerted a powerful influence on how biblical texts were henceforth read.[33]

Secondly, the recasting of scriptural traditions in BW was influenced by foreign epic traditions. For example, as VanderKam has explained, the portrait of Enoch reflected in BW has been shaped by the Sumerian tradition about Enmeduranki, typically the seventh king in antediluvian Sumerian king lists known for his skill in divination.[34] The connection between Enoch and Enmeduranki is already present in Gen 5:21-24, but in BW the implications of this link are developed further and help to explain the characterization of Enoch as a figure who associates with the Watchers and receives heavenly revelation.[35] In turn, this accounts for the connection between Enoch and Baalam observed in the opening lines of the Blessing of Enoch (*1 Enoch* 1:1-2), since Balaam, like Enoch, is depicted as a diviner.[36] Moreover, according to Hanson, the account of the Watchers' descent from heaven and intercourse with the women derives from Hurrian and Ugaritic myths about rebellion in

---

[32]   See VanderKam, *Generations*, 63-182; J. C. VanderKam, "1 Enoch, Enochic Motifs, and Enoch in Early Christian Literature," in J. C. VanderKam and W. Adler (eds.), *The Jewish Apocalyptic Heritage in Early Christianity* (CRINT 3.4; Assen: Van Gorcum; Minneapolis: Fortress, 1996) 33-101.

[33]   The interpretive tradition present in BW continues to shape the reading of the Hebrew Bible. For instance, in P. J. Achtemeier (ed.), *Harper's Bible Dictionary* (San Francisco: Harper & Row, 1985), under "Nephilim," one reads "the offspring of daughters of men and divine beings" (p. 696), an identification made only in BW, not in the biblical text.

[34]   VanderKam, *Growth*, 23-51.

[35]   VanderKam, *Growth*, 43-45.

[36]   VanderKam, *Growth*, 115-19.

heaven,[37] a connection which probably accounts for the extremely negative evaluation of the Watchers' deed in BW in contrast to the neutral attitude toward it in Gen 6:1-4. Likewise, the material about Asael's revelation of forbidden arts to the women, a deed not mentioned in Gen 6:1-4, appears to reflect broader ancient near eastern ideas about culture heroes, perhaps best known in the form of the Greek tradition about Prometheus.[38]

It is evident, then, that themes from foreign mythic and epic traditions inspired some of the recasting of Scripture in BW. The influence of foreign ideas on Israelite or Jewish literature was, of course, not a new development, but the Hellenistic matrix of early Jewish literature provided a fertile setting for the interplay of various traditions. It is difficult to be certain whether the amalgamation of Jewish and foreign traditions indicates an unwitting assimilation of foreign influence or, more likely, an attempt by the author to claim widely known traditions and heroes from the Hellenistic Near East for Jewish history.[39] The latter strategy is attested in *Ps.-Eupolemus*, which maintains that Enoch, not the Babylonians or Egyptians, discovered astrology and that while the Greeks say it was Atlas, Enoch and Atlas are the same.[40] Thus, while Jewish traditions were reshaped by elements and heroes from foreign epic traditions, the new Jewish tradition was probably meant to supplant those foreign stories. In *Ps.-Eupolemus* this cultural usurpation is explicit; in BW, it is implicit, since the foreign influence is embedded in the intertextual relationships.

The first two observations pertain to the portions of BW that employ the interpretive technique of rewritten Bible. My third observation concerns how allusions to other narrative elements in the Hebrew Bible function. In BW, narrative traditions are not cited with a view to their significance within their original narrative con-

---

[37] Hanson, "Rebellion in Heaven," 202-18.

[38] Hanson, "Rebellion in Heaven," 226-32; see also VanderKam, *Growth*, 126-28; Nickelsburg, "*1 Enoch* as Scripture," 336.

[39] J. J. Collins ("The Place of Apocalypticism in the Religion of Israel," in P. D. Miller Jr., P. D. Hanson, and S. D. McBride [eds.], *Ancient Israelite Religion: Essays in Honor of Frank Moore Cross* [Philadelphia: Fortress, 1987] 543) suggests the latter.

[40] For text and translation of *Ps. Eupolemus*, see C. A. Holladay, *Fragments from Hellenistic Jewish Authors: Volume I: Historians* (SBLTT 20; Chico: Scholars Press, 1983) 175.

text, but abstracted from that context in order to serve as symbols of eschatological realities. This use of allusions can rightly be labelled typological.[41] For instance, Mount Sinai has been abstracted from its narrative context in which it marks the location of God's appearance to establish his covenant with Israel and appropriated as an evocative symbol for God's awe-inspiring coming to render eschatological judgment on everyone.

Other allusions to narrative traditions function in a similar way. Hence, the story of the flood and its aftermath prefigure eschatological judgment and restoration. The Tree of Life is uprooted from its location in the Garden of Eden and replanted near the mountain throne of God where it symbolizes the anticipated eschatological reward of the righteous, who will draw forth from it long and blissful life when it stands outside the eschatological temple. Abel's complaint against the descendants of Cain represents the voice of righteous victims of oppression and violence who cry out for justice against their oppressors until the final judgment. And Jerusalem's role as the capital city of the Judah and Jewish life is set aside; now the city and its adjacent valleys provide the place of ultimate judgment upon the wicked as the righteous look on and bless God.[42] Even the figure of Enoch as depicted in BW has typological value in that he becomes a herald of eschatological punishment, a role alien to the characterization of Enoch in the biblical text. In each case, then, a fragment from the epic traditions of Israel functions to characterize some aspect of the eschatological situation. In other words, the author's hermeneutical approach is consistently that of typology.

Fourthly, although passages from various sections of the Hebrew Bible contribute to the description of scenes in BW, with two exceptions the narrative traditions cited come from Genesis 1–9.[43] The focus is clearly on the portion of the Hebrew Bible devoted to primeval history. Why is this so? One possibility would be that the author was attempting to avoid anachronisms by having the antediluvian figure Enoch refrain from mentioning events that occurred

---

[41]   Cf. P. D. Hanson, "Rebellion in Heaven," 197; Hartman, "Jewish Exegesis," 20-21.

[42]   The function of the reference to the Tree of the Knowledge of Good and Evil in the Garden of Righteousness (Eden), as noted above, is unclear.

[43]   The Tree of Life, the Garden of Eden, Cain and Abel, the story of the Watchers, the flood story, and Enoch himself are all found in Genesis 1–9.

long after his own time. Yet this seems unlikely for several reasons. For one, Enoch speaks of Mount Sinai and refers to the city of Jerusalem, though never using the latter's name, both exceptions to the preference for events from primeval times. Moreover, according to BW Enoch is very well informed about events in the distant future, that is, eschatological matters; this, however, was not perceived as anachronistic. Furthermore, in other books of the Enochic tradition, such as the Apocalypse of Weeks, which is roughly contemporary with BW, and the Animal Apocalypse, composed about a half a century later, Enoch does know about future historical events. It is not clear why only in BW would anachronisms be a concern. Accordingly, if avoiding anachronisms does not qualify as the reason why allusions are limited primarily to primeval history, we must seek some other reason for the author's preference for them.

In my judgment, a more plausible reason for the dominance of primeval materials is the author's overall rhetorical strategy of grounding the message of BW in realities that transcend the traditions associated with the particular history of the Jewish people. As a result, we see the author appealing to the structure of the cosmos as the standard of morality, to the voice of God as a basis for judgment and reward, and to heavenly phenomena as confirmation for the impending judgment, since the places of final punishment are revealed as already prepared. In a similar manner, primeval events, while not fully transcendent, nonetheless lie outside the particular history of Israel. Hence, by appealing to primeval traditions, the author's point is based on world events rather than the national history of Israel—or put another way, it is grounded in a more ancient, universal, and fundamental source of truth.

Perhaps we can account for this strategy by recognizing that in the hellenistic setting of early Judaism, knowledge of the national traditions of other peoples would have relativized Israel's own traditions as a basis for making claims about the fate of the cosmos. In other words, in a pluralistic cultural environment it would no longer do to assert a universal claim on a parochial foundation. Thus, one's message had to be based in traditions that predated one's particular national or ethnic culture or be grounded in supra-historical realities. A similar rhetorical tactic appears in other Jewish works from the same general milieu. For example, Ben Sira identifies Israel's Torah with the pre-existent wisdom of God (Sirach 24), and *Jubilees* refers to the Law of God inscribed on heavenly tablets (e.g. *Jub.* 3:10, 31).

In each case, the truth value of the Torah is anchored in a reality that transcends the historical events in the history of Israel. For the same reason then, the message of BW appeals to transcendent phenomena and to primeval traditions from Genesis 1–9.

On the whole, then, primeval events determine and symbolize eschatological affairs, thereby reflecting a view of history where *Urzeit* models *Endzeit*.[44] An important consequence of this schema, however, is that it renders the history of Israel superfluous for determining the ultimate fate of the cosmos. This helps explain why allusions to those historical traditions are nearly absent in BW. Even in the two instances where locations associated with the history of Israel are mentioned (Mount Sinai and Jerusalem), as noted above, they function typologically, without regard to their significance in the history of Israel. This attitude toward the history of Israel could be construed as merely the unintentional consequence of the author's strategy of grounding the message of BW in primeval events. On the other hand, perhaps the author viewed the history of Israel negatively, as a record of Israel's failure to live as a righteous and holy people, and therefore an illegitimate source for deriving the truth about eschatological realities.[45] That only the eschatological temple, not the actual second temple, plays a role in BW supports this second option.[46] Nonetheless, for whichever reason, because the end times are already determined and explained by events in the primeval age, the history of Israel loses its relevance.

My final observation pertains to the relationship between BW and the literature of the Hebrew Bible.[47] We may begin by noting that J. T. Milik's proposal that BW served as a source for Gen 6:1-4 has been widely rejected.[48] Thus, the direction of use flows from biblical

---

[44]   Cf. Nickelsburg, "*1 Enoch* as Scripture," 335.

[45]   Cf. P. A. Tiller, *A Commentary on the Animal Apocalypse of* I Enoch (SBLEJL 4; Atlanta: Scholars Press, 1993) 15-20, for a discussion of the nature of history according to the Animal Apocalypse (*1 Enoch* 85–91), a mid-second century BCE Enochic work, where the history of Israel is viewed more negatively than primeval history (p. 18).

[46]   Similarly, the Animal Apocalypse rejects the validity of the Second Temple (see Tiller, *Commentary*, 38-40).

[47]   For a recent treatment of this topic for all of *1 Enoch*, see Nickelsburg, "Scripture in *1 Enoch*."

[48]   For Milik's view, see *The Books of Enoch*, 30-31; for rejection of his view, see VanderKam, *Growth*, 113-14; Nickelsburg, "Scripture in *1 Enoch*,"

literature to BW, not the reverse.[49] Beyond this, however, the subject gets increasingly complicated for several reasons.[50] For one, we do not know the precise status of the Hebrew Bible, or parts of it, in Jewish communities at the time of the composition of BW. Was it simply traditional literature or was it understood as uniquely authoritative, and if so, how fixed was its content and text? And what terminology should be used to distinguish these different perceptions of the biblical text (traditional, scriptural, canonical?)?[51] Moreover, since the level of authority ascribed to traditional literature is always a function of a religious community's perception, different Jewish communities may have ascribed divergent levels of authority to the writings in the Hebrew Bible. Nevertheless, while recognizing these complicating factors, we may examine BW for what is implied about its relation to the Hebrew Bible and seek to draw some tentative conclusions.

To begin, BW never explicitly quotes from the biblical text using a citation formula, such as "it is written," a practice which would confirm that the author understood biblical writings as Scripture or canon. In fact, biblical texts are not quoted at all; they are paraphrased, though sometimes closely. In addition, the authority of BW does not rest on its connection to biblical texts, but on the claim that it represents divine revelation (*1 Enoch* 1:2; 13:8; 14:1).[52] On the other hand, as the scripture profile demonstrates, BW makes extensive use of the Hebrew Bible, rewriting it, using its language and motifs, and alluding to it directly and indirectly. Not surprisingly, these data have been interpreted differently. Hanson argued that "by means of a close paraphrase of the Genesis text . . . it seems that the

---

334-35.

[49] It is, however, probable that more extensive traditions about Enoch and about the Watchers stand behind the present text of Genesis, traditions that may have influenced BW as well.

[50] See R. A. Kraft, "Scripture and Canon in Jewish Apocrypha and Pseudepi-grapha," in M. Saebø (ed.), *Hebrew Bible/Old Testament: The History of Its Interpretation. Volume I: From Beginnings to the Middle Ages. Part 1: Antiquity* (Göttingen: Vandenhoeck & Ruprecht, 1996) 199-216, for a brief discussion of the complexities involved.

[51] See M. S. Jaffee, *Early Judaism* (Upper Saddle River: Prentice-Hall, 1997) 57-61, who attempts to sort out the relevant terminology associated with these different levels of authority and fixity.

[52] Nickelsburg, "Scripture in *1 Enoch*," 344-46.

intended purpose is to invoke scriptural authority for the exposition
...."[53] In contrast, Nickelsburg, with respect to *1 Enoch* as a whole,
speaks of the "diminution of the authority of the Tanakh and celebration of the Enochic authority."[54]

What can we deduced from the evidence? On the one hand, the
deep indebtedness of BW to the biblical writings implies that its
author understood these writings as more than *a* tradition. They
constituted *the* tradition in the sense that the biblical literature
provided the raw materials for discourse in the author's community.
It was primarily, though not exclusively, the biblical tradition that
supplied the language, codes, and symbols for discourse (in the form
of words, phrases, motifs, stories, persons, places, and events). This
in itself bespeaks a level of authority for the biblical writings
presumed by the author. On the other hand, the absence of biblical
quotations and the explicit claim that it constitutes divine revelation
show that BW did not depend on the Hebrew Bible for its own
authority. BW claimed independent authority, not derivative authority.

This last point raises related questions. If BW possessed independent authority vis-à-vis the biblical text, was it a competing authority,
perhaps meant to supplant the biblical version of things.[55] This is
possible, but unlikely in view of the heavy reliance on biblical
materials.[56] Was it then understood to have equal authority with the
Hebrew Bible? And then we must ask, equal authority for whom?
Within Jewish circles connected with the Enochic tradition, Nickelsburg contends that works such as BW attained authority equal to or
greater than the Hebrew Bible.[57] Similarly, VanderKam argues that
at Qumran the Enoch booklets, including BW, were considered
canonical.[58] It is more difficult to judge this matter with respect to
BW in its compositional setting, since we do not know from which
Jewish group it emanates. Nevertheless, if the author asserts that the
contents of BW present heavenly visions and in *1 Enoch* 14:24–16:4
presumes to repeat the very voice of God from the divine throne, it

---

53   Hanson, "Rebellion in Heaven," 198.
54   Nickelsburg, "Scripture in *1 Enoch*," 342.
55   Nickelsburg, "Scripture in *1 Enoch*," 346-47, raises this question.
56   Nickelsburg, "Scripture in *1 Enoch*," 346.
57   Nickelsburg, "Scripture in *1 Enoch*," 342, 347-49.
58   VanderKam, *Generations*, 183-85.

is difficult to conclude that its authority could have been construed as less than that of biblical literature. However, since biblical writings, at least the Books of Moses and the prophets, claimed the same source for their own authority—direct divine revelation, we should hesitate to posit a higher authority for BW in the eyes of its author and first readers.

We can thus summarize our fifth observation by saying the following. The writings of the Hebrew Bible provided the arena of discourse for BW, furnishing the language, codes, and symbols used. This suggests that the biblical writings possessed a level of authority beyond that of mere tradition. But BW claimed independent, not derivative authority, so that we should refrain from asserting that its author viewed the Bible as canon in the sense that this term would later obtain. Furthermore, it seems that for its author the authority of BW would be *theoretically* equal to that of the biblical writings, since both derived their authority from direct divine revelation, even if in circles that preserved the Enochic writings the authority of BW might have been *functionally* superior.

Finally, let me suggest that we should also take account of how authority flows between the Hebrew Bible and BW. Specifically, while the Hebrew Bible provided the arena of discourse for BW, a state of affairs that presumes a certain level of authority for the biblical text, it is also true that the composition and use of BW by a living community would impart additional authority to the biblical texts, if only because BW presents biblical traditions as existentially relevant. In this way, BW enhances the authority of the biblical texts it cites. This reciprocal relationship between the Bible and early Jewish documents that interpreted and applied biblical texts for their contemporaries may help to explain why the Bible eventually achieved canonical status—works like BW continued to make it existentially meaningful.

CONCLUSION

The scripture profile of BW showed which texts of the Hebrew Bible were invoked and how they are employed. Based on this profile, I made five observation: (1) through a series of interpretive moves, BW presents a radical recasting of Scripture, a recasting that nevertheless formed a lens for subsequent readings of the biblical base texts; (2) this recasting of Scripture was influenced by other

traditions from the Hellenistic Near East, perhaps in an attempt by
the author to incorporate these foreign traditions into the Jewish
heritage; (3) allusions to narrative elements in the Hebrew Bible
functioned typologically in BW in that they were abstracted from
their original narrative context to serve as symbols of eschatological
realities; (4) allusions to narrative traditions from primeval history
predominate in BW as part of the author's rhetorical strategy to
ground his message in realities that transcended Jewish history, a
strategy that rendered Jewish historical traditions superfluous; and
(5) while biblical literature provided the arena of discourse for BW,
BW nevertheless claimed independent and equal authority for itself
vis-à-vis the Bible, even as it in turn ultimately enhanced the
authority of the biblical writings.

PART THREE

TEXT AND CANON

THE FIRST TESTAMENT[1]
ITS ORIGIN, ADAPTABILITY, AND STABILITY

Lee Martin McDonald

ADAPTABILITY AND LIFE:
SANDER'S CONTRIBUTION TO THE NOTION OF CANON

For more than a hundred years scholars have seriously examined the scope of the biblical canon in its final stages, but James Sanders was one of the first to focus on the origins and the pre-history of the biblical canon in ancient Israel. In a very perceptive essay, he has asked some of the most penetrating and enduring questions about the nature and chief characteristics of the notion of canon that have become foundational for all subsequent canon inquiry.[2] He contends that the nature of canon has to do with its repetition in believing communities and its ability to change to meet the variable circumstances of the community of faith (adaptability). The primary function of canon, he observes, is to aid the community of faith in its own self definition (who are we) and to offer to it guidelines for living (what are we to do). Adaptability alone is not sufficient for writings to be recognized as canon. He contends that those traditions that eventually became canon for ancient Israel also had to empower that community for life, that is, they had to give hope even in hopeless situations (the exile) and bring life to the community (Israel).

---

[1]   This is the term that James Sanders prefers over "Old Testament," since the latter suggests that these Scriptures are outdated, surpassed, or irrelevant. It is also a less offensive term to our Jewish colleagues. First Testament is preferable to "Hebrew Scriptures" since there is nothing special about something being written in Hebrew and, of course, some portions of the Old Testament were not written in Hebrew but in Aramaic. Although I shall occasionally use "Old Testament" for convenience, "First Testament" is what I have in mind.

[2]   J. A. Sanders, "Adaptable for Life: The Nature and Function of Canon," in Sanders, *Magnalia Dei: The Mighty Acts of God: Essays on the Bible and Archaeology in Memory of G. E. Wright.* (New York: Doubleday, 1976) 531-60; repr. in Sanders, *From Sacred Story to Sacred Text* (Philadelphia: Fortress Press, 1987) 9-39.

The literature that may have spoken to the needs of one generation, but was unable to be interpreted or adapted to meet the needs of later generations, simply did not survive in Judaism or Christianity. The survivability, or endurance, of sacred literature has to do with its ability to be interpreted afresh to new communities and in new circumstances. Its ability to be re-interpreted in both Judaism and Christianity underscores its adaptability and ultimately canonicity, since, as Sanders has argued, "the major characteristic of canonical material is its adaptability—not its rigidity."[3] He acknowledges the eventual stabilization of the biblical text, but he notes that the need for such a fixed tradition in the believing community comes much later in the canonical process.[4]

Sanders has argued that at the heart of the earliest canon of the Jews was a story (or *mythos*) about a people who migrated from Egypt to Canaan under the guidance and protection of Yahweh, even though other elements were later added to the beginning and the ending of that story (the Genesis story, the prophetic tradition, and the history of the fall of the nation). The earliest development of the story did not include a Decalogue or other lists of divine commandments, but it consisted of the telling of God's calling a people to a land and his preservation of those people through his mighty acts. The response to these acts of preservation or salvation was the monotheizing move of the people to recognize the one true God and also the need for their obedience to his call. There are many examples of this story, or *mythos* as Sanders calls it, in the Old Testament Scriptures, especially in the Prophets, for example, in Amos 2:9-11; 3:1-2; 4:10-11; 5:25; 9:7, 11. There are other early summations of that story in Deut 26:5-9 and Joshua 24. In the New Testament that story is also preserved to some extent in several key texts (Acts 7:2-53 and to some extent also in 1 Cor 10:1-11; Heb 3:5-19). The story was clearly expandable and, after the exile of Israel to Babylon, the Jews reconsidered their story from the perspective of the classic prophets whose witness to that story gave them life and hope. In the message from Ezekiel, for example, the people could, through the faithfulness of Yahweh, look forward to the resurrection of the nation following its death (Ezekiel 36–37). In the exilic sojourn, Ezekiel began to echo the vision of Jeremiah who also spoke of the

---

3   Sanders, *From Sacred Story*, 22.
4   Sanders, *From Sacred Story*, 22.

reforming of the nation (Jer 18:1-11).[5]

After Israel had lost everything in terms of its national identity, especially its temple and cultus in the terrible destruction of 586, what was it that enabled the Jewish people to continue their identity? Why not like many nations before them and after them simply merge with other nations and become extinct as a people with a separate identity who served Yahweh? Merger with and assimilation into other nations and cultures with the consequent loss of separate national identity would have been most natural and also would have many parallels in the ancient world, but instead of that the nation of Israel was reborn. What was it that kept them alive as a nation when all of the things that identified them as a nation had been taken away from them, namely, their land, sovereignty-rulership, temple, cultus, and language? Sanders contends that only that which was indestructible, commonly available, adaptable, and portable could keep this people from extinction. The only thing that fits this description, he claims, was a *story* that could be transported to Babylon and adapted to the new circumstances of the nation in captivity.[6] Sanders further argues that it was especially during the exile that a remnant remembered the witness of the prophets who had predicted accurately what would happen to the nation. As these individuals realized that the prophets had told the truth regarding the fate and story of Israel, it was then, according to Sanders, that they realized that the message of the judgmental prophets before the exile also had a story that could offer them hope and allow them to survive the terrible judgments that had been inflicted upon them. Unlike other nations that saw in their defeat in battle also the defeat of their gods, the Jews accepted the message of the prophets, took responsibility for their failure as a nation, and accepted their captivity and destruction as a judgment of Yahweh for their own misdeeds. In this context, the prophets were remembered and their story was repeated. When the prophets had earlier proclaimed this story warning the people of the consequences of their behavior, they were accused of being "madmen, unpatriotic, blasphemous, seditious, and traitorous" (note, for example, Jer 29:26),[7] but now they were remembered precisely because what they had said actually came to pass. It was concluded that the core of the

---

5   Sanders, *From Sacred Story*, 15-29.

6   Sanders, *From Sacred Story*, 18-19.

7   Sanders, *From Sacred Story*, 28.

prophetic message was a story that was contained in the Torah. This notion was eventually expanded to include the Former and then the Latter Prophets and finally the Writings, but the core of the story that gave life (John 5:39) and identity to Israel was the Law. As the Jews returned from Babylon, the canon of the community of Israel—that which gave it an identity and purpose with guidelines to follow—was the laws of Moses.

In the repetition of this story within context (a feature of canon), life and hope were found for the remnant. The fluidity of the transmission of this story continued well into the time of Jesus when the very lack of a fixed or stabilized tradition was a contributing factor to the existence of the variety of Judaisms that flourished in the first century CE (e.g. Sadducees, Pharisees, Essenes, Christians). After the destruction of the temple and its cultus in 70 CE and later the failure of the messianic movement in the Bar Kokhba rebellion of 132–135, the two most important Judaisms that survived these traumatic events were Rabbinic Judaism and early Christianity. The stabilization of the collection of First Testament Scriptures developed over a long period of history that began with a fluid and adaptable story in the pre-exilic period that became fixed in the third and fourth centuries CE.

A similar story can be told about the emergence of the New Testament canon. What first gathered the Christian community together, gave it its identity, and reason for being and for mission was a story about God's acting in Jesus of Nazareth. The story was first told in preaching (Acts 2:17-36) and teaching (1 Cor 15:3-8) and eventually through the medium of writing. In time the story of God's activity in Jesus and its implications for humanity was expanded and expressed in a variety of forms (epistles, gospels, historiography, apocalyptic, and sermon). The movement toward a stabilization of the writings which faithfully told that story began in the second century but was especially pronounced in the late third or early fourth century after its canonical (stabilized or fixed) status was widely accepted. Almost at the same time, the Scriptures of the First Testament (Old Testament) were also moving toward the final stages of their stabilization in the Christian community and in Judaism.

The adaptability of these Scriptures to new circumstances was in part due to the creative genius of the surviving community that re-interpreted and applied this story of Yahweh's activity to the new circumstances in which they found themselves. This genius is what

Sanders calls the employed hermeneutics that grew out of the need "to keep a stabilized tradition adaptable"[8] and the ability to see in the literature something that was not only adaptable, but also highly relevant and useful for the community of faith. Some literature in both the Christian and rabbinic communities eventually fell away from the sacred collections because, for whatever the reasons, its usefulness and adaptability to the communities was no longer recognized. For example, the ancient prophecy about Eldad and Medad was an authoritative resource for some early Christian communities of the first two centuries (see Hermas, *Vis.* 2.3.4) along with other apocryphal and pseudepigraphal writings. *Enoch* was used by the author of the *Assumption of Moses*, the apocryphal book of *Jubilees*, the *Apocalypse of Baruch* (*ca.* 70 CE), the author of the *Testaments of the Twelve Patriarchs,* and even by the canonical book of Jude. In the Christian era, the author of *Epistle of Barnabas* cites *Enoch* some three times, and in two of those instances he employs scriptural designations when referring to *1 Enoch* (see 4:3, which begins "it was written as Enoch says"; and 16:5, citing *1 Enoch* 89:55, 66, 67, beginning with the words, "For the Scripture says"). It appears what was considered an offense in Jude in the fourth century was not that Jude made use of *Enoch,* as other Christian writers had done, but that he referred to the writing specifically by *name.* The use of *1 Enoch* in the second century was in the bounds of acceptable behavior in the church. The continued use of Sirach and Wisdom in the Jewish communities in the fourth and fifth centuries tells of a certain persistent ambiguity about the precise parameters of the Scripture collection at that time.

Whatever the reasons for the pseudepigrapha falling into disrepute in the third century and later in the Christian communities, as well as in the Jewish communities represented by rabbinic Judaism, our point is still valid. The fluidity of the textual tradition in the Christian communities was far more prominent in the longest period of the development of that tradition (second through fifth centuries). After that (fourth to fifth centuries), there was more focus on the hermeneutics that continued to adapt the story of that textual tradition, even after it was rapidly becoming more fixed, to the ever new and changing circumstances of the church. This fluidity of the textual tradition was also present in rabbinic Judaism in roughly the same

---

8   Sanders, *From Sacred Story,* 25.

period. Some of the Amoraim were still discussing the authority of
the Wisdom of Solomon and Sirach, that is, whether they "defiled the
hands," well into the fourth and fifth centuries of the Common Era.
Since the reading of a text in worship and teaching it in a religious
community implies the recognition of its sacredness and authority
for a believing community, forbidding the reading of a document in
public conversely suggests that it was not yet viewed as sacred. The
exception to this may be the writings that were reserved for the
spiritual elite as in the case of 4 Ezra 14:43-47. The writings excluded from public reading by some rabbis included the Song of
Songs (see *m. Yad.* 3:5; *b. Meg.* 7a), Ecclesiastes (*m. Yad.* 3:5; *b.
Šabb.* 100a; see also Jerome on Eccl 12:14), Ruth (*b. Meg.* 7a),
Esther (*b. Sanh.* 100a; *b. Meg.* 7a); Proverbs (*b. Šabb.* 30b), and
Ezekiel (*b. Šabb.* 13b; *Hag.* 13a; *Menaḥ.* 45a).

Again, the literature that survived in the canon was precisely that
which was perceived to have continuing viability for Judaism and
also for Christianity. The Law's ability to be re-interpreted and
adapted for a new era and in new circumstances gave to it a canonical identity. It was the remnant of Jews in the Diaspora, who defined
their identity in terms of the Law, however they adapted it to their
needs. They were the ones who survived assimilation into the other
societies and cultures of their neighbors. As the Law was adapted to
the new life of the community (Neh 8:1-8), it also brought new life
and hope to the people. The viability of the current biblical canon
has much to do with the genius of the interpreters of this literature
for the contemporary communities of faith. Scripture interpretation
and application continues unimpeded in both the Jewish and Christian
communities and, as the production of many new commentary series
demonstrates, there is no sign of discontinuing the process of
adaptability of the ancient Scripture to ever new circumstances.

The story which gave Israel its identity, hope, and direction
eventually became fixed in specific traditions that were no longer
fluid. The period of fluidity clearly existed through the Hellenistic
period when the land of Israel was dominated by Hellenized states
and heavily influenced by Hellenistic language and culture (at least
through the Maccabean period). As a result of two traumatic events
in the first and second centuries, namely, the destruction of
Jerusalem and with it the Temple and its cultus in 69–70 CE, and the
Bar Cochba rebellion in 132–135 CE with equally disastrous
consequences, the *story* and its specific traditions attained a more

stabilized form first for the synagogue, but then also for the church. The finalizing or stabilizing of the sacred Scriptures of Israel occurred during the height of the Roman Empire, especially in the third and fourth centuries when uniformity in religious devotion was demanded, at two major moves toward conformity in the empire: the first was the Diocletian persecution of the church (303–313); the second, just as compelling, was Constantine's push for religious unity and conformity within the Christian communities with the threat of banishment for those who did not comply.[9]

Sanders' challenging scholars to re-examine the origins of the biblical canon has yielded several valuable results, including a better understanding of the nature of canon itself and its chief characteristics. His work has made the origins of the biblical canon and the move toward its stabilization more comprehensible. He was certainly correct, when he concluded that "we cannot deal adequately with the question of the structure of canon, or what is in and what is out, until we have explored seriously and extensively the question of the function of canon. It is time to attempt to write a history of the early canonical process."[10] Sanders' challenge will be taken up, at least in a brief sketch in the remainder of this essay.[11]

THE EMERGENCE OF THE FIRST TESTAMENT

A. The Problem of Identity: When Do Canons Exist? A part of what complicates an inquiry into the origins of the biblical canon is the lack of agreement among scholars on what constitutes a biblical canon. What precisely is a biblical canon and how sure are we that such notions existed before, during, or immediately after the time of Jesus? Do biblical canons exist whenever an ancient book is cited in another source? Should we infer that the cited text or texts comprised the ancient writer's biblical canon?[12] It is difficult to find any

---

9   For a more complete discussion of this, see L. M. McDonald, *Formation of the Christian Biblical Canon* (Peabody: Hendrickson, 1995) 170-90.

10   Sanders, *From Sacred Story*, 11.

11   See McDonald, *Formation*.

12   Roger Beckwith ("Formation of the Hebrew Bible," in M. J. Mulder [ed.], *Mikra: Text, Translation, Reading and Interpretation of the Hebrew Bible in Ancient Judaism and Early Christianity* [CRINT 2.1; Assen: Van Gorcum; Philadelphia: Fortress, 1988] 46, 48-49) suggests this without stating it when he simply adds the references a writer made to earlier sources and called that his biblical canon. Interestingly, however, when he deals with Jude's citing of *1 Enoch* (Jude

such discussions in antiquity and recently Jacob Neusner has questioned whether the issue of a closed biblical canon ever reached
closure among the sages of late antiquity.[13] As a result of an awareness of this scarcity of information about these matters and also the
challenge not to draw conclusions from what we cannot show from
the ancient sources, scholars are beginning to make more cautious
comments about the formation of the biblical canon. We are on the
threshold of new advances in canonical studies that will change our
perceptions of the canonical process, if not the way in which we
define the notion of canon and the books that will be included within
it, though I do not think that the current shape of the Christian Bible
will be much affected in the church at large.

Since canons tend to be adaptable to the changing life of the
believing community, the continuing usefulness of the current
biblical canon gives witness its ability to be relevant to the ever new
circumstances of the synagogue and the church. Canons often change,
however, and most typically by expansion, though sometimes also by

---

14 cites *1 Enoch* 1:9), he equivocates on this understanding and asks more of Jude
than other New Testament writers when they cite or quote sacred texts. The very
criteria he used with other texts to establish a canon, namely, citing it in an authoritative manner, is rejected for New Testament writers if they cite other than the Old
Testament literature. He acknowledges that later Barnabas (*Ep. Barn.* 4:3 and 16:5)
cited *1 Enoch* as Scripture, but that has no effect on his conclusions about Jude.
See his *The Old Testament Canon of the New Testament Church* (Grand Rapids:
Eerdmans, 1985) 401-403, where he claims that Jude is only referring to *1 Enoch*
and the *Assumption of Moses* because they were edifying literature but not
canonical! Besides this inconsistency, I contend that claims of canon assumed by
early Christian writers are dubious. How certain are we that the notion of a fixed
biblical canon was present in this early period? What happens if we simply delay
the notion of a closed or fixed scriptural canon until we see it discussed or clearly
presented as we do in the fourth to the sixth centuries? Perhaps the notion of an
unclosed biblical canon is present, even though the Fathers did not yet have a term
to describe it.

13   J. Neusner, *Judaism and Christianity in the Age of Constantine* (Chicago
and London: University of Chicago Press, 1987) 128-45. See also Neusner's
Midrash in Context: Exegesis in Formative Judaism (Philadelphia: Fortress, 1983)
1-22. In the formative years of Judaism, he claims that the notion of Torah was
expanded to include the Mishnah, Tosefta, the two Talmuds, and the various
midrashim. A canon was constructed by defining Torah in a new way that encom-
passed all the literature that followed it. It was tied together through exegesis. The
notion of a biblical canon, however, is not *prominent* in second century rabbinic
Judaism or even later.

reduction. For example, *Hermas* and *Barnabas* eventually dropped away from the church's sacred Scriptures even after having been included for centuries. Codex Sinaiticus (א) that comes from the middle to late fourth century included these two books in its collection. Later in Codex Constantinoplitanus (C) includes *1* and *2 Clement, Barnabas,* the *Didache,* and an interpolated text of the letters of Ignatius. As the Jewish community developed, there was a time when some rabbis apparently recognized Sirach and the Wisdom of Solomon as sacred along with other writings besides those that made up the Hebrew Scriptures. As the church grew and developed, the early Christians accepted at first the words of and about Jesus as their final norm even though they clearly acknowledged the authority of the Old Testament Scriptures. The Old Testament Scriptures were employed by the church primarily as a predictive witness to the Christ event, but also as an authority on Christian conduct as we see throughout *1 Clement.* As the church developed, however, it became obvious that written Gospels and eventually the letters of Paul were also of value in the ongoing life of the community. Among the others that were added to the New Testament collection, *Hermas* and *1 Clement* were the commonly welcomed Scriptures but eventually were rejected by the majority of Christians. When some writings ceased being relevant to the religious needs of the Christian community, that is, they were unable to be repeated with relevance, life, and hope in new circumstances, they also ceased being canon to that community. In this regard, we should observe that Paul "decanonized"[14] much of the Old Testament's emphasis on the Law, especially its focus on clean and unclean foods or ritualistic cleansings, and sabbath laws because such things were no longer deemed by him to be relevant to faith. Dunn makes the point that the Old Testament can never function as canon for Christians in the same way that it does for the Jews. For the Christian, the New Testament always functions to some extent as *the* canon within the biblical canon.[15] Paul (Gal 3:15-22) and later Justin (see *Trypho* 16.2; 27.2-4; and 46.5; *ca.* 160) were the first to deal with the problem of accepting the Law as a part of their authoritative Scriptures while at the same time rejecting its prescriptions for

---

[14]   This is Dunn's expression in his *The Living Word* (Philadelphia: Fortress, 1987) 156.

[15]   Dunn, *Living Word,* 156.

conduct. For Paul, promise and faith preceded the Law, but for Justin the regulations were given because of the hardness of heart and rebellion among the Jews and such prescriptions are no longer needed by the church. The solution for many Christians later was found in the adoption of an allegorical hermeneutic that found secondary spiritual meaning in the various laws. Marcion, followed by the gnostic Christians, eventually rejected the Law and its traditions altogether, but the church condemned that option and taught that this literature also revealed the truth and will of God.

B. The Problem of Definition: Canon 1 and Canon 2. When we speak of canon in reference to the literature of the First Testament or the Old Testament, we are specifically talking about that limited collection of writings that was recognized by Jews and Christians to be inspired by God and consequently to have divine authority in those communities' life and ministry. As such these writings were also believed to reveal the truth and will of God.

A large part of the difficulty in canonical studies, as we have noted above, has to do with identifying two levels of canon. In a very perceptive discussion of this question, Gerald Sheppard has shown two ways of understanding the notion of canon in the ancient world.[16] The first, "canon 1," is essentially when a writing or story functions in an authoritative manner in a community, that is, as rules, regulations, or guides, but the tradition is not yet attached to a fixed or stabilized text or tradition. In other words, canon 1 traditions could grow and be modified. The essential feature here is that the text or tradition was accepted as an authority, even though it was also flexible or fluid in a given community and could, and often was, modified or adapted to meet the needs of the community.[17]

The other understanding of canon, what Sheppard calls "canon 2," comes when a canon 1 authority has become so well established that its text becomes stabilized or fixed in a community, that is, it becomes that to which nothing can be added or taken away (Deut 4:2; Rev 22:7-9, 18-19). Canon scholars often attribute to an ancient writer a "canon 2" understanding when in fact only a "canon 1" notion is in view, that is, an authority that is more fluid and open to

---

[16]   G. T. Sheppard, "Canon," in M. Eliade (ed.), *The Encyclopedia of Religion*, vol. 3 (New York: Macmillan, 1987) 62-69.

[17]   An example of this modification may be seen in the use of Ps 68:18 in Eph 4: 8. Notice how the original text is changed from "received" to "gave" gifts.

change even though it is functioning as an authority in a believing community. For example, the Prophets (*Nebi'im*) and the Writings (*Ketubim*) were accepted in a canon 1 fashion well before they were finally acknowledged as a fixed part of the Hebrew Scriptures (the Old Testament). There were many canon 1 texts that eventually were not received into fixed Scripture canon. Undoubtedly, for some in Israel and for some of the early Christians, these canon 1 texts included many of the apocryphal and pseudepigraphal writings. In the case of the Old Testament, only the Law and the Prophets clearly fall under the category of canon 2 before the time of Jesus' ministry. Perhaps the Psalms were well on their way, but how much is not certain. In the case of the New Testament, only a few books were *generally* accepted in a canon 2 fashion by the end of the second century CE. Even in this case, however, it is not certain that these texts were inviolable as the many second century textual changes in these writings (Gospels especially) show.

C. The First "Canon 2" Texts. There are numerous contexts in the Old Testament where a prophet spoke a word of admonition to ancient Israel but could have strengthened his case considerably by citing a text from the Law. Amos, for instance, could easily have enlisted texts from the law to support his accusations against Israel (see 2:6-16; 5:1-6:14; and the five visions in 7:1-9:15) had they been circulating in some canonical (authoritative) fashion in the eighth century, but he did not. Hosea could have cited texts from the Decalogue about having other gods before the Lord (Exod 20:4-6) and considerably strengthened his case, but he did not. He referred to Israel' unfaithfulness to Yahweh (2:11-13 and 4:1-11) and did say that the people had violated the Law of God (4:6), but it is not clear that the Decalogue was in his mind. There is no specific part of the law invoked here even though the first commandment could have been used with significant affect. In 6:7 and 8:1 an "agreement" is mentioned, but is this the same as the Decalogue in Exodus 20 or Deuteronomy 5? Nathan the prophet could also have been more specific about David's adultery and the murder of Uriah, with significant advantage, when he charged him with a violation of the law of God, had he quoted "thou shalt not commit adultery" or "thou shalt not kill" from the Decalogue (Exod 20:13-14) to reinforce his case against David (2 Sam 12:1-15). He does say that David has broken the word of the Lord (12:9), but does not say what that word is. Was this Nathan's own perception of the will of God? It is difficult to read into this passage a reference to a codified law that prohibited such conduct. But even if such a text did stand behind the prophet's message, citing a specific violation of a sacred Scripture or code that was well recognized by the people would have greatly added to the impact of the writer's message. Joshua appeals to the keeping of the "Book of the Law" (1:8), but this kind of reference is rare and not as obvious in Judges (see a reference to the word of the prophet in 6:8-11, without any clear recollection of a sacred text) and elsewhere in the Old Testament.

What inferences may be reasonably drawn from this absence of citations from the Law? At the least, the role of a fixed textual canonical authority was not an important part of the authoritative structure of the people of Israel at that time. Had the Torah then already been formed in its present condition? If it had, and there is no reason to doubt that the early mythos/story (Deut 26:5-9) existed in some form, the laws themselves apparently did not make a significant impact on the movers and shapers of Israel's pre-exilic traditions. If the Law had been received and functioned as canon or absolute authority in the nation of Israel earlier, why does it not function as canon more prominently before the reforms of Josiah in 621 BCE (2 Chr 34:14-33)?[18] Only at the end of the first Temple history is there a concerted effort to show the relevance of the laws of Moses to the people and the absolute importance of observing those laws, that is, acknowledging them as canon 2.[19] With the reforms of Ezra there is a clear call to obedience to and observance of the laws of Moses (Neh 8:1-8), but at this point, it is not evident that the "laws of Moses" were the same as the Five Books of Moses, the Pentateuch.

The Former Prophets were probably also a recognized authority in the time of Ezra, especially when the people of Israel believed that they had been judged by God because they had failed to listen to the prophets who witnessed to or proclaimed the message of the Law

---

[18]   J. Barr (*Holy Scripture: Canon, Authority, Criticism* [Philadelphia: Westminster, 1983] 6-8) argues the point that in the earlier stages of Israel that its religion is not yet the scriptural religion that it later became. It is also probable that only the Deuteronomic code is behind the reforms of Josiah. Only in the later stages of the religion of Israel do we find a concern about the interpretation of a former prophetic writing, as in the case of Dan 9:2 focusing on the meaning of the seventy years of Jer 29:10.

[19]   See Ezra 10:2-3 and Neh 8:1-8.

(Ezra 9:10-15.).[20] In the time of Ezra, however, only the Mosaic code was given a canon 2 type of recognition, and the prophets themselves were not yet brought into that arena even though they were mentioned occasionally. All references to the prophets in the postexilic writings of Ezra-Nehemiah have to do with the prophets' public proclamation pertaining to the Temple, but there is nothing said about their literary productions (see Ezra 5:1-2, where Haggai and Zechariah are mentioned and also Ezra 9:11; Neh 6:7, 14; 9:26, 30, 32). If the Prophets as a written collection had been recognized as sacred Scripture (canon 2) in the days of Ezra, this would have been a perfect opportunity to introduce them to the people, but only the Books (or laws?) of Moses were so presented by Ezra.

Canon 2 texts, though a permanent part of the sacred collection, are not always inviolate texts. In the Qumran community, for instance, it was not uncommon during the Hellenistic times for scribes to make changes in spelling, orthography, and even delete sentences from the Torah and Prophetic scrolls found at Qumran. These changes suggest to D. J. Silver that the Law, Prophets, and Psalms carried much authority in the pre-rabbinic times, but they had not yet been elevated to the rank of inviolable Scripture that we see in later rabbinic times in which every word and even every letter had to be presented accurately and copied faithfully.[21] Sanders has informed us that even though the Psalter was widely accepted in the first century BCE, still the scribes at Qumran felt free to make significant additions to the text, provide elaborations, and even revisions.[22] This all suggests that for those at Qumran the Scriptures, perhaps including Torah, had not yet become canon 2, that is, fixed or inviolate. The inviolability of Scripture that is seen in Matt 5:18 (cf. Deut 4:2; Rev 22:18-19) in the last quarter of the first century cannot be found among the scribes at Qumran, or at the least, they did not believe, as the rabbis later did, that one could not make such

---

[20]   The prophets witnessed to or reminded the people of the Law of Moses in regard to intermarriage (cf. Exod 34:15-16 and Deut 7:1-5). Judgment came as a result of failure to listen to the message from Moses, not their own. Moses' message was viewed as canon 2, but it is not clear that other writings were thus viewed at that time.

[21]   D. J. Silver, *The Story of Scripture: From Oral Tradition to the Written Word* (New York: Basic Books, 1990) 141.

[22]   J. A. Sanders, "Cave 11 Surprises and the Question of Canon," *McCQ* 21 (1968) 284-317.

changes in the Scripture collection.

Evidence that the Prophets had not been moved into a canon 2 category by the late third century BCE is the fact that when the LXX was produced (*ca.* 250–225 BCE), the Law alone was translated into Greek. Only later (*ca.* 150–130 BCE) were the Prophets circulating in a collection, as the Prologue to Sirach suggests, and the Writings were circulating in a more loose form until sometime later in the second or first century BCE when they and other religious texts were also translated into Greek and added to the LXX. It is difficult to know the precise contents of the LXX in the first century BCE or CE since no copies exist from that period, but that the LXX was eventually expanded to include the Prophets and the Writings is obvious. The New Testament writers, for instance, use the LXX in more than eighty percent of their references to the Old Testament and these came from each of the three categories of the Hebrew Scriptures (the Law, Prophets, and Writings). This should not suggest that these categories were complete nor that the New Testament writers were uninformed by other sacred texts as well. Luke 24:44 shows that the canonical categories were not complete at this time. The authority attributed to the LXX in antiquity is obvious from the sensational description of its translation in the legendary *Letter of Aristeas* (*ca.* 190 BCE–35 CE).[23] For the author of that letter, the Law of Moses was unquestionably accepted as canon 2 and at that time the books of the Pentateuch were the primary if not the only writings accepted as canon 2. Again, if the Prophets and Writings had already obtained that status when the LXX was produced, it is puzzling that they were not also included in the translation.

Well into the fifth century CE there was a higher place of priority given to the accurate translation of the Law of Moses and to the actual handling of the sacred scrolls themselves. Jews were not allowed to divide or separate the Torah scrolls and they reserved a special place in the synagogues for keeping the Torah (the *tevah*). Whatever the views about the scriptural status of the Prophets and the Writings, the priority of the Torah was indisputable. Only the books of the Law were regularly read through annually as an essential part of the Sabbath liturgy. Whatever else this means, there

---

[23]   It is difficult to establish the date of origin for the *Letter of Aristeas* with any precision. It may not have been written as early as 150 to 100 BCE, but the termination date is 35 CE since Philo refers to it.

was not an equal acceptance of all of the literature of the *Tanak*. Priority was always given to the Law (Pentateuch).

With regard to the pre-Christian texts, there is a tendency among some canon scholars to interpret these Jewish texts (e.g. Prologue to Sirach; Philo, *Contemplative life*; 4QMMT) and the events and writings of the first century as a whole anachronistically, from the perspective of the second century rabbinic sages or later, and also from the vantage point of the church fathers from the fourth and fifth centuries. The same could be said about citing one text from the second century and claiming that the views of the one citing the text were everywhere present in both the first and second centuries. For instance, some scholars cite the late second century *baraita* found in *b. B. Bat.* 14b as evidence for an understanding of the state of the biblical canon in the Land of Israel in the first century CE. There is no compelling evidence that this tradition was a widely held view *even in the second century* Jewish communities either inside or outside the land of Israel. Nor is it certain that all baraitot, including *b. B. Bat.* 14b, are second-century predictions.[24] Unfortunately, however, some scholars have not restricted themselves to what they can show from the traditions they examine and they have frequently drawn unwarranted conclusions from this passage about what obtained in the first or second century.

We will now proceed to a few summarizing comments about the early recognition and growth of the Scripture tradition in Israel.

EXPANSION AND STABILIZATION OF THE FIRST TESTAMENT

A. Early Stages of Recognition. There are several important texts that are generally cited to support the growth and eventual stability of the First Testament canon. These texts are not as precise as some scholars insist, but they do support the notion of the growth of the biblical canon from earlier stages when only the laws of Moses were acknowledged as authoritative and literarily assembled into place of prominence in what would become the sacred Scriptures. The following texts will illustrate the development that leads to a broader collection.

1. Sirach 49:8-10. In time (400–200 BCE), similar authority—but

---

24   See S. Friedman, "Baraiyta," in R. J. Z. Werblowsky and G. Wigoder (eds.), *Oxford Dictionary of the Jewish Religion* (Oxford and New York: Oxford University Press, 1997) 98.

never the same authority—that had first been given to the laws of
Moses and subsequently to the Pentateuch was also conferred upon
the Prophets, probably the Former prophets at first, and consequently also upon the Latter Prophets.[25] When did that conferral or recognition take place? In regard to the recognition of the Prophets, or at
least some of them (Sir 49:8-10), scholars suggest a *terminus ad
quem*, namely, 180 BCE since they are referred to in Sir 49:8-10. In
this text, Sirach shows an awareness of the books of Ezekiel and Job,
as well as the "Twelve Prophets." But this passage and its broader
context do not focus on a collection of the writings of the Prophets,
or writings at all for that matter, but focuses on the heroes of faith
who were the prophets of Israel. This passage comes at the end of
Sirach's "History of Famous Men" (Sir 44:1-50:24) in which he
shows an awareness of the contents of some of the books of the
prophets. He tells the story of the famous persons in his list, but the
focus is not on famous texts or books.

We may still ask, whether the reference to the "Twelve Prophets"
(49:10) is a reference to the Minor Prophets as a collection?
Whatever the case may be, *knowledge* of the books of the Former
and Latter Prophets and of the book of Job seems almost certain in
this passage. Possibly there is a canon 1 recognition of some sacred
literature here, but it is unlikely that we see as yet a canon 2 notion
since no specific texts are cited from this literature, nor is there a
mention of the existence of that literature with the possible exception
of the "Twelve." Books are simply not emphasized[26] and the great
persons were not described by Sirach as *writers* but, as Orlinsky has
correctly observed, as *activists*.[27] Awareness of the existence of the
Prophets, however, cannot be equated with any conferral of canonical authority (canon 2) upon them even though that step is probably
not far away. A stabilized sacred tradition, however, is not as clear

---

[25]   This is suggested by the citing of the prophet Jeremiah by a later prophet
(Dan 9:2).

[26]   Sirach likely shows an awareness of the contents of the books of Joshua
(46:1-6), Samuel (46:13–47:11), and the Kings (47:12–49:3), including David and
Solomon. He also mentions Hezekiah and Isaiah (48:20-25), as well as Josiah
(49:1-4), Jeremiah (49:6), Ezekiel, Job, and the Twelve Prophets (49:9-10), which
suggests that the twelve minor prophets were already circulating in Israel by this
time (200–180 BCE).

[27]   H. M. Orlinsky, "Some Terms in the Prologue to Ben Sera and the Hebrew
Canon," *JBL* 110 (1991) 483-90, here 487.

in the main text of Sirach as what we find in the later Prologue.

2. *Prologue to Ben Sirach.* When Sirach's grandson, or someone else,[28] wrote the Prologue to Sirach (*Ecclesiasticus*) and translated Sirach into Greek for those in Alexandria (*ca.* 130 BCE), he identified the literature that had already been translated for them into Greek as the "Law and the Prophets and the *others* that followed them." In a subsequent paragraph of the Prologue, and while describing the difficulty of translating from Hebrew into Greek, he states that there are differences that remain in the translation of the "Law itself, the Prophecies, and the rest of the books" as well as in the translation of his grandfather's work. What were those "other books" or "rest of the books" that he was speaking about? We do not know for sure since he does not say.[29] In fact, we cannot be certain about what comprised the "prophecies" either since they are not specifically identified. What were the contents of this collection that he identifies? It is common for some canon scholars to read back into the ancient times circumstances and views that only later obtained widespread acceptance in Israel. In this case, some contend that the traditional three-fold canon of Scriptures was intended by the Prologue's author, but that is not clear from the passage itself. We should emphasize that the proverbs of Sirach were also translated for the Alexandrian community just as the other literature, and the author of the Prologue does not make a clear distinction drawn between them. How was the use of Sirach qualitatively different from the use of the Law, Prophets, and others in that community? Nevertheless, we may see the beginnings of a three or four part collection of sacred Scriptures emerging among the Jewish people even though we are not certain what was in those parts. Philo, for example, referred to the holy books of the Therapeutae and Essenes that these people took with them into their sacred shrines or holy places in Egypt. These included "the laws and the sacred oracles of God enunciated by the holy prophets, and hymns, and psalms, and all kinds of other things by reason of which knowledge and piety are increased . . . ." (*Contemplative Life* 3.25). Again, it is impossible to deduce from these references that there were three specific and well

---

28   The authorship of the Prologue is not certain.

29   It is tempting to assume that they were the same as the third part of the twenty-two books that Josephus describes in *Against Apion* 1.8 §37-43 or perhaps identical to those in *b. B. Bat.* 14b. It may also be that the "other books" resembled the "70" books described in 4 Ezra 14:44-48, but we do not know.

defined collections of sacred Scriptures, let alone what was in them. The fact that there were other books besides those of the Tanak found at or near Qumran in the sacred collection of a group akin to the Essenes (other than the Therapeutae in Egypt) should give cause for caution before automatically equating them with the books that eventually made up the Hebrew Bible or the Protestant Old Testament canon.

3. 4QMMT (Miqṣat Maʿaśeh ha-Torah). In the recently translated Qumran text, 4QMMT (*ca.* 150 BCE), there is a reference to three or possibly four categories of sacred writings. In part the text reads: "we have [written] to you so that you may study (carefully) the *book of Moses and the books of the Prophets and (the writings of) David [and the events of] ages past.*"[30] In this text the three or four categories of sacred writings are only vaguely described and even the "prophets" are not clearly identified. Does the third category, "David," refer to the Psalter as we now have it or is it more or less than that? Does the fourth category—the "events of ages past," or "day to day chronicles"[31]—refer to Chronicles and Ezra-Nehemiah, and possibly also to Esther, as other scholars contend?[32] Neither

---

[30] Italics added. The translation is taken from E. Qimron and J. Strugnell, *Qumran Cave 4: V. Miqṣat Maʿaśe Ha-Torah* (DJD 10; Oxford: Clarendon, 1994) 59. For somewhat different translations, see B. W. W. Dombrowski, *An Annotated Translation of Miqṣat Maʿaśeh ha-Torah (4QMMT)* (Krakow and Weenzen: Enigma Press, 1993) 13-14; F. García Martínez, *The Dead Sea Scrolls Translated* (Leiden: Brill, 1994) 84. E. E. Ellis also supplies a translation in his *The Old Testament in Early Christianity: Canon and Interpretation in Light of Modern Research* (Grand Rapids: Baker, 1992) 10. Because of the poor condition of the text, several words have to be supplied. For our purposes, the above translations are not unreasonable and they allow us to conclude that there were at least three and probably four categories of sacred texts mentioned.

[31] As translated by Dombrowski, *An Annotated Translation of Miqṣat Maʿaśeh ha-Torah*, 14.

[32] Ellis, *Old Testament in Early Christianity*, 9-11; and F. F. Bruce, *The Canon of Scripture* (Downers Grove: InterVarsity, 1988) 32. It should be mentioned that the book of Esther has not yet been identified among the thousands of fragments from Qumran. J. Finkel ("The Author of the Genesis Apocryphon Knew the Book of Esther," in Y. Yadin and C. Rabin [eds.], *Essays on the Dead Sea Scrolls in Memory of E. L. Sukenik* [Jerusalem: Shrine of the Book, 1962] 163-82 [Hebrew]) attempted to prove that at least one of the scribes of the Dead Sea Scrolls was familiar with the book of Esther. More recently, J. T. Milik ("Les modèles araméens du livre d'Esther dans la grotte 4 de Qumrân," *RevQ* 15 [1992] 321-99 + pls. I-VII) renewed the discussion by concluding that 4Q550^{a-f} (which he names

Philo's text nor 4QMMT present us with a clear and crisp statement about the contents of what is later identified in rabbinic writings as the *Ketubim* or Hagiographa (Sacred Writings). They do show us, however, that both the Therapeutae in Egypt and the addressees of the 4QMMT text from Qumran had three or four categories of writings that probably, though not certainly, are like the writings we later hear about in Josephus in a more precise threefold division of the Scriptures.

We must be cautious, however, in deciding whether we have found in either 4QMMT or Philo a collection of sacred Scriptures that had clearly defined and fixed boundaries. Scholars often make the point that of all of the writings of the Old Testament canon, only Esther, was not found at Qumran. They infer from this that all the Jewish sects adopted this same canon.[33] But what *other* literature was also found in the same caves at or near Qumran and how can we—or should we—distinguish that literature from the canonical literature of later rabbinic Judaism?[34] Scholars know that the caves at Qumran included much more literature than the twenty-four book biblical canon of the Hebrew Bible less Esther. There were more psalms found there than currently exist in the Hebrew Scriptures, as Sanders has shown,[35] along with writings such as the Damascus Document, the Temple Scroll, *Jubilees*, and other noncanonical writings that did not obtain the canonical status of the later rabbinic collections.[36]

4QprEsth ar[a-f]) attests an Aramaic prototype of the tradition underlying Esther. S. Talmon ("Was the Book of Esther Known at Qumran?" *DSD* 2 [1995] 250-67), exposing the deficiencies of the arguments of Finkel and Milik, offers more convincing evidence that Esther was known to some of the scribes of the Dead Sea Scrolls but had not yet attained the status of Holy Scripture.

[33]   Bruce, *Canon*, 40-41.

[34]   Y. Yadin, for instance has argued that the Temple Scroll found at Qumran was both preserved and used in a scriptural-like manner indistinguishable from the later canonical literature found there. See his impressive three volume work on this scroll, *The Temple Scroll* (Jerusalem: Israel Exploration Society, 1983). See also his "The Temple Scroll—The Longest and Most Recently Discovered Dead Sea Scroll," *BARev* 10.5 (1984) 33-49.

[35]   Sanders, "Cave 11 Surprises and the Question of Canon," 284-317.

[36]   W. W. Klein, C. L. Blomberg, and R. L. Hubbard (*Introduction to Biblical Interpretation* [Dallas: Word, 1993] 57) argue that all of the books of the Old Testament except Esther were found at Qumran and only one book of the Apocrypha (Tobit) was found there. This is incorrect and misleading. From the Apocrypha we also have Sirach (2QSir, 11QPs[a], MasSir) and Epistle of Jeremy (7Q2). From the

There is currently no way to distinguish this literature from the
canonical literature either in use or esteem.

   3. Luke 24:44 and a three-part canon. In the New Testament, Jesus
made reference to a three part collection of sacred Scriptures that
included "the Law, the Prophets, and the psalms ['Psalms'?]" (Luke
24:44). Whether the latter category called the Psalms should also be
taken to include all of what later came to be known as the *Ketubim*
or Hagiographa, as some scholars insist, is a disputed matter.
Scholars have observed for some time that in the rabbinic writings
the term "Fifths" (Hebrew, חומשים, *ḥōmašim, ḥōmašin*) sometimes
refers not to the five books of the Pentateuch, but rather to the five
parts of the book of Psalms. In the Rabbinic tradition of the third
century and following, it also refers to the whole of the Hagiographa.[37] If all of this is correct and if it was widely understood in

---

so-called Pseudepigrapha we have *Jubilees, Enoch,* and *Testatments of the Twelve
Patriarchs.* Other documents were also found at or near Qumran, namely, the
Damascus Document (4QD = CD or Zadokite Document), the Manual of Discipline
(1QS), the Messianic Rule (1QSa), Book of Blessings (1QSb), War Scroll (4QM),
the Hymn Scroll (1QHodayot), the Genesis Apocryphon (1QapGen), and the
Temple Scroll (11QT). How can one with any assurance say what the limits of
Qumran's canon were, especially if we are not sure that a cave 12 or 13 or more
does or does not exist somewhere in the Judean wilderness? Neusner (*Midrash in
Context: Exegesis in Formative Judaism* [Philadelphia: Fortress, 1983] 6) speaking
of the other writings found at Qumran, correctly concludes that "those documents at
Qumran appear side by side with the ones we know as canonical Scripture. The
high probability is that, to the Essenes, the sectarian books were no less holy and
authoritative than Leviticus, Deuteronomy, Nahum, Habakkuk, Isaiah, and the
other books of the biblical canon they, among all Israelites, revered."

   37   Beckwith, in an attempt to equate Jesus' reference to Psalms in Luke 24:44
with the whole of the Hagiographa, shows how in the Talmudic literature that
"fifths" sometimes refers to the "Psalms" and to the whole of the "Hagiographa."
One of his supporting passages is the following: "In a scroll of the Law, the space
of the two finger-breadths must be left (between columns), but in scrolls of the
Prophets and in scrolls of the Fifths the space of one thumb-breadth. In the lower
margin of a scroll of the Law the space of a hand-breadth is left, and in the upper
margin two thirds of a hand-breadth, but in scrolls of the Prophets and the Fifths
three finger-breadths in the lower margin and two finger-breadths in the upper"
(*Sepher Torah* 2.3-4; *Sopherim* 2.4). See Beckwith, *Old Testament Canon,* 438,
but see also pp. 111-14. Beckwith also shows how the Hagiographa are referred to
as the "Fifths" (חומשים) in *t. Kelim B. Meṣ.* 5.8, which reads: "The Book of Ezra, if
it comes out (of the Temple), makes the hands unclean; and not the Book of Ezra
alone [Torah], but the Prophets and the Fifths. But another book makes the hands

the first century—and there is no evidence that it was, then it may be possible to say that Jesus endorsed the whole Hebrew biblical canon as we currently have it.[38] This inference, however, has no support whatever in the first century and scholars who draw this conclusion must acknowledge that it is not consistent even in the rabbinic traditions themselves.

We cannot be sure if texts that date considerably *after* the time of Jesus can clarify to us what Jesus, or Philo, or 4QMMT meant by the reference to "psalms." The terms *Ketubim* and *Hagiographa* are not found in the first century as references to the third part of the Hebrew Scriptures and the term "Fifths" is not used in reference to any part of the biblical canon *at that time*. We also cannot be sure that "psalms" in the first century ever referred to anything more than psalmic literature.

We conclude, therefore, that there is no *first century* evidence that shows that "psalms" ever stood for the whole of what was later called the Hagiographa.[39] Although Luke 24:44 suggests that a third part of the Hebrew Scriptures was emerging in Israel by the middle to late first century CE, there is no clear statement from the first century indicating what was in that third part. All references to it in the period before, during, and after the time of Jesus are imprecise. The evidence presented thus far leads us to conclude that the composition

---

unclean if it is brought in there." See Beckwith, *Old Testament Canon*, 438. If "Fifths" is used as a reference to the Psalms and if the term "psalms" is also used for the third part of the Hebrew Bible, because it stood in the first place in the Hagiographa, as Beckwith claims, then the reference to Psalms in Luke 24:44 may stand for the whole collection of Writings. However, these are big, unsubstantiated "ifs."

38   Beckwith (*Old Testament Canon*, 114-15, 118-20) reasons that since Jesus also cites the book of Daniel (see, for example, Dan 4:26 in Matt. 4:17; and Dan 7:13 in Mark 14:62), which was a part of the Hagiographa, then he surely must have intended the whole of the Hagiographa when he mentioned "psalms" in this passage. See also Bruce, *Canon*, 31, who agrees with this argument. But again there are too many unsubstantiated assumptions involved that prevent us from drawing his conclusions, not the least of which is his interpretation of first century sources through the eyes of the second and third century rabbinic sages.

39   J. P. Lewis ("Some Aspects of the Problem of Inclusion of the Apocrypha," in S. Meurer [ed.], *The Apocrypha in Ecumenical Perspective* [UBS Monograph Series 6; New York: United Bible Society, 1991] 161-207, here 176) correctly claims that of the above cited passages "no text defines explicitly the contents of 'the rest of the books' or 'the psalms'."

of the third part of the Hebrew Scriptures was still imprecise in the
first century and that it had not yet stabilized either in Judaism or in
early Christianity.

   5. Josephus, Against Apion 1.8 §37-43. The most frequently cited
text to support the theory of an early (first century) closing of the
third and final part of the Old Testament canon is Josephus' well
known polemical apology for the Jews, *Against Apion* 1.8 §37-43.
The passage is regularly cited as evidence that such a canon existed at
the beginning of the early church.[40] The most commonly cited
portion of this well known text is as follows:

> "Our books, those which are justly accredited, are but two and twenty, and
> contain the record of all time. of these, five are the books of Moses,
> comprising the laws and the traditional history from the birth of man down
> to the death of the lawgiver. This period falls only a little short of three
> thousand years. From the death of Moses until Artaxerxes, who succeeded
> Xerxes as king of Persia, the prophets subsequent to Moses wrote the
> history of the events of their own times in thirteen books. The remaining
> four books contain hymns to God and precepts for the conduct of human
> life. . .
>
>   We have given practical proof of our reverence for our own Scriptures. For
> although such long ages have now passed, no one has ventured either to add,
> or to remove, or to alter a syllable; and it is an instinct with every Jew, from
> the day of his birth, to regard them as decrees of God, to abide by them, and,
> if need be, cheerfully to die for them" (*Against Apion* 1.8 §37-43 [LCL]).

   Notice, that this text describes the third part of Josephus' collection
of sacred Scriptures as "hymns to God and precepts for the conduct
of human life." It is difficult to argue from this description that the
third part of his collection, which clearly included psalmic literature,
would also have included the Chronicles, Ezra-Nehemiah, Esther,
and Daniel. Further, it is not at all clear that the *Ketubim* began with
the Psalms as Beckwith and Bruce assume.[41] We agree with Orlinsky

---

   [40]   Bruce (*Canon*, 23, 32-34) and Ellis (*Old Testament in Early Christianity*, 7-
8) argue this point, as does Beckwith ("Formation of the Hebrew Bible," 50), who
acknowledges that there may be some exaggeration on the part of Josephus in his
account, but dismisses the notion that he may have misrepresented the actual state
of affairs at the end of the first century CE. He contends that Josephus reflects
instead a rather long standing biblical canon tradition within the Jewish community.

   [41]   Beckwith believes that the deciphering of Josephus' canon is relatively
easy, but there are too many "probably's" or "could be's" in his explanation to be
convincing. Essentially, he includes in Josephus' "Prophets" Chronicles, Ezra-
Nehemiah, Daniel and Esther. See his *Old Testament Canon*, 119. Klein, Blom-

that at the end of the first century CE only the Law and the Prophets were clearly defined and that the third section, the Writings, were still in need of definition.[42] It is likely that the references to the word "psalms" in 4QMMT, Philo (*Contemplative Life* 3.25), and Luke 24:44, refer only to the "psalms" which, along with the Law and the Prophets, comprised most of that which was generally recognized as canonical and fixed (canon 2) in the first century CE. Generally speaking, in the New Testament itself Scriptures were noted with the designation the "Law and the Prophets" (see, for example, Matt 7:12; 22:40). With the addition of the "psalms," we probably have an early indication of the emerging expansion of a stabilized canon in the first century, even though that canon had not yet reached a final stage.[43]

---

berg, and Hubbard (*Introduction to Biblical Interpretation*, 57) following Beckwith, also believe that deciphering Josephus' canon is relatively easy and with confidence say what comprises each part of that collection. They assert that the books of the Prophets can be "reconstructed from later Jewish lists," but never specify what those "lists" are. The only list that has any proximity to Josephus is *b. B. Bat.* 14b, but it does not break down the Prophets and Writings in this manner and it also has a familiar twenty-four book list, not the twenty-two book collection.

[42]   Orlinsky, "Some Terms," 488-89.

[43]   Bruce (*Canon*, 31) believes that he can detect the order of the Hebrew biblical canon from Luke 11:49-51 when Jesus spoke of the first (Abel) and last (Zechariah) prophets to be killed. He says that Zechariah (*ca.* 800 BCE; cf. 2 Chr 24:20-24) was the last canonical prophet to be killed since his death is reported in 2 Chronicles, the last book in the Hebrew Scriptures. Bruce claims that these comments in Luke 11:49-51 were intended by Jesus to cover the whole of the Hebrew Scriptures from Genesis to 2 Chronicles. Beckwith (*Old Testament Canon*, 170 n. 29) acknowledges that Jerome's Old Testament canon does not conclude with Chronicles, and that he only has a twenty-two book canon. He theorizes that if Jerome had listed a twenty-four book canon it might have followed the above order which concludes with 2 Chronicles! This argument leads him to conclude that Jesus was endorsing the whole collection of canonical Scriptures. On the other hand, the most commonly cited Hebrew text today, the Aleppo Codex, considered by Maimonides to be the most exact representative of the Masoretic tradition, places Chronicles at the *beginning* of the third division of Scriptures and Ezra-Nehemiah at the end. We should also note that the concluding sentences of 2 Chronicles 34 are the same as the opening sentences Ezra 1. It would appear that the writer/editor of this collection of sacred books at least wanted to have Chronicles in first place and Ezra-Nehemiah in last place. Also, if there had been no other books between Chronicles and Ezra, the parallel sentences at the end of 2 Chronicles and at the beginning of Ezra 1 would have been unnecessary. These passages are what some call "canonical glue" that were intended to bind other books together into a sacred collection. Jerome's reference to the Old Testament Scriptures in the fifth century

Historically, Josephus appears to have been the first to argue that the number of sacred books in the Hebrew Scriptures was limited or complete. The second century tradition, *m. Yad.* 3:5, shows that the status of Song of Songs and Qohelet was still being disputed in the rabbinic community. This suggests at least that the third part of the Hebrew Bible had not been settled for all of the religious leaders in Israel in the second century. The Alexandrian community, where Philo lived and wrote his *Contemplative Life*, and the community to which the grandson of Sirach addressed the Prologue to Sirach, produced the LXX, but it never produced a clearly defined tripartite biblical canon.[44]

This text, however, argues for a widely accepted and long standing three part biblical canon of twenty-two books among the Jews. Ellis argues that Josephus contradicts any views about an undetermined biblical canon in the first century, and that this well known passage was "a closely reasoned polemic against *inter alia* the work of an erudite Alexandrian grammarian, and he could not afford to indulge in careless misstatements that could be thrown back at him."[45] He adds that Josephus did not just present the views of his own Pharisaic party, but that of all the Jewish people.[46]

There are two other important observations that we should make about this reference: the first is that Josephus' twenty-two book canon did not eventually obtain in Judaism but rather the twenty-four book canon that was popular even in Josephus' own day (see 4 Ezra 14:44-48);[47] second, and perhaps more important for our purposes, it is well known that Josephus was given to exaggeration. In recent times several scholars have questioned the reliability of Josephus'

---

preserves the three-fold division of the Hebrew Bible, but he has Job in first place in the third category of Hebrew Scriptures, Chronicles, in seventh place, followed by Esdras (Ezra-Nehemiah) and concluding with Esther. See his "Helmeted Prologue" (*Prologus Galeatus*). Although *b. B. Bat.* 14b has Chronicles at the end of the collection, Ruth stands at the beginning, and not Psalms. We should also observe that whatever books made up Josephus' canon, Chronicles, by his own description, could not have stood last in the last category in his collection since in no way could the Chronicles be considered psalmic literature.

44   Orlinsky ("Some Terms," 490) argues this point.

45   Ellis, *Old Testament in Early Christianity*, 39.

46   Ellis, *Old Testament in Early Christianity*, 39.

47   The actual number of books is not as important since the number evidently only affected the way writings were grouped together and not the actual number of books involved in the canonization process.

comments on the extent of the Jewish biblical canon at the end of the first century CE. Leiman, for example, points out that the above passage was written in an apologetic context that is "a vigorous rebuttal" not only against Apion, but also against all who denied the antiquity of the Jews and their sacred literature. He claims that Josephus was contending for the accuracy of the Hebrew Scriptures as reliable history and that he was not arguing for them as sacred Scripture.[48] Leiman further argues that Josephus' comment that "no one has ventured to add, or to remove, or to alter a syllable" is simply without justification since "it is inconceivable that Josephus was unaware of the wide range of textual divergency that characterized the Hebrew, Greek, and Aramaic versions of Scripture current in first century Palestine."[49] The assertion itself only points to their sacredness, that is, their inviolability (see Deut 4:2; Rev 22:7-9, 18-19). But how do we account for the exclusive language about the contents of the Hebrew Scriptures in Josephus? Leiman says that this rhetoric has several parallels in classical historiography and that Josephus need not be taken literally.[50]

Louis Feldman is even more critical of Josephus' reliability in this matter citing several examples of exaggeration and propagandizing, especially in the defense of Judaism—which, of course, is the context of *Against Apion*.[51] He reviews the prejudices and inaccuracies of Josephus and concludes that "he is far from infallible" in his conclusions about the canon of Scripture at the end of the first century.[52] On the other hand, he believes that Josephus is quite reliable in the areas of topography and geography of the land of Israel and also in matters of economics, but he is nonetheless a propagandist in the defense of Judaism against the pagan intellectuals of his day.[53] Silver concludes that Josephus' assertions about a twenty-two book canon

---

[48]   S. Z. Leiman makes this observation in, "Josephus and the Canon of the Bible," in L. Feldman and G. Hata (eds.), *Josephus, The Bible, and History* (Detroit: Wayne State University, 1989) 50-58, here 51-52.

[49]   Leiman, "Josephus," 52.

[50]   Leiman, "Josephus," 52-53. He notes that Maimonides (d. 1204) and Joseph Albo (fifteenth century) also have similar statements in an apologetic context.

[51]   See L. Feldman, "Introduction," in Feldman and Hata (eds.), *Josephus, His Bible, and History*, 3-47.

[52]   Feldman, "Introduction," 46-47.

[53]   Feldman, "Introduction," 47.

revealed his wish rather than the actual state of affairs and he rightly observes that there were many other sacred texts circulating in that time with a claim to canonical authority "with more appearing all the time."[54] Since Josephus argued that the exact succession of prophets ceased with Artaxerxes, the son of Xerxes, whom he identifies in *Ant.* 11.6.1 §184 as Ahasuerus from the book of Esther, it is understandable why he concluded his biblical canon as early as he did. But this view was not the only view about prophecy among the Jews of the first century.[55]

Although Leiman acknowledges that in his writings Josephus frequently exaggerated, he still believes that Josephus spoke of a standardized biblical canon that could be independently verified. He reasons: "Even if one allows for exaggeration on Josephus' part, he could hardly lie about the extent or antiquity of the canon; any Roman reader could inquire of the nearest Jew and test the veracity of Josephus' statement."[56] This sounds plausible, but it assumes that "any Jew" would know the contents of the biblical canon, or would be interested in the question at all, and finally that all Jews would agree on the matter. It is precisely this kind of questioning that Melito, bishop at Sardis at the end of the second century, could have done in his own community where there was a large Jewish population and synagogue, but evidently he could not find sufficient awareness of the scope of the biblical canon in his own city. He therefore made a special trip to the East (Palestine? or Jerusalem?) to discover the contents of the Hebrew Scriptures or Christian Bible (Eusebius, *Hist. Eccl.* 4.26.13-14). If the church had received a closed biblical canon from Jesus, it is odd that the bishop of a large church at the end of the second century did not know the books that made up his Bible. This would be strange indeed if the matter had been settled for a long period in the church, but not so strange if the matter was still unsettled. How certain are we and what evidence is there that any Roman could have verified Josephus' comments about the extent of

---

[54] D. J. Silver, The *Story of Scripture: From Oral Tradition to the Written Word* (New York: Basic Books, 1990) 134. 4 Ezra 14:44-48 is one such example.

[55] Leiman ("Josephus," 51) makes this point. It is ironic to note that some of the strongest opponents of the legitimacy of Josephus' claims in his apology, *Ag. Apion*, are rabbis and the strongest endorsers of Josephus' canon are Christian scholars who use it to argue for a closed biblical canon in or before the time of Jesus!

[56] Leiman, "Josephus," 54.

the Hebrew Bible by asking "the nearest Jew"? If the church had received a closed biblical canon from Jesus, it is incomprehensible that a prominent bishop some 150 years later was unable to inform his parishioners of its contents? If such a canon existed, not one example of it or even a discussion of it has survived in the history of the church. Given the importance attributed to such a canon in the first century by some scholars, this silence is all the more amazing.

6. *Jubilees 2:22-24.* Where did Josephus get his understanding of the biblical canon if it was not widely held information in his day? Did he invent it or take it from an earlier source, or from the Greek model by using the alphabet as a means of dividing and identifying its sacred literature?[57] Ellis[58] and Beckwith[59] have noted that a *later* text of *Jub.* 2:23-24 is the first reference to a twenty-two book Scripture canon and may be behind the reference in Josephus, *Against Apion* 1.8 §37-43. The original text of *Jubilees* was probably written *ca.* 150 BCE, but it has been corrupted in transmission. Several versions of *Jub.* 2:23-24, including the Ethiopic text, were known in antiquity. Beckwith observed that R. H. Charles believed

---

[57] The equation of the Hebrew alphabet with the canon of Scriptures was not a novel idea in the first century and it is possible that its popularity could account for a later editing of *Jubilees* to include the Hebrew Scriptures in the text. The idea of the use of the alphabet to distinguish the parts of a religious canon did not originate with the Jews, but rather with the Greeks who regarded Homer's *Iliad* and *Odyssey* as canonical in the sense that only the gods found therein were objects of worship. The *Iliad* and *Odyssey* were divided into sections by the twenty-four letters of the Greek alphabet unlike other writings whose authors used *numbers* to designate parts or divisions of books. This division is preserved in the LCL Greek text and translation of Homer. This practice spoke for the Greeks of the sacredness attributed to the text. The use of the alphabet by the Greeks for identifying sacred writings probably also influenced the Jews. For example, observe the structure of several Psalms according to the letters of the Hebrew alphabet (e.g. Psalms 25, 34, 119) and the recognition of the number of books in their scriptural canons with the number of letters in the alphabet. We probably see for the first time the focus on the letters of the Hebrew alphabet after the Greek domination of Palestine, and it is interesting that the number that survived among the Jews was the twenty-four book canon, the same number as the letters of the Greek alphabet. It is probably not by coincidence that the risen Christ in the Book of Revelation is called the "Alpha and the Omega" (Rev 1:8), undoubtedly a divine reference. For a more complete discussion of this phenomenon, see D. N. Freedman, "The Symmetry of the Hebrew Bible," *ST* 46 (1992) 83-108, here 100-107.

[58] Ellis, *Old Testament in Early Christianity*, 10, 33.

[59] Beckwith, *Old Testament Canon*, 235-40.

he had recovered the original form of the text through an examination of the church fathers, particularly the one preserved in Epiphanius' *De mensuris et ponderibus* 22, which mentions in the grouping of twenty-two's that there were twenty-two books, presumably in the Hebrew Scriptures. Epiphanius mentions the twenty-two number tradition in Israel and includes the reference to the twenty-two books of the Hebrew Scriptures. He writes: "As there were two and twenty letters and two and twenty books and two and twenty heads of mankind from Adam to Jacob, so there were two and twenty kinds of work until the seventh day."[60]

The earliest form of *Jub.* 2:22-24, however, does not have the reference to the twenty-two books. This reference constitutes an insertion placed in the text during a time when the notion of a twenty two book canon had gained currency in Israel. But the tradition of the twenty-two books was also known among the church fathers who frequently referred to it.[61] This tradition circulated apparently in the church longer than in the rabbinic traditions. Whatever the source of this twenty-two book canon, it is difficult to substantiate Josephus' claim that his canon was as widespread and inviolable as he contends.

The focus on the number of letters in the Hebrew alphabet is an important stage in the development of the Hebrew Bible, a practice that had its roots in Hellenism and was likely borrowed by the Jews from the Greeks. What makes it likely that Jews borrowed from the Greeks is that Jews finally settled on a twenty-four book canon, the number of letters in the Greek alphabet, and not on a twenty-two book canon which would more easily represent the Hebrew alphabet. See, for example, 4 Ezra 14:44-47 and *b. B. Bat.* 14b, which mention

---

[60]   Beckwith, *Old Testament Canon*, 235-40. The early ninth century Georgius Syncellus text reads similarly: "All works are together twenty-two, equal in number with the twenty-two Hebrew letters and the twenty-two Hebrew books and the twenty-two founding fathers from Adam to Jacob." It is not clear whether there was some relationship between these two texts. For a careful discussion of this passage and others in *Jubilees*, see J. C. VanderKam and J. T. Milik, "The First *Jubilees* Manuscript From Qumran Cave 4: A Preliminary Publication," *JBL* 110 (1991) 243-70; for the quotation above, see 259-60 and 267-68. The Qumran form of this text does *not* include the mention of twenty-two books.

[61]   For example, Origen, referred to it according to Eusebius in his *Hist. Eccl.* 6.26.1, 2. If the tradition were a late first century invention, it is easy to see how a reference to it by Josephus would impact Christian writers of the fourth century who had high respect for Josephus and even made insertions into his writings that included references to Jesus.

twenty-four books in their sacred collections. The correspondence of the Scripture canon to the alphabet in Judaism is difficult to date with any certainty before the end of the first century CE (Josephus).

B. Use of Noncanonical Writings in Early Christianity. Although some scholars have tried to show that the corpus of the Hebrew Scriptures was completed no later than the second century BCE and was endorsed by Jesus,[62] this does not square with the attitude of the earliest Christians toward many of the noncanonical writings (apocryphal or pseudepigraphical) nor with the writings which survive the first two centuries of early Christianity (i.e. the New Testament, the so-called "Apostolic Fathers," and the writings of the second-century apologists). Christians were also informed in their theologies by the apocryphal writings, including pseudepigraphal writings (as seen in the case of Jude, which cited *1 Enoch*). Other examples include Mark 10:19, which makes use of Sir 4:1, along with Exod 20:12-16 and Deut 5:16-20. The author of 2 Timothy cites Sir 17:26, along with Num 16:5. Paul appears to make use of Wis 14:22-31 in Rom 1:24-32, and possibly also Wis 2:23-24 in Rom 5:12-21. In 1 Cor 2:9 he cites as "Scripture" either the *Ascension of Isaiah* 11:34 or a now lost Elijah apocalypse derived from Isa 64:3.

Christians readily accorded an authoritative status to noncanonical writings soon after the time of Jesus. This suggests that the scriptural canon was not complete in Jesus' day. The point is hardly debatable because of the many references to noncanonical literature in the Apostolic Fathers, some of them even referring to apocryphal literature as "Scripture."[63] If the Old Testament Scriptures were already current in a fixed form in the first century CE, why do the first writings that identify this canonical literature, Melito of Sardis, as reported in Eusebius, *Hist. Eccl.* 4.26.12-14, and the tradition in *b.*

---

[62]   See Ellis, *Old Testament in Early Christianity*, 36; and W. S. LaSor, D. Hubbard, and F. Bush, *Old Testament Survey* (Grand Rapids: Eerdmans, 1983) 17.

[63]   See E. Oikonomos, "The Significance of the Deuterocanonical Writings in the Orthodox Church," *The Apocrypha in Ecumenical Perspective* (UBS Monograph Series 6; New York: United Bible Societies, 1991) 18-23, who lists a number of examples of this. In the same volume P.Stuhlmacher ("The Significance of the Old Testament Apocrypha and Pseudepigraha for Understanding of Jesus and Christology," 1-15) adduces several examples from the New Testament that show awareness or dependence of the New Testament writers on the apocryphal literature.

B. Bat. 14b, provide different lists? Also, why do *Hermas* and *Barnabas* cite as Scripture noncanonical literature in the first half of the second century? Did the scope of the biblical canon in fact become blurred in the church in the second century and only later were lists constructed to deal with this failure of memory? What context in the early church would have given rise to such a "blur-ring"? Furthermore, if the matter had been settled earlier in the time of Jesus or before his time, how is it possible that there are so many variations in the canonical lists of Old Testament books that were drawn up by the Christians in the fourth, fifth, and sixth centuries? If we assume that the earliest Christians had a well defined canon of Old Testament Scriptures, we would have to conclude that subse-quent generations of Christians lost it! But how? What circumstances gave rise to such loss of memory in such a relatively short period of time? No one yet has found a satisfactory answer and the amount of time when such a change in attitude or understanding could take place simply is not there.[64]

C. The Jamnia Question. If the contents of the Writings were not fixed before or during the first century CE, when did they achieve a firm definition in Israel? Over the last eighty years or more, the most popular view has been that the third part of the Hebrew Scriptures was defined or closed at a "council" that took place at Jamnia (Yavna/Javneh) at the end of the first century CE.[65] Although

---

[64] Klein, Blomberg, and Hubbard (*Introduction to Biblical Interpretation*, 55) do not see a problem in the notion that the early Christians lost sight of their biblical canon. They account for the early Church's use of the apocryphal writings by saying: "One should remember that Roman and Eastern belief in some of these works as authoritative stems from a later period, removed by at least a couple centuries from the New Testament era, when Christianity had largely lost sight of its Jewish roots." This is, of course, pure conjecture. But it is a natural conclusion if one argues, as they do, that the Old Testament was closed and recognized as a biblical canon before the time of Jesus. When Marcion tried to cut the Jewish roots of Christianity, the Church rejected his position and continued to argue against it for the next 100 years. There is simply no support anywhere for the view that as the Church became more distanced chronologically from its Jewish roots and became more Gentile that it lost the scope of its inspired Scriptures.

[65] H. E. Ryle, *The Canon of the Old Testament* (London: Macmillan, 1914). At almost the same time F. Buhl (*Kanon und Text des Alten Testaments* [Leipzig: Akademische Buchhandlung, 1891]) appeared to espouse a similar view, which apparently originated with H. Graetz, in a brief excursus entitled "Der Alttestament-liche Kanon und sein Abschluss," in his *Kohelet oder der Salmonische Prediger*

popular for a long time and still held by some scholars today, J. P. Lewis and others have reasonably argued that this view does not have any credibility. Therefore, some scholars argued that if the Jamnia theory was set aside, then the most reasonable alternative for a time when the third part of the Hebrew Bible was fixed had to be earlier than Jamnia. Sid Leiman, for example, claims that the third part of the Hebrew Bible reached its present form no later than the time of Judas Maccabees (*ca.* 165 BCE) who collected the Hebrew Scriptures after Antiochus Epiphanes had tried to destroy them.[66] Beckwith agrees that the threefold division of the Hebrew biblical canon was probably initiated by Judas Maccabeus (2 Macc 2:14-15) and he goes on to state precisely how he made those divisions, namely, by compiling a list in which all three sections have narrative books. He says that this grouping was initiated by Judas and was completed no later than the time of the writing of the Prologue to Sirach *ca.* 130 BCE.[67] Adequate evidence for this view is lacking. The evidence suggests that the finalization of the Hebrew Scriptures took place *after* Jamnia and not before.

D. The Final Stages of Stabilization *ca.* 200–400 CE. Several important conclusions emerge from this brief sketch. We suggest that the third part of the Hebrew Bible, the Protestant Old Testament Canon, was not stabilized until well after the time of Jesus. Stabilization became a significant concern of Judaism close to the end of the second or the early third century CE, and reached its closure at the end of the fifth or the sixth century. For the Christians this came

---

(Leipzig: Winter, 1871) 147-73. Graetz may have depended on Spinoza. See P. Schäfer, "Die sogenannte Synode von Jabne," *Judaica* 31 (1975) 54-64, 116-24; repr. in Schäfer, *Geschichte und Theologie des rabbinischen Judenthums* (AGJU 15; Leiden: Brill, 1978) 45-64; and more recently D. E. Aune, "On the Origins of the 'Council of Javneh' Myth," *JBL* 110 (1991) 483-90.

66 S. Z. Leiman (*The Canonization of the Hebrew Scripture: The Talmudic and Midrashic Evidence* [Hamden: Archon, 1976] 29) says that Judas Maccabees' activity was a response to Antiochus' attempts to destroy the Hebrew Scriptures and that his collecting the scattered and remaining Scriptures provides the most obvious place of termination for closing the collection of Hebrew Scriptures. Even though according to 1 Macc 1:56-57 only the Law was destroyed, Leiman (*Canonization*, 151 n. 138) believes that the passage refers to all Scriptures of the Hebrew Bible. It is not clear from this passage, however, how the third part of the Bible was completed as a result of Judas Maccabees' activity.

67 Beckwith, "Formation," in Mulder (ed.), *Mikra*, 56-58.

sometime in last half of the fourth century and following. Our reasons for this conclusion against any first century or earlier fixation of the canon is based on the following special texts and arguments.

1. 4 Ezra 14:44-48. The apocryphal 4 Ezra 14:44-48 (*ca.* 90–100 CE) retains a tradition about the scope of the Bible in at least one sect of Judaism by the end of the first century that included not only 24 books, the identity of which is not given, but also seventy other books that were deemed both inspired by God and authoritative. According to the tradition, these seventy other books were transmitted by God to Ezra and his scribes, according to 4 Ezra 14:19-48, and were reserved for wise individuals—a reference to their special holy nature and spiritual insight. At any rate, if they were not considered scriptural or inspired, would the author of 4 Ezra have indicated that they were also transmitted by God (14:22-26) or that they were to be read only by the wise among them "for in them [the seventy books] is the spring of understanding, the fountain of wisdom, and the river of knowledge" (14:48 NRSV)? We know that many of the early Christians welcomed this book into their sacred collections and even made significant additions to it by transforming parts of the legend into a Christian text. This would be strange indeed if their biblical canon had been settled before the time of Christ.

2. Baba Bathra 14b. The text *b. B. Bat.* 14b, which is the first rabbinic text to identify specifically the books of the Hebrew Bible, is a *baraita*, i.e. an extraneous mishnah written toward the end of the second century CE and not included in the mishnaic traditions codified at the end of the second century. That *baraita* has no parallels in the second century, apart from Melito's similar but not identical list of Old Testament books noted above. We would nevertheless not dispute that some second century sages held to the canon in *b. B. Bat.* 14b, even though we have no clear evidence of it.

3. The Problem of Determining the Canon of Jesus. Many scholars have tried to establish the canon of Jesus by tabulating the Scriptures he cites. This is not a bad procedure, if we are mindful of the *way* he cites them and what he says about these sources.[68] But what do we

---

68 For example, he clearly cites Daniel in a Scripture-like manner in Matthew 24:15. I am aware of the arguments against the view that Jesus made this statement, but this is not the place to debate that matter. The reference in this passage illustrates

say about biblical books to which he does not refer, for example, Judges, Song of Songs, Ecclesiastes, and Esther? Should we only rely on references he quotes to establish his canon, or do we rely on the fact that he quoted passages from all three divisions of the biblical canon that were not yet clearly defined in the first century? This might be a fair way of arguing if we knew for certain the contents of the biblical canon at that time and if we knew what the absence of a citation from some Old Testament books means in terms of Jesus' canon. Since we have no *complete* record of all that Jesus said (observe John 20:30), and what we do have is often related to concrete situations (for the most part, Jesus' teachings were *ad hoc* sayings), how can we know for sure what his comprehensive biblical canon was? As a result, the argument from his citations and quotations, as well as from his silence, has two edges, a fact which those who use the argument do not sufficiently consider.

4. Continuing Variations in Rabbinic Judaism. The imprecise boundaries of the biblical canon among the Amoraim (third century CE and later) is seen in the fact that several of the canonical writings (Song of Songs, Esther, Ecclesiastes, Proverbs, and Ezekiel), were still disputed and sometimes excluded as late as the fourth and fifth centuries CE,[69] even if in an informal manner, and without any

---

my point at least for the author of Matthew in the last quarter of the first century.

[69] For Song of Songs, see *m. Yad.* 3:5; *b. Meg.* 7a; for Ecclesiastes, see *m. Yad.* 3:5; *b. Šabb.* 100a; for Esther, see *b. Sanh.* 100a; *b. Meg.* 7a; for Proverbs, see *b. Šabb.* 30b; for Ezekiel, see *b. Šabb.* 30b; *b. Ḥag.* 13a; *b. Menaḥ.* 45a. Beckwith ("Formation," 58-60) acknowledges this point, but argues that the disputes were among a minority of Jews when the majority had already accepted the contents of the Hebrew Bible as we have it today. What evidence is there, however, that a majority of religious leaders acknowledged all of the books of the current Hebrew Bible and no others at that time? See the following studies by S. Talmon, who has questioned the notion that there is evidence in Jewish sources for the assumption of the existence of "formal bodies" that decided on the inclusion of a book in the so-called biblical canon: "Heiliges Schrifttum und kanonische Bücher aus jüdischer Sicht—Überlegungen zur Ausbildung der Grösse 'Die Schrift' im Judentum," in M. Klopfenstein, U. Luz, S. Talmon, and E. Tov (eds.), *Mitte der Schrift? Ein jüdisch-christliches Gespräch: Texte des Berner Symposions vom 6.-12. Januar 1985* (Bern: Peter Lang, 1987) 45-80; idem, "Oral Tradition and Written Transmission or the Heard and Seen Word in Second Temple Judaism," in H. Wansbrough (ed.), *Jesus and the Oral Gospel Tradition* (JSNTSup 64; Sheffield: JSOT Press, 1991) 121-58; idem, "Between the Bible and the Mishnah," in Talmon, *The World of Qumran from Within* (Jerusalem: Magnes, 1989) esp. 21-45.

reference to an earlier time when these writings were accepted or "canonized." Sirach, on the other hand, was cited by several rabbinic sages as literature that "defiled the hands," i.e. Scripture (see *y. Ber.* 11b; *y. Nazir* 54b; *Gen. Rab.* 91.3 [on Gen 42:4-5]; *Qoh. Rab.* 7:11 §1; *b. Ber.* 48a).[70] This points to a lack of clear definition of the contents of the Hebrew Bible, at least in regard to the books on the "fringes."[71] What adds credibility to this argument, as we have noted above, is that the first Christian list of Old Testament books comes from Melito at the end of the second century CE.[72] He omits Esther from that list but includes Wisdom of Solomon without any commentary or explanation. If Esther is missing and Wisdom is included, how could the collection of Scriptures have been fixed among Jews? Which Jews (or Christians?) from the east gave this canon to Melito?

5. *The Acceptance of the Dual Torah.* It is probable that the framers of the Mishnah were among those involved in the finalization or stabilization of the Hebrew canon of Scriptures. While such matters were openly discussed at the end of the second century, the mishnaic tradition itself was gaining an authoritative status. The Amoraim soon thereafter began interpreting it in way somewhat analogous to the interpretation of Scripture. The act of interpretation itself strongly suggests its authority in the rabbinic community. The Amoraim clearly accepted the authority of the Mishnah and gave scriptural support for its prescriptions. Eventually the Jews also accepted in an authoritative fashion the *Tosephta, Genesis Rabbah, Leviticus Rabbah,* the two Talmudim, and the various midrashim of rabbinic Judaism. The expansion of the Torah-based canon to include not only the rest of the Hebrew Scriptures (*Nebiʾim* and *Ketubim*) but also these other writings took place when the myth of the oral Torah became a part of the sages' teaching. In the fourth century, when the sages mentioned the Torah, they no longer only spoke of a scroll of the laws of Moses, but of both the written and oral teaching that was

---

[70] See S. Friedman, "The Holy Scriptures Defile the Hands—The Transformation of a Biblical Concept in Rabbinic Theology," in M. Brettler and M. Fishbane (eds.), *Minḥah le-Naḥum: Biblical and Other Studies Presented to Nahum M. Sarna in Honour of His 70th Birthday* (JSOTSup 154; Sheffield: JSOT Press, 1993) 117-32.

[71] For further discussion and examples, see McDonald, *Formation* (1995) 55-94.

[72] This is preserved in Eusebius, *Hist. Eccl.* 4.26.13, 14.

revealed to Moses at Sinai (the "whole Torah").[73] This eventually included all that the rabbis taught about the Law, as well as the Law (now *Tanak*) itself.[74] This dual Torah was the codification of both what was written and what was believed to have been given orally to Moses at Sinai. There is no question that the Law of Moses, the Pentateuch, was at the heart of that Torah tradition and took priority over all other portions of the Torah tradition including the prophets and the Hagiographa, but the finalization of the Torah story must also take into consideration the inclusion of more than the Scriptures of the Hebrew Bible.

6. *"Writing Without Scripture."* Strangely, the framers of the Mishnah do not appear to have been very interested in the scope of their Scriptures since the matter does not occupy much space in their second century deliberations.[75] Even more interesting is the fact that the framers of the Mishnah felt no need to support the various prescriptions and proscriptions for holy living with references to the Hebrew Scriptures. How is it that the Mishnah focuses on personal salvation or sanctification without reference to Scripture? This is not what one would expect from a community that is willing to die for its Scriptures as Josephus had claimed. Neusner calls this absence of any reference to Scripture in the Mishnah "writing *without* Scripture."[76] This all changed later when the Amoraim supported the admonitions of the Mishnah with references from the Hebrew Scriptures in order to support the Mishnah's demands. This was the Amoraim's way of showing that both the written and oral dimensions of Torah were the same and did not contradict each other. Responding to this phenomenon with its appropriate inference, Neusner

---

[73]   This is not to say that the rabbis did not differentiate between the written and oral Torah.

[74]   For more in-depth discussion of this, see both D. Kraemer, "The Formation of Rabbinic Canon: Authorities and Boundaries," *JBL* 110 (1991) 613-30; and J. Neusner, *Midrash in Context*, 135-36; idem, *Judaism and Christianity in the Age of Constantine*, 128-43, as well as his and W. S. Green's *Writing With Scripture: The Authority and Uses of the Hebrew Bible in the Torah of Formative Judaism* (Minneapolis: Fortress, 1989).

[75]   *m. Yad.* 3:4-5 hardly qualifies as a significant debate or inquiry into the issue, and at any rate it does not address all divisions or books of the Hebrew Bible but only the status of the Song of Songs and Qoheleth (Ecclesiastes).

[76]   Neusner, *Writing With Scripture*, 1-2. See also Neusner, "Rabbinic Judaism in Late Antiquity," in R. Seltzer (ed.), *Judaism: A People and Its History* (New York: Macmillan, 1989) 75-76.

denies that the Hebrew canon was ever closed until after the two
Torahs (written and oral) became one and the "whole Torah" became
the canon of Judaism.[77] Kraemer is probably more correct in saying
that the basic contours of the Hebrew Bible were eventually defined
in the late second century CE,[78] even though at the same time the
canon of the rabbinic sages was expanding as we can see by the
Amoraim's supporting nearly all of the passages of the Mishnah with
texts from the Hebrew Scriptures. This practice has some parallels in
the early church. There was no significant discussion of the contents
of a biblical canon in the second century CE, or about canonization
per se, except that the canon or *rule of faith* (*regula fidei*) was
regularly employed in that period to deal with the heretical challenges facing the church. The New Testament and Old Testament
writings as well as apocryphal and pseudepigraphal writings were
cited by the church fathers to deal with the problems and heresies
that were confronting the church, including the questions raised
about the nature of Christ. There was no listing of the Old Testament
Scriptures, however, nor were there long discussions about the contents of scriptural collections at that time. The fact that Melito, a well
known bishop of the church at Sardis, did not know the contours of
his own biblical canon (Eusebius *Hist. Eccl.* 4.26.13-14), suggests
that this matter was not important to the church as a whole in his
time. Further, since only one Hebrew text in the second century
mentions the contents of the Hebrew Scriptures (*b. B. Bat.* 14b), this
was not a very important item on the agenda of rabbinic Judaism
either.

7. An appropriate term. The absence of an appropriate term to
describe a collection of Scriptures both before and immediately
following the time of Jesus suggests that such notions were not the
current *lingua franca* in that ancient context. In the second century
CE, Jews employed a category called "defiling the hands"[79] to

---

77 Neusner, *Midrash in Context* 135-38.

78 Kraemer ("Formation of the Rabbinic Canon," 626) disagrees with Neusner's view that there was no qualitative difference between the Hebrew Scriptures
and the Talmudim since both of the Talmudim "often seek to justify rabbinic
traditions by reference to scriptural proof. Why do so if what is scriptural is not
distinct and authoritatively superior?"

79 The meaning of this term is somewhat obscure and scholars debate its
meaning, but apparently it refers to the fact that the books were considered holy and
to touch them, according to D. J. Silver (*A History of Judaism* [2 vols., New York:

describe and identify their sacred texts, and it was then that the debate finally *started* about whether and which books ritually "defile the hands." In terms of context when such matters became topics of discussion and debate in Judaism, it appears that it is only with the secularization of the scribal profession, which took place in Judaism in the second and third centuries CE, that it became important on a wide scale to distinguish between the sacred and the secular writings, namely, the writings that "defile the hands" and those that do not.[80] This begins to take place in Judaism in the context of the Tannaitic writers of the late second century.[81] Christians never used that term "defiling the hands" to refer to the writings that were included in their sacred collection of Old Testament or New Testament Scriptures—a fact that in itself suggests a second century CE origin of the term. But in the fourth and fifth centuries they adopted relevant terms of their own that expressed the sacredness of their Scriptures, namely, "canonical," "canon," or the "encovenanted Scriptures" (αἱ ἐνδιαθήκαι γραφαί).[82]

Basic Books, 1974-80] 1.217-18), was to "receive their holiness into one's hands and to accept a ritual obligation to wash off this holy residue before engaging in any mundane task. In this ceremonial way the divine inspiration of these books was made clear for all to see." See also *m. Yad.* 3:2-5 and 4:6 for a discussion of the term in the Mishnah. The term may have come from the first century CE, but that is not clear and scholars disagree on the date. There is no question, however, that it was used in the second century.

80   This observation comes from M. Bar-Ilan ("Writing," in Mulder [ed.], *Mikra*, 28) who cites several examples of the secularization of the scribal profession. Since all scribal writing was held to be sacred, so he claims, there was a prohibition of the writing down of prayers, oral traditions, and legends until the third century CE. When the prohibition ceased, there was a need to distinguish between what was and what was not sacred.

81   The shift in the meaning of Torah from a reference to a scroll of the Pentateuch to the inclusion of all that the sages had to say about the Torah also began to take place during this time. By the fourth century the notion is complete that the Torah was given two-fold to Moses, namely, that which was written and that which was oral or committed to memory. This change is significant since it effectively and considerably expands the Hebrew canon of authoritative writings.

82   See, for example, Eusebius, *Hist. Eccl.* 5.8.1. G. A. Robbins has a helpful discussion of these terms in his "Eusebius' Lexicon of 'Canonicity'," in E. A. Livingstone (ed.), *Studia Patristica*, vol. 25 (Leuven: Peeters and Leuven University Press, 1993) 134-41.

IV. CONCLUSION

We have seen that canonical literature in Israel comes from an adaptable, expandable, and highly fluid story that gave identity, marching orders, and life to the people of Israel. In time—a long period of time, that tradition was stabilized in rabbinic Judaism and also in the church. A major problem with assuming an early date for the closure of the Hebrew biblical canon is how to account for what may have been a larger collection of Scriptures circulating among the Essenes of the first century, but also among the early Christians who freely used noncanonical writings in a scriptural manner?[83] If the earliest followers of Jesus, had received an endorsed biblical canon from Jesus, they left no certain traces of it in their surviving literature and nowhere did they discuss it or show any awareness of a closed canon of Scripture. The evidence does not lead us to conclude that Jesus endorsed the Old Testament collection or any collection of Scriptures, but that he employed in a canonical manner the Scriptures that had received widespread approval in Judaism in the first century CE. We have no problem acknowledging that the earliest Christians followed Jesus' lead in matters related to Scripture and the biblical canon,[84] but it is not clear that Jesus endorsed a fixed or closed biblical canon. If his followers had received a canon from him that approximates or is equal to our current Protestant biblical canon, then they apparently lost it since they never refer either to it or to Jesus' endorsement of it. That conclusion, however, is highly unlikely and lacks in support.

---

[83] For examples of this, see Oikonomos, "Deuterocanonical Writings in the Orthodox Church," 18-23. See also Appendix A in McDonald, *Formation* (1988) 172-77.

[84] In their discussion of the Old Testament canon of the early church, Klein, Blomberg, and Hubbard (*Biblical Interpretation*, 57) agree that the earliest Christians followed Jesus' example in the matter of the scope of their sacred Scriptures, but they say that "the liberals" "insist that we simply cannot know which books he would have had embraced." Although that position is held by several scholars in terms of a number of books acknowledged by the Christians, we are at a loss to understand why that is a "liberal" position if it is an historically accurate one! Such comments appear both uninformed and insensitive. Since Jesus never made any statements on the scope of a biblical canon, how can we be sure that we know all that he considered authoritative? Further, since the early Christians did not claim that he had passed on an endorsed biblical canon, why are some scholars so convinced that he did and that they know precisely what is in it ?

When the church fathers and church councils began to deliberate the scope of their canon of Scriptures in the fourth century, they never attributed any of their lists to a tradition derived from Jesus or to some other tradition passed on by him through the apostles. This leads us to conclude that early Christianity, like Judaism, was simply not interested in *closed* biblical canons the way that Christians were in later church history. Imposing such notions on individuals or churches of those times is, I believe, anachronistic. Jesus and the traditions (stories) about who he was, what he did, and what he said formed the central canon of the earliest Christian church along with a loosely defined collection of Scriptures that were widely but not uniformly acknowledged in the Judaisms of the first century CE.

How did the Christians arrive at their collection of Scriptures? It is most likely that the first Christians adopted as their own the sacred Scriptures that were recognized in wide circles of Judaism before the time of their separation from the synagogue, namely, before 70 CE.[85] The prevailing collections of Scriptures at that time most naturally became the Scriptures of the first Christians. Those Scriptures were only somewhat fixed and well recognized, especially the Law and the Prophets, but the matter of the final decisions about the Writings and the use of apocryphal writings had not yet been determined for Pharisaic Judaism in the first century. Widespread use of the apocryphal and pseudepigraphal writings in early Christianity is obvious and understandable, even in the New Testament writings themselves.[86] Metzger is undoubtedly correct when he concludes that "for early Jewish Christians the Bible consisted of the Old Testament and some Jewish apocryphal literature. Along with this written authority went traditions (chiefly oral) of sayings attributed to Jesus."[87] This represents the collection of sacred writings adopted by the earliest Christians.

---

85   The final separation was after 135 CE when the Jewish Christians were excluded from the synagogue in Palestine because of their failure to support the Bar Cochba rebellion.

86   See Appendixes A and B of McDonald, *Formation* (1995).

87   B. M. Metzger, *The Canon of the New Testament: Its Origin, Development, and Significance* (Oxford: Clarendon Press, 1987) 72. My only qualification here would be that I do not believe that the Old Testament was that firmly fixed at this time, but I do not deny that probably all of the writings of the current Old Testament and many of the apocryphal writings made up the loosely defined Bible of the early Christians.

There was no single normative Judaism with a universally fixed and accepted Scripture in the first century. That view is a misunderstanding of the literature that survives from that period and is a wrong inference drawn from the literature that was produced in the second century and later. As the stabilization of the Scripture canons of both the church and synagogue emerged, biblical hermeneutics continued to flourish as the two emerging communities of faith continued to find life, hope, purpose, and direction from their sacred literature.

THE COMMUNITY OF ISRAEL AND THE COMPOSITION OF THE SCRIPTURES

Eugene Ulrich

James Sanders has been one of the leading voices in the last third of this century reflecting on the relationship between the text and canon of the First Testament, and I thank him for being a catalyst, teacher, and conversation partner for my own thinking.[1] The purpose of this paper is to reflect further on the interrelationships between a number of topics for which he has made contributions. Can we gain further focus on the interrelationships between customary questions such as: How did the scriptures come to be, how were they composed? What is the text of Scripture, what form of the text do we seek in the text-critical endeavor or when translating "The Holy Bible"? What do the Qumran scrolls teach us about the nature of the scriptural text at the time of Hillel the Elder and Jesus Christ? And a question I do not think I have ever heard asked: does the way that the scriptures were *composed* have a bearing on the text form we present as Scripture?

THE COMMUNITY THAT COMPOSED THE SCRIPTURES
AND ITS METHOD OF COMPOSITION

The community of Israel (בני ישראל) composed the Scriptures over the course of approximately a millennium, from the time of the early monarchy to within a generation or so of the fall of the Second Temple. The name בני ישראל, originally probably a socio-political designation, eventually became a religious designation, as the people became identified as a political unit and the political unit became

---

[1]   See especially, J. A. Sanders, *Torah and Canon* (Philadelphia: Fortress, 1972); idem, *Canon and Community: A Guide to Canonical Criticism* (Philadelphia: Fortress, 1984); and idem, *From Sacred Story to Sacred Text* (Philadelphia: Fortress, 1987).

identified with its established religion and its God. Even after the
united monarchy split into Israel and Judah, and after the Assyrian
imperial greed and cruelty put an end to Israel as a state, the citizens
of Judah continued to be called Israel with respect to their religious
identity. In this paper I will be dealing explicitly with the Hebrew
Scriptures, but much will be true and transferable to the traditions
and writings of that part of the בני ישראל that eventually came to be
called Christians. As continuing Christian tradition attests, Israel
remained a spiritual designation for the Christian community, just as
it did for the Rabbinic community.

The Torah. During the monarchy, and according to the classical
Documentary Hypothesis even during the early monarchy, authors or
tradents produced something of a national epic—much like Rome's
Aeneid and Finland's *Kalevala*[2]—that was a blend of historical,
tribal, folk, religious, and national-identity literature. The theory
that dominated the first three quarters of this century was that four
main "authors/compilers," each from four different periods in
Israel's life before God and life in the volatile Near East, used partly
the same, partly different sources, to teach the Israelites how God's
word needed to be heard in their own generation. These were four
different messages, each in their drastically changed historical situations. Each, using a selection of mostly familiar sources, sought to
help the Israelites remember the ancient story of their ancestors with
their God. They offered "model stories" that portrayed the character
of the people, instilled national pride and traditional values, and
served indirectly as instruction concerning how to act and how not to
act.[3]

For our purposes, it does not matter whether the medium of the
literature was oral or written, for the dynamics and function are
identical.[4] Our focus is on the *method* by which the liberature was

---

2   *The Kalevala; or, Poems of the Kaleva District* (compiled by E. Lonnrot; tr.
F. P. Magoun, Jr.; Cambridge: Harvard University Press, 1963).

3   The origins and growth of the Pentateuch, of course, are bewilderingly
more complicated than this brief description can indicate, even as the Kalevala had
not one but three "finished" versions of the collection of adapted sources: the first in
1833, a second in 1835, and a third, the "New Kalevala," in 1849.

4   The cultural traditions of some modern peoples still remains oral.
Cambodia, for example, almost lost its age-old music and dance traditions—which

produced. The authors took national or folk traditions, individual stories told and remembered for certain purposes—sometimes recoverable now, sometimes not—and wove a series of such stories together with many other components into a narrative that can be viewed as a national epic. Whether we imagine authors or tradents or schools, such as J and P, along the lines of the Documentary Hypothesis, or whether we attempt revised hypotheses,[5] one is most likely left with this conclusion: the narratives and the law codes that now constitute the Torah were composed through a repeated process of older traditions being retold in a new context and in a new form, with the resulting composition on the one hand faithful to the spirit of the old traditions and their intent, and on the other creatively revised to teach the people and help guide their future destiny.

The Deuteronomistic History. In the late monarchy, probably during the reign of King Josiah (640–609 BCE), one or more Deuteronomistic authors/tradents (Dtr) produced the largest complex that has come down to us as a biblical unit: the Deuteronomistic History (the books from Deuteronomy through Kings). The analysis and description of this composition is as fascinating as that of the Torah.[6] But again, the method by which Dtr composed this opus was one of largely faithful recital of numerous older traditions creatively and richly imbued with a theological perspective. The History[7] selected myriad sources, arranged them in a framework that is both chronological and at least partly theological,[8] and presented the new

---

had been transmitted and were alive only in the memories of the trained performers—due to the purges of Pol Pot.

[5]   See, e.g. J. Blenkinsopp, *The Pentateuch* (New York: Doubleday, 1992); R. Rendtorff, *The Problem of the Process of Transmission in the Pentateuch* (Sheffield: JSOT Press, 1990); J. Van Seters, *Abraham in History and Tradition* (New Haven: Yale University Press, 1975); idem, *Prologue to History: The Yahwist as Historian in Genesis* (Louisville: Westminster/John Knox, 1992).

[6]   See esp. M. Noth, *Überlieferungsgeschichtliche Studien* (Tübingen: Niemeyer, 1943); F. M. Cross, *Canaanite Myth and Hebrew Epic* (Cambridge: Harvard University Press, 1973) 274-90; G. Knoppers, *Two Nations Under God: The Deuteronomistic History of Solomon and the Dual Monarchies* (HSM 52-53; Atlanta: Scholars Press, 1993).

[7]   "History" is perhaps an apt term if viewed in its own era, although perhaps today it is better styled a theological interpretation of the people's history.

[8]   One example of theological arrangement is the recurrent prophecy-

composition as a theological reflection on the people's history that is at once simple to characterize and rich as an example of ancient religious instruction. The major edition of this large opus was probably composed in the reign of Josiah, but after the failure of Josiah's dreams and the destruction of Jerusalem and exile of Judah's leadership, the work underwent a revised edition during the exile for a double purpose. It was important both to bring the history up to date by including the subsequent events and to offer a rationale for the destruction and exile by underscoring at numerous loci throughout the narrative the "curse" dimension that characteristically accompanied the "blessing" attendant upon Israel's choice of fidelity or infidelity. Again, the Deuteronomistic History is a vast repository of diverse national literature composed by scores of anonymous creative "authors."

The Latter Prophets. Also during the monarchy and continuing through the post-exilic period, the words of certain prophets were remembered and transmitted, probably already in adapted and rearranged form by the time they were first committed to writing. These collected sayings also encountered a series of new editions as they traversed the centuries. For example, the collected "Words of Amos" were eventually reedited by the Deuteronomists, probably after the destruction of the altar of Bethel by Josiah in 622, to serve—a century after the fall of the Northern Kingdom which Amos had excoriated—as a warning against a similar possibility for the Southern Kingdom. Yet a third major new edition was produced after the exile, seen principally in the oracles of salvation placed at the end (Amos 9:11-15). The purpose of this new edition was to impart much-needed hope to the despairing people in the gloom of the fallen monarchy and temple, but at the same time it dramatically changed the overall perception of "The Book of Amos."

The Books of Isaiah, Jeremiah, and indeed virtually all the prophets evolved through a similar process into the editions that we encounter. The process entailed both faithful repetition of older text and creative reshaping for new historical and theological contexts. That creative reshaping was achieved through augmentation with

---

fulfillment motif. It is uncertain how much of the arrangement of sources was done by Dtr and how much may already have been found in the sources taken up by Dtr.

additional material, rearrangement, rewording, and contemporizing the theological viewpoint dependent upon the new situation in which the בני ישראל now found themselves. Although the process may not have been frequent for major new forms or editions of a book in general, the frequency of the process in smaller additions, e.g. for the Book of Isaiah, was beyond counting.

Considerable editorial activity can be seen in the Book of Daniel as well, which is being treated in this section because it was considered a prophetic book by both Jews and Christians in the first century.[9] It has been transmitted in one edition in 𝔐, and in an expanded edition (with "the Additions") in 𝔊. So far, the Daniel MSS from Caves 1, 4, and 6 at Qumran all attest to the edition as in 𝔐, although the possibility must remain open that the reason that no fragments of the expanded edition have been identified is because there is no Hebrew/ Aramaic version of the expansions extant, and thus no Semitic text for easy comparison in the identification process. But prior to the form of the edition as found in 𝔐, there was a lengthy history of composition. At the earliest stages, even prior to any *collection* of stories, individual stories probably circulated, as suggested at Qumran by 4QPrayer of Nabonidus (4Q242). It is difficult, however, to know whether it and texts such as 4Qpseudo-Daniel ar[a-c] (4Q243–245) were isolated texts or already part of a cycle.[10] Subsequently, to form the book as we now know it there was probably an early collection of the Aramaic chaps. 2–6 in the Ptolemaic period, then augmented by chap. 7 and expanded with chaps. 8-12 at the time of Antiochus IV Epiphanes.[11]

The Writings. It has also long since been recognized that the Books of Psalms and Proverbs are the results of long and multi-staged editing processes. We will return later to look more closely at the

---

9   See E. Ulrich, "The Bible in the Making: The Scriptures at Qumran," in E. Ulrich and J. VanderKam (eds.), *The Community of the Renewed Covenant: The Notre Dame Symposium on the Dead Sea Scrolls* (Notre Dame: University of Notre Dame Press, 1994) 77-93, esp. 81-82.

10   See J. J. Collins, "*Pseudo-Daniel* Revisited," in F. García Martínez and É. Puech (eds.), *Hommage à Józef T. Milik = RevQ* 17 (1996) 111-35; and P. W. Flint, "4Qpseudo-Daniel ar[c] (4Q245) and the Restoration of the Priesthood," in *Hommage à Józef T. Milik*, 137-50.

11   See J. J. Collins, *Daniel* (Hermeneia; Minneapolis: Fortress, 1993).

variant editions of the Book of Psalms.

Another example of a book in which the editing process has produced dramatically altered views is the Book of Job. It is notoriously perilous, especially in short compass, to present views on the composition of Job. But it is clear at a minimum for our purposes that two different traditions, the tale in the Prologue-Epilogue and the Dialogue with the YHWH Speeches, have been juxtaposed in marvelous tension in the final edition of the book as transmitted. Each breathes an easily discernible theology regarding suffering, wisdom, and the divine-human relationship, and the two theologies stand defiantly opposed to each other.

In sum, the various books of the Bible were produced through a complicated series of editorial stages by a process that included two major thrusts: the faithful repetition or retelling of important traditions, and the creative reshaping of those traditions in new theological directions often as a response to the pastoral needs of the people of Israel as perceived by major editors or tradents whom we call the biblical authors. The composition of the Scriptures was dynamic, organic. It was in a sense evolutionary, insofar as the traditions remained static for a period and then in a burst of creativity leapt to a new form, a new literary edition, due to the creative adaptation effected by some religious leaders, usually in response to a new situation.

THE QUMRAN BIBLICAL MANUSCRIPTS: CONTINUATION OF THE SAME PROCESS

Direct evidence for the biblical text begins to appear in the latter half of the Second Temple period. The manuscript evidence shows that the same process which characterized the composition of the Scriptures from the earliest times was still continuing through the Hellenistic, Hasmonaean, and Herodian periods.

Our earliest evidence for biblical manuscripts was found at Qumran. The Great Isaiah Scroll (1QIsaª) was the first and most dramatic biblical MS to gain widespread fame, and especially because the text displayed multifaceted disagreement with the Massoretic *textus receptus*, an assumption was made that it was a (specifically) Qumran text of Isaiah. When the biblical texts continued to surface and continued to show pluriformity of textual character, the view continued to prevail that those texts were "sectarian" or "vulgar." The assumption apparently was that the biblical text as preserved in the Massoretic *textus receptus* had already become standard in the Hasmonean period, and insofar as any text in the late Second Temple period varied from it, that text was aberrant or substandard.

But the biblical texts from Qumran, just as most of the nonbiblical, are general Jewish texts, representative of the shape of the Scriptures elsewhere. There are certain nonbiblical works which do reflect the theology of a specific group within Judaism which probably had one of its centers at Khirbet Qumran, but a number of the works are clearly a part of the general Jewish literature of the day, and it is arguable that the majority of them were probably representative of general Jewish literature.[12] Similarly, the biblical texts from Qumran are representative of the shape of the Scriptures elsewhere in Judaism. There is nothing in the biblical texts to suggest that they are specific to Qumran or to any particular group within Judaism. In fact, everything we know about the biblical text prior to the end of the first century CE—e.g. the Samaritan Pentateuch, the Septuagint, Philo, Josephus, the New Testament, Rabbinic quotations, as well as in 𝔐—indicates that the text was pluriform.

The Samaritan Pentateuch,[13] the Septuagint,[14] and Josephus,[15]

---

[12]   The fact that the texts are representative of the broad spectrum of Second-Temple Judaism is probably one of the factors that led Norman Golb to leap to the opposite extreme, claiming that the texts were brought from Jerusalem (presumably all on a single occasion) and were simply hidden at the (uninhabited?) site.

[13]   Contrast the text of SP and that of MT especially for Exodus and Numbers; see also 4QpaleoExod^m in P. W. Skehan, E. Ulrich, and J. E. Sanderson, *Qumran Cave 4. IV: Palaeo-Hebrew and Greek Biblical Manuscripts* (DJD 9; Oxford: Clarendon Press, 1992) 53-130; and 4QNum^b in E. Ulrich and F. M. Cross, with J. R. Davila, N. Jastram, J. E. Sanderson, and E. Tov, *Qumran Cave 4: VII. Genesis to Numbers* (DJD 12; Oxford: Clarendon Press, 1994) 205-67.

[14]   The books of Jeremiah and Daniel are two of the most dramatic examples of variant literary editions documented in the Septuagint; see Tov, "Some Aspects of the Textual and Literary History of the Book of Jeremiah," in P.-M. Bogaert (ed.), *Le livre de Jérémie: Le prophète et son milieu, les oracles et leur transmission* (BETL 54; Leuven: Leuven University Press, 1981) 145-67; and Ulrich, "The Canonical Process, Textual Criticism, and Latter Stages in the Composition of the Bible," in M. Fishbane and E. Tov (eds.), *"Sha'arei Talmon": Studies in the Bible, Qumran, and the Ancient Near East Presented to Shemaryahu Talmon* (Winona

demonstrate bountifully that there were variant literary editions of the books of Scripture in the late Second Temple period. The evidence for a series of variant literary editions of the biblical books now documented in the MSS found at Qumran has been described in a long list of publications. Some of the first-hand evidence confirms the parallel literary editions already known from the SP (4Qpaleo-Exod[m], 4QNum[b]),[16] the LXX (4QJer[b,d]),[17] and Josephus (4QSam[a]).[18] Yet more MSS supply the evidence of the same phenomenon for other books, such as Joshua,[19] Judges,[20] Psalms,[21] Canticles, etc.[22]

Lake: Eisenbrauns, 1992) 283-87. But the phenomenon is more widespread, including sections or passages of books, e.g. the David-Goliath narrative in 1 Samuel 17–18. For the detailed characteristics of those two variant editions, see D. Barthélemy, D. W. Gooding, J. Lust, and E. Tov, *The Story of David and Goliath: Textual and Literary Criticism: Papers of a Joint Research Venture* (OBO 73; Freiburg: Éditions Universitaires; Göttingen: Vandenhoeck & Ruprecht, 1986).

[15]   The priest Josephus (*Vita*, 418) had books from the Temple allowed to him by Titus. His text for Joshua–2 Samuel is a developed form of the Old Greek, not the MT; see A. Mez, *Die Bibel des Josephus untersucht für Buch V–VII der Archäologie* (Basel: Jaeger und Kober, 1895); and E. Ulrich, *The Qumran Text of Samuel and Josephus* (Missoula: Scholars Press, 1978). The latter demonstrates that Josephus was using a text-type represented in Hebrew by 4QSam[a] and in Greek by a slightly developed form of the OG, in contrast to the text transmitted in the MT.

[16]   See P. W. Skehan, "Exodus in the Samaritan Recension from Qumran," *JBL* 74 (1955) 182-87; J. E. Sanderson, *An Exodus Scroll from Qumran: 4QpaleoExod[m] and the Samaritan Tradition* (HSS 30; Atlanta: Scholars Press, 1986); Skehan, Ulrich, and Sanderson, *Qumran Cave 4: IV*, 53-130; N. Jastram, in Ulrich and Cross, with Davila, Jastram, Sanderson, and Tov, *Qumran Cave 4: VII*, 205-67.

[17]   See E. Tov, in DJD 15 (forthcoming) 172.

[18]   See F. M. Cross, "The History of the Biblical Text in the Light of Discoveries in the Judaean Desert," *HTR* 57 (1964) 281-99; and E. Ulrich, *The Qumran Text of Samuel*.

[19]   Ulrich, "4QJoshua[a] and Joshua's First Altar in the Promised Land," in G. J. Brooke with F. García Martínez (eds.), *New Qumran Texts and Studies: Proceedings of the First Meeting of the International Organization for Qumran Studies, Paris 1992* (STDJ 15; Leiden: Brill, 1994) 89-104 and pls. 4-6. See also L. Mazor, "The Septuagint Translation of the Book of Joshua," *BIOSCS* 27 (1994) 29-38.

[20]   J. Trebolle Barrera, "49. 4QJudg[a]," in E. Ulrich and F. M. Cross, with S. W. Crawford, J. A. Duncan, P. W. Skehan, E. Tov, and J. Trebolle Barrera, *Qumran Cave 4: IX. Deuteronomy, Joshua, Judges, Kings* (DJD 14; Oxford:

From a historical point of view, the text of each book as in the MT was simply one form of that book as it existed in antiquity. In fact, the principal evidence we have for confirming that the texts of the books as found in the medieval MSS of the Massoretic Bible are closely faithful to ancient texts is the evidence from Qumran. And that evidence from Qumran, when seen in perspective, demonstrates that there were multiple editions of the biblical books in antiquity—one form of which survives in each of the books of the MT collection, while other forms may or may not have had the good fortune to survive in the SP, the LXX, at Qumran, or elsewhere.

Thus, we can see at Qumran, but it is evidence for Judaism in general, that the scribes and their predecessors were at work along two lines. First, they often simply copied the individual books of the Scriptures as exactly as humanly possible. But secondly, sometimes the scribes intentionally inserted new material which helped interpret or highlight for their contemporary congregation in a new situation the relevance of the traditional text. These creative biblical scribes were actively handing on the tradition, but they were adding to it, enriching it, and attempting to make it adaptable and relevant. They knew explicitly what they were doing, just as the redactors of the JEDP material, the exilic Dtr[2], and the compilers of the prophetic material, the psalmic and proverbial literature, etc. knew what they

---

Clarendon Press, 1995) 161-64; and idem, "Textual Variants in 4QJudg[a] and the Textual and Editorial History of the Book of Judges," in F. García Martínez (ed.), *The Texts of Qumran and the History of the Community: Proceedings of the Groningen Congress on the Dead Sea Scrolls (20–23 August 1989): 1. Biblical Texts* = *RevQ* 14 (1989) 229-45.

21   J. A. Sanders, *The Psalms Scroll of Qumrân Cave 11 (11QPs[a])* (DJD 4; Oxford: Clarendon Press, 1965); idem, *The Dead Sea Psalms Scroll* (Ithaca: Cornell University Press, 1967); idem, "Variorum in the Psalms Scroll (11QPs[a])," *HTR* 59 (1966) 83-94; idem, "Cave 11 Surprises and the Question of Canon," *McCQ* 21 (1968) 1-15 (reprinted in S. Leiman [ed.], *The Canon and Masorah of the Hebrew Bible: An Introductory Reader* [New York: Ktav, 1974] 37-51); idem, "The Qumran Psalms Scroll (11QPs[a]) Reviewed," in M. Black and W. A. Smalley (eds.), *On Language, Culture, and Religion: In Honor of Eugene A. Nida* (The Hague and Paris: Mouton, 1974) 79-99; and P. W. Flint, *The Dead Sea Psalms Scrolls and the Book of Psalms* (STDJ 17; Leiden: Brill, 1997).

22   E. Tov, "Three Manuscripts (Abbreviated Texts?) of Canticles from Qumran Cave 4," *JJS* 46 (1995) 88-111.

were doing.

Insofar as the scribes were handing on the tradition, they became part of the canonical process. Handing on the tradition is a constitutive factor of that process, and Sanders labels it the "repetition" factor.[23] Each repetition confirms that this material is important to the scribe and to the congregation, with importance from the past, importance in the current situation, and importance for the future. The texts were authoritative texts, and through the repetition they were being rendered more authoritative.

Insofar as the scribes were also updating the tradition and making it relevant to the current situation, they were also contributing to the canonical process. They were giving it another constitutive canonical characteristic, a complementary factor that Sanders terms "resignification."[24] The tradition now proves itself adaptable, capable of having new significance in this new particular situation. The word, heard in earlier times with significance in that situation, is now heard with revived significance in this new situation.

Thus, the same process which characterized the composition of the Scriptures from their beginnings was still continuing all the way through the Second Temple period. The process becomes visible and documented through the Qumran MSS starting around the middle and late third century BCE. When and why the period of pluriformity in the biblical text ended is still uncertain, although the first half of the second century CE is a plausible suggestion. Though the Greek Minor Prophets Scroll[25] shows that there were efforts toward bringing the Old Greek translation back to closer agreement with the Hebrew text, or at least with a Hebrew text, made apparently in the latter part of the first century BCE, most of the evidence points toward pluriformity at the time when both Christianity and Rabbinic Judaism were in their formative stages. It appears that the organic or developmental process of the composition of the Scriptures was brought to a halt only due to two factors: (1) the fact that Rome

---

[23]   J. A. Sanders, *Canon and Community*, 22.

[24]   J. A. Sanders, *Canon and Community*, 22.

[25]   E. Tov, with R. A. Kraft, *The Greek Minor Prophets Scroll from Naḥal Ḥever (8ḤevXIIgr)* (The Seiyâl Collection 1; DJD 8; Oxford: Clarendon Press, 1990).

posed such a threat to the continued life of Judaism, and (2) the growing tension between those Jews on the one hand who looked principally to the Torah, minimized apocalyptic and eschatological themes, and used the Scriptures in Hebrew, and those Jews on other hand who followed Jesus, looked to the larger Gentile world, and used the Scriptures in Greek. The second century moreso than the first, i.e. closer to the Second Revolt than to the First Revolt, appears to be a more likely setting for the crystallization of the view that a single form of the text was a necessity.

THE "ORIGINAL TEXT" OF SCRIPTURE AND AN ALTERNATE VIEW

If the text of the scriptures was pluriform and organic at the time when both Christianity and Rabbinic Judaism were in their formative stages, then the question must be raised: What form of the text should be the object of our search? At the start one might think that this question may well be answered in one way by Jewish scholars and in another way by Christians, and perhaps in different ways by Catholic and Protestant scholars. On the contrary, however, are we not all eventually drawn to base our denominational views on the clearest and best historical evidence we can attain? Thus, theoretically we would all come to a uniform conclusion based on the evidence, if the evidence is reasonably clear.

What form of the text, then, should be the object of our search? "The original text" is commonly listed as the object of textual research, the object of text criticism, and the object of those who produce translations of The Holy Bible for religious, literary, and historical purposes. But when one presses in detail to find out what precisely is "the original text" for the sum of all the passages of a biblical book, there is a bewildering array of meanings, differing phrase by phrase through the text. Possibilities are:[26]

(1) The "original text" of the *source* incorporated by an early author or tradent (e.g. the Canaanite or Aramean stories incorporated by J).

---

[26] For further discussion, see Ulrich, "Jewish, Christian, and Empirical Perspectives on the Text of Our Scriptures," in R. Brooks and J. J. Collins (eds.), *Hebrew Bible or Old Testament? Studying the Bible in Judaism and Christianity* (Christianity and Judaism in Antiquity 5; Notre Dame: University of Notre Dame Press, 1990) 69-85, esp. 73-77.

(2) The "original text" of the work produced by an early author or tradent (J, Dtr, P).

(3) The "original text" of the *complete book*, recognizable as a form of our biblical book, as it left the hand of the last major author or redactor (e.g. the Book of Exodus or Jeremiah).

(4) The "original text" as it was (in developed form) at the stage of development when a community accepted it as an authoritative book.

(5) The "original text" as the consonantal text of the Rabbinic Bible (the consonantal text that was later used by the Massoretes).

(6) The "original text" as the original or superior form of the MT as interpreted, vocalized, and punctuated by the Massoretes.

(7) The "original text" as fully attested in extant MS witnesses.

(8) The "original text" as reconstructed from the extant testimony insofar as possible but with the most plausible conjectural emendations when it is generally agreed that no extant witness preserves a sound reading.

Our imagination is a powerful tool in our learning and specifically in our reconstruction of history. But our imagination, when not properly disciplined, can also mislead us, or at least paint the details of a historical reconstruction quite differently from the way those details actually were. One thinks of the artistically great, but historically inaccurate, settings of Italian or Dutch renaissance paintings of biblical or classical scenes, or of Albert Edelfelt's powerful painting of Christ and the Magdalene, in which Christ is clearly Scandanavian, and the scenery quintessential Finland. So, when we move from art to history, it is important to discipline our imaginations.

Emanuel Tov has recently discussed "The Original Shape of the Biblical Text" and made a proposal concerning the form of the text that is the goal of textual criticism.[27] His argument rests on such a comprehensive set of data and such a nuanced discussion that I fear I cannot do it justice in a small section of a short article. But I think that it may be a useful step in the on-going discussion to present briefly an alternative idea here. Tov makes a preliminary conclusion that

> At the end of the process of the composition of a biblical book stood one textual entity (a single copy or tradition) which was considered finished at

---

27   E. Tov, *Textual Criticism of the Hebrew Bible* (Assen: Van Gorcum; Philadelphia: Fortress, 1992) 164-80.

the literary level, even if only by a limited group of people, and which at the same time stood at the beginning of a process of copying and textual transmission.[28]

He then proposes a conclusion based on the previous one:

> Since only one finished literary composition is in our mind when we deal with textual issues, textual criticism aims at that literary composition which has been accepted as binding (authoritative) by Jewish tradition, since textual criticism is concerned with the literary compositions contained in the traditional Hebrew Bible. This implies that the textual criticism of the Hebrew Bible aims at the literary compositions contained in 𝔐, to the exclusion of later (midrashic) literary compilations such as the Hebrew text behind several sections in 𝔊, viz. sections in 1–2 Kings, Esther, and Daniel . . ., and earlier and possibly parallel compositions, such as 𝔊 of Jeremiah, Joshua, Ezekiel, and sections of Samuel . . . .[29]

No one in our generation has contributed more than Emanuel Tov to our understanding of the textual criticism of the Hebrew Bible, especially in light of the scrolls. But I am sure he would agree that it will take time for us to assimilate all this new evidence and achieve a fully balanced perspective. I think that a check on the scene imagined here may help move the discussion forward, and so I suggest that we revise our imaginative scene to include the diachronic complexity of the text, and then test both formulations. First, insofar as the argument of this paper has validity, there would normally have been, at any one time, not one but two or possibly more editions of many of the biblical books in circulation. Was there really an "end of the process of the composition of a biblical book" that was anything more than the abrupt interruption of the composition process for external, hostile reasons (the Roman threat or the Rabbinic–Christian debates)? And clearly, for some books two variant editions "stood at the beginning of a process of copying and textual transmission."

Secondly, I think the time has come to question the traditional assumption that "only one finished literary composition is in our mind when we deal with textual issues." That has, of course, been the assumption, but it derives from the period when we had only a single witness to each book of the Hebrew Bible (since the Samaritan Pentateuch was not seriously considered as a text of Scripture). And

---

28 Tov, *Textual Criticism*, 177.
29 Tov, *Textual Criticism*, 177.

Part II of this paper suggests that, in contrast to an earlier era when there was an assumption of "normative Judaism," the acceptance "as binding (authoritative) by Jewish tradition" appears to be a slightly later phenomenon. Is the proof there at a sufficiently early date to warrant such a claim for Judaism? And, even if warranted for Judaism, is the proof there that general Judaism had a clearly defined single text of each book at a sufficiently early date to warrant such a claim for Christianity?

Insofar as I understand the evidence, neither warrant is in place. I have been searching, without result, for over a decade for any evidence that any group prior to the Second Revolt consciously selected a certain text-type on the basis of textual comparison. There seems to be no evidence that texts were compared for text-critical purposes to select a single text that would become standard. Then, like now, so it appears, the text was not subject to sectarian polemics. The text was pluriform, and creativity was allowed, but only for natural development, not for ideological polemics. If that be so, is the following a legitimate way to pose the question, both from a historical point of view and from a religious—Jewish and Christian—point of view: If the text was indeed pluriform and still developing near the end of the first century CE and perhaps into the second century, should not the object of the text-critical endeavor be the text as it truly was? That is, should not the object of the textual criticism of the Hebrew Bible be, not the single (and textually arbitrary?) collection of Massoretic texts of the individual books, but the organic, developing, pluriform Hebrew text—different for each book—such as the evidence indicates?

A historical example involving the honoree of this volume can illustrate the need for a revised view. Thirty years ago and perhaps still today, James Sanders stood in the minority in claiming that the Psalms Scroll (11QPs[a]) was truly a form of the Psalter, while a number of weighty voices declared that it was a secondary, post-biblical and non-biblical composition.[30] This demonstrates the need to refine the criteria for understanding the biblical text in the period of the formation of Rabbinic Judaism and Christianity. The case for the biblical character of that scroll has been strongly made now by

---

[30]   See note 21 above.

Peter Flint, made freshly in light of the gains in understanding the nature of the biblical text and in light of the full evidence of the Psalms material from the Judaean Desert.[31]

Thus, because the text of each book was produced organically, in multiple layers, determining "the original text" is a difficult, complex task; and arguably, it may not even be the correct goal. Historically, was there ever such a thing? Theologically, how do we decide which to select of the many layers that could claim to be the "original reading"? Often the more powerful religious meanings in a text are those which entered the text at a relatively late or developed stage; do we choose the "original" but less powerful reading or the later, more profound reading? In contrast, if a profound religious insight in an early stage of the text is neutralized later by a conventional formula, which do we select?

It is tempting to continue exploring the difficulties of seeking "the original text," by considering the relationship of text and canon.[32] One suggestive observation to consider here is that, beyond those books we now retrospectively consider Scripture, the בני ישראל were composing a wide library of religious literature, some of which was undoubtedly considered as serious, as holy, as some of those books which subsequently were included in the canons of the various heirs to the בני ישראל. One thinks of *Enoch* and *Jubilees*, *Sirach* and *Tobit*, and other books which were considered Scripture by some. All were composed in similar ways; the difference is due to later, reflexive judgments. But canon is a category of tradition, not of Scripture. Scripture, of course, began as tradition and only gradually *became* "Scripture"; and the collection of the Scriptures becomes canon retrospectively only through the historical developments of the

---

[31]   See the 4QPsalms editions by P. W. Skehan, E. Ulrich, and P. W. Flint in DJD 16 (forthcoming); P. W. Flint, *The Dead Sea Psalms Scrolls*; and E. Ulrich, "Multiple Literary Editions: Reflections Toward a Theory of the History of the Biblical Text," in D. W. Parry and S. D. Ricks (eds.), *Current Research and Technological Developments on the Dead Sea Scrolls: Conference on the Texts from the Judean Desert, Jerusalem, 30 April 1995* (STDJ 20; Leiden: Brill, 1996) 78-105, esp. 99-101.

[32]   For discussion, see Sanders, *Canon and Community*; idem, *From Sacred Story to Sacred Text*; Ulrich, "The Canonical Process"; idem, "The Bible in the Making."

community's on-going trajectory of life, thought, and controversy that eventually gets labeled "tradition."

BIBLICAL AUTHORITY, CANONICAL CRITICISM, AND GENERATIVE EXEGESIS

BRUCE CHILTON

At the close of his detailed and elegant work, *The Authority of the Bible and the Rise of the Modern World*, Henning Graf Reventlow describes the dilemma posed by the very notion that the Bible is authoritative for modern consciousness. His descrition is of the position reached by the eighteenth century in England, but his point is that it applies to the modern West more generally:

> . . . the Bible lost its significance for philosophical thought and for theoretical constitutional foundations of political ideals, and ethical rationalism (with a new foundation in Kant's critique) proved to be one of the forces shaping the modern period, which only now can really be said to have begun.[1]

Reventolow traces the development of an historical reading of the Bible, which grew out of a revival of interest in the ancient world during the Middle Ages. Curiously, however, history proved to be a corrosive agent when applied to received notions of the Bible's status. Historical study might illuminate the meaning of Scripture, and for that reason it was embraced by Protestants, but it also revealed that the Bible was a composite product, not a coherent body of revelation in the nature of a discourse.

The shock of what the Bible is *not* has yet to wear off. In the United States, Fundamentalism arose as an attempt to limit the claims of history upon the reading of Scripture. The Bible was generally declared to be free of error, so that the only reading permitted was that which showed it was an harmonious message concerning the end of the world by means of Jesus' judgment. History was therefore marginalized in two senses: (1) as a method, it could not argue against the message of the Bible, and (2) as a series of events, history was to be canceled by the second coming.[2] In order to achieve their

---

[1]   H. G. Reventlow, *The Authority of the Bible and the Rise of the Modern World* (London: SCM, 1984) 414.

[2]   See S. E. Ahlstrom, *A Religious History of the American People* (New Haven: Yale University Press, 1972) 808-16.

aims, of course, Fundamentalists must explain away contradictions and inconsistencies and factual mistakes in the Bible; their method is anything but a literal reading.

Fundamentalism is not a generalized form of conservatism, but a response to the claims of history in particular. A different form of conservatism evolved in England, in response to the refinement of historical inquiry which had taken place in Germany. It is ably described by John Rogerson:

> At the end of the nineteenth century, German critical Old Testament scholarship had triumphed in England, albeit in a form adapted to Evangelical and Catholic versions of progressive revelation.[3]

Where the Fundamentalists have banished history from theology, liberals have simply baptized the historical process itself. Indeed, one might argue that the English acceptance of German biblical scholarship is a consequence of embracing a Hegelian view of history.[4]

However, Fundamentalists have seen more accurately than liberals that the evaluation of the Bible's authority in the West is inextricably related to the issue of what one makes of history. Because Fundamentalism is a reaction against specifically Western, and post-Enlightenment, conceptions of history, to speak of "Muslim fundamentalism" is usually misleading. A systematic denial of change in doctrine might be called "integrism" (from the French *intégrisme*), in order to reserve the term "fundamentalism" for an integrism which also denies history as a method and a final reality. Although a Fundamentalist denial of history is only rarely maintained in scholarly circles, there is widespread agreement that the issues of biblical authority and history are inextricably related.

History itself has been the focus of intense discussion for as long as it has driven an intense skepticism regarding all received forms of authority (the Bible, law, political figures, teachers, priests, and so on). In a masterful survey of theories of history, Bernard Lonergan

---

[3]   J. Rogerson, *Old Testament Criticism in the Ninetheenth Century: England and Germany* (London: SPCK, 1984) 288. The stance he describes is still current; cf. A. T. Hanson, *The Living Uttterances of God: The New Testament Exegesis of the Old* (London: Darton, Longman & Todd, 1983) 217: "We value the Old Testament primarily for its account of salvation history."

[4]   See Rogerson, *Old Testament Criticism*, 69-71, 104-107. Hegelian views still find enthusiastic adherents; cf. G. Theissen, *Biblical Faith: An Evolutionary Approach* (London: SCM, 1984); J. Kovel, *History and Spirit: An Inquiry into the Philosophy of Liberation* (Boston: Beacon, 1991).

concluded that "historical narrative at every step is justified by evidence," but that "history differs from natural science, for its object is in part constituted by meaning and value, while the objects of the natural sciences are not."[5] We might pursue the distinction between history and science further: the necessary medium of history, whether we mean history as events or history as narratives, is meaning. Only what is meaningful is remembered as history; only an account of its meaning is related as history. Arguments concerning the relation of histories to realities considered more objective may or may not be fruitful, but the association of history's beginning and end with meaning is apparent.

In 1984 Krister Stendahl brought out a collection of articles under the title *Meanings*,[6] and treated in the first major essay of the interface between history and authority. He argues that the canon is their point of reconciliation:

> The question as to the meaning of the Bible in the present—as distinguished from the meaning in the past as stated by descriptive biblical theology— receives its theological answer from the canonical status of Scripture. In its most radical form, the question was: do these old writings have any meaning beyond their significance as sources for the past? On what basis could it be valid to translate them into new modes of thought? on what basis could such an original—and such a translation—have a normative function for the life of the church? Such questions can be answered only within the consciousness of the church. The answer rests on the act of faith by which Israel and its sister by adoption, the church, recognizes its history as sacred history, and finds in these writings the epitome of the acts of God.[7]

Stendahl's model of the canon as a lens of a particular consciousness has been worked out in detail by Brevard Childs.[8] Indeed, Childs has

---

5   B. J. F. Lonergan, *Method in Theology* (New York: Herder and Herder, 1972) 175-234, 219.

6   K. Stendahl, *Meanings: The Bible as Document and Guide* (Philadelphia: Fortress, 1984). It might be mentioned in passing that the title could have been applied to Harry Emerson Fosdick's Beecher Lectures at Yale in 1924, during which he (*The Modern Use of the Bible* [London: SCM, 1924] 123) said: "An important part of the modern preacher's responsibility is thus to decode the abiding meanings of Scripture from outgrown phraseology."

7   Stendahl, *Meanings*, 40. The essay is entitled "Biblical Theology: A Program" (pp. 11-44), and was first published as "Biblical Theology, Contemporary," *IDB* 1.418-32.

8   Cf. B. Childs, *Introduction to the Old Testament as Scripture* (Philadelphia: Fortress, 1979); idem, *The New Testament as Canon: An Introduction* (Philadel-

been understood as locating the authoritative meaning of the texts not in their historical meanings (which he does not deny), but in the pattern produced by the contextual relationship of the texts overall. He has been criticized for subverting a literary and history reading with an appeal to the canon as hermeneutical key, when in fact it is the product of the choices of particular communities.[9]

The heat with which Childs's approach is often attacked is a function of the extent to which a commitment to history as revelatory has been embedded within liberal theology. Likewise, his appeal to Fundamentalists is predictable, insofar as they may read his approach as a denial of history. Neither his detractors nor his Fundamentalist boosters have read him correctly. Childs is accepting of the historical reading of biblical literature: indeed, exegesis as usually practiced generally produces the meanings with which he deals. Then, however, Childs relates the meaning of one document to the other, assuming that the appropriation of Scripture by the Church *in any age* is the product of faith, the character of which comports with the pattern of the canon. In other words, the act of believing has a logic which is articulated by the object of its belief: the final form of the text.

Once Childs is understood to be an expositor of the decision to believe in Scripture, as well as of those Scriptures in their autonomy, his approach appears well-defined, critical, and convincing. Indeed, in its attendance to the issue of biblical authority in the midst of historical inquiry, his contribution is one of the most effective of this century. In some ways, it is comparable to that of Rudolf Bultmann, although the terms of reference are different. Bultmann proceeded from the understanding that the rule for recovering the authoritative message of Scripture was to determine what was relevant to his existentialist conception of human being:

> I may assume, I think, that the appropriate question with respect to the Bible—at least within the church—is the question about human existence, which is a question I am driven to ask by the existential question about my

phia: Fortress, 1984); idem, *Old Testament Theology in a Canonical Context* (Philadelphia: Fortress, 1986); idem, *Biblical Theology in the Old and New Testaments: Theological Reflections on the Christian Bible* (London: SCM, 1992).

    [9]   See C. M. Tuckett, *Reading the New Testament: Methods of Interpretation* (Philadelphia: Fortress, 1987) 168-74, 172; R. Morgan with J. Barton, *Biblical Interpretation* (Oxford Bible Series; Oxford: Oxford University Press, 1988) 213-14.

own existence . . . If hearing God's word in faith can only be the work of the Holy Spirit effected by understanding decision, understanding of the text can take place only by methodical interpretation, and the conceptuality guiding such interpretation can be acquired only by the kind of profane reflection that is the business of a philosophical analysis of existence.[10]

Where Bultmann must presuppose that existential *Angst*, liberating decision, and philosophical exegesis are all the principal terms of reference of faith,[11] Childs directly inquires into the logic implicit in accepting the Scriptures as the Bible. Several other recent proposals also involve an appeal to a supra-historical or meta-historical level of Scripture's meaning. In a book on preaching, Bernard Brandon Scott has appealed to a structuralist understanding of the Bible, in which the aim is to perform the meanings implicit within the relations (the structure, in that sense) among the words and concepts and stories and poems and speeches and letters and images of the texts.[12]

The abrupt decline in interest in a structuralist interpretation of Scripture is explicable with reference to two factors. First, in literary circles deconstruction has largely displaced structuralism,[13] and there is some tendency for fashions in theology to follow fashions in literature. Second (and more importantly), deconstruction has exposed a nearly solipsistic view of reality within many literary readings:

The most radical deconstructive critique of language posits that language is entirely turned in on itself, self-referential, like some house of cards each of which has not reference to any external reality, but only to the other cards

---

10   R. Bultmann, "On the Problem of Demythologizing," in Bultmann, *New Testament and Mythology and Other Basic Writings* (ed. and trans. S. M. Ogden; London: SCM, 1985) 95-130, 106-107.

11   On the decline of Bultmann's influence; cf. C. A. Evans, "Life-of-Jesus Research and the Eclipse of Mythology," *TS* 54 (1993) 3-36.

12   B. B. Scott, *The Word of God in Words: Reading and Preaching* (Fortress Resources for Preaching; Philadelphia: Fortress, 1985). For a useful introduction to structuralism, see Tuckett, *Reading the New Testament*, 151-166. Greater detail in regard to both Bultmann and structuralism (in various forms) is available in A. C. Thiselton, *The Two Horizons: New Testament Hermeneutics and Philosophical Description with Special Reference to Heidegger, Bultmann, Gadamer, and Wittgenstein* (Exeter: Paternoster, 1980).

13   Deconstruction itself, however, has perhaps seen its day. Cf. D. Lehman, *Signs of the Times: Deconstruction and the Fall of Paul de Man* (New York: Poseidon, 1990); P. S. Peterson, *Literary Pedagogics after Deconstruction: Scenarios and Perspectives in the Teaching of English Literature* (Dolphin 22; Aarhus: Aarhus University Press, 1992); J. T. Nealon, *Double Reading: Post-Modernism after Deconstruction* (Ithaca: Cornell Univeristy Press, 1993).

within the confines of the deck. Through language, we philosophically construct a world, but the world is neither a parallel reality to the one in which we live, nor any valid indicator of a transworld reality.[14]

Deconstruction more consistently and explicitly than structuralism engages the interpreter in choosing the context within which interpretation will take place, and then makes that context determinative of meaning. It justifies the critic's freedom in the name of play, while structuralism invokes the power of an associative pattern within language. But both approaches assert the power of the general over the particular, the contextual over the textual.

Of lesser influence, but perhaps also noteworthy, is the appeal to the theological value of reading Scripture as narrative. George Stroup argued that the Church ("the Christian community") could claim it had "heard God's word within this narrative history."[15] With less sophistication, David Clines blandly argues that his thematic Pentateuch is really a story, and as such "functions as reality from beginning to end." Enthused by the inerrancy of story, he proceeds: "No awkward historical questions about the material of the Pentateuch stand in the way of its efficacy in creating a 'world' or in drawing its readers into participation in that world."[16] That statement is a classic instance of using a modern category ("story") to homogenize the multi-layered composition of Scripture. But the fallacy comports well with Clines's attempt to urge, without argument, that Scripture be taken as a privileged horizon.[17]

Canonical interpretation, existential exegesis, structuralism, deconstruction, and narrative theology have been adapted largely in order

---

[14]   M. H. Suchocki, "Constructing Theology in a Deconstructive Age," in R. Farmer (ed.), *Religion and the Postmodern Vision: 1991 Paine Lectures in Religion* (Columbia: University of Missouri at Columbia Press, 1991) 37-47, 38. Suchocki's own orientation is along the lines of the Alfred North Whitehead's *Process and Theology*; cf. W. A. Beardslee, *Margins of Belonging: Essays on the New Testament and Theology* (American Academy of Religion Studies in Religion 58; Atlanta: Scholars Press, 1991).

[15]   Cf. G. W. Stroup, *The Promise of Narrative Theology* (London: SCM, 1981) 242.

[16]   Cf. D. J. A. Clines, *The Theme of the Pentateuch* (JSOTSup 10; Sheffield: JSOT Press, 1978) 104.

[17]   As I have discussed elsewhere, Clines appears to appropriate the hermeneutical model of Thiselton's *Two Horizons*; cf. B. Chilton, *Profiles of a Rabbi: Synoptic Opportunities in Reading about Jesus* (BJS 177; Atlanta: Scholars Press, 1989) 164-66.

to address the dichotomy between authority and history. In each case, a supra-historical context (the canon, the existential question of being, the power of language, the interpretative possibility, the story) is urged upon us as the solution to the doubts which a strictly historical reading might involve. Authority becomes a matter of method or approach; but because fashions have changed so quickly, authoritative interpretation has not been an agreed result of recent methodological discussion.

Moreover, the debate has proceeded in a way which seems to preclude engagement with modern people in their actual conditions. The latter point has especially disturbed Walter Wink:

> If, as proposed here, we join Teilhard de Chardin in locating spirit at the very heart of matter—if we see it as the "within" of actual people, institutions, the state, nature—then the establishment of the material basis for the full and free development of people must be an indispensable aspect of our vision of God's Reign.[18]

It would take us too far afield of our topic to enter here into a discussion of the recent revival of process theology and the relationship it postulates between nature and God. But what is of immediate relevance to our consideration is that those who seek to develop an engaged reading of the Bible (such as Beardslee, Kovel, and Wink) generally do so on a philosophical basis, rather than on the foundation of recent theories of interpretation. Supra-historical readings do not provide grounding for engagement in historical conditions.

In the remainder of this essay, I will argue that the authority of Scripture is to be defined in infra-historical, not supra-historical, terms. But the history which might become the medium of authority is a more complex phenomenon than even recent commentators have assumed:

> A text has no life of its own. It "lives" only as an electric wire is alive. Its power originates elsewhere: in a human author . . . However powerful the author's act of creation, the text lies impotent until it also comes into contact with a human reader.[19]

Robert Morgan's insistence—against some fashions—upon an historical reading of Scripture might be welcomed, but there is no reason to react against such fashion with a view of history which itself

---

18 W. Wink, *Naming the Powers: The Language of Power in the New Testament* (The Powers 1; Philadelphia: Fortress, 1984) 125.

19 Morgan, *Biblical Interpretation*, 269.

reverts to a heroic model of authorial intent. The pluralism of
meanings which (as we will see) Prof. Sanders describes is a more
suitable point of departure.

Serious scholarship does not support the model of a single meaning
of Scripture, which is then transmitted to the reader. The reader,
even after an adjustment to the differing languages and cultures of
the biblical text, must appreciate the variety *within and among the
communities which produced the Bible.* There is no agreed "Moses"
or agreed "Jesus" who gave a body of teaching which was then
passed on. Just that recognition was the point of departure of James
Sanders in *Canon and Community.*[20] Unfortunately, since Sanders,
"canonical criticism" (or "canon criticism"), has been more ideological than historical in its orientation, for reasons which have already
been discussed.

Quite aside from the considerable degree of interpretation to
which the most basic traditions of the Bible were subjected, the new
communities which arose and contributed to the biblical traditions
themselves developed substantially new institutions, practices, and
meanings. There are worlds of difference involved as one moves
from Abram in Canaan to his putative progeny in Egypt, from the
time of incursion into the promised land to the establishment of a
monarchy and a preeminent Temple, from a single kingdom to a
divided, dispersed Judah, from the exile to the Hasmonean state,
from the accomodation to the Romans to the failed revolt which
resulted in the burning of the Temple. And the concerns of Jesus within
that Temple, some forty years before its destruction in 70 CE (see
Matt 21:12-16; Mark 11:15-18; Luke 19:45-48), are not those of a
Paul, whose global ambitions included an itinerary to Spain (see Rom
15:28-29), as far west of the Temple as most Jews could have
imagined.

A critical exegesis of the Bible must be sensitive to the shifts of
meaning involved as one moves from culture to culture among the
communities which produced the texts, sometimes over a period of
many generations, orally and/or in writing. Sanders articulates that
awareness as a guiding principle in exegesis:

> A primary character of canon is its *adaptability* as well as its *stability.* These
> two qualities must be seen together and in the same light. The concept of

---

[20]   J. A. Sanders, *Canon and Community: A Guide to Canonical Criticism*
(Philadelphia: Fortress, 1984) esp. xvii.

canon in terms of its *function* in the believing communities puts in relief the rather amazing fact of *repetition*. Repetition of a community value in a context other than that of its "original" provenance (the main stress of biblical criticism until recently) introduces the possibility, some would say the necessity, of *resignification* of that value to some limited extent. One may have been able to repeat the value . . . "accurately," meaning in this instance verbatim, but the very fact that the later context involved different ears, questions, and concerns means the high likelihood that a somewhat different meaning was derived from rereading the text (*relecture*, the French call it).[21]

By definition, a change of cultural context, even when a tradition remains verbally the same, will involve a change of meaning.

Sometimes the change seems to be a matter of emphasis, in which case we might speak of a fresh *construal* of the tradition. But sometimes the change is of a nature to demand the awareness that it is a *transformation* of the earlier tradition.[22] An example of a construal is the way in which, in Matthew, Jesus' teaching of forgiveness is put in the context of the organization of churches, which only existed after his time (Matt 18:15-20). An example of a transformation is the casting of Jesus' teaching about the Temple, an institution in which he took an active interest,[23] into an elaborate prophecy of the destruction of the Temple (see Matthew 24–25; Mark 13; Luke 21). Such changes are facilitated when translation and substantial creativity are involved in the formation of traditions (orally and in writing), as was the case both in Israel and in the primitive Church.

A critically viable reading of the Bible must therefore involve a *generative exegesis of texts*, that is: an exegesis which is sensitive to the ways in which changes in culture correspond to changes in meaning as traditions develop into texts.[24] (Had "canonical criticism" been widely understood along the lines of Sanders' program, that is the category I would be using now. But that phrase is now applied to a more ideological reading than I find productive,[25] so that a new category, "generative exegesis," is called for.) Generative exegesis

---

21   Sanders, *Canon and Community*, 22.

22   On the distinction between construal and transformation; cf. Chilton, *Profiles of a Rabbi*, 139-82.

23   Cf. Chilton, *The Temple of Jesus. His Sacrificial Program Within a Cultural History of Sacrifice* (University Park: Penn State Press, 1992).

24   Cf. B. Chilton, *A Feast of Meanings: Eucharistic Theologies from Jesus through Johannine Circles* (NovTSup 72; Leiden: Brill, 1994).

25   Sanders (*Canon and Community*, 24-25, 31) elegantly sets out his differences from Childs.

by itself has nothing whatever to do with the authority of Scripture in a theological sense. But it is a necessary prelude to the reading of Scripture as authoritative, because generative exegesis is the means by which the religious meanings of Scriptures within the contexts and phases of their developments may be defined. Prior to any claim of authority, the Bible's meanings within the many religious communities which produced it must be understood.

Generative exegesis provides us with an account of how meanings developed, but no key to how those meanings are to be ordered. It may reveal contradictions, major gaps in understanding, prescriptions from and for former cultural contexts which seem out of place in our own, as well as rich resources for the description of God and his ways which are resonant with our experience.[26] That, indeed, is the tension which believers commonly refer to when they consider the historical meaning of the Bible in comparison with claims made on the Bible's behalf within their faith. The purpose of generative exegesis is *not* to alleviate that tension, as is the case of appeal to progressive revelation, alleged Fundamentals, existential decision, structuralism, narrative theology, and deconstruction. The aim is rather to permit the meanings of diverse religious systems to come to expression from within the text, to confront—rather than to evade—the challenge of critical history.

Once that challenge is confronted, how might it be addressed? More than ten years ago, a monograph was published in which I related Jesus' teaching to tradition contained with the Aramaic Targum of Isaiah.[27] My argument was not that Jesus had read the Targum, since the document only came into existence after his time (and he himself may well have been illiterate). But he quoted renderings of Isaish which were later incorporated into the Targum and he alluded to that folk tradition, its wording, motifs and contexts in Aramaic.

The proposed dating of the Targum has been confirmed by subsequent discussion, and the link between targumic traditions and Jesus'

---

26   The unsystematic quality of the religious meanings of Scripture puts us in the sort of position which Beardslee ("Whitehead and Hermeneutics," in *Margins of Belonging*, 117-23) describes. The metaphysical aspects of his argument are simply beyond our purview.

27   Cf. B. Chilton, *A Galilean Rabbi and His Bible: Jesus' Use of the Interpreted Scripture of His Time* (GNS 8; Wilmington: Glazer, 1984); also published with the subtitle, *Jesus' own Interpretation of Isaish* (London: SPCK, 1984).

teaching has generally been granted. In a work published in 1982, I had suggested that the Targum of Isaiah should be understood to have developed in two principal stages.[28] A version—no doubt incomplete—of Isaiah in Aramaic was composed by an interpretative community which flourished between 70 and 135 CE. That work was completed by another community, asociated with Rabbi Joseph bar Ḥiyya of Pumbeditha, who died in 333 CE.[29] Throughout the process, insofar as individuals were involved, they spoke as the voice of synagogues and of schools.[30] Given the periods of development of the Isaiah Targum, the argument that agreements between the targumic renderings and Jesus' sayings are simply a matter of coincidence appear strained. Scholarly review has confirmed the link between Jesus and the targumic tradition of his period.[31]

The discovery of the targumic connection provides a foundation for understanding Jesus' use of Scripture.[32] Jesus' method should not be described as midrash, since there is no general or systematic plan of commentary evident within his sayings. Rather, Jesus employed

---

[28]   Cf. *The Glory of Israel: The Theology and Provenience of the Isaiah Targum* (JSOTSup 23; Sheffield: JSOT Press, 1982). It might be mentioned, in the interests of accuracy, that the date printed on the title page is an error. (Churgin's work suffered a similar fate, although the error involved misplacing his book by a decade! Cf. P. Churgin, *Targum Jonathan to the Prophets* [Yale Oriental Series; New Haven: Yale Univeristy Press, 1927]). In a condensed form, my conclusions are available in *The Isaiah Targum: Introduction, Translation, Apparatus, and Notes* (ArBib 11; Wilmington: Glazier; Edinburgh: T. & T. Clark, 1987) xiii-xxx.

[29]   Chilton, *The Glory of Israel*, 2, 3; idem, *The Isaiah Targum*, xxi. For the sections of the Targum most representative of each meturgeman; cf. Chilton, *The Isaiah Targum*, xxiv.

[30]   The model developed for the case of the Targum of Isaiah is applied in D. J. Harrington and A. J. Saldarini, *Targum Jonathan of the Former Prophets* (ArBib 10; Wilmington: Glazier; Edinburgh: T. & T. Clark, 1987) 3; R. Hayward, *The Targum of Jeremiah* (ArBib 12; Wilmington: Glazier; Edinburgh: T. & T. Clark, 1987) 38; S. H. Levey, *The Targum of Ezekiel* (ArBib 13; Wilmington: Glazier; Edinburgh: T. & T. Clark, 1987) 3-4; K. J. Cathcart and R. P. Gordon, *The Targum of the Minor Prophets* (ArBib 14; Wilmington: Glazier; Edinburgh: T. & T. Clark, 1989) 12-14. Levey's acceptance of the paradigm is especially noteworthy, in that he had earlier argued that Targum Jonathan (especially Isaiah) should be placed within the period of the ascendancy of Islam; cf. S. H. Levey, "The Date of Targum Jonathan to the Prophets," *VT* 21 (1971) 186-96.

[31]   See, for example, the reviews of M. McNamara in *CBQ* 47 (1985) 184-86; 48 (1986) 329-31; and I. H. Marshall in *EvQ* 58 (1986) 267-70.

[32]   Cf. Chilton, *A Galilean Rabbi*, 148-98.

Scripture, scriptural imagery, and scriptural language (all in the popularly received form which would later be crystallized in the Targumim) by way of analogy. That implicit but powerful analogy —involving both similarities and critical distinctions—was always between what was said of God in Scripture and what Jesus claimed of God as a matter of experience.

The last third of *A Galilean Rabbi* is devoted overtly to the theological implications of Jesus' instrumental usage of Scripture. The book was in fact written to some extent with a view to continuing debated concerning authority within the Church, and was published by an Anglican house as well as by a Catholic publisher.[33] The meanings of Scripture may only be discovered by historical means (at least, within the cognitive context of the contemporary world and its predominant cultures); the appropriation of such meanings as authoritative is only possible by means of analogy.[34] The analogy is rooted in the sensibility that a given biblical text, from the level of whatever constituent community, is describing just the God we experience. Without the sensible link between the generative community of the text and the experiential community of the reader, analogical authority cannot be developed. Such a direct claim upon his hearer's experience on the basis of God's reality in the Bible is characteristic of Jesus' message.

The experience of God as biblical, however, is only the beginning, or the occasion, of the Bible's authority. Jesus refused to limit himself to the repetition of the biblical text: he was noted (and notorious) for departing from agreed norms in order to speak of God. In addition to being experiential in reference to Scripture, he was also critical. His critical perspective, of course, was not historical; rather, his creative adaptation of biblical language and imagery evidences an awareness that God in the text and God in experience do not entirely coincide.

Because the God of the Bible is experienced, and yet—as experienced—may not be contained by the biblical text, the trademark of Jesus' instrumental use of Scripture is "fulfillment." By referring to

---

[33]   In the same year, Prof. Sanders' *Canon and Community* appeared. My present effort is to define the sort of analysis which we have independently promoted, and to give it focus under the category of "generative exegesis."

[34]   Analogy may therefore function for us in the way that typology and allegory once did for the early Church. Cf. R. M. Grant, *A Short History of the Interpretation of the Bible* (New York: Macmillan, 1972).

Scripture as fulfilled, Jesus claimed to resolve the tension between the coincidence with and the distance of the biblical God from his own experience. When, for example, Jesus says in the synagogue in Nazareth, "Today this scripture has been fulfilled in your ears," he does not literally mean that he did everthing referred to in the passage from Isaiah he has just read (see Luke 4:16-21).[35] The significance is rather that the present experience of God, although identified as such by the Bible, itself represents a fuller disclosure of God than what the text says. The Bible is not a vessel which contains God, but an index of how God might be experienced in his fullness.

The authority of the Bible, then, is not inherent in its texts, nor is it a matter of a particular mode of reading them. The authority which the Bible exerts is rather by means of its analogy to our experience of God. Scripture helps us to identify and define that experience, but also to see it as distinctly our own experience, and not a simple repetition of biblical norms. In the field of tension between the Bible, with the religious meanings involved within it, and our experience, framed according to our cultural contexts, there emerges—in the readings of some passages, with some meanings, some of the time—a consensus.

That consensus is not simply legislated by either the biblical text or our current experience. Text and experience are rather fulfilled in consensually pointing to the God of whom text, experience, and much else are themselves functions. The authority of the Bible emerges when the meanings which generated it illuminate the meanings which speak to us of God, and the textual and the experiential together orient us to their common, divine matrix. The task of biblical theology is to identify those meanings isolated by generative exegesis which can explain most fully both the senses of Scripture and the senses of our lives.

---

35 For a full treatment of the passage, see B. Chilton, *God in Strength: Jesus' Announcement of the Kingdom* (SNTU 1; Freistadt: Plöchl, 1979; repr. BibSem 8; Sheffield: JSOT Press, 1987) 123-77.

KERYGMATIC CENTRALITY AND UNITY
IN THE FIRST TESTAMENT?

Eugene E. Lemcio

INTRODUCTION

Quite obviously, one cannot do justice to such a difficult, contro-
verted, and significant subject as the unifying center of the First
Testament (FT) in the course of a single essay. And the question
mark at the end of the title makes clear how tentative my own
suggestion will be. I proceed only because of the freedom which this
genre of writing allows for responsible pot-boiling. It's the sort of
exercise that our friend, colleague, and honoree would approve of,
having turned up the heat on recipes new and old once or twice
himself. Furthermore, an emerging climate within our discipline in
general and the particular character of this volume of essays (concentrating on the text *qua* text as they do) provide a context for reopening and re-invigorating a debate which after two hundred years
has been declared impossible to resolve at the historical level and
irrelevant for doing theology.

But why this harsh, two-part verdict against the quest to identify
the unifying center of the FT, and, for that matter, the Second Testament (ST) as well? As one examines the surveys of research charting
the history of these efforts, it is possible to infer a number of reasons
for the current impasse.[1] First, the proposals made seemed alien to
the spirit of the text. They used terminology which bore little
resemblance to the idiom of the Scriptures. The categories suggested
appeared to be externally-imposed rather than emerging from within
the biblical materials. At times, trans-textual realities were invoked:
"the living God," "the experience of Israel," etc. These and other
schemas sometimes lacked formality and concreteness, tending more
towards the abstract and inferential. To the extent that single themes,
such as love, grace, righteousness, etc. were proposed, to that extent

---

[1]   G. Hasel, *Old Testament Theology: Basic Issues in the Current Debate* (4th
ed; Grand Rapids: Eerdmans, 1991) 139-71; idem, *New Testament Theology:
Basic Issues in the Current Debate* (Grand Rapids: Eerdmans, 1978) 140-70.

they minimized (or could not accommodate and integrate) the multiple and diverse character of the documents and their pluriform motifs. Furthermore, there arose the suspicion that some, if not most, of the preceding were a function of the scholar's own subjectivity, either as a matter of individual prejudice or ecclesiastical commitment. The latter would bring with it a particular point of view and means of expression (Calvinist, Lutheran, Roman Catholic, and in more recent years, the ideology of various -isms).

Methodological differences tended to reduce the possibility of consensus even further. Scholars have been unable to agree on the literary-descriptive or reconstructive-historical *nature of the task*. In other words, there is currently no common mind as to whether one is to look for that which is unifying and central within the documents of the canon as canon, or whether one should search for these features among the traditions and persons who subsequently produced the documents which were later canonized. In the former, if an answer is to be found, one needs to look within the texts; in the latter, it is to be found behind them.[2]

Moreover, even those who confined their search to the writings have not agreed upon the *scope* of the investigation. There is the quantitative question. How much of the canon needs to be represented? Will a simple majority do? Would a substantial minority satisfy? Then, of course, there is the qualitative issue. Because neither the texts themselves, nor the communities which produced and preserved them, define or identify "central" and "unifying," one had to appeal to significance and consequence. But these categories were not free of a high level of subjective interpretation, especially in the absence of agreed-upon criteria for methodological control. Therefore, by the end of the nineteenth century, the search for a unifying, central core to the FT produced no consensus.

With the flourishing of form criticism in this century, the quest was made more problematic as scholars focused on the diverse

---

[2]   Of course, one need not view these projects as mutually-exclusive. In fact, the history of research shows that writers sometimes opted for a combination of both. Each activity is legitimate and important. However, a substantial case can be made that, unless the final redaction and literary composition are fully understood, all (traditio-) historical study is premature and its results therefore at risk. Ideally, if literary conclusions match historical ones, then any thesis becomes doubly confirmed.

communities which handed on traditions orally.[3] Prospects for successfully identifying the axis around which all else in the FT revolves became even less likely after the Second World War. Redaction critics demonstrated how diverse are the points of view exhibited by individual biblical writers functioning as author-theologians and not merely as preservers of oral tradition. In fact, there was a series of articles in *Interpretation* during the sixties which attempted to identify the particular kerygma (usually understood as "message" or "theme") of select biblical writings.[4] Although it could be argued that some, if not most, of the claims for diversity were overstated, the main point became firmly established. Hence, the search for unity and centrality would seem more daunting even to the most intrepid explorer.

Apart from these technical barriers, there is the current, prevailing mood or mindset within the guild of biblical scholars itself. The concern persists that the quest for unity and centrality may signal a desire to return to some form of anti- or ahistorical dogmatic theology. Moreover, researchers worth their salt want to steer clear of anything which even hints at apologetics, both because that is an unworthy motive for doing scholarship and also because of the stigma which the fraternity of scholars attaches to such activity. For example, *Neutestamentler* Hans Conzelmann allegedly dismissed Oscar Cullmann's thesis of a unifying *Heilsgeschichte* as being particularly congenial to ecclesiastical authorities.[5] And J. I. H. MacDonald attributed the initial popularity of C. H. Dodd's thesis of

---

[3]   For an example from the ST of how such analyses had direct impact on the structure and content of a New Testament theological work, see Wilhelm Heitmueller's article, "Zum Problem Paulus und Jesus," *ZNW* 13 (1912) 320-37 and its appropriation by Rudolf Bultmann in *Theology of the New Testament* (2 vols., New York: Scribner's, 1951-55) 1.vii-viii; 2.v-vi.

[4]   R. E. Murphy, "The Kerygma of the Book of Proverbs," *Int* 20 (1966) 3-14; J. M. Myers, "The Kerygma of the Chronicler," *Int* 20 (1966) 259-73; G. M. Landes, "The Kerygma of the Book of Jonah," *Int* 21 (1967) 3-13; M. Barth, "The Kerygma of Galatians," *Int* 21 (1967) 131-46; R. E. Brown, "The Kerygma of the Gospel According to John," *Int* 21 (1967) 387-400; M. Rissi, "The Kerygma of the Revelation to John," *Int* 22 (1968) 3-17; W. Brueggemann, "The Kerygma of the Deuteronomistic Historian," *Int* 22 (1968) 387-402; F. F. Bruce, "The Kerygma of Hebrews," *Int* 23 (1969) 3-19. See Brown, above, who defines the kerygma as "its central salvific message" (p. 387).

[5]   He reportedly lamented to Old Marburgers that form and redaction criticism, as practiced in Germany, was not done elsewhere(!).

a kerygmatic center within the ST[6] to a flaw in character: "Such widespread acceptance of a hypothesis that was by no means exhaustively argued suggests that it spoke to some psychological need on the part of the English-speaking theological public."[7] Furthermore, there is the more subtle constraint upon those who want to reconsider the question: unity and centrality do not resonate with the spirit of the age which values diversity and pluralism.

DEFINITIONS, ASSUMPTIONS, AND METHOD

Consequently, one will have to work especially hard at examining the impulses which drive (and inhibit) such an effort, including my own. A way of proceeding is to distinguish between the *motives* of an investigation and the *uses* to which results are put. So long as apologetic intentions do not dictate the outcome in advance, one can reduce the chances of ideological readings of the text. And we must be even-handed. Should objections, say, to a Lutheran interpretation of scripture be any more serious than against an ideological one? Finally, all who value truth must reject bowing the knee to the *Zeitgeist*, whose reign is temporary, local, and often demagogic.

Since the volume of essays honoring Jim Sanders has as its dominant approach the investigation of intertextuality, it already circumscribes the arena of the discussion: the texts of the canonical FT. So, one ought not make any apologies or offer disclaimers for a study that is primarily literary in scope. Consequently, my own contribution will bear these features, too.[8] Furthermore, the focus will be less on how texts *per se* are handled by various authors than on the manner by which biblical writers work with their primal story, which I shall refer to as the "*kerygma.*" This term will signify an announcement, recital, or narrative. From among the variety of stories available, the task is, of course, to identify the basic, primal,

---

[6]   C. H. Dodd, *The Apostolic Preaching and Its Developments* (London: Hodder & Stoughton, 1936).

[7]   J. I. H. MacDonald, *The Articulation and Structure of the Earliest Christian Message* (SNTSMS 37; Cambridge: Cambridge University Press, 1980) 3.

[8]   To keep this investigation manageable, I shall confine my attention to the thirty-nine canonical writings of the Hebrew Bible, knowing that eventually the deuterocanonical documents of the Roman Catholic and Eastern Orthodox traditions need to be included. My suspicion is that an analogous phenomenon can be detected.

or central one which unifies and integrates the whole.[9]

Given the history of research summarized above, why do I not speak of a central, unifying *theme*? The reason is simple. One of the major points of contention among scholars lies in the variety of topics proposed: virtually equivalent to the number and diversity of interpreters. Furthermore, themes are static. They often resemble categories found in the table of contents of a *systematic* theology, which the Bible clearly is not. Subjects tend to be treated exclusively and singularly, rarely reflecting the more complex, multiple, diverse, and inclusive character of biblical expression. *Narrative*, on the other hand, *embraces* themes. The following statement will serve as an example of the difference: "In remembering his promise to Abraham and Sarah, God graciously redeemed his people with a mighty hand." Within this sentence, there are the subjects of fidelity, grace, salvation, power, and community. Systematic or dogmatic theology, as historically practiced, has usually converted qualifying elements into nouns, extracted them from the story, separated them, and then organized all within a schema of varying degrees of artificiality. (Ironically, biblical theologians, though decrying such an approach, have sometimes taken a similar tack). However, recital accommodates multiple and diverse topics, orders them (allowing some flexibility), and then relates all according to the integrative character of the story line. Consequently, an attempt to develop a fully-biblical theology (and a biblically-oriented systematic theology) might try employing a kerygmatic (i.e. narrative) approach to organizing its component parts.[10]

In addition to these more narrow considerations, one can say that the very nature of Scripture itself is narrative, a point almost too

---

9   While some might object that "kerygma" is a proclamation made to outsiders, I need only recall that Jesus preached the near-arrival of the Kingdom of God to his own—the people of God (Mark 1:14-15). The Greek herald announced news to his community. "Creed" or "confession" functions in a complementary way. It expresses one's response to the story: "I believe / confess that . . . [kerygma related]." The community commits itself to the truth of the recital and pledges allegiance to God, its protagonist. Each is the flip-side of the same coin. One is declaration; the other, assent.

10   Hasel (*Old Testament Theology*, 133-38) reports the shift in discussion which occurred when John Barton and James Barr sought to move attention from history to story, from tradition to narrative. I support such an emphasis, going further to suggest a particular story which unifies and centers the FT.

obvious to make these days. While aware of the excesses of what might be called "narrativism," one may still make the following incontrovertible points. Quantitatively speaking, story abounds. Furthermore, much of non-narrative (ethical codes and cultic manuals) is framed by it. Speaking more qualitatively, one can show that recital lies at the foundation of statutes and commandments. The rationale for obeying them ("why these statutes?") comes from an account of the community's origins. Other material (some wisdom literature) presupposes it . If these definitions, assumptions, and methodological approaches be allowed for the sake of argument, then I shall proceed to show why I am inclined to answer affirmatively the question posed by my title.

THESIS AND ABSTRACT

There is an eight-member "form" which recites God's promise to the patriarchs and his delivering Israel from Egypt. This archipelago identifies the range of mountains and foothills on the ocean floor which constitute the unifying center of the FT. The back-bone of island-peaks may be named with the well-established, though contested, term, "kerygmatic" (either the act or content of heralding). Regarding it as "unifying" and "central" can be justified by the following considerations, beginning with *quantitative* ones. The bifocal recital can be found in all of Tanakh's major and minor canonical sub-units (with heavy concentration in Torah) and in every major era of Israel's salvation history: ancestral call and wanderings, liberation from Egypt, wilderness dereliction, conquest and settlement, monarchy (united and divided, north and south), exile, and restoration. Thus, pervasiveness becomes a criterion for centrality and unity.

Furthermore, this narrative *in nuce* may be regarded as central and unifying because of certain *qualitative* factors. An extreme example of the need to move beyond numbers might help. Simply by its frequency, "and" could be regarded as the key. However, it is without consequence. Thus, significance is a clue to centrality. By this I mean that the outline of promise and deliverance appears in connection with the most fundamental aspects of the community's life. The elemental story is told at covenant making and renewal ceremonies both on the verge of Israel's entry into the Promised Land and in the wake of its return from exile in Babylon. Recital of

Yahweh's foundational promise to the "fathers" and subsequent rescue from Egypt of their descendants lies at the heart of Israel's response in worship at major, annual, cultic events as well as on unique occasions such as Solomon's prayer at the Temple's dedication. Subsequently, its highlights were sung during Temple worship. The elemental story provides the ground of ethics, the keeping of the Great Commandment and the commandments. Centrality is indicated, too, by the kerygma's appropriation of the widespread, foundational myth of the world's creation and of Israel's deliverance. Thus, when quantity (frequency) and quality (significance) go hand in hand, it is possible to speak of unity and centrality with a lesser degree of subjectivity than might otherwise be the case.

The advantages of this narrative approach to the centuries-old, elusive quest for centrality and unity are numerous. It transcends the limitations of using thematic and topical categories. While the latter are static, unitary, and exclusive, recital includes multiple and diverse themes, integrating them within a dynamic story-line. Furthermore, the text-based nature of this proposal reduces the transtextual (and, therefore, elusive) character of other suggestions (e.g. "the living God," "the experience of Israel"). Internal, native, and natural, it should limit the imposition of external and ideological categories foreign to the text but at home in ecclesiastical dogma or the current spirit of the age. The "form's" own idiom could help to minimize the use of artificial, technical terminology. By being formal and concrete, it reduces the subjectivity which bedevils abstract reconstructions of tradition and history.

THE "FORM"

Arguing for unity and centrality is easier if one can demonstrate a degree of formality in the proposal. In other words, without demanding an inflexible sequence, it is reasonable to expect that certain items recur. And this informal formality ought to occur within a circumscribed amount of text and within discrete documents rather than to range over several chapters and among several books. Otherwise, such defusion increases the already-easy drift into deep subjectivity. The "form" which I propose has eight components, two halves reciting the themes of promise and deliverance:

(1) God
(2) promised / swore

(3) land / covenant fidelity
(4) to Abraham, Isaac, and Jacob / forefathers.
(5) God
(6) delivered / led up / led out
(7) his people / our (fore-) fathers
(8) from Egypt.

ITS SCOPE: THE QUANTITATIVE CASE

This pattern can be found numerous times in fifteen (just over one third) of the protocanonical documents, a significant minority judged by the following considerations. All of the major and minor canonical units of the Hebrew Bible contribute instances. Torah is represented most fully; and Tanakh provides substantial testimony. Examples from the Former Prophets appear in Joshua, Judges, and 1–2 Kings. The pattern occurs among the Latter Prophets: Isaiah and two members of the "Scroll of the Twelve," Hosea and Micah yielding their testimony. From the Writings come Psalms, Nehemiah, and 2 Chronicles. Furthermore, each significant epoch of the biblical story contains the "form." And it is imbedded in the major literary genres: narrative, prophetic oracle, and poetry.

TORAH

Genesis

One would not have expected to find in Genesis examples of both the promise and the deliverance, since the latter only begins to be told in Exodus. Yet, as early as chap. 15, Yahweh confirms the original promise (12:1-3) made to the heirless Abraham (vv. 5-7). Further assurance of its fulfilment in future deliverance (vv. 13-15) is interwoven with an account of the establishment of a covenant sealed with sacrifices offered by Abraham but initiated by God (vv. 9-11, 17-18). Near the end of the book, in 50:24-25, the dying Joseph declares that God will indeed bring Israel out from the land of Egypt into the land which he swore to Abraham, Isaac, and Jacob.

Exodus

Although partial examples of the pattern occur in 3:6-8, 16-17 (no reference to land or covenantal obligations) and 33:1-2 (Moses rather than God leads them out), the full outline appears on two occasions. In what amounts to a second commisioning, Yahweh recites the account of his appearances to each of the three patriarchs with whom he established a covenant to give them the land in which they have been sojourners. He has heard the cries of his people and promises to bring them out from Egyptian bondage (6:2-8). Later, when liberated Israelites incur God's wrath from their orgiastic worship of the golden calf (32:1-11), Moses uses the eight-membered narrative to dissuade him from destroying them (vv. 12-14).

Leviticus

This configuration subsequently becomes the means of assuring later generations who find themselves exiled because of covenant violations (26:38-41). Confession and repentance will cause Yahweh to remember his covenant with Jacob, Isaac, and Abraham. He will remember the land. The covenant made with their ancestors whom God brought out of Egypt remains inviolate (vv. 42-45).

Numbers

Numbers 14:13, 23 parallels Moses' intercession for the people when they committed idolatry at the foot of Mount Sinai. At 32:10, God's wrath is not abated against the generation which came up out of Egypt. Except for Caleb and Joshua, no one twenty years or older will see the land which he swore to Abraham, Isaac, and Jacob (vv. 11-12).

Deuteronomy

By far, the greatest number of complete occurrences of the "form" are found in Deuteronomy. In some cases, instead of promising land, Yahweh expresses his love for the fathers (4:37-40; 7:6-8; 10:14-22) and swears to be the people's God (29:13-28). The first instance of the pattern promising land belongs to the Shema. Having achieved what God swore to Abraham, Isaac, and Jacob, they are not to forget the Lord, who brought them out of the land of Egypt, the house of bondage (6:10-12). Moreover, this memory is to be passed on to children when they ask about the origins of the statutes given by Moses (vv. 20-23). He again reminds the Israelites of this legacy as they prepare to cross the Jordan River (9:26-28; 11:8-10). Finally, this narrative of promise and deliverance is to be recited at the Feast of Firstfruits. After setting the basket before the altar, one is to "do the tell" about the Ancestor, a wandering Aramaean who went down to Egypt (26:1-15).[11]

THE FORMER PROPHETS

Joshua

In the covenant renewal ceremony at Shechem, Joshua on God's behalf begins the patriarchal narrative with Terah, Abraham's father, an idolater. To the son, Yahweh "gave" Isaac while in Canaan. To Isaac, he "gave" Jacob and Esau, to whom he gave Mt. Seir for a possession. Under Moses and Aaron, he brought the fathers of the present generation out of Egypt (24:1-6). After marvelous acts of deliverance, God led them into a land for which they had not labored (vv. 7-13). In response to Joshua's admonitions and warnings (vv. 14-15), the people swear their loyalty (vv. 16-18).

Judges

After less-than-successful efforts at settling the land, an angel of the Lord confronts the Israelities at Bochim for their failure to abide by the strictures against co-existence and their compromise with the inhabitants (2:2-3). This brief litany of complaints is introduced by the even more succinct statement of the now familiar story: "I made you go up out of Egypt, and have brought you to the land which I swore to your fathers; and I said I will never break my covenant with you" (v. 1).

1 Kings

At the Temple's dedication, Solomon opens and closes his prayer citing God's deliverance from Egypt (8:16, 51-53). In between, however, the King refers to the land given by God to the fathers. That this is not simply a general reference to Israel's ancestors is evident in the attention given to the foreigner, the alien whose prayer Yahweh will answer so that "all the peoples of the earth may know thy name and fear thee, as do thy people Israel" (vv. 40-43). The purpose of the covenant established with Abraham and Sarah seems

---

[11]   The expression, "doing the tell," comes from the final scene of a book and movie which appeared in the mid-eighties (cf. J. D. Inge, *Mad Max: Beyond Thunderdome, a Novelization* [New York: Warner Books, 1985]). A colony comprised mainly of children, having found refuge in a Sydney devastated by worldwide nuclear war, gathers regularly to preserve their sense of identity and provide hope for a future. A young teenage girl begins each session by narrating the events which led to their life together.

on the verge of fulfillment.

2 Kings

Although in the land, and long-since free of threats from native populations, the people of God experience the trauma of civil war and the hostility of their neighboring states. In the regime of Jehoahaz of Samaria, Syria rather than Egypt oppresses Israel. Nevertherless, the author explains that the people escaped destruction and loss of the Lord's presence; he showed them graciousness, compassion, and respect because of the covenant made with Abraham, Isaac, and Jacob (13:22-23). Thus, promise is invoked to interpret deliverance which occurred between bondage in Egypt and exile in Babylon.

THE LATTER PROPHETS

Isaiah

With the destruction of the southern kingdom, the prophet comforts the people of God in Babylon, both with a metaphoric reminder of their ancestral heritage and by a mytho-poetic account of their original deliverance:

> Look to the rock from which you were hewn, and to the quarry from which you where digged. Look to Abraham your father and to Sarah who bore you; for when he was but one I called him, and I blessed him and made him many (51:1-2).

> Awake, awake, put on strength, O arm of the Lord; awake, as in days of old, the generations of long ago. Was it not thou that didst cut Rahab in pieces, that didst pierce the dragon? Was it not thou that didst dry up the sea, the waters of the great deep; that didst make the depths of the sea a way for the redeemed to pass over? (vv. 9-10).

The original Exodus experience and its grounding in the patriarchal promises become the foundation of the prophet's hope for a second Exodus: "And the ransomed of the Lord shall return, and come to Zion with singing" (v. 11).

Hosea

The foregoing appeal by a prophet of the southern kingdom had earlier antecedents in the north. During the reign of Jereboam II, the word of the Lord came to and was "empersonated" by Hosea. God's case against Israel begins with the experience of its namesake, the patriarch Jacob, whom God favored through struggle with his angel

(12:3-4). In Syria, he served for a wife by keeping sheep. By a prophet, the Lord brought Israel out of Egypt (vv. 12-13).

Micah

Initially directing his critique both to Samaria and Jerusalem, Micah closes his book with confidence that God will be true to Jacob and show mercy to Abraham as pledged to the fathers long ago (7:20). As in the days of the generation which came up out of Egypt, Yahweh will yet perform wonders for his people (v. 15).

THE WRITINGS

Psalms

Singing the praises of Yahweh's wonderful deeds occupies Psalm 105, whose author recounts the salient events of promise and deliverance from the times of the patriarchs through the Exodus. God has remembered the covenant made and confirmed with Abraham, Isaac, and Jacob to give them and a thousand generations the land of Canaan (vv. 1-11). Though few in number, the original families enjoyed protection from the resident nations among whom they were aliens (vv. 12-15). Through Moses and Aaron, Yahweh ravaged Egypt with signs and wonders, finally bringing his people out with the wealth of their captors (vv. 16-38). Because of the promise made to Abraham, all of their needs were met on the way to the lands inhabited and "developed" by heathen nations (vv. 39-44). This was the purpose of observing his statutes and keeping his laws (v. 45).

Nehemiah

That they did not and suffered the consequences is graphically chronicled in several summaries which appear in exilic and post-exilic literature. The one bearing most on this thesis occurs in the covenant renewal ceremony under Ezra. After acknowledging God as the Creator (9:6), its recital of the people's history begins with the choosing of Abram from Ur of the Chaldees and renaming him Abraham (v. 7). His faithfulness led Yahweh to make a covenant bequeathing the land of several peoples to the patriarch's descendants (v. 8). Its fulfillment followed liberation from Egypt and instruction at Sinai (vv. 9-15).[12]

---

[12]   Although no complete instance of the recital in question occurs in Ruth, a canonical neighbor of Nehemiah in the Writings, important echoes of it do occur. In

2 Chronicles

It is fitting that the last book of Tanakh should maintain those elements of the story which the first set forth. There is here (6:5, 25, 31-33) a virtual replica of Solomon's prayer at the Temple's dedication in 1 Kings 6. In a document so concerned with royal commitment to liturgical correctness and Israel's identity as a separate people, it is noteworthy to find included that openness to the foreigner, the subject of universal blessing promised to Abraham and Sarah.[13]

ITS SIGNIFICANCE: THE QUALITATIVE CASE

Having attempted to make the case for centrality and unity from primarily quantitative perspectives (its pervasiveness), it is necessary to move towards more qualitative ones. By the latter, I mean that the primal narrative appears in the most significant eras of the people's history and community life, as the following endeavor to show.

KERYGMA AND COVENANT

That the eight-part form is found in the promise made to Abraham where it is called "covenant" (Gen 15:5-7, 13-16, 18) is another witness to its centrality. Kerygma and covenant are linked in Yahweh's assurances to Moses after Pharaoh doubled the burden of Israelite slaves (Exod 6:1-8, esp. vv. 4-5). Furthermore, the promi-

---

place is the Mosaic legislation regarding gleaning and the transmission of property, wherein the Moabitess plays such an important role. In the end, the hope is that she will build up the house of Israel, just as Rachel and Leah, the wives of Jacob, did. Boaz's house is to be like that of Perez, whom Tamar bore to Judah, the patriarch's son from whom kings were to come. And Ruth became the great-grandmother of king David himself (4:11-22). That this foreigner (whose race originates from the incestual union of Lot and his daughters!) could play such a significant role is a testimony that the goals of the Abrahamic Covenant, as reflected in Solomon's prayer, are being met. Consequently, the patriarchal, Sinaitic, and royal elements of the story converge.

13   While I have not cited any example from wisdom literature, it is the case that Proverbs, Ecclesiastes, and the Song of Songs have internally (redactionally?) and canonically been linked to Solomon, who did recite the narrative at the Temple's dedication, according to 1 Kings 8 and 2 Chronicles 6. Thus, one can say that the kerygma attracts themes and literatures which themselves do not contain the pattern per se.

nent place and repeated use of the divine name in this connection (vv. 2, 6, 7, 8: אני יהוה) also underscores how central these issues are.

Centrality is in evidence at covenant renewal ceremonies on the verge of Jordan under Joshua (24:1-18) and on the brink of Israel's restoration in Judah under the leadership of Ezra (Neh 9:7-11). The high moments of entering the promised land and returning to it are fittingly marked by a recitation of those earlier, foundational events that had made the subsequent ones possible. Kerygma and covenant belong together. On both occasions of covenant renewal, a written testimony was produced for subsequent generations (Josh 24:25-27, Neh 9:38).

KERYGMA, THE COMMANDMENT, AND CODES

That the kerygma should be identified with The Commandment certifies its foundational character. In Deut 6:4-5, the Shema testifies not only to the unity of God, but to the duty to love and obey him alone with one's entire being. This is, of course, an expansion of the first word of the Decalogue (v. 14; cf. 5:7). Sandwiched by these variations on the theme lies the elemental story about the promises made to Abraham, Isaac, and Jacob, on the way to being fulfilled by the deliverence from Egypt (6:10-12).

Likewise, such faithfulness must extend to all of the "testimonies, statutes, and ordinances." These are to be taught and spoken of from dawn to dusk and in every place, aided by physical reminders (6:6-9). When rationale and meaning for such observance are sought by subsequent inquisitive (and, perhaps, incredulous?) generations who were not part of nor privy to the original events, one is to tell one's "son" about the deliverance from Egypt into the land promised to the people's ancestors (vv. 20-23).

KERYGMA, CULTUS, AND CALENDAR

It will be useful to distinguish two kinds of cultic acts: those performed *ad hoc* or occasionally and those which occur regularly. To the former belong instances of covenant making and renewal, the recitation of the Shema, and the son's instruction. Of separate and unrepeated cultic acts which might be cited, Genesis 15, mentioned above in connection with covenant, heads the list. Here the covenant is sealed with sacrifices initiated by God himself. The foundational story is integrated with worship (vv. 9-11, 17-21).

One of the more dramatic and public occasions of the kerygma's link with the cult occurs during Solomon's prayer at the Temple's dedication recorded in 1 Kings 8 and 2 Chronicles 6 (thus straddling two canonical units: both Former Prophets and Writings, and two traditions: both the pre-exilic, royal and the post-exilic, priestly). Animals beyond counting had been sacrificed (8:62-63). More significantly, the cloud of Yahweh's glory weighed so heavily on the premises that the priests could not perform their service (vv. 10-11). In the 2 Chronicles account, divine fire ignited the sacrificial victims (5:6, 13-14; 7:1-7).

If we use the classic (but still useful?) form critical notion of *Sitz im Leben* (not simply the moment of a form's emergence, but the context of its *continuous* or at least *regular* use), what does one find? It happens that our proto-narrative occurs in instances of annual, community worship. Thus, during the annual Feast of Firstfruits or Weeks (Deut 26:1-4, 10), after setting the basket before the altar, one is to tell about the Ancestor, a wandering Aramaean who went down to Egypt . . . (vv. 5-9, 15). The dual motifs of Abrahamic promise and Mosaic deliverance also appear in Psalm 105:7-15, 42 and 23-38, respectively. The psalm, by definition, was to be sung (in the shrine?) repeatedly--although it is not clear on precisely which occasion.

KERYGMA AND KINGSHIP

That king Solomon himself presides over the Temple's dedication and prays thus (1 Kings 8; 2 Chronicles 6) links the establishment of the monarchy to the two-part, foundational story. In each instance, the covenant made with David privately (cf. 2 Sam 7:14-16) is reiterated publicly in this mometous, liturgical setting. Furthermore, the recital of promise and deliverance occurs at the covenant renewal ceremony in Jerusalem for the community returning from Exile in Babylon. In the narration of God's dealings with Israel, the litany of sins underscores the failure of Israel's *kings and princes* to make good on all that God had accomplished earlier in her history and on her behalf. Although Ezra, the priest, officiates at this occasion, the account is recorded by Nehemiah, the *political* head of the community (who nonetheless shows extreme zeal for the religious well-being of God's people. See 9:34 and chap. 13).

KERYGMA AND CHARISMA

The formality and stability of this kerygmatic form does not militate against the flexibility and freedom enjoyed by those who transmitted it, as evidenced in the prophetic tradition, especially, where both the Abrahamic call and the Exodus from Egypt are retained. However, any claim by God, mediated by the prophets, to be doing a "new thing" is not absolutely novel; it is grounded upon the old. As we saw in (Second) Isaiah, the announcement terminating the Babylonian captivity adapts the very Exodus motif which it adopts. However, it does so by reworking the motif of Yahweh's conquering the dragon. In the prophet's hands, it can either celebrate God's act of creation (Ps 74:12-17) or it can anticipate final, eschatological victory (Isa 27:1; cf. Revelation 12).

KERYGMA AND COSMIC MYTH

Significantly, this is itself an adoption (stability) and adaptation (flexibility) of motifs common in the ancient Near East.[14] So far as the Exodus portion of the pattern is concerned (Isa 51:1-2, 9-11), the ' fact that a primal myth which dealt with such foundational matters as cosmic and historical origins is a sure indicator of its centrality. That it enjoyed international and cross-cultural distribution also testifies to its fundamental character. This kerygma deals with archteypal issues.

KERYGMA AND CANON-BEHIND-THE CANON

In thus promoting the existence of a formal kerygma which centers and unites the FT, I am not advocating a canon-*within*-the-canon. To regard the kerygma as central is not a value judgement any more than saying that the axle is central to the wheel. Materially speaking, axle, spokes and rim, diverse in shape and function as they are, together make up a wheel (although it might be said that an axle is a proto-wheel). So far as their role is concerned, spokes direct motion away from the center while the rim contains the motion within boundaries, returning it to the center by means of the same spokes. One originates, another transmits by adaptation, and the other stabilizes. Centripetal forces balance centrifugal ones, thereby making "wheelness" possible. It might be more correct and modest to

---

[14]   A. Y. Collins, *The Combat Myth in the Book of Revelation* (HDR 9; Missoula: Scholars Press, 1976).

suggest that the basic recital served as a canon-*behind-* the-canon, the measuring rod by which multiple and diverse documents were acknowledged as integral and complementary. It is the meta-story which I have in view. This is not to be confused with the plot of an "historical" work such as 1 Kings. Rather, I am referring to that story-behind-the-story upon which the plot hangs. The questions to be asked are, "Which recital gave the community its origin and which carried it through? Whose story began generating the tradition(s) and the literature(s)? Which kerygma best explains the emergence of canon at all?"

---

15 My attempts to identify a kerygmatic, unifying center for the ST have detected a six-member "form" in nineteen of the twenty-seven writings representing the Gospels, Acts, Pauline and catholic letters, and Revelation. This kerygmatic skeleton differs from the one proposed here in several significant ways. No mention is made of the commitment to Abraham and rescue from Egypt. The second half calls for a response. Although heavily theocentric (God originates the saving event and is the subject of the response), the agent of salvation is Jesus. See the Appendix in my monograph, *The Past of Jesus in the Gospels* (SNTSMS 68; Cambridge: Cambridge University Press, 1991) 115-31. This chapter combines the results of two earlier studies, "The Unifying Kerygma of the New Testament," *JSNT* 33 (1988) 3-17 and 38 (1990) 3-11.

However, there are significant traces of the FT phenomenon here and there. It is intriguing to find how Matthew, in a very short space, alludes to, adapts, and gives an ironic twist to the themes which I have been treating in the present article. Jesus is identified early on as the "Son of Abraham" (1:1) who, because his own people oppose the prospect of his kingship, force Joseph, Mary, and their Child to flee for refuge to that former land of bondage (2:1-14). When the coast becomes clear, the holy family settles in Galilee, fulfilling Hosea's prophecy (11:1), "Out of Egypt have I called my Son" (2:15). In Hebrews, more attention is given to Abraham and Moses in that citation of faithful heroes and heroines than to any others. (See 11:8-12, 17-22 and 23-29 for the parallels). A fuller development of the eight-member kerygma is to be found in Stephen's speech (Acts 7:1-36). Of course, other ST authors, especially Paul, deal with Abraham and Moses. However, the emphasis is less on land, in the case of the former, and more on Sinai, so far as the latter is concerned. Were I to press the alliteration *ad nauseum*, analysis of these texts could be labeled, *Kerygma and Christ* and *Kerygma and Kirk*.

THE ONCE AND FUTURE TEXT

Paul E. Dinter

On a recent summer trip from Atlanta to New York, motoring inland on Interstate 81, I detoured to visit the Civil War battlefield at Gettysburg, Pennsylvania. The location of a terrible slaughter wrought in and around it in July, 1863, Gettysburg became fixed in American memory by Abraham Lincoln's Address at the dedication of its national cemetery later that year. Intrigued by what I had seen there, I took up Garry Wills's *Lincoln at Gettysburg: The Words that Remade America*. In it the author argues that Lincoln's brief 272-word speech changed the course of democracy in this country. Its cogency caused my interest in biblical intertextuality to lurch forward nineteen centuries. It alerted me afresh to the powers of suggestive language, to the social and cultural weight of textual re-signification, and to the enduring importance of the habit of intertextuality that developed centuries ago among the Bible's earliest tradents.

Twenty-five years ago, when I first studied with Jim Sanders, the tools that today help us describe the inter-generational canonical process were only just being developed. While some studied the Bible and, detective-like, uncovered clues to the historical meaning of the text, Jim's classes were about different discoveries. Ranging backwards and forwards through the Bible, illuminating its textured layers, highlighting its convergences, and unearthing its divergencies, he showed us how to grasp it as a polymorphous yet synchronic whole. His reading method made us confront anew its discomfiting character as a *two-testament* collection that harbored a riot of typologies, a host of dynamic analogies, and a record of contending interpretive modalities. Learning to read the Second Testament with First Testament sensitivies, to listen to familiar Christian phrases with Hebraic ears, and to see on the page, not a simple text, but a complex intertext ruined most of us for life. Taking his course on text criticism made us masters of suspicion, no longer trustful of doctrinal harmonies, nor content with *textus recepti*. The only place to go for comfort was back to the text in its multivalent loveliness. There we would have to learn to ring the changes again so as to let the canonical words speak afresh. That much, it seems, Abraham Lincoln knew and too many of us had forgotten.

As my contribution to celebrating the impact of Jim Sanders's scholarship on his students and colleagues, as well as "the field" itself, I wish to begin with highlighting the phenomenon of intertextuality as it made of a classic funeral address an old form with a very new meaning, so as to take up an old interpretive question from the new perspective of intertextuality. The old question involves the Catholic-Protestant debate on Scripture and Tradition as it was irenically treated by the Second Vatican Council's *Dei Verbum (Dogmatic Constitution on Revelation)*; the new treatment of it will argue that intertextuality reveals something about the authority of the Bible for both Catholic and Protestant interpreters. For both, "tradition" is no set body of doctrines, and "interpretation" is not merely a key to unlock hidden secrets. Both tradition and interpretation are alternative names for the intertextual endeavors that drive the engine of theological affirmation forward (often in spite of itself).

Lincoln's speaking style preceding the Gettysburg Address already evidenced his mastery of the intertextual forays common in nineteenth-century Unitarian and Transcendentalist reading of the Bible. Combining biblical with classical rhetoric was the surest way to communicate the ideas that "transcended" a particular age, ideas that the Constitution (known for its political compromises) failed to enshrine but that had been encoded in the founders' Declaration of Independence.[1] This perspective allowed Lincoln to employ the language of spiritual regeneration in his oratory opposing the Kansas-Nebraska Act of 1854 when he declared, "Our republican robe is soiled, and trailed in the dust. Let us re-purify it. Let us turn and wash it white, in the spirit, if not in the blood of the Revolution." If "all Americans," he urged, would re-adopt the Declaration of Independence and work for an end to slavery, then "millions of free happy people, the world over, shall rise up and calls us blessed

---

[1]   G. Wills, *Lincoln at Gettysburg: The Word That Remade America* (New York: Simon & Shuster, 1992) 102-103.

to the latest generations."[2] The language of the *Magnificat* could not but seem appropriate for describing the highly favored United States at its best.

At Gettysburg, Lincoln wove together a complex intertext, calling on classical funeral rhetoric (going back to Pericles' oration), on Romanticist nature-imagery and its melancholia in the face of death, as well as on biblical images to evoke a chosen nation's consecration, suffering and resurrection. Concentrating for our purposes on his use of the Bible, we should note the playfulness involved in his famous opening "Fourscore and seven years ago." Psalm 90:10, which pondered the everlastingness of God and the shortness of mortal life, measured a long life as "threescore and ten years, and if by reason of strength they be fourscore" (KJV). Lincoln punned on the sacrality of the measurement in his opening phrase, thus signaling how at peril was the survival of what "our fathers" had wrought. These anonymous ancestors themselves continued his biblical evocation by reference to the eponymous patriarchs of biblical history. What these worthies had done was to have *"brought forth . . . a new nation conceived* in Liberty and *dedicated"* a series of images recalling the births of Samson, John the Baptist, and Jesus. This chosen nation was set apart by its dedication (cf. Jer 1:5 and Gal 1:15) to the "proposition that all men are created equal"—in effect linking the tradition of annunciation and nativity with the creation account as surely as Matthew 1 or John 1 had made that intertextual link.

Lincoln's brief but packed text connected the day's dedication of the cemetery to the very purpose of the "great civil war" that was testing the truth of the nation's dedication. Because those who died there "gave their lives" that the nation might live (cf. John 11:50), Lincoln declared in solemn liturgical language: "It is altogether fitting and proper that we should do this" [i.e. dedicate the burial ground] drawing on the prefatory dialogue response of the Roman Canon *vere dignum et justum est* (together with canons of Greek rhetoric) as justification for his actions.[3] At the same time that he carefully chose his few words on that occasion, he deprecated those same words: "The world will little note, nor long remember, what we do here, but it can never forget what they did here" paradoxically

---

2   Wills, *Lincoln at Gettysburg*, 88-89.
3   Wills, *Lincoln at Gettysburg* 273 n. 41.

invoking Moses' "remember and do not forget" invocations throughout Deuteronomy. To conclude, he called on those present "highly [to] resolve that these dead shall not have died in vain [cf. 1 Cor 15:17] — that this nation, under God, shall have a new birth of freedom," recalling the nation's miraculous birth and the "born again" imagery of John 3:3-7 so central to the two Great Awakenings in American religious history. The result of this re-birth would be that the people, and their government—again foregrounding the transcendental ideas of the Declaration of Independence and its proposition of universal liberty—would not "perish from the earth."[4]

As a result of Lincoln's mastery of text and context, Wills argues that "the Civil War is, to most Americans, what Lincoln wanted it to mean."[5] The narrative he wove (via intertextuality) structured both the popular and scholarly reception of a complex series of bloody and unnecessary *bruta facta* of war. Historians have tirelessly reconstructed the battle which, as a battle, was a turning point of the fortunes of General Lee's army. But at Gettysburg the battle took on its unique meaning in and through the narrative appropriation that Lincoln's Address gave to it, effecting nothing less, says Wills, than an "intellectual revolution" calling up "a new nation out of the blood and trauma" of Gettysburg.[6]

* * *

Wills's construal of both Lincoln's intertextual artistry and its impact presents us with as good a secular case of the development of doctrine as we are going to find. It demonstates well the historical and social dynamics by which canonical ideas are re-appropriated textually by becoming part of the on-going dialectic of interpretation at the heart of all doctrine, religious and secular. It can also serve as the occasion of our re-visiting an old-new issue: the role of the

---

[4]   Wills, *Lincoln at Gettysburg*, 37: "His speech hovers far above the carnage. He lifts the battle to a level of abstraction that purges it of grosser matter—even 'earth' is mentioned as the thing from which the tested form of government shall not perish."

[5]   Wills, *Lincoln at Gettysburg*, 38. Concerning Lincoln's rhetoric, Wills affirms, "'Plain speech' was never less artless. Lincoln forged a new lean language to humanize and redeem the first modern war" (174).

[6]   Wills, *Lincoln at Gettysburg*, 175.

biblical canon in the ongoing formulation of Christian belief. Lacking a method that specifies adequately *how* God is said to "speak" through the Bible, most Christians are left floundering with little more than the formulation that the Bible is the Word of God, understood as everything from a weak metaphor to a strong identification. The result is substantial confusion in the matter of the authority of the Bible in both Protestant and Catholic circles, producing renewed assaults on and defenses of the integrity of the canon.[7]

Thirty years ago, the Second Vatican Council sought to update Catholicism's doctrine of the Bible against the background of centuries of anti-Protestant polemic and a small but significant twenty-year opening to new methods of biblical study inaugurated by Pius XII in *Divino Afflante Spiritu* (1943).[8] The Council's Constitution (despite its title *Dei Verbum*) avoided any simple identification of the Bible with the Word of God, considering it as part of the mystery of divine revelation: *that* God communicates with humanity is more basic a truth than *how* God has communicated. What God communicates is not mere words, but the Divine Self and the effects of that Self-giving ("the eternal decrees of his will" concerning human salvation; §6). God Self-communicates, not first in written messages, but through events. These are called "divinely revealed realities, which are contained and presented in the text of sacred Scripture" (§11), e.g. the choice of Israel, the covenants, or the "economy of the Old Testament" (§15).

But the Self-disclosure of God occurs chiefly through the *event* of "Christ the Lord, in whom the entire Revelation of the Most High God is summed up." God's revelation, then, reaches its peak in the Person of Christ, whose resurrection and exaltation became available to humanity not through appearances or visual evidence (except to a relatively small number of disciples), but through the preaching of the Gospel. In turn, this preaching was "committed . . . to writing"

---

7   F. Kermode, "The Argument about Canons," in *An Appetite for Poetry* (Cambridge: Harvard University Press, 1990). The recent attempt by the Jesus Seminar to insert the *Gospel of Thomas* into the operative canon of the gospels also reflects confusion about the role of the biblical canon.

8   Cf. G. Moran, *Scripture and Tradition: A Survey of the Controversy* (New York: Herder and Herder, 1963); G. Fogarty, *American Catholic Biblical Scholarship: A History from the Early Republic to Vatican II* (San Francisco: Harper & Row, 1989) 281-350.

and "handed on" (as "tradition") to the successors of the apostles in such a way that both Scripture and Tradition are together "like a mirror, in which the Church, during its pilgrim journey here on earth, contemplates God" (§7). More basic than any unwritten or written text, then, the *activity of communicating God's Self-communication* continues to be the heart of divine revelation and underlies any adequate theory of biblical hermeneutics.

Though *Dei Verbum* paralleled Scripture and Tradition as making up a "single sacred deposit of the Word of God" (§10), it also distinguished them as well. The one is a fixed body of written books, the other includes them as they are part of the entire body of "what was handed on by the apostles" (i.e. the Church's body of teaching as well as her life and worship). In other words, the Council's definition of the "deposit of faith" is a dynamic rather than a static one. It comprises all manner of activity by which "the Tradition which comes from the apostles makes progress in the Church" through "growth in insight into the realities and words that are being passed on . . . in various ways" (§8). The document goes on to list modes of the ongoing transmission of the revelation as contemplation, study, the intimate sense of spiritual realities, and preaching. Through these activities, Scripture and Tradition "communicate one with the other" for the first is "the speech of God as it is put down in writing" and the latter transmits the speech-act of God's Self-communication "enlightened by the Spirit of Truth" (§9).

In sum, the constitution preserved continuity with Catholic teaching on the "plus" factor in revelation, but avoided simplistic notions of both tradition and the literal inspiration, inerrancy, and indefectability of the Bible. It did this by accepting a basically critical perspective which required that the variety of literary forms be taken into account when interpreting a text. But it also affirmed the unity of the whole based on the Bible's divine inspiration and the way its true meaning is communicated by "the Tradition of the entire Church and the analogy of faith" (§12). In other words, the historical sense of ancient inspired texts has to be sought in the same manner as any ancient text is interpreted, i.e., by exegesis. But the contemporary reference of the text (its meaning in the fuller sense) continue to be created by re-engaging it in the evolving teaching, worship, and life of the church.

Adopting (albeit mildly) a historical-critical perspective, the Council could not affirm that there are "two sources of revelation" (the title of the first rejected schema), for it was not possible to pretend that Tradition comprised a body of written material on precise analogy with the Bible. Some might have wanted to elevate Denzinger's collection of magisterial statements to quasi-canonical status, but that would have defined Tradition as static, unchanging content. Instead, Tradition (even when written with an upper case "T") is understood as a *dynamic process* wherein the "realities and words passed on" are said to be subject to growth in understanding "until eventually the words of God are fulfilled" (§8). This means that the norm by which "the People of God live their lives in holiness and increase their faith" is not just the Bible, but all that was "handed on" by the apostles and continues to be "handed on" in the teaching, life and worship of the church. According to Vatican II, it is this *traditioning activity* that continues to make available to later generations the encounter between God and the believing community which the canon enshrines. This activity occurs typically in the proclamation, preaching and worship of our Sunday congregations, in the study of the Bible both academically and pastorally, and only then in formal declarations of the episcopal or papal teaching offices. While this might seem to claim a great deal for Sunday worship, it appears to be a clear implication of the Council's insistence that the "Magisterium is not superior to the Word of God, but is its servant"(§10).

To the extent that *Dei Verbum* is itself a document of Roman Catholicism's official Magisterium, it is among the best examples of how a teaching authority serves the Word of God or the mystery of God's Self-communication. It does so by placing the Bible and its ongoing interpretation into a worship-and-life context rather than seeking to give it a status outside of historical time. At the same time, the Council's constitution only made tentative suggestions about the complex task of hermeneutics, being content with its own version of the "intentional fallacy." Because it was still fighting for the task of historical investigation, it declared that "the interpreter of sacred Scripture, in order to see clearly what God wanted to communicate to us, should carefully investigate what meaning the sacred writers really intended, and what God wanted to manifest by means of their words."[9] Still its insistance that any reading and interpretation take

---

9   R. E. Brown ("Hermeneutics," *Jerome Biblical Comentary,* 606) was still taking this cautious position in the 1960s: "The principal task of interpretation centers around the author's intended meaning." But more recently (*The Critical*

place in the light of "the content and unity of the whole of Scripture" and "the living tradition of the whole church," modifies its naively historical standard regarding the range of meaning of bibical texts.

As mentioned above, the question concerning *how* the Bible continues to communicate God's Self-revelation has produced renewed debates over the authority of the canon and over biblical hermeneutics. For the most part, the canon is either taken for granted as an historical artifact or excused away before its content is mined for either doctrinal or historical material of interest.[10] In this essay I wish to develop an insight from Jim Sanders's writings that argues for linking the Bible's authority to its proper interpretation. This means that the biblical canon cannot be viewed as a sacred historical artifact but as itself a renewable matrix for and ongoing process of encountering revelation. In this matter, Sanders is one with *Dei Verbum* in his insistence that the Bible and the Word of God are separable.

> Hermeneutics, therefore, is as much concerned with the contexts in which biblical texts were and are read or recited as with the texts themselves. It is in this sense that one must insist that the Bible is not the Word of God. The Word is the point that is made in the conjunction of text and context, whether in antiquity or at any subsequent time . . . Hermeneutics is the midpoint between the Bible's stability and adaptability as canon.[11]

According to Fr. Dominique Barthélemy, Sanders's notion of the bi-polarity of canon as stable and adaptable best reconciles historical criticism with canon (the Bible as the church's book). Because he details the ways in which Tradition as a process ("the holy Scriptures . . . actualized in the Church" *DV,* §8) is critically accomplished,[12]

Meaning of the Bible [New York: Paulist, 1981] 19) he has contended "that one cannot be satisfied with the literal meaning of Scripture," adding in a note: "the literal sense is larger than the author's intent." He coined the term "biblical meaning" to take the whole canonical tradition into account.

10   See n. 7 above. S. Schneiders (*The Revelatory Text: Intepreting the New Testament as Sacred Scripture* [San Francisco: HarperSan Francisco, 1991] 102) uses the term "paschal imagination" to describe a comprehensive New Testament hermeneutics. She combines a dogmatic treatment of the New Tetsament as a medium of revelation with a hermeneutical treatment of how we get at what a text means today dependent on the hermeneutics of Paul Ricoeur.

11   J. A. Sanders, *From Sacred Story to Sacred Text* (Philadelphia: Fortress Press, 1987) 65-66.

12   D, Barthélemy ("La critique canonique," *Revue d'Institut Catholique de*

Sanders's "canonical hermeneutics" highlights the way that the ancient process of canon formation has actual material continuity with
what continues to go on in faith communities today, despite the
formal discontinuity created by the "canonization" (i.e., closure) of
the Bible itself. By developing Barthélemy's judgment, I wish to
consider whether the concept of intertextuality can help us better
describe an important dynamic in faith's hermeneutical challenges as
we enter the post-modern era.

The technical basis for Sanders's dissociation of written Bible and
Word of God has been undergirded by the magisterial work of
Michael Fishbane in his *Biblical Interpretation in Ancient Israel*. For
the author has demonstrated how the historical and textual dynamics
that produced the First Testament make it a complex *intertext*. He
shows that any approach that seeks to uphold "the mystique of the
authority of revelation" at the price of ignoring how an on-going
process of *traditio* relativized the older *traditum* (finally becoming
one with each other as "entwined and inextricable") cannot
understand the genius of the Bible as "a variety of teachings and
responses."[13] For, in it we find "an ongoing interchange between a
hermeneutics of continuity and a hermeneutics of challenge and
innovation" that shows the Bible to be a "complex blend of *traditum*
and *traditio* in dynamic interaction, dynamic interpenetration, and
dynamic interdependence."[14] Fishbane's investigations into the
layered texture of the legal, haggadic (narrative), and mantological
(prophetic) material in the Tanak (and its consequent doctrinal
plurality) has implications for addressing the post-critical authority
of the Bible. Over against attempts to isolate a single layer of
tradition or a single amalgamated whole as authoritative for all time,
approaches that seek to discover the inner dynamics of the Bible's
varied materials promise to help us formulate other criteria for the
canon's authority which are not dependent upon dubious historical
reconstructions or an unhistorical dogmatism. This promise is some–
what paradoxically confirmed by another student of the literature

---

Paris [1991] 211-220) contrasts the work of Brevard Childs, whose "très origi-
nales" views risk opposing canon and criticism. The Latin text of *Dei Verbum* 8
defines tradition as that by which *ipsaeque Sacrae Litterae in ea penitus intelliguntur
et indesinenter actuosae redduntur.*

13   M. Fishbane, *Biblical Interpretation in Ancient Israel* (Oxford: Clarendon,
1985) 15, 440.

14   Fishbane, *Biblical Interpretation*, 428, 543.

whose approach at first would seem completely inimical to Fishbane's "genetic" search for the scribal authors' methods. Declaring most source-criticism of the Hebrew Bible "fruitless," Meir Sternberg's *Poetics of Biblical Narrative* sees in the *poesis* of biblical narratives (rather than the specifics of its *genesis*) a singularly non-didactic approach to doctrine (or ideology). Instead, biblical story-telling consciously "generates ambivalence:"

> The characterization is complex, the motives mixed, the plot riddled with gaps and enigmas, behavior unpredictable, surprises omnipresent, the language packed and playful, the registration of reality far more governed by the real and realistic than by the ideal.[15]

There is coherence in the bibical narrative, but it is a "difficult coherence regulated by the manuevering between truth and the whole truth," what he also calls "the told and the withheld" which constitutes the narrative's theocentric world picture.[16] In it God's "leading role shines through the drama of indeterminacy" so much so that the Bible encourages the tendency to assimilate character to type mainly "with a view to its ultimate discomfiture." Its rhetoric is uniquely harmonized to its ideology, seeking to get its readers to "adopt a world picture that both transcends and threatens" them, to accompish the task of persuasion without dwarfing, betraying, or compormising the object of persuasion."[17]

These characteristics of the narrative portions of the biblical text correspond to Fishbane's analysis that "as a form of instruction" the received canon of Scripture "is quintessentially an aggadic trope." Both studies demonstrate that the ancient Israelites developed their

---

[15]   M. Sternberg, *Poetics of Biblical Narrative: Ideological Reading and the Drama of Literature* (Bloomington: Indiana University Press, 1985) 38. Among his affirmations of the "poetic originality" of the Bible are the following, "The Bible goes out of its way to complicate our enlightenment: to produce curiosity, wonder, even skepticism about God's disposition in order to trap us into faith on the backswing" (p. 99). "One can hardly think of a biblical narrative that might not be profitably reduced—or lends itself to adequate explanation as it stands—by reference to a narrator with a purely doctrinal interest or viewpoint" (p. 138). "The Bible . . . has created *ex nihilo* a poetics of ambiguity, with reticence taking the place of confidence, in order to fix rather than blur the line of demarcation between heaven and earth: unless the reader undergoes the drama of knowledge himself, the whole tale will have been told in vain" (p. 163).

[16]   Sternberg, *Poetics of Biblical Narrative*, 250, 322.

[17]   Sternberg, *Poetics of Biblical Narrative*, 348, 483.

religious culture by balancing its continuous and its discontinuous elements, by seeing its stable *traditum* as adaptable *traditio*, by embracing indirection and ambiguation rather than by eliminating the interplay of truth through rigid ideology. These considerations of the inner-biblical dynamics behind the canonizing of the Bible (whichever version) can help us recast the authority of the Bible in terms of its own categories rather than in philosophical or ideological terms alien to it. It allows us to rehabilitate what is in fact "an ancient hermeneutical insight: the Bible can be read as a self-glossing book."[18] Thus, its own textured and intertextual content is the best spring board for our attempts to understand it afresh. Efforts to "interpret" it by extracting truth from it as one extracts marrow from bones will fail because the Bible's *message* (content) is inseparable from its *medium* (its hermeneutics). Because "the whole orientation of Scripture is toward its future, not toward its past," says Gerald Bruns, one cannot understand the Bible by divining some intention in it, but rather "by appropriating it anew."[19]

This recovered perspective on the dynamics at work in the biblical canon also provides us with an alternative to the Romantic notion of biblical inspiration still prevalent today. This notion saw inspiration occurring in the more or less tortured soul of an individual wrestling with divinely inspired thoughts. Instead, the intertextuality of the Bible allows us to take account of the social construction of its texts as well as the social nature of its inspiration. Because the Bible as a canonical intertext reveals the inter-dependency of the generations of successive tradents whose managing of the vicisssitudes of history made their efforts sporadic, unsystematic, and contextual, we can understand its revelation as radically incarnational and, as such, as a measure (*kanon*) of how God "speaks." This shift from the *what* to the *how* of the Bible means that it is not the definitive transcript of a past conversation where we can overhear something essentially lost.

This mode of understanding the interpretation of the Bible as a continuous re-contextualizing is a specification of the literary and

---

18   G. L. Bruns, "Midrash and Allegory: The Beginnings of Scriptural Interpretation," in R. Alter and F. Keremode (eds.), *The Literary Guide to the Bible* (Cambridge: Belknap Press, 1987) 26.

19   L. Bruns, "Midrash and Allegory," 27: "the Bible effectively blocks any attempt to understand it by reconstruction of its textual history and a working back to an original, uninterpreted intention."

social phenomenon of intertextuality. Daniel Boyarin defines intertextuality as having three accepted senses: first, that texts are comprised of mosaics of conscious and unconscious elements because every author, speaker (and human being for that matter) is made up of all the discourses he or she has ever heard or read; secondly, that texts are themselves implicit or explicit dialogues with the past; and, thirdly, that since all texts are produced or constrained by cultural codes, there is no such thing as "a true, objective mimesis of reality in language. Reality is always represented through texts that refer to other texts, through language that is a construction of the historical, ideological, and social system of a people."[20]

But, unlike authors who distinguish strongly between the Bible (First Testament) and post-biblical midrash (of which much of the New or Second Testament is a variant), both Boyarin and Fishbane see the Bible and midrash as genetically connected by similar intertextual reading practices. By correlating text to text, reflecting earlier texts in later ones, citing itself, and interpreting itself, the Bible's long-term presumption is that God communicates indirectly.[21] Its texts do not specify, they symbolize. This means that the very gaps, repetitions, contradictions, and heterogeneity of the Bible must be read as central, not incidental, to the way its makes any truth claims. Its indeterminacy is not an enemy of its system of meaning, but its ally because it compels readers to enter into dialogue with the texts and even with its "gaps," i.e., those silences within the text that cry out for interpretation. Boyarin's final point about midrashic intertextuality stresses the extent to which, in Judaism, midrash "was experienced as revelation itself." The rabbis so presumed that the Bible had only one Author that, to read it at all, required a strong reading to bridge the gaps and explain repetitions, ambiguites, and the texts' many figurative symbols.[22] This made the whole of the Bible (and the interpretation of it) a system of independent elements that could be recombined "to generate its meanings—its original

---

20   D. Boyarin, *Intertextuality and the Reading of Midrash* (Bloomington and Indianapolis: University of Indiana Press, 1990) 12-14.

21   Boyarin, *Intertextuality*, 15, 40, 128: "Midrash is best understood as a continuation of the literary activity which engendered the Scriptures themselves . . . the Bible is characterized aleady by a degree of self-reflexivity, self-citation, and self-interpretation . . . ." See also Fishbane, *Biblical Interpretation,* 277.

22   Boyarin, *Intertextuality*, 148, 53-54.

meanings—in ever new social and cultural situations."[23]

This perspective on the intertextuality of the Bible and the biblical tradition in Judaism has strong analogies with what we saw above in Vatican II's unitary view of the way that Scripture and Tradition are "like a mirror, in which the Church, during its pilgrim journey here on earth, contemplates God" (DV §7) and that Scripture and Tradition make up a "single sacred deposit of the Word of God" (DV §10). These magisterial statements can be seen as variants of Boyarin's "The Book has only one Author," and of the rabbinic practice of recreating Scripture (as Oral Torah) while continuing to give pride of place to the written Scripture. Equally, they show that the Tradition does not just reflect history, but generates it (as theology) intertextually. The Bible's original authority is located in its internal workings. Its own intertextual dynamics spawned more than a millenium of rabbinic commentary and patristic-monastic theology. Our recovery of these dynamics (with the added awareness of the important role of historical context in the Bible's overall formation) can help us retrieve the religious import of the interplay of text and context for articulating an old-new perspective on the Bible's ongoing authority.

*   *   *

From the beginning of the historical critical period (ca. 1770s), conservative Protestantism has increasingly sought refuge from the fracturing of the unity of the Bible in concepts of biblical inerrancy (or infallibility), while acounting for any diversity through the practice of private interpretation. For its part, Catholicism tended to limit the access of the faithful to any personal investigation of the Bible and to stress the need for an "authentic interpreter" of Scripture, a role claimed increasingly for the Magisterium, but rarely if ever employed. While not surrendering these cautionary claims, Vatican II (DV §10) sought to recover the central role of the Bible in the life of faith and so rose above the older formulations to create the new synthesis out of Scripture and Tradition that we have seen above. So far, I have detailed how intertextuality characterizes the

---

23   Boyarin, Intertextuality, 28, 39. Sanders (Sacred Story, 180) speaks of the "bad news and good news" of textual stabilization and its atomization: "A frozen text written for one set of problems can create new ones when read in a totally different situation."

Bible itself as well as the midrashic appropriation of the Bible, and have observed a similarity in structure between the role of midrash in traditional Judaism and Vatican II's notion of Scripture and Tradition. In addition, I have observed that *Dei Verbum* professed that the papal and hierarchical Magisterium served rather than dominated the Word of God.

In the rest of this essay I would like to argue that we post-modern Christians of all stripes best continue to participate in Tradition (i.e. the *traditio* or *paradosis*) principally through liturgically intertextual activity and the study of faith that emerges from it. Thus, the relatively late idea in Roman Catholicism that church authorities somehow constitute a unitary hierarchical Magisterium, despite all its self-advertisement, is today seriously overblown. At best, it has a subsidiary role of "oversight" or judgment over the whole tradition-ing process, not *the* defining role that has been claimed for it. It neither inaugurates it or controls it because "the word of God is not chained" (2 Tim 2:9) nor does it have any other Magister except the Messiah (Matt 23:10).[24] Equivalently, just as we have come to see that the inspiration of Scripture is more socially complex than the way Romantic notions of inspiration conceived of it, so we can note the peril in both (Protestant) personal models of the "inspired knowledge" of God's will and (Catholic) ecclesiastical models of "authentic interpretation" of Scripture by the hierarchy.

For all their differences in confessional politics, both private and magisterial interpretation depend on an uncritically appropriated imitation of certain naive characterizations in the Bible of how God "communicates." Both presume that either the individual inquirer or a semi-inspired hierarchical official have direct access to what God wants to manifest by means of the scriptural words either in them-selves or as they are part of the traditioning process. Both also depend, then, on an early modern, if not Cartesian, understanding of the self-presence of the self in thought that does not accurately represent the actual dynamics of the traditioning process. This understanding of the religious knower's immediate self-presence (upon which God's communication is predicated) takes it for granted that "in consciousness there is no gap between the knower and the

---

24   Schneiders (*Revelatory Text*, 85) argues for the appropriateness of the pastoral magisterium acting as a "final court of appeals" that realizes its limits so as to avoid degenerating into "autocracy."

known. I am immediately present to myself, without needing any representation to mediate the presence." In this scheme the subject's unthematized (and non-linguistic) presence to itself is said to guarantee a human being's openness to the absolute, hence a believer's ability to be grasped by God directly in a communicative act and so respond with understanding and faith.[25]

Yet again, for all their differences, the practicioner of private interpretation and of magisterial authority fundamentally hold a position that anticipates the kind of knowing that St. Paul assured us would be operative in the future when "I will know fully, even as I am known." Unlike how it will be "then," he presumes that *now* we see in a mirror dimly . . . *Now* I know only in part" (1 Cor 13:12). Paul's perspective that, before we "see face to face," our knowledge is composed of clues, incomplete in themselves but symbolically revelatory, was thematized in Western Christianity by St. Augustine. Paradoxically, it has been confirmed by the work of Sigmund Freud. For both of them, the proliferation of symbolic, hence, *non self-interpreting* images (both in the Bible and in the unconscious) argues that we only get at truth via a structure of indirection. Any knowledge that we have of our depths is indirect because of "some precise event . . . the development of some geological fault across a hitherto undivided consciousness: for Freud, it is the creation of the unconscious by repression; for Augustine, it is the outcome of the Fall."[26] While Augustine the Platonist never abandoned his premise that all knowledge stems from divine inspiration, when God "called" him, the medium was both his desire and a *text* that a boy's voice told him to "take up and read" (*Conf.* VIII,12). Hence, all our knowledge is mediated to us: This side of the Eschaton, there is no *immediate* (i.e. unmediated) knowledge of self, of other, or of God. Rather, the Christian experience of grace is always mediated in and through limited historical contexts, and this is no less true when we are engaged in the traditioning process. Like all interpreters of the Bible, we encounter it partially, as fragmentary, wrestling with itself, as it were, via affirmations and denials that do not easily add up. Rather, the more familiar one becomes with it, the greater the

---

25   A. Dulles, *The Craft of Theology: From Symbol to System* (New York: Crossroad, 1992) 36.

26   P. Brown, *Augustine of Hippo* (Berkeley: University of California Press, 1969) 261.

gaps, its incompleteness, and the interstices or unmatched seams by which it achieved its "difficult coherence."

This means that we know what we know of God's truth from Scripture from the clues that the whole traditioning process has bequeathed to us, not by some direct, unambiguous grasp of them.[27] Because there is no complete linguistic or propositional representation of the whole truth of revelation, it follows that the dynamics of the traditioning process must be placed in contexts more social than the scholar's study or the reader's desk and more responsive to ongoing change than the committee rooms of Vatican congregations have shown themselves to be. Today, most theologians recognize that the dynamics of symbolic communications are most readily discovered in the encounter of the believing community with God in worship.[28]

Without idealizing the setting of worship, as if it were somehow exempt from the historical conditioning that modernity affirms affects all private believers or magisterial functionaries, we still must recognize worship as the primary place of hermeneutical encounter. This stems from various pre-modern factors that are strangely post-modern as well. The setting of worship is, first of all, transpersonal and communitarian, and most redolent of the "suspension of disbe-lief" that disarms seekers of truth and allows them to be "found" rather than be actively in charge of the matter they are seeking. When so engaged in, worship disposes its participants for conversion or transformation by lulling them into a "space" where they can be aware of, yet not undone, by their silly, sinful desperation or by shocking them into an unexpected confrontation. For this to happen, the space into which the Word is spoken should be sufficiently playful as well as unstiflingly traditional. For if worship is a privi-leged setting, it is paradoxically so. This is because preaching and doxology confront believers today with gaps and interstices between the Bible's affirmations and the community's questions (as well as the Bible's questions and the community's ideology). Indirectly, through

---

27   Dulles (*Craft*, 10) affirms that "postcritical theology treats the Bible in its totality as a set of clues."

28   Dulles (*Craft*, 19) says that "the Christian religion is a set of relationships with God mediated by the Christian symbols." Therefore, a privileged locus for apprehending the theological tradition "is the worship of the Church, in which the biblical and traditional symbols are proclaimed and 're-presented' in ways that call for active participation (at least in mind and heart) on the part of the congregation."

seeming mismatches and via our puzzled questions, the Word obliquely enter our lives. The way that this will most likely occur is through the dynamics of intertextuality where we encounter the recognition that "events do indeed seem to repeat or half-repeat each other, calling up the past even as they lead into the future."[29]

Because worship is inherently "traditional" it calls upon the languages and images of the Bible and tradition, but adapts them both consciously and unconsciously so that they speak in familiar-yet-new ways to a community's identity-in-God. In other words, all worship is structured as an intertextual encounter with a tradition in which the affirmations of a community's faith are an active interplay between their ancestors' faith and their own. The words may be the same (as in the Apostle's or Nicene Creed, the Lord's Prayer, or any of the canonical texts used), but their meaning and significance shift along a spectrum that either confirms or challenges the congregation's faith. In this process, it is *paradoxically the inadequacy of the canonical texts to say everything there is to say* that propels contemporary inquirers of God (midrashists or intertextualists) to dig deeper, look more broadly, or reach higher to apprehend where and how the two-edged sword of the Word is cutting—and in which direction. In this matter, worshipful affirmation and response itself shares in the dynamics of canonical stability and adaptability.

Today, preachers (and liturgists too) have the responsibility for animating a properly critical intertextuality that refuses either to turn its back on the *traditum* or to divinize or fetishize it. Critical intertextual work commits itself to a *traditio* that is more inclusive and sensitive to the disharmonies and inadequacies of our liturgical and theological God-talk. For instance, feminist scholars have today discovered that between Jesus' prayer to *Abba,* and his teaching that we pray likewise and the prayer formula *Omnipotens et sempiterne Deus* of Western liturgy, there is a gap in the *traditio* to which believing communities need to attend. As scholar-believers like Elizabeth Johnson have shown, the gaps between the Bible's setting

---

29   G. Josopovici, *The Book of God: A Response to the Bible* (New Haven: Yale University Press, 1988) 151. According to Josopovici, "liturgy . . . makes accessible in our daily selves a memory which is alive [bridging the gap between "A consciousness devoid of meaning and an unconsciousness which is fully meaningful, 'alive'], which is quite other than the historian's memory" (pp. 149-150).

and the setting of women today open us up to a new setting in which
to attend to elements in the textual *traditum* that have been "under-
played" in an historically male-oriented *traditio*. Hence, believing
communities today must listen again to the *traditum*'s disharmonies,
recover its ignored voices, and re-read them to produce a more
inclusive intertext for prayer and life. Unlike other critics who wish
to excise elements of the *traditum*, Johnson does not exclude, but
rounds out and expands our doxological repertory through a faithful
traditioning process.

Hearing anew the Bible's affirmations about Hokhma/Sophia
(Wisdom), a revealed symbol of God's creative wholeness, she has
discovered in the Bible's intertextual creativity new evidence of how
God's Spirit is revealed in friendship, how Christ's humanity is more
than his maleness, and how Trinitarian faith grounds God's maternal
implication.[30] None of these images stands complete in themselves as
the whole revelation. They are all part of "a vast system unrevealed"
(Cardinal Newman) which is at the heart of God's Self-Revelation,
the "dark lights" by which faith seeks to understand the Mystery
rather than to control it. Today we stand poised, not unlike the
audience at Gettysburg, in grave need of a performative intertextuality, able to recite the old words with insight into their new potential.
For old canons, if they are truly canonical, never die. They are
revived when revisited by those alive to their unsettled issues, their
deeply questioning resonances, their creedal harmonies and living
disharmonies. For no text of prayer or faith achieves canonicity until
it has been sung again in a foreign land. When it is so performed, it
becomes an intertext, capable of saying more through its constant,
yet variable, recital. Critical intertextuality, practiced by congregations at prayer and by their servant-scholars, represents our best tool
to re-appropriate God's Self-revelation, to listen to the revealing
Voice of the Spirit, as we move into the twenty-first century.

---

[30]   E. A. Johnson (*She Who Is: The Mystery of God in Feminist Theological
Discourse* [New York: Crossroad, 1992] 125-87. L. T. Johnson ("Something
Fundamental is Afoot," *Commonweal* 120.2 [29 January 1993] 19) adjudged this
work "the most substantial and sophisticated effort yet undertaken to connect
'feminist and classical wisdom' in a synthesis at once bold and discerning, critical
and doxological . . . ."

THE HISTORICAL SIGNIFICANCE OF
SECONDARY READINGS

Alexander Rofé

Textual criticism is a historical discipline. This applies in the first place to our endeavors at restoring primary readings. Here we are led by arguments drawn from the realm of history, be it political, geographical, linguistic, literary or religious. All these facets determine our conscious or unconscious decisions as to which readings are primary and which should be considered secondary.

However, there is an additional aspect to the historical character of textual criticism: it lies in the contribution the discipline can make to historical knowledge. This is mainly obtained by the study of textual transmission. Especially in the case of religious texts, the way they were handled while being copied sheds light on the circumstances of the transmission. In other words, the opinions of the copyists, their intellectual milieu, affected their work and its end-product, the text. This amounts to saying that changes introduced by the scribes into the manuscripts i.e. secondary readings, sometimes have considerable historical significance. The proposition will be discussed at the hand of several examples.

We start with the issue of sectarian corrections in Biblical manuscripts, a well known subject, since it was already explored by Abraham Geiger in the middle of the nineteenth century. Among other things, Geiger drew attention to the textual divergence between the MT and LXX in Prov 14:32.[1] The MT submits:

> The wicked man is felled by his own evil;
> the righteous man finds shelter in his death (בְּמוֹתוֹ).

The LXX reads instead of בְּמוֹתוֹ: τῇ ἑαυτοῦ ὁσιότητι, which probably reflects a Vorlage reading בְּתֻמּוֹ. The whole verse in the LXX, when retroverted into Hebrew, would translate:

---

[1]   A. Geiger, *Urschrift und Uebersetzungen der Bibel in Ihrer Abhaengigkeit von der Innern Entwicklung des Judentums* (2nd ed., Frankfurt am Main: Madda, 1928) 175.

> The wicked man is felled by his own evil;
> the righteous man finds shelter in his own integrity.

Thus construed the verse conveys a fine antithetical parallelism, the hallmark, in this case, of a superior reading. Geiger argues that the reading of MT is not due to graphical metathesis (במותו – בתמו), but a deliberate correction: במותו introduced the concept of retribution in the afterlife into the proverb. The text has been manipulated out of a theological concern which can be defined as Pharisaic or Proto-Pharisaic, since the Pharisees, among the religious movements of the Second Commonwealth, were those who upheld the belief in afterlife and retribution therein.

An opposite case, of a Sadducean manipulation of a Biblical text, is extant in the LXX to 1 Samuel. If I am not mistaken, I had the privilege of first recognizing it, some years ago, while reading with my students the first chapters of the Book of Samuel. I refer to the passage in 1 Sam 7:6. The MT reads:

> They assembled at Mizpah, drew water and poured it out before the Lord;
> they fasted on that day and confessed their sins to the Lord.

"Before the Lord" is said about a ritual act: the water is presented to Him, presumably upon the altar. The Greek closely follows the Hebrew text, but having translated the words "and poured it out before the Lord," it adds three words, ἐπὶ τὴν γῆν, which equal one word in Hebrew, אָרְצָה ("onto the earth"). This is self-contradictory. One does not pour water "before the Lord" onto the earth; a proper dedication requires pouring it on the altar. Obviously, the LXX at this point runs a secondary text. Its origin will become evident once we recall the divergences between Pharisees and Sadducees concerning the libation of water during the festival of Sukkot. The Pharisees prescribed a proper oblation on the altar while the Sadducees denied its legitimacy, throwing, whenever they could, the water down to the floor. This explains the inconsistency present in the LXX. The words "onto the earth" were inserted here by a Sadducean scribe bent on denying the Pharisees any support from Scripture for their custom of water-libation on the altar during the fall festival. The addition was plausibly penned in Hebrew by a Palestinian scribe familiar with the details of worship at the temple of Jerusalem. A Greek translator or copyist would scarcely be interested in what were for him ritual minutiae.[2]

The historical implications of this secondary reading cannot be exaggerated. In the first place, we have gained evidence to the existence of a class of Sadducean scribes who were involved in the task of copying the sacred books. One wonders if it is not against the activity of such people that their opponents, the Pharisees, came forth with the ruling that "the sacred books defile hands", thus thwarting the everyday handling of these books by the priestly-Sadducean circles.[3]

No less significant are the implications of this LXX reading for the history of the Jewish sects. Since the Greek translation of the Book of Samuel was made at about the end of the third century BCE, and its Vorlage certainly contained the 'Sadducean' correction, here is a piece of evidence, small but revealing, that in the third century, well before the crisis of Antiochus IV, the divergences that in time would come to characterize the Sadducean-Pharisaic polemics, already existed in Jerusalem. The schism that featured Hasmonean times was already latent in the early Hellenistic period.

Essenians too contributed their share to the correction of Biblical manuscripts. About forty years ago Isac Leo Seeligmann dedicated a detailed study to Isa 53:11 where the LXX rendering δεῖξαι αὐτῷ φῶς is supported by two Qumranic Biblical manuscripts, 1QIsa[a] and 1QIsa[b], which read יראה אור instead of the MT יִרְאֶה. Seeligmann demonstrated the superiority of MT in this passage and argued that the concept of "light" as parallel to "knowledge" (σύνεσις, דַּעַת), belonged to the stock of ideas of the Qumran people and found its way to circles in Alexandrian Jewry.[4] The addition of "light" was meant to insist on the divine source of knowledge, as against human

2   A. Rofé, "The Onset of Sects in Postexilic Judaism: Neglected evidence from the Septuagint, Trito-Isaiah, Ben Sira and Malachi," in J. Neusner et al. (eds.), *The Social World of Formative Christianity and Judaism* (Essays in Tribute to H. C. Kee; Philadelphia: Fortress, 1988) 39-49. References in Rabbinical literature are quoted there.

3   E. Rivkin, "Defining the Pharisees: the Tannaitic Sources," *HUCA* 40-41 (1969-70) 205-249, on p. 233: "The *sofrim*-Pharisees were thus, it seems, using the technicalities of the laws of ritual purity to discourage priestly handling of Holy Scriptures . . . ."

4   I. L. Seeligmann, "δεῖξαι αὐτῷ φῶς," *Tarbiz* 27 (1957-58) 127-41 = idem, *Studies in Biblical Literature* (ed. A. Hurvitz et al., 2nd ed., Jerusalem: Magnes, 1996) 411-26 (Hebrew).

wisdom, gained by experience or through the teaching of elders.

The fact that a "Qumranic" correction entered a manuscript that reached Alexandria and influenced, perhaps even served as, the Vorlage of the LXX to Isaiah proves, if I am right, that the circles peripheric to the Qumran *Yaḥad* were rather wide. This conclusion is confirmed by the wide circulation enjoyed by books kindred to the Qumranic religion, such as *Jubilees* and *Enoch*. As against them, there existed an esoteric Qumranic literature, comprising the *sĕrakim*, the *hodayot*, the *pĕšarim*, the Damascus Document, the Temple Scroll which did not circulate outside the Essenian denomination and therefore were not afterwards translated into Greek.[5]

The number of "sectarian" corrections in the textual witnesses of the Hebrew Bible is limited. I doubt if one can add many more to those recorded here.[6] This situation changes, of course, if one counts the Biblical *lemmata* in the *pĕšarim*.[7] But we may rightly question whether these were exact quotations from extant manuscripts or reworded ones, done ad hoc for the sake of the *pešer*.[8] All in all, the evidence yields that by the time of the emergence of the three Jewish sects, in the mid-second century BCE, copyists of biblical manuscripts usually abstained from modifying the texts according to their creeds. Let us recall in this context the early date suggested above for the Proto-Sadducean addition in LXX 1 Sam 7:6. The other "sectarian" modifications cannot be dated, though it is probable that they too

---

[5]   The Damascus Document seems to be an exception to this group, since it first surfaced in the Cairo Geniza. A plausible explanation is that the Geniza manuscripts were copied from scrolls discovered in a cave by Qumran in the eighth century CE. Cf. J. T. Milik, *Ten Years of Discovery in the Wilderness of Judaea* (SBT 28; London: SCM, 1959) 19 n. 2. Here perhaps belongs the note of al-Qirqisani concerning the sect whose writings were discovered in a cave; cf. L. Nemoy, "Al Qirqisani's Account of the Jewish Sects and Christianity," *HUCA* 7 (1930) 317-97, esp. 326-27, 363-64; B. Chiesa and W. Lockwood, *Ya'qub al-Qirqisani on Jewish Sects and Christianity* (Judentum und Umwelt 10; Frankfurt am Main: Lang, 1984) 102, 134-35.

[6]   Is Isa 9:14, attested by all textual witnesses, a polemical actualization inserted by a sectarian scribe? Cf. M. Goshen-Gottstein, "Hebrew Syntax and the History of Bible Text," *Textus* 8 (1973) 100-106.

[7]   See S. Talmon, "Yom Hakkippurim in the Habakkuk Scroll," *Bib* 32 (1951) 549-63, esp. 554.

[8]   See, however, C. Rabin, "Notes on the Habakkuk Scroll and the Zadokite Documents," *VT* 5 (1955) 148-62. On p. 152 Rabin pointed out that the sectarian reading *hon* in Hab 2:5 also appears paraphrased in CD 8:7.

preceded the formation of the sects themselves.

Thus it appears that in Hasmonean times a complex situation obtained: on the one hand, a variety of text-types were in use side by side, as witnessed by the Qumran libraries; on the other hand, respect for the biblical text (as an ideal) and attention in the process of copying it were already becoming the rule in the learned circles of the Jewish people. This may be considered as a first stage in the stabilization of the text.[9]

The situation just described does not apply to the Samaritan schism. It is well known that their copies of the Pentateuch contain a series of expansions asserting the sanctity of Mount Gerizim. I refer to the insertion of the words מול שכם in Deut 11:30 and especially to the additional commandment, appended to the Ten Commandments in Exodus 20 and Deuteronomy 5, enjoining the erection of an altar on that mountain. This precept has been forged with elements from Deut 11:29-30 and 27:2-7 where the Samaritan Pentateuch (= SP) reads Gerizim instead of Ebal extant in the MT. As a by-product of the addition of this new Tenth Commandment, all passages in Deuteronomy that mention the Lord's future choosing of a place "to set His name there" have been turned by the SP from imperfect (יבחר) to perfect (בחר).[10]

In my view, all these deviations of SP from the MT represent secondary Samaritan revisions. This applies to Deut 27:4 as well where the Vetus Latina corroborates SP by reading *Garzin* as against Ebal of the MT.[11] Suffice it to say that Mount Gerizim never appears as a holy site in the patriarchal legends nor in the historical books of the Bible. The sacred place of Elon Moreh (Gen 12:6-7) was near Shechem (Tel Ballaṭah), situated on the lowest slopes of the opposite mountain, Ebal. And the *temenos* containing the grave of Joseph (Josh 24:32) and the pillar erected by Jacob (Gen 33:19-20)[12] was in

---

9   S. Talmon, "The Old Testament Text," in P. R. Ackroyd and C. F. Evans (eds.), *The Cambridge History of the Bible*, vol. 1 (Cambridge: Cambridge University Press, 1970) 159-99, esp. 165-66.

10   Cf. J. A. Montgomery, *The Samaritans – The Earliest Jewish Sect: Their History, Theology and Literature* (Philadelphia, Winston, 1907) 234-39.

11   Cf. E. Tov, *Textual Criticism of the Hebrew Bible* (Assen/Maastricht: Van Gorcum; Minneapolis: Fortress, 1992) 95 n. 67. In his opinion, בהר גריזים in SP Deut 27:4 reflects the original reading.

12   Cf. J. Skinner, *A Critical and Exegetical Commentary on Genesis* (2nd ed., ICC; Edinburgh: T. & T. Clark, 1930) 416.

front of the city (Gen 33:18) i.e. on its outskirts, either on the slopes of Mount Ebal or down in the valley. Thus it appears that the sanctuary on Mount Gerizim was a *parvenu* among the holy places in the area of Shechem, a fact which explains why the Samaritan community felt the need of inserting the election of Mount Gerizim into the holy of holies, the Ten Commandments. Seen in this context, the composition of this literary-textual layer appears as a legitimization of Gerizim against competing Samarian sites, rather than a defiance against the supremacy of Jerusalem.

It is difficult to tie the composition of the "Gerizim-layer" in the SP to any specific episode. A superb Samaritan temple on Mount Gerizim, founded in the times of Antiochus III the Great (*ca.* 200 BCE), has been unearthed at the site.[13] But excavating beneath that stratum, the archeologist Dr. Yitzhak Magen has recently reached the remains of a former temple, dating to the late fifth or early fourth century BCE.[14] It is possible, indeed, that building activities coincided with scribal ones, but archeology does not offer a clue to a more specific identification. The Persian era as the time of composition of the SP "Gerizim-layer" is to be excluded, since at that time the Torah was still in the process of its formation. A low date in Hasmonean times is not very plausible, if one infers from the analogy of the paucity of sectarian corrections as discussed above. Of course, one might argue that the state of affairs in Jerusalem did not apply to Shechem while Jewish scribes preceded their Samaritan colleagues in developing a conservative attitude towards text transmission. All in all, a date at the end of the third century BCE, shortly preceding the building of the large sanctuary under Antiochus III, seems the most plausible. This would, up to a point, also take into account the paleographical character of the script in the Samaritan Pentateuch.[15]

A similar type of correction was introduced into biblical manuscripts by another dissident group. I refer to the mention of a city "in the Land of Egypt speaking the language of Canaan and taking

---

[13]   Y. Magen, "Mount Gerizim and the Samaritans," in F. Manns and E. Alliata (eds.), *Early Christianity in Context. Monuments and Documents* (Studium Biblicum Franciscanum, Collectio Maior; Jerusalem: Franciscan Press, 1993) 91-148, esp. 104. Cf. also U. Rappaport, "The Samaritans in the Hellenistic Period," *Zion* 55 (1989-90) 373-96 (Hebrew).

[14]   Oral communication by Dr. Y. Magen. I hereby thank him for his kindness.

[15]   See J. D. Purvis, *The Samaritan Pentateuch and the Origin of the Samaritan Sect* (HSM 2; Cambridge: Harvard University Press, 1968).

oath by the name of the Lord" in Isa 19:18. For the name of that city we have a number of variants:

עיר ההרס MT

עיר ההרס MT^{MSS} 1QIsa^a LXX^S (πόλις ασεδ ἡλίου) et al.

עיר הצדק LXX (πόλις-ασεδεκ)

Plausibly, the primary text ran עִיר הַחֶרֶס, hinting at the Egyptian city Heliopolis which was greatly populated by Jews. No sanctuary is mentioned in the verse in connection with the city. Later on, when a sanctuary was established in Leontopolis by the fugitive high-priest Onias III or his son Onias IV, the mention of the city in this verse was adapted to the name of Onias' family, Ṣadoq: עִיר הַצֶּדֶק, city of justice. Jerusalemite circles responded with a derogatory appellative: עִיר הַהֶרֶס, city of destruction.[16] In this case we have an exceptional instance of theological modifications introduced into the Biblical text as late as the second century BCE.

The study of secondary readings is instructive for the history of Jewish *aggadah*, especially concerning its very beginnings. Most significant in this context is the Qumran scroll of Samuel known as 4QSam^a which still awaits publication. This contains a text that at times departs from all other textual witnesses, such as the MT and the LXX. One such deviation is a large plus which obtains right in the middle of 1 Sam 10:27. The passage runs in English rendition: (completions are not marked here):[17]

> And Nahash king of the Ammonites sorely oppressed the Gadites and the Reubenites and gouged out all their right eyes and struck terror and dread in Israel. There was not left one among the Israelites in Transjordan whose right eye was not gouged out by Nahash king of the Ammonites; only seven thousand men fled from the Ammonites and entered Jabesh Gilead. About a month later . . .

I still adhere to my opinion, expressed about a decade ago, that the extra-sentences of 4QSam^a in this passage, also known to Josephus,

---

16   In another way, I. L. Seeligmann, *The Septuagint Version of Isaiah: A Discussion of its Problems* (Leiden: Brill, 1948) 68. Concerning the identity of the founder of the temple at Leontopolis, see his excursus: "Onias III and the Onias Temple in Heliopolis," 91-94.

17   F. M. Cross, "The Ammonite Oppression of the Tribes of Gad and Reuben: Missing Verses from 1 Samuel 11 Found in 4QSamuel^a," in H. Tadmor and M. Weinfeld (eds.), *History, Historiography and Interpretation* (Jerusalem: Magnes 1983) 148-58.

are a secondary *midrash aggadah*.[18] Indeed the additional story bears
an evident hallmark of midrash: one trait of a biblical hero is
exaggerated to the point of becoming his permanent property. Here
Nahash, the Ammonite king, is transformed into an inveterate eye-
gouger. Thus, midrash has entered into this biblical manuscript as a
kind of supplement to one of its stories.[19]

I believe we can even reckon the approximate date of the composition of this midrash. At the end of the Book of Samuel, in the story
of the consecration of the altar on Araunah's threshing floor (2
Samuel 24), 4QSam[a] again deviates from the MT. 4QSam[a] runs a text
similar to 1 Chronicles 21, a secondary text vis-à-vis the MT of 2
Samuel 24, since it solves the queries contained in that narrative one
by one.[20] A Samuel text similar to the one in 4QSam[a] was before the
Chronicler, which amounts to saying that it took shape before the
composition of the book of Chronicles in the mid-fourth century
BCE. In other words, stories such as the Nahash-midrash were
composed in the Persian period. The year 350 BCE is to be considered as a date *ante quem* for the beginnings of the Jewish midrash.

On our trail backwards to uncover earlier historical information
by the evidence of secondary readings, we now come to the question
of the double text of Jeremiah. There is a longer text, mainly
represented by the MT, and a shorter one, which presumably served
as Vorlage to the LXX of Jeremiah, and has been very partially
retrieved in the manuscript 4QJer[b].[21] I believe that the relation
between these two should not be explained on the basis of the routine
ruling *brevior lectio potior est*; rather both texts must be looked into
in detail, in order to find out the possible reasons for their
differences.

---

[18]   Cf. A. Rofé, "The Acts of Nahash according to 4QSam[a]," *IEJ* 32 (1982)
129-33.

[19]   For further arguments, cf. J. A. Sanders, "Hermeneutics of Text Criticism," *Textus* 18 (1995) 1-26, esp. 22-26.

[20]   For further details I refer the reader to my study: "4QSam[a] in the Light of
Historico-Literary Criticism: The Case of 2 Sam 24 and 1 Chr 21," in A. Vivian
(ed.), *Biblische und Judaistische Studien* (Festschrift für P. Sacchi; Frankfurt am
Main: Lang, 1990) 100-119.

[21]   J. G. Janzen, *Studies in the Text of Jeremiah* (HSM 6; Cambridge: Harvard
University Press, 1973). E. Tov ("Three Fragments of Jeremiah from Qumran
Cave 4," *RevQ* 15 [1992] 531-42) has recently introduced a distinction between
three separate scrolls, 4QJer[b,d,e].

A case in point is the divine epithet צְבָאוֹת.[22] In the MT of Jeremiah it appears eighty-two times; in the LXX it is represented sixteen times only, most of them in two well defined collections: the book of restoration (Jeremiah 30–33; LXX 37–40) and the prophecies against the nations (chaps. 25; 46–51; LXX 25–32). How can this phenomenon be explained?

In my opinion, it should be considered in conjunction with the absence of the epithet צְבָאוֹת from the books Genesis–Judges and Ezekiel and the traces of its being erased from several passages in Samuel and Kings: certain editors of biblical books endeavored to obliterate this appellation of the Lord from the sacred books. Apparently, they took offense to the "Hosts" (צְבָאוֹת), because they sensed in it a recognition of the "Host of Heaven." Actually, polemics against the worship of astral deities is clearly preserved in Hos 13:4 according to the LXX and one Qumran manuscript (4QXII^c):[23]

> But I am the Lord your god, who establishes the heaven and creates the earth, whose hands have created all the host of heaven; but I did not show them to you that you would go after them . . .

The reading is undoubtedly secondary. However, it joins the editorial operations mentioned above in documenting an opposition to astral worship at a certain phase of the formation of the biblical canon. Thus we reach the conclusion that astral religion, far from being limited to the times of the Assyrian supremacy (2 Kgs 21:3-5; 23:5, 11), still troubled observant Jews in the late Persian days. The interpolation in Hos 13:4, together with the editorial deletions from biblical books, particularly from Jeremiah, have led us to this result.

The shorter, sometimes secondary, text of Jeremiah presents, by its very omissions, some substantial information even about the sixth century BCE, i.e. late Babylonian and early Persian era. LXX Jeremiah 52 lacks all three mentions of the exile of Zedekiah's people contained in the MT (vv. 15, 27b, 28-30). How is this difference to be construed? As far as I can see, the reports about exiles at the fall of Jerusalem in 586 BCE were deleted from Jeremiah 52 in order to deny Zedekiah's people any survival: they were all and sundry wiped

---

22   I summarize here the arguments presented in "The name YHWH ṢEBAʾOT and the Shorter Recension of Jeremiah," in *Prophetie und geschichtliche Wirklichkeit im alten Israel* (Festschrift für S. Herrmann; Stuttgart: Kohlhammer, 1991) 307-15.

23   4QXII^c frag. 8 has recently been published; cf. R. Fuller, "A Critical Note on Hosea 12:10 and 13:4," *RB* 98 (1991) 343-57.

out.[24] The same lot befell the vessels of the temple that had remained after the first despoilment with Jehoiachin's exile. According to the MT Jer 27:19-22 they would one day be restored from Babylon; according to the LXX in this passage (34:19-22), they were never to be returned![25] These allegations accord with those Deuteronomistic speeches announcing salvation to the exiles of the first deportation as against annihilation to the remainder (Jer 24:1-10; 29:10-14, 16-20). These speeches, and later the deletions in LXX Jeremiah 27 and 52, reflect the mutual aversion of two Jewish factions in the exilic and early postexilic periods,[26] an antagonism that can hardly be dated later than the fourth generation after the fall of Jerusalem.

Thus, if I see it right, the shorter text of Jeremiah submits important data for the history of Israel in a period for which the documentation at our disposal is extremely scanty.

The corollary of the present discussion is that in the study of the texts of sacred literature secondary readings frequently are more revealing than primary ones, since secondary readings can be used as a source for the history of the community that preserved the holy writings.

One additional conclusion is in order as to the principal aim of biblical text-criticism. It is not the recovery of a presumed original text,[27] but rather the pursuit, step by step, of the history of the text. The task is to follow, as far as possible, the various phases of the transmission of the texts, in order to extract from them all possible information concerning the religious community which preserved and transmitted the sacred books.

---

[24]   See A. Rofé, "Not Exile but Annihilation for Zedekiah's People: The Purport of Jeremiah 52 in the Septuagint," in L. Greenspoon and O. Munnich (eds.), *VIII Congress of the International Organization for Septuagint and Cognate Studies: Paris 1992* (SBLSCS 41; Atlanta: Scholars, 1995) 165-70, where the argument is made in detail.

[25]   This point was brought to my attention by Prof. Christopher Seitz, Yale University, at my lecture there in April 1994.

[26]   These conclusions also affect the date of Ezek 11:14-21. In another way, M. Greenberg, *Ezekiel 1–20* (AB 22; Garden City: Doubleday, 1983) 203-205.

[27]   See Tov, *Textual Criticism*, 288, where he writes: " . . . textual criticism aims at the 'original' form of the biblical books as defined by scholars." However, further on he admits: "it is now possible to formulate the aims of the textual criticism of the Bible. The study of biblical text involves an investigation of its development, its copying and transmission and of the processes which created readings and texts over the centuries" (pp. 289-90).

CONTRASTING AS A TRANSLATION TECHNIQUE
IN THE LXX OF PROVERBS

Johann Cook

INTRODUCTION

The translator of the Septuagint version of Proverbs has correctly been classified as a unique translator by Gerleman, Brock, Gammie, Tov, and others.[1] The essence of the uniqueness of this translation is found in the creative way in which the translator renders his parent text on various levels; on the level of semantics, syntax as well as issues of style. In addition he does not refrain from adding extensively to this parent text. He actually added some 17 strophes to 9:12 and 18 in connection with Dame Folly.[2] I am also of the opinion that the translator is responsible for the nuanced addition of the simile on the bee[3] in the context of that of the ant in Prov 6:8, which again represents a rather extensive addition of three clusters of strophes in comparison to the MT.

In order to be able to evaluate these rather extensive additions, as well as other smaller ones, it is necessary to take a holistic approach to variant readings. As is commonly known there are two distinguishable methods[4] as far as the textual criticism of the Hebrew Bible

---

[1]   S. P. Brock, "The Phenomenon of Biblical Translation in Antiquity," in S. Jellicoe (ed.), *Studies in the Septuagint: Origins, Recensions, and Interpretations* (New York: Ktav, 1974) 551; E. Tov, "Recensional Differences between the Massoretic Text and the Septuagint of Proverbs," in H. W. Attridge et. al. (eds.), *Of Scribes and Scrolls, Studies on the Hebrew Bible, Intertestamental Judaism, and Christian Origins Presented to John Strugnell* (Lanham: University Press of America, 1990) 43-56; G. Gerleman, *Studies in the Septuagint. III. Proverbs* (N.F. 1.52. Nr 3; Lund: Lunds Universitets Arsskrift, 1956) and J. G. Gammie, "The Septuagint of Job: Its Poetic Style and Relationship to the Septuagint of Proverbs," *CBQ* 49 (1987) 16.

[2]   J. Cook, "זרה אשה (Proverbs 1–9 Septuagint): A Metaphor for Foreign Wisdom?" *ZAW* 106 (1994) 470-74.

[3]   See R. L. Giese, "Strength through Wisdom and the Bee in LXX-Prov 6,8a-c," *Bib* 73 (1992) 404-11.

[4]   This distinction was evident yet again at one of the sessions set aside for

is concerned. The one, which is characteristic of the Cross school, concentrates on individual variants, searching for the original readings. The other prefers to look at the broader picture. The UBS Bible project is an appropriate example of this approach. James Sanders[5] is by far the most prominent exponent of the latter approach. Although he is a brilliant and well versed textual critic,[6] he consistently chooses to account for the larger context. To him the *story*,[7] and not the *individual variant*, is of primary importance. In what follows I pay tribute to this outstanding biblical scholar by endeavouring, as he does, to understand the larger picture of a translation unit, in this instance the Septuagint version of Proverbs. As will become apparent in due course, it is an interesting and significant picture, quite different from that of the Hebrew version (MT).

Of crucial importance for our endeavours to understand this specific translation unit is the overriding role specific ideological/religious perspectives play in the translator's rather free and creative rendering of his *Vorlage*. He consequently does not "adapt" his parent text[8] solely on the basis of stylistic semantic, or syntactic considerations. In many instances he has some "ideological" perspective in mind when adapting his *Vorlage*. One such decisive

---

text criticism at the recent SBL meeting in Philadelphia. Sanders was alone in his more encompassing approach, over against F. M. Cross, E. Ulrich and E. Tov, the other members of the panel.

5   Another scholar who has consistently proposed an emcompassing approach towards variants is S. Talmon. See his contributions in F. Cross and S. Talmon, *Qumran and the History of the Biblical Text* (Cambridge: Harvard University Press, 1975), and his more recent work, *The World of Qumran from Within* (Jerusalem: Magnes Press; Leiden: Brill, 1989). A. van der Kooij can also be grouped here; see his "Accident or Method? On 'Analogical' Interpretation in the Old Greek of Isaiah and 1QIsa," *BO* 43 (1986) 366-76.

6   See his outstanding publication of the Psalm Scroll from Qumran cave 11, *The Dead Sea Psalm Scroll* (Ithaca: Cornell University Press, 1967), which he completed in a much shorter period of time than any of the other editors had done in respect of Qumran material assigned to them.

7   Hence his interest in story telling. See his work with the significant title, *From Sacred Story to Sacred Text* (Philadelphia: Fortress, 1987).

8   I am of the opinion that this parent text does not differ extensively from the MT; see my arguments in *The Septuagint of Proverbs: מִשְׁלֵי and/or παροιμίαι?* (VTSup 69; Leiden: Brill, 1997), which concern the Hellenistic coloring of LXX Proverbs.

"theological" concept is to this translator *contrasts* or *dualisms*. In practically each chapter he concentrates on such contrasts which he finds in his parent text. And, as I will shortly indicate, he then emphasizes these dualisms even more explicitly than the parent text. This is not a totally novel perspective. That the translator of Proverbs had a predilection for antithesis has already been observed by Gerleman.[9] However, the extent to which this translator actually applies "religiously" orientated contrasts is so conspicuous that it can be seen as a translation technique followed by him. From this statement it should already be evident that I have a more encompassing view of the issue of translation technique, which should not be restricted exclusively to the area of linguistics, as is done, for instance, by the Helsinki school,[10] but is applicable also to the level of exegesis.[11]

In this contribution I shall therefore concentrate on the issue of contrasts as found in specific passages, choosing evidence from chaps. 1, 2, 11, and 31. I need to remind the reader that Proverbs in the Septuagint is subject to unique problems. The fundamental problem is that it has not yet been published in the Göttingen series. Therefore we do not have an Old Greek text available. In addition, the LXX of Proverbs contains a multitude of double translations, doublets, and later Hexaplaric additions. As a matter of fact, this text has an extremely complicated transmission history. The possibility of inner Greek corruptions must therefore consistently be in the mind of the researcher who is studying Proverbs.

CONTRASTS IN PROVERBS CHAPTERS 1 AND 2

The translator creatively approaches his parent text on three levels—those of semantics, syntax, and style:

(1) On the semantic level. A close reading of this chapter provides clear evidence that the translator endeavoured to make his parent text as clear as possible. It would seem as if this Hebrew text did not differ extensively from the MT. On a lexical level he used Greek

---

[9]   Gerleman, *Studies in the Septuagint. III. Proverbs*, 18.

[10]   See A. Aejmelaeus, *On the Trail of the Translators (Collected Essays)* (Kampen: Kok, 1993) 2.

[11]   This contribution was completed during my stay at the University of Leiden while on sabbatical leave in 1995. In connection with a larger project I had many fruitful discussions with Arie van der Kooij on exegetical methodology.

words which are intended to express the nuance of the Hebrew as he understood them. Very few, if any, stereotypes were identified in this chapter. The creative approach of the translator is the primary reason for this situation. Consequently a Hebrew lexeme such as חָכְמָה is rendered variously by the Greek translator. σοφία is used in most cases, but other equivalents are γνῶσις, ἐντολάς, πηγὴ ζωῆς, and προσεχόντως. The Greek noun, σοφία, in its turn, is used as the rendition of various Hebrew lexemes: חכמה, דעת, תבונה, בינה, מוסר, מחשבת, and שׂכל. חָכְמָה is the most common rendering.

A characteristic of this specific translator is his application of "explicative" additions to express the meaning of a Hebrew term. The adjectives νέος in v. 4 and χρύσεον in v. 9 are telling examples. Similarly, he also uses specific word combinations. In v. 3 מוּסָר הַשְׂכֵּל is explicated by στροφὰς λόγων, and in v. 6 by σκοτεινὸν λόγον in connection with מְלִיצָה.

(2) On the syntactical level. That the translator has a creative attitude towards his parent text is clear not only from the lexical items which he applies, but also from the syntactical constructions. Verses 2, 3, 4, and 6 commence with an infinitive construct in MT. But the LXX uses infinitives in vv. 2 and 3 in order to render motive clauses, in v. 4 the particle ἵνα plus a subjunctive, in v. 5 a participle together with the particle γάρ, and an indicative in v. 6. This creative approach results in part from the fact that the translator had a different understanding of the syntactical coherence of these first seven verses.

There are also other syntactical constructions which he understood differently from the MT. Whereas the MT has a conditional clause in v. 10, the Greek translator interpreted the verse somewhat differently, in line with his creative attitude. The verse is not opened with a conditional statement as in the MT, but with a negative command. In the second stich, which in the MT is the beginning of v. 11, the translator indeed does use a conditional clause similar to that in the MT. Verse 17 is explicitly translated as a rhetorical question by the nuanced addition of the negating particle οὐ.

A major difference between the MT and LXX on a syntactic level occurs in v. 22. The Hebrew has a temporal clause in the first stich which the translator has changed into a conditional clause using the particle ἄν. Also the apodosis (οὐκ αἰσχυνθήσονται) has no equivalent in the Hebrew text. Verse 23 is connected to v. 22 by changing the subject of the sentence from 2nd to 3rd person plural.

Verse 26 is the apodosis of the conditional clause that commences in v. 24. The Hebrew particle גַּם is used in the MT whereas the Septuagint used τοιγαροῦν ending the conditional phrase in a final clause. The beginning of the conditional clause in v. 24 is also expressed differently in the LXX. For the particle יַעַן the translator used ἐπειδή. The Hebrew particle expresses causality,[12] whereas the Greek equivalent is aimed at temporal nuances. Also the following conditional clause in v. 27 is rendered differently in the LXX. In the MT an infinitive plus a preposition בְּבֹא as introduction to the protasis occurs twice. In the Greek the particles ὡς ἄν plus a subjunctive is used as equivalent. The apodosis in v. 28 is expressed in the MT by means of the particle אָז plus an imperfect, which the translator rendered by the Greek phrase ὅταν ἐπικαλέσησθε.

The translator's different view on v. 32 has implications for the macro-structure of practically the whole passage. He made a nuanced and significant connection between v. 32 and the previous verses. The term κακοί of vv. 28 and 33, which in the final analysis goes back to and also includes the "fools" (οἱ δὲ ἄφρονες) of v. 22, is made to refer also to those who wronged the innocent. These fools are then killed, and not the innocent, as seen by the MT. The Greek translator thus followed the syntax of the Hebrew to some extent, but expressed the individual clauses in a typically Greek linguistic manner. In some instances he brings about nuanced changes in order to deliberately express specific meanings. This is the case in vv. 22, 23, and 32 where he clearly structured his translation so as to emphasize a religious theme, the contrast between the good and the bad.

(3) Style. That the translator is thoroughly versed in the Greek language is, *inter alia*, demonstrated in his translation of the first chapter. He applies the Greek particles creatively. The particle τε is used only in the first six verses and is in most cases added for stylistic effect. The particle δέ is used abundantly in the entire chapter and again is in most cases added in order to attain stylistic fluency. The word combinations to which I already referred are another stylistic characteristic. In addition to their semantic implications they also balance the Greek text stylistically. The rendition of the noun חַטָּאִים in v. 10 by the phrase ἄνδρες ἀσεβεῖς is an appropriate example. Rhyme certainly also played a part in the translator's construction of

---

12   P. Joüon and T. Muraoka, *A Grammar of Biblical Hebrew* (Rome: Biblical Institute Press, 1991) 637.

these verses. The ending of the infinitives in vv. 2 and 3, as well as the ending of the word παροιμίαι in v. 1 seems to me more than just coincidence. And again the ending of specific words are conspicuous. The ending -ωμεν in vv. 11, 12 (2x), and 13 is caught by the eye and the ear. The endings -αι and -ει are conspicuous in vv. 20-22. In v. 23 alliteration appears to have played a role. In the second stichos the long vowel -ῇ jumps in the ear (eye) in ἰδοὺ προήσομαι ὑμῖν ἐμῆς πνοῆς ῥῆσιν. This could be one of the reasons why ῥῆσιν was added. The same argument could also apply to the third stich, διδάξω δὲ ὑμᾶς τὸν ἐμὸν λόγον, where the Hebrew is rendered somewhat differently. The plural דְּבָרַי is translated by means of the singular τὸν ἐμὸν λόγον. In my view the translator considered two issues: On a semantical level he opted for the interpretation of רוּחִי ("my spirit") by means of ἐμῆς πνοῆς ῥῆσιν. It is also possible that religious considerations came into play. He also structured these two stichs stylistically as I indicated.

The same stylistic considerations seem to have been taken into account in the expression of negative nuances in v. 24. The MT has the verb מֵאֵן in the first hemi-stich and the particle for non-existence, אֵין, in the second hemi-stich. The Greek translator followed his own way by using the negative particle in both cases, οὐχ ὑπηκούσατε and οὐ προσείχετε. In v. 25, on the contrary, the translator opts for a Greek verb (ἠπειθήσατε) without the negating particle, in order to express the negative nuance of the Hebrew construction לֹא אֲבִיתֶם. This interpretation is underscored by the fact that the translator rendered the verb אָבָה by using the negative particle in v. 30 (οὐδὲ ἤθελον).

Harmonization is another stylistic feature applied by the translator. It certainly was a contributing factor in the translation of ἐμῆς πνοῆς ῥῆσιν (v. 23), where the translator probably took the third stich into account. I think that this also explains the lexeme λόγους used for יְדִי in v. 24.

In my opinion the translator of Proverbs in the final analysis was guided by religious motivations in the rendering of his text. This becomes apparent in his nuanced application of the above mentioned combination of words. In v. 3, for example, he used the phrase στροφὰς λόγων to explicate מוּסַר הַשְׂכֵּל, and in v. 6 σκοτεινὸν λόγον in connection with מְלִיצָה. These difficult terms all appear in a religiously pregnant context, namely that of righteousness, justice, wise words, etc. The most convincing example is found in vv. 10 and

11, where the translator contrasts the two clearly religious groupings of the ἀνὴρ δίκαιος and the ἄνδρες ἀσεβεῖς. In both instances the MT has only one word, הַחַטָּאִים, which in v. 10 is translated by means of ἄνδρες ἀσεβεῖς, and בְּקִי in v. 11 by ἄνδρα δίκαιον. Another pertinent example occurs in vv. 20-23, where the translator applied alliteration with the aim of giving the Hebrew text a religious thrust. Also the addition of the noun ῥῆσιν in the phrase, ἰδοὺ προήσομαι ὑμῖν ἐμῆς πνοῆς ῥῆσιν, is in the final analysis religiously motivated.

(4) Moralizing dualisms. Contrasts or dualisms abound in this chapter. On the one hand, there are the ἄκακοι (vv. 4 and 22); παιδοὶ νέοι (v. 4); σοφοί (v. 6); the ἀνὴρ δίκαιος (v. 11); and νηπίοι (v. 32). On the other hand, the translator refers to ἀσεβεῖς (vv. 7, 22, 32); ἄνδρες ἀσεβεῖς (v. 10); ἄνδροι παρανόμοι (v. 18); ἄφρονες (v. 22); and κακοί (v. 28).

The use of contrasts and dualisms seems to me to be one of the important techniques of this translator. As can be clearly observed, he stresses antipoles more extensively than the MT. The same trend is found in other chapters in Proverbs. Chapter 2 is divided neatly into two parts by the use of the exclamation particle ὦ in v. 13, to bring about this significant dichotomy. He then applies dualisms in order to contrast the good and the evil. Prominent contrasts in this chapter are ὁδοὶ δικαιωμάτων (v. 8) and ἄξονοι ἀγαθοί (v. 9); ὁδοὶ εὐθείας and ὁδοὶ σκότοι (v. 13); τρίβοι σκολιαί and καμπύλαι αἱ τροχιαί (v. 15); ὁδὸς εὐθείας in v. 16 and τρίβοι εὐθείας in v. 19 and τρίβοι ἀγαθαί and τρίβοι δικαιοσύνης in v. 20. The negative poles are ὁδὸς κακός (v. 12); ὁδοὶ ἀσεβῶν and οἱ παράνομοι in v. 22. Other highly significant contrastive terms are καλὴ βουλὴ in v. 11 and κακὴ βουλὴ in v. 17.

This chapter also has its quota of good and evil personages. As far as *the good* grouping goes, the translator speaks about the upright (τοῖς κατορθοῦσι) in v. 7; χρηστοί (upright), ἄκακοι (innocent), εὐθεῖς (upright), and ὅσιοι (holy) in v. 21. The negative poles of this grouping (*the bad*) are (ἀνὴρ) λαλοῦντος μηδὲν πιστόν (a man who speaks untruth) in v. 12; οἱ ἐγκαταλείποντες ὁδοὺς εὐθείας (those who forsake straight ways), in order "to follow dark ways" (τοῦ πορεύεσθαι ἐν ὁδοῖς σκότους) (v. 13). They rejoice in evil (οἱ εὐφραινόμενοι ἐπὶ κακοῖς καὶ χαίροντες ἐπὶ διαστροφῇ κακῇ) (v. 14). Their paths are crooked (τρίβοι σκολιαί) and their ways are devious (καμπύλαι αἱ τροχιαί) (v. 15); they are ultimately the ungodly (ἀσεβῶν) and the transgressors (οἱ δὲ παράνομοι) (v. 22).

They have all been mislead by the bad advice (κακὴ βουλή) (v. 17).

It is not difficult to see the religious, moral content in these dualisms. To me it is clear that this "theological" aspect actually plays a determinative role in their application by the translator, who takes into account religious considerations when adapting his parent text. As already said, in adapting his parent text he has mostly a specific religious motif in mind, and not any other reason.

I shall now present evidence that he goes even further than this. For when he deems it necessary he even brings about major structural changes on account of religious, dualistic considerations.

THE DIFFERENT STRUCTURE OF CHAPTER 31

Towards the end of Proverbs the major differences emerge in the sequence of some chapters as compared to the MT.[13] Whereas the first 23 chapters are in the same order as in the MT, the order of the last eight chapters differs.

LXX:[14] I-III		MT: 1:1–24:1-22
VI, part 1	30:1-14	(The words of Agur, 1st part)
IV	24:23-34	(Words of the wise)
VI, part 2	30:15-33	(The words of Agur, 2nd part)
VII	31:1-9	(The words of Lemuel, 1st part)
V	25–29	
VIII	31:10-31	(The words of Lemuel, 2nd part)

Chapter 31 is found in the Septuagint in two places. The first nine verses follow immediately after 30:9, which is then followed by chaps. 25–29. Directly after chap. 29 follows the rest of chap. 30. This interpolation has been interpreted differently. Scholars have argued that as all the other differences also the different sequence of the chapters reflects a deviating Hebrew *Vorlage*. Mezzacasa[15] and Eissfeldt[16] accept this possibility. Tov speaks of a recensionally different Hebrew text for "When the book of Proverbs was translated into Greek, presumably in the second century BCE, a scroll was used that contained an editorial stage of the book differing from the

---

[13] Interestingly enough no such differences occur in the first nine chapters.

[14] E. Tov, *Textual Criticism of the Hebrew Bible* (Assen: Van Gorcum; Minneapolis: Fortress, 1992) 337.

[15] G. Mezzacasa, *Il libro dei proverbi di Salomone: studio critico sulle aggiunte Greco-alessandrine* (Rome: Biblical Institute Press, 1913) 2-3.

[16] O. Eissfeldt, *Einleitung in das Alte Testament* (Tübingen: Mohr [Siebeck], 1956) 472.

one now contained in the MT."[17] Swete presents a nuanced perspective.[18] He considers the possibility that the translator was responsible for the changes, but also deems it possible that he could have used a recensionally different parent text.

It must also be considered that these textual differences are the result of mechanical factors, namely inner Greek corruptions. The end of chap. 29 and 31:10 agree to some extent, as I will shortly indicate. Consequently, one could argue that a later revisor actually combined these two passages. Tov offers an interesting explanation for the order in the LXX.[19] He correctly observed that not all the sayings in chap. 30 are actually the words of Agur. Similarly, chap. 31 is made up of two clearly distinguisable parts. On the one hand, the introduction, vv. 1-9, and on the other hand, the last passage (vv. 10-31) which consists of an acrosticon praising the virtuous housewife. Interestingly enough it is exactly here where the order of the chapters differ. Tov argues that in the final analysis the arrangement of the LXX is more logical than that of the MT.

In order to solve this problem it is necessary to take a closer look at the relationship between Proverbs 29 and 31. The proverbs in chapter 29 are predominantly structured in antithetic parallelism,[20] contrasting various groupings; the righteous and the wicked, the scoffers and the wise, etc. The last couple of verses pertain to the upright and the wicked. Verse 27 reads as follows:

תּוֹעֲבַת צַדִּיקִים אִישׁ עָוֶל וְתוֹעֲבַת רָשָׁע יְשַׁר־דָּרֶךְ

The unjust are an abomination to the righteous, but the upright are an abomination to the wicked.

The Greek of this verse is:

βδέλυγμα δικαίοις ἀνὴρ ἄδικος
βδέλυγμα δὲ ἀνόμῳ κατευθύνουσα ὁδός

An unrighteous man is an abomination to a righteous man, and the direct way is an abomination to the wicked.

The Septuagint of Prov 31:10 reads:

γυναῖκα ἀνδρείαν τίς εὑρήσει;

---

17   Tov, "Recensional Differences," 53-56.

18   H. B. Swete, *An Introduction to the Old Testament in Greek* (Cambridge: Cambridge University Press, 1902) 241.

19   Tov, "Recensional Differences," 54.

20   W. McKane, *Proverbs: A New Approach* (London: SCM, 1970) 632.

τιμιωτέρα δέ ἐστιν λίθων πολυτελῶν ἡ τοιαύτη.

Who shall find a virtuous woman?
For such a one is more valuable than precious stones.

There seems to be a direct relationship between the last verse in
chap. 29 and 31:10 which follows upon it. The phrase ἀνὴρ ἄδικος
can certainly be seen as the antecedent of γυναῖκα ἀνδρείαν, even
though the contrast is of a different order from some of the other
categories I have discussed. It would therefore be appropriate to
argue, on the one hand, that in the process of translating, the
translator became aware of the fact that these two verses fit together
better than the beginning of chap. 30 and therefore simply changed
the sequence. As I mentioned earlier, it is also possible that a later
hand could have brought about this change.

On the other hand, it is true that also in the Hebrew these verses
are related. Chapter 29 speaks about the אִישׁ עָוֶל, whereas chap. 31
contrasts this with the reference to the אֵשֶׁת־חַיִל. However, it must be
remembered that in the MT and all versions these verses are separated by chap. 30 and the first 9 verses of chap. 31! It would mean
therefore, theoretically at least, that these changes could have come
about in the *Vorlage.* We do of course have no textual evidence,
other than the LXX, of such a different text. It is not easy to decide
the case. If one would argue from the perspective of a free translator, such as the translator of Proverbs certainly is, then one would
ascribe these differences to him. There is, fortunately, a decisive
argument in this regard.

As I have demonstrated abundantly, one of the characteristics of
the Greek translator is that he contrasts specific entities even more
than the MT. Tov has given many examples of the way this translator
contrasts certain groupings.[21] For example, in 11:16, the Hebrew
reads אֵשֶׁת־חֵן and the LXX γυνὴ εὐχάριστος. The rest of the verse
in the LXX, however, contains an antithesis of this *graceful woman,*
namely the woman that hates (γυνὴ μισοῦσα) righteousness, which
has no equivalent in the MT. The MT of Prov 11:16 reads:

אֵשֶׁת־חֵן תִּתְמֹךְ כָּבוֹד וְעָרִיצִים יִתְמְכוּ־עֹשֶׁר

The Greek reads:

γυνὴ εὐχάριστος ἐγείρει ἀνδρὶ δόξαν
θρόνος δὲ ἀτιμίας γυνὴ μισοῦσα δίκαια

---

21   Tov, "Recensional Differences," 46.

πλούτου ὀκνηροὶ ἐνδεεῖς γίνονται
οἱ δὲ ἀνδρεῖοι ἐρείδονται πλούτῳ

The Septuagint contains two stichoi that have no equivalent in the MT. Tov correctly ascribes these additions to the translator.[22] Taking this explanation as a lead, as well as the evidence of chaps. 1–2, which I presented above, I would argue that by the same token the translator also changed his parent text in 31:10, by simply rearranging it in order to contrast the ἀνὴρ ἄδικος and γυναῖκα ἀνδρείαν as I described above.

To me it is therefore clear that this translator went to rather great pains in order to explicate his parent text. There are of course more than just this one example of a chapter that has a different position in LXX compared with the MT. I do not imply that the translator is actually responsible for all the differences in the sequence of chapters, because I still need to study all the other examples. However, if my analysis of Proverbs 31 is correct, it must have implications for the extent to which translators would be prepared to adapt their parent texts. The translator of Proverbs actually changed the sequence of the chapters, probably for contextual reasons. The difference between the sequence of the two parts in chap. 31 should therefore not be seen as the result of another edition, based on a different recension.

CONCLUSION

Taking the work of Jim Sanders as a lead, I endeavoured to look at the broader picture of the Septuagint version of Proverbs. In some four chapters I showed that the translator actually stresses more extensively contrasts that are found in the Hebrew (MT). This is done on various levels. In some cases he renders these dualisms by adding small explicative adjectives. The addition of the adjective νέος in the combination παιδὶ δὲ νέῳ (Prov 1:4) is a pertinent example. In other instances he makes use of word combinations in order to underscore the contrastive contents of a Hebrew lexeme. The combination ἄνδρες ἀσεβεῖς for חַטָּאִים is one example. In 11:16 the translator even added two stichs in regard to the graceful woman, so as to contrast her with her opposite, the hateful woman. The fundamentally religious concept of contrasts (dualisms), was so important to this translator that he even changed the order of one chapter in compari-

---

22   Tov, "Recensional Differences," 47.

son with the MT. For this reason I think it appropriate to define his contrasting activity as a translation technique. This is, however, only one of the characteristical techniques used by this translator in order to explicate his parent text. To me it is clear that his text did not differ too extensively from the MT. Significant are also all the dualisms which this translator employed, a technique which is characteristic of apocalyptic literature. The translator's presumed polemical stance[23] towards Hellenism of the day ties in neatly with this perspective. However, I will address this issue in another context.

---

23   Cook, "אשה זרה (Proverbs 1–9 Septuagint)," 474-75.

PART FOUR

THE FIRST TESTAMENT IN THE SECOND

FROM "HOUSE OF PRAYER" TO "CAVE OF ROBBERS" JESUS' PROPHETIC CRITICISM OF THE TEMPLE ESTABLISHMENT

Craig A. Evans

JESUS IN THE TEMPLE PRECINCTS

Shortly after entering Jerusalem Jesus demonstrated in the Temple precincts. This important and disputed episode is presented in Mark 11:15-18 as follows:

15 Καὶ ἔρχονται εἰς Ἱεροσόλυμα. καὶ εἰσελθὼν εἰς τὸ ἱερὸν ἤρξατο ἐκβάλλειν τοὺς πωλοῦντας καὶ τοὺς ἀγοράζοντας ἐν τῷ ἱερῷ, καὶ τὰς τραπέζας τῶν κολλυβιστῶν καὶ τὰς καθέδρας τῶν πωλούντων τὰς περιστερὰς κατέστρεψεν, 16 καὶ οὐκ ἤφιεν ἵνα τις διενέγκῃ σκεῦος διὰ τοῦ ἱεροῦ. 17 καὶ ἐδίδασκεν καὶ ἔλεγεν αὐτοῖς, Οὐ γέγραπται ὅτι Ὁ οἶκός μου οἶκος προσευχῆς κληθήσεται πᾶσιν τοῖς ἔθνεσιν; ὑμεῖς δὲ πεποιήκατε αὐτὸν σπήλαιον λῃστῶν. 18 καὶ ἤκουσαν οἱ ἀρχιερεῖς καὶ οἱ γραμματεῖς καὶ ἐζήτουν πῶς αὐτὸν ἀπολέσωσιν, ἐφοβοῦντο γὰρ αὐτόν, πᾶς γὰρ ὁ ὄχλος ἐξεπλήσσετο ἐπὶ τῇ διδαχῇ αὐτοῦ.

15 And he enters Jerusalem. And going into the Temple he began to throw out those who were selling and buying in the Temple, and he overturned the tables of the money-changers and seats of those selling the doves. 16 And he was not permitting anyone to carry a vessel through the Temple. 17 And he was teaching and saying to them, "Is it not written, 'My house shall be called a house of prayer for all the nations'? But you have made it a 'cave of robbers.'" 18 And the ruling priests and the scribes heard it and were seeking how to destroy him, for they feared him, for the whole crowd was amazed at his teaching.

This passage raises at least two intriguing questions. The first and most demanding inquires into the grounds for Jesus' criticism. To describe the Temple as a "cave of robbers," which alludes to Jer 7:11, constitutes severe criticism. But on what basis has Jesus made this charge? Was it simply the money-changing and the trafficking in sacrificial animals that angered him? But were not these activities necessary and legitimate, if the pragmata of the Temple cultus were to be observed, as commanded in the Torah? In what way did these activities undermine the vision of Isa 56:7, so that the Temple could not be termed a "house of prayer for all the nations"? Jesus' angry criticism seems to be imply that the Temple had become in some sense disqualified from its divinely appointed purpose. These questions require careful consideration.

This last point gives rise to the second question that concerns us. In what sense did Jesus think of the Temple as a house of prayer for the nations?[1] Why was that important to him? Did concern for the nations form part of his agenda?[2] Did Jesus entertain hopes that the Temple someday might become the religious capital of the world, with the nations dutifully making pilgrimages? It will be proposed below that Jesus' concern with the nations was an integral part of his restorative hopes and that his appeal to Isa 56:7 offers an important clue into his self-understanding.

We are also confronted with the question of the authenticity of the passage. E. P. Sanders has little doubt of the historicity of the Temple action in general terms. But he questions the authenticity of Mark 11:17, where fragments of Isa 56:7 and Jer 7:11 appear. He also doubts that v. 16, where Jesus does not permit people to carry vessels through the precincts, reflects genuine reminiscence of what transpired. He suspects that an early Christian scribe has attempted to

---

[1]   It is not always easy to determine the sense of τὰ ἔθνη. Often it refers to "the nations," as distinct from the nation or people of Israel. Other times τὰ ἔθνη refer to "the Gentiles," as distinct from the Jewish people (see BAG; *TDNT* 2.369-72). "Nations" is probably the correct nuance for Isa 56:7. There is no compelling reason to think that at Mark 11:17 Jesus understood the epithet differently.

[2]   Some scholars, such as H. Kasting (*Die Anfänge der urchristlichen Mission: Eine historische Untersuchung* [BEvT 55; Munich: Kaiser, 1969]), trace the Gentile mission to Paul and the Hellenistic Church. M. Hengel ("The Origins of the Christian Mission," in Hengel, *Between Jesus and Paul: Studies in the Earliest History of Christianity* [London: SCM; Philadelphia: Fortress, 1983] 48-64, 166-79) believes the Gentile mission grew out of Jesus' conduct. Some older German work (e.g. F. Spitta, *Jesus und die Heidenmission* [Giessen: Töpelmann, 1909]; A. Schlatter, *Der Evangelist Matthäus* [6th ed., Stuttgart: Calwer, 1963]) argued that this mission was part of Jesus' conscious intention. For a more recent statement of this view, see E. Schnabel, "Jesus and the Beginnings of the Mission to the Gentiles," in J. B. Green and M. Turner (eds.), *Jesus of Nazareth: Lord and Christ. Essays on the Historical Jesus and New Testament Christology* (I. H. Marshall Festschrift; Carlisle: Paternoster; Grand Rapids: Eerdmans, 1994) 37-58. The results of the present study support Schnabel's conclusion.

cast Jesus into the light of a reformer, as opposed to that of a radical prophet who believes the Herodian-built Temple must be destroyed, in order to make way for the new, eschatological Temple.[3] But his interpretation encounters several difficulties. It is more probable that Mark's description of what Jesus did and said represents an incomplete, but genuine fragment of authentic tradition.[4] It will be shown that the allusions to Isaiah 56 and Jeremiah 7 support this position.

Both problems, that of the nature of Jesus' criticism of the Temple establishsment and his reasons for it, and that of the place of the nations in his program, will be addressed in this study. We begin with the second.

From Mark 11:15-18 one might infer that Jesus' mission included the nations, or Gentiles. After all, Jesus believes that God's house is supposed to be a "house of prayer for all the nations." But before making such an inference we must also take into account other passages that could suggest that Gentiles did not have a place in Jesus' mission. The three most important passages are Matt 10:5-7; 15:24; and Mark 7:24-30.[5] It will be helpful to cite them in the order just mentioned:

5 Τούτους τοὺς δώδεκα ἀπέστειλεν ὁ Ἰησοῦς παραγγείλας αὐτοῖς λέγων, Εἰς ὁδὸν ἐθνῶν μὴ ἀπέλθητε καὶ εἰς πόλιν Σαμαριτῶν μὴ εἰσέλθητε· 6 πορεύεσθε δὲ μᾶλλον πρὸς τὰ πρόβατα τὰ ἀπολωλότα οἴκου Ἰσραήλ. 7 πορευόμενοι δὲ κηρύσσετε λέγοντες ὅτι Ἤγγικεν ἡ βασιλεία τῶν οὐρανῶν.

5 These twelve Jesus sent out, charging them, saying, "Go nowhere among the Gentiles, and enter no town of the Samaritans, 6 but go rather to the lost sheep of the house of Israel. 7 And preach as you go, saying, 'The kingdom of heaven is at hand.'"

---

3   See E. P. Sanders, *Jesus and Judaism* (London: SCM; Philadelphia: Fortress, 1985) 61-76, 363-69.

4   See C. A. Evans, "Jesus' Action in the Temple: Cleansing or Portent of Destruction?" *CBQ* 51 (1989) 237-70; B. D. Chilton, *The Temple of Jesus: His Sacrificial Program Within a Cultural History of Sacrifice* (University Park: Penn State Press, 1992) 91-111. On the authenticity of the reference to the nations, see Z. Kato, *Die Völkermission im Markusevangelium* (Frankfurt and Bern: Lang, 1986) 109-11; R. Pesch, *Das Markusevangelium* (2 vols., HTKNT 2.1-2; 4th ed., Freiburg: Herder, 1991) 2.198-99.

5   These passages and other related ones are reviewed by J. Jeremias, *Jesus' Promise to the Nations* (SBT 24; London: SCM, 1958) 19-32; the first is treated by T. W. Manson, *Only to the House of Israel?* (London: Athlone, 1955; repr. Philadelphia: Fortress, 1964).

24 ὁ δὲ ἀποκριθεὶς εἶπεν, Οὐκ ἀπεστάλην εἰ μὴ εἰς τὰ πρόβατα τὰ ἀπολωλότα οἴκου Ἰσραήλ.

24 "I was sent only to the lost sheep of the house of Israel."

24 Ἐκεῖθεν δὲ ἀναστὰς ἀπῆλθεν εἰς τὰ ὅρια Τύρου. καὶ εἰσελθὼν εἰς οἰκίαν οὐδένα ἤθελεν γνῶναι, καὶ οὐκ ἠδυνήθη λαθεῖν· 25 ἀλλ' εὐθὺς ἀκούσασα γυνὴ περὶ αὐτοῦ, ἧς εἶχεν τὸ θυγάτριον αὐτῆς πνεῦμα ἀκάθαρτον, ἐλθοῦσα προσέπεσεν πρὸς τοὺς πόδας αὐτοῦ· 26 ἡ δὲ γυνὴ ἦν Ἑλληνίς, Συροφοινίκισσα τῷ γένει· καὶ ἠρώτα αὐτὸν ἵνα τὸ δαιμόνιον ἐκβάλῃ ἐκ τῆς θυγατρὸς αὐτῆς. 27 καὶ ἔλεγεν αὐτῇ, Ἄφες πρῶτον χορτασθῆναι τὰ τέκνα, οὐ γάρ ἐστιν καλὸν λαβεῖν τὸν ἄρτον τῶν τέκνων καὶ τοῖς κυναρίοις βαλεῖν. 28 ἡ δὲ ἀπεκρίθη καὶ λέγει αὐτῷ, Κύριε, καὶ τὰ κυνάρια ὑποκάτω τῆς τραπέζης ἐσθίουσιν ἀπὸ τῶν ψιχίων τῶν παιδίων. 29 καὶ εἶπεν αὐτῇ, Διὰ τοῦτον τὸν λόγον ὕπαγε, ἐξελήλυθεν ἐκ τῆς θυγατρός σου τὸ δαιμόνιον. 30 καὶ ἀπελθοῦσα εἰς τὸν οἶκον αὐτῆς εὗρεν τὸ παιδίον βεβλημένον ἐπὶ τὴν κλίνην καὶ τὸ δαιμόνιον ἐξεληλυθός.

24 And from there he arose and went away to the region of Tyre and Sidon. And he entered a house, and would not have any one know it; yet he could not be hid. 25 But immediately a woman, whose little daughter was possessed by an unclean spirit, heard of him, and came and fell down at his feet. 26 Now the woman was a Greek, a Syrophoenician by birth. And she begged him to cast the demon out of her daughter. 27 And he said to her, "Let the children first be fed, for it is not right to take the children's bread and throw it to the dogs." 28 But she answered him, "Yes, Lord; yet even the dogs under the table eat the children's crumbs." 29 And he said to her, "For this saying you may go your way; the demon has left your daughter." 30 And she went home, and found the child lying in bed, and the demon gone.

The Matthean passages may very well reflect the theology of the evangelist or that of his tradition. The parallels in Mark (6:7; cf. 1:15) and Luke (9:1-2; 10:3, 9) do not contain the saying that prohibits the Twelve from going among Gentiles. Our suspicion of redactional activity is confirmed when we observe the insertion of a similar saying in the Markan story of the Syrophoenician woman. Matthew adds, by way of explaining Jesus' initial rebuff of the woman: "I was sent only to the lost sheep of the house of Israel" (Matt 15:24).

But we should not assume that Matt 10:5-6 and 15:24 derive from the Matthean evangelist. It is more probable that this is traditional material which the evangelist has used as he saw fit. Nowhere else does the evangelist talk about Samaritans, so why, if he created this material, does he here? If the prohibition from going among Gentiles was part of his understanding of salvation history (i.e. the gospel goes first to Israel, then to the Gentiles), the evangelist has not made himself very clear. If the saying derives from Jesus, what could it have meant? If it is understood in connection with Jesus' ministry to the marginalized of Israel, to the "sinners" and tax collectors, then it could mean that Jesus enjoined his disciples to follow his example and go to the "lost sheep *within* the house of Israel." Here, the genitive οἴκου 'Ισραήλ is taken in the partitive sense.[6]

The Markan passage smacks of realism and surely cannot be assigned to Christians. It is hard to imagine the early Church, which was admitting Gentiles into its membership early on, generating the saying found in Mark 7:27: "Let the children first be fed, for it is not right to take the children's bread and throw it to the dogs." Adding weight to our suspicion that the entire pericope reflects authentic tradition is the fact that the woman, in a certain sense, bests Jesus in argument. Although initially refused, her request is granted. This point only adds to the improbability that the story originated in the early Church.[7]

Elsewhere in Matthew we find sayings that could be interpreted as being unsympathetic to a Gentile mission. One thinks of Jesus' injunction that the unrepentant and unresponsive member of the community be viewed "as a Gentile and a tax collector" (Matt 18:17); or Jesus' admonition that his followers show compassion even to their enemies: "If you greet only your brothers, what more do you do than others? Do not even Gentiles do the same?" (Matt 5:47). The Gentiles are singled out as greedy (Matt 6:32) and as poor examples in prayer (Matt 6:7).

But how much of this is dominical and how much is Matthean? In any event, there are several sayings in Matthew that suggest that the Gentiles are part of Jesus' mission, whether he himself fulfills this mission, or his apostles fulfill it. As the Missionary Discourse continues, the Twelve are told that they will be brought before

---

6   See the discussion in D. C. Allison, Jr., and W. D. Davies, *The Gospel According to Saint Matthew* (3 vols., ICC; Edinburgh: T. & T. Clark, 1988-97) 2.550-51; R. H. Gundry, *Matthew* (2nd ed., Grand Rapids: Eerdmans, 1994) 185. D. A. Hagner (*Matthew 1–13* [WBC 33A; Dallas: Word, 1993] 270-71) takes the genitive as epexegetical and so understands the "lost sheep" as all of Israel.

7   See B. D. Chilton, *A Galilean Rabbi and His Bible* (GNS 8; Wilmington: Glazier, 1984) 64-77; R. H. Gundry, *Mark* (Grand Rapids: Eerdmans, 1993) 380-81.

governors and kings for Jesus' sake, "for a testimony to them and to
the Gentiles" (10:18). Even the quotation of Isa 42:1-4 in Matt
12:18-21 carries with it promise of mission to the Gentiles. The task
of the servant is to "proclaim justice to the Gentiles" (Isa 42:1 = Matt
12:18) and "in his name the Gentiles will hope" (Isa 42:4 = Matt
12:20). Matthew's citation of this passage from Isaiah implies that the
Gentiles are part of the mission of Jesus the messianic servant. In the
eschatological discourse Mark's "gospel must first be preached to all
Gentiles" (Mark 13:10) becomes in Matthew "this gospel of the
kingdom will be preached throughout the whole world, as a
testimony to all Gentiles" (Matt 24:14). Mark's "first" is omitted, for
Israel, not the Gentiles, receives priority in Matthew. But the
Gentiles are still to hear of the good news of the kingdom. The
Gentiles will be gathered before the Matthean "son of man" (Matt
25:32) and are the object of the so-called Great Commission (Matt
28:19-20).

The sayings, "You are the salt of the earth" and "You are the light
of the world" (Matt 5:13a, 14a), are suggestive of a universal perspective. The second one may reflect Isa 49:6: ". . . to raise up the
tribes of Jacob and to restore the preserved of Israel; I will give you
as a light to the nations, that my salvation may reach the end of the
earth." In my judgment, these sayings are probably authentic, for
they advance no distinctive Christian doctrine,[8] while the second
saying merely reflects an idea drawn from Isaiah, which in various
forms appears in Jewish texts of late antiquity (e.g. *T. Levi* 14:3;
Apoc. Abr. 9:3; *b. Ber.* 28b = *'Abot R. Nat.* B. 25.1; *b. B. Bat.* 4a).
The sayings reflect the importance Jesus attached to his mission and
to that of his followers. They also suggest that Jesus' mission was
expected to have a major impact that would reach far beyond the
borders of Israel.

Most of what has just been considered is Matthean; very little of it
is dominical, at least in the form and context extant in Matthew. The
evangelist believes that the good news of the kingdom is to go to the
Gentiles, but Israel still receives priority. The upshot is that for all
its interest in Gentiles, Matthew reveals very little about the attitudes
the historical Jesus may have had with respect to the Gentiles.

More suggestive is the encounter with the Syrophoenician woman.

---

[8]   This is not to deny the editorial activity of the Matthean evangelist, which
throughout Matthew 5 is in evidence.

Jesus' initial rebuff should be taken as clear evidence of Israel's priority. "Let the children first be fed, for it is not right to take the children's bread and throw it to the dogs" (Mark 7:27). But by acceding to the woman's request, Jesus has indicated that messianic blessings can in fact extend to Gentiles.

The Lucan evangelist wishes to drive home this point in a masterful rewrite of Mark's account of Jesus' preaching in Nazareth (Mark 6:1-6). According to Luke, the people of Nazareth are offended not because he is known to them (as in Mark's version) but because Jesus has promised messianic blessings to Gentiles, even to Israel's enemies (Luke 4:16-30).[9] But how much of this theology, including the exegesis of the Elijah/Elisha narratives, derives from Jesus is difficult to say.[10]

The place of Gentiles in Jesus and the Gospels is somewhat ambiguous. This is largely so because of the differing assessments each evangelist offers. The Matthean evangelist, who mentions the Gentiles some fourteen times, tends to be critical, viewing the Gentiles much as many first-century Jews did. Nonetheless, he anticipates their inclusion in the kingdom (cf. 8:11-12; 10:18-19; 21:43; 24:14; 25:31-46; 28:18-20). The Lucan evangelist, who mentions the Gentiles some ten times, is more positive in his views (see esp. Luke 2:32; 24:47). Mark's perspective is less clear. Gentiles are referred to only five times, and most of these references, if not all of them, are traditional (Mark 10:33, 42; 11:17; 13:10).[11] The Marcan evangelist does not appear to have any axe to grind. The appearance of the quotation of Isa 56:7 in the Temple action (Mark 11:17) and the reference to the need of the good news of the kingdom being first preached to all the nations/Gentiles (Mark 13:10) are two very important passages that must be considered. If these two passages derive from Jesus, we may have telling evidence that Gentiles played

---

9   On the cause of offense in Jesus' Nazareth sermon, see J. A. Sanders, "From Isaiah 61 to Luke 4," in C. A. Evans and J. A. Sanders, *Luke and Scripture: The Function of Sacred Tradition in Luke-Acts* (Minneapolis: Fortress, 1993) 46-69.

10   Elijah/Elisha tradition is present elsewhere in the dominical tradition. The possibility therefore that Luke 4:25-27 derives from Jesus, if even in a context different from the one in which Luke has placed this material, cannot be ruled out.

11   Mark's ἔθνος ἐπ' ἔθνος in 13:8 probably means "nation against nation," not "Gentile against Gentile." The τὰ ἔθνη of Mark 11:17 and 13:10 is best translated "the nations," but their non-Jewish ethnicity seems to be the primary point.

a role in Jesus' program.

Before this question can be pursued further it is necessary to consider Isa 56:7 and Jer 7:11 in their full traditional contexts. Both texts were interpreted in interesting ways. Certain aspects of this interpretive tradition may shed light on Jesus' demonstration in the Temple precincts.

A HOUSE OF PRAYER FOR ALL THE GENTILES

Jesus is said to have quoted the last part of Isa 56:7. The passage as a whole is potentially very significant and deserves to be reviewed. The MT reads:

כֹּה אָמַר יְהוָה שִׁמְרוּ מִשְׁפָּט וַעֲשׂוּ צְדָקָה	1
כִּי־קְרוֹבָה יְשׁוּעָתִי לָבוֹא וְצִדְקָתִי לְהִגָּלוֹת	
אַשְׁרֵי אֱנוֹשׁ יַעֲשֶׂה־זֹּאת וּבֶן־אָדָם יַחֲזִיק בָּהּ	2
שֹׁמֵר שַׁבָּת מֵחַלְּלוֹ וְשֹׁמֵר יָדוֹ מֵעֲשׂוֹת כָּל־רָע	
וְאַל־יֹאמַר בֶּן־הַנֵּכָר הַנִּלְוָה אֶל־יְהוָה	3
לֵאמֹר הַבְדֵּל יַבְדִּילַנִי יְהוָה מֵעַל עַמּוֹ	
וְאַל־יֹאמַר הַסָּרִיס הֵן אֲנִי עֵץ יָבֵשׁ	
כִּי־כֹה אָמַר יְהוָה לַסָּרִיסִים אֲשֶׁר יִשְׁמְרוּ אֶת־שַׁבְּתוֹתַי	4
וּבָחֲרוּ בַּאֲשֶׁר חָפָצְתִּי וּמַחֲזִיקִים בִּבְרִיתִי	
וְנָתַתִּי לָהֶם בְּבֵיתִי וּבְחוֹמֹתַי יָד וָשֵׁם טוֹב	5
מִבָּנִים וּמִבָּנוֹת שֵׁם עוֹלָם אֶתֶּן־לוֹ אֲשֶׁר לֹא יִכָּרֵת	
וּבְנֵי הַנֵּכָר הַנִּלְוִים עַל־יְהוָה לְשָׁרְתוֹ	6
וּלְאַהֲבָה אֶת־שֵׁם יְהוָה לִהְיוֹת לוֹ לַעֲבָדִים	
כָּל־שֹׁמֵר שַׁבָּת מֵחַלְּלוֹ וּמַחֲזִיקִים בִּבְרִיתִי	
וַהֲבִיאוֹתִים אֶל־הַר קָדְשִׁי וְשִׂמַּחְתִּים בְּבֵית תְּפִלָּתִי	7
עוֹלֹתֵיהֶם וְזִבְחֵיהֶם לְרָצוֹן עַל־מִזְבְּחִי	
כִּי בֵיתִי בֵּית־תְּפִלָּה יִקָּרֵא לְכָל־הָעַמִּים	
נְאֻם אֲדֹנָי יְהוִה מְקַבֵּץ נִדְחֵי יִשְׂרָאֵל	8
עוֹד אֲקַבֵּץ עָלָיו לְנִקְבָּצָיו	

1   Thus says the Lord, "Safeguard justice, and do righteousness; for my salvation is about to come, and my righteousness to be revealed."

2   Blessed is the man that does this, and the son of man that holds it fast; that observes sabbath, not profaning it, and keeps his hand from doing any evil.

3   Neither let the son of a foreigner, that has joined himself to the Lord, speak, saying, "The Lord will surely separate me from his people"; neither let the eunuch say, "Behold, I am a dry tree."

4   For thus says the Lord to the eunuchs that keep my sabbaths, and choose the things that please me, and hold fast my covenant:

5   "To them will I give in my house and within my walls a memorial and a name better than of sons and of daughters; I will give them an

everlasting name, that shall not be cut off.

6   Also the sons of a foreigner that join themselves to the Lord, to minister to him, and to love the name of the Lord, to be his servants; every one that observes sabbath from profaning it, and holds fast my covenant;

7   even them will I bring to my holy mountain, and make them joyful in my house of prayer. Their burnt-offerings and their sacrifices shall be accepted upon my altar; for my house shall be called a house of prayer for all peoples."

8   The Lord God, who gathers the outcasts of Israel, says, "Yet will I gather others to him, besides his own that are gathered."

Apart from a few minor spelling variants, 1QIsaiah[b] agrees with the MT.[12] However, a few interesting variants are found in the Great Isaiah Scroll (i.e. 1QIsaiah[a]). The parallel passage reads (with departures from the MT italicized in the English):[13]

כיא כוה אמר יהוה שמורו משפט ועשו צדקה	1
כיא קרובה ישועתי לבוא וצדקתי להגלות	
אשרי אנוש יעשה זואת ובן אדם יחזיק בה	2
שומר שבת .חללה ושומר ידיו מעשות כול רע	
אל יואמר בן הנכר הנלוא אל יהוה	3
לאמור הבדל יבדילני יהוה מעל עמו	
ואל יואמר הסריס הנה אנוכי עץ יבש	
כיא כוה אמר יהוה לסריסים אשר ישמורו את שבתותי	4
ויבחורו באשר חפצתי ומחזיקים בבריתי	
ונתתי להמה בביתי ובחומותי יד ושם טוב	5
מבנים ומן בנות שם עולם אתן להמה אשר לוא יכרת	
ובני הנכר הנלויים אל יהוה להיות	6
לו לעבדים ולברך את שם יהוה ושומרים	
את השבת מחללה ומחזיקים בבריתי	
והביאותים אל הר קודשי ושמחתים בבית תפלתי	7
עולותיהמה וזבחיהמה יעלו לרצון על מזבחי	
כיא ביתי בית תפלה יקרה לכול העמים	
נואם אדוני יהוה מקבץ נדחי ישראל	8
עוד אקבץ עליו לנקבציו	

1   Thus says the Lord, "Safeguard justice, and do righteousness; for my

---

12   1QIsa[b] 9:15-26 = Isa 56:1-7. For text, see E. L. Sukenik, *The Dead Sea Scrolls of the Hebrew University* (Jerusalem: Magnes, 1955) pl. 11.

13   1QIsa[a] 46:10-22 = Isa 56:1-7. For text, see M. Burrows, *The Dead Sea Scrolls of St. Mark's Monastery.* Volume I: *The Isaiah Manuscript and the Habakkuk Commentary* (New Haven: American Schools of Oriental Research, 1950) 64; J. C. Trever, *Scrolls from Qumrân Cave I* (Jerusalem: Albright Institute of Archaeological Research, 1974) 53 (pl. 46).

salvation is about to come, and my righteousness to be revealed."

2 Blessed is the man that does this, and the son of man that holds it fast; that observes sabbath, not profaning it, and keeps his hand*s* from doing any evil.

3 Neither let the son of a foreigner, that has joined himself to the Lord, speak, saying, "The Lord will surely separate me from his people"; neither let the eunuch say, "Behold, I am a dry tree."

4 For thus says the Lord to the eunuchs that keep my sabbaths, and choose the things that please me, and hold fast my covenant:

5 "To them will I give in my house and within my walls a memorial and a name better than of sons and of daughters; I will give them an everlasting name, that shall not be cut off.

6 Also the sons of a foreigner that join themselves to the Lord, *to be his servants, and to bless the name of the Lord*, that observe *the* sabbath from profaning it, and hold fast my covenant;

7 even them will I bring to my holy mountain, and make them joyful in my house of prayer: their burnt-offerings and their sacrifices shall be accepted upon my altar; for my house shall be called a house of prayer for all peoples."

8 The Lord God, who gathers the outcasts of Israel, says, "Yet will I gather others to him, besides his own that are gathered."

The text of 1QIsaiah[a] matches the MT closely. In v. 2 we find the plural "hands," instead of the singular "hand." Because the plural is found in the LXX and Targum also, it is possible that the MT's singular is not original. The major variation, however, is found in v. 6. 1QIsaiah[a] omits "to minister to him" and presents the remaining elements in a different order.

MT וּבְנֵי הַנֵּכָר הַנִּלְוִים עַל־יְהוָה לְשָׁרְתוֹ וּלְאַהֲבָה אֶת־שֵׁם יְהוָה
לִהְיוֹת לוֹ לַעֲבָדִים כָּל־שֹׁמֵר שַׁבָּת מֵחַלְּלוֹ וּמַחֲזִיקִים בִּבְרִיתִי

Also the sons of a foreigner that join themselves to the Lord, to minister to him, and to love the name of the Lord, to be his servants; every one that observes sabbath from profaning it, and holds fast my covenant.

1Q ובני הנכר הנלויים אל יהוה להיות לו לעבדים ולברך את שם יהוה
ושומרים את השבת מחללה ומחזיקים בבריתי

Also the sons of a foreigner that join themselves to the Lord, to be his servants, and to bless the name of the Lord, that observe the sabbath from profaning it, and hold fast my covenant.

We see that not only does "to minister to him" (לְשָׁרְתוֹ) drop out, "to *love* the name of the Lord" (לְאַהֲבָה אֶת־שֵׁם יְהוָה) becomes "to *bless* the name of the Lord" (לברך את שם יהוה), and "to be his servants" moves into first place, following "that join themselves to the Lord." The significance of this revision,[14] as J. R. Rosenbloom has suggested,[15] is to avoid the impression that foreigners could become priests.[16] The Great Isaiah Scroll makes it clear that the foreigner who joins himself to the Lord becomes his servant, blesses his name, keeps the sabbath, and holds fast to the covenant.

The LXX represents a fairly literal translation of the Hebrew, with only a few minor variants. The text reads (with departures from the MT italicized in the English):[17]

1 Τάδε λέγει κύριος· Φυλάσσεσθε κρίσιν, ποιήσατε δικαιοσύνην· ἤγγισε γὰρ τὸ σωτήριόν μου παραγίνεσθαι, καὶ τὸ ἔλεός μου ἀπο-καλυφθῆναι. 2 μακάριος ἀνὴρ ὁ ποιῶν ταῦτα καὶ ἄνθρωπος ὁ ἀντ-εχόμενος αὐτῶν καὶ φυλάσσων τὰ σάββατα μὴ βεβηλοῦν καὶ διατηρῶν τὰς χεῖρας αὐτοῦ μὴ ποιεῖν ἀδίκημα. 3 μὴ λεγέτω ὁ ἀλλογενὴς ὁ προσκείμενος πρὸς κύριον· Ἀφοριεῖ με ἄρα κύριος ἀπὸ τοῦ λαοῦ αὐτοῦ· καὶ μὴ λεγέτω ὁ εὐνοῦχος ὅτι· Ἐγώ εἰμι ξύλον ξηρόν. 4 τάδε λέγει κύριος· Τοῖς εὐνούχοις, ὅσοι ἂν φυλάξωνται τὰ σάββατά μου καὶ ἐκλέξωνται ἃ ἐγὼ θέλω καὶ ἀντέχωνται τῆς διαθήκης μου, 5 δώσω αὐτοῖς ἐν τῷ οἴκῳ μου καὶ ἐν τῷ τείχει μου τόπον ὀνομαστὸν κρείσσων υἱῶν καὶ θυγατέρων, ὄνομα αἰώνιον δώσω αὐτοῖς καὶ οὐκ ἐκλείψει. 6 καὶ τοῖς ἀλλογενέσι τοῖς προσκειμένοις κυρίῳ δουλεύειν αὐτῷ καὶ ἀγαπᾶν τὸ ὄνομα κυρίου τοῦ εἶναι αὐτῷ εἰς δούλους καὶ δούλας καὶ πάντας τοὺς φυλασσομένους τὰ σάββατά μου μὴ βεβη-λοῦν καὶ ἀντεχομένους τῆς διαθήκης μου, 7 εἰσάξω αὐτοὺς εἰς τὸ ὄρος τὸ ἅγιόν μου καὶ εὐφρανῶ αὐτοὺς ἐν τῷ οἴκῳ τῆς προσευχῆς

---

14   And in this instance 1QIsaiah[a] probably does represent a deliberate revision, for both 1QIsaiah[b] and the Vulgate agree with the MT. The Vulgate does attest a minor variant: *Et filios advenae, qui adhaerent Domino, ut colant eum, et diligant nomen ejus, ut sint ei in servos; omnem custodientem sabbatum ne polluat illud, et tenentem foedus meum* (= Also the sons of the foreigner that adhere to the Lord, to serve him, and to love his name, to be his servants; every one that keeps sabbath, not to profane it, and that holds fast my covenant). "To love the name of the Lord" becomes "to love his name."

15   J. R. Rosenbloom, *The Dead Sea Isaiah Scroll: A Literary Analysis. A Comparison with the Masoretic Text and the Biblia Hebraica* (Grand Rapids: Eerdmans, 1970) 62-63.

16   שרת and כהן occur together some two dozen times in the Hebrew Bible; for example: "And the priests the sons of Levi shall come forward, for the Lord your God has chosen them to minister to him and to bless in the name of the Lord" (Deut 21:5).

17   Text based on J. Ziegler, *Septuaginta: Vetus Testamentum Graecum*. Vol. XIV: *Isaias* (Göttingen: Vandenhoeck & Ruprecht, 1939) 330-31. Translation is my own, but cf. R. R. Ottley, *The Book of Isaiah according to the Septuagint* (2nd ed., Cambridge: Cambridge University Press, 1909) 287.

μου· τὰ ὁλοκαυτώματα αὐτῶν καὶ αἱ θυσίαι αὐτῶν ἔσονται δεκταὶ ἐπὶ τοῦ θυσιαστηρίου μου· ὁ γὰρ οἶκός μου οἶκος προσευχῆς κληθήσεται πᾶσι τοῖς ἔθνεσιν, 8 εἶπεν κύριος ὁ συνάγων τοὺς διεσπαρμένους Ἰσραήλ, ὅτι συνάξω ἐπ' αὐτὸν συναγωγήν.

1 Thus says the Lord: "Safeguard judgment, practice righteousness; for my salvation is come near to be present, and my *mercy* to be revealed. 2 Blessed is the man who does *these* things and the person who holds them fast, and safeguards *the* sabbaths, not to profane them, and keeps his hand*s* from doing unrighteousness. 3 Let not the stranger who attaches himself to the Lord say, "The Lord will surely separate me from this people"; and let not the eunuch say, "I am a dry tree." 4 Thus says the Lord to the eunuchs, as many as keep my sabbaths, and choose the things in which I take pleasure, and hold fast my covenant: 5 to them will I give in my house and within my wall an honorable place, (it is) better than sons and daughters. I will give them an everlasting name, and it shall not fail. 6 And to the strangers that attach themselves to the Lord, to serve him, and to love the name of the Lord, to be his servants *and handmaids*; and all that safeguard *the* sabbaths, not to profane them, and that hold fast to my covenant, 7 I will bring them to my holy mountain, and make them rejoice in the house of my prayer. Their whole-burnt offerings and their sacrifices shall be acceptable upon my altar; for my house shall be called a house of prayer for all the *Gentiles*, 8 said the Lord that gathers the dispersed of Israel, "For I will gather to him a congregation."

In v. 1 the LXX reads "my mercy" (ἔλεός μου) instead of "my righteousness" (צִדְקָתִי). The translator may have felt that "mercy" was a more suitable parallel for "salvation." The plurals of v. 2 constitute minor variants (though, as already mentioned, the plural "hands" may be original and the MT's singular "hand" the variant). The translator expands the Hebrew's "servants" to "servants and handmaids [*or* female servants]" (δούλους καὶ δούλας). In v. 7 the Hebrew's "peoples" (הָעַמִּים) becomes "nations"/"Gentiles" (τὰ ἔθνη), rather than the more literal "peoples" (λαοί). But the LXX frequently translates עַם and גּוֹי with ἔθνος, so this is not especially significant.

The paraphrase found in the Isaiah Targum introduces significant variants. The text reads (with departures from the MT italicized in the English):[18]

---

[18] The text is taken from A. Sperber, *The Bible in Aramaic* (5 vols., Leiden: Brill, 1959-73) 3.112-13; J. F. Stenning, *The Targum of Isaiah* (Oxford: Clarendon, 1949) 187, 189. The English translation is based on B. D. Chilton, *The Isaiah Targum* (ArBib 11; Wilmington: Glazier, 1987) 109; but I have departed from this rendition in a few places to offer a slightly more literal reading.

1   כדנן אמר יהוה טרו דינא ועבדו צדקתא

     ארי קריב פרקני למיתי וזכותי לאתגלאה

2   טובי אנשא דיעביד דא ובר אנש דיתקף בה

     יטר שבתא מאחלותה ויטר ידוהי מלמעבד כל ביש

3   ולא יימר בר עממין דמתוסף על עמיה דיהוה

     למימר אפרשא יפרשינני יהוה מעל עמיה

     ולא יימר סריסאה האנא כאע יביש

4   ארי כדנן אמר יהוה לסריסיא דיטרון ית יומי שביא דילי

     ומתרען ברצבינא ומתקפין בקימי

5   ואתין להון בבית מקדשי ובארע בית שכינתי אתר ושום טב

     מבנין ובנן שום עלם אתין להון דלא יפסוק

6   ובני עממיא דמתוספין על עמיה דיהוה לשמשותיה

     ולמרחם ית שמא דיהוה למהוי ליה לעבדין

     כל דיטר שבתא מאחלותה ומתקפין בקימי

7   ואיתינון לטורא דקודשא ואחדינון בבית צלותי

     עלותהון ונכסת קדשיהון ותסקון לרעוא על מדבחי

     ארי בית מקדשי בית צלו לכל עממיא

8   אמר יהוה אלהים דעתיד לכנשא מבדרי ישראל

     עוד אקריב גלותהון לכנשא יתהון

1 Thus says the Lord, "Safeguard justice and do righteousness, for my salvation is about to come, and my *virtue* to be revealed."

2 Blessed is the man who will do this, and a son of man who will hold it fast, who *will* keep *the* sabbath from profaning it, and *will* keep his hand*s* from doing evil.

3 Let not a son of *Gentiles* who has *been added to the people of* the Lord say, "The Lord will surely separate me from his people"; and let not the eunuch say, "Behold, I am *like* a dry tree."

4 For thus says the Lord, "To the eunuchs who keep *the days of the* sabbaths *that are mine*, who *are pleased* with the things that I *wish* and hold fast my covenants,

5 I will give them in my *sanctuary* and within *the land of the house of* my *Shekinah* a *place* and a name better than sons and daughters; I will give *them* an everlasting name which shall not *cease*.

6 And the sons of *Gentiles* who *have been added* to *the people of* the Lord, to minister to him, to love the name of the Lord, and to be his servants, every one who *will* keep *the* sabbath from profaning it, and hold fast my covenants—

7 these I will bring to *the* holy mountain, and make them joyful in my house of prayer; their burnt offerings and their *holy* sacrifices will *even go up* for *my pleasure* on my altar; for my *sanctuary will be* a house of prayer for all the peoples.

8 Thus says the Lord God who *is about to* gather the outcasts of Israel, yet will I *bring near their exiles, to* gather *them*."

The Aramaic paraphrase offers a few interesting contributions of its own. The rephrasing found in vv. 3 and 6 ("Gentiles who have been added to the people of the Lord") is probably intended to make it clear that these foreigners, who "minister" to the Lord, are in fact proselytes and not simply Gentile visitors. Understood in this sense, the translator does not object to their ministering to the Lord (as apparently did the scribe of the Great Isaiah Scroll). Secondly, the importance of the Temple is intensified. The Hebrew's "house" becomes "house of my sanctuary" (בית מקדשי), while "within my walls" becomes "within the land of the house of my Shekina" (בארעא בית שכינתי). "Walls" have apparently been understood as alluding to the boundaries of the land of Israel. The purpose of this modification may have been to avoid the suggestion that foreigners will be permitted entry into the Temple itself. Finally, and for our purposes probably the most important interpretive element, the meturgeman renders the Hebrew's "yet will I gather others to him, besides his own that are gathered" with "yet will I bring near their exiles, to gather them." The meturgeman elsewhere assigns to the Messiah the task of regathering the exiles (גלות) of Israel. The Lord's "servant, the Messiah" (*Tg.* Isa 52:13) will "bring our exiles near . . . he will take away the rule of the Gentiles from the land of Israel . . . they shall see the kingdom of their Messiah" (*Tg.* Isa 53:8, 10).[19] The hope of the eschatological gathering of Israel's dispersed and exiled people finds expression in the liturgy of the ancient synagogue (cf. *Amida* §10; Sir 51:12f [in the Hebrew version]), a liturgy that also longs for the appearance of the Davidic Messiah (cf. *Amida* §14; Sir 51:12h [in the Hebrew version]). Later midrashim state: "They should not attempt to go up from the diaspora by force. For if they do, why should the King Messiah come to gather the exiles [גליותיהן] of Israel?" (*Song Rab.* 2:7 §1); "For what purpose will the royal

---

[19] The "holy seed" of Isa 6:13 is expanded in the Aramaic to read: "So the exiles of Israel will be gathered and they will return to their land." At 27:6 the text is completely rewritten in the Targum, again to emphasize the regathering of the exiles: "They shall be gathered from among their exiles and they shall return to their land." In 35:10 the Hebrew's "ransomed of the Lord" in the Aramaic are "gathered from among their exiles." The Aramaic paraphrase of Isa 42:1-9 seems to envision a messianic deliverance of exiles (v. 7: "to bring out their exiles, who resemble prisoners, from among the Gentiles, to deliver from the slavery of the kingdoms those who are jailed as prisoners of darkness"). On this theme in the Isaiah Targum, see B. D. Chilton, *The Glory of Isrel: The Theology and Provenience of the Isaiah Targum* (JSOTSup 23; Sheffield: JSOT Press, 1982) 28-33, 132-34.

Messiah come, and what will he do? He will come to assemble the exiles [גליותיהן] of Israel" (*Gen. Rab.* 98.9 [on Gen 49:11]).

Later midrashim offer a few points of interest. In one exegesis Isaiah 56 is connected with the messianic age: "And the proof that charity brings speedily the days of the Messiah and the days of redemption? The verse 'Safeguard justice, and do righteousness; for my salvation is about to come, and my righteousness to be revealed' [Isa 56:1]" (*Eliyyahu Zuṭa* §1 [171]). But most interpretations are more interested in who will be gathered in Zion, in fulfillment of Isaiah 56.

Whereas Isaiah speaks of foreigners being brought to the Temple Mount, the midrashists, often ignoring the context, apply the oracle to Israel. For example, in one midrash God promises to comfort Israel in the same ways he afflicted them: "Jeremiah said, 'Let all their wickedness come before you [Lam 1:22]; Isaiah said, 'even them will I bring to my holy mountain' [Isa 56:7]" (*Lam. Rab.* 1:2 §23). Here the foreigners are understood as estranged Israelites. In another midrash those brought to God's holy mountain, whose sacrifices are acceptable to the Lord, are proselytes. For example, "It says, 'Neither let the son of a foreigner, that has joined himself to the Lord, speak, saying, "The Lord will surely separate me from his people" [Isa 56:3]. That refers to the foreigners who are circumcised" (*Exod. Rab.* 19.4 [on Exod 12:43], commenting on "no foreigner shall eat of it"). Following a similar line, Isa 56:3-5 is appealed to as exemplifying one type of convert among several (*Seder Elijah Rabbah* §27 [146]). "and the proselytes are called servants, as it says, 'to be his servants' [Isa 56:6] . . . (acceptableness) is used of proselytes, for it says, 'Their whole-burnt offerings and their sacrifices shall be acceptable upon my altar' [Isa 56:7] . . . (ministering) is used of the proselytes, for it says, 'Also the foreigners that join themselves to the Lord, to minister to him' [Isa 56:6]" (*Num. Rab.* 8.2 [on Num 5:6]). These interpretations apparently reflect a concern to qualify the passage. However, in Mekilta we find a very generous, ecumenical interpretation of Isa 56:1-7 (cf. *Mek.* on Exod 22:20-23 [*Nezikin* §18]).

Isaiah 56 proves to be a significant oracle that caught the attention of ancient tradents, translators, and interpreters. The oracle concerns the coming of God's salvation, a time when divine righteousness will be revealed (v. 1). According to the MT, at this time the marginalized, including foreigners, will be welcomed into God's house and will be permitted to minister to the Lord (vv. 6-7). Their sacrifices will be accepted. Indeed, God's house will be called a house of prayer for all the nations. This optimistic oracle is qualified somewhat in the Great Isaiah Scroll. The foreigner may become servants and bless the Lord, but not "minister" to him, as might priests. The Targum qualifies the oracle still further by making it clear that these foreigners have become proselytes. They will be accepted into the land of Israel, but not into the Temple itself. The Aramaic version ends on the happy note that Israel's exiles will be gathered, which elsewhere in the Isaiah Targum and some of the midrashim is a task for the Messiah.

How much of this interpretive tradition was in circulation in the time of Jesus is impossible to determine. His appeal to Isa 56:7b and his association with "sinners," toll collectors, and others of dubious standing with respect to the cultus and popular piety, suggests that Jesus' interpretation of the oracle may have been at variance with those of a more qualified and restrictive perspective, as illustrated by the versions and midrashim just reviewed. Because elsewhere we find Jesus' understanding of Isaiah similar to interpretive tendencies preserved in the Isaiah Targum, we may be permitted in this instance to suspect that Jesus may have been reacting to the Aramaic's interpretive orientation in Isa 56:1-8.[20] Thus, it is plausible to suppose that Jesus' more inclusive stance was somewhat in tension with the Aramaic's later and more exclusive orientation.

Whereas his appeal to Isaiah 56 hints at Jesus' conception of what the Temple establishment was supposed to be, his appeal to Jeremiah 7 makes clear what he thought it had become. The appeal to Jeremiah may also have hinted at the Temple's doom.

A CAVE OF ROBBERS

In the MT Jer 7:11-15 reads:

הַמְעָרַת פָּרִצִים הָיָה הַבַּיִת הַזֶּה אֲשֶׁר־נִקְרָא־שְׁמִי   11
עָלָיו בְּעֵינֵיכֶם גַּם אָנֹכִי הִנֵּה רָאִיתִי נְאֻם־יְהוָה

כִּי לְכוּ־נָא אֶל־מְקוֹמִי אֲשֶׁר בְּשִׁילוֹ אֲשֶׁר שִׁכַּנְתִּי שְׁמִי שָׁם בָּרִאשׁוֹנָה   12
וּרְאוּ אֵת אֲשֶׁר־עָשִׂיתִי לוֹ מִפְּנֵי רָעַת עַמִּי יִשְׂרָאֵל

וְעַתָּה יַעַן עֲשׂוֹתְכֶם אֶת־כָּל־הַמַּעֲשִׂים הָאֵלֶּה נְאֻם־יְהוָה וָאֲדַבֵּר אֲלֵיכֶם הַשְׁכֵּם   13

---

[20]   On the dictional and thematic points of contact between Jesus and the Isaiah Targum, see Chilton, *A Galilean Rabbi and His Bible*.

וְדַבֵּר וְלֹא שְׁמַעְתֶּם וָאֶקְרָא אֶתְכֶם וְלֹא עֲנִיתֶם

14 וְעָשִׂיתִי לַבַּיִת אֲשֶׁר נִקְרָא־שְׁמִי עָלָיו אֲשֶׁר אַתֶּם בֹּטְחִים בּוֹ וְלַמָּקוֹם
אֲשֶׁר־נָתַתִּי לָכֶם וְלַאֲבוֹתֵיכֶם כַּאֲשֶׁר עָשִׂיתִי לְשִׁלוֹ

15 וְהִשְׁלַכְתִּי אֶתְכֶם מֵעַל פָּנָי כַּאֲשֶׁר הִשְׁלַכְתִּי אֶת־כָּל־אֲחֵיכֶם
אֵת כָּל־זֶרַע אֶפְרָיִם

11 "Has this house, which is called by my name, become a den of robbers in your eyes? Behold, I myself have seen it," says the Lord.

12 "Go now to my place that was in Shiloh, where I made my name dwell at first, and see what I did to it for the wickedness of my people Israel."

13 "And now, because you have done all these things," says the Lord, "and when I spoke to you, rising up early and speaking, you did not listen, and when I called you, you did not answer,

14 therefore I will do to the house which is called by my name, and in which you trust, and to the place that I gave to you and to your fathers, just as I did to Shiloh."

15 "And I will cast you out of my sight, as I cast out all your kinsmen, all the seed of Ephraim."

The Greek version of Jer 7:11-15 renders the Hebrew literally; it reads:

11 μὴ σπήλαιον λῃστῶν ὁ οἶκός μου, οὗ ἐπικέκληται τὸ ὄνομά μου ἐπ' αὐτῷ ἐκεῖ, ἐνώπιον ὑμῶν; καὶ ἐγὼ ἰδοὺ ἑώρακα, λέγει κύριος. 12 ὅτι πορεύθητε εἰς τὸν τόπον μου τὸν ἐν Σηλωμ, οὗ κατεσκήνωσα τὸ ὄνομά μου ἐκεῖ ἔμπροσθεν, καὶ ἴδετε ἃ ἐποίησα αὐτῷ ἀπὸ προσώπου κακίας λαοῦ μου Ἰσραήλ. 13 καὶ νῦν ἀνθ' ὧν ἐποιήσατε πάντα τὰ ἔργα ταῦτα, καὶ ἐλάλησα πρὸς ὑμᾶς καὶ οὐκ ἠκούσατέ μου, καὶ ἐκάλεσα ὑμᾶς καὶ οὐκ ἀπεκρίθητε, 14 καὶ ποιήσω τῷ οἴκῳ τούτῳ, ᾧ ἐπικέκληται τὸ ὄνομά μου ἐπ' αὐτῷ, ἐφ' ᾧ ὑμεῖς πεποίθατε ἐπ' αὐτῷ, καὶ τῷ τόπῳ, ᾧ ἔδωκα ὑμῖν καὶ τοῖς πατράσιν ὑμῶν, καθὼς ἐποίησα τῇ Σηλωμ. 15 καὶ ἀπορρίψω ὑμᾶς ἀπὸ προσώπου μου, καθὼς ἀπέρριψα τοὺς ἀδελφοὺς ὑμῶν πᾶν τὸ σπέρμα Εφραιμ.

11 "Is my house, which is called by my name, a cave of robbers in in your sight? And behold, I have seen it," says the Lord. 12 "Go to my place that is in Shelom, where I caused my name to dwell before, and see what I did to it on account of the wickedness of my people Israel. 13 And now because you have done all these things, and I spoke to you and you did not hear me, and I called you and you did not answer, 14 I shall also do to this house, which is called by my name, in which you trust, and to the place that I gave to you and to your fathers, just as I did to Shelom. 15 And I will cast you out of my sight, just as I cast away your brothers, all the seed of Ephraim.

There is only one variant in the Greek. It constitutes the omission of λέγει κύριος in v. 13 (cf. v. 11).

The Aramaic paraphrase of Jer 7:11-15 reveals some interesting features. The Targum reads (with departures from the Masoretic Text italicized in the English):[21]

11   הכבית כנישת רשיעין הוה ביתא הדין דאתקרי שמי
עלוהי בעיניכון אף קדמי כין גלו אמר יוי

12   ארי איזילו כען לאתר בית מקדש דבשילו דאשריתי שכינתי תמן בקדמיתא
וחזו ית דעבדית ליה מן קדם בישות עמי ישראל

13   וכען חלף דעבדתון ית כל עובדיא האלין אמר יוי ושלחית לותכון ית כל
עבדי נבייא מקדים וממליל ולא קבילתון ואתנביאו לכון ולא תבתון

14   ואעביד לביתא דאתקרי שמי עלוהי דאתון וחיצין ביה ולאתרא
דיהבית לכון ולאבהתכון כמא דעבדית לשילו

15   ואגלי יתכון מארע בית שכינתי כמא דאגליתי ית כל אחיכון
ית כל זרעא דישראל

11   "Was this house, which is called by my name, *like a house of an assembly of wicked* men in your eyes? *They*, too, *are revealed before me like this*," says the Lord.

12   "But go now to *the* place *of the house* of my *sanctuary* which was in Shiloh, where I made my *Shekina* dwell formerly, and see what I did to it because of the wickedness of my people Israel."

13   "And now, because you have done all these things," says the Lord, and I have *sent* to you *all my servants the prophets*, rising up early and speaking, but you did not heed *them*; and *they prophesied* to you, but you did not repent,

14   so I will do to the house, which is called by my name, in which you trust, and to the place which I gave to you and to your fathers, as I did to Shiloh."

15   "And I will *exile* you from *the land of the house of my Shekina*, as I *exiled* all your brothers, the whole seed of *Israel*."

The oracle of Jer 7:11-15 has the Lord complain of the wickedness that now takes place in his house, the house on which he has bestowed his name (cf. 7:10, 30; 32:34 [= LXX 39:34]; 34:15 [= LXX 41:15]).[22] In essence, God feels insulted. He has lent his name to the Temple of Jerusalem, but instead of being the center of justice and righteousness,

---

[21]   For text, see Sperber, *The Bible in Aramaic*, 152-53. The English translation is based on R. Hayward, *The Targum of Jeremiah* (ArBib 12; Wilmington: Glazier, 1987) 70-71.

[22]   The phrase, "which is called by my name," renders נִקְרָא־שְׁמִי עָלָיו in Hebrew, דאתקרי שמי עלוהי in Aramaic, and οὗ ἐπικέκληται τὸ ὄνομά μου ἐπ' αὐτῷ in Greek. The *niphʿal* of קרא carries with it the connotation of ownership; cf. BDB 896. On ἐπικαλοῦμαι, see BAG 293-94; *TDNT* 3.496-500; C. Spicq, *Theological Lexicon of the New Testament* (3 vols., Peabody: Hendrickson, 1994) 2.44.

it has become a "cave of robbers" (v. 11). The priests and people of Jerusalem should abandon the false notion that the city is safe because of the presence of the Temple. Saying "It is the Temple of the Lord" (v. 4) offers no guarantee of security. Indeed, appealing to the Temple as the "Lord's" but not observing his commandments only provokes the Lord further. The inhabitants of Jerusalem need only gaze on the ruins of the house of God that at one time stood at Shiloh (cf. Judg 18:31; 21:19; 1 Sam 1:3, 24; 4:3) to know that the inviolability of the Jerusalem Temple is not guaranteed.

This oracle is not preserved in the Scrolls from Qumran (4QJer[a] preserves small portions of the latter part of Jeremiah 7). The LXX's rendering of the oracle is quite literal. But the Targum introduces a few interesting readings. The Hebrew's colorful "cave of robbers" (מְעָרַת פָּרִצִים) in the Aramaic becomes "house of an assembly of wicked men" (בית כנישת רשיעין). Reference to the כנישה modernizes the passage, giving the oracle a contemporary focus.[23] In v. 13 the Hebrew's "I spoke to you" (אֲדַבֵּר אֲלֵיכֶם) in the Aramaic becomes "I have sent to you all my servants the prophets" (ושלחית לותכון ית כל עבדי נבייא).[24] Because of their sin, the people will be sent into exile and will be cast out of the land where God's shekinah dwells (v. 15).

There are two important parallels that draw together Isaiah 56 and Jeremiah 7: (1) Both passages speak of the Temple as God's "house" (Isa 56:5, 7 ["my house"]; Jer 7:2, 10, 11, 14 ["this house ... called by my name"]). (2) The complementary nature of the two passages is enhanced in the Aramaic tradition. In the targums both passages speak of Israel's exile (in Jeremiah the people go into exile; in Isaiah they return from exile). Moreover, in the targums both passages speak of "the house of (God's) shekinah." In Jeremiah 7 the people will be exiled from this house of God's presence; in Isaiah 56 it will be given to them.

This complementary relationship of the two passages, especially as seen in the Aramaic tradition, is potentially significant for understanding the point that Jesus was trying to make when he alluded to

---

23   Indeed, בית כנישת could be translated "synagogue." For another instance of modernization in *Tg.* Jeremiah 7, see esp. v. 4.

24   Here I follow Hayward (*Targum of Jeremiah*, 70-71) who accepts the longer reading (cf. *Tg.* Jer 35:17). Some mss read only ושלחית לותכון ("I have sent to you").

Isaiah 56 and Jeremiah 7. The juxtaposition of these two oracles may
have run deeper than merely the common theme of God's "house."
The threat of destruction and exile, on the one hand, and the hope of
return from exile and renewal of God's presence in Jerusalem, on
the other, may very well represent the substance of Jesus' message.

The tradition history of these prophetic oracles coheres with other
aspects of Jesus' teaching. The tendency observed in the Great Isaiah
Scroll, to qualify, if not limit participation in the Temple precincts
seems to stand in tension with Jesus' more inclusive orientation.[25]
This tension coheres with the stricter halakic interpretations of the
sectarian Scrolls, on the one hand, and with Jesus' much more lenient
halakah, on the other.[26] Another interesting point of comparison lies
in *Tg.* Jer 7:13's reference to the sending of the prophets. We think
of the saying in Q, "O Jerusalem, Jerusalem, killing the prophets and
stoning those who are sent to you" (Matt 23:37a = Luke 13:34a), as
well as the allegorical allusion to the prophets in the Parable of the
Wicked Vineyard Tenants (Mark 12:1-12; cf. vv. 2-5: "he sent a
servant to them . . . and he sent to them another . . . and many
others"). It is important to observe that both of these passages are
directed against the Jerusalem establishment, as is Jeremiah 7.[27]

One may ask if Jesus' prophetic pronouncement related in any way
to his messianic objectives. In Mark 11 he rides into Jerusalem
mounted on a donkey, apparently a deliberate acting out of Zech 9:9.
Accompanying this entrance into the city are shouts anticipating the
coming of the kingdom of David. On some occasion Jesus assured his
disciples that they would sit on twelve thrones judging the twelve
tribes of Israel (Matt 19:28 = Luke 22:28-30). Throughout his
ministry he told parables illustrating aspects of the kingdom of God.
Indeed, the evangelist Mark summarizes Jesus' message as a call to
repentance in light of the nearness of the kingdom (Mark 1:14-15).
This royal messianic dimension coheres with Jesus' crucifixion as
"king of the Jews" (Mark 15:2, 9, 12, 18, 26, 32 ["king of Israel"]).
Pilate's inscription (Mark 15:26 par.) confirms Jesus' messianic

---

[25]   See the Parable of the Pharisee and the Publican (Luke 18:9-14).

[26]   See Mark 2:23-28; 3:1-6; 7:1-23. See also P. Sigal, *The Halakah of Jesus
of Nazareth according to the Gospel of Matthew* (Lanham and New York: University Press of America, 1986).

[27]   It is important to remember that one Jesus ben Ananias alluded to Jeremiah
7 to pronounce woe on Jerusalem and the Temple. The aristocracy tried to silence
him. See Josephus, *J.W.* 6.5.3 §300-309.

recognition, at least on the part of some of his following (see also Mark 8:29). All of these elements suggest that Jesus' appeal to the oracles of Isaiah and Jeremiah, at the time of his demonstration in the Temple precincts, was part of a messianic agenda and not simply an ad hoc response to an objectionable practice. The role of Israel's kings in preserving the nation's cultic fidelity offers a measure of general support to this suggestion (e.g. David's establishment of Jerusalem as the religious center of Israel; Solomon's replacement of Abiathar with Zadok and his building of the Temple; the reforms of Jehoash, Hezekiah, and Josiah).[28] But Jesus' appeal to Isaiah 56 and Jeremiah 7 may lend specific support to it. To this possibility we now turn.

SOLOMON'S PRAYER OF DEDICATION

It is interesting to observe in Isa 56:1-7 and Jer 7:11-15 allusions to Solomon's prayer of dedication of the Temple (1 Kgs 8:41-43). The allusions are noted in square brackets:

> 41 "Likewise when a foreigner [הַנָּכְרִי], who is not of your people [מֵעַמְּךָ] Israel, comes from a far country for the sake of your name [שְׁמֶךָ] 42 (for they shall hear of your great name, and your mighty hand, and of your outstretched arm), when he comes and prays [וְהִתְפַּלֵּל] toward this house [הַבַּיִת הַזֶּה], 43 hear in heaven your dwelling place, and do according to all for which the foreigner [הַנָּכְרִי] calls [יִקְרָא] to you; in order that all the peoples of the earth may know your name and fear you, as do your people Israel, and that they may know that this house which I have built is called by your name [שִׁמְךָ נִקְרָא עַל־הַבַּיִת הַזֶּה]."

We find important parallels at several points: (1) the "foreigner" who comes to the Temple seeking the Lord parallels Isa 56:3, 6-7. (2) God's "people" parallels Isa 56:3; Jer 7:12. (3) References to God's "name" appears in all three passages. (4) The association of "this house" with prayer parallels Isa 56:7. (5) The foreigner "calls" to God, but in Jer 7:13, when God called to his people, they did not listen. (6) The Temple as "this house . . . called by (God's) name" parallels Jer 7:10, 11, 14.

---

28   In reference to David, see 2 Sam 6:12-19; 7:1-2 (1 Chr 15:1–17:2; 21:18–23:32; 28:1–29:22); in reference to Solomon, see 1 Kgs 2:27, 35; 5–8 (2 Chronicles 2–7); in reference to Jehoash, see 2 Kgs 12:4-16 (2 Chr 24:2-14); in reference to Hezekiah, see 2 Kgs 18:3-7 (2 Chr 29:3–31:21); in reference to Josiah, see 2 Kgs 22:2–23:25 (2 Chr 34:2–35:19; 1 Esdras 1:1-23).

Although offering a fairly literal rendition, the targum of 1 Kgs 8:41-43 introduces elements that draw the passage even closer to the oracles of Isaiah and Jeremiah. The text reads (with departures from the Hebrew italicized):[29]

> 41 And also one *from a son of the peoples* that are not from your people Israel and he comes from a far-off land on account of your name, 42 for they will hear of your great name and your mighty hand and your *raised-up* arm, and he will come and pray *toward* this house, 43 *may you receive from the heavens, from the place of the house of your shekinah*, and act according to all *the son of the peoples will pray before you*, in order that all the nations of the earth may know your name to *fear before you* like your people Israel and to know that your name is called upon this house that I have built.

Two features of the Aramaic paraphrase call for comment. (1) The epithet in v. 43, "house of your shekinah" (בית שכינתך) parallels God's reference to "house of my shekinah" (בית שכינתי) in *Tg*. Isa 56:5. (2) Another expression in v. 43, "the son of the peoples will pray before you" (דיצלי קדמך בר עממין), is similar to the reference "the house of prayer for all peoples" (בית צלו לכל עממיא) found in *Tg*. Isa 56:7.

Josephus' paraphrase of Solomon's prayer (*Ant.* 8.4.3 §116-117) is also instructive and may have relevance for our concerns. The text reads:

> 116 "And this help I ask of you not alone for the Hebrews who may fall into error, but also if any come even from the ends of the earth or from wherever it may be and turn to you, imploring to receive some kindness, do listen and give it to them. 117 For so would all people know that you yourself desire that this house should be built for you in our land, and also that we are not inhumane by nature nor unfriendly to those who are not of our country, but wish that all people equally should receive aid from you and enjoy your blessings."[30]

Josephus emphasizes the Temple establishment's commitment to ecumenicity, implying that it had lived up to the ideals expressed by Solomon. It is probably against this idea that we should understand Josephus' recounting of the speech of former High Priest Jesus ben Gamala, who says that the Temple "is revered by the world and

---

[29] Translation based on D. J. Harrington and A. J. Saldarini, *Targum of the Former Prophets* (ArBib 10; Wilmington: Glazier, 1987) 230.

[30] Translation based on H. St. J. Thackeray and R. Marcus, *Josephus*, vol 5. (LCL 281; London: Heinemann; Cambridge: Harvard University Press, 1934) 635.

honored by foreigners from the ends of the earth who have heard of its fame" (*J.W.* 4.4.3 §262). These words apparently allude to Isa 56:7 and imply that Jerusalem, at least under ben Gamala's leadership, had lived up to the ecumenical obligation expressed in Solomon's prayer of dedication. Later midrashim elaborate on the theme of the Temple's great value for the Gentile world.[31]

JESUS, THE TEMPLE, AND THE GENTILES

When he demonstrated in the Temple precincts (Mark 11:17) Jesus is remembered to have alluded to Isa 56:7 ("My house shall be called

---

31   One midrash states: "Had the nations of the world realized what a benefit the Temple was to them they would have built fortifications around it in order to safeguard it. For it was a greater benefit to them than to Israel; as appears from the prayer which Solomon composed: 'Likewise when a foreigner, who is not of your people Israel' [1 Kgs 8:41]; and he goes on to write, 'and do according to all for which the foreigner calls to you' [1 Kgs 8:43]" (*Num. Rab.* 1.3 [on Num 1:1]). Other midrashim provide some interesting interpretations of Isa 56:1-8: "And the proof that charity brings speedily the days of the Messiah and the days of redemption? The verse 'Safeguard justice, and do righteousness; for my salvation is about to come, and my righteousness to be revealed' [Isa 56:1]" (*Eliyyahu Zuṭa* §1 [171]); "It says, 'Neither let the son of a foreigner, that has joined himself to the Lord, speak, saying, "The Lord will surely separate me from his people" [Isa 56:3]. That refers to the foreigners who are circumcised" (*Exod. Rab.* 19.4 [on Exod 12:43]); "It says, 'Neither let the son of a foreigner, that has joined himself to the Lord, speak, saying, "The Lord will surely separate me from his people" [Isa 56:3]. That refers to the foreigners who are circumcised" (*Exod. Rab.* 19.4 [on Exod 12:43], commenting on "no foreigner shall eat of it"); "And the proselytes are called servants, as it says, 'to be his servants' [Isa 56:6] . . . (acceptableness) is used of proselytes, for it says, 'Their whole-burnt offerings and their sacrifices shall be acceptable upon my altar' [Isa 56:7] . . . (ministering) is used of the proselytes, for it says, 'Also the foreigners that join themselves to the Lord, to minister to him' [Isa 56:6]" (*Num. Rab.* 8.2 [on Num 5:6]); "He (Solomon) began reciting his prayers and said: 'Sovereign of the World, when someone from Israel comes to pray in the future and asks for sons or for something else, if he is worthy, give it to him; but if not, do not give it to him . . . But if a foreigner should come to pray there, give to him whatever he asks . . . For perhaps, if you do not do for him all that he asks, he will talk and say to himself: "So it is with this house of Solomon. I have gone from one end of the world to the other and have been worn out from so many journeyings. Then I came and prayed in here and have found nothing tangible in here, just as I did not find it in idolatry"'" (*Midr. Tanḥ. Toledot* 6.14 [on Gen 27:28]); translation based on J. T. Townsend, *Midrash Tanhuma* (Hoboken: Ktav, 1989) 159.

CRAIG A. EVANS

a house of prayer for all the nations"). As suggested above, this prophetic tradition probably alludes to Solomon's prayer of dedication
of the Temple (1 Kgs 8:41-43). If it does, it could imply that Jesus'
action in the Temple was informed by Solomonic, or son of David,
tradition.[32] As son of David, Jesus has taken messianic action in the
Temple, criticizing the Temple establishment for failing to live up to
the expectations expressed in Isaiah 56, especially in reference to
strangers, or "nations" as in the LXX, or "peoples" as in the Targum.
Because of this failure, Jesus warns that the fateful words of Jeremiah
apply to the Temple and so hint at the Temple's impending doom.
Jesus' believed that he could invoke the witness of these prophetic
traditions, because he was the anointed descendant of David. Indeed,
when he cited Isa 56:7, "My house . . .," he may have implied that
the Temple was his house, or his responsibility, by virtue of his
messianic authority.[33]

If this interpretation is correct, then we may have here an important piece of evidence that suggests that Jesus' messianic mission
included the Gentiles and that part of his criticism of the Temple
establishment was in response to its failure to maintain a proper
witness for the Lord (cf. Isa 43:10: "You are my witnesses").

Another potentially important piece of evidence that Jesus included
Gentiles in his mission is Mark 13:10: "the gospel must first be
preached to all the Gentiles." Many critics have maintained that Mark
13:9-13 is a potpourri of inauthentic materials reflecting the *Sitz im
Leben* of the early Church, a Church experiencing persecution and

---

[32] There is evidence elsewhere in the Gospels that Jesus compared himself to
Solomon, the son of David: "The queen of the south will rise up at the judgment
with this generation and condemn it; for she came from the ends of the earth to hear
the wisdom of Solomon; and behold, something greater than Solomon is here"
(Matt 12:42 = Luke 11:31). When approaching Jerusalem, the blind man hails
Jesus as "son of David" (Mark 10:47, 48). The Matthean evangelist asserts that
Jesus' exorcistic success led his contemporaries to assume that Jesus was indeed
the awaited "son of David" (Matt 12:22-23). Although clearly a redactional contribution, it probably reflects accurately how many saw Jesus. Josephus passes on
some interesting tradition about Solomon's abilities to exorcize and heal (*Ant.* 8.2.5
§45-47; cf. Thackeray, *Josephus*, vol. 5, 595). The late first-century *Testament of
Solomon* is devoted to the subject of demons and exorcisms. Taking action in the
Temple precincts is consistent with the portrait in *Pss. Sol.* 17:30, 36 of the Davidic
Messiah who will purge Jerusalem and drive out sinners.

[33] See Gundry, *Mark*, 640, 644-45.

domestic quarrels and divisions.[34] Although the combination and context of these materials may be secondary and a certain amount of editing in the light of the events of the 40s–60s is probable, principal components of this material should not be too quickly dismissed as inauthentic.[35]

Jesus probably did envision a place for Gentiles in his messianic program for the following four reasons: (1) It was the messianic task. Israel's Messiah was expected to deal with the Gentiles (Isa 8:23 [E 9:1]; 11:1-10; 42:1, 6; 49:6; Ps 2:1-8; *Pss. Sol.* 17:22-25, 31, 34). Are we to believe that Jesus had no thoughts about the Gentiles? As the human being (or "son of man") of Daniel 7, Jesus would have to take into account Israel's relationship to the nations.[36] The "son of man" is given dominion and kingdom over "all peoples, nations, and languages" (Dan 7:14). Self-understanding in terms of Daniel would therefore require taking a position with respect to Gentiles. (2) Jesus' concept of "gospel" (בשׂר) derives from Second Isaiah (esp. 40:1-9; 52:7; 61:1-2). Isaiah envisions the "gospel" and the "light" of Israel (Isa 49:6; 56:1-8) extending to the Gentiles. We should expect that this idea would form a part of Jesus' thinking also. (3) Gentiles came from afar to see and hear Solomon, the son of David. Jesus, the son of David, who has followed the example of Solomon, alludes to this passage (Matt 12:42). The implication is that the nations are to benefit in some way with the appearance of Israel's Messiah and the kingdom of God. (4) The Gentile mission was early and enjoyed the support of the Jerusalem Church, as is attested in Galatians 1–2 (cf. Acts 8–15). Not long after his death and resurrection many of Jesus' followers were evangelizing Gentiles (see Matt 28:19; Luke 24:47;

---

34   The Fellows of the Jesus Seminar, for example, regard the entire section as inauthentic; cf. R. W. Funk and M. H. Smith, *The Gospel of Mark Red Letter Edition* (Sonoma: Polebridge, 1991) 195-97; R. W. Funk and R. W. Hoover (eds.), *The Five Gospels: The Search for the Authentic Words of Jesus* (New York: Macmillan, 1993) 110. As usual, the Seminar fails to distinguish the later contextualization of the early community from the earlier setting and somewhat different meaning the material had in the *Sitz im Leben Jesu*.

35   See Gundry, *Mark*, 767.

36   This is not the place to argue the point, but I believe that the evidence is compelling that Jesus understood himself as the "son of man" (i.e. human) depicted in Daniel 7, to whom God gave authority and the kingdom. It is improbable that this identification arose in the early Church, given the fact that it plays no role in the christology that we see developing in Paul or other early Christian literature.

Acts 1:8; John 20:21).[37] Where did this impulse come from? It is easier to understand this early development, if we suppose that such a mission had its roots in Jesus' teaching and example.[38] Had Jesus taught that the gospel was for Israel alone, the early mission to the Gentiles becomes problematic and not easily explained.

Jesus' allusion to the oracles of Isaiah 56 and Jeremiah 7, at the time of his action in the Temple precincts, is consistent with the factors summarized above. From this I conclude tentatively that Jesus' action was in part motivated by his criticism of the Temple establishment for its failure to live up to its obligations toward, among others, the Gentiles. I further conclude that the appeal to Isaiah 56 and Jeremiah 7 reflected aspects of Solomon's prayer of dedication. I suggest that this criticism on the part of Jesus arose from understanding himself as the Davidic Messiah who, as such, assumed responsibilities for promoting religious reform.

---

[37]   Note also the issue of table fellowship involving Paul (vs. Peter) in Gal 2:15-16 and in Jesus (Mark 2:16-17; Matt 11:19 = Luke 7:34). On purity, see Rom 14:14 in comparison with Mark 7:15 and 20-23 (as well as the evangelist's comment in Mark 7:19).

[38]   Jesus ministered to the Roman centurion at Capernaum (Matt 8:5-13 = Luke 7:1-10), as well as to many considered "marginal" (such as "sinners," "toll collectors," lepers, and others who were infirm).

PAUL AND THE NEW EXODUS

W. D. Davies

It gives me great pleasure to contribute to a collection of studies dedicated to honoring the life and work of James A. Sanders, a distinguished scholar, a gentleman, a stimulating teacher, and a man of faith. Professor Sanders has always been interested in the function of sacred tradition in the life of the believing community. A very rare scholar of the Hebrew Bible and of rabbinics, he is also keenly interested in the use of the Old Testament (or "First Testament," as Professor Sanders prefers to say) in the New (or "Second") Testament. It is a delight for me to return to a discussion that I know will be dear to his heart. In doing so, I conjoin with him his lifelong helpmeet, and memories of years of happy colleagueship in Union Theological Seminary, New York City.*

I wish to speak to the use of sacred tradition in the theology of the Apostle Paul. This sacred tradition comes to the apostle in two important streams: the Scriptures of Israel and the words of Jesus. I shall treat aspects of this tradition under two headings: (1) the Christian dispensation as a new exodus, and (2) echoes of the Jesus tradition in the letters of Paul.

THE CHRISTIAN DISPENSATION AS A NEW EXODUS

There is much to indicate that a very significant part of the conceptual world in which Paul moved, *as a Christian*, was that of the Exodus. It is clear that, as for Matthew and other New Testament writers, so for Paul, there was a real correspondence between the Christian Dispensation and the Exodus of Israel from Egypt. The redemption of the Old Israel was the prototype of the greater

---

*   I should like to thank four people for their help in the publishing of this essay. First, I cannot sufficiently praise the care and imagination which Dr. Craig A. Evans, in collaboration with my old friend Dr. Shemaryahu Talmon, brought to the preparation of this chapter. I am also grateful for the very helpful comments of Dr. D. C. Allison, and to Sarah Freedman for her ready and unfailing competence.

redemption from sin wrought by Christ for the New Israel. This has been much recognized in recent scholarship.[1]

One of Paul's most important passages relating to this subject, 1 Cor 10:1-10, reads as follows:

> I want you to know, brothers, that our fathers were all under the cloud, and all passed through the sea, and all were baptized into Moses in the cloud and in the sea, and all ate the same supernatural food and drank the same supernatural drink. For they drank from the supernatural Rock which followed them, and the Rock was Christ. Nevertheless with most of them God was not pleased; for they were overthrown in the wilderness. Now these things are warnings for us, not to desire evil as they did. Do not be idolaters as some of them were; as it is written, "The people sat down to eat and drink and rose up to dance." We must not indulge in immorality as some of them did, and twenty-three thousand fell in a single day. We must not put the Lord to the test, as some of them did and were destroyed by serpents; nor grumble, as some of them did and were destroyed by the Destroyer.

The interpretation of the Christian life as a counterpart of the Exodus is here made quite explicit; note especially that the experience of the New Exodus, like that of the first, demands the forsaking of immorality (1 Cor 10:8); that is, the taking up of the yoke of Christ, although this is not expressly so stated. Again, Paul's understanding of the Eucharist is largely covenantal; it is for him the institution of the New Israel, the counterpart of the Old (1 Cor 11:20-34).[2] This is reinforced in 1 Cor 5:7, where Christ is referred to as a Passover lamb slain for Christians, and in 1 Cor 15:20, where

---

[1]   See, for example, P. Dabeck, "Siehe, es erschienen Moses und Elias," *Bib* 23 (1942) 175-89; E. Sahlin, "The New Exodus of Salvation," in A. J. Fridrichsen (ed.), *The Root of the Vine* (Westminster: Dacre, 1953); R. Schnackenburg, "Todes- und Lebensgemeinschaft mit Christus: Neue Studien zu Rom. vi. 1-11," *TZ* 6 (1955) 32-35; J. Manek, "The New Exodus and the Book of Luke," *NovT* 2 (1957) 8-23; H. M. Teeple, *The Mosaic Eschatological Prophet* (Philadelphia: SBL, 1957); G. H. Williams, *Wilderness and Paradise in Christian Thought* (New York: Harper, 1962); D. Daube, *The Exodus Pattern in the Bible* (London: Faber and Faber, 1963); U. Mauser, *Christ in the Wilderness: The Wilderness Theme in the Second Gospel and its Basis in the Biblical Tradition* (SBT 39; Naperville: Allenson, 1963); and now especially the extraordinarily rich work of D. C. Allison, *The New Moses: A Matthean Typology* (Philadelphia, Fortress, 1993).

[2]   See my *Paul and Rabbinic Judaism: Some Rabbinic Elements in Pauline Theology* (2nd ed., London: SPCK, 1955; repr. Philadelphia: Fortress, 1980) 250-54.

Christ is the first fruits. This last contains a side-glance at the ritual of the Passover; Christ is the first fruits of a new redemption. Out of the passages where Paul roots the imperative in the indicative (1 Thess 2:10-11; 4:7, 8; 5:5-11; 1 Cor 5:7; Gal 5:1, 25; 2 Cor 8:7; Rom 6:2-4; Col 3:1), two certainly, and a third possibly, are influenced by the thought of the Christian as having undergone a new Exodus. This is so as we saw in 1 Cor 5:7 and the motif of freedom in Gal 5:1 owes something to the motif.[3] Moreover, if our argument elsewhere be accepted that the Pauline concept of dying and rising with Christ is to be understood in terms of a New Exodus,[4] then another passage, Rom 6:2-11, from the six referred to, also contains this idea of the Christian Dispensation as a counterpart to the first Exodus. Among the metaphors used by Paul to expound his experience in Christ is that of "redemption," which, we cannot doubt, was intimately bound up in his mind with the thought of the emancipation of the Old Israel from Egypt (Exod 6:6; 15:13; Deut 7:8; 15:15).[5] In 2 Cor 6:16 the presence of God in the temple of the New Israel, the Church, is expressly understood, we may assume, as

---

[3]   On this, see D. Daube, *The New Testament and Rabbinic Judaism* (London: Athlone, 1956) 282. The whole chapter on "Redemption" (see pp. 268-84) is illuminating.

[4]   Davies, *Paul and Rabbinic Judaism*, 102-108. The language of "dying and rising with Christ" in Paul, particularly in European and continental theology, has been traditionally explained in terms of Hellenistic Mystery religions, whose ideas influenced the Early Church, partly consciously and partly unconsciously. This traditional explanation was subjected to exhaustive examination by A. J. M. Wedderburn in his truly classic work *Baptism and Resurrection: Studies in Pauline Theology Against Its Graeco-Roman Background* (WUNT 44; Tübingen: Mohr [Siebeck], 1987). He concludes that this language finds "no true parallel" in the soteriology of the mysteries (p. 342). He turns instead to "the obvious parallel" in the Mishnaic text relating to the Passover, *m. Pesaḥ.* 10.5, and refers (p. 344) to my own work in *Paul and Rabbinic Judaism*, 102-104, where this is discussed, and even more sympathetically to Jewish ideas of "corporate personality" in the references to Adam. See Wedderburn's rich discussion in pp. 342-348. He finds that while "Davies has rightly perceived the *Grundstruktur* of Paul's thought . . . . Davies was wrong to specify these ideas as peculiarly connected with the Exodus; rather they are basic ideas, ways of looking at things, to which the Jews had given classic expression in their Passover liturgy" (344 n. 9). It still seems to us that it was in that liturgy—with which Paul, as a Pharisee, must have been highly familiar—that he was most directly exposed to the ideas concerned, although the precise form of that liturgy in Paul's day eludes us.

[5]   Davies, *Paul and Rabbinic Judaism*, 268-75.

the realization of the promise made to Moses, as for example in Exod 25:8: "And let them make for me a sanctuary that I may dwell in their midst," or again in Exod 29:43-5: "There will I meet with the people of Israel, and it shall be sanctified by my glory; I will consecrate the tent of meeting and the altar . . . and I will dwell among the people of Israel, and will be their God." This is in agreement with the view that in 2 Corinthians the thought of Paul is largely governed by the understanding of the Christian life in terms of a new covenant (2 Cor 3:1-18) and of the sojourn in the wilderness (2 Cor 5:1-5). Moreover, the reference in 2 Cor 6:14: "or what fellowship has light with darkness?"[6] reminds us that Christians for Paul are children of the day. Thus, in Col 1:12-13, we read ". . . giving thanks to the Father who has qualified us to share in the inheritance of the saints in the light. He has delivered us from the domination of darkness and transferred us to the kingdom of his beloved Son, in whom we have redemption, the forgiveness of sins." It is possible that here the Exodus motif is again apparent in the use of the term "inheritance." In Deuteronomy this term is closely connected with the deliverance from Egypt,[7] and it may be that for Paul it also suggests the eschatological redemption, through the death and Resurrection of Christ, parallel to that wrought at the Exodus. Certainly the motif of "light and darkness" which occurs in the same passage suggests this. In 1 Pet 2:9, 10 this motif occurs in a context which recalls the Exodus, and especially Exod 19:4-6. In *m. Pesaḥ.* 10:5 we read in the Passover service: "Therefore we are bound to give thanks, to praise, to glorify, to honor, to exalt, to extol, and to bless him who wrought all these wonders for our fathers and for us. He brought us out from bondage to freedom, from sorrow to gladness, and from mourning to a festival day, *and from darkness to great light* and from servitude to redemption; so let us say before him the *Hallelujah*" (my emphasis). Specific references to darkness and light are clear in the Exodus story itself. In Exod 10:21-23 we read: "Then the Lord said to Moses, 'Stretch out your hand toward

---

6   The use of the "darkness and light" motif in Paul can be connected perhaps also with the kind of dualism we find in the Dead Sea Scrolls; see S. Wibbing, *Die Tugend- und Lasterkataloge im Neuen Testament* (Berlin: Töpelmann, 1959) 61-63. On 2 Cor 3:1-18; 5:1-2, see *Paul and Rabbinic Judaism*, 106-108, 309-20.

7   The Greek verb "to inherit" (κληρονομεῖν) and its corresponding substantives have a long association with the Exodus, the land of Canaan being the "inheritance" of Israel, as in, for example, Deut 4:20, 21, etc.

heaven that there may be darkness over the land of Egypt, a darkness to be felt.' So Moses stretched out his hand toward heaven, and there was a thick darkness in all the land of Egypt three days; they did not see one another, nor did any rise from his place for three days; but all the people of Israel had light where they dwelt." The parallelism between Old and New Israel there may not be pressed, however because the Old Israel did not strictly pass from darkness, although they were surrounded by it (Exod 12:23). Nevertheless, the symbol of a passage from darkness to light was taken up by Deutero-Isaiah and employed to describe redemption (Isa 42:16)—"I will turn the darkness before them into light, the rough places into level ground," a redemption which was a New Exodus. Paul in Col 1:12-14 may be governed by the same concept.

So far, however, we have only pointed to passages where the concept of Exodus, as the type of Christian redemption, has been employed by Paul in a general sense. In many of the passages cited above as containing the New Exodus motif, while there is an appeal, implicit or explicit, to its consequences in good conduct, there is none to any specific commandment as such which characterizes the New Exodus. Are we then to conclude that it was in the character of the Exodus, almost solely as deliverance, rather than as also imposing a demand, in the giving of the Law, that Paul found it pertinent for the interpretation of the Gospel? In other words, did anything in his understanding of the New Exodus "in Christ" correspond to those events in the total complex of the Exodus that transpired *particularly* at Sinai? It is our contention that there was, and that on grounds which may not be equally cogent but which are all worthy of attention. They constitute the second category of consideration which we mentioned above as specifically suggesting that the words of Jesus were important for Paul.

ECHOES OF THE JESUS TRADITION IN THE LETTERS OF PAUL

We begin with the assertion that it has been insufficiently recognized how frequently the Epistles of Paul echo the Synoptic Gospels, even as it has been too readily assumed that the Apostle was indifferent to the Jesus of history, his works, and especially for our purpose, his words. Two factors are relevant: first, there is clearly traceable in the Epistles a process whereby reminiscences of the words of the Lord Jesus himself are interwoven with traditional material; and, secondly, there is strong evidence that there was a collection of sayings of Jesus to which Paul appealed as authoritative. In this connection 1 Cor 7:25 is particularly instructive. The data we have provided in detail elsewhere; we here merely reiterate that the tables presented by Alfred Resch in his work *Der Paulinismus und die logia Jesu* demand serious evaluation.[8]

It might be observed that whereas Resch found 925 parallels with the Synoptic Gospels in nine Pauline letters, Victor Furnish found only eight which he believed could with any confidence be identified as dominical.[9] According to J. D. G. Dunn in a recent study, "that there can be such a disparity at once tells us how subjective the whole exercise has been and still is."[10] Some of the parallels discussed by Dunn include the following:

Rom 12:14   *"Bless those who persecute you, bless* and do not *curse"*
Luke 6:27-28   "Love your enemies...*bless* those who *curse* you"
Matt 5:44   "Love your enemies and pray for *those who persecute you"*

1 Cor 13:2   "if I *have* all *faith* so as to move (μεθιστάναι) *mountains"*
Matt 17:20   "if you *have faith* . . . you will say to this *mountain,* 'Move from here to there and it will move (μεταβήσεται).'"

1 Thess 5:2, 4 "You yourselves *know* well that the day of the Lord is *coming* like a *thief* in the night...you are not in darkness that the day will surprise you like a thief"
Matt 24:43   "Know this that if the householder had *known* at what watch the *thief* was to *come,* he would have watched."

---

[8]   A. Resch, *Der Paulinismus und die logia Jesu in ihrem gegenseitigen Verhältnis untersucht* (TU 12; Leipzig: Hinrichs, 1904). See Davies, *Paul and Rabbinic Judaism,* 136-38. Cognate to this field of study is Paul's usage of the Old Testament, both explicit and allusive. See the important work by R. B. Hays, *Echoes of Scripture in the Letters of Paul* (New Haven: Yale University Press, 1989), and discussion of this work in C. A. Evans and J. A. Sanders (eds.), *Paul and the Scriptures of Israel* (JSNTSup 83; SSEJC 1; Sheffield: JSOT Press, 1993).

[9]   V. P. Furnish, *Theology and Ethics in Paul* (Nashville: Abingdon, 1968).

[10]   J. D. G. Dunn, "Jesus Tradition in Paul," in B. D. Chilton and C. A. Evans (eds.), *Studying the Historical Jesus: Evaluations of the State of Current Research* (NTTS 19; Leiden: Brill, 1994) 155-78. See also A. M. Hunter, *Paul and His Predecessors* (London: SCM, 1961) 47-51; D. C. Allison, "The Pauline Epistles and the Synoptic Gospels," *NTS* 28 (1982) 1-32; F. Neirynck, "Paul and the Sayings of Jesus," in A. Vanhoye (ed.), *L'Apôtre Paul* (BETL 73; Leuven: Peeters, 1986) 265-321.

1 Thess 5:13 *"live at peace among* yourselves" (εἰρηνεύετε ἐν
ἑαυτοῖς)

Mark 9:50   *"live at peace with* one another" (εἰρηνεύετε ἐν ἀλλήλοις)

Rom 16:19   "I want you to be *wise* (σοφούς) in regard to what is good
and *innocent* (ἀκεραίους) in regard to what is bad."

Matt 10:16 "Be *wise* (φρόνιμοι) as serpents and *innocent* (ἀκέραιοι)
as doves."

1 Thess 5:6 "So then, let us not sleep as others do, but let us *keep
awake* (γρηγορῶμεν) and be sober"

Matt 24:42 *"Keep awake* (γρηγορεῖτε) therefore" (cf. Luke 21:34-36)

1 Thess 5:16 *"Rejoice* (χαίρετε) at all times"

Luke 10:20 *"Rejoice* (χαίρετε) that your names have been written in
heaven"

With the echoes of the teaching of Jesus in his epistles it must be
assumed that Paul refers to a law of the Messiah.[11] This is not a mere
overhang from a pre-Pauline Jewish-Christian legalism unrelated to
the essentials of Paul's thought. In addition to what we have noted in
another work, the evidence seems to suggest that the interpretation of
the teaching of Jesus as a New Law was not necessarily aboriginal in
primitive Jewish-Christianity but only comes into prominence in
later Jewish-Christianity after the fall of Jerusalem in A.D. 70.[12] Nor
again is the phrase "the law of Christ" to be explained away as a
vague equivalent to an immanent principle of life like the Stoic law
of nature.[13] Moreover, though there are places where Paul seems to
understand the law of the Messiah as fulfilled in the law of love, this
last also does not exhaust the meaning of the phrase. Almost certainly
it is a comprehensive expression for the totality of the ethical

---

[11]   1 Cor 9:21; Gal 6:2. See Davies, *Paul and Rabbinic Judaism*, 142; C. H.
Dodd, "Ἔννομος Χριστοῦ," in W. C. van Unnik et al. (eds.), *Studia Paulina in
honorem Johannis de Zwaan* (Haarlem: Bohn, 1953) 96-110.

[12]   See M. Simon, *Verus Israel* (Paris: Éditions E. de Boccard, 1948) 100-103,
whose treatment, however, also shows that there were anticipations of the later
interpretation of Christianity, as a New Law in the New Testament itself, for example, Jas 1:25; Gal 6:2; Heb 7:12. The notion of a New Law is closely associated
with that of a new people (see Simon, pp. 102-103); J. Daniélou (*Théologie du
Judeo-Christianisme* [2 vols., Paris: Desclée, 1958] 1.216-18) notes how Christ
became not only a New Law but the New Covenant.

[13]   C. H. Dodd, *The Bible and the Greeks* (2nd ed., Naperville: Allenson,
1954 [orig. 1935]) 37; the view is retracted in "Ἔννομος Χριστοῦ." See also H.
Schürmann, "'Das Gesetz des Christus' (Gal. 6:2)," in J. Gnilka (ed.), *Neues
Testament und Kirche* (Freiburg: Herder, 1974) 282-300.

teaching of Jesus that had come down to Paul as authoritative. Paul's vocabulary at several points makes it clear that he regarded himself as the heir of a tradition of ethical, as of other, teaching, which he had received and which he had to transmit. He was the servant of one who had criticized the tradition of the fathers as obscuring the true will of God; he himself violently attacked the same tradition. Nevertheless, he turns out on examination to be the steward of a new tradition.[14]

The *content* of this tradition can be broadly divided into two groups:

(1) That which deals with Christian preaching where the tradition is identified with the gospel or the apostolic message itself. The chief passages are as follows (my emphasis):

"For I *delivered* to you as of first importance what I also *received,* that Christ died for our sins in accordance with the scriptures, that he was buried, that he was raised on the third day in accordance with the scriptures, and that he appeared to Cephas, then to the twelve. Then he appeared to more than five hundred brethren at one time, most of whom are still alive, thought some have fallen asleep. Then he appeared to James, then to all the apostles. Last of all, as to one untimely born, he appeared also to me. For I am the least of the apostles, unfit to be called an apostle, because I persecuted the church of God. But by the grace of God I am what I am, and his grace toward me was not in vain. On the contrary, I worked harder than any of them, though it was not I, but the grace of God which is with me. Whether then it was I or they, so we preach and so you believed" (1Cor 15:3-11).

"For I would have you know, brethren, that the gospel which was preached by me is not man's gospel. For I did not *receive* it from man, nor was I taught it, but it came through a revelation of Jesus Christ" (Gal 1:11-12).

"As therefore you *received* Christ Jesus the Lord, so live in him, rooted and built up in him and established in the faith, just as you

---

[14]   For what follows, see these pivotal works: O. Cullmann, "The Tradition," in A. J. B. Higgins (ed.), *The Early Church* (London: SCM, 1966) 59-104; L. Cerfaux, "La tradition selon Saint Paul," in *Recueil Lucien Cerfaux* (2nd ed., Gembloux: Duculot, 1954) 253-82; H. Riesenfeld, *The Gospel Tradition and its Beginnings* (Oxford: Blackwell; Philadelphia: Fortress, 1970); P. Neuenzeit, *Das Herrenmahl* (Munich: Kösel, 1960) 77-88; J. Waggenmann, *Die Stellung des Apostels Paulus neben den Zwölf* (Giessen: Töpelmann, 1926) 464-73.

were taught, abounding in thanksgiving. See to it that no one makes a prey of you by philosophy and empty deceit, according to human *tradition*, according to the elemental spirits of the universe, and not according to Christ" (Col 2:6-8).

(2) Tradition concerned strictly with rules or orders for the Christian life, as in 1 Cor 11:2: "I commend you because you remember me in everything and maintain the *traditions* which you were taught by us, either by word of mouth or by letter." (See also 1 Cor 7:10, 12, 40; 11:14; 1 Thess 4:15.)

The *forms* of the terminology employed to describe the reception and transmission of all forms of the traditions in both (1) and (2), while they appear in Hellenistic sources,[15] almost certainly have their origin for Paul in a Jewish milieu. Note the following: "hold to the tradition" (1 Cor 11:2; 15:2; compare Mark 7:18); "stand in the Gospel which you have received" (1 Cor 15:1; in the traditions, 2 Thess 2:15). Most striking, however, is the use of "receive" and "deliver" (1 Cor 11:2, 23; 15:3; 1 Thess 2:13; 2 Thess 2:15; 3:6; Gal 1:9, 12; Phil 4:9; Col 2:6, 8), which translate the Hebrew *qibbel min* and *masar le* respectively.

Thus, the *terminology* used by Paul was customary in Judaism. Are we to conclude from this that he regarded the Christian tradition as similar in its nature to that handed down in Judaism, or was there an essential difference between them? In other words, is there a "rabbinic" element in the Pauline understanding of tradition, that is, the conception of a tradition of a prescribed way of life transmitted from "authority" to "authority"? The question revolves around Paul's understanding of the source of the Christian tradition with which he was concerned. And in the first group of material, mentioned above, the tradition is explicitly stated to have been derived, not from men but directly from God. In 1 Thess 2:13 it constitutes the message *of God*; and while in 1 Cor 15:1-11 its exact source is not described, both in Gal 1:11-12 and Col 2:6-8 the tradition is deliberately, and very forcefully, set over against the tradition of men. Thus, so far as the content of his Gospel as such is concerned, that is, if we may so express it, as kerygma, Paul insists that it was given of God himself, who was its soul source. However, while in 1 Cor 15:1-11 Paul does not describe the source of the

---

15   J. Dupont, *Gnosis* (Paris: Gabalda, 1949) 59-60.

tradition, he clearly presents it in non-Pauline terms,[16] in a form molded by the Church probably at Jerusalem, so that in one sense he can be claimed to have received it from men. But this is true for him only of the form; the substance of the tradition was God, as his call was from God. While Paul could not but be aware of human agencies who had been at work in the precise formulation of the tradition containing his Gospel, his emphasis was not on this aspect of the matter, which was entirely secondary. What intermediaries there were in themselves were not significant. Paul's emphasis was on the Gospel as born of the divine initiative in Christ. As far, then, as what we may call the primary content of the kerygma was concerned, the tradition was not understood by Paul in a rabbinic manner. This is as true of 1 Cor 15:1-11, as of Gal 1:11-12. Even though in 1 Cor 15:1-11 he might seem at first sight to be quoting authorities, as does *Pirqe Abot* 1:1-2, this is, in fact, not the case. The authorities in 1 Cor 15:1-11 are not teachers transmitting an interpretation of a primary deposit, the one to another, but witnesses severally of a primary event. In *Abot* 1:1-2 we find a chain of successive authorities; in 1 Cor 15;1-11 a series of "original" witnessess. The chronological sequence in *Abot* denotes authorities increasingly removed from contact with the original deposit, and increasingly dependent on the preceding secondary authorities, but the chronological sequence in 1 Cor 15:1-11 is intended merely to describe the order in which the "immediacy" of the event was experienced by each witness; that is, it is not a rabbinic sequence. The source of Paul's Gospel is God himself, who took the initiative in revealing himself in Jesus Christ, and, through his Resurection, created witnesses to Jesus Christ in the world. Thus Jesus Christ is not strictly the source of the kerygmatic tradition but its content: Jesus of Nazareth, crucified, buried, and risen is the primary deposit of the Christian tradition, given by God himself. In 2 Corinthians Paul contrasts the Christian ministry with that of the Old Covenant, and it is of the highest significance that it is Paul himself, not Jesus, who is set in parallelism with Moses: Jesus is rather parallel to the Law, that is, the revelation granted to Moses. Jesus is not the first link in a chain of teachers, no new Moses, but rather a new "Law."[17]

---

16   J. Jeremias, *The Eucharistic Words of Jesus* (London: SCM, 1966) 101-105.

17   Davies, *Paul and Rabbinic Judaism*, 148-50.

As far, then, as those passages which deal with the kerygma as a tradition are concerned, Paul does not think of himself as a Christian rabbi dependent upon teachers, the first of whom was Jesus. But what of those in the second group, isolated above, concerned with the tradition of teaching? Is there here another emphasis in which Jesus is thought of as a New Moses? In 1 Corinthians 10 the implication is unmistakable that Jesus is such: incorporation into Christ, the Rock, who is distinguished from the first Moses, is, nevertheless, parallel to that into Moses, and here the moral reverence of the incorporation is made clear. The passages in which Paul cites the words of the Lord as authoritative would seem to support this implication. But here there is a complication. Paul in 1 Cor 10:1–11:1 uses the term, not Jesus, but Christ: elsewhere he speaks neither of a law nor of a word "of Jesus," but "of Christ" and "of the Lord." Is this significant? Oscar Cullmann thinks that it is. While recognizing that there were words *of Jesus* in the tradition, by concentrating his attention on a passage which we omitted from our classifications above, because it demands separate treatment, Cullmann comes to a striking conclusion. The passage concerned is the following in 1 Cor 11:23-24: "For I received from the Lord what I also delivered to you, that the Lord Jesus on the night when he was betrayed took bread, and when he had given thanks, he broke it and said, 'This is my body which is for you. Do this in remembrance of me.'"

Here the source of a particular tradition—not, however, an ethical one—is declared to be "the Lord," which refers so Cullmann maintains, neither to God, the ultimate source of the kerygma, nor to the Jesus of history, but to the Risen Lord. This can only be reconciled with the fact that we have previously noted, that Paul had received tradition from others, by claiming that the Lord, the exalted Christ, was himself the transmitter of his own words and deeds. Thus in 1 Cor 7:10, "Unto the married I command, yet not I but the Lord," "*it is the exalted Lord who now proclaims to the Corinthians, through the tradition, what he had taught his disciples during his incarnation on earth.*"[18] Elsewhere in Col 2:6 the Lord is the content of the tradition. The Lord is, therefore, both author and content of the tradition; the genitive in the phrase "the Gospel of Christ," in Rom 15:19 and elsewhere, is a subjective genitive: "the exalted Christ is

---

18   O. Cullmann, *The Early Church* (Philadelphia: Westminster, 1956) 68. His emphasis.

Himself originator of the Gospel of which He is also the object."[19] While, as we noted above, the tradition is connected with the Jesus of history, Cullmann insists that we owe the tradition really to the exalted Lord. On 1 Cor 11:23 he writes: "The designation *Kyrios* not only points to the historical Jesus as the chronological beginning of the chain of tradition as the first member of it, but accepts the exalted Lord as the real author of the whole tradition developing itself in the apostolic Church. Thus the apostolic *paradosis* can be set directly on a level with the exalted *Kyrios*."[20] The use of the aorist in 1 Cor 11:14 indicated how the exalted Lord who *now* commands in 1 Cor 7:10 and probably in 1 Thess 4:15 is the same as the Jesus who walked on earth. "The exalted One Himself after His resurrection delivers the words which He has spoken." In this way, although Cullmann does not ignore the historical Jesus in this matter, he virtually relegated him to the background and elevated the *Kyrios* to supreme significance. It agrees with this that it is necessary for the exalted Lord to repeat what he had declared on earth. Moreover, Cullmann is thus able to connect the tradition with the activity of the Spirit, because the *Kyrios* is closely related to, if not identified with, the Spirit in Paul.[21] The conclusion is that tradition in Paul is opposed to the rabbinic principle of tradition in Judaism in two ways: "Firstly, that the mediator of the tradition is not the teacher but the *Apostle* a the direct witness, secondly, the principle of succession does not operate mechanically as with the rabbis, but is bound to the Holy Spirit."[22] Cullmann refuses to treat the two groups of material distinguished above as different kinds of tradition: they are both to be understood as derived, as an undifferentiated whole, from the Lord, so that not only the kerygmatic tradition that Paul received and transmitted, but also the didactic is to some extent removed from the historical Jesus, and any analogy between Christian and Jewish tradition is obviated. Jesus as teacher, or Jesus as counterpart of Moses, has little significance for the tradition, but only Jesus as Lord. The Christ of Paul is not easily recognizable as the Jesus of the Mount, as Matthew understood him.

---

[19]   Cullmann, *The Early Church*, 69.

[20]   Cullmann, *The Early Church*, 62.

[21]   Cullmann, *The Early Church*, 70-72. See Davies, *Paul and Rabbinic Judaism*, 182, 196.

[22]   Cullmann, *The Early Church*.

But is Paul so to be interpreted? Is the sharp distinction between the exalted Lord and the Jesus of history which Cullmann finds really present in Paul? Certain considerations are pertinent.

(1) The exegesis of certain texts suggested by Cullmann is questionable. Thus in 1 Cor 7:10, 12, is it correct to interpret the verse to mean that the exalted Lord is now commanding (v. 10) or refusing to command (v. 12)? In 1 Cor 9:14 the past tense is used of a command of the Lord and it is probable that the reference in the former two passages is also to a commandment given by Jesus in the past, which is in force in the present. When Shakespeare wrote of the pound of flesh, he did not mean Shylock to imply that the particular law referred to was there and then enacted, although he used the present tense. So too Paul in 1 Cor 7:10, 12 merely claims that a past commandment of Jesus is still in force.

Again the very passage on which Cullmann leans most, 1 Cor 11:23-6, points not to a distinction between Jesus and "the Lord," but to their identity. In 11:26 we read: "For as often as you eat this bread and drink the cup, you proclaim the Lord's death until he comes."[23] Clearly the "Lord's" death can only refer to the death of the historical Jesus, which probably takes the place in the "Christian Passover" or Eucharist of the historical event of the Exodus in the Haggadah of the Passover. The Jesus remembered and proclaimed is also the present Lord and the Lord to come. Past, present, and future meet in the name "Lord," because "the Lord" is "Jesus." That very Holy Spirit to which Cullmann appeals in support of his position testifies to this very truth. While "no one speaking by the Spirit of God ever says 'Jesus be cursed!'," it is equally valid that "no one can say 'Jesus is Lord,' except by the Holy Spirit" (1 Cor 12:3).

(2) It has been claimed that Paul never refers to a word of Jesus as a commandment. This, however, is debatable.[24] In any case, the claim might be countered by the statement that nowhere does Paul regard the Spirit, the connection of which with "the Lord" Cullmann rightly emphasizes, as the source of ethical commandments, although

---

[23]   The force of "proclaim" here is "to make haggadah of it"—as was the Exodus "proclaimed" in the Passover Haggadah. See Davies, *Paul and Rabbinic Judaism*, 252-53; G. B. Gray, *Sacrifice in the Old Testament* (Oxford: Clarendon, 1925) 395. For another approach, see Neuenzeit, *Das Herrenmahl*, 128-30.

[24]   See the fuller discussion of this material in Davies, *The Setting of the Sermon of the Mount* (Cambridge: Cambridge University Press, 1964) 341-66.

it is that of moral power. The term "law" in Rom 8:2 ("For the law of the Spirit of life in Christ Jesus has set me free from the law of sin and death") denotes not so much commandments as "principle."

(3) A factor which is not clear in Cullmann's discussion is the exact meaning which he ascribes to the term "Lord." Does he mean the "Risen Lord" and the "Exalted Lord" to refer to the same phenomenon? He uses the two terms apparently interchangeably and rather sharply sparates both the Risen Lord and the Exalted Lord, whom he seems not to distinguish, from the historical Jesus. The improbability that this separation should be accepted appears when we set Paul's understanding of the didactic role of the Lord, as Cullmann understands it, over against the data in the rest of the New Testament. Mark's conception of the activity of the Risen Lord we cannot certainly determine, either because the end of his Gospel has been lost, or, if he did finish it at 16:8, because he does not tell us anything about this activity. If we follow R. H. Lightfoot and others, and find in Mark 16:8 the expectation of an almost immediate Parousia to be enacted in Galilee, then no didactic activity of the Risen Lord can have been contemplated by Mark.[25] Clearly Mark cannot help us in our quest into the functions of the Risen Lord. Matthew, however, is rich in significance just at this point. It is probable that for Matthew the Resurrection is coincident with the glorification of Jesus as Lord. "All authority in heaven and on earth *has* been given to Him": the aorist tense in 28:18 is to be taken seriously. Jesus as Risen is in heaven, that is, glorified. But the ethical instructions which he issues are identified with those which he had given to his own while on earth, and, we may assume, particularly those recorded in Matthew's "Sermon on the Mount."[26] The Jesus of history had initiated an ethical paradosis which the glorified Christ reaffirms; the latter neither initiates the Christian paradosis nor repeats what, as the historical Jesus, he had previously delivered on earth: he needs merely to refer to the tradition of the latter. When we turn to Luke there is a significant change. The Risen Christ instructs his own (Luke 24:27, 44-49; Acts 1:6-8), although no explicit reference is made to any moral

---

[25]   R. H. Lightfoot, *Locality and Doctrine in the Gospels* (London: Hodder and Stoughton, 1938) 1-48; idem, *The Gospel Message of St. Mark* (Oxford: Clarendon, 1950) 80-97.

[26]   Lightfoot, *Locality and Doctrine*, 66-68 (on Matt 28:16-20). He does not do justice to the didactic factor in the passage.

teaching he may have given. After forty days, however, the Risen
Christ ascended into heaven, where he was glorified. Contact with
him, of a direct kind such as had been theirs hitherto, is now denied
his disciples until he comes again "in the same way as you say him go
unto heaven" (Acts 1:11). the Risen Christ taught the things concerning himself (Luke 24:44-48) and gave commands (Acts 1:2) and
spoke of the Kingdom of God (Acts 1:3)—all of which possibly[27]
implies ethical instruction—with a reference to what he had taught
on earth. But the impression given is that the *glorified* Christ did not
teach. This is the emphasis in Acts 2:32-6; 3:13-21, which reflect
perhaps the earliest Christian preaching, and, by implication possibly, in Acts 13:30-31. On the other hand, in Acts 10:40-41 the
Resurrection alone is to the fore, there being no emphasis on any
Ascension. A didactic function is ascribed to the Risen Christ. Luke
would seem to confine teaching whether ethical or other to the latter.
the Lord of Glory is not directly available for such.[28] In the Fourth
Gospel there is a reference to the Ascension implied in 20:17, but
emphasis is laid most on the Risen Christ. Moreover, for John the
real glorification of Jesus had already occurred in the crucifixion.[29]
It follows that there is nothing in the Fourth Gospel comparable to
Matt 28:16-20 because, essentially, the Resurrection could add nothing to the glory of the crucifixion. For John it is neither the Risen
Jesus nor the Exalted Lord who exercises the task of teaching in the
Church, but the Holy Spirit, to which this function is not thus directly applied in Paul. The content of the teaching of the Spirit, however, is rooted in teaching already given by the historical Jesus. "But
the counsellor, the Holy Spirit," so we read, "whom the Father will
send in my name, he will teach you all things, and bring to your remembrance all that I have said to you" (John 14:26).

For our purpose what is significant in all the above is that,
however the relation between the Risen Christ and the glorified or
exalted Lord be conceived in the rest of the New Testament, whether
in terms of Ascension or not, the teaching asribed to both figures

---

27   The exact content of the teaching in Acts 1:2-3 is difficult to assess. It is too
precarious to claim on this basis that the Risen Lord gave ethical instructions. But
this does not invalidate the distinction we make in the text between the Risen and
Glorified Lord in Acts.

28   In Matthew there is no statement on the Ascension as such.

29   See, for example, John 17:1.

always has reference to the teaching of the historical Jesus, both in ethical and other matters. The presumption, therefore, is that Paul also, unless he was quite removed from the main currents of the Church, intended the same reference. This is particularly reinforced by the fact that Paul's understanding of the Risen Christ seems to be closest to that of Matthew. He does not mention any Ascension, but only appearances of the Risen Christ, who becomes the object of worship of the Church. The Resurrection would appear to be for him the glorification.[30] That the glorified one was the Risen Jesus would therefore have been central to Paul. That he called him the Lord does not mean that he was removed from the Jesus or history, with whom he is indeed identical.

(4) This last leads us to what should never have been questioned, namely, that the term "Lord" stands in Paul for the historical Jesus in 1 Cor 11:23. The last phrase, "you proclaim the Lord's death until he comes," in 1 Cor 11:26 *must* refer to the historical Jesus and any distinction between "the Lord" and "the Lord Jesus" in 1 Cor 11:23 is unlikely. In Acts 9:5, 13, 17, 27, 22:8, 19; 26:15 the Risen Lord is make to refer to himself as Jesus, and "Lord" is used of Jesus 80, 18, 103, 52 times respectively in Matthew, Mark, Luke, John. Early Christianity thought of the historical Jesus as "Lord," and so did Paul.[31]

Paul then inherited and transmitted a tradition which has two elements, a kerygmatic and didactic. How are these elements related in his thought? Were they sharply differentiated, as Cerfaux holds, on being conceived as from God and the other having its *point de départ* in the historical Jesus, so that there are two sources for the tradition? Or is Cullmann[32] justified in claiming that both elements issue from the Risen or Exalted Lord, who took the place of all Jewish parado-

---

[30] It agrees with this that the Resurrection of Christ is the inauguration of the New Age, not of an age preliminary to this; see Davies, *Paul and Rabbinic Judaism*, 285-320; and more recently D. C. Allison, Jr., *The End of the Ages Has Come: An Early Interpretation of the Passion and Resurrection of Jesus* (Philadelphia: Fortress, 1985; repr. in Studies of the New Testament and Its World; Edinburgh: T. & T. Clark, 1987).

[31] For a balanced statement, see L. Cerfaux, *Christ in the Theology of St. Paul* (New York: Herder and Herder, 1959) 179-89, esp. pp. 187-88.

[32] On Cullmann's understanding of "the Lord," see *The Christology of the New Testament* (London: SCM, 1959) 195-97. Surprisingly he does not develop his understanding of the Lord as a designation of "the tradition" in this volume.

sis? Cullmann makes too sharp a distinction between the Lord as the source of all paradosis, and the historical Jesus as, at least, the source of the didactic *paradosis*. Cerfaux makes too rigid a distinction between the two kinds of paradosis. But he does greater justice to the texts by giving due place to the historical Jesus as an initiator of one aspect of the tradition. Jesus as Lord and Jesus as teacher were both one for Paul. He may have dwelt more in his epistles on the former, but this is not because he did not recognize the significance of the teaching of Jesus, which to him was authoritative.

And this brings us to the final point, the possibility that for Paul the Person and the Words of Jesus had assumed the significance of a New Torah. In addition to the evidence for this supplied above, we refer to our treatment elsewhere.[33] The objections to this view have been many. But too much weight should not be accorded to the claim that, since Paul was indifferent to the life of Jesus, he was also indifferent to his moral teaching. Nor need the absence of as explicit claim that Jesus is the New Torah be taken as decisive.[34] The same motives which may have led Paul to avoid the use of the term *Logos*, the fear of being misunderstood by Hellenists, may have led him to avoid the description of Christ as the New Torah, which might have been misleading, in discussions with Jewish-Christian and Jewish opponents. Most serious is the objection that the concept of Christ as the New Torah contradicts Paul's radical criticism of the Law and his insistence on salvation as a free gift of grace in the epistles. The Law is there conceived of as a preliminary, provisional discipline, whose term the coming of Christ has closed.[35] Indeed does not the Law for Paul come to fulfill functions ascribed by Judaism to Satan himself?[36] Thus, that Paul thought of Christ in terms of the Law is unlikely; more likely was he to view the Law in terms of Christ.

Full force must be given to these objections. But while, in ascribing to Paul the concept of Christ as the New Torah we are going outside Paul's *explicit* words or formulae, we are hardly going beyond his implicit intention, if we can judge this form his use of

---

33 See Davies, *Paul and Rabbinic Judaism*, 147-76.

34 Contrast at this point L. Cerfaux, *Christ in the Theology of St. Paul*, 274 n. 36; and W. Manson, in his review of my *Paul and Rabbinic Judaism*, in *SJT* 1 (1948) 217-19, esp. 218-19.

35 I have summarized this in Davies, "Law in the New Testament," *IDB* 95-102.

36 G. B. Caird, *Principalities and Powers* (Oxford: Clarendon, 1956) 41.

Jesus' words and life in is ethical exhortations and from his application to Jesus of those categories that Judaism had reserved for its hightest treasure, namely, the Torah, that is, preexistence, agency in creation, wisdom. To be "in Christ" was for Paul to have died and risen with him in a New Exodus, and this in term meant that he was to be subject to the authority of the words and Person of Christ as a pattern. The historical circumstances of Paul's ministry, set as it was in a conflict against Judaizers, has given to this aspect of his interpretation of the Christian Dispensation a secondary place, a fact further accentuated by the violence of Paul's personal engagement with the Law in Judaism not strictly as "Law" in the sense of moral demand only but as a whole cultural or social system which ad the effect of cutting him off from the fascinating Gentile world.[37] But, though Paul attacked Judaizers and avoids referring to himself or to Christians as "disciples," at no point is he free from the constraint of Christ's example: he has as a Christian "learnt Christ,"[38] and this we may understand in a twofold way. He has learnt his words as formerly he did those of the Torah,[39] and he has become an imitator of Christ,[40] as formerly he had doubtless been an imitator of Gamaliel. The process of learning in Judaism had a twofold aspect— the learning of teaching and the imitation of a life, that of the rabbi. The concept of the rabbi as living Torah and, therefore, as the object of imitation would be familiar to Paul, as it would have been to Philo,[41] who regards the patriarchs as living the Law before it was

---

[37]   See C. H. Dodd, *New Testament Studies* (Manchester: University of Manchester Press, 1953) 72. That Luther's struggle over Law and Gospel was also sociologically conditioned is noted by W. Joest, *Gesetz und Freiheit* (Göttingen: Vandenhoeck & Ruprecht, 1951) 135; and E. Benz, "Das Paulus-Verständnis," in *ZRGG* 4 (1951) 289-91.

[38]   On the expression to "learn Christ" (Eph 4:21), see W. Manson, *Jesus the Messiah* (Naperville: Allenson, 1943) 54.

[39]   This is implied in his use of the citation to which we have already referred.

[40]   1 Cor. 11:1; 1 Thess 1:6; Phil 2:5.

[41]   See my volume, *Torah in the Messianic Age and/or The Age to Come* (SBLMS 7; Philadelphia: SBL, 1952). It is not irrelevant to restate the fact that the Law itself has a "personal" character for Philo; see J. Daniélou, *Théologie du Judeo-Christianisme*, 1.217. For Judaism, see my essay, "Law in First Century Judaism," *IDB* 89-95; repr. in Davies, *Jewish and Pauline Studies* (London: SPCK; Philadelphia: Fortress, 1984) 3-26; now see E. P. Sanders, *Paul, the Law and the Jewish People* (Philadelphia: Fortress, 1983); idem, *Jewish Law from Jesus to the Mishnah: Five Studies* (London: SCM; Philadephia: Trinity Press

given. When Paul refers to himself as an imitator of Christ he is doubtless thinking of Jesus as the Torah he has to copy—both in his words and deeds. A passage in Rom 6:15-17 suggests the formative power of the teaching of Jesus in Paul's conception of the Christian life, and reveals his understanding of this teaching in relation to grace. It reads: "What then? Are we to sin because we are not under law but under grace? By no means! Do you not know that if you yield yourselves to any one as obedient slaves, you are slaves of the one whom you obey, either of sin, which leads to death, or of obedience, which leads to righteousness? But thanks be to God, that you who were once slaves of sin *have become obedient from the heart to the standard of teaching to which you were committed*, and, having been set free from sin, have become slaves of righteousness" (my emphasis).

The precise meaning of the words "have become obedient from the heart to the standard of teaching to which you were committed . . ." in Rom 6:17 has been disputed. F. W. Beare's comment, however, is to be treated seriously. He finds Paul to be claiming that "the Christian Didache, when it is followed with a wholehearted obedience, imparts to our lives a specific character and pattern, moulding them into the likeness of Christ. St. Paul speaks more often, it is true, of the power of the Spirit as the transforming influence in the Christian life; but it is quite wrong to imagine that he thinks of the leadings of the Spirit as a succession of formless impulses or vagrant illuminations. Here, in correlation with the call for obedience, he thinks naturally enough of the specific moral instruction in which the guiding of the Spirit is given concrete expression (Phil 4:8-9). For all his faith in the Spirit, the Apostle thinks of the Christian life as disciplined and ordered in keeping with clear and concrete instruction given by precept and example. Such teaching is here conceived as the die or pattern which shapes the whole of the life which yields it it, in conformity with the will of God. No antithesis with the Law or with other (non-Pauline) "forms" is implied or suggested. He is thinking simply of the *didache* which belongs to the Gospel, the teaching concerning the way of life which is worthy of the Gospel of Christ, considered as a mould which gives to the new life its appro-

---

International, 1990); idem, "Law in Judaism of the NT Period," *ABD* 4 (1992) 254-65; and Allison, *The New Moses*, 228-30, where Allison discusses the tradition of Moses himself as Torah.

priate shape or pattern."[42] The Christian life as Paul understood it
was lived within a normative ethical tradition. This tradition is not
an isolated deposit, however, but part and parcel of what Paul understands by the Christian Dispensation, and, therefore, seen, not in opposition to grace, but as a concomitant of it. At no point is Paul
without law (*anomos*); he is always with law (*ennomos*). To this extent Paul is at one with Matthew who also places the law of Christ in
a context of the grace of Christ. This is nowhere clearer than in a
section which is usually quoted in proof of the succor of Christ, but
which also contains within itself the demand of Christ. "Come to me,
all who labor and are heavy-laden, and I will give you rest. Take my
yoke upon you, and learn from me; for I am gentle and lowly in
heart, and you will find rest for your souls. For my yoke is easy and
my burden is light" (Matt 11:28-30). The "yoke of Christ" stands
over against the yoke of the Law. The upshot of all this is that Paul,
who is usually set in antithesis to matthew, would probably not have
found the Matthaean emphasis on the "law of Christ" either strange
or uncongenial. He, too, knew of the same law, although the circumstances of his ministry demanded from him greater concentration on
other aspects of the Gospel.[43]

We may now sum up. In the light of the above, it can be urged that
Paul had access to a tradition of the words of Jesus. This he had
"received" and this he "transmitted"; to this, whenever necessary and
possible, he appealed as authoritative, so that this tradition
constituted for him part of the "law of Christ." Caution is, however,
necessary in making this claim. Out of the epistles as a whole, the
passages where this emerges are few and the use that the Apostle
made of a catechesis derived possibly from a non-Christian
Hellenistic-Jewish tradition, into which he introduced few, if any,
express words of Jesus, makes it doubly clear that he did not
formulate a "Christian-rabbinic" casuistry on the basis of the words
of Jesus that he had received. Whether the reason for the paucity of
evidence in this matter is due to the historical fact that Paul during
his ministry had to contend with "judaizing" tendencies, as was

---

[42]   F. W. Beare, "On the Interpretation of Rom. vi. 17," *NTS* 5 (1959) 206-
10. We should emphasize, as Beare does not, the role of the words of Jesus in the
tradition. Beare refers to the other interpretations that have been suggested. We find
his the most plausible, with the qualifications mentioned.

[43]   Compare Cullmann, *The Early Church*.

suggested above, is uncertain. Nevertheless, it is not going too far to claim that part of the being "in Christ" for Paul was standing under the words of Jesus. Paul, like Matthew, appealed to these words as authoritative. As for Matthew, so for Paul, there was a real corresondence between the Christian Dispensation and the events of the Exodus. The redemption of Israel from Egypt was the prototype of the greater redemption from sin wrought by Christ. Thus Christ for Paul also had the lineaments of a new and greater Moses. He shared with Matthew a common understanding of Christ and his words. Like Matthew, Paul too can speak of a law of Christ, partly, at least, composed of Jesus' words; he was governed by a tradition. Like Matthew, Paul too can speak of a law of Christ, partly, at least, composed of Jesus' words; he was governed by a tradition.[44]

---

44   The notion of Christ as the New Torah in Paul—a phrase which he himself never explicitly used—has been widely criticized. See E. P. Sanders, *Paul and Palestinian Judaism* (London: SCM; Philadelphia: Fortress Press, 1977) 479; studies by S. Westerholm, in P. Richardson and S. Westerholm (eds.), *Law in Religious Communities in the Roman Period: The Debate over Torah and Names in Post-Biblical Judaism and Early Christianity* (Studies in Christianity and Judaism 4; Waterloo: Wilfrid Laurier University Press, 1991) 54-55, 80-85; F. Thielman, *From Plight to Salvation: A Jewish Framework for Understanding Paul's View of the Law in Galatians and Romans* (NovTSup 62; Leiden: Brill, 1989) 11. Allison (*The New Moses*) is more sympathetic. For my attempt to accept criticisms and respond to them also, see my "Canon and Christology in Paul," in Evans and Sanders (eds.), *Paul and the Scriptures of Israel*, 18-39, esp. 35-39; and my *Paul and Rabbinic Judaism* (4th ed., Philadelphia: Fortress, 1980) xxvii-xxxviii, where I deal with the works of the honoree of this volume in his *Torah and Canon* (Philadelphia: Fortress, 1972) xxviii-xxx, and of E. P. Sanders, xxix-xxxviii, the former being more sympathetic or receptive than the latter. In a seminar John Barclay made it clear that in Gal 6:2, in his judgment, it is unwise too quickly to turn to the Rabbinic parallel for the "law of Christ." See also his rich work *Obeying the Truth: A Study of Paul's Ethic in Galatians* (Edinburgh: T. & T. Clark, 1988) *ad rem.*

PAUL'S UNDERSTANDING OF THE TEXTUAL CONTRADICTION BETWEEN HABAKKUK 2:4 AND LEVITICUS 18:5

J. Louis Martyn

In Gal 3:11 and 3:12 Paul quotes from Hab 2:4 and from Lev 18:5.[1] He knows that these two texts do not at all say the same thing. Both speak of future life (ζήσεται), but whereas Hab 2:4 says that faith leads to life, Lev 18:5 says that the route to life lies in observance of the Law. We will call the form displayed in Gal 3:11-12 a Textual Contradiction.

Ancient instances of the Textual Contradiction fall into two broad types. The first consists of traditions that display abstract rules developed in scholastic discussions lacking a genuine polemical cast. This type of Textual Contradiction is of limited help in illuminating the line of thought in Gal 3:11-12, for Paul does not compose those verses in order to put himself at ease by showing how a mind-troubling contradiction between two scripture texts can be resolved.[2] On the contrary, these verses fit well into the section begun at 3:6, by continuing the real-life polemic in which Paul pits his own exegetical argument quite specifically against that of the Christian-Jewish evangelists whose work in his Galatian churches has brought his blood to a boil (I refer hereafter to these persons as "the Teachers").[3]

---

[1]   Remaining instructive on Hab 2:4, an early work of J. A. Sanders, "Habak-kuk in Qumran, Paul, and the Old Testament" (*JR* 39 [1959] 232-44), has been updated and reissued in C. A. Evans and J. A. Sanders (eds.), *Paul and the Scriptures of Israel* (JSNTSup 83; SSEJC 1; Sheffield: JSOT Press, 1993) 98-117.

[2]   The materials collected in the classic essay of N. A. Dahl, "Contradictions in Scripture," *Studies in Paul* (Minneapolis: Augsburg, 1977) 159-77, provide needed assistance. They are, however, largely of the abstract type, the result being Dahl's assumption—in effect—that the contradiction between Hab 2:4 and Lev 18:5 may have kept a lonely Paul awake at night until he "solved" it. See also G. A. Kennedy, *New Testament Interpretation through Rhetorical Criticism* (Chapel Hill: University of North Carolina Press, 1984) 149.

[3]   On the nomenclature "the Teachers," see J. L. Martyn, "A Law-Observant

Truly significant parallels are found, therefore, in a second type of
Textual Contradiction, one that reflects actual conflict between two
parties—often in the setting of a courtroom—the first of whom finds
support for his position in one of the law's statements, whereas the
second supports his position by citing a contradictory statement from
the law. It is the strength of a recent study by J. S. Vos to have
provided this truly comparable material, drawing it both from the
rhetorical recommendations made by Cicero, Quintilian, and other
rhetoricians, and from Jewish sources as well.[4] Two factors are of
particular importance, and they lead to a reasonably well-defined
form.

(a) Although we will continue to call the form a Textual Contradiction, we also note that *the point of departure* from which it is
constructed is not the contradiction between two laws or texts, but
rather, as noted above, the substantive conflict between assertions
made by two parties who are in actual disagreement with one
another. The parties' citation of contradictory texts is secondary to
their voicing of contradictory assertions.

(b) Because both parties take for granted that the law (or
Scripture) cannot ultimately be in conflict with itself (Quintilian,
Inst. Orat. 7.7.2), one or the other of the parties must be able to find
a resolution that affirms both texts.

The resulting form shows five steps:

1. An assertion (in Jewish traditions a *halaka*) is made by Party A.

2. Party A cites an authoritative text in support of that assertion.

3. A contradicory assertion (in Judaism a *halaka*) is made by Party B.

4. Party B cites an authoritative and contradictory text in support of that
assertion.

5. One of the parties wins the debate by giving a new interpretation to his
opponent's text, being thereby able not only to honor both texts as aspects
of the indivisible law, but also to show that, correctly read, both texts
support his own assertion.

Philo's treatise on the unchangeableness of God provides an
excellent example, for as Vos points out, the pertinent discussion

---

Mission to Gentiles: The Background of Galatians," *SJT* 38 (1985) 307-24; idem,
Theological Issues in the Letters of Paul (Edinburgh: T. & T. Clark, 1997) 7-24.

[4]   J. S. Vos, "Die hermeneutische Antinomie bei Paulus (Gal 3.11-12; Röm
10.5-10)," *NTS* 38 (1992) 254-70.

there reflects an actual conflict.[5] One can represent it in the form given above:

1. Philo asserts that God is not like a human being.

2. In support of that assertion he cites Num 23:19, "God is not like a human being."

3. Persons known to Philo make a contradictory assertion: God is like a human being (note "some persons" [τινες] in *Quod Deus Imm.* 52).

4. These persons support (or Philo knows that they can support) their assertion by citing Deut 8:5, "Like a human being he [God] shall train his son."

5. Philo then victoriously solves the textual contradiction by showing that, at the level of intention, both Num 23:19 and Deut 8:5 support his assertion. Deut 8:5 speaks not of God's own nature, but rather of God's concern to provide instruction, something definitely needed by the masses who think that God is like a human being (the "body lovers").

It is no long step from this example to Gal 3:11-12, provided we begin with a likely hypothesis: As Paul composes these two verses, he anticipates the Teachers' reaction to his assertion in 3:11a—"Before God no one is being rectified by the Law"—and to his citing Hab 2:4 in support of it (3:11b). In a word, given the tradition of the Textual Contradiction, Paul can be confident that, upon hearing his letter, the *Teachers* will employ that tradition, in order to say something like this:[6]

1. As Paul's messenger read his letter aloud, we noted his lethally misleading assertion: Before God no one is being rectified by the Law.

2. To undergird that assertion he cites a text from the Law itself, specifically from the prophet Habakkuk: "The one who is rectified by faith will live."

3. We assert, on the contrary, that one is indeed rectified by observing the Law.

4. And we find clear support for our assertion in the same divinely given Law from which Paul draws his text, for in the book of Leviticus it says: "The one who does the commandments will live by them."

5. We can say in conclusion, then, that, being the word of the one God, the Law does not really contradict itself. At the level of intention, the text quoted

---

5   *Quod Deus Imm.* 51-73. Together with related ones, this passage was cited and discussed by Dahl ("Contradictions," 166-68), but without the insight into its polemical cast that is now added by Vos.

6   (a) The breadth of the comparative material collected by Dahl, "Contradictions," and Vos, "Antinomie," and (b) the fact that the five-step form of Textual Contradiction is both simple and reflective of common sense indicate that we can assume both the Teachers and Paul to have known it as a relatively fixed tradition.

by Paul and the text quoted by us actually say the same thing. Habakkuk's reference to life by faith is God's assurance of life to the one who faithfully observes God's commandments, as stated in Leviticus.[7]

Paul's line of thought now emerges when we put Gal 3:11-12 itself in the form of the Textual Contradiction:

1. On the basis of the truth of the gospel I make a fundamental assertion: Before God no one is being rectified by the Law.

2. I then undergird that assertion with a quotation from Scripture: "The one who is rectified by faith will live."

3. In light of the way in which the Teachers quote from the Law, I must add a second assertion: the Law does not have its origin in faith.

4. Finally, given that second assertion, I cite a text from the Law that does not have its origin in faith—I think it is one of the Teachers' favorite texts— "The one who does the commandments will live by them."

Here three factors are truly revealing, Line 4 (Paul's citation of the text from Leviticus), Line 3 (Paul's second assertion), and the absence of Line 5.

Line 4. Paul's citation of Lev 18:5 is a pre-emptive strike. Confident that the Teachers will cite it if he does not do so first, he adheres to the form of the Textual Contradiction by allowing his opponents' text to make up line 4.

Line 3. It is important to note that Paul could have followed the standard form in this line as well, reproducing the assertion he knows the Teachers to be making. In Line 3, that is, he could have said, "Those who are troubling your minds are saying, to be sure, that one is rectified by observing the Law" (note Line 3 in the example from Philo). And given the mental agility we know Paul to have possessed, we can be sure that, after stating the Teachers' assertion in Line 4, he could have completed the form of the Textual Contradiction with a fifth line in which he showed that Hab 2:4 and Lev 18:5 are to be harmonized in favor of his own assertion in the first line.[8]

---

7   Cf. the interpretation of Hab 2:4 in 1QpHab 8: "Interpreted, this [text] concerns all those who *observe the law* in the House of Judah, whom God will deliver from the House of Judgment because of their suffering and because of *their faith* in the Teacher of Righteousness" (translation by G. Vermes, emphasis added).

8   Neither Dahl nor Vos argues in precisely this way. But, assuming that Paul means to affirm both Hab 2:4 and Lev 18:5, these interpreters manage to find the essence of Line 5 in the later verses of Galatians 3. Dahl ("Contradictions," 172-73) credits Paul with demonstrating the validity of Lev 18:5 by arguing in Gal 3:19-25 that "the entire law of Moses itself [was] . . . a provisional, interim ararangement,

That is not at all Paul's way of using the tradition of the Textual Contradiction. One notes that in Line 3 he formulates a second assertion of his own: The Law extolled and quoted by the Teachers does not have its origin in the faith about which Habakkuk speaks, the faith elicited in Abraham by God's promise, and the faith that has now arrived with the advent of Christ (Gal 3:6, 25).[9] By taking over Line 3 for a second assertion of his own, Paul accomplishes several things.

(a) Addressing the issue of origin only for the Law represented in Lev 18:5 and not for the scriptural promise represented in Hab 2:4, Paul distinguishes the two from one another, but he also does more. He creates an imbalance in which it is only the Law that is placed in question, the divine origin of the promise being taken for granted. (b) Paul's assertion that the Law does not have its origin in the faith of

---

valid only for pre-messianic times." But, as R. B. Hays (*The Faith of Jesus Christ: An Investigation of the Narrative Substructure of Galatians 3:1–4:11* [SBLDS 56; Chico: Scholars Press, 1983] 221) points out, Paul gives no indication in 3:19-25 that he is explaining how Lev 18:5 can be affirmed.

Crediting the apostle, in effect, with Quintilian's dictum that the law cannot finally stand in contradiction with itself, Vos ("Antinomie," 265) assumes that Paul found both Hab 2:4 and Lev 18:5 in the substantively indivisible Law of God. For Vos ("Antinomie," 265), therefore, the tension between Paul and the Teachers is "der Konflikt zweier Parteien, die sich jeweils auf verschiedene Stellen *derselben Schrift* berufen" (my emphasis). In short, in Vos's view, Paul argues as follows: True enough, the promise (Hab 2:4) and the Law (Lev 18:5) seem to contradict one another, the first supporting my gospel, the second supporting the gospel of the Teachers. In fact, however, when one considers both the letter of the Law and the intention of the Law-giver, God, one sees that there is no contradiction. For although Lev 18:5 says literally that the observer of the Law will live, one finds that God had something else in mind when he gave it: the Law should serve the cause of life in a quite indirect way. Placing the whole of humanity under the power of Sin (3:22), the Law paved the way for the fulfillment of the Abrahamic promise.

Although gladly indebted to Vos for the comparative material mentioned earlier, I am compelled for reasons that will emerge in the following analysis to disagree with his conclusions.

9   In making this change, Paul employs, to be sure, a motif at home in the tradition of the Textual Contradiction. As Vos points out, the rhetoricians recommend that under certain conditions one should ask about the origin of a given law (Hermogenes, Περὶ Στάσεων [ed. H. Rabe; Leipzig: Teubner, 1913] 87). Paul thus speaks of the origin of the Law to which the Teachers appeal, preparing the way for his assertion in Gal 3:19-20 that angels instituted that Law in God's absence!

which Habakkuk speaks does not suggest merely that Paul considers the Law of Lev 18:5 to be inferior. It shows that Paul does no adhere to a major presupposition of the Textual Contradiction, the assumption that the two texts, Hab 2:4 and Lev 18:5, have their origin in a monolith that is larger and more fundamental than either of them. (c) The foundational place of such a comprehensive monolith is given by Paul to the faith that is elicited by God's promise, as one sees it in Hab 2:4. Thus the benchmark from which all else must be judged is not a harmony that can be discerned between two texts drawn from the same source. That benchmark is quite simply the faith elicited by God's promise. (d) Far from thinking, then, that Hab 2:4 is itself drawn from the Law, Paul uses it to disqualify the Law before he quotes from the Law. The result: not having its origin in the benchmark of faith, the Law speaks a false promise when it says "The one who does the commandments will live by them."[10]

Line 5. The absence of this line cannot now come as a surprise. The fundamental premise of the Textual Contradiction, that the law (or Scripture) cannot ultimately be in conflict with itself, has for Paul no pertinence to the contradiction between his text from Habakkuk and the Teachers' text from Leviticus. From the time of Paul's own "participation" in the crucifixion of Christ (Gal 2:19), he has been unable to assume in a simple way the integrity of a Law that contains both the blessing uttered by God and the curse spoken by the Law. Or, as noted above, although Paul continues to believe that there is a benchmark from which all else is to be judged, he can no longer identify that benchmark as a Law in which one can find both his text ans the text of the Teachers. The benchmark is God's own blessing, the promising gospel spoken to Abrahan ahead of time (Gal 3:8) and thus the faith elicited by that gospel.[11] In Hab 2:4 Paul hears nothing other than that blessing promise and that elicited faith. In Lev 18:5, however, he hears nothing other than the voice of the Law, that, failing to have its origin in faith, can utter only a false promise, doubtless one means by which it enacts its universal curse (Gal 3:10).

---

10   Arguing on the basis of Gal 3:21b and Rom 8:3, Hays also concludes that Paul considered Lev 18:5 to be "unconditionally false" (*Faith*, 221).

11   This promise (Gal 3:8) was spoken to Abraham by Scripture, functioning on God's behalf. There is here, then, a hint of Paul's view that the Law has two distinguishable voices, indeed two modes of existence (see Comment #48 in my forthcoming Anchor Bible commentary on Galatians). Prior to Gal 4:21; 5:3, 14; 6:2, however, one finds at most a hint of this view. See n. 13 below.

It follows that Paul is not at all concerned to "solve" the contradiction between two texts he considers to have been drawn from the same Law, showing thereby that they can be harmonized in favor of his original assertion (Line 1). On the contrary, he is concerned to emphasize the contradiction between the two texts. He sees that God's promise in Hab 2:4—rectifying faith will lead to life—is the truth of the gospel. And given the work of the Teachers in his Galatian churches, he also sees that the Law's promise in Lev 18:5—observance of the Law will lead to life—is the falsification of the gospel.[12] The contradiction between these two texts is altogether essential. For it is the result of the gulf between the voice of the cursing Law and the voice of the blessing God, and that gulf is not to be hidden. It is to be emphasized, until one sees that, in the cross, gulf became contradiction, and contradiction became collision, and collision became defeat for the Law's curse and victory for God's blessing (3:13).[13] In the final analysis, then, Paul's use of the tradition of the Textual Contradiction in Gal 3:11-12 reflects his concern to distinguish one spirit from another.[14] We might even credit Paul

---

[12] In Gal 3:21a, Paul says categorically that the Law is unable to grant life. Taken together with the way in which he uses the tradition of the Textual Contradiction, that bald assertion seals the case against Lev 18:5. To Paul it is a false promise, for in his daily work among the Gentiles he sees that it does not prove true (cf. Deut 18:22). That this shocking reading of Lev 18:5 is the one intended by Paul is also suggested by his interpretation of that same text in Rom 10:5. There, having drawn a strict distinction between two rectifications—the one that comes from God (Rom 10:3, 6) and the one that comes from the Law (10:5a)—Paul cites Lev 18:5 as the voice of the latter (cf. Phil 3:9). The wording Paul uses for Lev 18:5 in Rom 10:5 is somewhat uncertain; there are textual variants. It may very well be, however, that in this case he changes the final phrase of that text from "will live by them" to "will live by *it*," thus referring to the nomistic rectification that he has just distinguished from the rectification that comes from God (see, e.g. U. Wilckens, *Der Brief an die Römer* [3 vols., Neukirchen: Neukirchener, 1978-82] 2.224).

[13] Paul's concern to portray a *conflict* that issues in defeat for the Law's curse and victory for God's blessing could remind one that Quintilian asks which of two conflicting laws is the stronger (*Inst. Orat.* 7.7.7). That is indeed a question fundamental to the argument Paul formulates in Gal 3:15, 17, and 21a, where, far from saying that the Law's impotence to grant life merely puts it at a disadvantage (Vos, "Antinomie," 266: "im Nachteil"), Paul says that the Law is doubly impotent: It cannot grant life, and it is unable effectively to oppose God's promise in the sense of being strong enough to annul that promise.

[14] Cf. E. Käsemann, *Commentary on Romans* (Grand Rapids: Eerdmans,

with an emended form of 1 John 4:1:

> Beloved [Galations, in light of the Teachers' work in your midst], do not
> believe every spirit [or every text], but test the spirits [and the texts] to see
> whether they are from God.

*   *   *

Although the positive view of the Law that emerges in Galatians 4,
5, and 6 cannot be discussed in detail here, a few hints can be
offered. In 4:21 Paul no longer speaks of the blessing God and the
cursing Law. On the contrary, he clearly asserts that *the Law itself*
has two voices, one being the cursing voice of Deut 27:26/Lev 18:5,
the other—speaking in God's behalf—being the promissory voice
that is to be heard in Gen 12:3; Hab 2:4; Genesis 16–21; and Isa 54:1.
Particularly striking is the fact that, in Gal 5:14, Paul even succeeds
in hearing the guiding voice of God in Lev 19:18: "You shall love
your neighbor as yourself." That Paul should find in Leviticus both a
false promise (Lev 18:5) and the positive statement of God's true
guidance for the church's daily life (Lev 19:18) is clear indication of
his conviction that, with the coming of Christ, the two voices of the
Law have been brought out into the open, thus being now distinguished from one another throughout the whole of the Law.

In the second and third centuries, the drawing of distinctions
within the Law became an important motif among Christian Jews,
gnostics, and "orthodox" Christians.[15] In the five books of Moses,
Ptolemy found (a) the Law of God (itself composed of three sub-
parts), (b) the additions of Moses, and (c) the traditions of the elders.
Perhaps influenced both by Galatians itself and by Ptolemy, the
author of the *Didascalia* spoke repeatedly of a clean distinction
between the eternally valid first Law, which "consists of the Ten
Words and the Judgements," and the *deuterosis*, the punitive Second
Legislation with its cursing bonds of circumcision etc. Similarities

---

1980) 286: "The apostle is not afraid to apply *to scripture* . . . the distinguishing of
spirits demanded of the prophets in 1 Cor 12:10" (emphasis added).

[15] See especially the theory of false pericopes in the *Kerygmata Petrou*: E.
Hennecke and W. Schneemelcher (eds.), *New Testament Apocrypha* (2 vols.,
Philadelphia: Westminster, 1965) 2.118-21. See also the *Letter of Ptolemy to Flora*
(W. Foerster, *Gnosis* [Oxford: Clarendon, 1972] 154-61); Irenaeus, *Heresies*
4.24-9; and R. H. Connolly (ed.), *Didascalia Apostolorum* (Oxford: Clarendon,
1929).

and differences between these writings and those of Paul warrant more investigation than they have received.

Some important *similarities* should be mentioned. Three motifs in *the Letter of Ptolemy to Flora* and the *Didascalia* can be compared with motifs in Galatians: (1) The distinction(s) internal to the Law have been *revealed by Christ*: "The words of the Saviour teach us that it [the Law] is divided into three parts" (Ptolemy 4.1); "He teaches what is the Law and what is the Second Legislation" (*Didascalia*, p. 218); "If one accepts his [the true prophet's] doctrine, then will he learn which portions of the Scriptures answer to the truth and which are false" (*Kerygmata Petrou*).[16] (2) Christ came in order to destroy the second law, with its injustice, thus *setting us loose from its curse* (Ptolemy 5.7; *Didascalia*, p. 224). (3) In his act of making distinctions in the Law and of liberating us from the second Law, Christ fulfilled, *restored*, and *perfected* the Law of God (Ptolemy 5.3, 9; *Didascalia*, p. 224).

Two *differences* are also noteworthy: (a) Over against the second law, Ptolemy and the author of the *Didascalia* place not the singular Abrahamic promise, but rather the plural Decalogue, as its commandments were perfected by Christ (a view that is literally foreign to Galatians, but very close to the perspective of 1 Cor 7:19 and Rom 13:8-10). (b) For the Catholic author of the *Didascalia*, God is expressly identified as the author both of the first Law and of the Second Legislation, whereas Ptolemy attributes only part of the Law to God, considering the laws of divorce and corban to have come from Moses and the elders.

One may wonder: In writing Galatians, does Paul come close to preparing the way for Ptolemy?[17]

---

16   As in Hennecke and Schneemelcher (eds.), *New Testament Apocrypha*, 2.119.

17   See J. L. Martyn, "The Crucial Event in the History of the Law (Gal 5:14)," in E. H. Lovering, Jr., and J. L. Sumney (eds.), *Theology and Ethics in Paul and His Modern Interpreters: Essays in Honor of Victor Paul Furnish* (Nashville: Abingdon, 1996) 48-61; idem, *Theologial Issues*, 235-50.

"THE PERFECT LAW OF LIBERTY" (JAMES 1:25)[1]

Robert W. Wall

James introduces the law motif by the phrase "the perfect law of liberty" (νόμον τέλειον τὸν τῆς ἐλευθερίας; 1:25), and later in the same section (1:22–2:26) encourages obedience to the "royal law" (2:8), which stands at the center of the "whole law" (2:10). In my view, all three uses of law are metaphors of the biblical Torah,[2] and

---

[1]   This essay is excerpted from my forthcoming *The Community of the Wise: The Letter of James* (NTC; Valley Forge: Trinity Press International).

[2]   The term "biblical Torah" is multivalent and no one technical use of "law" (νόμος) is found in Scripture. Moreover, the specific meaning of "law" in James remains contested between scholars. Thus, for example, P. H. Davids, *Commentary on James* [NIGTC; Grand Rapids: Eerdmans, 1982] 50) following a more conservative line takes "law" as a Christian reference to the "law of Christ," consisting of his moral teachings like those gathered in Matthew's Sermon on the Mount. Especially in light of 2:8 and under the pressure of Pauline usage, others are more inclined to take "law" as a vague allusion to the "law of neighborly love" (as in R. P. Martin, *James* [WBC 48; Waco: Word, 1988] 51). I take "law" in James as a metaphor of the "biblical Torah." The primary clue for this reading comes from 2:10-11, where the "whole law" (2:10) is illustrated by references to the Decalogue (2:11). Clearly, James does not take "whole law" literally, as a reference to the 600+ laws that make up the Torah's legal code. Rather, in a way similar to Jesus and other Jewish contemporaries who reduced the extensive rules of right conduct and ritual purity to a few principles, James defines the Torah's moral code in terms of the Decalogue and the "royal law" of neighborly love (2:8); see L. T. Johnson, *The Letter of James* (AB 37A; New York: Doubleday, 1995) 30-32. If considered within the wider frame of a theology of the "word," with which James identifies the law (1:18, 21, 22-23), the connection between law and Scripture is more certain: the "word" in James refers to Scripture (Davids, *James*, 89). Close parallels are found in 1 Pet 1:23-24, where the "word" is rooted in the writings of the biblical prophets; and in 2 Tim 2:15, where the content of the institutionalized "word of Truth" is scriptural (2 Tim 2:16). However, I find no evidence in James for narrowing the meaning of the biblical word (and by implication the biblical law) to its christological (so J. H. Ropes, *A Critical and Exegetical Commentary on the Epistle of St. James* [ICC; Edinburgh: T. & T. Clark, 1916] 178-80) or kerygmatic content. In James, the divine word is summarized by Scripture's proverbial

are pregnant *Stichwörter* that nevertheless perplex interpreters to this day. The purpose of this essay is to reprise the issue of law in James by attending to the meaning of the "perfect law of liberty," the first and most significant reference to law in this composition.

The primary interpretive problem considered by the present study is a theological one: what is the meaning of the law's "perfection" in James and in what sense does the law "liberate," whom and from what? The problem of theological definition is made more difficult when the full context is extended to include the entire field of New Testament literature. Within this setting, the biblical James is found alongside the biblical Paul, who is clearly ambivalent about the law's continuing role in guiding the community's life.[3] The significance of

---

wisdom of 1:19 (see commentary), by which the community's "quick hearing" (= doing) of the law is prescribed.

[3]   The critical debate over the authorship of James is waning for lack of interest and agreement. What seems rather more significant about the name "James," whether added by the pseudepigraher in his "letter's" opening greeting (1:1) or by the church in its superscription, is that this writing came to be identified with the person of James and his Jacobean tradition: that is, this composition envisages the theological interests of the Palestinian Jewish Christianity which came to be associated with James. Further, while I am convinced that much of the raw material for this book comes from a pre-Pauline period, perhaps from memories of James himself, it final canonical shaping took place during the post-Pauline era and is the work of a redactor who "knew" of Paul and perhaps even of the biblical Paul (cf. Davids, *James*, 2-22). The use of a common "Christian" vocabulary suggests that the author of James edited his traditions in order to engage the emergent Pauline tradition in a conversation that may be viewed either as prophetic (to correct dangerous distortions to Jewish faith prompted by Pauline preaching) or pastoral (to sharpen the readers understanding of their own faith which is currently tested by various trials).

In any case, a critical approach to exegesis requires the interpreter to recognize that the New Testament canon consists of different voices, sometimes sounding dissonant notes. The biblical teaching concerning the Torah is at the very least the sum of these various sounds; to elevate one or to exclude the other is theological myopia and surely distorts the Scripture's teaching about the relationship between the believer and the Torah. In fact, to presume the simultaneity between every part of the whole, without also adequately discerning the plain meaning of each in turn, undermines the integral nature of Scripture and even distorts its full witness to God.

The approach of this essay to Scripture's own theological diversity recognizes that different notes, no matter how dissonant, belong to the same Scripture which bears witness to "one Lord, one faith, one baptism, one God and Father of all." This sovereign and living object of Scripture's witness demands that the interpreter

their apparent disagreements over the law are intensified when considered by the current faith community that reads both James and Paul as parts of its canonical Scriptures. This seems especially true within the Protestant church, for whom the Pauline writings provide its principle theological justification and subject matter.[4] For many Protestant interpreters, it is its positive view of the law that "has made James most famous."[5]

LAW AND THE NEW TESTAMENT *JAKOBUSBILD*

Ralph Martin appeals to this phrase as an important reason not to accept direct association of this letter with the historical James.[6] According to Martin, the characterization of the law as freeing the believer to serve God's will does not square with James whose "attitudes recorded in Acts and Galatians suggest a more legalistic frame of mind." Martin seems reluctant to find in this expression a polemic against Paul in support of nomistic Christianity and actually champions a Pauline interpretation. In my view, the meaning of this phrase agrees with the portraits of James in Acts and Galatians and suggests a contrary (although perhaps complementary) understanding of the biblical Torah to that of Paul.

Three narratives about James in the New Testament anticipate the idea of law found in James.[7] The first two are narrated by Luke in Acts, which functions as the NT's own "authorized" introduction to the New Testament letters and their "apostolic" writers. The Evangel-

---

"put the text back together in a way that makes it available in the present and in its (biblical) entirety—not merely in the past and in the form of historically contextualized fragments" (J. D. Levenson, *The Hebrew Bible, The Old Testament, and Historical Criticism* [Louisville: Westminster/John Knox Press, 1993] 79). It is under the light of these methodological interests, then, that the disagreements between Jacobean and Pauline over the Torah will help to form a complementary whole.

4   Cf. R. W. Wall, "Law and Gospel, Church and Canon," in R. W. Wall and E. E. Lemcio, *The New Testament as Canon: A Reader in Canonical Criticism* (JSNTSup 76; Sheffield: JSOT Press, 1992) 208-49; B. S. Childs, *Biblical Theology of the Old and New Testaments* (Minneapolis: Fortress, 1993) 559.

5   Davids, *James*, 47.

6   Martin, *James*, lxx-xxi.

7   See "Introduction" in Wall and Lemcio, *Canon*, 15-25, for a brief discussion of my methodological interest in the New Testament as a context for reading New Testament writings.

ist's narrative of the Jerusalem Synod in Acts 15:13-21 introduces
the reader to the biblical James as the second generation leader of
Palestinian Christianity (cf. 12:17). His midrash on Amos 9:11-12
supplies the necessary compromise that settles the conflict between
the church's law-observant Jewish and law-free Gentile missions.[8]
While the intentions of James' midrash and resulting decree remain
contested, what seems clear is that he retains a pharisaical concern
for table fellowship, including obedience to the "law of unclean
foods." Later in Acts 21:15-26, these same concerns are extended to
include ritual purity. In this second episode, Paul takes a nazirite
vow of purification to allay the suspicions of those belonging to
James, who were "zealous for the law."

The third narrative is found in Galatians 2:11-18, where Paul
describes his response to James, a so-called "pillar" of the Jewish
church. In particular, Paul tells of his disagreements with Peter who
was persuaded to oppose Paul's teaching in Antioch by those "who
came from James" (2:12). In the context of his narrative apologia,
Paul identifies James with those who define the "Israel of God"
(6:16; cf. 2:15) in terms of the "works of the law" rather than by the
"faith of Jesus Christ" alone (2:16; cf. 6:12-16).

I am inclined to agree with James D. G. Dunn's construction of the
original Sitz im Leben of this passage as well as his definition of the
catchphrase, "works of the law."[9] According to Dunn, Paul's protest
is against those Jewish believers who draw social boundaries around
their community's life in ways that demonstrate their continuing
loyalty to ancestral religion. In this setting, then, the "works of the
law" include those religious rites and public practices that preserve a
community's social identity rather than its salvation. In addition to
the instructions in Torah concerning personal and interpersonal conduct, with which Paul would certainly agree (cf. Rom 2:6-10; 7:7-
12; 1 Cor 7:17-24), these "works" include those more public rituals
(dietary and cultic) and rites of passage (circumcision) prescribed by
Torah, which are distinctively Jewish and whose motive is

---

[8]   By "law/Torah-free," I do not mean that Paul denied the pertinence of the
biblical Torah; clearly he does not. Rather, Paul makes clear the distinction between
faith-righteousness and law-righteousness when defining the membership requirement of spiritual Israel.

[9]   J. D. G. Dunn, *Jesus, Paul and the Law* (Nashville: Westminster/John
Knox, 1990) 129-214.

nationalistic and cultic in keeping with the current requirements of mainstream messianic Judaism. Thus, according to Dunn, Paul is neither disparaging the "doing of the law" nor advocating the complete and radical separation from Judaism. Rather, he is advocating a new social marker which is the community's confession that Jesus from Nazareth is the Christ of God.

Certainly, Dunn's interpretation would seem to posit the Pauline Paul against the more Jewish *Paulusbild* of Acts currently being advanced by Jacob Jervell and others! Paul's theological interest in Galatians seems rather to define Christian faith by his theocentric and christological convictions rather than in terms of Judaism's nationalistic and cultic practices. Yet, I disagree with Dunn's suggestion that Paul's protest against those who practice the "works of the law" on gentile turf is not motivated by his soteriological commitments. On this score, I tend toward the side of E. P. Sanders,[10] who finds in Galatians and Romans a Pauline polemic against a Judaic "covenantal nomism," where the catchphrase, "works of the law," represents a discrete pattern of salvation. In this case, Torah observance forms a Jewish identity which bears public witness to its covenant with God. While the Reformation may have been incorrect in defining "works of the law" as the "good works of self-achievement," to use Bultmann's phrase, or in understanding that in Galatians Paul describes two mutually exclusive kinds of justification, one by faith in Christ alone and the other by good works, surely the Reformation is right in supposing that the plain meaning of Paul's polemic is against a *via salutis* that requires in some sense the community's obedience to the law. On this issue, the biblical Paul apparently disagrees with the biblical James.

This brief discussion prepares the reader for two important aspects of the idea of the law in James, especially when considered within the context of the whole New Testament.[11] First, both Acts and Galatians reflect disagreements, however edited by their authors, between apostolic traditions over the role the biblical Torah continues to play in defining what it means to be the true Israel and to do the true

---

10 E. P. Sanders, *Paul and Palestinian Judaism: A Comparison of Patterns of Religion* (London: SCM; Philadelphia: Fortress, 1977) 447-523.

11 Although outside the scope of this essay, the biblical narratives of James and Paul especially in Acts yields an important hermeneutical clue for relating their different theologies of Torah together.

Israel ought to do. Second, the narratives of Acts and Galatians, whose central characters are Paul and James, depict James in conflict with Paul over issues related to the role of the law in Christian faith. James contends (if only for certain Jewish believers) that Torah observance is necessary for covenant membership and for blessings to come. If "covenantal nomism" supplies James a critical aspect of its organizing calculus, then the reader is prepared to engage a writing whose theological conception is quite different than that found within the Pauline writings.[12]

THE IDEA OF LAW IN JAMES

Thematic studies of biblical texts are artificial, if they fail to take into account the substantial hermeneutical issues raised by the texts themselves.[13] Every literary text is created by certain compositional strategies according to which its most important themes unfold and are ultimately understood by the interpreter. Even so, the more facile dimensions of James' understanding of law are apparent by observing its use in three key passages (1:22-27; 2:8-13; 4:11-12), and agree with the antecedent narratives of James in the New Testament.

1. *The Torah is valid today.* Unlike the Pauline description of law, there is no ambivalence in James about the importance or permanence of the biblical Torah. The mirror metaphor (1:23-24) reproves those who do not continue to stand before the law; it is not removed to a prior dispensation of salvation's history. In fact, the "whole" of biblical Torah is valid (2:10). It is given by God and enshrines God's will (4:11-12). There is no sense in James, as in Paul, that the law has ended or its demand already satisfied by Christ for those who are "in him." Rather, Jesus is portrayed in 2:1-4 as a

---

[12] This perspective on James agrees with second century Jewish Christianity as enshrined within Ebionism, where Torah observance maintained a Jewish way of life and where James was Jesus's successor in leading a Mosaic reformation of Israel. In this sense, neither Jesus nor James was a sage, but rather a prophet whose way was of Torah and not of wisdom.

[13] There is a sense in which my analysis of James shares methodological interests with those who believe that the text itself yields its own meaning—rather than its author/editor. Certainly, the interpreter, who is contextualized by and made sensitive to the text's meaning, contributes to (perhaps even collaborates in) its meaning.

prophetic exemplar of its performance.[14]

Ironically, the reference to Jesus in 2:1 is combined with a plea to preclude favoritism, since Jesus exemplifies "impartial" treatment of rich and poor alike. Yet, in Rom 2:11, the same word (προσωπο-λημψία) is used of divine judgment as preface to Paul's criticism of the law observant Jew (Rom 2:17-29). Surely the status of law in Jacobean Christianity is different, since divine approval (2:8) and judgment (2:12-13) are conditioned upon observance of the law.

2. *The Torah must be performed.* The teaching of the whole law is observed (2:10-11). The legal vocabulary of James includes "doing" and, implicitly, "works," which underscores the requirement of a Torah observant faith (1:25). Unlike Paul, James mentions neither the Spirit's leading in doing God's will, nor the spiritually debilitating effect of performing the law on one's own. God's will, articulated by the biblical Torah, is performed as an act of the human will devoted to God and enabled by God's word (1:18, 21, 22-3).

Even though perhaps implicit in the language of a "whole" law, there is no mention in James of circumcision or of sabbath and food laws; the letter's exhortation keeps to the moral essentials that both Jewish and Gentile believers could accept in principle. The social role of the law is to draw moral boundaries around the faith community, to keep it pure from outside contaminants (1:27), especially those that afflict the wealthy outsiders. The biblical Torah also provides the community's social boundaries, to facilitate acts of mercy toward other believers, especially its poor and powerless members. When paired with wisdom, the Torah gives shape to a psychology that passes the test of faith by resisting those passions that might prevent an active piety.

3. *The Torah of James is delimited by the levitical laws of holiness.* For James, God's will is codified in the biblical Torah (2:8-13; 4:11-12) rather than in its specific commands (in which case ἐντολή would be used). However, James seems to have a discrete unit of the biblical Torah in mind—a "canon within the Canon." In particular, according to L. T. Johnson, parts of James form a halachic midrash on Lev 19:12-18.[15] In fact, the comparison in Jas 1:26-27 between

---

14   Cf. Wall and Lemcio, *Canon*, 257-61.

15   L. T. Johnson, "The Use of Leviticus 19 in the Letter of James," *JBL* 101 (1982) 391-401—although Johnson (*James*, 30) notes the absence in James of an explicit connection between "law" and "works," as in Pauline polemics, or between

religious practice (1:26) and ethical conduct (1:27), which requires
social responsibility and moral purity, may well allude to the moral
code of Leviticus. It is by this levitical rule (or select sections of it),
that God determines a "pure and undefiled religion" (1:27).

4. *"Doing Torah" is an eschatological idiom.* If God's will is
disclosed in the biblical Torah, then God's future judgment is determined by whether or not one complies with its stipulations (4:11-12).
While the doer of the law is blessed by God (1:25) and is granted the
promised "crown of life" (1:12), God reserves a merciless judgment
for those who have failed the law's precept of mercy (2:13). Significantly, the connection between 1:25 and 1:12 that is fashioned by
their common use of the important catchwords, "blessing" and "endurance" (ὑπο-μένειν/παρα-μένειν), suggests that the performance
of Torah demonstrates a community's love of God which in turn
leads to the fulfillment of the biblical promise of life according to
both Torah (Exod 20:4-6; Deut 5:29; 6:1-9; 7:9; 12:28; cf. Isa 51:6;
60:21; Eze 43:7) and James (1:12).

The various prophetic exemplars mentioned by James, Jesus (2:1-
4), Abraham (2:21-4), Rahab (2:25), Job (5:9-11), Elijah (5:16b-8)
all commend a pious life of faithfulness to God, according to which
God will determine the believer's participation in God's coming
reign. Jesus, Abraham and Rahab are all "approved" by God on the
basis of their merciful treatment of others—that is, because they
observed the "royal Torah" (2:8).

5. *Torah is paired with wisdom.* James continues Scripture's own
depiction of wisdom as independent upon Torah, especially exemplified by the biblical Solomon (cf. 1 Kgs 2:1-9; 3:10-14) and later,
more pervasively, in Sirach: the way of wisdom is both justified and
explicated by its relationship to Torah.[16] The interchange of verbs in

---

law and ritual purity.

[16]   The interdependency of the traditions of biblical Torah and biblical wisdom
is defended by G. T. Sheppard in a significant body of published work, the most
important of which is his *Wisdom as a Hermeneutical Construct* (BZAW 151;
Berlin: de Gruyter, 1980). See also, idem, "The Role of 'Wisdom' in the
Interpretation of Scripture," in T. Fabiny (ed.), *Acta Universitatis Szegediensis de
Attila Jozsef Nominatae*, vol. 4 (Szeged: Attila Jozsef, 1992) 187-201; idem, "The
Role of the Canonical Context in the Interpretation of the Solomonic Books," in G.
T. Sheppard (ed.), *Solomon's Divine Acts: Joseph Hall's Representation of
Proverbs, Ecclesiastes and Song of Songs (1609), with Introductory Essays*
(Boston: Pilgrim Press, 1991) 67-107; idem, "The Relation of Solomon's Wisdom

1:23-25, where the wise man "observes" (1:23; κατανοεῖν) wisdom rather than Torah (cf. Ps 119:15, 18) and "sees" (1:25; παρακύπ-τειν) Torah rather than wisdom (cf. Sir 14:23; 21:23) suggests that Torah and wisdom are paired in some strategic way. In fact, the very word that bids the believer to "quick hearing" (1:19) actually points to the Torah as its subject matter: the wise quickly "hear" and there-fore "do" the teaching of Torah.

It is no doubt true that this initial pairing of two biblical traditions, Torah and wisdom, envisages the author's own "canon conscious-ness." That is, James is written by and for believers, who have main-tained the status of the biblical Torah as the essential rule of faith for its religious life, similar to those addressed by Sirach. The author's interpretation and application of wisdom, then, is made more persua-sive when paired with Torah.[17]

THE "PERFECT LAW" IN JAMES

1. *The intertextuality of the "perfect law."* The entire composition is only one part of the text's full literary context, which also includes its various subtexts.[18] The interpreter realizes that most biblical texts are composed in a theological light cast by biblical traditions recalled by their writers. The profoundly biblical environment of these writers shaped texts that must be read with other biblical texts in

---

to Biblical Prayer," *TJT* 8 (1992) 7-25; and F. A. Spina's unpublished paper, "*In But Not of* the World: Reflections on Solomonic Wisdom in 1 Kings 1–11."

17 For this use of "canon consciousness," see Sheppard, *Hermeneutical Construct*, 110-19, who demonstrates that wisdom writings, while retaining their own vocabulary and sensibility, use biblical traditions of Torah and the prophets to authorize its own "voice" and to supply some its conceptual freight prior to canoni-zation. In Sheppard's mind, for example, Ben Sira's "canon consciousness" facilitated the integration of his biblical tradition (i.e. Torah and prophets) with a non-canonical way of thinking of faith and life (i.e. wisdom).

18 S. Talmon ("Emendation of Biblical Texts on the Basis of Ugaritic Parallels," in S. Japhet [ed.], *Studies in the Bible* [Jerusalem: Magnes Press, 1986] 279-300) has called attention to less known "exegetical rules of the sages" which provide important background to the kind of internal textual interpretation suggested by this essay. Especially appropriate is the rule where, according to Talmon, "one verse may help in ascertaining the sense of another" (p. 280). Such texts are linked together by similar phrases or subject matter (so pp. 281-87). This strategy, of course, is deeply rooted in the conviction that "diverse components of the biblical anthology share a common world view, (where) innumerable strands link together the constitutive units (to form) a literary and ideological entity" (p. 279).

mind. As a result, the Bible in its final form, despite its rich diversity, can be read as a "self-glossing" book. Common or synonymous words found in different parts of the biblical canon draw these texts together and into a reflexive conversation.[19] In this sense, as is characteristic of all midrashic literature, I understand James to be an *intertext*, whose meaning is substantially "thickened" by the dialogue between the text and its various (but especially biblical) subtexts.

The programmatical meaning of law for James is introduced in 1:25, where a cluster of important words signify the biblical Torah's abiding importance. Of these various words, pride of place goes to *teleios* which stands in predicate relationship to law to assert its perfection. This phrase has been variously understood; yet most scholars recognize the importance of its OT roots, particularly in the Torah Psalm 18:7 [19:7] (cf. Psalms 1 and 119) where it is used as an idiom of praise for the Mosaic revelation of God's will. In this setting, the perfection of the Torah is clearly disclosed by the spiritual benefits it yields within the observant community.

The importance of the intertext is clarified when considering the entire frame of Ps 18:7 (19:7) commendation of Torah's perfection: ὁ νόμος τοῦ κυρίου ἄμωμος, ἐπιστρέφων ψυχάς ("the law of the Lord is perfect, converting souls").[20] The Psalmist's celebration of the law because it "converts souls" recalls the theological calculus of Jas 1:21, which claims that the "implanted word" (i.e. wisdom) is able σῶσαι τὰς ψυχὰς ὑμῶν ("to save your souls"). This passage anticipates Jas 5:20 where the same phrase is used with ἐπιστρέφειν. In continuity with the Psalm, James is concerned with the conversion of the soul; indeed, the full meaning of the exhortation to listen to and act upon the "perfect Torah" no doubt includes those who are at

---

[19]   D. Boyarin, *Intertextuality and the Reading of Midrash* (Bloomington: Indiana University Press, 1990) 1-21. Sheppard (*Hermeneutical Construct*, 100-102), among others, catalogues the various kinds of linguistic connections between texts as follows: (1) citation (with or without alteration); (2) paraphrase; (3) key words or phrases; (4) allusions; (5) metaphors or biblical images which allow for "free associations."

[20]   Note that Ps 18:7 uses the priestly ἄμωμος ("blameless") instead of τέλειος to underscore Torah's spiritual or religious effect. If this verse from the Psalm provides the subtextual meaning of "perfect law," then the substitution of τέλειος for ἄμωμος in James may well intend a somewhat different and expanded (i.e. "Christian") meaning of Torah's perfection than is found in the Psalm, which is best recovered by inter/intratextual analysis (below).

present spiritually disaffected and are in need of conversion.[21]

2. *The intratextuality of the "perfect law."* Discrete layers of a thickened meaning are mined by the interpreter who is sensitive to how a particular word or idea unfolds within its entire compositional field. In this sense, the full context of a word is discerned at an *intratextual* level, where important catchwords are repeated but in different compositional contexts.[22] While a new linguistic environment changes the meaning of words, old meanings are retained. The result is that words acquire an ever-enlarging meaning by their subsequent usage, while at the same time their prior uses alert the interpreter to possible meanings that may well be obscured by their new literary and linguistic context. In my view, this literary characteristic of James is especially important, since its intratextuality provides a kind of compositional coherence within a paraenesis that seems rather disjointed to many readers. In this sense, the meaning of law in James unfolds in an intratextual fashion. That is, the meaning of law in its first use in 1:22-27 carries over to its second

---

21   In his *Restoring the Diaspora: Discursive Structure and Purpose in the Epistle of James* (SBLDS 144; Atlanta: Scholars Press, 1993), T. B. Cargal utilizes Greimasian semiotics to contend that the purpose of James is best envisaged by relating the opening address to the "diaspora" (1:1) with the concluding exhortation to those who have "wandered from the truth" (5:19-20). Within these structural "brackets," then, the reader finds advice for converting a spiritually disaffected Christian diaspora. In light of the composition's own rhetorical structure, then, the "perfection" of the "word," which is defined in 1:2-21, sets forth the subject matter of a message whose yield is the "salvation of the soul." My analysis agrees substantially with Cargal's, although our interpretive strategies differ. I would also equate the "word" with the way of Torah; thus, following Cargal's lead, James is here arguing that the spiritual effect of "perfect Torah" is to convert the disaffected Christian.

22   "Intratextuality" is defined variously by scholars who have different interests in the text itself. In my use, the composition itself is presumed to be a privileged medium of interpretation. The interpreter must make sense of words and ideas that are prized within (i.e. "intra") the "world" created by the text itself. Further, I suspect that the final editor was himself sensitive to how words and ideas developed within the literary world he had shaped. If he was informed by strategies of rabbinical exegesis as many commentators suspect, then this kind of literary strategy which recalls catchwords for later use and expanded meaning takes its cues from *gezera šawa* (i.e. the rule of equivalence) by which one passage is used to interpret another when similar words link the two. Of course, these literary techniques are deeply rooted in theological convictions about the perspicuity and coherence of sacred traditions.

use in 2:8-13, both explaining and expanding the meaning of law found there. This expanded meaning of law in turn prepares the reader for its final use in 4:11-12, and helps to explain its relationship to the paraenetic traditions to which it is joined in 4:1–5:6.[23]

Suffice it to say that a variety of scholars have assigned different meanings to "perfect law," either to indicate the Torah's ethical value or its salvation-historical role. Davids, following Davies, even suggests the word carries a messianic freight, so that the "perfect law" refers to Jesus' messianic interpretation of his biblical Torah.[24] In this meaning of the phrase, Jesus' teaching ministry fashions a "new Torah" that defines the life of "surpassing righteousness" (Matt 5:20), which is lived to perfection (cf. Matt 5:48) and which Jesus himself perfectly performed and embodied.

Yet, what is often overlooked in interpreting this phrase is the prior use of τέλειος in 1:2-21. In fact, according to 1:4, τέλειος is a critical ingredient of the author's restatement of his thesis.[25] The eschatological requirement for passing the test of faith is termed the ἔργον τέλειον—a "perfect work" which is claimed for the believer's heroic patience during various trials. In turn, the eschatological result of this perfect work is τέλειος, which is coupled with "completion" (ὁλο-κλῆρος; cf. the phrase, ὅλον τὸν νόμον, in 2:10) to describe the realization of a restored creation where nothing lacks for those who dwell therein.[26]

This eschatological meaning of perfection is next imported into the phrase, "every perfect (τέλειος) gift," used in 1:17 as a critical feature of the author's restatement of the opening thesis. Here, James

---

[23]   The primary references to the biblical Torah in James fall within the section marked off by 1:22–2:26, which is a halachic midrash on "quick to listen," the first member of triadic proverb found in 1:19-20. The hermeneutical environment for interpretation includes the situation of the readers who first read the text. That is, the big ideas of any composition unfold in a way that interpret the faith and life of its first audience. In this case, the crisis that requires James's commentary on "quick listening" is the oppression of the community's poor (2:1-7).

[24]   Davids, *James*, 99-100.

[25]   Following (although modifying) the lead of F. O. Francis ("The Form and Function of the Opening and Closing Paragraphs of James and 1 John," *ZNW* 61 [1970] 110-26), I take Jas 1:2-21 to be a "double opening," pairing 1:2-11 and 1:12-21, whose rhetorical role is to introduce the author's organizing themes (e.g. testing, eschatological blessing, wisdom, jubilary reversal) in a nuanced and more persuasive manner.

[26]   F. Mussner, *Der Jakobusbrief* (HTKNT 13; Freiburg: Herder, 1964) 66-7.

corrects the foolish deception that God is responsible for our difficult trials (1:13-16). In fact, the Creator's will is for a restored
creation (1:18); and toward that end God provides the perfect gift of
wisdom (1:17, 19-20), which empowers the community's patience
and ensures the prospect of a perfected existence at the triumph of
the Creator's reign (1:21).

It is this unfolding idea of τέλειος within the thesis statement of
James that is then posited with νόμος in 1:25: like wisdom, Torah is
also a "perfect gift of God" and it too guides the community through
its trials and toward the τέλος of God's reign. Before the fool is
deceived about God's goodness (1:13-16); in this new setting, the fool
is deceived in reducing the wisdom of "quick hearing" (cf. 1:19) into
a simple matter of merely listening to its sage advice without then
following it (1:22). Such a deception is readily exposed by pairing
wisdom with Torah, which must be both observed and performed.
Under the light of a Torah interpretation of the wisdom tradition,
one's eschatological blessing (τέλειος) results from quickly *obeying*
the divine word: in this sense, the way of wisdom must be the same
as the way of Torah, which must be obeyed. More basic than the
skills of knowing wisdom is its performance. Like the perfect Torah,
the perfect gift of wisdom envisages the pattern of eschatological
religion, which must be followed in order to receive God's promised
blessing.

The point of asserting that Torah is "perfect," then, is not to indicate the divine quality of its revealed words nor the moral outcome
of its observance. Rather, the use of τέλειος with νόμος within this
compositional context reminds the reader that Torah is God's perfect
gift (cf. 1:17) for those undergoing testing (cf. 1:3-4). At the same
time, it warns the reader not to respond foolishly by merely glancing
at what it says: the biblical Torah discloses God's eschatological
requirement, which must be obeyed and not merely heard, if the
community is to participate in God's coming salvation (cf. 1:4, 18).[27]

THE "LAW OF LIBERTY" IN JAMES

1. *The intertextuality of the "law of liberty."* With its intertextuality in mind, let me explore the meaning of the second and more

---

27 Interpreter made even more sensitive to the pairing of wisdom and law by
noting the repetition of τέλειος and ὅλο (-κλῆροι), used together in 1:4 to introduce
wisdom in 1:5, and τέλειος and ὅλος, used to introduce Torah in 1:25 and 2:10.

difficult adjective, "liberty" (ἐλευθερία), whose attributive relation to νόμος points us to its subject matter. I am aware of the substantial source critical problems pertaining to the pre-literary history of James in general and this word in particular. While the Torah's perfection is known from Jewish literature (see above), the Torah's "liberty" is not and we can only speculate about its possible sources.[28]

Three possible interpretations of "liberty" have been proposed. (1) The law's liberating effect may well be paradoxical. Following Jewish and Jesus tradition (cf. Matt 11:29-30), the "yoke of the law" may actually liberate the observant to serve the interests of God. R. Fabris contends that Jewish tradition would understand this liberation in terms of a spiritual and inward experience rather than eschatological and cosmic.[29] While James is certainly concerned about inward struggle, the pairing of "law of liberty" with human blessing in 1:25 would seem to argue against understanding liberty in this way. (2) Many scholars appeal to contemporary hellenistic philosophy, especially Stoic, to define "liberty" as the present experience of the wise person's efforts in maintaining personal control over one's destiny by submitting to the "law of nature." The pairing of law and proverbial wisdom in this passage, coupled with an exhortation to "do" what is heard, makes this an attractive interpretation. (3) Still others find here a Christian reference to the "new Torah" of Jesus' messianic reign, which is certainly concerned—as James is—with the moral essentials of Christian community (Matt 5). Paul's spiritualizing of the law in Rom 8:2 seems less likely here, especially in light of Rom 6:15-23 where the moral dimension of the Christian life is possible only in liberty *from* the enslaving power of the law.

The strange tone the combination of "law" and "liberty" sounds is muted somewhat for readers who recognize the same combination in Paul. However, another problem immediately arises when they realize that the Pauline relationship between law and freedom is a negative one: faith in Christ liberates the believer *from* the law (Rom 6:15-23; 7:6-8:2; Gal 2:4; 4:21-31; 5:1,13), while only the Spirit

---

[28]   Cf. Davids, *James*, 99-100. Suggested sources include Jewish (e.g. wisdom, Qumran, etc.), Jacobean (i.e. some version of hellenized Jewish Christianity, although still perhaps a Palestinian province), pre-/post-/anti-Pauline depending on date and interpretation), Jesus of Gospel, Jesus of pre-gospel, Jesus of Q, or Jesus of pre-Q.

[29]   R. Fabris, *Legge della libertà in Giacomo* (RivBSup 8; Brescia: Paideia, 1977).

empowers compliance with God's will. Thus, while the tone sounded by this phrase is not strange, it is dissonant: according to James, "true religion" (1:27) does not result from being "liberated from the Torah" but rather from being liberated by the Torah.[30] There is a Jewish slant to the notion of law in James that would surely unsettle the Pauline Christian. Because of the notable disagreements between the biblical James and Paul,[31] some scholars suppose the Jacobean "law of liberty" is a catchphrase from a Jewish polemic against Paulinizing "sola fideism."[32] In this case, the Torah's "liberty" refers to its spiritual effect: Torah observance actually frees the believer from sin to enjoy a more profitable relationship with God (cf. Matt 5:17-20).

Yet, the interpreter may be able to recover a more textured meaning of "liberty" from its subtextual layer. In light of this methodological interest, I suggest that "liberty" functions in this difficult phrase as a metaphor of the levitical Jubilee (Leviticus 25). Yes, the *text* of James does not cite any of the legal or prophetic idioms for the Jubilee year. However, the phrase, "law of liberty," may well facilitate a "free association"[33] with a cluster of themes and concerns found within the levitical ordinance of the Jubilee year (Leviticus 25; cf. Deut 15:1-11). Especially the prophetic references to an eschatological Jubilee (e.g. Isa 61:1-2) were well-known to messianic Jews of the Second Temple period, which no doubt included the author and first auditors of James. Even so, when the current "canonical audience" considers the trials of the community's poor according to Jas 1:26–2:11, bracketed as it is by James' double

---

30   Scholars struggling with the apparent conflict between James and Paul over the importance of Torah sometimes claim that whatever anti-Pauline polemics are included in James are focused by a mistaken understanding of Paul's teaching. In any case, James is probably responding to the "real" (rather than stated) and even logical outcome of Paul's teaching found in Romans 3–4 and Galatians 2–5, which continues to form the core convictions of a "folk Paulinism" even to this day.

31   See now M. Goulder, *A Tale of Two Missions* (London: SCM, 1994).

32   So J. T. Sanders, *Schismatics, Sectarians, Dissidents, Deviants* (Valley Forge: Trinity Press International, 1993) 222-23. In Pauline thought, the Spirit's in-filling is a liberating event, and in James wisdom is on par with Paul's Spirit. In some sense, then, one might suppose that the incursion and joining of wisdom with law liberates the law from its deadly legalism. Wisdom applies the example of Christ to life in a way that accords with God's will.

33   Cf. Sheppard, *Hermeneutical Construct*, 102.

reference to the "law of liberty" (cf. 1:25; 2:12), it would recognize an allusion to the biblical Jubilee when "liberty" is granted to the oppressed and indigent poor. Sharply put, the "law of liberty" associates with (perhaps even with the "volume" of an allusion) the levitical ordinance of Jubilee, which demands a socio-economic expression of holiness that is embodied in the treatment of the poor and powerless neighbor. Sharply put, the "law of liberty" refers to the biblical Torah injunctions for the year of Jubilee, specifically for the justice of the oppressed.

The crucial word used in the jubilee code is actually ἄφεσις rather than ἐλευθερία; nevertheless both words are conceptually similar:[34] aphesis is the priestly equivalent of ἐλευθερία. Further, they are used in similar settings within Scripture. For example, ἐλευθερία is used in Lev 19:20—part of James' "torah within the Torah"—with λύτρον ("redemption") in speaking of clemency for the slave. In a parallel text within the jubilary code dealing with slaves (25:39-46), λύτρον is paired with ἄφεσις in specifying their freedom from oppression. In this case, the concepts of "freedom" and "forgiveness" envisage a similar "redemption" from oppression that results from observing the Torah's demand. In addition, the levitical passage expresses concern for the poor "brother" (cf. ἀδελφός in Lev 25:39) as does James (2:5, 15)—for believers, who in both contexts have need for liberation from the oppression of those in power (cf. the "rich" in Jas 2:2-7; par. Lev 25:46).[35]

The pairing of ἐλεύθερος (instead of ἄφεσις) and λύτρον is also

---

[34]   See J. P. Louw and E. A. Nida, *Greek-English Lexicon of the New Testament Based on Semantic Domains* (2 vols., New York: United Bible Societies, 1988) 1.487-89, where ἄφεσις (§37.132: "the process of setting free or liberating") and ἐλευθερία (§37.133: "the state of being free or liberated") are members of the same subdomain as lexically similar words.

[35]   The story behind Jas 2:2-7 remains difficult to tell. In my opinion, the rich of 2:2-3 and 2:6-7 are able to exploit their legal powers over the poor and powerless members of this Christian synagogue. Perhaps they are extorting payment in exchange for "protection," and it is this payment to the rich outsider that funded the community's welfare to the poor insider. In this case, the foolishness of not siding with those poor insiders whom God has elected to be rich in faith (2:5) is understood against the wisdom of obeying Torah's command (2:8), since obedience issues in God's favorable verdict at the end of the age (2:13). The allusion to jubilee "thickens" this calculus: a jubilary concern for the liberation of the poor from those who impoverish them heralds the coming triumph of God and indicates their devotion to God and fitness to participate in the Lord's reign.

used in the deuteronomic legislation of the sabbatical year, again for "freeing" slaves (Deut 15:12-13, 18; cf. Exod 21:2-6), in a text that is parallel to the levitical ordinance for sabbath/jubilary years. In fact, these two traditions are typically held together in the literature of the Second Temple period. Given their biblical use, then, the word association between ἐλεύθερος and ἄφεσις seems a logical one for James to create, and is especially apropos if the author has Paul's ἐλεύθερος in mind to counteract a de-Judaizing (and perhaps even de-canonizing) Pauline *Tendenz* within his community (see above).

Finally, James' understanding of Jubilee is more prophetic and typological of the sociology of God's coming reign (cf. Isa 61:1-2; *Jub.* 1:21-5; Luke 4:14-30; 6:20-38; 11:2-4). In fact, the use of Jubilee as a prophetic typology of the coming kingdom would have been sufficiently familiar to the author and first auditors of James so that a clearer allusion or even citation of the Jubilee year would not have been necessary. In this prophetic sense, then, the "law of liberty" prescribes a jubilary justice that liberates the oppressed neighbors from their economic woes as faithful witness to the coming era of prosperity and social justice. The sort of material detachment envisaged by James' piety of poverty motif (2:5; 4:1-17) is a matter of expectant faith in the coming reversal of fortune (1:9-11).[36]

In my reading, the conceptual similarity and plausible linguistic links between the "preferential option for the poor" of Jubilee and the setting of this particular crisis in James (cf. Jas 5:1-6; par. Lev 25:39-46) is highly suggestive of a jubilary subtext in defining the fuller meaning of the phrase, "the law of liberty." To be sure the subject matter of the law is clarified by what follows in Jas 1:26–2:12;[37] however, what follows in James does not point to the fulfillment of Jeremiah's "law written on the human heart"[38] nor

---

36   There are other jubilary themes found in James; cf. R. W. Wall, "James as Apocalyptic Paraenesis," *RestQ* 32 (1990) 11-22. For example, a jubilary eschatology might include the cycle of time mentioned in 5:7-18; cf. G. W. Buchanan, *The Book of Revelation* (Lewiston and Queenston: Mellen, 1993) 7-14; or the reversal theme in 1:9-11; 5:1-6; cf. M. Dibelius and H. Greeven, *James* (Hermeneia; Philadelphia: Fortress, 1976) 39-45, 84; emphasis on an active faith in 2:14-26; cf. R. B. Sloan, *The Favorable Year of the Lord* (Austin: Schola, 1977) 7-27; and the Lord's parousia in 5:7-9.

37   So Martin, *James*, 51.

38   *Contra* L. Goppelt, *Theology of the New Testament*, vol. 2 (Grand Rapids:

even to Jesus' interpretation of Jewish law in a way that transformed it into Christian "gospel."[39] Rather, "liberty" in this rhetorical setting is a catchword that gathers to itself the images of neighborly love for poor and oppressed believers found in the levitical laws of holiness, and especially within its jubilee ordinance.

2. *The intratextuality of the "law of liberty"*. The repetition of the phrase "law of liberty" in 2:12 brackets off 1:26--2:11, which in turn contemporizes the meaning of the phrase. Now when the reader comes to the phrase again, additional points have been scored since its first reference that supply important ingredients of a hermeneutical environment which enables the reader to better understand its significance for James. A close reading of this material lies outside the purview of this essay; however, three brief observations will suffice to clarify my point.

(a) While the story behind 2:1-7 is impossible to construct with any precision, it would seem to tell of the presence of class strife between rich outsiders and poor insiders, evinced both in a synagogue-court (2:2-4) and in a law-court (2:6-7) where justice is expected but not found.[40] Almost certainly, the form of partiality is more material than according rich guests preferential seating in the assembly (2:3); in fact, such seating may have biased the proceeding in favor of the rich. The description of the wealthy in this passage suggests they are bankers, whose disagreements with the poor are financial.[41] The prejudicial seating of these wealthy bankers, then,

---

Eerdmans, 1982) 203-208, who is followed by Martin, *James*, 51.

[39] So Mussner, *Der Jakobusbrief*, 107; also, Davids, *James*, 100.

[40] For the various possibilities, see P. U. Maynard-Reid, *Poverty and Wealth in James* (Maryknoll: Orbis, 1987) 48-67. Whether to consider the references to rich and poor as social categories of outsider ("rich") and insider ("poor") remains contested, although R. B. Ward's argument ("Partiality in the Assembly: James 2:2-4," *HTR* 62 [1969] 87-97) in favor of a Christian setting is convincing. However, elsewhere in James, including 2:6-7, the struggle between "rich" and "poor" classes seems to place Christian poor against non-Christian rich. If both belong to a common group, then both are Palestinian Jews (but not necessarily Christian) and subject to a common juridical tradition. This solution retains continuity with 2:6-7, where the rich are obviously non-Christians. Paul's advice in 1 Cor 5:9–6:11 envisages a similar distinction within his Gentile mission, where a church-court (cf. Jas 2:2-3) is called for instead of a pagan law-court (cf. Jas 2:6-7) to settle differences between believers and "so-called" believers who are actually outsiders to the Christian faith (1 Cor 5:11-12).

[41] Maynard-Reid, *Poverty and Wealth in James*, 59-61, 63-64.

hints at a negative verdict for the poor, who no doubt remained poor or worse.

The community's partiality toward the rich at the expense of the poor is condemned as "evil" in the text's apodosis (2:4) for the two reasons given in what follows in 2:5-7. First, a preferential option for wealthy financiers fails the testing of the community's faith in God (cf. 1:3), who favors the poor and promises them a portion of the coming kingdom (2:5). The reader is well aware from earlier material in James (cf. 1:13-15) that such theological failures are rather foolish because they exchange the pragmatism of a quick-fix for an eschatological blessing that endures (cf. 2:13). Second, foolish still, their preferential option for the wealthy evinces the contradiction of taking the side of those who harass them in law-courts (2:6), perhaps even as an instrument for extorting money dedicated to their poor, and who seek to impugn Jesus' reputation (and so their own) within this Jewish context (2:7). It is this terrible irony that only deepens the sense of injustice.

If this construction approximates the story behind the text, then the application of jubilary justice is explicable. In this setting, it is the "law of liberty" rather than the synagogue-court or law-court which discloses God's choice of the poor and defends the poor against the rich.

(b) Significantly, the author not only pairs Torah with wisdom but also with Jesus tradition in 2:1.[42] At the very least, the allusions to

---

42   The important phrase, "the faith of Jesus Christ," in 2:1 cues the reader to the pairing of Jesus and Torah. Johnson links the "no partiality" phrase in 2:1 to Lev 19:15, which James posits at the core of the "faith of Jesus." Johnson does not go on to suggest, however, that Lev 19:15 includes the vocabulary of the poor and evil judgment (also 19:18; cf. S. Laws, *The Epistle of James* [HNTC; San Francisco: Harper & Row, 1980] 93-4) which recalls James 2:2-4 (cf. Davids, *James*, 110). In this sense, 2:1-4 is a christological midrash on Lev 19:15. The questions of genre that Johnson raises in his essay are important. If James is midrashic literature (rather than hellenistic paraenesis) and therefore intertextual, then the sources the interpreter attends to when analyzing the text will also shift. That is, if midrashic literature, then the primary sources are biblical rather than the moral traditions of the Greco-Roman world.The allusions are to tradition preserved in Luke's gospel: Jas 2:2-4 allude to Luke 14:7-14; and Jas 2:5 to Luke 6:20. The seems apropos since it is Luke, more than any other New Testament writer, who preserves a jubilary interpretation of Jesus's messiahship.

One final point in this regard. Since the date of James remains contested, the identity of these pre-gospel traditions of Jesus, used in Jas 2:1-5, remain contested

the biblical Torah in 2:1-4 and citation from it in 2:8 envisage the author's "canon consciousness," and give authority and additional substance to his memories of a pre-canonical Jesus. Further, these biblical allusions and citation are from a discrete portion of the biblical Torah (the levitical laws of holiness) by which Jesus tradition is interpreted. In this sense, a particular portion of Torah is normative for the author's interpretation of Jesus Christ, whose exalted status as "glorious Lord" is justified by his observance of the Torah's commitment to the poor.

Again, I do not suppose that James' appeal to Jesus' faith in 2:1 is as authoritative interpreter of wisdom or a new Torah. Rather, the reference to "the faith of the glorious Lord Jesus Christ" in 2:1 cues up the memory of his ministry among the poor (cf. Jas 2:2-4 par. Luke 14:7-14; Jas 2:5 par. Luke 6:20[-36]) alluded to in the following passage, a ministry that demonstrates his exemplary obedience to the "royal Torah" of love (2:8).[43] In fact, the "impartiality" of Jesus' faith must be viewed in this context as ironical, since the rich are non-Christians and rejected, while the poor comprise God's "true" Israel and loved.[44]

---

as well. The pairing of Jesus and traditional Jewish wisdom (1:19-20) constructs a different Jesus than is found within Christian gospel tradition. Especially in Matthew (i.e. Q, QMatt, Matt), Jesus is a *prophetic* sage who sponsors a messianic reformation of Jewish wisdom. In my mind, the allusions to the Jesus tradition in 2:2-5 (cf. Luke 14:7-14 par. Jas 2:2-4; Luke 6:20 par. Jas 2:5), which define "the faith of the Lord Jesus Christ" (2:1), are rooted in biblical Torah and wisdom. In this sense, the author's understanding of Jesus's faith follows the teaching of biblical Torah and wisdom: he is the glorious exemplar of doing the levitical law of holiness, whose love of his poor and powerless neighbors bears witness to his messiahship.

43   I have argued (in Wall and Lemcio, *Canon*, 260) that the curious addition of the articular δόξα ("the glory") to Jesus's title in 2:1 may refer to God's approval of Jesus's messiahship ("Lord Jesus *Christ*") and exaltation to Lord ("*Lord* Jesus Christ") results from his love of the poor and powerless neighbor (cf. καλῶς ποιεῖτε; 2:8b). A. F. Segal ("Conversion and Messianism," in J. H. Charlesworth [ed.], *The Messiah* [Minneapolis: Fortress Press, 1992] 332-35) offers the intriguing suggestion that δόξα in 2:1 is an idiom for the כָּבוֹד of the Lord, recalled from Ezekiel's vision of a human figure who is called "the Glory of God" (Ezek 1:29), and expresses God's human appearance. Within the apocalypticism of James, such an idiom might mean that Jesus embodied the values of God's coming reign.

44   Paul's own vision of Christ's "impartiality," in response to questions about theodicy, is more missiological than sociological. Thus, claims of God's impartial-

(c) Finally, the meaning of the anarthrous νόμον βασιλικόν ("royal law"), which is "fulfilled" (τελεῖτε; cf. 1:25) by observing Lev 19:18 (cf. 2:8), is clarified in relationship to the "law of liberty."[45] Virtually all commentators understand that both νόμον βασιλικόν and the levitical "love command" are coextensive with the poor, and that their combined use here intends to condemn the community's preferential option for the rich (2:9; cf. Lev 19:15). However, the precise meaning of βασιλικός to define the biblical Torah remains obscure. The critical majority seems to assign four aspects to the adjective's meaning: (1) it is a euphemism for God; (2) whose will is disclosed in OT law; and (3) then interpreted for Christians in the teachings of the synoptic Jesus, (4) whose epitome is the "love command."[46] Davids contends that the teaching of Jesus which figures into this phrase is not ethical but theological, pertaining to "the sovereign rule of God's kingdom."[47] Yet, I do not find this calculus entirely convincing. While Jesus does include the poor within God's reign, his own midrash on the levitical love command focuses on those outside of the faith community, on the poor and sinful "enemy" of the rich and righteous "neighbor." In my view, James' midrash on the levitical law is more traditional and less prophetic than Jesus': James is more concerned to love the insider.[48]

---

ity are directed to opponents of his Gentile mission: God has called Gentiles as well as Jews out of the world and into Christ's "body" to share equally in the promised blessings of grace (Rom 15:8-12; cf. 3:29-30). Moreover, God's impartiality will be disclosed at the Lord's coming triumph, when all will be judged by the same criteria which are met by all through their participation with Christ Jesus (Rom 2:5-16).

45   Johnson ("The Use of Leviticus 19 in the Letter of James," 399) agrees that the "law of liberty" and the "royal law" refer to the same biblical material (in his view, Lev 19:12-18); however, rather than mere equivalents (pace Martin, James, 67), they serve different roles: the "law of liberty" judges Christians, whereas the "royal law" guides the conduct of Christians (399).

46   Mussner (Der Jakobusbrief, 124) adds "darum scheint mit dem Ausdruck 'königliches Gesetz' nur gesagt zu sein, dass das Gebot von Lv 19, 18 königlichen Rang unter den anderen Geboten hat."

47   Davids, James, 114.

48   I agree with Ben Witherington ("Wisdom's Legacy: From Q to James," in Jesus the Sage [Minneapolis: Fortress Press, 1995] 211-47) who contends that James's appropriation of the Jewish sapiential materials is quite early and more traditional than is found in the Jesus tradition (whether Q or synoptic Gospels). According to Witherington, the book of James envisages a community with "care-

Let me return to a point scored by the critical consensus with which I do agree: "law of liberty" and "royal law" are mutually-glossing phrases, especially within a common compositional environment where the latter phrase concentrates material bracketed off and interpreted by the former. If "liberty" is a metaphor of jubilary justice and heralds the coming sociology of God's reign, then perhaps "royal" carries a similar freight: the νόμος βασιλικός discloses the rule of the coming βασιλεία θεοῦ. In turn, the eschatological force of the conditional τελεῖτε becomes apparent: only if the community orders its life by the rule of the coming kingdom (νόμος βασιλικός) will it receive a favorable verdict when διὰ νόμου ἐλευθερίας κρίνεσθαι ("judged by the law of liberty;" see under 2:12-13).

CONCLUSION

According to the thesis of James, wisdom is the word of truth that enables the believer to know how to pass the testing of faith; and it is wisdom's way to lead the believer through such testing and ultimately into God's future blessing. In Jas 1:25, the wisdom of "quick to hear" (1:19) is held together with the biblical Torah, which supplies both its justification project as well as its content. According to this text, then, the Torah tradition actually defines the way of wisdom: wisdom "heard" is the whole Torah observed.

The importance of a Torah observant wisdom is introduced in 1:25 by two adjectives, each of which is an important theological catchword, together clarifying core convictions about the Torah role within the Christian community. First, the Torah is "perfect"; that is, it purposes an eschatological and redemptive effect for those who obey its command. Second, Torah's more specific demand is defined by the second adjective, "liberty," which is not an article from some Jacobean anti-Pauline polemic but rather privileges the ordinance of the Jubilee year found in the levitical laws of holiness, which funded an important prophetic typology of the coming age. In anticipation

---

fully controlled boundaries," to serve as "sacred space" for believers within a spiritually hostile world. Jesus, on the other hand, reaches out beyond the community in "free association with sinners" to produce a "counter order" with new and different boundaries in witness to the *present* inbreaking of God's eschatological reign. It would seem to me that James's interpretation of Torah parallels his handling of biblical wisdom.

of their participation in the coming triumph of God's reign, then, the congregation must address the financial trials of its oppressed poor by nurturing a Jubilee-like social world in which all prejudice and the harsh treatment of its poor and powerless "neighbors" ends.

THE *VESTIGIA TRINITATIS* IN THE OLD TESTAMENT

Reginald H. Fuller

During the six years in which I was privileged to have James A. Sanders as a colleague at the Union Theological Seminary in New York (1966-72) I gained from him important insight. This is that texts have a life of their own in the community of faith. Their meaning was not fixed once and for all by the original author. Rather, they constantly acquire new meaning in the light of later experiences.

This insight is frequently denied by historical critical scholarship. I remember how at Cambridge, back in the 1930s, it was customary to laugh at the chapter headings of the Authorised (or King James) Version, such as "Sufferings of Christ," printed at the head of Isaiah 53. In a similar vein, John Bowden has recently poured scorn on the way passages from the Hebrew Scriptures are read at the beloved service of Nine Lessons and Carols broadcast throughout the world each Christmas Eve from King's College Chapel.[1] These lessons suggest that the authors of Genesis and Isaiah actually had the birth of Christ in mind when they wrote: "I will put enmity between thee and the woman, and between thy seed and her seed; it shall bruise thy head, and thou shalt bruise his heel" (Gen 3:15 KJV). And again: "Behold, a virgin shall conceive, and bear a son, and shall call his name Immanuel" (Isa 7:14 KJV). Bowden protests that today only the historical-critical interpretation of these texts is acceptable, and that they have nothing to do with the birth of Christ.

Just as earlier Christian interpreters discovered the doctrine of the incarnation and atonement in these two passages so too did they discover the doctrine of the Trinity in other passages of the Hebrew Scriptures. It was customary to speak of the *vestigia trinitatis*, i.e. adumbrations of the Trinity in the Old Testament. Such adumbrations were found in the following passages: "Let us make humankind in our own image, according to our likeness" (Gen 1:26). There is a story told of Dean Burgon, a 19th-century cleric of the Church of

---

[1]   J. Bowden, *Jesus: The Unanswered Questions* (London: SCM, 1988) 13.

England, who was notorious for opposing every innovation in his own day. He had been scheduled to preach the University sermon in St. Mary's, Oxford one Trinity Sunday. It was at a time when the admission of women to the University was being canvassed. Seeking a text that would cover both themes, he chose Gen 1:26. In the first part of his sermon he expounded the plural, "us" and "our" as an allusion to the three persons of the Trinity. In the second part he interpreted "man" so as to exclude women (!). Modern scholars of course interpret the "we" and "our" as a dialogue between God and the divine or angelic beings that constitute God's heavenly court.[2] And it goes without saying that "man" includes woman.

Another adumbration of the Trinity was found in the Aaronic blessing. Note the three-fold mention of the LORD: "The LORD bless you and keep you; the LORD make his face to shine upon you and be gracious unto you; the LORD lift up his countenance upon you, and give you peace" (Num 6:24-26). Anyone who has ever attended a German Lutheran service will recall how the liturgy invariably closes with the pastor standing at the altar, pronouncing the Aaronic blessing with a huge sign of the cross, thus clearly indicating its trinitarian character.[3] Another indication of the trinitarian understanding of the Aaronic blessing was the appointment of Num 6:22-27 as the Old Testament reading for Trinity eve in the 1928 Prayer Book of the Protestant Episcopal Church in the United States.

A third vestige of the Trinity was sometimes found in the story of the three men who appeared to Abraham. First, we are told, it is Yahweh himself who appears (Gen 18:1). Then it is three men (vv. 2, 3, etc.). Finally, it is again Yahweh himself who was the subject of the apparition; "And the LORD went his way, when he had finished speaking to Abraham" (v. 33). The mysterious oscillation suggested the three Persons of the Trinity.

The last instance of an adumbration of the Trinity to be noted here is the best known one. It occurs in Isaiah's call vision (Isaiah 6). Here

---

[2]   Thus, e.g. H. G. May and B. M. Metzger (eds.), *The Oxford Annotated Bible with the Apocrypha* (New Revised Standard Version; New York: Oxford University Press, 1991) 2.

[3]   Jürgen Moltmann has shown how the cross, the Trinity, baptism and the sign of the cross in baptism and in the pronouncement of the benediction, as well as the invocation of the Trinity at the beginning of the liturgy, have a close theological relation. See J. Moltmann, *The Crucified God* (New York: Harper & Row, 1974) 240-49.

the three-fold "Holy, holy, holy, suggested the Trinity, an idea expressed poetically in Reginald Heber's well-known hymn, probably sung in every Angelican church throughout the world on Trinity Sunday:

> Holy, holy, holy, LORD God Almighty . . .
> God in three Persons,
> Blessed Trinity.

Modern commentatios do not even bother to mention this idea, and one of them, John McKenzie, states roundly in his article, "Trinity," in *Dictionary of the Bible*: "The OT does not contain suggestions or foreshadowing of the trinity of persons."[4] Similarly, our former doctoral student at Union Theological Seminary, Thomas W. R. Longstaff, in the corresponding article in *Harper's Bible Dictionary*, writes: "Attempts to trace the origins [sc. of the doctrine of the Trinity] still earlier (to the OT literature) cannot be supported by historical-critical scholarship."[5] We agree with this statement as it stands, and the instances we have given are not only untenable in the light of modern scholarship, but are in fact quite trivial.

This, however, is not the end of the matter. If the doctrine of the Trinity is true, as Christian orthodoxy, both Catholic and Protestant, claim it to be, God did not as it were wake up after Pentecost and say "Now I am a Trinity, three persons in one God." God must have been Trinity all along. That being so, it is not unreasonable to take another look at the God of the Hebrew Scriptures and ask ourselves whether there is anything there to suggest that the God of those texts was indeed the kind of deity who could later be seen as having a three-fold aspect to the unity which those Scriptures so strongly assert. Perhaps after all, the Church Fathers showed a true instinct in looking for such *vestigia*, even if the way they exercised that instinct seems to us both trivial and exegetically impossible.

Now the doctrine of the Trinity was required in order to make sense of the incarnation and the experience of the Holy Spirit. This experience had to be squared with the Old Testament insistence on the one God—which the Christian community inherited from the Hebrew Scriptures and Judaism without question. So the prior

---

4   J. L. McKenzie, *Dictionary of the Bible* (Milwaukee: Bruce, 1965) 900 s.v. "Trinity."

5   *The HarperCollins Bible Dictionary* (ed. Paul J. Achtemeier; San Francisco: HarperCollins, 1996) 1178-79.

problem is whether the doctrine on the incarnation is in any way adumbrated in, or at the very least is not incosistent with, the Old Testament and Jewish understanding of God. Was the God of the Hebrews the kind of God about whom incarnation might later be affirmed? Or was that God the kind of God about whom any idea of incarnation would be inappropriate?

In speaking of the incarnation, the Nicene creed asserst that the eternal Son "came down from heaven." It is interesting and significant that Yahweh in the Hebrew Scriptures is precisely a God who "comes down" from heaven at important moments in salvation history. That idea first appears in connection with the story of Babel: "The LORD came down to see the city and the tower, which mortals have built" (Gen 11:5). Then, a little later, Yahweh says: "Come, let us go down, and confuse their language there" (v. 7). The whole story is clearly very primitive, for Yahweh is depicted in highly anthropomorphic terms. God has to go down in order to see what is happening! The plural "us" probably refers to the heavenly court of divine beings as in Gen 1:26. Here, however, is the germ of a later, more sophisticated belief that God, though transcendent, intervenes in history. Some degree of sophistication is reached in the story of the theophany of Moses at the burning bush. Here Yahweh accounces to Moses:

> "I have observed the misery of my people who are in Egypt; I have heard their cry on account of their taskmasters. Indeed, I know their sufferings, and I have come down [Heb. אֵרֵד] to deliver them from the Egyptians, and to bring them up out of that land . . ." [Exod 3:7-8].

Here we have the picture of a God who condescends to be concerned with the suffering of human beings, who becomes directly involved in those sufferings, who identifies with them, and who acts in order to liberate them. To do this, God "comes down" (ירד), that is to say, as a transcendent deity God enters into the immanent world without abandoning transcendence. The God of the exodus does not yet become incarnate, but that God exhibits a mode of being and action with which incarnation would later be consistent—the same move from transcendence into history in order to act redemptively. This action is not as it were accomplished merely from the outside, but from inside, through direct involvement, yet without forfeiting transcendence.

The same understanding of God, again in reference to the exodus, is found in the book of Nehemiah, in Ezra's recital of Israel's salvation history. When he reaches the giving of the law, he says of Yahweh: "You *came down* (יָרַדְתָּ) also on Mount Sinai, and spoke with them" (Neh 9:13). Thus the exodus events—both the deliverance from Egypt and the giving of the law—are conceived to be acts in which God "comes down," both of them acts of redemption and revelation.

The same picture of Yahweh is reflected in psalmody: "He bowed the heavens, and came down" (2 Sam 22:10 = Ps 18:9). It is not clear what event this psalm was originally referring to, or indeed whether it had any particular event in salvation history in view. As it now stands in 2 Samuel (and probably also at the canonical level in the psalter, as a "Psalm of David") it is interpreted as reference to the whole of David's career, especially the inauguration of the monarchy. This is again a crucial event in Israel's salvation history when God "came down."

There is one more psalm that speaks of God's "coming down." This is Psalm 144, which has affinities with Psalm 18, and which, like the earlier psalm, was later designated a psalm of David. Here the psalmist prays again in almost identical words:

> Bow your heavens, O LORD, and come down;
> touch the mountains so that they smoke [Ps 144:5].

Interpreted at the canonical level, David is praying for a divine intervention at some point in his career. Once again, God is asked to "come down," probably at a significant moment in the establishment of the Davidic monarchy.

The last passage to be noted in the Hebrew canon occurs in Trito-Isaiah. Here the unknown prophet cries out:

> O that you would tear open the heavens and come down . . .
> to make your name known to your adversaries,
> so that the nations might tremble at your presence [Isa 64:1-2].

Deutero-Isaiah had looked forward to the return from exile as a new exodus (e.g. Isa 40:3-5). But the return proved a disappointment. Now another prophet in the Isaianic tradition continues the call for Israel's restoration in a new exodus event. But that event never fully happened. So the prayer was shelved, as it were, for an eschatological future. In Christian perspective that new exodus which the Isaianic prophet had anticipated found its fulfillment in the Christ event, in which God "came down" decisively.

There is one more passage that need to be looked at, this time from the apocryphal/deutero-canonical Wisdom of Solomon. Here, in a sophialogical *relecture* of Israel's salvation history we read:

> "For while gentle silence enveloped all things,
> and night in its swift course was now half gone,
> your all-powerful word *leaped* [ἥλατο] from heaven,
> from the royal throne,
> into the midst of the land that was doomed,
> a stern warrior [Wis 18:14-15].

The specific reference in this passage is to the slaughter of the first-born of Egypt (Exod 12:29-30) as we can see from Wis 18:12. In the original story, as narrated in the Book of Exodus, God had intervened directly in the slaughter of the first-born (Exod 12:29) or through a destroying angel. In the *relecture* Yahweh intervenes through his word,[6] who leaped down just as Yahweh had "come down" in person in original narrative. As a boy chorister in the Church of England 70 years ago, the present writer remembers singing a Victorian anthem on Wis 18:15, sung at Evensong every Christmas Day. The actual words of the anthem were:

> While all things were in quiet silence,
> and the night was in the midst of her course,
> the almighty Word of the LORD *came down*
> from his royal throne.

I learned much later that these were the words of the antiphon on the Magnificat for the first vespers of Christmas. So we see how the church later reinterpreted the scriptural language of Yahweh's coming down. It is also significant that in the later thought of Hellenistic Judaism God no longer comes down directly and in person, but rather, through his Word.

Typological exegesis has no need to claim that the later interpretation was the original intention of the author. The Isaianic authors would not have denied the reality of the Exodus in appropriating the language of Yahweh's "coming down" for the return from Babylon. The Christian church was therefore following Old Testament-Jewish precedent when it appropriated the language of "coming down" for the Christ event, and thus subjected the Hebrew Scriptures to yet another *relecture*.

Looking back on the Hebrew Scriptures from the perspective of

---

6   This reinterpretation is also found in *Tg. Ps.-J.* Exod 12:29 (so *The Jerome Biblical Commentary* [ed. R. E. Brown et al., Englewood Cliffs: Prentice Hall, 1968] 567, on Wis 18:15).

Christian faith we may therefore claim, not that the Old Testament affirmed or intended to affirm the incarnation, but that the God of the Hebrew Scriptures is a *deus incarnandus*,[7] the kind of God whose nature and action were such that incarnation would be appropriate for that God, and consistent with that God's earlier activity. It is important to note that in "coming down" Yahweh does not abandon transcendent existence.[8] In the mythical language of Scripture God is "in heaven" at the same time and active in history. Yahweh can be both transcendent, and yet can intervene in salvation history. This is an important insight which will later be developed in the doctrine of the Trinity. In the language of Yahweh's "coming down" we thus have an adumbration of the doctrine of the Trinity so far as the first and second Person are concerned.[9]

But what of the third Person? Of course there are abundant references to the "spirit" (רוּחַ) of Yahweh in the Hebrew Scriptures (Gen 1:2; 6:3 and frequently). But as yet there was no distinction between the spirit and other divine intermediaries including God's Wisdom, or even the angels. It would be more helpful if we could find something analogous to the picture of Yahweh's "coming down" that would provide a foundation for the Christian doctrine of the Spirit as the third Person of the Trinity. Perhaps we might look for this in the language of Yahweh's indwelling in the chosen people. As

---

7   I owe this expression to the late Professor Adolf Köberle, who in his lectures on "Dogmatik I" in the University of Tübingen, summer semester 1939, suggested that in the Hebrew Scriptures we encounter the *logos incarnandus*, and only in the New Testament the *logos incarnatus.*

8   It is regrettable that the late John A. T. Robinson, in his epoch-making book, *Honest to God* (London: SCM, 1963) 45-49, recommended the abandonment of the metaphor of a God "up there" and "coming down." Instead, argued Robinson, we should substitute Tillich's metaphor of God in the depths, God as the ground of being. Unfortunately this results in the loss of God's transcendence, which is crucial to biblical faith.

9   I am aware that there is disagreement among scholars as to whether such entities, as Wisdom, the Logos, and the Shekinah were thought of as hypostases— so H. Ringgren, *Word and Wisdom* (Lund: Ohlssons, 1947) 89-128. Others regard such concepts as mere "poetical personifications"—so J. D. G. Dunn, *Christology in the Making* (Philadelphia: Westminster, 1980) 174. Whichever view is correct, it remains true that in intertestamental Judaism there was an advance in the direction of recognizing distinctions within the being of God. Dunn would confine the word hypostasis to the later trinitarian definitions worked out in the patristic period. It is perhaps sufficient to speak of personified aspects of God's being and activity, so far as Hellenistic Judaism is concerned.

well as being a God who intervenes at decisive moments in salvation history, like the exodus, the establishment of the monarchy, and the return from exile, we also find a continuous presence of Yahweh in the people resulting from these interventions. Some seventeen references to this divine indwelling are listed in the NRSV concordance. Of these, the following passages merit particular attention:

> And they shall know that I am the LORD their God, who brought them out of the land of Egypt that I might dwell among them [Exod 29:46].

This shows that Yahweh's dwelling among the people of Israel is the end and goal of the divine intervention ("coming down") in the exodus event. This adumbrated the New Testament affirmation that the continuous indwelling of the Holy Spirit in the Christian community is the direct consequence of the divine intervention in the Christ event. The Pauline, Lucan, and Johannine writings all agree that the mission of the Spirit is a direct consequence of the Christ event.

Next, there is some suggestion in the prophetic writings that at the time of the exile God had withdrawn the divine presence from the chosen people:

> Go now to my place that was at Shiloh, where I made my name dwell at first ... And now, because you have done all these things, says the LORD, and when I spoke to you persistently, you did not listen, and when I called you, you did not answer, therefore I will do to the house that is called by my name ... and to the place that I gave to your ancestors, just what I did at Shiloh [Jer 7:12-14].

Note that the term "name" replaces the word "spirit." There is no firmly fixed language for the adumbration of the third Person, any more than there is for the second Person.

The return from exile carries with it the hope that God will renew the former indwelling among the restored people:

> Sing and rejoice, O daughter of Zion! For lo, I will come and dwell in your midst, says the LORD. Many nations shall join themselves to the LORD on that day, and shall be my people; and I will dwell in your midst [Zech 2:10-11].

This passage calls for three comments. First, it is Yahweh in person rather than an intermediary, such as the spirit or name, that is said to dwell in the people. We saw the same variation of language in those contexts which speak of the divine intervention. Second, this divine indwelling is again the result of God's intervention in salvation history: the passage continues with an announcement that Yahweh "has aroused himself from his holy habitation" (v. 13)—an image closely akin to that of "coming down." Third, the hope for national restoration contains a further, universalist element ("many nations"), a hope that obviously went beyond what at the time of the return could reasonably be expected, and that was therefore bound to be shelved for eschatological fulfillment at a later date. These additions to the third vision of Zechariah paved the way for the hope of a new Jerusalem to be extablished in the last days when the presence of God would dwell definitively in the redeemed people.

We have now discovered an understanding of God in the Hebrew Scripture that has the potentiality of developing into the doctrine of the Trinity as a consequence of the Christ event. The God to whom the Hebrew Scriptures bear witness is a God who is transcendent, prior to, above and beyond creation and history, and yet a God who from that transcendence intervenes to create, to redeem, and to establish the chosen people, yet without abandoning that transcendence. This is a God who "con-descends" (Luther: *Herablassung*). This God in turn perpetuates and renews the effects of those decisive interventions. In other words, the God of the Hebrew Scriptures is the kind of God who in the light of the Christ event came to be seen as a God who in his unity was somehow three-fold. To our brothers and sisters of the first covenant the doctrines of the incarnation and the Trinity have always been the supreme *skandalon*, a denial of Israel's central belief in the unity of God: "Hear O Israel: The LORD our God, the LORD is one" (Deut 6:4, NRSV marg.). But already the Judaic tradition was moving in the direction of recognizing distinctions within the activity of God. These activities included creation, revelation/redemption, and indwelling presence. It was also moving in the direction of distinctions within the *being* of God, distinctions corresponding to these activities, ascribing them to the Wisdom or Word (*logos*) and the Spirit of God. Judaism did not go very far in this direction, but the direction was certainly established. The Christian community was impelled to move much further, though still in the same direction. Thus it eventually developed the doctrine of the Trinity. This development was not a deviation from the Hebrew Scriptures but a continuation of a process already begun. On the other hand, those who remained under the first covenant backtracked from this line of development (as indicated by their rejection of the apocryphal or deutero-canonical writings, and their neglect of Philo of Alexandria). Theirs was a different, though valid faith experience.

But the Christian experience was an equally valid development from the Hebrew Scriptures. It is along these lines that we would reformulate the patristic idea of the *vestigia trinitatis*. We would also hope that this is consistent with the insight of our honoree, who taught his students and colleagues that texts acquire new meanings in the light of later experiences of faith communities, though always meanings consistent with the original texts. We offer these reflections in gratitude to our former colleague to whom we are much indebted, among other things, for this insight.

PART FIVE

EARLY JEWISH AND RABBINIC INTERPRETATION

HAMMER ON THE ROCK: ONGOING JEWISH EXEGESIS

Elliot N. Dorff

In recent years, Professor James Sanders has concentrated on what archaeology can teach us about Jewish and Christian Scripture and tradition. But one of his early books, *Torah and Canon*, deals with the process by which the Jewish community came to define its Holy Scripture. Since that book has been reprinted many times and is used by the Bible Department of the University of Judaism, where I teach, to inform rabbinical students and others about that process, I hope that the present essay, which is about an offshoot of that topic and not about archaeology, will nevertheless please Professor Sanders and serve to express the honor and love that I have for him.

THE PROBLEM:
PRESERVING GOD'S AUTHORITY IN HUMAN INTERPRETATIONS

As Professor Sanders has demonstrated, the Bible as we know it is the product of conscious *decisions* which Jewish religious leaders made at various times that some books are holy and some are not. The theological way of describing those decisions—a way which certainly articulates how the leaders themselves understood what they were doing—is to say that they were determining which texts contain the word of God and which do not. Other texts, like the Wisdom of Ben Sira, may have been popular—so much so that Ben Sira is quoted in the Talmud—and still others may have been at least part of the liturgical basis for holidays in the Jewish cultic year, as the Book of Maccabees is for Hanukkah.[1] To be recognized as Holy Scripture,

---

In the following notes, *m.* = Mishnah (edited *ca.* 200 CE); *t.* = Tosefta (also edited *ca.* 200 CE); *y.* = Jerusalem (Palestinian) Talmud (edited *ca.* 400 CE); *b.* = Babylonian Talmud (edited *ca.* 500 CE); *M.T.* = Maimonides' *Mishneh Torah* (completed 1177 CE); and *S.A.* = Joseph Karo's *Shulhan Arukh* (completed 1565 CE).

[1] I say here "part of the basis" because although the Book of Maccabees tells the story of Hanukkah and no biblical book does, the Rabbis, writing several centuries later, reinterpreted its meaning. Instead of being primarily a celebration of the

however, the book had to be a revelation of God's word.

This concept makes the succeeding history of Jewish tradition theologically very perplexing, for Jewish theological and legal authorities consist of human beings—largely, rabbis—who interpret those texts and record their own legal decisions and attitudes toward life. Rabbinic literature, in fact, is hundreds of times as comprehensive as the Bible is. What happened to the Bible in all of this? And how or in what way is any of this interpretive tradition sacred as the word of God?

In essence, the problem is a familiar one in the history of both Christianity and Judaism. Paul wanted to replace observance of the Law with adherence to the Spirit,[2] but even he had to spell out the demands of the Spirit in rather legalistic terms when it became clear that the Galatians had no idea of what he meant by living by the Spirit.[3] The later Roman Catholic Church carried further these tendencies toward additional clarification and qualification by developing a body of canon law every bit as complex as Jewish law. The Protestant Reformation was, in part, a reaction to this and an attempt to get back to living by the Spirit through direct, unmediated reading of Scripture. At the same time, however, Protestant denominations developed their own interpretations of what living by the Bible means, and those often entail abiding by specific demands and prohibitions. In some cases Protestants have established rules governing life in its entirety, including the clothes one wears, the books one reads, the food one eats, and the people with whom one socializes—to say nothing of more distinctly "religious" matters like the service one gives to the community and the activities from which one refrains on the Sabbath. Southern Baptists, Puritans, Mormons, Amish, and Seventh Day Adventists come readily to mind, but the same is also true for most other Protestant sects, including "mainline" Protestantism, in one degree or another.

Hasmonean military victory over the Greeks as recorded in the Book of Maccabees, the Rabbis maintained that the holiday celebrates a miracle that God wrought—namely, that when the Hasmoneans returned from their military exploits to rededicate the Temple which the Greeks had defiled with their idolatry, there was only enough oil to burn for one day but it burned for eight days. In this way, the Rabbis shift the focus of Hanukkah from human military might to a miraculous act of God. See *b. Šabb.* 21b.

2   See Romans 7–9; Galatians 2–3.
3   See Galatians 5; cf. also Romans 13–15.

My point is not to call into question the seriousness of the Christian claim to live by the Word instead of by the Law. It is rather to stress that anyone who wants to live by the Word—Jew, Christian, or Muslim—must first *interpret* and *apply* it. Sometimes an ambiguity in the biblical text necessitates interpretation, and sometimes it is required because the Bible does not speak at all about a given situation.

Cases where the biblical command is unclear are easy to find. For example, when the Bible says that one must honor one's father and mother, what does that entail? Is it only that one must feel certain emotions toward them? Must we also treat them with respect in our interaction with them? Must we express that respect by fulfilling specific duties toward them? If so, does one fulfill the commandment by performing those duties, even if one detests one's parents? Are children who have been physically abused by their parents still commanded to honor them? On all of these questions, the demand in the Decalogue to honor one's parents is silent. Therefore further interpretation and application are necessary.

If that is true for an apparently clear command like to honor one's parents, it is even more so for some of the Bible's more puzzling or complicated laws and ideas. What is included, for example, in the biblical demand, "Justice, justice shall you pursue" (Deut 16:20)? And exactly what does being created in the image of God (Gen 1:27) mean—and what effect should that have on our lives?

Even when the meaning of a text is clear, its application to present circumstances may not be. To take an example from the New Testament, should Paul's pronouncements about the status of women[4] be understood as the inviolable Word of God, or are they merely a reflection of proper conduct as understood in his society with no divine authority for ours? Or when the Bible decrees that "a stubborn and rebellious son" should be stoned, should we do that on the basis of those biblical verses, or should we set the biblical directive aside, either through legal techniques, as the classical Rabbis did, or by claiming that all of the law has been superseded by the Spirit, as Paul maintained?[5] And do the biblical verses, from which both

---

4   See 1 Cor 11:1-16.

5   See Deut 21:18-21. For the Rabbis' treatment of this law, see *m. Sanhedrin* 8 and *b. Sanh.* 68b–72a. After developing all of the restrictions on the definition and operation of this law, the Rabbis conclude that "there has never been 'a stubborn and rebellious son' and never will be" (*b. Sanh.* 71a).

traditions derive the imperative to save lives, require us or not to use artificial nutrition and hydration for someone in an irreversible coma?[6]

Thus even if one is convinced that one should live by the Bible, doing so is not as simple as it may seem at first; interpretation and application are required. As the Rabbis said,

> "Is not My word like a hammer that breaks a rock in many pieces?" [Jer 23:29]. As the hammer causes numerous sparks to flash forth, so is a scriptural verse capable of many interpretations (b. Sanh. 34a).

But as soon as one admits that human beings must interpret and apply God's word, the divine authority of the results is at risk. For even if the interpreter links the interpretation directly to a biblical text, who is to say that an alternative explanation is not preferable? Canons of interpretation have been developed, but they rarely preclude an interpretation or even enable one to decide between alternatives because such rules generally do not give sufficient guidance in the all-important task of *weighing* the options.[7] Matters get even worse when reasonably plausible interpretations of biblical passages produce diametrically opposed results—unfortunately, not an uncommon occurrence. For example, when the Bible describes the creation of Eve out of Adam's rib, is that meant to attribute a secondary, subservient status to women because she was created after man and from a part of his body, or is it rather intended to convey the equality of men and women since Eve's creation out of Adam's rib makes her "bone of my bones and flesh of my flesh"? And how is one's interpretation of those verses related to the Bible's first creation story, where God created man and woman simultaneously?[8]

---

[6]   In the Jewish tradition, that imperative is derived from Lev 18:5: "You shall keep My laws and rules and live by them," which the Rabbis interpreted to mean "and not die by them." The resultant imperative of *pikkuah nefesh*, saving one's own life, takes precedence over all but three commandments, namely, the prohibitions of murder, adultery/incest, and idolatry (see b. Sanh. 74a). The requirement to save other people's lives is derived from Lev 19:16: "Do not stand idly by the blood of your neighbor" (see b. Sanh. 73a).

[7]   For a description and explanation of classical Jewish rules of exegesis, and for Karl Llewellyn's masterful demonstration that canons of interpretation never determine the outcome of the law, see E. N. Dorff and A. Rosett, *A Living Tree: The Roots and Growth of Jewish Law* (Albany: State University of New York Press, 1988) 198-213.

[8]   The story of Eve's creation out of Adam's rib is found in Gen 2:21-23. The

Whenever there is even the slightest disagreement about the meaning of a verse, humans inevitably must decide what it means, and then one must wonder whether it is the word of God that one is hearing or the word of a human being.

BIBLICAL ATTEMPTS TO IDENTIFY GOD'S WORD

This problem is difficult enough with regard to the Torah, which the Jewish tradition accepts without question as the word of God. But does the word of God end with Torah? If it does, where is God now, and why is the Eternal refusing to communicate with us? Indeed, a number of biblical passages construe a refusal by God to communicate with humanity as a form of punishment.[9] On the other hand, if God does continue to speak to us, how are we to discern what is an authentic message of God and what is not?

The Bible itself has difficulty discerning a true prophet from a false one, with Deuteronomy suggesting two different criteria for knowing which is which. According to Deut 13:26, one can tell a false prophet by the content of his or her words: a prophet who tells you to follow God's already established commandments is to be believed; one who tells you to follow another God (and presumably other commandments) is to be shunned—even if the sign or portent the prophet provides to support his/her authenticity comes true. The problem with that approach, however, is that it freezes the religion in its biblical form. Moreover, prophets considered in the Bible to be true ones themselves announce new rules. Jeremiah, for example, says for the first time that carrying objects within the public domain or from private to public property constitutes a violation of the Sabbath (Jer 17:19-27), and Isaiah (58:13-14) and Nehemiah (10:32; 13:15-22) declare that doing business is not allowed on the Sabbath. We also learn from the last two sections of the Hebrew Bible, the Prophets and Writings, customs which are not recorded in the Torah. From some narrative passages the following rules may be derived: work is prohibited on the New Moon (1 Sam 20:18-19; Isa 1:13); one should pray three times a day (Daniel 6:11; Ps 55:18); sales of goods have to be done in a specific way (Ruth 4:7-12; Jer 32:6-15, 42-44); and mourning over the death of a person entails specified rites (2 Sam 1:11-12; 13:30-31; 14:1-2; Jer 9:16-17; Ezek

---

story of the simultaneous creation of man and woman is found in Gen 1:27.

9   For example, Amos 8:11-12; Mic 3:4, 6, 7; Jer 18:18; 23:29-40; Ezek 7:26.

24:15-18; Job 1:18-20). In some instances the practice is not proclaimed as a rule but rather just reported as the custom, and none of
the Torah's rules is invalidated in other biblical books. Nevertheless,
we are hearing of new customs and laws which God did not declare
in the Torah.

The Torah's second suggestion for recognizing a true prophet, in
Deut 18:9-22, is even more problematic. It says that we are to distinguish a true prophet from a false one by the criterion of whether his
or her predictions come true. But according to Deuteronomy 13 we
are never to believe a prophet who asks us to follow another god,
even if his or her predictions come true. Furthermore, some of the
predictions of people recognized as true prophets in the Bible did *not*
come true. For example, Jeremiah (22:19-23) proclaimed that King
Jehoiakim would die in disgrace, but the historical account in 2
Kings (23:36–24:6) belies that. Ezekiel predicted the destruction of
Tyre by Nebuchadnezzar (Ezek 26:7-14), but he himself later
acknowledges that Nebuchadnezzar's siege of the city was unsuccessful (Ezek 29:17-20). Both Haggai (2:21-23) and Zekhariah (4:6-7)
thought that Zerubbabel, governor of Judah, would have glorious
success in rebuilding the fallen Temple, but that never happened.[10]
Jonah's prophecy of the destruction of Nineveh was reversed, just as
he had feared (Jonah 3:4, 10; 4:1-3). To make matters worse, a true
prophet may be misled by a false one (1 Kings 13), and God may
even mislead a prophet to deliver a false message (1 Kgs 22:21-23;
Ezek 14:9-11).

THE RABBINIC SUBSTITUTION OF STUDY FOR PROPHECY

In light of all of these difficulties, one can understand the frustra-
tion involved in identifying true and false prophets. It was partly for
this reason that one of the last biblical prophets foresees a time when
people will be downright embarrassed to claim a prophetic gift—
indeed, when their own parents will kill them for doing so:

> In that day, too—declares the Lord of Hosts—I will erase the very names of
> the idols from the land; they shall not be uttered anymore. And I will also
> make the "prophets" and the impure spirit vanish from the land. If anyone
> "prophesies" thereafter, his own father and mother, who brought him into the

---

[10]   He is not, for example, mentioned as even being present at the dedication
ceremonies of the Temple (Ezra 6:14-18). Cf. B. Porten, "Zerubbabel," *EncJud*
16.1000-1001.

world, will say to him, "You shall die, for you have lied in the name of the Lord"; and his own father and mother, who brought him into the world, will put him to death when he "prophesies." In that day, every "prophet" will be ashamed of the "visions" [he had] when he "prophesied" (Zech 13:2-4).

This reaction to prophecy arose not only because of the problems inherent in discerning an authentic communication from God but also because in the period after the destruction of the First Temple in 586 BCE. Jews no longer felt that God was present among them so that prophecy could be forthcoming. After all, God had commanded the Israelites to "make Me a sanctuary that I may dwell among them" (Exod 25:8). Therefore, once the Temple was destroyed, God apparently was no longer present.

These two factors, then—the problems of distinguishing true from false prophecy, and the feelings of distance from God after His dwelling place had been destroyed—made Jews skeptical of any new claims to prophecy. The Rabbis later express this forcefully in the following story of a disputation between sages:

We learned elsewhere: If he cut it [the material for an oven] into separate tiles, placing sand between each tile, Rabbi Eliezer declared it pure, and the Sages declared it impure . . . .

On that day Rabbi Eliezer brought forward every imaginable argument, but they [the Sages] did not accept them. Said he to them: "If the law agrees with me, let this carob tree prove it." At that moment the carob tree was torn a hundred cubits out of its place—others maintain that it was four hundred cubits. "No proof can be brought from a carob tree," they answered.

Again he said to them: "If the law agrees with me, let the stream of water prove it." At that moment the stream of water flowed backwards. "No proof can be brought from a stream of water," they retorted.

Again he urged: "If the law agrees with me, let the walls of the academy prove it," at which point the walls inclined to fall. But Rabbi Joshua scolded them saying: "When scholars are engaged in a legal dispute, what right have you to interfere?" Therefore they did not fall in honor of Rabbi Joshua, nor did they resume their upright position, in honor of Rabbi Eliezer, and they remain inclined to this day.

Again he said to them: "If the law agrees with me, let it be proved in Heaven." At that moment a Heavenly Voice cried out: "Why do you dispute with Rabbi Eliezer? In all matters the law agrees with him!" But Rabbi Joshua arose and exclaimed: "It is not in heaven" [Deut 30:12]. What did he mean by this? Rabbi Jeremiah said: "That the Torah had already been given at Mount Sinai; therefore we pay no attention to a Heavenly Voice. For You have long since written in the Torah at Mount Sinai, 'One must follow the majority'" [Exod 23:2] [and God does not have a vote!]

Rabbi Nathan met Elijah (the Prophet) and asked him: "What did the Holy

One, blessed be He, do in that hour?" "He laughed with joy," he replied, "and said, 'My children have defeated Me, my children have defeated Me'" (b. B. Meṣ. 59a–59b).[11]

This is clearly a story which was very popular and was told around the fire over and over again. Trees uprooting themselves—with disputes as to just how far (!)—and streams of water flowing backward and walls responding to the honor of two conflicting rabbis are surely the product of a long tradition of a beloved and significant tale. Its fanciful quality, though, should not disguise the serious implications for the development of law and theology and for one's understanding of revelation. Legally and theologically, it means that the law is not to be determined by new revelations in the form of voices, signs, or the like; it is to be decided exclusively in each generation by the rabbis charged with that task.

Furthermore, the story manifests an important shift in the understanding of revelation. Note that nobody in the story questions the authenticity of the voice from heaven as a true revelation from God. *Even so*, such revelations were no longer to be given any authority, for that was only to be determined by the rabbis' interpretation of the one accepted revelation, the Torah. As the Rabbis say in another place, revelation in the form of direct verbal or visual communication with God had ceased after the destruction of the First Temple (b. Sanh. 11a). Even before that time the authenticity and authority of the revelation to Moses (i.e. the Five Books of Moses known as the "Torah") was superior to all other revelations because the other Prophets "looked through nine lenses whereas Moses looked only

---

[11] Someone in San Francisco, whose name I do not remember, suggested to me a nice, alternative explanation of the last words of this passage, *nizhuni banai, nizhuni banai*. Instead of "My children have overcome [defeated] Me, My children have overcome Me," based on the verb, *nazeah*, he suggested translating (on the basis of the root *nezah*, "eternal"), "My children have eternalized Me [or given Me eternal life], My children have eternalized Me." That powerfully conveys that the process of interpreting and applying the Torah anew in every generation makes it an eternal document, one relevant to Jews for all time.

Rabbi Avram Kogen suggests yet a third possibility which is somewhat more fanciful, but makes the same point beautifully. Based on the root of *lamenazeah*, a word used in the superscriptions of 55 psalms (e.g. Ps 4:1) which may mean "to conduct" or "to direct" an instrumental ensemble or a choir, God may be saying, "My children have directed Me, My children have directed Me." It is, in other words, as if God wrote the symphony of Jewish law, but He wants human beings to determine its tempo and cadence.

through one; they looked through a cloudy lens while Moses looked through a clear one" (*Lev. Rab.* 1.14 [on Lev 1:1]).

This did not mean, however, that it was now impossible to determine what God wants of us. To be sure, one could no longer know this through prophecy, but one could discern God's will in another way which was, in fact, superior to prophecy in respect to divine authenticity and fidelity—namely, through *interpretation* (*midrash*) of the original, authoritative revelation contained in the Torah.

> Rabbi Abdimi from Haifa said: Since the day when the Temple was destroyed, the prophetic gift was taken away from the prophets and given to the Sages.—Is then a Sage not also a Prophet?—What he meant was this: although it has been taken from the prophets, it has not been taken from the Sages.
>
> Amemar said: A Sage is even superior to a prophet, as it says, "And a prophet has a heart of wisdom" [Ps 90:12]. Who is (usually) compared with whom? Is not the smaller compared with the greater? (*b. B. Bat.* 12a).

Indeed, the sage who interprets the Torah is to be trusted more than prophets ever were. Thus, while Deuteronomy 13 requires that the prophet provide a sign of his or her authenticity, the sage needs no such warranty:

> To what are a prophet and a sage to be compared? To a king who sent two ambassadors to a state. For one of them he wrote, "If he does not show you my seal, do not believe him." For the other he wrote, "Even if he does not show you my seal, believe him." Similarly, in regard to a prophet, it is written, "If he gives you a sign or a portent" [Deut 13:2], but here [on Deut 17:11, concerning judges] it is written, "You shall act in accordance with the instruction which they shall give you" [even without a sign] (*y. Ber.* 1.4).

This means that the authority of determining God's word no longer rests in the written text itself but rather in the appointed, human interpreter's understanding of it. The Rabbis did not flinch from this. They asserted that in addition to the Written Torah, God gave at Sinai an Oral Torah, which consists of the interpretations of the sages and the practices of the Jewish people over the generations —what lawyers would call "the common law." For the rabbis this Oral Torah clearly depends upon human beings, as the following story makes crystal clear:

> It happened that a heathen came before Shammai and asked him, "How many Torahs do you have?" He answered, "Two—the written and the oral." He [the heathen] said, "With respect to the written Torah I will believe you, but not with respect to the Oral Torah. Accept me as a convert on condition

that you teach me the former only." Shammai rebuked him and drove him out with contempt. He [the heathen] came before Hillel with the same request, and he accepted him. The first day he taught him the [Hebrew] alphabet in the correct order, but the next day he reversed it. The heathen said to him, "Yesterday you taught it to me differently!" Hillel replied, "Do you not have to depend upon me for the letters of the alphabet? So must you likewise depend upon me for the interpretation of the Torah" (b. Šabb. 31a).

At the same time, the Oral Torah has the stamp of God's authority on it, for God Himself empowered the judges of each generation to define and apply the law (Deut 17:8-13). None of it is left with God in heaven, and one may not disobey contemporary rabbis on the grounds that their knowledge and stature may not be as great as those of the rabbis of the past, for God has given us both the qualities and the personnel to make such decisions. Indeed, the rabbis apply the law to God Himself:

It is written, "For this commandment . . . is not in heaven" [Deut 30:11-12]. Moses said to the Israelites, "Lest you should say, 'Another Moses will arise and will bring us another Torah from heaven,' therefore I make it known to you now that 'it is not in heaven.' Nothing is left of it in heaven." Rabbi Hanina said: "The Torah and all the implements by which it is to be carried out have been given, namely, modesty, beneficence, uprightness, and reward" (Deut. Rab. 8.6 [on Deut 30:11-12]).

Scripture says, "And Samuel said to the people: It is the Lord who made Moses and Aaron" [1 Sam 12:6], and it says [in the same passage] "And the Lord sent Jerubaal and Bedan and Jephthah and Samuel" [1 Sam 12:11]. Jerubaal is Gideon . . . Bedan is Samson . . . Scripture thus places three light ones of the world ["lightweights"—namely, Gideon, Samson, and Jephthah] on the same level as three of the heavy ones of the world ["heavyweights"] to show that Jerubaal in his generation is like Moses in his generation, Bedan in his generation is like Aaron in his generation, Jephthah in his generation is like Samuel in his generation, thus teaching you that the most worthless, once he has been appointed a leader of the community, is to be accounted like the mightiest of the mighty. Scripture says also: "And you shall come to the priests, the Levites, and the judge who shall be in those days" [Deut 17:9]. Can we imagine that a person should go to a judge who is not in his days? This shows that you must be content to go to the judge who is in your days. It also says, "Say not that the former days were better than these" [Eccl 7:10] (t. Roš. Haš. 1.18; b. Roš. Haš. 25a–25b).

Nobody should say, "I will not observe the precepts of the elders [i.e. the Oral Torah] since they are not of Mosaic authority [literally, contained in the Torah]. For God has said, "No, my son, but whatever they decree for you, you must perform," as it says: "According to the Torah which they [i.e. the judges in days to come] shall teach you must you do" [Deut 17:11]. Even for

Me do they make decrees, as it says, "When you [i.e. the judges] decree a command, it shall be fulfilled for you" [i.e. by God himself—a playful interpretation of Job 22:28] (*Pesiq. R.* 3.1).

This method of determining the substance and application of God's Word, of course, can be chaotic. Dependence upon interpretation of texts—even if the texts interpreted are well defined and restricted—opens the door to a variety of different readings, and that can make squirm all those who like clarity and order.

While such a reaction is understandable, Judaism has taken the opposite tack: it has actually relished lively debate about the proper understanding of its sources—to the extent that a standard Jewish joke is that wherever there are two Jews, there are at least three opinions! Such feistiness and pluralism help Judaism avoid authoritarianism, and these traits of the tradition encourage all Jews to take religion seriously and to get into the habit of discerning God's word through the study and application of the Torah and later, rabbinic literature.

RETAINING THE CONSISTENCY AND COHERENCE OF TRADITION

The price that a tradition like Judaism pays for tolerating and even encouraging openness and pluralism is that it then cannot easily preserve consistency and coherence: a multitude of interpretations inevitably means that some will disagree with each other, at least in emphasis, and the resulting disputes ultimately challenge the integrity of the tradition and its ability to speak in one voice. This is a serious matter, of course, for if the tradition cannot say one, clear thing on any given matter, its value as a way of looking at the world and of acting in it is seriously undermined. That is, much of the guidance in thought and action which people seek in religion in the first place seems to disappear when every Jew may—and should—study the text to discern God's word. After all, with such an approach, each person may and, in practice, often does differ with others who are studying the same text. Where, then, is the clear word of God—or a clear word at all?

The Rabbis responded to this very real problem in several ways. First, tradition would remain coherent despite the many variations of opinion because they all derive from one God:

Lest a man say, "Since some scholars declare a thing impure and others declare it pure, some pronounce a thing forbidden and others permitted, some disqualify an object while others uphold its fitness, how can I study Torah under such circumstances"? Scripture says, "They are given from one shepherd" [Eccl 12:11]: One God has given them, one leader [Moses] has uttered them at the command of the Lord of all creation, blessed be He, as it says, "And God spoke *all* these words" [Exod 20:1]. You on your part must then make your ear like a grain receiver and acquire a heart that can understand the words of the scholars who declare a thing impure as well as those who declare it pure, the words of those who declare a thing forbidden as well as those who pronounce it permitted, and the words of those who disqualify an object as well as those who uphold its fitness . . . Although one scholar offers his view and another offers his, the words of both are all derived from what Moses, the shepherd, received from the One Lord of the Universe (*Num. Rab.* 14.4 [on Num 7:48]; cf. also *b.* '*Erub.* 13b).

In other words, however much the opinions of various rabbis may vary, they are all interpretations of one document, the Torah, and they will all be cohesive because God, the Author of that document, can be presumed to be consistent.

Second, the tradition will be cohesive because there is a sense of continuity within tradition itself. There is a famous story in the Talmud which illustrates that. When Moses visits the academy of Rabbi Aqiba, who lived some 1400 years after him, he does not even understand what Rabbi Aqiba is saying (let alone agree with it). Nevertheless, Moses is comforted when Rabbi Aqiba cites one of the new laws in Moses' name because that indicates that there is a sense of continuity in the tradition, although it has changed much in form:

Rabbi Judah said in the name of Rav: When Moses ascended on high, he found the Holy One, blessed be He, engaged in affixing crowns to the letters [of the Torah]. Moses said: "Who stays Your hand?" [i.e. is there anything lacking in the Torah so that additions are necessary?] He answered: "There will arise a man at the end of many generations, Aqiba, son of Joseph, by name, who will expand upon each decorative marking heaps and heaps of laws." "Lord of the universe," said Moses, permit me to see him." God replied: "Turn around." Moses went and sat down behind eight rows [of Rabbi Aqiba's students and listened to the discussions of the law]. Not being able to follow their arguments, he was ill at ease, but when they came to a certain subject and a student said to the teacher, "From where do you know this?" and the teacher replied, "It is a law given to Moses at Sinai," he [Moses] was comforted. Thereupon he returned to the Holy One, blessed be He, and said, "Lord of the universe, You have such a man, and You give the Torah by me?!" (*b. Menah.* 29b)

This sense of continuity is dependent, of course, on having people who have studied the tradition sufficiently to carry on its spirit and substance in new settings, and the Rabbis were keenly aware of what happens to the law's coherence when those to whom it is entrusted do not know it thoroughly:

> When the disciples of Shammai and Hillel who had not sufficiently studied with their teachers increased, dissensions multiplied in Israel and the Torah became like two Torahs (b. Soṭa 47b).

But they were also convinced that the continuity and consistency which they sensed were real, that the law in its present form, however different from the Torah, is the direct extension of it:

> Moses received the Torah from Sinai and handed it down to Joshua, and Joshua to the elders, and the elders to the prophets, and the prophets handed it down to the men of the Great Assembly [later known as the rabbis] (m. ʾAbot 1:1).

> When the Holy One, blessed be He, revealed Himself on Sinai to give the Torah to Israel, He delivered it to Moses in order—Scripture, Mishnah, Talmud, and Aggadah [that is, the Torah and all of its later legal and non-legal interpretations] (Exod. Rab. 47.1 [on Exod 34:27]).

Third, Jewish law would retain its coherence because it includes a way of making decisions. All opinions could be aired in discussion, and, in fact, all are to be considered "the words of the living God," but in the end a decision must be made:

> Rabbi Abba stated in the name of Samuel: For three years there was a dispute between the School of Shammai and the School of Hillel, the former asserting, "The law is in agreement with our view," and the latter contending, "The law is in agreement with our view." Then a Heavenly Voice announced, "The utterances of both are the words of the living God, but the law is in agreement with the rulings of the School of Hillel." Since, however, "both are the words of the living God," what was it that entitled the School of Hillel to have the law fixed in agreement with its rulings? Because they were kind and modest, they studied their own rulings and those of the School of Shammai, and they were even so humble as to mention the opinions of the School of Shammai before their own (b. ʿErub. 13b).

Normally, however, legal decisions were made not through heavenly bodies but through judicial rulings, and everyone, including members of the court itself who may disagree, was required to abide by the ruling of the majority of the court.[12] This gave coherence to

---

12   A particularly poignant case demonstrating the authority of the court over its own members is recorded in m. Roš. Haš. 2:8-9, where Rabbi Joshua, Vice-President of the Sanhedrin, was ordered by its president, Rabban Gamliel, to appear before him in regular, weekday clothes on the day which Rabbi Joshua thought was the Day of Atonement, the most sacred day of the Jewish liturgical year, but which was ruled by Rabban Gamliel and the majority of the Sanhedrin to

Jewish law while yet permitting lively debate.

That method of regularizing the law was not applied to matters of belief. Since Judaism defines Jewish identity in legal terms, it needed to be reasonably clear about what was required to be a Jew (namely, to be born by a Jewish woman or converted according to the established procedures) and which divine commandments a Jew was obligated to fulfill. Since action thus defined Jewish identity, Judaism could be, and was, considerably more liberal in matters of belief. It is not until the Middle Ages that lists of binding Jewish beliefs were formulated. Even then the lists were devised by individual Jewish philosophers, and none of them gained universal acceptance. This is in sharp contrast to the catechisms coming out of Church councils from the fourth century on. There were clearly some beliefs which were construed to be antithetical to Judaism—e.g. that Jesus was Christ or that there was no ultimate divine justice, at least in an afterlife[13]—but diversity was definitely the mode in matters of belief. Thus in the rabbinic interpretation of non-legal passages of the Bible one understanding of them is followed immediately by another, introduced simply by "another opinion" (*davar aher*), with no attempt whatsoever to reconcile them. One could easily describe mainstream Jewish beliefs of the classical rabbinic period, but one would always have to stipulate that the specific character of those beliefs was always open for debate and sometimes even the very existence of a given belief. In other words, Judaism defined itself in terms of actions and was therefore quite liberal in matters of thought, precisely the opposite of Christianity.

However, in respect to both law and thought it is clearly the rabbis who shape the tradition through their ongoing interpretations of the Bible and of the progressive, post-biblical development. For this reason many texts of interpretation are developed in Judaism, and the Bible is seldom directly quoted outside an exegetical context. As the Rabbis put it:

> "For your beloved ones are better than wine" [Song 1:2]. This means that the words of the beloved ones [the Sages] are better than the wine of Torah. Why? Because one cannot give a proper decision from the word of the Torah since the Torah is ambiguous and consists entirely of headings . . . From the words of the Sages, however, one can derive the proper law because they

---

be a day earlier.

[13]   The closest that the classical rabbis get to formulating dogmas is found in *m. Sanhedrin* 10 (= chap. 11 in editions of the Babylonian Talmud).

explain the Torah (*Song Rab.* 1:2 §2).

THE INTERACTION BETWEEN THE BIBLE
AND LATER TRADITION

In the process of interpreting the Bible, the biblical "statutory" text (the Written Torah) is theoretically more authoritative than the later, "precedential" discussions and decisions (the Oral Torah). The Bible is believed to be the written record of God's word, while the Oral Torah, despite its roots at Sinai, is the way in which the Bible was interpreted and applied by human beings. Laws based on the written Bible are thus known as *mi'deoraita*, "from the Torah," and have greater authority and more permanence than laws which derive *mi'derabbanan*, "from the rabbis." This preference of the written over the oral Torah reflects ultimately on the problem of this essay, namely, how can one discern God's word through human interpretation. The categories of *mi'deoraita* and *mi'derabbanan* express the Jewish traditional belief that the written Torah is to be given preference, being a more faithful and trustworthy record of God's word than the later tradition, for the former came directly from God at Sinai while the latter developed over the ages as rabbis discerned God's word through study. Consequently, even though the rabbis recognized fully that the rules and beliefs of the written Torah must be interpreted by human beings in order to be intelligible, the written Torah was nevertheless more clearly the word of God, even though the Oral Torah was God's word too. Laws in the Written Torah took precedence over those in the Oral Torah, and could be altered or adapted only with much greater difficulty.

In practice, though, the situation was exactly the other way around. That is, in reality, Jewish tradition in the later sources define the meaning of the Bible, which may well be different from the original meaning of the biblical text, as determined by linguistic and historical evidence, or from its interpretation in Christian, Muslim, or secular circles. Judaism, in other words, is very much the religion of the Bible *as defined and interpreted by the Rabbis*. In a similar way, it was the Church Fathers who decided which books were to be accorded the status of sacred Scripture in the Christian faith and then determined how those books were to be interpreted. Therefore, Christianity is the religion of the Bible as defined and interpreted by the Church Fathers and their successors. The same process occurred in Islam: The Koran includes the retelling of some biblical stories together with additions to serve in toto as the Muslim sacred scripture. Islam is then the religion of the Bible as retold, adapted, and interpreted by the imams throughout the centuries.

To take one example of this phenomenon, the Garden of Eden story is basically the same in the Jewish and the Christian Bible. But classical Christianity interpreted it as the foundation of the doctrine of Original Sin. In its Augustinian formulation this meant that people are born in sin and therefore cannot escape their deserved damnation except through the grace of God, a grace which cannot be earned through human actions but can only be freely given by God and only to a small number of people. In contrast, Jewish interpretations of the Garden of Eden story do not draw those conclusions. Classical Jewish sources see people born morally neutral, with desires for both good and evil, and God, as an expression of His goodness, giving us a book of instruction (the literal meaning of *"Torah"*) to help us choose the good. The Garden of Eden story, then, only explains why we are not born totally good; for the Jewish tradition, it does not establish that we are born absolutely and irrevocably evil.[14] It is the same story, but it means totally different things for Judaism and Christianity.

If the meaning of biblical texts depends on later tradition in theological matters, it does even more so with regard to the legal texts of the Bible. The two traditions not only differ sometimes on the interpretation of those texts, but more importantly, also on their status. Jewish tradition holds them to be binding on us to this day, while Paul and his disciples hold them to be superseded by the Spirit. The meaning and implications of these texts depend completely on the different ways in which they have been understood in the two traditions.

From a fundamentalist perspective, the situation is even worse: not only does the meaning of God's word as contained in the Bible depend on how human beings have interpreted it over the ages, but

---

[14] Moreover, the Rabbis maintain the ability of human beings to do good despite a later verse in the Noah story (Gen 6:5), according to which "every plan devised by the human mind was nothing but evil all the time," That verse, according to the Rabbis, may express God's exasperation with the evil abilities of human beings, but it does not declare that human beings are incapable of doing the good. Indeed, according to Ben Azzai, the most important verse in the Torah is Gen 5:1: "This is the record of Adam's line. When God created man, He made him in the likeness of God" (y. Ned. 9.4 [41c]).

in neither tradition can one say that a meaning was fixed once and for all in ancient times by those closer in time to the original revelation. On the contrary, it is the more recent sources which carry greater weight than the earlier ones in determining a specific rule or belief for the present time. *Hilkhitah ke'batra'ei*, "the law is according to the later ones," a medieval exegetical rule declares, and that was how it was also in the earlier times of the Talmud. Similarly, church law and beliefs are very much what contemporary ecclesiastical authorities say they are, and the same is true of Islam. It applies also to a secular legal system such as American law. Legal briefs rarely cite the Constitution; rather they rely on the most recent precedents relevant to the case.

In view of this process, one could think that it is simply a device of the Western religions to profess allegiance to the Bible and to base on it their claims to authority. The same could be said of a contemporary American court that asserts that its ruling is based on the Constitution when in fact it is based on the laws and precedents which developed later in the history of American law. One might, in other words, take a fundamentalist (or literalist) stance in one's attachment to, and understanding of, the constitutive text of a religion or a nation and maintain that all subsequent developments lack authority altogether or can be easily overturned by a ruling based directly on the Bible, the Koran, or the Constitution. Without this assertion, the fundamentalist would maintain, one loses all credible connection to God's authority as contained in the written word of the Bible—or to the original common agreements, and hence the authority of America's Founding Fathers.

In all four cases, however, that would be an incorrect way of construing the matter. To take the American case first: The reliance of courts on recent precedents does *not* mean that the Constitution has become irrelevant to American law. It continues to function as the foundation of later forms of American law, giving them their authority, the fundamental principles to which they must adhere, and the mode of operation through which they must be promulgated. Similarly, in Jewish law the Bible continues to be studied and understood as the basic norm which provides its essential standards, methodology, and authority. The same is true for the Christian Bible in Christianity and for the Koran in Islam.

Why, then, is contemporary belief and practice determined by recent interpretations and applications rather than by older ones in all four cases? In part, this results from the presumption that those who created the recent understandings of the text knew and took into account all previous developments of the tradition, and that therefore their understandings are ultimately based on the authority of the constitutive text. Those who wrote the recent interpretations had two advantages over their predecessors: they knew the history of the tradition—that is, how over the centuries the constitutive text has been interpreted and applied by the authorities of the community which holds them sacred. Moreover, the authors of recent interpretations had the advantage of knowing the nature of the contemporary community for whom, and the circumstances to which, the tradition must now be sensitively applied. Contemporary authorities, in other words, have the power to determine the way in which the tradition is going to be understood and practiced in their time because they know both the past and the present in their fullness. Therefore they are best equipped to define how the tradition should take form now.

Thus, in respect to American law and in all three Western religions, it would be misleading to assert that earlier sources are totally ignored when the tradition relies on more recent developments within the tradition. It would be equally misleading to assert that only the constitutive documents matter. The truth is that the constitutive documents and contemporary renderings of the tradition each have their claim to authority. Often they are in harmony, but sometimes they pull in opposite directions. When that happens, it is the *tradition* which prevails over the constitutive text. Since that text is still held sacred and studied as such, any discrepancies between it and the later tradition are subject to constant reevaluation in each generation. That is what it means that *both* a constitutive text and the later tradition are authoritative.

There is another way to think about this interaction between text and tradition. Professor Sanders has demonstrated convincingly that in Judaism the very formation and definition of the canon resulted from decisions by the rabbis concerning which texts contained the word of God and which did not. Those decisions, in turn, depended at least in part on how the Jewish community reacted to those texts. Thus the love poetry of Song of Songs, whch clearly does not pertain to God, was nevertheless made part of the canon. The rabbis found a justification for its inclusion through Rabbi Aqiba's interpretation of the text as a poem featuring the love between God and Israel and not just between two human lovers.[15] On the other hand, the sages delayed to the very last stages of the definition of the canon their decision about whether or not to include the Book of Ezekiel. That book clearly is about God, but the rabbis' indecision may have reflected a hesitancy which both they and the Jewish people of their time had about its authenticity as a revelation of God.[16]

What I am claiming in this essay is that just as the formation of the canon was a product of the interaction of the community, its religious authorities, and the texts which it accepted over time as sacred, so too the later development of the tradition grew out of that kind of interaction. Note that this will mean that in each age the historical *context* of the interpreters and their sense of *morality* will play vital roles in the ways in which they interpret God's word.[17] That may not please those who would like to have divine directions come from an authoritative, unambiguous, and unchanging text so that they

---

15   Professor Sanders (*Torah and Canon* [Philadelphia: Fortress Press, 1972] 113) notes that "The *Song of Solomon* . . . contains numerous love and wedding songs, of widely divergent dates of composition but collected in the early Hellenistic period in something like their present form, for the acceptable purpose of providing music for betrothals and weddings. Some of the love poems in the Song of Solomon may have originated in boldly erotic practices, but they all testify to the Old Testament's basic view that sex in its various expressions is a sensuous gift of God to be enjoyed in the measure that the gift is given and the law allows. That the Song of Solomon was later universally allegorized by both church and synagogue as the love between God and Judaism or between God and the church is as much a witness to Jewish and Christian freedom to ascribe sensuality to God as to confusions about sex in the acceptably pious Christian or Jew."

16   S. Z. Leiman, *The Canonization of the Hebrew Scripture: The Talmudic and Midrashic Evidence* (Hamden: Archon, 1976). On the question of the process of canonization and what role, if any, formal bodies may have played in it, see the studies by S. Talmon: "Heiliges Schrifttum und kanonische Bücher aus jüdischer Sicht—Überlegungen zur Ausbildung der Grösse 'Die Schrift' im Judentum," in M. Klopfenstein, U. Luz, S. Talmon, and E. Tov (eds.), *Mitte der Schrift? Ein jüdisch-christliches Gespräch: Texte des Berner Symposions vom 6.-12. Januar 1985* (Bern: Peter Lang, 1987) 45-80; idem, "Oral Tradition and Written Transmission or the Heard and Seen Word in Second Temple Judaism," in H. Wansbrough (ed.), *Jesus and the Oral Gospel Tradition* (JSNTSup 64; Sheffield: JSOT Press, 1991) 121-58; idem, "Between the Bible and the Mishnah," in Talmon, *The World of Qumran from Within* (Jerusalem: Magnes, 1989) esp. 21-45.

17   Cf. my article, "The Interaction of Jewish Law with Morality," *Judaism* 26 (1977) 455-66, for a presentation and discussion of some of the primary sources on this.

themselves would be relieved of any responsibility of judging what God wants of us in our time. But all three Western religions have functioned through a *tradition*, even when some exponents have wanted to deny that. They have all, in practice even though not in theory, recognized that it is only through ongoing interpretation and tradition that God's word can have meaning for us in our day.

The Jewish texts which I have brought to bear in this discussion demonstrate clearly that the Jewish tradition was consciously aware of this process from a very early stage. The hammer still strikes the rock to this day when contemporary Jews living under new conditions and with new sensitivities and concerns—in addition to many of the old ones—attempt to discern God's word for themselves in their time and place. This is what makes Judaism a living tradition.[18]

---

[18]   For further discussion and sources on the points of this section, see my article, "Judaism as a Religious Legal System," *Hastings Law Journal* 29 (1978) 1331-60; and see Dorff and Rosett, *A Living Tree*, 187-245.

"ORALLY WRITE THEREFORE AURALLY RIGHT"
AN ESSAY ON MIDRASH

Michael Fishbane

INTRODUCTION

An old tradition found in *Sifre Deuteronomy* §343 (on Deut 33:2) presents a powerful image of the giving of the Law: God's word appears as a fire that emerges from His right hand, encircles the nation, and returns; the fire is then transferred by God from His left hand to His right, whereupon it is inscribed upon the tablets of Moses.[1] In this way the sages gave mythic realism to the scriptural phrase, מִימִינוֹ אֵשׁדָּת לָמוֹ, "from His right hand [there emerged] a fiery law for them [the nation]" (Deut 33:2). Another passage, stating that קוֹל־יְהוָה חֹצֵב לַהֲבוֹת אֵשׁ, "the voice of the Lord carves out flames of fire" (Ps 29:7), is expressly added to indicate the world-encompassing power of divine speech. This line from the Psalms serves here to reinforce the main teaching that the tablets were chisled by tongues of fire (the verse was thus presumed to say that God's "voice . . . carves out *the Decalogue by* flames of fire"). Elsewhere, Rabbi Aqiba gave just this explication as an independent account of God's fiery words at Sinai.[2] The editor of our *Sifre* text has chosen to subordinate this teaching to his interest in the heavenly arm as an agent of the inscription.

In our midrashic myth God's word emerges from the divine

---

[1]   In the edition of L. Finkelstein, *Sifre on Deuteronomy* (Berlin: Gesellschaft zur Förderung der Wissenschaft des Judentums, 1939; repr. Jerusalem and New York: Jewish Theological Seminary of America, 1969) 399.

[2]   See *Mek.* on Exod 20:18 (*Yitro* §9); in the edition of H. S. Horovitz and I. A. Rabin, *Mechilta d'Rabbi Ismael cum variis lectionibus et adnotationibus* (Frankfurt am Main: J. Kauffmann, 1931; repr. Jerusalem: Bamberger & Wahrmann, 1960) 235. The first of the anonymous traditions in the *Sifre*, dealing with the arm, is attributed to Rabbi Simeon bar Yoḥai, in *Song Rab.* 1:2 §2; in this midrashic corpus the aforenoted Aqiban tradition is presented by Rabbi Berekhia, in the name of Rabbi Helbo, and the fire is said to have come directly to God's right hand.

essence as visable fire and takes instructional shape as letters and words on the tablets. The written law is thus an extension of divine speech—and not merely its inscriptional trace. This identification of God's utterance and Torah is the hermeneutical core of Judaism. Midrash works out the details.

The sages were alive to this point. In a teaching joined to a version of the aforementioned myth, Rabbi Azariah and Rabbi Judah bar Simon (in the name of Rabbi Joshua ben Levi) pondered the question of how much the Israelites actually learned at Sinai (*Song Rab.* 1:2 §2). They proposed that the people learned *all* the 613 (principal) commandments of (rabbinic) Judaism at that time. This interpretation links the ten Words of the tablets to all the teachings that will emerge through Jewish discourse. Such a notion is first found explicitly in Philo;[3] but something of it can already be found in Tannaitic teachings. Thus, in a variation of the teaching found in the passage from *Sifre* already mentioned, we learn that the meaning of the word יְבוֹנְנֵהוּ in Moses's song—"He [God] instructed him [Israel])" in Moses' Song (Deut. 32:10)—is that Israel learned "how much Midrash was in it [each Word], how much Halakhah was in it, how many *minori ad maius* arguments were in it, and how many textual analogies were in it."[4] Significantly, this phrase also appears in *Song Rabba* in connection with what the angel of the Law (according to Rabbi Yohanan), or the Word itself (according to the rabbis), addressed to each Israelite as they heard each of the Ten Commandments.[5]

The Decalogue is thus a paradigmatic text, and Sinai a pradigmatic moment, for Midrash: not only does something of the mysterious fulness of divine speech comprise the letters of the Decalogue, but its revelation is accompanied by a prolepsis of the achievement of rabbinic interpretation. The written text thus mediates between the verbal revelation of God at Sinai and the ongoing discourses of the sages. Paradoxically, the divine Word unfolds through human speech. As exegetical act and event, this human speech is Midrash.

And more: As a field of totality, the tablets metonymically represent the truths of the whole culture. They may therefore be

---

[3]   *De Decalogo* 19, and 154; also *De Specialibus Legibus* 1.1.

[4]   *Sifre Deut.* §313 (on Deut 32:10).

[5] This text adds that the Israelites were also informed of the judgments, punishments, and rewards consequent to obedience to the Law.

compared to the shield of Achilles which was fashioned for the hero by the god Hephaestus (*Iliad* 23). The sea-like border design indicates the boundaries of civilization, and the images on the various panels depict its achievements and values. The shield is therefore more than armour for a day: it is the world for which the hero fights, the symbolic order rescued from chaos by human industry and virtue.

Similarly, to understand the shapes on the tablets is to understand the truths of God's teachings for all generations—which are the truths of Judaism insofar as the tradition is truly founded upon a Scriptural foundation. As a fixed and final formulation, the tablets are therefore a canon-before-the-canon. That is to say: just as the closing of Scripture in later times meant that "all" was "in it" and nowhere else, so too is "everything" already on the tablets. In this sense, divine instruction was virtually complete at Sinai. Ongoing interpretations (of these or other Words) do not add to God's original voice, but merely give it historical and human expressions. This is an essential pre-understanding of the sages, and it is fundamental to the work of Midrash.[6]

I

Taken as a whole, biblical Scripture is a complex system of written signs whose original significations make sense through the interrelation of words in their primary context—beginning with the phrase and including the sentence, the paragraph, and so on. As an anthology of cultural materials spanning a millenium, a good many of the units were originally independent of each other, and they circulated in distinct circles of instruction and tradition (such as the priestly or wisdom schools). Because of the long period of literary development, many of the materials allude to predecessor traditions and rework them in a number of ways.[7] In these cases, a new network of inter-textual relations is produced, and the "context" of the second text is greatly explanded.

---

6   A classic formulation of this paradox is Targum Onqelos' transformation of the biblical statement that God spoke only the Decalogue at Sinai וְלֹא־יָסָף ("and no more") into the rabbinic truth that God's voice resounded "without end"; and cf. Rashi's gloss.

7   I have discussed such matters at length in my *Biblical Interpretation in Ancient Israel* (Oxford: Clarendon, 1985).

In the terms of structural linguistics, we may restate this as follows. The texts of Scripture derive from any number of conditioning linguistic factors; and these, as the set of open possibilities, constitute the potentials of biblical "language" (*langue*). By contrast, the realizations of these possibilities in actual expressions (and by this is meant the meanings constructed from the potentials through the conjunction of specific letters, words, or syntax) is biblical "speech" (*parole*)—though, of course, this does not mean oral speech only (even if the written text is derived from an oral expression, purports to quote it directly or indirectly, or has special status when recited aloud).[8] Naturally, as a document of great historical and cultural range, Scripture is made up of many such "speeches"—now collected in units and genres. The books (τὰ βιβλία) of these anthologies constitute the Bible.

The word "torah" is indicative of these matters. At one end of the spectrum it marks very specific, short instructions of law in the priestly sources, which are attributed to Moses as speaker of divine speech; but "Torah" also marks, eventually, the entire book of Deuteronomy as Moses's summary instruction of divine speech through him (along with historical details); and finally, by the post-exilic period, the "Torah of Moses" has an even more comprehensive designation (as in Mal 3:22).[9] In wisdom circles, the term "torah" originally indicated some didactic instruction—grounded in experience of the natural world—which was then written down as a cultural maxim. On the surface, such instructions have nothing whatever to do with Moses's divine speech. Indeed, the task of the moral teachings is to make one worldly-wise—not holy or pure. The incorporation of gnomic and priestly torahs in one Text shows just how diverse Scripture is.

The closure of the Scriptural canon (by the beginning of the common era) changes matters fundamentally. It is a transformative event, for with this closure there can be no new additions or supplementations to the Text from without. Indeed there is now an in and

---

8   For the relationship between *langue* and *parole*, see F. de Saussure, *Cours de linguistique générale* (Paris: Payot, 1900). For these terms in the wider context of structural poetics, see J. Culler, *Structuralist Poetics* (London: Routledge & Kegan Paul, 1975; New York: Cornell University Press, 1976).

9   The "Book of Moses" in 2 Chr 35:12-13 refers to the traditions found in the books of Exodus and Deuteronomy. See my discussion in *Biblical Interpretation*, 134-37.

an out, a within and a without. And since God's Word (*parole*) is deemed comprehensive and sufficient for human culture in all its historical diversity, it is only within the existent divine words that new meanings can arise. Accordingly, the effect of the closure is to transform the separate units (and contexts) of "speech" into the *one* speech (and context) of Scripture. Everything must be found in it.

The result is that the extended speech of Scripture is unified as the multiform expressions of divine revelation—beginning with the individual letters of its words, and including all the phrases and sentences of Scripture. These all become the constituents of possibility in the opening of Scripture *from within*. In the process, to return to our structuralist diction, the *parole* of Scripture becomes the *langue* of each and every midrashic *parole*. In other words, Scripture becomes a closed and unified system of language with particular possibilities for linking words and phrases. Midrash is the speech that arises from this system. Hence, just as each *parole* of Moses is an actualization of the divine *langue* through him, so each midrashic *parole* (properly) spoken by the sages is an actualization of the divine *langue* of the scriptural canon. Thus is the midrashic word inscribed within the language of Scripture.

The opening of Scripture from within radically transforms the grammaticality of the text: the ordinary connection between the letters of a word, and between the words of a sentence, is broken. These components now become extra-ordinary. Indeed, each letter has (virtual) anagrammatical significance; each word may encode numerous plays and possibilities; and each phrase has any number of potential correlations within Scripture. Midrash determines the sense of each component through extending the context of the component to the entirety of Scripture (thus original setting or sequence is often immaterial). Letters "here" may therefore be related to letters "there"; and words or phrases from one part of Scripture are revealed through midrashic methods to be speaking about the same thing as words and phrases elsewhere. The emergent "enchainment" (חֲרִיזָה) of possibilities thus dramatizes what is always the presupposition of midrashic exegesis: that all Scripture is one interconnected whole. Accordingly, the use of the word "torah" in the book of Proverbs not only means that its epigrams may be correlated with teachings of the "Torah of Moses," but also means that the divine elements in Moses' words are related to the wise words of Solomon. Both Solomon's Proverbs and Moses's Torah are aspects of the divine *langue*—which is Scripture.

Ezra is the first master of the midrashic *parole*—for he "inquires" (דְּרַשׁ) of the "Torah of the Lord" (in Ezra 7:10) as former generations "inquired" of God for a living oracle (2 Kgs 22:5, 8). His act (and those of his rabbinic heirs) thus conjures new meanings from God's *langue*.[10] No part is too small to become a whole. Come and hear.

II

The account of creation in the book of Genesis is framed by a prologue and epilogue. It opens with the words בְּרֵאשִׁית בָּרָא, "in the beginning" God "created" the heavens and the earth (Gen 1:1); and it concludes with the coda about the heavens and earth בְּהִבָּרְאָם "when they were created" (Gen 2:4a). Struck by the form of this last word, the midrash in *Genesis Rabba* (see 12.10 [on Gen 2:4]) ponders the agency of the divine creation. Grammatically, בְּהִבָּרְאָם combines the preposition בְּ (used in the temporal sense of "when") with an infinite absolute form of the verb בָּרָא (in the niphal form) and a plural suffix. And precisely because of this grammatical form, some sages intuited a parallel to the phrase בְּרֵאשִׁית בָּרָא in Gen 1:1.

Genesis 1:1 had long since been interpreted to suggest that God "created" (בָּרָא) the world "with" or "for the sake of" (בְּ) רֵאשִׁית (variously deduced as "Torah," "Throne of Glory," "Moses," and so on).[11] A similar anagrammatical construction (though of more esoteric import, as we shall see) was proposed for the word בְּהִבָּרְאָם in Gen 2:4a by Rabbi Abbahu in the name of Rabbi Yohanan. In his view, we may find (encoded) here the teaching that God "created" (בָּרָא) the heavens and earth "with" or "by means of" (בְּ) the letter ה. The meaning of this reading emerges from the whole teaching. It is reported as follows.

> בְּהִבָּרְאָם. Rabbi Abbahu (interpreted) in the name of Rabbi Yohanan: "with (the letter) ה He created them. Just as this ה is the only non-lingual letter (being merely aspirated), so did the Holy One blessed be He create His world merely 'with the word of יהוה' [Ps 33:6]—and immediately 'the

10 For the relationship between oraclular inquiry and exegesis, see my *Biblical Interpretation*, 245.

11 See *Gen. Rab.* 1.4 (on Gen 1:1); in the edition of J. Theodor and C. Albeck, *Bereschit Rabba mit kritischen Apparat und Kommentar* (4 vols., Berlin: Akademie, 1912-36) 1.6-7.

heavens were made' [Ps 33:6]."

Rabbi Yudan Neshiyya inquired of Rabbi Samuel bar Naḥman, and asked: "Since I have heard that you are an expert in haggadah, explain the meaning of (the phrase) 'Extol Him who rides the clouds; the Lord [בְּיָהּ] is His name' [Ps 68:5]." He answered: "There is no place in (all) His dominion [בְּיָהּ; Greek βία][12] without an appointed authority—(thus) the *ecdicus* (public prosecutor) is responsible for the dominion in his city,[13] (and) the *agba bastes* (apparitor) is responsible for the dominion in his city.[14] Similarly: Who is responsible for the dominion [בְּיָהּ] on High? בְּיָהּ is His name, בְּיָהּ is His name." (Rabbi Yudan) answered: "O woe for those (sages) who have died but are not forgotten!"; for I had (also) inquired of Rabbi Eleazar, and he did not explain it so, but rather (interpreted the word with reference to Isa 26:4) "for in YaH [בְּיָהּ] the Lord (יהוה) you have an everlasting Rock [צוּר עוֹלָמִים]." (Meaning:) With these two letters (i.e. י and ה of His name) the Holy One blessed be He created [בָּרָא; but rendering צוּר] His world."[15]

Now we do not know if this world was created with (the letter) ה and the world to come with the י; but on the basis of the way Rabbi Abbahu in the name of Rabbi Yohanan explained בְּהִבָּרְאָם as "with a ה He created them"

---

12   See the commentary of *Minḥat Yehudah*, in Theodor and Albeck, *Bereschit Rabba*, 1.108, and the gloss in the *Liqqutin*. See *Midr. Ps.* 114.3 (on Ps 114:1) קורא ביה אלא ביאה שמו ("read [not] '*Beyah*' but '*Bia* is his name'"); from S. Buber, מדרש שוחר טוב על תהלים (Vilna: Romm, 1891) 163. See also A. Kohut's *Aruch Completum* (Vindobona: Hebräischer Verlag Menorah, 1926) s.v. ביה (2.45a). These views are rejected by I. Wartski, "שימושי המלים היווניות בְיָה, בְיי, בי במדרשים [The Usage of the Greek Words βία, βίος, in Midrashic Literature]," *Tarbiz* 36 (1966-67) 239-56. W. G. Braude (*The Midrash on Psalms* [2 vols., YJS 13; New Haven: Yale University Press, 1959] 2.510 n. 7), renders "power" (Greek βία), so that it reads: "He who wields power" (βιαστής). Braude adduces the observation of S. Lieberman that this term is equivalent to Latin *defensor civitatis* or *defoensor loci*. This would link βία to other juridical functions mentioned in the text (see below). D. Sperber (*A Dictionary of Greek and Latin Terms in Rabbinic Literature* [Jerusalem: Bar Ilan University Press, 1984] 68-69) has adduced evidence to render "justice."

13   The Hebrew is אְגְדִיקוֹס, which reflects the Greek loan word ἔκδικος (lit. an avenger); see *Minḥat Yehudah* in Theodor and Albeck, *Bereschit Rabba*, 1.108; and lexical evidence in Sperber, *Greek and Latin Terms in Rabbinic Literature*, 32.

14   The Hebrew is אְגַב בָּסְטֵס, which reflects the Greek loan word ἐκβιβάστης (one who executes justice), though some versions read אְגוּסְטוֹס (Augustus); see S. Lieberman, *Tarbiz* 36 (1967) 401; and Sperber, *Greek and Latin Terms in Rabbinic Literature*, 31-32.

15   For the text and variants, see *Gen. Rab.* 12.10 (on Gen 2:4), in the edition of Theodor and Albeck, *Bereschit Rabba*, 107-109; also M. Mirqin, מדרש רבה (11 vols., Tel Aviv: Yavneh, 1986) 1.88-89.

[בְּהֵ"א בְּרָאָם], surely this world was created with the (letter) ה. And whereas from the (graphic) shape of this ה, which is closed on all (three) sides but open from below, we have an indication that all the dead descend to Sheol; (so too) from the tip on the upper side we have a hint of their resurrection; and from the spatial gap in the upper corner we may (also) learn (a lesson of hope) for penitents. (Thus we may conclude:) the world to come was created with the י. And just as its stature is bent over, so (will) the stature of evil-doers be bent over and their faces darkened in the world to come—as we read (in Scripture): "Then man's haughtiness shall be humbled" [Isa 2:17].[16]

This teaching appears as a typical midrashic construction, combining a variety of voices and opinions (let us call each of them a micro-form) into one integrated piece (let us call the whole a macro-form). First we have Rabbi Abbahu's (received) teaching that God created the world with the letter ה. This point is supplemented with the linguistic comment that ה is an aspirant. The point is apparently indicative of the ease of God's creation; but the prooftext (from Ps 33:6) adduced in support of this is perplexing, since it speaks of creation by the word. But appearances are deceiving in Midrash. I am inclined to suppose that this scriptural proof was initially cited to extend the view of creation through the letter ה. For a close reading of that phrase (in light of the ensuing discussion) suggests that it was understood quite concretely to mean that "the heavens were created (by God) by means of the (letters of the) word יהוה (the Lord)"—ה being one of those letters. And because this citation also goes on to say that "all the hosts (were created) by the breath of His mouth," the primary teaching was supplemented by a second one about aspirants. The prooftext now does double duty: it links Rabbi Abbahu's teaching to the discussion of the letters of God's name, and it mentions the hosts who reappear as the regents of God's dominion. As is typical, the midrashic teaching is laconic. It springs from Scripture and is reanchored in Scripture. Between these poles of authority the sage mediates his message.

The ensuing queries of Rabbi Yudan seem to be an abrupt *non sequitor* after Rabbi Abbahu's teaching—a shift which even the citation of Ps 33:6 (as meaning that God created the heavens with His name) only partially mitigates. Moreover, though Rabbi Samuel's

---

16   I have followed the *editio princeps* of Theodor and Albeck, *Bereschit Rabba*, 107-109. For manuscript variants and alternate suggestions concerning the names of the regents, see the *varia lectiones* and the commentary of *Minḥat Yehudah* on p. 108.

teaching of בְּיָה as a Greek homonymn is consistent with multi-lingual puns in the Midrash,[17] it is certainly irrelevant to this macro-form as a whole. The discussion of Ps 68:5 is adduced merely as a prelude to Rabbi Eleazar's exegesis. The editor then cleverly brings the discussion back to the opening teaching by reconciling Rabbi Eleazer's position (that God created the world with the letters י and ה) with that of Rabbi Abbahu (who asserted that the world was created with the one letter ה). The differentiation of the letters (one for this world, the other for the world to come), leads to a bit of graphology. The letters are now viewed as iconic forms—replete with religious significance. Thus does the midrashist follow God and inscribe theological truth into the depth of existence. Axiology recapitualtes ontology.

The teaching in *Genesis Rabba* thus appears as a hierarchy of voices—beginning with Scripture itself, and descending through a chain of teachers, to the anonymous editor. Indeed, beginning with the opening lemma (the word בְּהִבָּרְאָם) the string of teachings is knoted by several scriptural citations. The editor seems to direct this midrashic theatre with consummate legerdemain, introducing and resolving microforms to produce a teaching that begins with the creation and ends with eschatology. But we would hardly suspect the degree to which this editor has manipulated his traditions in the process. This editorial activity becomes clear when we examine the homily of Rabbi Abbahu and the exegesis of Rabbi Eleazer in *y. Ḥag.* 2.1, their original context.

In this Talmudic context the teaching of Rabbi Abbahu comes after traditions about the meaning and shape of the second letter ב, the first letter of the creation account. He offers a new proposal. In view of what may be learned about how Midrash is formed and re(-) formed, the matter deserves closer scrutiny.

> Rabbi Abbahu (said) in the name of Rabbi Yohanan: "With two letters were two worlds created—this world and the world to come: the one with ה, the other with י . What's the proof? 'For בְּיָה (with י / ה) the Lord צוּר עוֹלָמִים (formed, צְיַר, worlds; literally, is an everlasting Rock)' [Isa 26:4]. And

---

17   A striking example occurs in *Gen. Rab.* 56.4 (on Gen 22:7), in connection with the phrase "God will show him tne lamb (הַשֶּׂה) for the offering" in Gen 22:8. Deepening the irony of the father's answer, the sages played on the Greek pronoun σε ("you"). This pun sneaks back into the vernacular in the *Fragment Targum* (and cf. *Pirqe R. El.* §31). The conceptual basis for such puns is found in the teaching that God's word at Sinai divided into 70 languages (see *b. Šabb.* 88b).

(from this verse) we do not know with which letter he created which world. But since it is (also) written, 'These are the generations of the heavens and the earth בְּהִבָּרְאָם' [Gen 2:4], (we may infer that) He created them with ה. Thus: this world was created with ה, and the world to come was created with י . And whereas ה is open below, this is an indication to all creatures that they will descend to Sheol; (and) whereas ה has a point at its top, (this is to indicate that) from the moment they descend they (may) ascend; (and) whereas ה is open at (nearly) every side, so (God) opens a passage for penitents; (and) whereas י is bent, so will all He creates be bent over—(as is written), 'and all faces will turn pale' [Jer 30:6]. When David perceived this, he began to praise (God) with (the same) two letters: 'Hallelu-yah (Be praised, י and ה)! O servants of the Lord, give praise; praise the name of the Lord' [Ps 113:1]. Rabbi Yudan Neshiyya inquired of Rabbi Samuel bar Nahman: "What is (the meaning of) this scripture?: 'Extol Him who rides on the clouds; the Lord [בְּיָה] is His name. Exult His presence' [Ps 68:5]." He said to him: There is no place without an authority apppointed over its dominion [בְּיָה]. And who is responsible for the dominion of them all? The Holy One blessed be He: בְּיָה is His name, for Yah is His name." (Rabbi Yudan) replied: "Your master Rabbi (E)leazer did not interpret [דָּרַשׁ] so; but rather (explained it by way of a parable) of a king who built a palace in a place of sewers [בִּיבִין], dumps, and waste.[18] (Now) if anyone would come (by) and say that the palace is built in a place of sewers, dumps, and waste, would he not malign (both king and palace)? Just so: if one were to say that the world was originally water within water, he would surely malign the Garden of the King and the Roof built above it. He should therefore look and not touch.

It is clear that we have here two separate microforms: a teaching of Rabbi Abbahu regarding the two letters of the divine name used to create this world and the next; and teachings by Rabbi Samuel and Rabbi Eleazer regarding the lower and upper worlds. All three sages develop interpretations of the word בְּיָה, but they do so on the basis of different texts. Rabbi Abbahu uses Isaiah 26:4, and divides the letters anagrammatically, while the teachings of Rabbi Samuel and Rabbi Eleazer explain Ps 68:5 via Greek puns (βία, "dominion"; and οὐαί, "woe").[19] In many ways the macroform in y. Hagiga is more streamlined than the one in Genesis Rabba, and presents each of the microforms as a distinct exegetical unit. For example, Rabbi Abbahu's homily opens with a teaching about the letters ה and י , and

---

18 See *Gen. Rab.* 1.5 (on Gen 1:1).

19 See בְּיָא בְּיָא in *b. Yebam.* 97b; and the explanation of *Yelammedenu* Lev 13:24 in Kohut, *Aruch Completum* 2.44b-45a. There is an obvious pun as well on Hebrew בֵּיב.

procedes to ponder the specific employment of each (resolving the issue through reference to Gen 2:4). By contrast, the version in *Genesis Rabba* has separated Rabbi Abbahu's remark regarding the letter ה from its use to resolve the quandry as to which letter (ה or י) was used for the creation of which world (this one or the next).

On can see by reference to *y. Ḥagiga* that *Genesis Rabba* presents a total transformation of the tradition. For now (in *Genesis Rabba*) Rabbi Abbahu's teaching seems limited to a comment on Gen 2:4; and his interpretation of Isa 26:4 (in the *yerušalmi*) is given to Rabbi Eleazer (whose parable is totally dropped). Moreover, the ensuing query about which letter was used in the different worlds *now* seems to be the voice of the editor, since it invokes Abbahu's first teaching by name in order to clarify what is *now* presented as Rabbi Eleazer's exegesis. The subsequent theology of the letters also reappears as the editor's voice, and not part of the extended homily of Rabbi Abbahu as presented in the *yerušalmi*.

Obviously, the editor of *Genesis Rabba* desired to privilege Rabbi Abbahu's comment on the letter ה in the context of a midrash on Genesis; but this resulted in a total relocation of interpretations and the insinuation of his own voice into a prominent position. As distinct from the redactor of the *yerušalmi* pericope, whose voice is absolutely absent, the anonymous editor of *Genesis Rabba* 12.10 speaks loud and clear as an impressario of traditions. By dividing the original homily of Rabbi Abbahu in two, and transferring one part to the end, the teachings of Rabbi Samuel and Rabbi Eleazer are now incorporated into the discourse on the letters of the creation. In the *yerušalmi* they are simply subordinate interpretations of the word בְּיָהּ, included for the sake of the completeness of tradition. Thus while both macroforms show midrashic tradition as complex acts of tradition-building, they do so in different ways. On the one hand, the *yerušalmi* has grouped its traditions in a static chain of authorities. This stands in stark contrast with the more dynamic process of enchainment found in *Genesis Rabba*. Hereby, the voice of the editor actively enters the hermeneutical fray. Little wonder that he once spoke the words of Rabbi Abbahu right out of his mouth.

III

The hierarchical chain of voices that constitute midrashic pericopes is also a chain of memory. Scripture is remembered first and foremost—and then the teachers who are remembered by the anonymous editor, in their own name and that of their teachers. Thus Midrash swings between the temporal poles of a memorialized past of instruction and the present moment of re-presentation. Indeed, as a linear process time is marked by the teaching of Scripture. Meanings accumulate as one "other thing" (דָּבָר אַחֵר) after "another"— and these are even edited into stylized series and structures for the sake of further instruction. From the myriad phonetic and grammmatical possibilities of connection, passages throughout Scripture are combined in ever new ways: "as it is written" here, says one teacher; or "this is what Scripture says," notes another. Exegetical discourse thus speaks from the fulness of God's canonical *langue*, revealing ever-new iterations of its Truth. Our collections of midrashic *paroles* bear witness to this messianic project.

But the rabbinic sage also works under the sign of myth. For every Scriptural interpretation is a reenactment of 'Sinai'—the paradigmatic time of Instruction. Indeed each midrashic *parole* participates in God's canonical *langue* and revitalizes it for new generations. The divine "word is fire", reports the prophet Jeremiah, "like a hammer splitting a rock"; and his rabbinic heirs understood this as the Sinaitic sparks that are released from Scripture through human interpretation.[20] Every sage is thus a disciple of Moses, and may be compared to Ben Azzai, who was once interpreting Scripture "and a flaming fire encircled him". His colleague Rabbi Aqiba thought him to be in the heat of mystical passion, but Ben Azzai explained that he "was rather sitting and (exegetically) enchaining (חֹרֵז) the words of Torah, Prophets, and Writings to each other— and the words rejoiced as when they were given at Sinai, and pleasant as when they were first given" (to which tradition rejoined that they were given at Sinai in fire—when the mountain was enflamed, as Scripture states).[21] King Solomon seems to have had all this in mind, suggested an anonymous sage, when he spoke of his

---

[20]   See the interpretation of Jer 23:29 in *b. Sanh.* 34a, and the reading of Rabbi Samuel in the *Tosafot, ad loc.*, s.v. מָה.

[21]   *Song Rab.* 1:10 §2. According to traditions in *b. Ḥag.* 14a and *y. Ḥag.* 2.1, a fire descended as R. Eleazar ben Arak dealt with mystical matters. However also in the last source is an account of fire which descended while Rabbi Eleazer and Rabbi Joshua "were engaged" in studying Scripture and connecting verses one to the other. This tradition is stylistically similar to that in *Song Rabba* (but correct חֹזְרִים in the *Yerušalmi* passage to חֹרְזִים, "linking" or "enchaining").

beloved's "cheeks as beautiful in ringlets" (תֹּרִים; but he hinted at "the oral and written Torahs"), and her "neck in chains of gold" (saying חֲרוּזִים), but alluding to the process of linking the words of Scripture).[22] We may even perhaps perceive here something of the eros of midrashic exegesis, whereby the Bride (Torah) is adorned by her rabbinic lovers through re-citations of her very essence (the words) in endless combinations.

And to whom may Ben Azzai be compared? To Rabbi Berekhiah (in the name of Rabbi Jonathan), who linked the phrase "To the leader: concerning (עַל) עֲלָמוֹת לַבֵּן" in Ps 9:1 to the words of Ecclesiastes. Ecclesiastes said in 3:11 that God created each thing for its proper time, "and even put the world [הָעוֹלָם] in their hearts [בְּלִבָּם]." Reading הָעוֹלָם in the second passage as הָעֶלֶם ("the youth"), he reread Ecclesiastes to mean that God has even put fathers' "love for their children [עֲלָלִים] in their hearts." He thereby hinted that one should likewise understand David's words in the Psalm (that is: עֲלָמוֹת לַבֵּן could be midrashically construed as עֲלָמוֹת [בְּ]לִבָּן, "youth in their hearts"). Others, however, preferred to interpret Ecclesiastes as meaning that God "concealed [הֶעְלִים] the day of death [מָוֶת] and judgment from His creatures"—and thus likewise the words of David. That is, Ps 9:1 now midrashically means that "God (the Leader) has hid [הֶעְלִים] the time of (עַל) death (מָוֶת) from the hearts (לְבָן) of His creatures (לַבֵּן; "the son," construed as a collective noun).[23]

And to whom may Rabbi Berekhia be compared? to yet other teachers who taught David's words to refer to how God cleanses (מְלַבֵּן) the hidden (or secret) sins (הָעֲלֻמוֹת) of His sons (בֵּן) on the Day of Atonement; or with respect to the death (עַל הַמָּוֶת) decreed by God against Israel (His firstborn son, בֵּן; citing Exod 4:24) for their sins, but God then cleanses him (מְלַבְּנוֹ) of all iniquity when he (the son, Israel) returns in true repentance? Other sages added "another thing" when they suggested that these words even taught how God's own heart was cleansed of retributive anger with the atoning death of His sinning sons (who failed to repent in their lifetime).[24]

Surely in all these ways (and myriads of others) the words of

---

22 *Song Rab.* 1:10 §2.

23 *Midr. Ps.* 9.1 (on Ps 9:1); Buber, מדרש שוחר טוב, 79-80.

24 *Midr. Ps.* 9.4 (on Ps 9:1); Buber, מדרש שוחר טוב, 82.

Scripture are renewed through new correlations, redivision, and repointing. And surely this process also reanimates the consonants of Scripture with new sounds and senses drawn from like-minded scriptures. The enchainments thus dramatize the unity of Scripture and *reveal it as a rabbinic work.* Indeed, this is ultimately the great achievement of midrashic exegesis. For in endless variations the sages show that the Written Text is one, interconnected instruction; and that all the values of rabbinic Oral Tradition (as for example here: divine providence and justice, sin and judgement, or repentance by deed or death) are present in it, explicitly or implicitly. By activating the *langue* of Scripture, rabbinic *paroles* keep the fiery speech of Sinai aflame. What is more: re-animated by human breath, the old words rejoice. And not least because they reveal the "laughing face" of God (*Pesiq. Rab Kah.* 12.25).

IV

The messianic dimension inherent in the midrashic desire to reveal the fulness of the divine *langue* leads to a last question. Is there a limit before the End?

The answer is three-fold, at least. First and foremost let us mention the limitations imposed by spiritual or intellectual capacity. This may be enunciated through Rabbi Aqiba's reply to Rabbi Ishmael's query as to how his (Aqiba's) hermeneutical techniques could help him explain the meaning of the seemingly senseless accusative particles in Gen 1:1 (since by his own principles and tradition such elements could be interpreted).[25] Rabbi Aqiba answered by way of Deut 32:47, "For it (Scripture) is not something [דָּבָר] of little-worth [רֵק] for you [מִכֶּם]"—meaning, as he pointedly says, that "if it is senseless [רֵק], it is your fault (lit. "from you"; מִכֶּם)—for you do not (therefore) know how to interpret"! By cleverly playing on the noun דָּבָר as the "word" of Scripture, and semantically restructuring the clause, Rabbi Aqiba hermeneutically rebukes his interlocutor and meta-communicates the truth that the horizon of interpretation is extended both by sufficient exegetical techniques and by the individual ability to use them. The limits of the *langue* are inscribed by the *parole*.

---

[25] See *Gen. Rab.* 1.14 (on Gen 1:1). I have followed the sequence of interlocutors as reconstructed by the *Minḥat Yehudah.* See the discussion in Theodor and Albeck, *Bereschit Rabba, ad loc.*

Another limitation to Midrash lies between the poles of mean-spirited and potentially anarchic readings of Scripture. The first of these two is what the sages call הַגָּדוֹת שֶׁל דּוֹפִי, midrashic interpretations which are designed to malign or mock the teachings or teachers of Scripture (b. Sanh. 99b).[26] Jeroboam is the paradigmatic offender, and his like is silenced lest they use the tradition to traduce it. Quite otherwise are those who show little self-restraint for their position as teachers, or those who push theology to its public limits. One thinks here of Rabbi Pappius, whose exegeses hang on gnostic horns. Rabbi Aqiba senses the danger, and issues a recurrent command of "Enough!" (דַּיֶּיךְ; e.g. Mek. on Exod 14:22 [Bešallaḥ §7]).[27] The fact that other times and teachers might regard the interpretations as acceptable, is irrelevant. The principle of דַּיֶּיךְ (like the danger of דּוֹפִי) is always a matter for social regulation.

A final consideration may be offered here by way of conclusion—and that is the limits which sin places on faithful interpretation. Indeed, this factor subverts the very possibility of Midrash. Come and hear: When the Holy One blessed be He gave the tablets to Moses on Sinai, their physical weight was lightened because of the holy letters inscribed thereon. Only thus could Moses bear their heavenly weight—until the moment the people sinned before the Golden Calf. Descending with God's Law to see the people's apostasy, the letters flew off the tablets and ascended to their heavenly source. The stones were then too heavy for Moses to bear, and the fell from his hands to the earth, as it is written, "And he cast the tablets from his hands, and he broke them at the base of the mountain" (Exod 32:19).[28]

For the sages, the fiery words of God's speech transform the world of nature—elevating it towards their supernatural source. But sin fashions other shapes, and the letters fly upward. Their loss is not

---

26   The opposite of such exegeses are the praiseworthy haggadot meshubbaḥot; cf. Mek. on Exod 15:22-26 [Vayissaʾ §1]; see Horovitz and Rabin, Mechilta d'Rabbi Ismael, 157.

27   See in Horovitz and Rabin, Mechilta d'Rabbi Ismael, 112, and many other places. M. Cahana has reviewed and presented important manuscript evidence in his study, "Mahadurot Ha-Mekilta de-Rabbi Yishmael Le-Shemot Be-Reʾiy Qiteʾei Ha-Genizah," Tarbiz 55 (1987) 499-515. His arguments are compelling.

28   I have woven together the variously similar accounts in y. Taʿan. 4.4; Tanḥuma, כי תשא §26 and §30. Cf. also ʾAbot R. Nat. A, as presented in S. Schechter, אבות דרבי נתן (New York: Feldheim, 1945) 11; and Ps.-Philo, Bib. Ant. 12.5.

only the end of revelation, but of all the traditions to come. One may suspect that this myth was told with a shutter.

THE GERIZIM-SAMARIAN COMMUNITY IN AND BETWEEN
TEXTS AND TIMES: AN EXPERIMENTAL STUDY

Ziony Zevit

The living Samaritan community has a history documented in varied sources extending from the middle ages, but for the periods of late and early antiquity, both the quality and quantity of documentation decreases. Under these circumstances, the onus on historians becomes greater because in the absence of clear contexts, it is obligatory to hypothesize responsibly about developments in the large gaps between documents and attested factules.

My objective in this essay is to outline a history of the Samaritan community in its "becoming" through texts critically analyzed in terms of their own cultural contexts. This enables situating the community within its historical context. In addition, I presuppose overtly in this study that the Samaritans are not to be considered a religious group exclusively, but an ethnic community as well. The contribution of this sociological dimension to an analysis of their past is its ability to clarify some developments in their history and to suggest a solution to a perennial question in Samaritan studies: When did the schism between Samaritanism and Judaism occur?

It is a pleasure to offer this essay as a tribute to my friend and colleague James A. Sanders whose insights into the creative, transforming tensions between sacred texts and religious communities, past and present, have increased our understanding of both.

I

Two major sources bear on Samaritan origins. Unfortunately, it is not quite clear exactly how these texts bear on their origins. Each may be interpreted plausibly as relevant or irrelevant; each may be considered significantly biased, and neither has been substantiated by any additional documentation.

The first, and certainly the better known of the two, is 2 Kings 17 describing events that transpired *ca.* 721–705 BCE. This chapter is the basis of what may be labeled, "the Jewish explanation." The following salient points in this chapter form the basis for discussion:

1. Samaria was destroyed and Israel exiled to Halah, Habor and the cities of the Medes (v. 6).

2. The original population was replaced by people from Babylon, Kuthah, Avva, Hamath, and Sepharvaim (v. 24). (But see additional groups mentioned in Ezra 4:9-10).

3. Some of these newcomers were killed by lions, apparently in numbers not explicable as pure happenstance. They interpreted these killings as an omen indicating the displeasure of the local numen. Recognizing that they did not know the law/custom, מִשְׁפָּט, "of the god(s) of the land," i.e. the proper manner of propitiation and placation, they appealed to the king of Assyria to remedy the situation (vv. 25-26).[1]

4. At the command of the king, a priest from among those Israelites who had been exiled from Samaria came, settled at Bethel, and taught the newcomers how to fear YHWH (v. 28).[2]

5. Each of these groups of newcomers established their own (old country) deities at the cult places, בָּמוֹת, that had been constructed by the exiled Samarians, appointed their own priests, and they also "feared YHWH" (vv. 29-32).

6. "YHWH they were fearing, and their gods they were serving according to the law/custom [מִשְׁפָּט] of the peoples that exiled them from there [אֲשֶׁר־הִגְלוּ אֹתָם מִשָּׁם]" (v. 33).[3]

---

[1]   A similar rash of man-attacking and man-eating mountain lions was noted in Southern California during the early 1990s. It was attributed to overpopulation in the feline community and the incursion of human suburbs and joggers into their shrinking habitats

[2]   The discovery of jar handles stamped with a למלך seal at Jebaᶜ, a village about 10 km north of Jerusalem and at the site of ancient Bethel about 10 km further north indicates that Bethel was not destroyed at the time of the Assyrian conquest of the northern kingdom. The למלך seals were used *ca.* 705–701 BCE in Judah as part of an inventory system in the royal administration. Bethel must have fallen into Assyrian control after the beginning of the seventh century BCE and was destroyed by Josiah *ca.* 622. Cf. H. Eshel, "Samaria—From the Destruction of the City of Samaria Until the Beginning of the Second Temple Period," in *Judea and Samaria Research Studies. Proceedings of the First Annual Meeting—1991* (Jerusalem: Reuben Mass, 1991) 28-29 (Hebrew); and Y. Kamisky, "A למלך Stamp from the Village of Jebᶜ in Benjamin?" in Z. H. Erlich (ed.), *Samaria and Benjamin 3* (Israel: College of Judea and Samaria, 1993) 101-102 (Hebrew).

[3]   This translation reflects the ambiguity of the Hebrew.

7. "Unto this day they do like the former laws/customs, they do not fear YHWH and do not do like their ordinances [חֻקֹּתָם] and like their law and like the teaching and like the command that YHWH commanded the children of Jacob, who made his name Israel" (v. 34).

The time frame of the authorial voice in v. 34 must be prior to the early exilic period since the Samaritans of the post-exilic period were not involved in pagan or quasi-pagan activities or theologizing; cf. Ezra 4:2-3, where such a charge might have been leveled against the northern petitioners easily and justifiably but is not. Thus, a person writing *ca.* 560–530 BCE described the origins, almost two centuries earlier, of what appeared to be a remarkably odd doxological-cultic situation.

As far as the proto-Rabbinic and Rabbinic groups of the late Second Temple and following periods were concerned, 2 Kings 17 provided an accurate, historical explanation for the origins of the Samaritans. In Rabbinic sources, they usually referred to them as "Kuthim," the name of one of the foreign groups who were brought into the land, and at times by the sobriquet גֵּרֵי אֲרָיֹות, "proselytes of lions," an allusion to the situation described in vv. 25-28. Furthermore, it is clear that those who used the expression גֵּרֵי אֲרָיֹות considered them to be Jews in some manner like themselves. And therein lies the question: How, when, and why did these foreigners integrate into Israel initially and evolve into a category of Jew centuries later?

The sobriquet clearly ignores the information provided by vv. 29-34 which may be understood to communicate that once the lion problem was over, so was any need for the "gods of the land." Once the cats were away the people could pray to whomever they wished. Verses 29-34 cannot be taken as indicating that these foreigners integrated any manner of the YHWH cult into their worship or that they did anything which the Deuteronomistic historian considered acceptable. Nothing in their activities approaches the schizophrenic piety of Naaman who skillfully grounded his minimal Yahwism in an isolated cultic activity, prostration on earth from YHWH's turf (2 Kgs 5:17-19).

There are a few possible exegetical strategies for bridging the gap between the new residents of Samaria and its environs as described in 2 Kings 17 and the Kuthim of the Rabbinic period: (1) The negative statements in vv. 29-34 are polemical additions to the text and are not correct; (2) the religious situation portrayed in vv. 29-34 was correct at the time the verses were penned, but ceased to be so afterwards as Yahwism evolved into proto-Judaism; (3) The Kuthim of the Rabbinic period have nothing to do with the peoples of 2 Kings 17.

The first and second strategies may or may not be useful, and dependence on them poses some difficulty. Although v. 33a corresponds with and amplifies v. 32 slightly, v. 33b, translated above, makes little sense without emendation; while v. 34 flatly contradicts both vv. 32 and 33a. In fact, v. 34 segues into a typical Deuteronomistic harangue against Israelites who engage in non-Yahwistic worship, vv. 35-41, a discourse that is totally irrelevant when addressed to a non-covenanted people touched by a tad of Yahwism.

Many of these difficulties are alleviated and cast into a different perspective when it is observed (1) that vv. 34-40 continue the Deuteronomistic discourse from v. 23, and (2) that the notice about the origins of the Samaritans in vv. 24-33 + 41 is revealed to be an interruptive insertion into this discourse (cf. the expression, "unto this day," in vv. 23, 34, 41). This reframes the first strategy and blunts the force of the stark contradictions in the extant text: they are not original but rather are the accidental result of an editorial insertion from another source noting the odd cult of the newcomers while condemning the exiled old timers (v. 33b, however, remains difficult). The polemic is only apparent, but not real, the accidental result of juxtaposed texts in an era without punctuation.[4]

Accordingly, chap. 17 may be considered a redacted collage: vv. 1-6, a standard Deuteronomistic summary with its regular synchronistic notations based on Judahite sources; vv. 7-23 + 34-40, Deuteronomistic sermonics; vv. 24-33 + 41, a slight recasting by a Deuteronomistic redactor of a northern, Ephraimitic document.[5]

---

[4] For a different analysis leading to a similar conclusion; cf. F. Dexinger, "Limits of Tolerance in Judaism: The Samaritan Example," in E. P. Sanders et al. (eds.), *Jewish and Christian Self-Definition*, vol. 2 (Fortress: Philadelphia, 1981) 89-91.

[5] S. Talmon ("Polemics and Apology in Biblical Historiography—2 Kings 17:24-41," in R. E. Friedman [ed.], *The Creation of Sacred Literature: Composition and Redaction of the Biblical Text* [Berkeley: University of California Press, 1981] 57-68, esp. 60-62) considers the following verses fragments of the Ephraimitic chronicle: (3-4), 5-6, 24, 29-31. I accept part of his general arguments but not

The text, in its own clumsy way after some ham-handed editing, speaks negatively about the cultic practices of the exiled northerners from the area of Samaria, the similar practices of non-exiled Israelites in other regions, as well as the quite different practices of those exiled into the land.[6] The הַזֶּה הַיּוֹם, "this day," to which v. 41 refers is self-evidently one generation after the third generation of newcomers. Allowing 25 years for each generation, this etiological note may be dated *ca.* 622–605 BCE, with a date closer to 605 being more reasonable. By then, the experimental application of Deuteronomic ideology as royal policy had taken place under Josiah; the implementor was dead, killed in battle, his achievements had been set aside and the *status quo ante* restored; and the military and political threat of Babylon to Judah, an obvious sign of divine displeasure, had become obvious.

The literary observations reframe the second strategy also, since the newcomers were actually more like Naaman than the impression caused by the combined text might lead us to believe. They might have evolved directly and become more like their southern neighbors in the ensuing periods. If so, Jer 41:5, in which men from Samaria, Shechem, and Shiloh coming to sacrifice at the site of the destroyed Temple in Jerusalem are murdered at Mizpah by the treacherous Ishmael son of Nethaniah may be significant. Jerusalemites would have no truck with ethnically foreign northerners who may have chosen to act like Israel, but who were not Israel.[7] The observations have no bearing whatsoever on the third exegetical strategy.

Higher critical analysis which solves the problem rather satisfactorily was not, however, a methodological option available to the Rabbis and their predecessors. Furthermore, it sidesteps the following

---

all of his specific ones and their concomitant textual implications. An expanded, corrected, and annotated version of this study will appear in a Hebrew volume to be published by the Y. Ben Zevi Institute. I thank Professor Talmon for allowing me to read the manuscript of his forthcoming study.

6 A similar intersplicing of distinct yet thematically related narratives is attested in the confusing story about the quail and the judicial/administrative system of Israel in Numbers 11. These narratives are linked by the theme of complaint and dissatisfaction in the wilderness.

7 According to attested P legislation, there was nothing cultically offensive in the piety of these northern pilgrims. Their death may have been due either to the violence of the times or perhaps because their act was perceived by the Jerusalem patriots as politically meaningful and aggressive against their interests.

questions: Assuming that the editor who inserted the notice of origins was linguistically competent and that he read over what he had written, didn't he understand that he was creating the impression of an anti-newcomer polemic? And if so, was it done willfully? (Shades of the first strategy proposed above rise again.) No answer to these questions is forthcoming.

II

A second source of information is the *Samaritan Chronicle II*, a reflection of Samaritan traditions about their own history written in Hebrew. According to J. MacDonald who published the part of the chronicle dealing with the Biblical period, it is written in a late form of Biblical Hebrew and may have achieved its extant shape sometime after the Muslim conquest of Palestine.[8] It is the basis for what may be called "the Samaritan explanation." Since this is neither well known nor readily available to most biblicists, I will summarize its major points somewhat expansively.

1. According to *Chronicle II*, the group originated after Israel was settled in the land as a result of tension between the priest Eli, a descendent of Ithamar, and Uzzi, the high priest, who was a descendent of Phineas.

2. Eli, overseer of the treasury, was much older than Uzzi. Desiring the office of high priest for himself, he allied many to his cause arguing that as the oldest of claimants to Phineas' office, he merited it by reason of seniority, not the younger Uzzi. One day, Eli accidentally omitted salt from an offering that he made and was rebuked by Uzzi. When Eli reported the incident to his supporters, a public break occurred between the two. Joseph tribes followed Uzzi and Judahites followed Eli. Then the Ephraimites and Manassites drove Eli and his community away from the chosen place, "Mount Gerizim Bethel."

3. Eli and his community settled in the territory of Judah at Shiloh, made an ark, altar, and all the cultic appurtenances that looked exactly like those in the tent on Mount Gerizim, but put into the ark scrolls written in the version of his own ancestor Ithamar which contained the same words as the authentic text but "in a different order." Eli went on sacrificing the offerings on the altar

---

    8   J. MacDonald, *Samaritan Chronicle II (or Sepher Ha-Yamim) from Joshua to Nebuchadnezzar* (BZAW 107; Berlin: de Gruyter, 1969) 5-9, cf. 73.

that he had made and every one of his festivals was in accord with the commandments of the holy law.[9]

4. Uzzi and his community adopted a live and let live attitude, even joining Israel in battles against the Philistines. But Saul, encouraged by Samuel who had been raised by Eli, halted cultic activities on Mount Gerizim for 22 years. Relations between the two groups were hostile and the sundering of the united monarchy into two kingdoms eventually culminated in the formation of four divisions of Israelites:

> The first division believed in Mount Gerizim Bethel—for it was the mount of blessing, the chosen place, the mount of inheritance and the Divine Presence; they were the community of the *šmrym ʿl h'mt*, keepers/guardians of the truth, who were the descendants of Phineas the son of Elazar the priest and the descendants of Joseph—along with some Levites and some from the rest of the tribes who were associated with them—a small number.

The second division consisted of those who substituted the Temple in Jerusalem for Mount Gerizim; the third consisted of people in the city of Pirʿaton who followed strange gods;[10] and the fourth consisted of the rest of the tribes who followed Jeroboam. He moved away from the holy city of Shechem to Samaria and erected two golden calves, one in Samaria and one in Dan.[11]

5. *Chronicle II* follows the community's vicissitudes until their exile with other citizens of the northern kingdom, and then their return. The published portion ends at the same point as does 2 Kings.

What is most significant, however, about this telling of their story, along with other similar versions, is its maintaining that those who "guarded the truth" were an ignored, oppressed minority in the northern kingdom throughout its existence and that their rise to prominence occurred only after their return from exile when their numbers became significant and there was no opposition to them.

---

9   MacDonald, *Samaritan Chronicle II*, 112-14.

10   The significance of this reference to apostasy in a single community has not been examined either as an historical or as a polemical reference. The few mentions of this site in the MT (Judg 12:13, 15; 2 Sam 23:30; 1 Chr 11:3; 27:14) locate it in the territory of Ephraim. The Judge Abdon and Benaiah, one of David's heroes, came from there. In the Samaritan chronicle *Kitab Al-Tarikh of Abu'l Fath* (trans. with notes by P. Stenhouse; Sydney: Sydney University Press, 1985), a place Faraʿtaʾ is mentioned. It was the site of major idolatry by pagans who learned magical rites from Israelites and then tried to use these to curse Israel (p. 47, and notes p. xi, §162).

11   MacDonald, *Chronicle II*, 157-58.

According to Samaritan tradition, it was only as they acquired some political power that significant enmity developed between them and the post-exilic Jewish community gathered around Jerusalem.

In light of the ideology of *Chronicle II*, the enmity was born in competition for priestly office. The Samaritans were permanently estranged from the rest of those who considered themselves Israel over the matter of who was a proper priest and the location of the proper place for the divinely ordained sacrificial cult, and that is all.

The significance and usefulness of this information and of the chronicle has been challenged legitimately on linguistic and historical grounds.

A colophon dates the manuscript to 1026 A.H., after Hijra, according to the Muslim calendar, corresponding to 1616 CE. In a significant review of this volume for which he utilized unpublished sections of *Chronicle II*, Z. Ben-Hayyim demonstrated that there was an error in the colophon. Both linguistically and stylistically the material published by MacDonald was identical with unpublished sections that continued the history of the Samaritan community through the end of the 19th century and described specific events while providing exact dates. Furthermore, the author identified himself as the son of a person known to have died in 1898 CE. Accordingly, Ben-Hayyim concluded that the author accidentally omitted the words "three hundred" in providing the date A.H. and that the whole composition was written in 1908 by one of a known group of Samaritan scholars who translated older documents into Hebrew for sale to European scholars.[12]

Ben-Hayyim, however noted that even though *Chronicle II* was young, it and other similar documents might be of value since the modern writers may have used good manuscripts of ancient documents written close to the time of the events they purported to describe. He continued however, "but certainly they are without

---

[12] Z. Ben-Hayyim, "A Samaritan Text of the Former Prophets?" *Leš* 35 (1970-71) 296-97 (Hebrew). His analysis of the relevant data and the conclusions that he drew are accepted by western Samaritan scholars. Cf. J. M. Cohen, a student of MacDonald who published another section of Chronicle II, *A Samaritan Chronicle: A Source-Critical Analysis of the Life and Times of the Great Samaritan Reformer, Baba Rabbah* (Leiden: Brill, 1981) 185-87; P. Stenhouse, "Samaritan Chronicles," in A. D. Crown (ed.), *The Samaritans* (Tübingen: Mohr [Siebeck], 1989) 223.

value with regard to events in the Biblical period."[13]

None of the other known Samaritan chronicles is dated prior to the tenth century CE. and to the extent that they relate the history of the Biblical period, their story is essentially the same as that found in *Chronicle II*.[14] This material is useful for understanding how the Samaritans viewed their history during the periods covered by the books of the Former Prophets in the MT, but Ben-Hayyim's statement precludes considering its statements about these early periods as deriving from the periods themselves.

Accepting these criticisms ostensibly leaves little to pursue: a historical tradition about the origins of a community attested in a few linked but distinctively medieval chronicles all emanating from a close knit, rather scrupulously observant community. Granting the lateness of the language and the cast of the tradition, it nevertheless cannot be discarded casually as a late concoction with regard to its information, just as MT Chronicles cannot be dismissed as an exercise in manufactured history.[15]

The Samaritans were always linked geographically to a small section of ancient Israel. Despite their own diaspora communities,

---

[13]   Ben-Hayyim, "A Samaritan Text," 298. Cohen (*A Samaritan Chronicle*, 176; cf. pp. 188-92) cites Ben-Hayyim approvingly and dates the composition of the underlying text to the 14th century.

[14]   Stenhouse, "Samaritan Chronicles," 218-24; cf. Stenhouse, *Kitab Al-Tarikh*, 47-48. This is the oldest known complete chronicle. It was composed in 756 A. H.= 1355 CE at the request of the High Priest and has been known in the west since 1653 (p. xxiv; and cf. Stenhouse, "Samaritan Chronicles," 221). The core story of the origin is also found in the Samaritan *Book of Joshua*, an Arabic composition, perhaps based on Hebrew manuscripts, that was purchased from Samaritans in Egypt in 1584. The older parts of this manuscript were written in the 14th century, and the younger parts were written in 1513 (Stenhouse, "Samaritan Chronicles," 220; J. Bowman, *The Samaritan Problem* [Pittsburgh: Pickwick Press, 1975] 15-16). A putative Hebrew original of Joshua, published by Moses Gaster in 1908 was demonstrated to have been written in 1902 and based on the Arabic *Book of Joshua* and the *Kitab al-Tarikh* (Ben-Hayyim, "A Samaritan Text," 297-98) though A. D. Crown argued in 1972 that it is antecedent to the Arabic composition (cf. Stenhouse, "Samaritan Chronicles," 220). Ben-Hayyim ("A Samaritan Text," 298) argues that the "Joshua" parts of *Chronicle II* are identical to Gaster's Hebrew Joshua despite MacDonald's asseveration on p. 5 to the contrary.

[15]   R. J. Coggins, *Samaritans and Jews, the Origins of Samaritanism Reconsidered* (Atlanta: John Knox, 1975) 121. Coggins does not deal with the linguistic problem, only with the overtly partisan nature of the narrative.

there is no reason to assume that they lost their own traditions and then had to make up new ones. They were a distinct ethnic group known from varied written sources over a period of 1000 years before their earliest extant chronicles were written. So, it is worthwhile exploring if some kernels of probable historical memory underlie information in these chronicles.

The following discussion focuses on the Samaritans not only as a religious community, but also as an ethnic group. Objectively, members of ethnic groups comprise a distinct population whose members are bound, or are perceived by themselves and others to be bound, by shared features such as ties of origin, kinship, norms and behavior standards, language, religion, shared lore and technical knowledge, beliefs, laws, and customs. Ethnic groups may function economically as a unit independent of other local groups, and may undergo economic development as a community; they intermarry among themselves according to accepted norms to preserve the group whose continuity is perceived as a self-evident good; they define themselves as distinct vis-a-vis other groups, and they have standards for interactions on various social and economic levels with other similar groups. These features, not all of which may be highlighted the same way in ethnic self-awareness at the same time, implicitly define their circles of "we." Finally, ethnic self-awareness often originates through historical experiences of shared struggle, tragedy, or oppression.[16]

III

It is unlikely that Samaritan stories relating to these events in what we call "the biblical period" were concocted totally in the medieval period, or even in late antiquity. By then they were a well organized, ancient people whose beliefs, practices, and confessions were known beyond the confines of their own community. Were that the case, in light of the overt and, in the medieval period, rancorous split between Jewish and Samaritan communities, we might have expected,

---

[16]   This understanding of ethnic groups is adapted loosely from G. Baum, "Ethical Reflections on Nationalism," *The Economist* 1.3 (1994) 44-47; W. G. Dever, "Cultural Continuity, Ethnicity in the Archaeological Record and the Question of Israelite Origins," *EI* 24 (1993) 31; D. A. Hollinger, "How Wide the Circle of 'We'? American Intellectuals and the Problem of Ethnos since World War II," *American Historical Review* 98 (1993) 329.

after musing about an answer to the question "Whose good is served by this tale?" that the Samaritans could have provided themselves with a more interesting and glorious past than they did. But that is not the case with this story. Or, had the origin stories been told with the Jewish stories and documents in mind (or in hand) or had they been born in an atmosphere clouded with polemics, we might have expected that the Samaritan stories would comprise a counter-history in which the essential details of the Jewish version would have been preserved and engaged but recast with a positive Samaritan spin, an effective form of rebuttal. But that too is not the case. The version presented above provides an unapologetic tale that with regard to its gross, general information by and large parallels but is not congruent with the biblical one.[17]

The Samaritan explanation maintains that the Samaritan community originated in a dispute over the legitimate priesthood and the legitimate place of worship. Formulated abstractly, the dispute revolved around two questions: (1) Are purificatory and celebratory rites effective and acceptable to YHWH if done properly by anybody who designates himself a priest, or are they effective only if done properly by one who is a legitimate priest? (2) Are such rites effective if done by a legitimate priest at an illegitimate shrine or must they be performed only at a legitimate shrine? These are not only late concerns in Israelite religion, but early ones also.

The issue of priestly legitimacy comprises the sub-text in the story of Korah's rebellion (Numbers 16–17). The etiologic objective of this narrative was to explain and demonstrate that divine favor

---

17   *Kitab Al Tarikh* conflates the conquest of Israel with that of Judah, but distinguishes between the exile of dwellers in Sebastia (= Samaria) and those in Nablus (= Shechem). Then "men came from the foreign nations and dwelt in the land of Canaan instead of the sons of Israel" (cf. Stenhouse, *Kitab Al Tarikh*, 73-75, 77). Counter-history, as defined above, abounds in other stories.

Chronicle II places the conquest in the days of Hezekiah and Hoshea ben Elah. The "guardians of truth" were sent to exile in Harran. The chronicle matter of factly explains that the Assyrians brought men from the land of Babylon to dwell in the land of Canaan—and not Samaria as in MT—in place of the Israelites (cf. Cohen, *A Samaritan Chronicle*, 182-83, 186).

MacDonald (*Samaritan Chronicle II*, 14) explains the many verbatim citations of biblical historical books in *Chronicle II* and the general order of of events that parallel the MT's articulation of events as being due to the fact that the chronicle is a heavily redacted version of a biblical text to which material was added as well as deleted.

determined which of the Levitical families was designated as priestly. It determined that only descendants of Aaron could be priests. This was the tradition at the Jerusalem Temple. However, at Dan, the priesthood was descended from Jonathan the son of Gershom son of Moses, a Levite though not an Aaronide (Judg 18:30).[18] In addition non-Levites functioned as priests: Micah, an Ephraimite, consecrated on of his own sons to be a priest at a private shrine (Judg 17:5); later he hired a Levite from Bethlehem to fill this function (Judg 17:12). Samuel, From Mount Ephraim, functioned as a priest on at least one occasion (1 Sam 7:9-10). (His inclusion in the Levitical genealogy of 1 Chr 6:7-13 is a form of post-exilic apologetic midrash contradicting 1 Sam 1:1 that classifies him as an Ephrathite of the tribe of Judah [cf. 1 Sam 17:12; Ruth 1:2; 4:11].) David appointed his sons, Judahites, to serve as priests (2 Sam 8:18). He also appointed Zadoq to be a priest (2 Sam 8:17), while Solomon later elevated him to head priest, an office in the royal cabinet. Unfortunately, in Samuel which usually tracks the tribal origins of the main characters, Zadoq's genealogy is unclear at best. A genealogical note in 1 Chr 5:27-41 (= English 6:1-15) corrects the "oversight" of Samuel providing him with an Aaronide origin.[19] In 1 Kgs 4:4, Zadoq and Abiathar, an Aaronide priest, functioned as head priests together; but in 1 Kgs 2:26-27, Abiathar was dismissed from the court.

The cases of Micah, Samuel, and David's sons indicate that in some circles being a priest was a function of duties and administration rather than of genealogy.

Jeroboam, as part of his religious reform, installed non-Levites to be priests at cult places described as בֵּית בָּמוֹת, "house of bamot" (1 Kgs 12:31-32). The result was that within the territories that constituted the northern kingdom of Israel, there was a Levitical, non-Aaronic priesthood at Dan and non-Levitical priesthoods at other shrines. This according to the Biblical account. Such institutions continued even after the Israelian kingdom was destroyed, its territo-

---

[18]   This interpretation ignores the suspended nun after the mem in Moses' name as an ancient scribal device to preserve Moses' reputation. So already Rashi *ad loc.*, Kimḥi *ad* Judg 18:6, and most moderns.

[19]   Cf. S. Japhet, *I & II Chronicles* (OTL; Louisville: Westminster/John Knox, 1993) 151-153. In his useful study of the history of the priesthood, F. M. Cross (*Canaanite Myth and Hebrew Epic* [Cambridge: Harvard University Press, 1975] 198-215) reconstructed the text in 2 Sam 8:17 providing Zadoq with an Aaronide genealogy there also.

ries divided into Assyrian provinces, and foreign elements settled in various sections. During Josiah's campaign into these territories, almost a century after the kingdom was destroyed, he attacked בָּתֵּי הַבָּמוֹת located in the cities around Samaria, slaughtered their priests, and burnt human bones on their altars (2 Kgs 23:19-20). Jeroboam's legacy was undone.

Some conclusions may be reached on the basis of this brief survey. The Korah story, from the Jerusalem P school, indicates that at some time there was conflict between Levitical groups. At Jerusalem, the inner-Levitical priestly conflict was resolved during the time of Solomon in favor of the Aaronides—despite the problem, acknowledged above, with regard to Zadoq—possibly in reaction to the ancient Moses priesthood at Dan. Jeroboam's actions, an explicit reflection of policy, indicate that Levitical ascendency was not to his liking, and for his political purposes, he would have no part of them.[20] Consequently, although Jeroboam was already stuck with the well established Moses Levites at Dan who predated the ascendancy of Levitical priests in Jerusalem, he did not appoint other Levites to institutions over which he exercised control. Therefore, he followed the old tradition in which a priest was one who functioned like one, and named priests from among the northern tribes. In aggregate, these data indicate that the time of conflict and resolution extended from the pre-monarchial period into the early years of the Divided Monarchy.[21]

---

[20]   One reason for this may have been that under the Davidic house, Levites in their cities that bordered Israel's inhospitable neighbors apparently functioned as the equivalent of military border guards and civil engineers. Their loyalty was to Jerusalem, site of the Temple and its treasury, and the king whose administration controlled their remuneration. Jeroboam would not have been interested in people who had no stake in the aspirations of those among whom they lived and who could have formed a potential fifth column. If 2 Chr 11:13-17 does not contain an authentic tradition not found in the Dtr composition about northern Levites migrating into Judah because they were excluded by Jeroboam from certain appointments (which they would have had no theological qualms accepting), they reflect a realistic reconstruction of what most likely occurred given the role of Levites in the north under David and Solomon. Cf. B. Mazar, "The Cities of Priests and Levites," VTSup 7 (1960) 193-205.

[21]   R. E. Freedman (Who Wrote the Bible? [New York: Summit, 1987] 37-48, 120-24, 157-60), extending Cross's analysis, artfully portrays the tensions in priestly politics as various groups became enmeshed in political struggles of various sorts.

To complicate this sacerdotal soup even more, M. Haran argues
that various allusions to בֵּית יהוה, or בֵּית אֱלֹהִים, or to places where
the biblical text indicates that somebody stood or ministered or was
crowned לִפְנֵי יהוה, "before YHWH," refer to a temple. Accordingly,
he concludes that there were temples at Beersheba, Bethlehem, Gibea
of Saul, Gibeon, Gilgal, Hebron, Micaiah's temple in Mount Ephraim
(Judges 17–18), Mizpeh in Benjamin, Mizpeh in Gilead, Nob, and
Ophrah in Manasseh.[22] Presumably, each of these had their own
historical traditions, cultic myths, priestly family of officiants, some
of whom may have been Levites. When Shiloh, Dan, Jerusalem, and
Bethel are added to this list, along with some sites known only from
archaeological excavations, e.g. Arad, Hazor, and Megiddo, and
considered in light of the biblical data adduced above about conflict,
the Samaritan portrayal of their origins is congruent with the
historical picture emerging in critical scholarship.

Furthermore, their contention that a place on Mount Gerizim had
been the focus of all Israelite cultic culture prior to the defection of
Eli and the rise of Shiloh may be exaggerated but is not implausible.
The political and cultic importance of Shechem in the history of
northern tribes may have developed prior to the period of the
monarchy, possibly as the northern equivalent of Hebron (see the
Deuteronomistic story of Joshua's covenant at Shechem [Joshua 23–
24] and the reference to the sanctuary there [Josh 24:26]). It was to
there that the elders of the northern tribes summoned and negotiated
with Rehoboam and there that they withdrew loyalty to the Davidic
house, and most likely to there that Jeroboam was summoned and
made king. Jeroboam, then "built the city" and turned it into his
capital; and from that city he initiated the establishment of Bethel and
Dan as cult places (2 Kings 12). Remarkably, Jeroboam's cultic
concerns did not extend to either Mount Gerizim or Mount Ebal,
both of whose shadows fell on his city, and both of which had a
cultic role in Israel's past:

> Cf. Josh 8:30-33: "then Joshua built an altar for YHWH, god of Israel, on
> Mount Ebal as Moses, servant of YHWH commanded the children of Israel
> as is inscribed in the scroll of the teaching of Moses . . . and he wrote there
> on the stones the repetition of the teaching of Moses . . . And all Israel and
> its elders . . . are standing on this and on that side of the ark of the covenant

---

[22]   M. Haran, *Temples and Temple Service in Ancient Israel* (Oxford: Clarendon, 1978) 26-39.

of YHWH . . . one half opposite Mount Gerizim and one half opposite Mount Ebal as Moses, servant of YHWH, commanded at first, that they should bless the children of Israel."

These verses describe a ceremony all of which took place on Mount Ebal with the people so situated that some faced Mount Gerizim across the valley of Shechem and others, presumably, the peak of Mount Ebal. They allude to Deut 27:1-8. But, whereas Deut 27:4 locates the setting up of stones on Mount Ebal, the Samaritan Pentateuch at that point reads: ". . . you shall set up these stones . . . on Mount Gerizim . . ." The "Gerizim" reading finds contextual support in the continuation of Deuteronomy 27 where the prescribed ceremony is slightly different from the one whose performance is described in Joshua 8.[23] In Deut 27:11-14 certain tribes are to stand

---

23   I. R. M. Bóid (*Principles of Samaritan Halachah* [SJLA 38; Leiden: Brill, 1989] 339-40) discusses the Old Latin version that preserves this reading also. A. Rofé ("The Editing of the Book of Joshua in the Light of 4QJosha," in G. J. Brooke [ed.], *New Qumran Texts and Studies* [STDJ 15; Leiden: Brill, 1994] 75-77) argues (1) that the original text of Deuteronomy 27 consisted of vv. 2-3, 4 + 8, 5-7 calling for the setting up of stones and writing on them as well as a prescription for the altar, (2) that the present text is garbled, and (3) that the extant garbled text is reflected in the text of Joshua. Thus, the entire Joshua ritual is built on that of the edited, garbled text of Deuteronomy and is not an authentic independent tradition but a made up scribal one trying to show that Joshua kept the law. In support he notes that the setting of the pericope in Joshua 8, after v. 29; or in the LXX after Josh 9:2; or in a Qumran fragment at the end of chap. 4 are all nonsensical since according to the inner logic of the story, Joshua is still located at Gilgal, nowhere close to Shechem. He argues that each of the different settings was motivated by the same desire to mark Joshua as a follower of the Deuteronomic commands who got around to them as soon as he established a foothold in the land.

Actually, the Deuteronomy text describes a ritual in which certain parts are preparatory for others: vv. 2-3 form an introduction to the prescribed complex of activities that focus on the stones. The first part unfolds in v. 4, setting up and preparing the stones; the second part consists of vv. 5-7, construction of an altar according to the altar laws of Exod 20 and sacrifice; and the third part is found in v. 8, the writing of the stone. The description in Joshua simply skips the first part. But the fact that the pericope "floated" doesn't deprive it of antiquity or of historical worth. Rofé's research deals with a lower critical problem from which he has drawn a historical conclusion. I am not asserting its factuality, but maintain that some form of the tradition that it represents was considered a true report at the end of the eleventh century BCE by certain groups who acted on it. True or not, they believed it to be true, and what they did as a result of this belief may be analyzed as a historical event. Logically, the pericope belongs somewhere toward the end of the book.

on Mount Gerizim to bless the people, while others are on Mount
Ebal to curse them as part of a covenant making ritual. Enough has
been changed and edited by Deuteronomic and Deuteronomistic
authors, but enough left, to suggest that the references in both Joshua
and Deuteronomy were originally to an altar on Mount Gerizim.[24]

There is a general consensus among biblicists that although the
extant Deuteronomy is a Jerusalem composition, its core originated
in northern Levitical circles and that the Shechem, Gerizim and Ebal
material in the book are authentic, pre-Deuteronomic, and ancient.[25]
The significance of this material, i.e. Deut 11:26-30; 27:1-8, 11-13;
28:3-6, 16-19, is that it attests to the intersection of Levitical, covenantal, and sacred place traditions at Mount Gerizim. This
convergence was part of northern cultic lore before the documents
through which we have traced it, as well as earlier documents whose
existence may be posited, were written.[26]

These conclusions are congruent with Samaritan claims in their
chronicles, with the suggestion made above that Jeroboam ignored
the mountain because he wanted to have nothing to do with Levites
and certainly not with Aaronides among them, and they provide a
background, albeit reconstructed, to the suggested Deuteronomic/
Deuteronomistic obfuscation of some verses in older texts, relocating
the altar to a mountain that nobody claimed was significant.[27] This

---

24   See the archæological and Qumran data analyzed by A. Kempinski, "'When
History Sleeps, Theology Arises': A Note on Joshua 8:30-35 and the Archaeology
of the 'Settlement Period' ," *EI* 24 (1993) 176-81 (Hebrew).

25   Cf. N. W. Porteous, *Living the Mystery: Collected Essay* (Oxford: Blackwell, 1967) 113-41; O. Eissfeldt, *The Old Testament: An Introduction* (New York:
Harper and Row, 1965) 223; G. Fohrer, *Introduction to the Old Testament* New
York: Abingdon, 1968) 170-77; R. E. Clements, "Deuteronomy and the Jerusalem
Cult Tradition," *VT* 15 (1965) 309-12; H. Cazelles, "Sur l'origine du mouvement
deuteronomique," *EI* 24 (1993) 13-15. Cazelles, arguing for the northern origin
among Levitic and scribal circles, discusses the origins of this notion in academic
circles during the last century. The notion is presented somewhat matter-of-factly in
a popular textbook, L. Boadt, *Reading the Old Testament: An Introduction* (New
York: Paulist Press, 1984) 354-55. Were it not part of a widely known, hoary
tradition, it is difficult to explain why the Deuteronomic circles in Jerusalem would
have included it since it contained information that could be used to argue against
the sacredness of Jerusalem.

26   A. Rofé, *Introduction to Deuteronomy*, Part I (Jerusalem: Akademon,
1975) 23-31 (Hebrew).

27   Arguments that Samaritans altered their texts and that the MT preserves the

was the all the result of late, pre-exilic inter-Aaronide conflict coupled with the rise of Jerusalem to political and economic prominence.

According to this reconstruction, the Gerizim community was a relatively unimportant sect during most of the Iron Age. Aside from the sectarian differences, its members were indistinguishable from other Israelians with regard to their piety, except for the fact that their cult may never have involved non-Yahwistic elements.[28] They were just a local group comprised of Aaronide priests, Levites, and families stemming from a few northern tribes that had its own particular place of worship and whose rituals most likely bore closer

---

original reading consider as significant the fact that Jews would have had no reason to change the text as both mountains were irrelevant to them (cf. J. A. Montgomery, *The Samaritans: The Earliest Jewish Sect* [New York: Ktav, 1968 [orig. 1907] 235 n. 133). However, if the change is ancient, representing inner Levitical conflicts during the last pre-exilic decades, it would have entered the main Jerusalem-Judahite-Jewish tradition and been preserved there in the post-exilic period when the Samaritans self-differentiated themselves from Jews. This is not to deny that the later Samaritans did indeed introduce tendentious changes into what became their literature in later periods (cf. R. T. Anderson, "Samaritan Literature," in Crown, *The Samaritans*, 404). E. Tov ("Proto-Samaritan Texts and the Samaritan Pentateuch," in Crown, *The Samaritans*, 401-405) discusses the "thinness" of the so-called "Samaritan" layer to the underlying text type that is known from Qumran.

Kitab Al Tarikh contains a polemical passage that presupposes that even in the Jewish Torah Deut 27:4 read "Gerizim," though elsewhere it accuses Ezra of changing the text (cf. Stenhouse, *Kitab Al Tarikh*, 86 and notes, xxii, §330). J. Purvis (*The Samaritan Pentateuch and the Origin of the Samaritan Sect* [Cambridge: Harvard University Press, 1968] 50-52, 67-69, 86-87) dated the sectarian Samaritan recension to the time of the Hasmoneans on a variety of grounds. The background to their sectarian recension may have been Hyrcanus' destruction of a temple on Mount Gerizim, *ca.* 128 BCE. Perhaps Hyracanus thought that he was reclaiming Gerizim for Zion and its adherents for Judaism and that he was a new Josiah at Bethel. Hyrcanus then moved south, conquered the Idumeans and forced them to be circumcised and accept Jewish customs. Hyrcanus' actions indicate that as far as Jewish standards were concerned, the Gerizim-Samarians were but misguided Jews whereas the Idumeans were errant children of Abraham who had to be reclaimed for the covenant that was their legacy.

28   This statement is based on the lack of references to any such cult in biblical texts. Samaritan sources would not have been expected to retain such information. Mention in late antiquity that Samaritans worshipped a dove are not relevant, and have to be measured in the balance along with the observations that the head of an ass was worshipped in Jerusalem. New discoveries, however, from the ongoing excavations atop Mount Gerizim could falsify this statement.

resemblance to what was practiced in Jerusalem than at Bethel, site of another Israelite cult.

Whatever may have actually happened to their shrine/tabernacle on the mountain, after the Babylonian destruction of the Jerusalem Temple, their situation was similar to that of their fellow Israelites. This clarifies why their religious development in the post-exilic period paralleled that of other Israelites as proto-Judaism began to evolve.

The thrust of this argument has implications for the identity of Zerubbabel's opponents in Ezra 4:2 *ca.* 520 BCE. According to the book, these identified themselves as foreigners in the land from the time of Esarhaddon wishing to forge a religio-political alliance with the Jerusalem community. They worshipped YHWH in some way, and may have represented non-Levitic traditions emanating from Bethel.[29] Their approach may have been encouraged by those supporting the sentiments of Zechariah *ca.* 520–518 BCE: ". . . People and dwellers in many cities will again come; and those dwelling in one (city) will go to another saying, "Let us go to entreat the face of YHWH and to seek YHWH of hosts . . . in Jerusalem . . ." (Zech 8:20-23). They were rebuffed.[30]

When rejected, they tried to frustrate and hinder affairs in Jerusalem but did not advance a program calling for the building of a new temple/tabernacle on Mount Gerizim. Hence, they should be distinguished from the Gerizim-Levitical community.[31] These

---

[29]   Their religion must have been affected somehow by Josiah's destruction of cult sites and clerics in the area of Samaria *ca.* 622, almost a century earlier, but it is impossible to gauge how. Their turn to Jerusalem, however, may reflect some acceptance of the notion that sacrifices should be offered to YHWH only at the single, legitimate shrine.

[30]   *Kitab Al Tarikh* claims that this discussion took place between Samaritans and Zerubbabel over the proper place to worship while still in exile. In their version, they acted against the Jews and were supported by the Mesopotamian king (Stenhouse, *Kitab Al Tarikh*, 85-98).

[31]   The articulation of episodes in Ezra makes it appear that the letter complaining to Persian authorities about construction in Jerusalem (Ezra 4:7-16) is a continuation of the anecdote in 4:2 about the building of the Temple. It is not. The opponents who authored the letter represent a different group of individuals, cf. the ethnic identities in 4:2 and 4:9, and a different social group in terms of authority. The concern of the complainants in Ezra is similar to those who opposed Nehemiah's work projects (Neh 4:6). Nehemiah's opponents were motivated by a desire to maintain authority and hegemony over against a weak Jerusalem; those

foreigners, living in the villages clustered near Samaria, comprised a loose confederacy of various ethnic groups and they defined themselves in terms of whom their ancestors had been elsewhere.[32] They lacked a clear sense of self—though not of shrewd self-interest—and tried to draw close to the Jerusalem Jews who had such a sense. Like themselves, many of the Jews in Jerusalem had experienced exile, and somehow the Samarians may have discerned a kinship rooted in a common adverse experience with them. Yet unlike the foreigners, the Jews returnees were rooted in the land and they were who their ancestors had been in their covenanted land. For the Samarians, the alliance would have expanded the mutuality of experiences and helped them achieve a sense of integrated, *Heimat*, ethnicity. Rejected by Jerusalem, for some, a second option was at hand.[33]

---

who approached Zerubbabel were attempting to forge an alliance out of a position of weakness. They were willing to commit to the religious authority of priests, Aaronides, and Jerusalem. An earlier attempt may have resulted in the murderous incident reported in Jer 41:5; cf. Dexinger, "Limits of Tolerance," 92-93. (I do not agree with that part of his analysis dependent on the assumption that the Chronicler is responsible for Ezra-Nehemiah. Cf. Japhet, *I & II Chronicles*, 3-5.)

Note the cautionary caveat of L. L. Grabbe, "Reconstructing History from the Book of Ezra," in P. R. Davies (ed.), *Second Temple Studies* (JSOTSup 117; Sheffield: JSOT Press, 1991) 105-106; and cf. L. L. Grabbe, *Judaism from Cyrus to Hadrian*, vol. 1 (Minneapolis: Fortress, 1992) 30-41.

32   A. Zertal (*The Manasseh Hill Country Survey: The Shechem Syncline* [Haifa: IDF and University of Haifa Press, 1992] 55-56 and 581) notes that there were 87 sites during Iron Age II (i.e. 1000–721 BCE) in an area delimited roughly by Nablus-Samaria-Dothan-Taanach-Jenin-Tell el Farʾa (North). In Iron Age III (i.e. 722–586 BCE) there were only 40 sites most of which clustered around Samaria. Eshel ("Samaria," 28-29) refers to archaeological and epigraphical data indicating the Mesopotamian origins of at least part of this population.

33   The ability of small or weak ethnic groups in contact with larger and stronger ones to maintain ethnic identity over extended periods of time should not be underestimated, and the American metaphors of homogenization, "melting pot" and "mosaic," should not be generalized. Intermarriage and assimilation are not necessarily an automatic, inevitable process. Among extant groups which have managed to retain ethnic identity in situations where assimilation into larger groups was possible are the following: the Armenian diaspora, Jews, Gypsies, Native Americans, the Amish people, Irish Protestants, groups in the Balkans, foreign laborers in Germany and other European countries; Lebanese Christians, and, of course, Samaritans. An example of the opposite tendency is the cultural Americanization of German speaking Lutherans in the U.S. in the course of this century.

Exiled Judahites maintained some sort of quasi-tribal structure as evidenced by

A few villages and clans of these Samarians may have allied themselves with the Gerizim community, accepting their social norms, Yahwistic practices, cultic authority, Levites, Aaronides, and Gerizim. From the perspective of observers in Jerusalem, the Gerizimization of the Samarians may have been perceived as the Samarianization of the Gerizim community. The effect was the blurring of distinctions between the two groups. So that depending on what one wishes to emphasize, the newly developing ethnic group could be considered Kutheans, or "proselytes of lions" (*b. Yeb.* 24b; *b. ʿAbod. Zar.* 26b–27a), or a strangely fixated cult of some sort, or a marginal, quasi-Jewish people. From the perspective of their own documentation and traditions, the Gerizim community absorbed some of the foreigners completely just as the Israelite tribes of the Early Iron Age had absorbed what was left of the identifiable Canaanite enclaves within two or three generations.

Contemporary genetic studies of the Samaritan community in Nablus, Holon, and a few other locales, reveal them to be a "genetic isolate," so distinct from other groups that genetic connections between them cannot be assumed. They are isolated from Ashkenazic, Babylonian, and North African Jews, from European populations and from other non-Jewish middle-eastern populations. Their genetic isolation from all other Jewish groups is not explained entirely by the history of diaspora Jewish population movements and inter-marriage, so that it has been concluded that the Samaritans have their own unique history.

B. Bonné-Tamir, who studied them,[34] suggests that they may

---

reference to the "elders of the exile" (Jer 29:1), "the elders of Israel" (Ezek 14:1; 20:1, 3), "the elders of the Judahites" (Ezra 5:5, 9; 6: 7, 8, 14) and "the heads of the (houses of the) fathers," i.e. extended families (Ezra 1:5; 2:68; 4:2, 3; 8:1; Neh 7:70). Babylonian texts indicates that in exile they apparently settled in enclaves known by the town of their origin in the homeland. This was also true of groups of Philistines, Phoenicians, and Egyptians (I. Ephʿal, "The Western Minorities in Babylon in the 6th–5th Centuries B.C.: Maintenance and Cohesion," *Or* 47 [1978] 75, 82-88]). The experience of maintaining and fostering ethnic identity and continuity in exile and of seeing assimilation did not provide an atmosphere within which foreigners, considered "them," would be welcomed into the "us" group. The reconstituted Jerusalem polity knew itself to be a minority within the Persian empire.

[34]   B. Bonné, "Are There Hebrews Left?" *American Journal of Physical Anthropology* (series 2) 24 (1966) 140-44; B. Bonné-Tamir, "The Samaritans: A Living Ancient Isolate," in A. W. Eriksson (ed.), *Population Structures and*

represent an isolated descendant populariont from parts of some Israelite tribe. From the absence of any significant connections to other middle eastern groups, I suggest that the genetic data support the following conclusions: The number of Samarians who underwent re-ethnicization was relatively small visà-vis the number of members in the original, compact Gerizim community, so much so that they have left no genetic trace that can be picked up by contemporary research.[35]

Practically, the expanded Gerizim-Samarians formed a strategic demographic arc extending from Shechem around the base of Mount Gerizim into some of the villages around Samaria and perhaps even into the city itself. The enlarged, vitalized community achieved a critical mass and distribution of people that could no longer be ignored in local politics. The process, begun *ca.* 520 BCE would have been concluded within three generations, *ca.* 445 BCE, a period coinciding with the missions of Ezra and Nehemiah to Jerusalem.[36]

The eyes of Gerizim were on Zion, and both of these foreign Jews had a significant influence on the newly emerged Gerizim-Samarian religious community. It perceived in Nehemiah's building activities a potential threat to its own recently emerged mini-hegemony and influence, and it attempted to frustrate his plans (Neh 2:10, 19-20; 3:33-35; 4:1-3; 6:1-19). The activities of northern leaders, as ineffective as they were in the long term, increased the store of shared historical experiences, victories and defeats in the northern community and helped to define its members as a religio-ethnic group vis-à-vis the Jews of Jerusalem. who became a "them."[37]

Genetic Disorders (London: Academic Press, 1980) 38-39.

[35] For examples of how genetic studies may corroborate historical analyses based on textual, linguistic, anthropological, and archaeological data, cf. the studies collected in the volume edited by Eriksson mentioned in the previous note, and for the application of recent advances to address these issues, cf. K. Kidd et al., "Nuclear DNA Polymorphisms and Populations Relationships," in B. Bonné-Tamir and A. Adam (eds.), *Genetic Diversity Among Jews. Diseases and Markers at the DNA Level* (New York: Oxford University Press, 1992) 33-42.

[36] This date corresponds to the dates of 445 BCE for Nehemiah and 443 BCE for Ezra proposed by A. Demsky ("Who Came First, Ezra or Nehemiah? The Synchronistic Approach," *HUCA* 65 [1994] 17-19) on the basis of quite different considerations and calculations.

[37] Assuming that the Persian statecraft operated realistically and not particularly ethically, their inability to carry the day in the Persian court against the obviously weak Jerusalem community indicates the even greater weakness of the

Ezra's activities also had a profound impact initially only on the priestly establishment of the core Gerizim community. Acting with royal authority, Ezra, a priest, and scribe-interpreter imposed on the Jerusalem community a series of cultic and behavioral norms based on a written Torah that reflected their teachings or that could be understood as they understood traditional teachings. I hypothesize that some time after Ezra departed, they too adopted a written Torah and with it the Ezra-like role of scribe-interpreter. They expanded the priestly office to include the roles of preservers and transmitters of divinely inspired written instructions, interpreters of said instructions, and administrators of many of the same said instructions through their hereditary authority. This was possible because Ezra was of the same line of priestly descent through the line of Phineas as they (Ezra 7:1-6), he was not of the Jerusalem establishment, and he had done nothing against the people of Gerizim. The adoption of a written Torah as the constitutional basis of the theocratic community along with their own tradition of interpretation furthered the development of ethnic pride.

IV

Although there remain considerable gaps in our knowledge, by the middle of the Second Temple period, their private piety was similar to that of Jews except that they rejected Jerusalem and its Temple.[38]

---

northern community.

[38]   This explains why *ca.* 400 BCE the Jews of Elephantine were comfortable addressing a letter to Bagohi, the Persian governor of Judea, and to northerners, the sons of Sanballat, governor of Samaria, asking for help in restoring their temple that had been built long before the Persians; cf. A. Cowley, *Aramaic Papyri of the Fifth Century B.C.* (Oxford: Clarendon, 1923) 108-19, papyrus no. 30, lines 13, 17-19, 29. From the vantage point of the Elephantine community, Bagohi, as a foreigner recognized that Jews had YHWH temples in more than one place—despite what may or may not have been said by the Jerusalem priests about the legitimacy of such establishments—and enlisted his good offices. An address to the Jerusalem priests had earned no response. Presumably, in asking for help from the northern community, the leaders from Elephantine assumed that the Gerizim-Samarians would give them a more sympathetic hearing. After all, they were Jews, like themselves, but with their own temple. There is no record of a response, but I doubt that the Gerizim priesthood would have sanctioned helping them. For a discussion of the nature of the Temple and problems in determining which of Sanballat's sons are addressed, cf. B. Porten, *Archives from Elephantine* (Berkeley: University of California Press, 1968) 109-22.

They were monotheists, accepted the Torah alone as canonical, had their own calendar that was determined by their priests, a lunar-solar calendar sufficiently similar to the Pharisaic one so that the Passover celebrations sometimes coincided; and their own standards of ritual purity as determined by their own traditions affecting clean and unclean animals, death, food, and so on, were similar to those of Pharisees (*t. Pesaḥ.* 2.1-3; *m. Roš. Haš.* 2:2; *b. Qidd.* 76a; *Masseket Kuthim*[39] 15, 17, 20, 24). They practiced circumcision and observed the sabbath (*m. Ned.* 3:10).[40] Most likely such considerations lie behind a statement recorded in the Jerusalem Talmud: "The land of the Kuthim is pure; its immersion pools are pure[41]; and its dwellings and roads are pure[42]" (*y. ʿAbod. Zar.* 44d; cf. *t. Miqw.* 6.1).

Some Tannaitic discussions that refer to the Kuthim indicate that they were considered Jews and as a community fastidious in their observance of these commandments that they observed (*t. Pesaḥ.* 2.3; *b. Qidd.* 76a; *b. Ber.* 47b; *b. Giṭ.* 10a). Despite their origins, as considered by the Tannaim who accepted the Biblical account in 2 Kings 17, they were adjudged converts and were therefore to be treated as Jews. They ate with Pharisees and shared some liturgy with them (*m. Ber.* 7:1; 8:1).

On the other hand, there are statements that they are like non-Jews (*t. Ter.* 4.12, 14), that their "Jewish" status is questionable and therefore marriage with them is proscribed (*m. Qidd.* 4:3), that they were lax concerning tithes but could be entrusted to respect tithed products on the assumption that they knew what it entailed (*m. Dem.* 3:4; *Masseket Kuthim* 9).[43]

---

39   *Masseket Kuthim* is a late collection of *mishnayot* and *baraitot* relating to the Samaritans. Although most of the material is found elsewhere in the Rabbinic corpus, it does contain new statements. Not part of the canonical Mishna, it is one of seven tractates printed at the end of *Nezikin*, the fourth order of the Talmud, in the oft reprinted Vilna edition. It may be dated to *ca.* 400 CE and attests to a Jewish attitude towards Samaritans in Palestine at that time. It contains two chapters, but is cited here according to the enumeration in Montgomery, *The Samaritans*, 196-203, which, to my knowledge, contains the only readily available English translation.

40   Like the Sadducees, the Samaritans take the word שַׁבָּת in Lev 23:11, 15, to refer to the Sabbath of Passover and not to the day of the holiday. Thus, even if Samaritans and Pharisees celebrated Passover on the same day, their celebration of Weeks/Shavuot would never coincide.

41   That is, they use the proper water for ritual bathing.

42   That is, one may be sure that there are no graves or corpses there.

43   G. Alon (*Studies in Jewish History*, vol. 2 [Jerusalem: Hakibutz Hameu-

In a very useful article, L. Schiffman studied the development and placement of various negative statements about them and concluded that it was Rabbi Judah ha-Nasi, *ca.* 155?–215? CE, who added anti-Samaritan material to the Mishna when he redacted it.[44] Rabbi Aqiba, *ca.* 50–135 CE, whose oral redaction of the Mishna underlies and was the basis for Rabbi Judah's written work, was of the opinion that "the Samaritans are true proselytes and the priests who became mixed up with them were fit priests" (*b. Qidd.* 75b). In a study of Josephus' attitudes toward them, L. H. Feldman points out that although Josephus (*ca.* 38–100? CE), who was committed to viewing them through 2 Kings 17, understood them to be of foreign origin and considered them a separate ethnos, in the observable reality that he saw, they acted like halakhic Jews.[45]

M. Mor and A. D. Crown trace the origins of clearly defined anti-Samaritanism to the period after the failure of the Bar Kokhba revolt in the early second century CE.[46] The change in Jewish attitude may be attributed to an altered worldview and to the social locations of the individuals whose views have been cited: Jerusalem/Judean vs. Galileean; Levitical descent vs. non-Levitical descent; Sadducee vs. non-Sadduceean loyalties; upper class and worldly vs. lower class. Each of these (somewhat artificial) corelative polarities of identification, each an independent variable, may have influenced attitudes with individuals identifying with the first term of each set tending to be more hostile and antagonistic. The first terms are all more

---

had, 1958] 4-10 [Hebrew]; idem, *Jews and Judaism in the Classical World* [Jerusalem: Magnes Press, 1977] 359-67) traced halakhic traditions presupposing that the Samaritans were descended in part from Canaanites. These traditions, although believed by some Jews in Late Antiquity, have no historical basis and will not be considered.

[44] L. Schiffman, "The Samaritans in Tannaitic Halakha," *JQR* 75 (1975) 329, 333, 339, 349-50.

[45] L. H. Feldman, "Josephus' Attitude Toward the Samaritans: A Study in Ambivalence," M. Mor (ed.), *Jewish Sects, Religious Movements, and Political Parties* (Omaha: Creighton University Press, 1992) 25, 26, 35, 37. Cf. I. R. M. Bóid's comment ("The Samaritan Halachah," 643): "On almost any particular point the Samaritan practice will be the same as that of some Jewish group or will be explicable as a stricter version of such practice." Cf. also, idem, *Principles of Samaritan Halachah*, 317-28.

[46] M. Mor, "The Samaritans and the Bar Kochba Revolt," in A. D. Crown (ed.), *The Samaritans*, 22-31; A. D. Crown, "Redating the Schism Between the Judaeans and the Samaritans," *JQR* 82 (1991) 17.

distinctive, defining, and exclusive than the latter. They serve to clarify the difference between Josephus who was an upper class priest of Levitical descent who was educated in Jerusalem, and Aqiba a non-priest, a Galileean, and a man who identified with the lower classes.

By the time of R. Judah ha-Nasi, Jerusalem and Judah had become "ideas" enshrined in the Galilee, and the Pharisees/Rabbis considered themselves *de jure* and had become *de facto* the new spiritual priests of Israel. The polarities enumerated above had partially collapsed into each other under the press of new concerns. As the perceived measure of common shared misfortune increased among Jews, and as a sense of powerlessness created by a diaspora worldview strengthened, the self-comprehension of the ethnic group constricted. Those who did not pain on the Ninth day of Ab when the destruction of the Temple was marked were no longer Israel.[47]

The above analysis suggests that we may consider the Gerizim-Samarians a pre-Pharisaic Jewish sect whose social and halakhic development paralleled a number of features attested in other Jewish halakhic systems. In other words, with regard to the principles by which they interpreted the Torah and applied it to their daily life, they were clearly part of the Jewish intellectual world of the Second Temple period.

Rabbi Aqiba's statement in *b. Qidd.* 75b, referred to above, approaches closely the reconstruction presented: the Kuthim were comprised of an authentic, Aaronide priesthood with a laity of those who had accepted divine Torah and most of the important halakhic practices observed by Jews of his time.[48]

If Josephus and his period represent a stepping stone toward the time of Bar Kokhba, and Bar Kokhba one toward the time of R. Judah ha-Nasi, then the Gerizim-Samarian people during the late Second Temple period were most likely considered by Jews an Israelite-Jewish sect with some troublesome genealogical elements and theological quirks; while they considered themselves the true, pure Israel, שַׁמְרִים עַל־הָאֱמֶת ("guarding the truth") and the Jews

---

47 This would have excluded Samaritans and Jewish Christians as well.

48 Aqiba's statement is cited in the Talmud in opposition to that of R. Ishmael: "Kutheans are proselytes of lions [i.e. they became Jews only under duress and hence their "conversion" is invalid] and the priests who became mixed up with them were unfit/illegitimate priests."

their erring brethren.

Viewed in this context, the term "Samaritan schism" refers neither to a political act or to an historical event but rather to a sociological process that affected perceptions of reality and awareness, defined and redefined schools of thought, practice, and belief in ways that led to both the inclusion and exclusion of various communities.[50] After the time of Bar Kokhba, there was no schism, in the sense of a rupture or break as the term is employed in church history; rather, there was again a redefinition of "we, us," and "you, them" as the groups drifted apart and became increasingly irrelevant to each other. The term "schism" makes sense only if applied to this extended process of irrelevantization.

---

[49]   This explanation sheds light on the restricted canon of Samaritan scripture, i.e. from Genesis through Joshua. Books of the Hebrew canon from Judges through Kings, in their extant Deuteronomistic form, speak about the decline and fall of an Israel to which the Samaritan community did not belong. Prophetic books in the collection from Isaiah through Malachi also address a community which in their eyes was not Israel, and refer to misdeeds which their community, according to Samaritan lights, had not committed. Their sentiments could be encapsulated in the saying attributed to a third-century CE Amora, Rabbi Adda ben Rabbi Hannina, who said, "Had Israel not sinned, they would have been given only the Pentateuch and (the book of) Joshua . . ." (*b. Ned.* 22b).

[50]   Coggins, *Samaritans and Jews*, 165.

JOSEPHUS' PORTRAIT OF JETHRO

Louis H. Feldman

INTRODUCTION

A major goal of Josephus' "rewriting" of the Bible is to make it more attractive to his primarily non-Jewish audience. As he himself says (*Ant.* proem 2 §5), he undertook his work in the belief that all Greeks would find it worthy of serious attention. The very fact that he cites the Septuagint as a precedent (*Ant.* proem 3 §10) is a further indication that according to Josephus it was intended primarily for non-Jews, inasmuch as the Septuagint was undertaken at the specific behest of Ptolemy Philadelphus (*Ant.* proem 3 §10).

Therefore, it should not be surprising that Josephus is particularly careful in his portrayal of non-Jewish personalities in the Bible, so as not to offend his pagan readers. Thus, he protects Pharaoh's reputation by remarking that he had wished to contract a legitimate marriage alliance with Sarai and not to commit an outrage against her in a transport of passion (*Ant.* 1.8.1 §165). Moreover, whereas in the Bible (Gen 46:34) Josephus instructs his brothers to say that they are keepers of cattle rather than shepherds, when the Pharaoh of his day asks them what their occupation is, inasmuch as in Josephus' version (*Ant.* 2.7.5 §185) every shepherd is an abomination to the Egyptians, Pharaoh asks Joseph what the occupation of the brothers is so that he, magnanimously, may permit them to continue in that work. Likewise, Josephus (*Ant.* 2.9.1 §201) is careful to place the blame not on the Pharaoh of the Exodus but on the Egyptians, who are described as voluptuous and lazy people. That this Pharaoh is not portrayed as being prejudiced against the Israelites is seen by Josephus' insertion of an extraordinarily long episode (*Ant.* 2.10.1–2 §238-253), completely unparalleled in the Bible, in which Pharaoh appoints Moses, an Israelite, as general of his army to halt an invasion by the much feared Ethiopians. As for Ahasuerus, Josephus (*Ant.* 11.6.9 §236) expands greatly in his depiction of that king's gentleness and his tender concern for Esther's wellbeing. Indeed,

Ahasuerus (*Ant.* 11.6.6 §216) is represented, in an extra-biblical addition, as the ideal ruler whose goal is peace and good government, which his subjects may enjoy forever. Even in the depiction of the wicked Balaam, sent to curse the Israelites, Josephus shifts the focus from Balaam's personality to the historical, military, and political confrontation between the Israelites and their enemies. Balaam's initial decision to desist from cursing the Israelites is presented as sincere; indeed, the blame for the reversal is actually put on God Himself (*Ant.* 4.6.3 §107).

One criterion of the importance of a given biblical figure for Josephus is the sheer amount of space that he devotes to one personality as compared with the attention which he gives to others.[1] Thus, the ratio for Josephus' account of Zedekiah is 7.45:1 compared with the Hebrew text, 3.41 for Korah, 2.46 for Joab, 2.45 for Eglon and Ehud, 2.31 for David, 2.19 for Saul, 2.17 for Solomon, 2.16 for Jeroboam, 2.09 for Balaam, 2.01 for Jehoshaphat, 2.01 for Jehu, 1.98 for Ahab, 1.93 for Jehoram of Israel, 1.87 for Samuel, 1.83 for Absalom, 1.71 for Josiah, 1.63 for Joseph, 1.58 for Jehoiachin, 1.52 for Samson, 1.52 for Elijah, 1.39 for Asa, 1.32 for Daniel, 1.30 for Noah, 1.22 for Ezra (0.72 compared with the Septuagint), 1.20 for Abraham, 1.17 for Moses, 1.11 for Elisha, 1.08 for Jacob, 1.04 for Isaac, 0.97 for Hezekiah, 0.94 for Jephthah, 0.91 for Manasseh, 0.90 for Gideon, 0.79 for Joshua, 0.67 for Jonah, 0.63 for Deborah, 0.62 for Aaron, and 0.24 for Nehemiah (0.18 compared with the Septuagint). In the case of Jethro, the Bible devotes fifty-six lines (Exod 2:16-21 [8 lines] and 18:1-27 [forty-eight lines]) to him; Josephus devotes 121 lines (*Ant.* 2.11.1–12.1 §257-264 and 3.3.1–4.2 §63-74), giving a ratio of 2.16 for Josephus in relation to the Hebrew, and 1.68 in relation to the Septuagint. This shows that for Josephus Jethro, like another non-Jew, Balaam, is definitely one of the more important biblical personalities.

---

[1]   For the Hebrew I have used the standard edition of the biblical text with the commentary of M. L. Malbim (New York: Friedman, s.a.). For the Septuagint I have used the text edited by A. Rahlfs, *Septuaginta*, vol. 1 (Stuttgart: Württembergische Bibelanstalt, 1935). For Josephus I have used the Loeb Classical Library text edited by H. St. J. Thackeray, *Josephus IV* (LCL 242; London: Heinemann; Cambridge: Harvard University Press, 1930).

THE TREATMENT OF JETHRO IN OTHER ANCIENT SOURCES[2]

It would appear that in antiquity there was a sharp difference of opinion in the evaluation of the personality of Jethro. There were those who elevated him, notably Demetrius, Artapanus, Ezekiel the tragedian, and Josephus; and those who basically denigrated him, notably Philo the philosopher; there were those who were divided on the issue, notably in the rabbinic tradition; and those who ignored him, notably the writers in the Apocrypha and Pseudepigrapha.

Demetrius, a chronographer, who apparently lived in Egypt during the latter half of the third century BCE,[3] notes (*ap.* Eusebius, *Praeparatio Evangelica* 9.29.1), in his summary of Exodus 2:15-21, that Moses fled to Midian, where he was married to Zipporah, the daughter of Jethro ('Ιοθώρ), whom he identifies as the son of Raguel. The fact that he then traces the ancestry of Jethro back to Abraham, through the latter's marriage to Keturah, clearly elevates the status of Jethro. It would also resolve the embarrassing problem of Moses' apparent intermarriage with Zipporah, a Midianite, since it turns out that both Moses and Zipporah are directly descended from Abraham. It will be recalled that the historian Cleodemus-Malchus, who apparently lived at some time between 200 BCE and 50 BCE,[4] likewise proudly reports that through Abraham's marriage with Keturah a son was born, whose daughter was married to the greatest Greek hero, Heracles (*ap.* Josephus, *Ant.* 1.15 §240-241). Moreover, the fact that Jethro is mentioned by Demetrius as the son of Raguel solves the problem of his name in the Book of Exodus, where it is first given in the Septuagint at Exod 2:16 (the Hebrew text does not give his name at this point), clearly Demetrius' source, as Jethro ('Ιοθώρ), and then (Exod 2:18) as Raguel ('Ραγουήλ; Hebrew Reuel). It also solves the problem of the apparent identity of Jethro with Hobab (LXX 'Ιωβάρ), who in Judg 4:11 is referred to as the

---

2   There has been no comprehensive treatment of the role of Jethro in ancient sources. J. R. Baskin (*Pharaoh's Counsellors: Job, Jethro, and Balaam in Rabbinic and Patristic Tradition* [Chico: Scholars Press, 1983] 45-74) discusses at some length his portrayal in rabbinic and patristic literature, while dealing only briefly with Philo (pp. 62-65) and Josephus (pp. 65-66). She does not mention at all the treatment of Jethro by the writers Demetrius, Artapanus, and Ezekiel.

3   So C. R. Holladay, *Fragments from Hellenistic Jewish Authors*, vol. 1: *Historians* (Chico: Scholars Press, 1983) 51-52.

4   So Holladay, *Fragments*, 246.

father-in-law of Moses, since Demetrius there says that Hobab was
the son of Raguel.

Perhaps a century after Demetrius, the historian Artapanus (*ap.*
Eusebius, *Praeparatio Evangelica* 9.27.19)[5] likewise aggrandizes
Jethro by referring to him as the chief (ἄρχων) of the region even
though the Bible (Exod 2:16) identifies him merely as "the priest of
Midian." In view of the apologetic nature of much of Artapanus'
work, it should not be surprising that he adds the extra-biblical detail
that Jethro, to whom he refers as Raguel, wanted to wage war against
the Egyptians in order to conquer the throne for his daughter and
son-in-law. Such a remark would clearly raise Jethro's stature in the
eyes of Jewish readers, who would feel grateful to him for his
concern. When, according to Artapanus, Moses declined to join in
this plan because of his regard for his own people, who presumably
would have been accused of lacking patriotism since one of their
number was waging war against the country where they were living,
Raguel ordered the Arabs to plunder Egypt.[6]

Ezekiel, the author of the tragedy *The Exodus*, dating from
perhaps the second century BCE,[7] considerably enhances the status of
Jethro. In one of the fragments (*ap.* Eusebius, *Praeparatio Evangelica* 9.28.4b) his daughter Zipporah refers to him as chief (ἄρχων) of
the state, as had Artapanus. Far from being merely a priest he is
called both ruler (τύραννος) and general (στρατηλάτης). He not
only rules (ἄρχει) but also judges (κρίνει) the people (the latter
attribute arises presumably from the fact that it is Jethro who gives
Moses advice as to how to set up a judicial system). Moreover,
Ezekiel (*ap.* Eusebius, *Praeparatio Evangelica* 9.29.4) truly glorifies
Jethro by presenting him in the role of interpreter of Moses' dream.

---

[5]   Artapanus' date is apparently somewhere between the middle of the third
and the middle of the second century BCE. See Holladay, *Fragments*, 189-90.
There is considerable debate among scholars, as Holladay (p. 189) remarks, as to
whether he was Jewish or pagan, with most concluding that he was Jewish, despite
the religious syncretism in much of his work.

[6]   There is some question as to the meaning of Artapanus' Greek here. For
alternate translations, see Holladay, *Fragments*, 238 n. 77.

[7]   This is the conclusion of the most exhaustive treatment of this playwright;
see H. Jacobson, *The Exagoge of Ezekiel* (Cambridge: Cambridge University
Press, 1983) 5-13, as well as of the most recent extensive discussion, that by C. R.
Holladay, *Fragments from Hellenistic Jewish Authors*, vol. 2: *Poets* (Atlanta:
Scholars Press, 1989) 308-12.

As Jacobson notes,[8] this is most remarkable, inasmuch as nowhere in the Bible do we find a non-Jew interpreting a dream for a Jew, but rather the reverse, as in the case of the dreams of Pharaoh and of Nebuchadnezzar. Furthermore, the fact that Jethro is able to interpret the dream without any mention of divine help offers a considerable contrast to the description of Joseph's and Daniel's actions. Jethro's announcement that the dream signifies that Moses will judge and lead mankind and it shall be given to him to see present, past, and future, is, of course, a tremendous compliment to Moses, but it also glorifies the interpreter for being able to perceive this. This portrayal of Jethro as ruler and interpreter of dreams, in effect, presents him in the image of Joseph, especially as elaborated by Josephus.[9] The fact that Jethro is portrayed as a military leader makes him a kind of Moses, as described in the Bible and especially as elaborated by Josephus.[10] The notion of a priest-ruler is surely reminiscent of the role of the Hasmonean priest-rulers, notably Simon and John Hyrcanus, as well as the mysterious Melchizedek (Gen 14:8).

What is striking in Philo's portrait of Jethro is that it is almost completely negative,[11] presumably because of his Midianite origin. The most severe criticism that Philo, the Platonist, can make of anyone is that he prefers appearances to actualities, conceit to truth. This is precisely the charge he makes against Jethro (*De Agricultura* 10.43), deriving these traits of character from the very name Jethro, which he says means "uneven" (περισσός).[12] Jethro, consequently,

---

8   Jacobson, *The Exagoge*, 92. Jacobson (pp. 37-38) notes several narrative details in which Josephus is similar to Ezekiel and concludes that he was familiar with the latter's play. Though the *argumentum ex silentio* is never conclusive, one must, however, express surprise, if Josephus did know the work of Ezekiel, that he does not mention Moses' dream and the interpretation by Jethro, especially in view of Josephus' great interest in dreams. See my "Josephus' Portrait of Joseph," *RB* 99 (1992) 394-400.

9   See my "Josephus' Portrait of Joseph," 379-417, 504-28.

10   See my "Josephus' Portrait of Moses," *JQR* 83 (1992-93) 13-28.

11   Baskin (*Pharaoh's Counsellors*, 62) notes only the unfavorable comments about Jethro in Philo; she neglects to cite *De Specialibus Legibus* 4.33.173-174, which speaks of the excellent (ἄριστα) and useful (συμφέροντα) advice given to Moses by Jethro.

12   This is the most common epithet applied to Jethro. Its meaning is "super-fluous" or "over-wise." F. H. Colson (*Philo II* [LCL 227; London: Heinemann; Cambridge: Harvard University Press, 1929]) translates it as "worldling" in *De*

stands for wavering and inconsistency. Jethro, he says (*De Mutatione Nominum* 17.104), "values the human above the divine, custom above laws, profane above sacred, mortal above immortal, and in general seeming above being." It is hard to imagine a more devastating attack, coming as it does from a Platonist. Again, he declares (*De Ebrietate* 10.36) that Jethro corresponds to a "commonwealth peopled by a promiscuous horde, who swing to and fro as their idle opinions carry them." He declares (*ibid.*) that the mythical Proteus, constantly changing form as he did, is most clearly typified by Jethro, who bows to the opinions of the multitude and will undergo any manner of transformation in order to conform with the ever-varying aspirations of human life. To a Platonist this is well nigh the ultimate sin.

Indeed, Philo (*De Mutatione Nominum* 17.104) completely perverts the biblical account of Jethro's visit to Moses. It is almost as if Philo's text of the Bible ended with the statement, "What you are doing is not good" (Exod 18:17). According to Philo, Jethro suggests to Moses that "he should not teach the only thing worth learning, the ordinances of God and the law, but the contracts which men make with each other, which as a rule produce dealings where the partners have no real partnership." He is accused of trying to convince Moses "to give great justice to the great, and small justice to the small." Rather than praise Jethro for giving such excellent advice to Moses, Philo describes him here (*De Mutatione Nominum* 17.105) and elsewhere (*De Ebrietate* 10.37) as "seemingly wise" (δοκησίσοφος) and as being actually concerned with little else than things human and corruptible. In enumerating four classes of children—those who obey both parents, those who obey neither, those who obey only the father (that is, right reason), and those who obey only the mother (that is, mere variable and unstable convention)—Philo says (*De Ebrietate* 9.35–10.36) that the last class, which, he explains, symbolizes those who bow to the opinions of the masses, is most clearly represented by Jethro. Indeed, Jethro, who in the Bible is depicted as dispensing excellent advice to Moses on how to administer his

---

Sacrificiis Abelis et Caini 12.50 and as "worldly-wise" in *De Gigantibus* 11.50. G. H. Whitaker (*Philo III* [LCL 247; London: Heinemann; Cambridge: Harvard University Press, 1930]) translates it as "uneven" in *De Agricultura* 10.43. Colson (*Philo V* [LCL 275; London: Heinemann; Cambridge: Harvard University Press, 1934]) renders it as "superfluous" in *De Mutatione Nominum* 17.103.

judicial system (Exod 18:17-23), is described by Philo (*De Mutatione Nominum* 19.110) as having seven daughters who represent the unreasoning element. When he condemns Jethro (*De Ebrietate* 10.37) as playing the demagogue, Philo undoubtedly has in mind Plato's allegory of the ship (*Republic* 6.488). Instead of welcoming Jethro's statement (Exod 18:11), "Now I know that the Lord is greater than all gods," Philo (*De Ebrietate* 11.41-45) vehemently condemns Jethro as a blasphemer, because the word "now" implies that he had never previously understood the greatness of God, and because he dares to compare God with other deities.

And yet, Philo is not completely negative in his portrayal of Jethro. We do see a favorable side of Jethro in the gratitude that he exhibits toward Moses for having aided his daughters whom the shepherds drove away when they were drawing water at the well. Indeed, Philo (*De Vita Mosis* 1.11.58-59) elaborates considerably on the scene. Jethro shows real exasperation that his daughters did not bring the stranger home so that he might be thanked for his kindness. "Run back," he tells them, "with all speed, and invite him to receive from me first the entertainment due to him as a stranger, secondly some requital of the favor which we owe to him." This overwhelming concern with showing hospitality to the stranger would surely have endeared Jethro to a Greek audience that worshipped Ζεὺς Ξένιος.

Again, in the treatise *De Specialibus Legibus* (4.33.173-174), Philo compliments Jethro for having given Moses excellent advice (ἄριστα συνεβούλευσεν) which was useful (συμφέροντα), namely to choose judges to adjudicate less important matters while attending to more important issues and thus giving himself time to rest. But this is secondary: in particular, we may note that Philo nowhere refers to Jethro as a proselyte to Judaism, as do the rabbis. In any case, the two sides of Moses' father-in-law may be reflected in his two names: Jethro having negative associations and Reuel (Raguel), meaning "the shepherding of God" (*De Mutatione Nominum* 17.105), evoking positive associations.

We may well wonder why in his *Biblical Antiquities* Pseudo-Philo does not mention Jethro at all, especially since he does ascribe to Miriam an extra-biblical prophetic dream (9:10). Perhaps this omission may be explained as arising from Pseudo-Philo's polemic against intermarriage (viz. Moses' marriage with the Midianite Zipporah [Exod 2:21] and with the nameless Ethiopian woman [Num

12:1]). This can be seen, for example, in his extra-biblical statement that Tamar's intent in having relations with Judah was to prevent her being joined with Gentiles (9:5), in his stressing on the incident of the Midianite women (and we must not forget that Jethro was a priest of Midian) who led the Israelite youths astray (18:13-14), and in the unique detail that the Levite's concubine of Judg 19:25 had transgressed against her husband by having relations with foreigners (45:3).

Unlike Philo, the rabbis were, on the whole, positively inclined toward Jethro, presumably because they found it hard to believe that Moses, the greatest prophet of Israel ever (Deut 34:10), would associate with anyone of less than high repute and, in fact, would marry the daughter of an idol-worshipper.[13] In fact, the sheer volume of comments about him in rabbinic literature is a sure indication of his importance in their tradition.

The rabbis were apparently troubled by the fact that Jethro was a pagan priest; and, indeed, we find a debate (*Mek.* on Exod 18:1 [*Yitro* §1])[14] as to whether the term כֹהֵן as applied to him (Exod 2:16) indicates that he was a priest or, more neutrally, that he was a chief—an appellation that we have already noted in Artapanus and Ezekiel. According to one view, he counselled Pharoah to throw Israelite baby boys into the Nile River but later repented (*Exod. Rab.* 27.6 [on Exod 18:1]). Another tradition relates that Pharaoh had three advisers—Balaam, Job, and Jethro; Balaam advised Pharaoh to cast the Israelite babies into the river, Job was silent, and Jethro fled (*b. Sanh.* 106a). Tradition holds that because he refused to join in the scheme, his descendants were privileged to sit in the Sanhedrin. It is true that Jethro was viewed by some as an idolater of the worst sort, so much so that it is said that there was not an idol on earth that he had not worshipped (*Mek.* on Exod 18:11 [*Bešallaḥ* §1])[15] and that he permitted his daughter Zipporah to marry Moses only on condition that their first son would be raised to worship idols (*Mek.* on Exod 18:3 [*Yitro* §1]).[16] On the other hand, we hear that even before

---

13   On the rabbinic attitude toward Jethro, see B. J. Bamberger, *Proselytism in the Talmudic Period* (Cincinnati: Hebrew Union College, 1939) 182-91; and Baskin, *Pharaoh's Counsellors*, 47-61.

14   See *Mek.* on Exod 18:1 (*Amalek* §3) in J. Z. Lauterbach, *Mekilta de-Rabbi Ishmael* (3 vols., Philadelphia: Jewish Publication Society of America, 1933) 2.166.

15   See *Mek.* on Exod 18:11 (*Amalek* §3) in Lauterbach, *Mekilta*, 2.176.

16   See *Mek.* on Exod 18:3 (*Amalek* §3) in Lauterbach, *Mekilta*, 2.168.

Moses came to Midian Jethro was excommunicated by his neighbors for giving up his idolatry (*Exod. Rab.* 1.32 [on Exod 2:15]).

The tradition is similarly divided in commenting on the reaction of Jethro to the miracles performed by God. One view, transmitted by the third-century Amora Rav, holds that he actually became a proselyte to Judaism (*Tanḥ.* B Exodus §71); that he became in fact a proselyte even before Moses came to his home (*Exod. Rab.* 1.32 [on Exod 2:15]). Indeed, he becomes the prototype of a proselyte (*Mišnat Rabbi Eliezer*);[17] and the very change of his name from Jether to Jethro ("enlarges") is cited to illustrate God's love for proselytes. In striking contrast to Esau, who though born of Israelite parents chose to abandon his ancestral beliefs, Jethro, although born a non-Jew, chose a life of piety (*Exod. Rab.* 27.2 [on Exod 18:1]). The fact that Jethro left his comfortable home in order to meet Moses in the desert, in the eyes of the rabbis (*Mek.* on Exod 18:1 [*Yitro* §1]),[18] proves his sincerity to go to any lengths in order to become a convert.[19] The other view, expressed by Rav's contemporary Samuel, holds that he felt sympathetic for the sufferings of the Egyptians (*b. Sanh.* 94a), and that he converted to Judaism only after he had heard what had happened to Amalek (*Exod. Rab.* 27.6 [on Exod 18:1]).

Jethro is so highly regarded that, according to one tradition (*Mek.* on Exod 18:1 [*Yitro* §1]),[20] the very Presence (*Shekhinah*) of God greeted Jethro when he came to visit Moses, and he was "taken under the wings of the Shekhinah"—another indication that Jethro became a convert, since this is the traditional term for conversion. One factor in the recognition of Jethro as a proselyte was apparently the concern that a non-Jew should have been responsible for the reorganization of the Jewish judicial system. The rabbis explain that Moses gave credit to Jethro for his advice (*Sifre Num.* §78 [on Num 10:29-36]),

---

17   See H. G. Enelow, *The Mishnah of Rabbi Eliezer or the Midrash of Thirty-Two Hermeneutic Rules* (New York: Bloch, 1933) 304.

18   See *Mek.* on Exod 18:1 (*Amalek* §3) in Lauterbach, *Mekilta*, 2.172.

19   Baskin (*Pharaoh's Counsellors*, 74), after surveying the evidence with regard to the treatment of Jethro in the writings of the Church Fathers, concludes that, aside from Aphraates and Cyril of Alexandria, Jethro remains a virtual nonentity in Christian exegesis. We may suggest that one reason for this neglect was that the Fathers may have been aware of the rabbinic tradition that Jethro became a proselyte to Mosaic Judaism, a type of Judaism which Christianity claimed to supersede.

20   See *Mek.* on Exod 18:1 (*Amalek* §3) in Lauterbach, *Mekilta*, 2.173.

although the changes had actually been commanded by God, in order
to give merit as a convert (*Sifre Num.* §80 [on Num 10:29-36]) to
Jethro and to his descendants and in order to enhance the status of
Jethro in the eyes of Moses and all Israel (*Mišnat Rabbi Eliezer*).[21]
Indeed, the fact that Jethro blessed God (Exod 18:10) shows him to
be superior to Moses and the rest of the Israelites who had failed to
bless Him before Jethro arrived. There is even a view that it was
Jethro who was responsible for the revelation of the Torah in its
complete form. God was afraid that after Jethro had been responsible
for the reorganization of the judicial system, the Israelites might
think that it was he who was the source of their whole system of law
(*Pesiq. R. Kah.* 12.11).

There is likewise a difference of opinion as to the reason for
Jethro's departure from Moses. On the one hand, the view is
expressed that Moses dismissed Jethro because he did not want him, a
non-Jew, to be present at the moment of revelation at Sinai (*Tanḥ.* B,
Exodus §75); on the other hand, we have the view justifying Jethro's
departure so that he might spread the knowledge of monotheism
among his fellow Midianites (*Tanḥ.* B, Exodus §73; *Mek.* on Exod
18:27 [*Yitro* §2]).[22] In effect, the contradictory views about Jethro
parallel the divergent views of the rabbis with regard to the
reception of proselytes. Side by side with the prevalent attitude of
welcoming them[23] was the view of those, who like Rabbi Ḥelbo
regarded them as being as injurious to Israel as a scab (*b. Qidd.*
70b).

JETHRO'S QUALITIES OF CHARACTER, ACCORDING TO JOSEPHUS

One of the charges most frequently raised against Jews in the
writings of pagan intellectuals is that they hate non-Jews. Even
Hecataeus (*ap.* Diodorus 40.3.4), who is otherwise well disposed
toward the Jews, describes the Jewish way of life as "somewhat
unsocial" (ἀπάνθρωπόν τινα) and hostile to foreigners (μισόξενον).
The Alexandrian Lysimachus (probably first century BCE) reflects
such a charge when he says that Moses instructed the Israelites "to

---

21   See Enelow, *The Mishnah of Rabbi Eliezer*, 304.

22   See *Mek.* on Exod 18:27 (*Amalek* §4) in Lauterbach, *Mekilta*, 2.186.

23   See especially Bamberger, *Proselytism in the Talmudic Period*; and W. G.
Braude, *Jewish Proselyting in the First Five Centuries of the Common Era: The
Age of the Tannaim and Amoraim* (Providence: Brown University, 1940).

show goodwill to no man, to offer not the best but the worst advice and to overthrow any temples and altars of gods which they found" (*ap*. Josephus, *Against Apion* 1.34 §309). Tacitus remarks that while the Jews are extremely loyal to one another and always ready to show compassion to their compatriots alone, they feel only hate and enmity toward all other peoples (*Hist.* 5.5.1). Juvenal goes so far as to attack the Jews for not showing the way or pointing out a well to anyone but a fellow Jew (*Satires* 14.103-104). According to Josephus' addition (*Ant.* 11.6.5 §212), Haman charges that the Jews refuse to mingle with others, are unsocial, and are by custom and practice the enemy of the Persians and, indeed, of all mankind.

Josephus, in his portrait of Jethro the non-Jew, is particularly eager to answer the charge that Jews hate non-Jews. Unlike Philo and the rabbis, who are, as we have seen, divided in their views of Jethro, Josephus presents a uniformly favorable picture of him. In the first place, when the reader is introduced to him, Jethro is described as a priest held in high veneration (πολλῆς ἠξιωμένου τιμῆς) by the people of the country (*Ant.* 2.11.2 §258). This is presumably intended to counteract the implication of the biblical text that the shepherds drove away Jethro's daughters (Exod 2:17), which, we may assume, they would not have done if they had had respect for Jethro himself. It would also counter the idea found in the rabbinic tradition, if, as seems likely, Josephus was acquainted with at least some of it,[24] that Jethro was *persona non grata* among his neighbors and was even excommunicated for giving up his idolatry. Again, when Jethro comes to Moses to congratulate him upon his victory over Amalek, the Bible states that he came accompanied by his wife and her sons (Exod 18:5); Josephus, seeking to build up the stature of Jethro, has him come alone so as to focus the spotlight upon him (*Ant.* 3.3.1 §63).

One of the cardinal virtues in antiquity and, indeed, the central theme of Plato's most influential work, *The Republic*, is justice, foremost in respect to humanity (φιλανθρωπία).[25] Connected with the quality of φιλανθρωπία is the virtue of showing gratitude, in

---

24 See my "Josephus' Portrait of Asa," *BBR* 4 (1994) 43-44 n. 5.

25 See Philo, *De Mutatione Nominum* 40. 225; *De Vita Mosis* 2.2.9; *De Decalogo* 30.164; and the discussion by H. A. Wolfson, *Philo, Foundations of Religious Philosophy in Judaism, Christianity, and Islam*, vol. 2 (Cambridge: Harvard University Press, 1947) 220 n. 146.

accordance with the definition of justice as rendering every man his due (Plato, *Republic* 1.332A). Thus Moses, in an extra-biblical addition, shows the way to exhibit gratitude in the manner in which he rewards the valiant soldiers after their victory over Amalek (*Ant.* 3.2.5 §59). Again, in his last speech to the people, in a supplement to the Bible (Deuteronomy 32), Moses renders personal thanks to God for the care which He had bestowed upon them, for the help which He had given him in his struggles, and for the graciousness which He had shown to him (*Ant.* 4.8.47 §315-316). Likewise, in his portrait of David, Josephus elaborates on the concern which David shows for the remnant of the house of Saul (2 Sam 9:1), adding, in particular, that besides all the other qualities that he possessed was the virtue of being ever mindful of those who had benefited him at any time (*Ant.* 7.5.5 §111).[26] Likewise, in reference to Jehoshaphat, while there is no indication in the Bible (2 Chr 19:4) that he expressed gratitude to God after he had managed to survive the rout of his forces by the Syrians, Josephus specifically declares that Jehoshaphat thereupon betook himself to giving thanks and offering sacrifices to God (*Ant.* 9.1.1 §2).

In the case of Jethro, Josephus elaborates considerably on the scene in which Jethro is represented as saying to his daughters after they tell him how Moses had delivered them from the shepherds and had drawn water for them (*Ant.* 2.11.2 §261), "Where is he? Why have you left the man? Call him, that he may eat bread" (Exod 2:20). In Josephus' version the shepherds' insolence (ὕβριν) is spelled out as such, as is Moses' beneficence (εὐεργετηθεῖσαι); and Jethro specifically bids his daughters not to allow such benevolence (εὐποιίαν) to be in vain or go unrewarded and to bring Moses to him so as to receive the gratitude (χάριτος) that was his due. He commends his daughters for their zeal (σπουδῆς) for their benefactor (εὐεργετη-κότα). In the Bible there is no statement that Jethro actually thanked Moses; we are merely told that Moses was content to dwell with Jethro (Exod 2:21). In contrast, in *Ant.* 2.11.2 §262 Jethro tells Moses, upon the latter's arrival, that his daughters informed him of the help which he had rendered and expresses admiration for his gallantry (ἀρετῆς). He adds that he did not bestow these meritorious services (ἀναισθήτους εὐεργεσιῶν) upon people who had no sense of gratitude but rather on persons well able to requite a favor,

---

26   See my "Josephus' Portrait of David," *HUCA* 60 (1989) 153-54.

"indeed to outdo by the amplitude of the reward the measure of the benefit." In fact, in a startling addition to the biblical text, Jethro (*Ant.* 2.11.2 §263) even adopts Moses as his son.[27] The key point is that while Jethro is actually identified as a barbarian; Josephus clearly emphasizes that far from being prejudiced against barbarians, Israel's greatest leader Moses actually married a barbarian and that he was even adopted by a barbarian. In terms of the startling impact upon a reader only the marriage of Alexander the Great with a Persian princess would be comparable. We may also add that not only does Jethro show gratitude but he appreciates it when others show it. Thus we are told that when he meets Moses he heaps eulogies upon the Israelites for their gratitude (εὐχαριστία) to Moses.

We may well ask what was the motive and what was the setting for Jethro's visit to Moses (Exod 18:1). In the Bible this comes immediately after the description of the Israelites' victory over the Amalekites (Exod 17:8-16); and we are told that Jethro heard of all that God had done for Moses and for Israel and, in particular, how God had brought the Israelites out of Egypt (Exod 18:1). In the rabbinic tradition there is a debate as to exactly when Jethro came to congratulate Moses (*b. Zebah.* 116a). Rabbi Joshua ben Hananiah, adhering to the order of events in the biblical text, expresses the view that Jethro heard of the battle with the Amalekites, which is mentioned immediately before this passage, as we have noted. Rabbi Eleazar ben Pedath opines that he heard of the miraculous dividing of the Red Sea, since the passage refers to God's leading the Israelites out of Egypt. Rabbi Eleazar of Modin maintains that Jethro heard of the giving of the Torah at Mount Sinai. The last view is clearly the most difficult to sustain, inasmuch as the account of the revelation at Sinai is reported only after Jethro's visit (Exodus 19–20), though it is perhaps alluded to in the statement that Jethro came to Moses in the wilderness, where Moses was encamped at the mountain of God (Exod 18:5). Significantly, in his effort to build up the stature of Jethro, Josephus goes out of his way and out of the biblical order in

---

27 S. Rappaport (*Agada and Exegese bei Flavius Josephus* [Vienna: Alexander Kohut Memorial Foundation, 1930] 100-101) notes that elsewhere (*Ant.* 1.7.1 §154) Josephus states that Abraham adopted Lot and that neither this adoption nor that by Jethro is mentioned in the Bible. He suggests that perhaps Josephus took over into the Bible an institution known from Rome.

prefacing the visit of Jethro with the remark that the Israelites had
reached Mount Sinai (*Ant.* 3.2.5 §62). This gives a more important
setting for the visit, since it puts Jethro in immediate juxtaposition
with the central event in Israelite history and makes of his visit more
than a mere congratulation for military victory. Likewise, whereas
the Bible says nothing about the feast which Moses arranged in honor
of his father-in-law, Josephus not only does so but adds further
honor to Jethro by remarking that the feast took place near the very
site where Moses had seen the burning bush (*Ant.* 3.3.1 §63).

One of the most delicate problems for Josephus must have been
how to deal with the scene in which Jethro criticizes the way in
which Moses had been administering justice (Exod 18:14). In the
Bible Jethro's criticism is blunt: "What is this that you are doing for
the people? Why do you sit alone?" Such criticism must have been
disconcerting for Moses, especially since there is no indication in the
biblical text that Jethro took Moses aside so as to avoid embarrassing
him in the presence of the Israelites. On the other hand, in Josephus'
version Jethro shows real sensitivity so as to avoid embarrassing his
son-in-law (*Ant.* 3.4.1 §67). We are told that when he sees the way
Moses administers affairs he holds his peace (ἡσυχίαν ἦγε; "kept
quiet") at the moment (τότε), reluctant to bar anyone from availing
himself of the talents of their chief. It is only after the tumult of the
crowd has subsided that he discreetly takes Moses aside and instructs
him in utter privacy (συμμονωθείς; "be alone in private with someone") what should be done.

THE ATTITUDE OF JETHRO THE NON-JEW TOWARD JEWS

In view of the frequent negative statements on the part of non-Jews
toward Jews, particularly with regard to theology, circumcision, the
Sabbath, dietary laws, credulity, begging, and alleged Jewish influence,[28] Josephus was particularly eager, notably in the essay *Against
Apion*, to demonstrate that there were famous non-Jews who appre-
ciated the virtues of the Jews in the realms of wisdom, courage,
temperance, and justice.[29]

Hence, we see a significant change in Josephus' account of Jethro's

---

[28]   See my *Jew and Gentile in the Ancient World* (Princeton: Princeton University Press, 1993) 149-76.

[29]   See my "Philo-Semitism among Ancient Intellectuals," *Tradition* 1 (1958-
59) 27-39.

meeting with Moses (*Ant.* 3.3.1 §63; cf. Exod 18:5). Whereas in the biblical version we read only that Jethro came with Moses' sons and his wife to Moses and are told nothing of his feelings in meeting his son-in-law, Josephus remarks that Raguel (i.e. Jethro) went with gladness (ἀσμένως; "with pleasure") and that he welcomed (δεχόμενος) Moses. One would have expected that since Jethro was visiting Moses it would be Moses who would go out to greet Jethro; and, indeed, this is what we find in the biblical text. There we are told that Moses went out to meet his father-in-law and did obeisance to him and kissed him (Exod 18:7). In Josephus' version, however, we are told that Moses rejoiced at the visit of his father-in-law, but there is no description of Moses actually greeting Jethro, and the stress is placed on Jethro's acknowledgment of the greatness of Moses.

THE ROLE OF GOD IN THE JETHRO NARRATIVE

Josephus states in his prooemium (*Ant.* proem 3 §14) that the chief lesson to be derived from a perusal of his history is that God rewards those who obey his laws and punishes those who do not. Because he presumably aimed primarily at a non-Jewish audience (*Ant.* proem 2 §5; 2 §9; 20.12.1 §262),[30] Josephus approaches the Bible as history rather than as theology, reserving the latter subject for a separate work (*Ant.* proem 4 §25; 1.10.5 §192; 3.5.6 §94; 3.6.6 §143; 4.8.4 §198; 20.12.1 §268) which he apparently was never able to complete.[31] Indeed, we may cite numerous instances of his paraphrase of the Bible, where he omits appeals to God, as for example, in Abraham's address to Isaac (*Ant.* 1.13.3 §228-231). Moreover, he omits mention of God in Jacob's angry exchange with Rachel (Gen 30:1-2; *Ant.* 1.19.7 §303) and in Rachel's statement

---

30   See my "Use, Authority and Exegesis of Mikra in the Writings of Josephus," in M. J. Mulder and H. Sysling (eds.), *Mikra: Text, Translation, Reading and Interpretation of the Hebrew Bible in Ancient Judaism and Early Christianity* (CRINT 2.1; Assen: Van Gorcum; Philadelphia: Fortress, 1988) 470-71.

31   H. Petersen ("Real and Alleged Literary Projects of Josephus," *American Journal of Philology* 79 [1958] 259-74) contends that we have all of Josephus' proposed works and that most of the references are to *Against Apion*. But while *Against Apion* does contain a discussion of the nature of God (2.19 §180; 2.22 §188-192; 2.23 §197) and of the Jewish code of laws (2.14–21 §145-187, etc.), this discussion is brief and, in any case, is not the central theme of that work. In the *Antiquities* (see especially 4.8.4 §198) we are told that the work is to be about these subjects.

(Gen 30:23; *Ant.* 1.19.7 §308) after she has given birth to Joseph. There is likewise a de-emphasis of the role of God in Josephus' version of the story of Joseph and Potiphar's wife (Gen 39:9; *Ant.* 2.4.2 §42-43). The most striking example of the diminution of the role of God may be seen in his version of the Ruth pericope. Whereas the biblical account refers to Him seventeen times, Josephus mentions God only at the very end of the episode (*Ant.* 5.9.1–9.4 §318-336).

In the case of Jethro, the biblical narrative six times mentions God (Exod 18:1 [*bis*], 9, 10, 11, 12) in noting what God had done for Moses and for the Israelites and in indicating Jethro's sacrifice of thanksgiving to God for these successes. Josephus, on the other hand, omits totally Jethro's rejoicing for all the good which God had done to Israel and his blessing God for delivering the Israelites from the Egyptians (*Ant.* 3.3.1 §63; cf. Exod 18:9-10). Indeed, Jethro speaks not of God's but of Moses' success, and he expresses admiration for Moses for the gallantry (ἀνδραγαθίας) which he had displayed in the salvation of his friends (*Ant.* 3.3.1 §65). Likewise, when Aaron and his company get Jethro to join them, they sing the praises of their general, Moses (*Ant.* 3.3.1 §64), whereas in the Bible Jethro blesses God (Exod 18:10).

Again, in the biblical version, where Jethro gives his counsel to Moses as to how to administer justice, he mentions God no fewer than three times within a single verse: "God be with you! You shall represent the people before God, and bring their cases to God" (Exod 18:19). He then tells Moses to choose men such as fear God as his subordinate judges (Exod 18:21). Indeed, lest the reader think that it is Jethro, the non-Jew, who is advising Moses what to do, the biblical Jethro is very careful to state that Moses is do what Jethro advises only if God commands him to do so (Exod 18:23). In other words, Jethro's suggestions required divine sanction. In place of all this spiritual advice, which may well raise the question whether Jethro is not superior to Moses, at least with respect to the administration of justice, Josephus' Jethro counsels Moses to select capable (ἀγαθούς; "good") Hebrews (*Ant.* 3.4.1 §68). Later he recommends the appointment of upright and just persons (ἀγαθοὶ καὶ δίκαιοι: *Ant.* 3.4.1 §72) and he specifically limits his advice to mundane (ἀνθρωπίνων; "human," "worldly") matters (*Ant.* 3.4.1 §70).

Indeed, in what follows, it now appears that Jethro, the ruler experienced presumably in military affairs, who had begun by giving judicial advice, gives military advice to Moses, since he tells him how to draw up (ἐξετάσεις) his army and how to divide it into groups of ten thousands, thousands, five hundreds, hundreds, and fifties (*Ant.* 3.4.1 §70). This is a portrait of one general talking to another, and the result would surely add greater appeal to Josephus' military-minded Roman readers.[32] In place of the biblical statement in which Jethro, as we have seen, after giving his advice to Moses, expressly declares that Moses should do so only if God commands him thus (Exod 18:23), Jethro omits the giving of veto-power for the reorganization to God. Instead, by organizing his judicial and military systems thus, says Jethro, Moses will have more time to spend in gaining the favor of God for the army (*Ant.* 3.4.1 §72).

JETHRO THE NON-PROSELYTE

During the very period that Josephus lived there is good reason to believe that the Jews were notably successful in converting many to Judaism. If Baron is at all accurate in estimating the number of Jews in the world in 586 BCE at the time of the destruction of the First Temple at 150,000 and their number by the middle of the first century at eight million, during a period when apparently the number of the people in the world generally had not increased,[33] only through postulating a tremendous number of converts to Judaism can we account for the vast increase in the number of Jews. That the proselyting movement was very successful is indicated from numerous comments in such works as the *Letter of Aristeas* (266), the pseudepigraphic *Testament of Levi* (14:4), Philo (*De Vita Mosis* 2.5.27), the New Testament (Matt 23:15), Horace (*Satires* 1.4.142-143), Tacitus (*Hist.* 5.5.1), Juvenal (*Satires* 14.96-106), and rabbinic literature (*b. Pesaḥ.* 87b, *Sifre Deut.* §313 [on Deut 32:10]).[34] The Jews' success in winning converts arouses bitter resentment, as seen

---

32 See my "Josephus' Portrait of Moses," 13-28.

33 S. W. Baron, "Population," *EncJud* 13 (1971) 869; idem, *A Social and Religious History of the Jews*, vol. 1 (2nd ed., New York: Columbia University Press, 1952) 370-72 n. 7.

34 See my "Was Judaism a Missionary Religion in Ancient Times?" in M. Mor (ed.), *Jewish Assimilation, Acculturation and Accomodation: Past Traditions, Current Issues and Future Prospects* (Lanham: University Press of America, 1992) 24-37; and S. McKnight, *A Light Among the Gentiles: Jewish Missionary Activity in the Second Temple Period* (Minneapolis: Fortress, 1991).

for example, in the remark of Seneca (*ap.* Augustine, *De Civitate Dei* 6.1): "The vanquished have given laws to the victors" (*victi victoribus leges dederunt*). It is seen also in the statement of Tacitus (*Hist.* 5.5.1), who stresses the economic factor: "The worst among other peoples, renouncing their ancestral religions, always kept sending tribute and contributing to Jerusalem, thereby increasing the wealth of the Jews." The fact that on at least two occasions (139 BCE and 19 CE) the Jews were expelled from the city of Rome, apparently because of proselyting activities,[35] indicates how much resentment had been aroused by the Jews' success in winning converts. In fact, at the very time when Josephus wrote the *Jewish Antiquities*, during the reign of Domitian, the proselyting movement was successful in converting none other than the Emperor's own cousin, Flavius Clemens, and his wife (the Emperor's niece), Flavia Domitilla, as well as others who had "drifted" (ἐξοκέλλοντες) into the practices of the Jews (Dio Cassius 67.14).

Josephus was clearly aware that the Romans were sensitive to the great expansion of the Jewish population, especially through proselytism.[36] For example, when Isaac blesses Jacob before sending him off to find a wife, the Bible invokes God's blessing to "make them fruitful and multiply thee, that thou mayest become a multitude of people" (Gen 28:3). Josephus omits this (*Ant.* 1.19.1 §278).

In the Bible, as we have noted, when Moses tells Jethro all that the Lord has done to Pharaoh and the Egyptians, Jethro rejoices for all the good which God has done to Israel, he blesses God for having delivered them from the Egyptians, he declares that he now knows that the Lord is greater than all gods because of His saving the Israelites, he offers a sacrifice to God, and Aaron comes with all the elders to eat bread with him (Exod 18:8-12). What is striking in this brief passage is that Jethro is brought into immediate juxtaposition with the mention of God no fewer than six times. It is not surprising, consequently, according to rabbinic tradition, especially in view of Jethro's outright statement that the Lord is greater than all gods, that Jethro is represented as having become a proselyte to Judaism. Con-

---

[35] See my *Jew and Gentile in the Ancient World*, 300-304.

[36] If we ask why, if he was so sensitive to Roman feelings about proselytism, Josephus inserted the long pericope (*Ant.* 20.2.1–4.3 §17-96) describing the conversion to Judaism of the royal house of Adiabene, we may suggest that Adiabene was outside the Roman Empire and hence not of direct concern to the Romans.

sequently, in his sensitivity to the proselyting movement, Josephus quite carefully omits Jethro's statement about God's greatness.

Moreover, the biblical narrative actually states that Jethro offered a burnt offering and sacrifices to God (Exod 18:12), an act that would seem to indicate, as some of the rabbis noted above deduced, that he had come to accept the belief in the Israelite God. Josephus, sensitive to the Roman opposition to proselytism by Jews, has quite obviously made a deliberate change in having Moses offer the sacrifice (*Ant.* 3.3.1 §63).[37]

Furthermore, in distinct contrast to Jethro's outright taking the lead in his blessing of God in the Bible (Exod 18:10) and his offering of sacrifices to God (Exod 18:12) and in contrast to the clearly subordinate role of Aaron in merely coming with the Israelite elders to eat bread with Jethro (Exod 18:12), Josephus, in the apparent realization that such a role would, in effect, make Jethro a convert to Judaism, makes Aaron the prime mover in chanting hymns to God as the author and dispenser of salvation and liberty to the Israelites (*Ant.* 3.3.1 §64). Jethro's role is clearly subordinate; Aaron merely gets him to join him (προσλαβόμενος).

"IMPROVEMENTS" IN THE STORY:
CLARIFICATIONS, INCREASED SUSPENSE, AND DRAMA

One basic reason for Josephus' writing of a paraphrase of the Scripture was that he sought to clear up obscurities and apparent contradictions in the biblical text.[38] In the case of Jethro, the reader is befuddled by the fact that Jethro seems to be called by no fewer than seven names—Jethro (Exod 3:1), Jether (Exod 4:18), Putiel (Exod 6:25), Reuel (Num 2:18), Hobab (Num 10:29), Keni (Judg 1:16), and Heber (Judg 4:11).[39] Aware of this, Josephus regularly

---

37 Augustine (*Locutionum in Heptateuchum* 82) suggests that perhaps Jethro handed over the sacrifice to Moses so that the latter might offer it to God. But there is no hint of this in the text.

38 Thus, for example, the Bible declares that God told Adam that he would die on the day that he would eat from the tree of knowledge (Gen 2:17). The fact is, of course, that not only did Adam not die but he lived until the age of 930. Josephus (*Ant.* 1.1.4 §40) resolves the problem by simply omitting the phrase "on the day" and by generalizing that if they touched the tree it would prove the destruction of Adam and of Eve.

39 W. F. Albright ("Jethro, Hobab and Reuel in Early Hebrew Tradition," *CBQ* 25 [1963] 1-11) resolves the problem by asserting that Reuel (Num 10:29) is

calls him Raguel, but remarks (*Ant.* 2.12.1 §264) that his surname was Ietheglaeus, that is, Jethro.

One means by which Josephus seeks to "improve" upon the biblical narrative is through providing better motivation and through increasing the plausibility of events.[40] We see an example of this in connection with Jehu. Whereas in the Bible we are not told why Jehu sent letters to the rulers of Samaria (2 Kgs 10:1-3), and we must conjecture as to the motive from the result, Josephus spells out the motive, telling us that Jehu sent these letters because he wished to test the feelings of the Samaritans toward himself—a wise move, indeed, because if they had not been well disposed toward him he would have had to plan a military campaign against them (*Ant.* 9.6.5 §126). In connection with Moses and Jethro, there is an improbability in the biblical text in that Moses asks Jethro for permission to return to Egypt even though he does not yet know (until the following verse) whether those who are seeking him are still alive (Exod 4:18). In Josephus' version the setting is more reasonable: it is only after learning that the Pharaoh from whom he had fled is dead that Moses asks Jethro for permission to return to Egypt (*Ant.* 2.13.1 §277).

---

the clan name of Hobab. He notes that in the Septuagint text of Gen 25:3 it actually appears as the name of the clan affiliated with Midian.

40   Thus, whereas Manoah's desire in the Bible to recall the angel is not well motivated (Judg 13:8), Josephus' elaboration (*Ant.* 5.8.3 §280) makes it more plausible, for he has Manoah's wife entreat God to send the angel again so that her husband may see him and thus allay the suspicions arising from his jealousy of the angel. Similarly, in order to remove the implausibility of the narrative, Delilah in Josephus, full of feminine wiles, uses Samson's love for her as a weapon against him; thus she keeps saying to him that she takes it ill that he has so little confidence in her affection for him as to withhold from her what she desired to know, "as though," she adds with typical strategy, "she would not conceal what she knew must in his interests not be divulged" (*Ant.* 5.2.6 §130). Again, the reader of the biblical narrative might well ask how Mordecai was able to discover the conspiracy of Bigthan and Teresh against King Ahasuerus (Esth 2:22). Josephus offers a plausible explanation which is found in no other source, namely that the plot was discovered by a certain Jew, Barnabazos, the servant of one of the eunuchs, who, in turn, revealed it to Mordecai (*Ant.* 11.6.4 §207). Furthermore, the reader might well ask how Harbonah was able to learn about the gallows which Haman had prepared for Mordecai (Esth 7:8). Josephus explains this by noting that he had discovered this from one of Haman's servants when Harbonah had gone to summon him to Esther's second banquet (*Ant.* 11.6.11 §261 and §266).

SUMMARY

To judge from the amount of space that he devotes to him, like another non-Jewish biblical figure, Balaam, Jethro was clearly of great interest to Josephus. Prior to Josephus his personality had occasioned a great deal of controversy. On the one hand, such Hellenistic-Jewish writers as Demetrius, Artapanus, and Ezekiel the tragedian had elevated his stature. Others, notably Philo, had for the most part denigrated him. The rabbis were divided in their opinions. Still others, notably the writers of the books of the Apocrypha and the Pseudepigrapha, had chosen to ignore him.

In his portrait Josephus presents a uniformly favorable picture of Jethro. He is particularly concerned to answer the frequently heard charge that Jews hate non-Jews. In an addition to the biblical text Jethro is presented as a priest who is held in high veneration by the people of his country. Josephus heightens the gratitude which Jethro expresses to Moses for helping his daughters when they were driven away by the shepherds. Not only does he give his daughter Zipporah in marriage to Moses, but he, who is termed a barbarian by Josephus, actually adopts Moses as his son. He shows remarkable sensitivity in not criticizing Moses openly for his failure to delegate authority, but rather takes him aside and advises him in private in order to avoid embarrassing him in the presence of the Israelites. Again, in reply to the frequent criticisms of Jews by non-Jews in pagan literature, Josephus depicts Jethro as welcoming Moses with gladness. Whereas in the Bible Jethro blesses God for the Israelites' successes, in Josephus he expresses admiration for Moses for his gallantry. In contrast to the Bible, where, in counselling Moses, Jethro mentions God several times—a factor that might well raise a question as to whether Jethro may not have God's ear, so to speak, to a greater degree than Moses himself—, in Josephus he presents his advice in human terms. Again, whereas in the Bible Jethro tells Moses that he is to listen to his advice only if God sanctions it, in Josephus he limits his advice to mundane matters. Indeed, a good deal of the advice is presented in terms of a recommendation to Moses to reorganize his people militarily; and instead of seeking God's sanction for this reorganization we are told that by doing so Moses will have more time to spend seeking greater favor from God for his army.

A major problem that confronted Josephus was what to do with the biblical passage in which Jethro mentions God over and over again and even acknowledges that he now knows that God is greater than any other god. That this passage could be and was interpreted to indicate that Jethro actually became a proselyte to Judaism would have been a source of great embarrassment to Josephus in view of the sharp antagonism that had been caused by the success of the Jews in his day in converting so many non-Jews to Judaism. To have Jethro offer sacrifices to God, as he does in the Bible, would, in effect, have indicated his conversion to Judaism. So Josephus, quite delicately, has Moses offer the sacrifice. For the same reason Jethro is likewise subordinated to Aaron in chanting hymns to God.

Josephus avoids apparent contradictions, notably in the many names of Jethro. He likewise avoids improbabilities, particularly in Moses' asking Jethro for permission to return to Egypt when he actually does not yet know whether those who were seeking to kill him are still alive. Josephus' version explains that he makes his request because he has learned that the Pharaoh who was seeking to kill him has died.

THE SEVENTY-WEEKS PROPHECY (DANIEL 9:24-27)
IN EARLY JEWISH INTERPRETATION

Lester L. Grabbe

In the view of many, biblical interpretation is simply an intellectual exercise or, as it might be phrased, a spiritual exercise. Those who study social history can attest, however, that it can be much more than this. People do not just interpret the Bible—they may also act on their interpretation. From the Maccabean martyrs to the Branch Davidians of Waco, what one thinks the Bible is is a matter of life and death. Scholarship may once have been "astonied in the face of apocalyptic,"[1] but not thousands of believing Jews and Christians. Apocalypticism has been an important motivating religious and social force at various time in history, not only in Jewish and Christian cultures, though probably more so in these traditions than many people are aware. Some books appearing in the last few years have revealed the intense apocalyptic speculation among even (staid?) Englishmen in certain historical periods, such as the time of the Civil War.[2]

Those expecting the imminent end of the world may respond in two ways. One is rather passive: to leave it in God's hands, though this may entail neglect of the ordinary preoccupations of everyday life and perhaps even withdrawal from society altogether—those who grab their bag of beans and bucket of yoghurt and head for the hills. Another response is to assist in bringing about the end by active paramilitary means: demonstrations, rioting, terrorism, guerrilla

---

[1]   This is one way of putting Klaus Koch's famous phrase, "ratlos vor der Apokalyptik," into "biblical" English: K. Koch, *Ratlos vor der Apokalyptik* (Gütersloh: Mohn, 1970); ET: *Rediscovery of Apocalyptic* (SBT 22, 2nd series; London: SCM, 1970).

[2]   See, for example, B. W. Ball, *A Great Expectation: Eschatological Thought in English Protestantism to 1660* (Studies in the History of Christian Thought; Leiden: Brill, 1975); K. R. Firth, *The Apocalyptic Tradition in Reformation Britain 1530–1645* (Oxford University Press, 1979).

warfare. It is this latter which has the greatest consequences for history and society at large. Yet recently, in the heartland of America itself, we have seen those who combine the two: not engaging (yet) in paramilitary activity now but stoked to the gills in assault rifles, bayonets, and bazookas, and training like Cox's army because they think they are going to be attacked.

Such people, under the conviction of divine backing, have often appealed to the prophetic and apocalyptic literature of the Bible. There are many passages which could be and have been so interpreted, but most are fairly general. Only a few passages of the Old Testament seem to give sufficient data to calculate the endtime. One of the most important of these is Dan 9:24-27, hence its relevance for the study of religious activity based on the imminent expectation of the end. In this paper I am primarily concerned with its interpretation in pre-70 Judaism and the consequences of that interpretation. Not unexpectedly, most early Christian writers give a Christological interpretation, ending the 70 weeks with the coming of Jesus. Not all do, however, and some of those may have an originally Jewish exegesis at their base. We shall look at a few of these as well.

It is not my purpose to delve into an exact understanding of what was meant by the original oracle.[3] Suffice it to say here that it is generally assumed to have been written sometime during the period of the Maccabean revolt, after the cessation of the daily sacrifice about 168 BCE but before its resumption in about the year 165.[4] Whatever the original writer intended by the prophecy, it was sufficiently obscure and ambiguous to lend itself to a variety of later interpretations. I shall proceed in roughly chronological order, though the date of some interpretations and texts is uncertain.

THE SEPTUAGINT VERSION

Probably the earliest commentary we have on the prophecy is the

---

[3]   For the most recent treatment, see J. J. Collins, *Daniel* (Hermeneia; Minneapolis: Fortress, 1994). For my own arguments about the origins of the prophecy, see "'The End of the Desolations of Jerusalem': From Jeremiah's 70 Years to Daniel's 70 Weeks of Years," in C. A. Evans and W. F. Stinespring (eds.), *Early Jewish and Christian Exegesis: Studies in Memory of William Hugh Brownlee* (Homage 10; Atlanta: Scholars Press, 1987) 67-72.

[4]   For justification of this dating, see my "Maccabean Chronology: 167–164 or 168–165 BCE?" *JBL* 110 (1991) 59-74.

version in the Septuagint. Most manuscripts of the Greek Daniel have the later translation/revision attributed to Theodotion,[5] but what is probably the original LXX is now known from a few MSS. It differs widely from the MT in several places:

Greek	Hebrew
24ἑβδομήκοντα ἑβδομάδες ἐκρίθησαν	שָׁבְעִים שִׁבְעִים נֶחְתַּךְ 24
ἐπὶ τὸν λαόν σου καὶ ἐπὶ τὴν πόλιν Σιων	עַל־עַמְּךָ וְעַל־עִיר קָדְשֶׁךָ
συντελεσθῆναι τὴν ἁμαρτίαν καὶ τὰς ἀδικίας	לְכַלֵּא הַפֶּשַׁע וּלְחָתֵם
σπανίσαι καὶ ἀπαλεῖψαι τὰς ἀδικίας	חַטָּאות וּלְכַפֵּר עָוֹן
[καὶ διανοηθῆναι τὸ ὅραμα]	
καὶ δοθῆναι δικαιοσύνην αἰώνιον καὶ συντελεσθῆναι	וּלְהָבִיא צֶדֶק עֹלָמִים וְלַחְתֹּם
τὸ ὅραμα καὶ εὐφρᾶναι ἅγιον ἁγίων.	חָזוֹן וְנָבִיא וְלִמְשֹׁחַ קֹדֶשׁ קָדָשִׁים:
25καὶ γνώσῃ καὶ διανοηθήσῃ καὶ εὐφρανθήσῃ	וְתֵדַע וְתַשְׂכֵּל 25
καὶ εὑρήσεις προστάγματα ἀποκριθῆναι	מִן־מֹצָא דָבָר לְהָשִׁיב
καὶ οἰκοδομήσεις Ιερουσαλὴμ πόλιν κυρίῳ.	וְלִבְנוֹת יְרוּשָׁלַ͏ִם
	עַד־מָשִׁיחַ נָגִיד שָׁבֻעִים שִׁבְעָה
(= LXX v. 27a)	וְשָׁבֻעִים שִׁשִּׁים וּשְׁנַיִם תָּשׁוּב
(= LXX v. 27a)	וְנִבְנְתָה רְחוֹב וְחָרוּץ וּבְצוֹק הָעִתִּים:
26καὶ μετὰ ἑπτὰ καὶ ἑβδομήκοντα καὶ ἑξήκοντα	וְאַחֲרֵי הַשָּׁבֻעִים שִׁשִּׁים 26
δύο ἀποσταθήσεται χρῖσμα καὶ οὐκ ἔσται,	וּשְׁנַיִם יִכָּרֵת מָשִׁיחַ וְאֵין לוֹ
καὶ βασιλεία ἐθνῶν	
φθερεῖ τὴν πόλιν καὶ τὸ ἅγιον μετὰ τοῦ χριστοῦ,	וְהָעִיר וְהַקֹּדֶשׁ יַשְׁחִית עַם נָגִיד
καὶ ἥξει ἡ συντέλεια αὐτοῦ μετ' ὀργῆς	הַבָּא וְקִצּוֹ בַשֶּׁטֶף
καὶ ἕως καιροῦ συντελείας·	וְעַד קֵץ
ἀπὸ πολέμου πολεμηθήσεται.	מִלְחָמָה נֶחֱרֶצֶת שֹׁמֵמוֹת:
27[καὶ δυναστεύσει ἡ διαθήκη εἰς πολλούς,]	וְהִגְבִּיר 27
καὶ πάλιν ἐπιστρέψει καὶ ἀνοικοδομηθήσεται εἰς πλάτος	(= MT v. 25b)
καὶ μῆκος· καὶ κατὰ συντέλειαν καιρῶν	(= MT v. 25b)
καὶ μετὰ ἑπτὰ καὶ ἑβδομήκοντα καιροὺς καὶ ἑξήκοντα	
δύο ἔτη [ἕως καιροῦ συντελείας πολέμου	
καὶ ἀφαιρεθήσεται ἡ ἐρήμωσις] ἐν τῷ κατισχῦσαι	
τὴν διαθήκην ἐπὶ πολλὰς ἑβδομάδας·	בְּרִית לָרַבִּים שָׁבוּעַ
καὶ ἐν τῷ τέλει τῆς ἑβδομάδος	אֶחָד וַחֲצִי הַשָּׁבוּעַ
ἀρθήσεται ἡ θυσία καὶ ἡ σπονδή,	יַשְׁבִּית זֶבַח וּמִנְחָה
καὶ ἐπὶ τὸ ἱερὸν βδέλυγμα τῶν ἐρημώσεων ἔσται	וְעַל כְּנַף שִׁקּוּצִים מְשֹׁמֵם
ἕως συντελείας, καὶ συντέλεια δοθήσεται	וְעַד־כָּלָה וְנֶחֱרָצָה תִּתַּךְ
ἐπὶ τὴν ἐρήμωσιν.	עַל־שֹׁמֵם:

---

5   The identification of this version as Theodotion has now been questioned by A. Schmitt, *Stammt der sogenannte "θ"-Text bei Daniel wirklich von Theodotion?* (NAWG, Phil.-hist. Klasse 8; Göttingen: Vandenhoeck & Ruprecht, 1966); regardless of whether his thesis is correct, there is agreement that only a few manuscripts have the original LXX version.

[24] Seventy weeks were determined upon your people and upon the city Zion for sin to be completed and to exhaust and wipe out the unrighteousness [and for the vision to be understood]

and eternal righteousness given and the vision completed and to gladden (the) holy of holies. [25] You will know and understand and rejoice, and you will find (the) commands to answer and to rebuild Jerusalem, the city of the Lord.

[26] After the 77 and 62 (years the) anointing will be removed and will not be. A kingdom of the nations will destroy the city and the holy (place) with the anointed one, and his end will come with wrath. And until the time of the end he/it will be fought with war. [27] [The covenant will hold power over many,] and it will turn again and be built with breadth and length. At the end of times, after the 77 times and 62 years [until the time of the end of war, the desolation will also be removed] to strengthen the covenant for many weeks. At the end of the week the sacrifice and oblation will be taken away, and an abomination of desolation will be upon the Temple until the end, and an end will be put to the desolation.

[24] Seventy weeks have been decreed for your people and your holy city until the measure of transgression is filled and that of sin complete, until iniquity is expiated,

and eternal righteousness ushered in; and prophetic vision ratified, and the holy of holies anointed. [25] You must know and understand: From the issue of the word to restore and rebuild Jerusalem

until the [time of the] anointed leader is seven weeks; and for sixty-two weeks it will be rebuilt, square and moat, but in a time of distress.

[26] And after those sixty-two weeks, the anointed one will disappear and vanish. The army of a leader who is to come will destroy the city and the sanctuary, but its end will come through a flood. Desolation is decreed until the end of war.

[27] During one week he will make a firm covenant with many. For half a week he will put a stop to the sacrifice and the meal offering. At the corner [of the altar] will be an appalling abomination until the decreed destruction will be poured down upon the appalling thing.

The problem is how to understand this translation. At times it seems to assume an underlying Hebrew text very close to the MT, despite some freedom in rendering, but in some places it is quite different. To reconstruct the Hebrew text presupposed by the LXX translation would be a difficult task, and I do not attempt it here. However, some comments would be in order. Part of the difference between the LXX and the MT can be explained as perhaps a misreading or corruption of the underlying Hebrew text. For example, "to gladden" in LXX v. 24 seems to be a misreading of מָשַׁח ("anoint") as

שָׂמַח ("rejoice"). The MT reading "seal (the) vision" in v. 24b presupposes the root חתם ("seal"), whereas the LXX evidently read the root תמם (*hiphʿil*; "to complete"; i.e. להתם instead of לחתם). In v. 26 the phrase "with a flood" (root שׁטף; "flood") in the MT is read as "with wrath" in the LXX; this is difficult but perhaps presupposes the root קצף "wrath." Similarly, "people of a prince" has עַם "people," but the LXX has read the same consonants as "with a prince" (Hebrew עַם "with"). The expression "distress of times" (root צוק "distress") in the MT of v. 25 is understood as "end of times" (Hebrew קץ "distress") in the LXX (= v. 27a). Finally, part of the missing text of v. 25 in the LXX is found in the portion of v. 27 for which the MT has no counterpart.

Most puzzling, though, is the additional number 77 in vv. 26 and 27. Where did it come from? What is its significance? The "seventy" (reading שִׁבְעִים) is often thought to be a misreading of the Hebrew word for "weeks" (שָׁבֻעִים). This is a reasonable explanation, but it does not explain the extra "seven" (in 77). F. F. Bruce has suggested that it is due to reinterpretation because the original prophecy was not fulfilled. The 77 and 62 add up to 139; it was the 137th year of the Seleucid era that Antiochus Epiphanes began to reign (1 Macc 1:10). An extra two years may have been allowed before the death of Onias III, the "anointed one" according to this interpretation. This is ingenious, but its very ingenuity makes it suspect. The question is why the interpreter switched from "weeks of years" simply to "years."

Thus, some of the differences between the LXX and MT can be explained by possible corruption. Yet it is not immediately clear that the LXX is secondary in every case nor that it comes from the MT. It may well be that both have a common origin in an earlier oracle.[6] Obviously, the LXX needs more study but is still problematic at the moment.

INTERPRETATIONS IN JOSEPHUS

It has also been suggested that other early interpretations can be found in passages in Josephus.[7] The first is in *Ant.* 20.10.3 §237. This concerns the succession of high priests. When Antiochus IV

---

6   As I have argued; see n. 3 above.

7   F. F. Bruce, "Josephus and Daniel," *ASTI* 4 (1965) 148-62, specifically pp. 152-53.

came to the throne in 175 BCE, the high priest was Onias III. Onias
was displaced by Jason who paid money to Antiochus not only for
the priesthood but also for the privilege of making Jerusalem into a
Greek *polis*. About 172 Jason himself was overthrown by Menelaus
who promised even more money to Antiochus; further, Menelaus
had Onias slain by trickery to eliminate him as a potential rival.
About 162 Alcimus became high priest, with Seleucid approval but
opposed by Judas Maccabaeus. At this point Josephus gives contradictory data. In *Ant.* 20.10.3 §237 he mentions a seven-year hiatus
between the death of Alcimus (*ca.* 159) and the beginning of
Jonathan's tenure as high priest.[8] According to Bruce's view the
seven-year interregnum was meant to correspond to the 70th heptad
in Daniel. Although the "anointed one" of Dan 9:27 who is "cut off"
is often identified with Onias III, Bruce's explanation here seems
rather subtle.

Another of Bruce's suggestions seems to have greater probability.[9]
Ant. 13.10.1 §301 states that the Hasmonaean Aristobulus I was the
first to take the diadem, 481 years and some months after the return
from the Exile. Since Aristobulus ruled only one year, Alexander
Jannaeus would have begun his reign very close to the beginning of
the 70th heptad (years 483-490) according to this reckoning. The
figures given by Josephus are, of course, completely wrong—about
50 years too long—and disagree with data given by him elsewhere.
Nevertheless, Josephus may have incorporated here another separate
interpretation into his account even though it did not mesh with his
other statements. The evidence is indirect, but this explanation of
Bruce's seems more of a possibility than his previous ones.

This interpretation is also remarkably similar to an explanation of
Eusebius of Caesarea in the *Demonstratio Evangelica*. Eusebius gives
a number of ways of calculating the 70 weeks. One of these begins
with Cyrus and ends with the death of Alexander Jannaeus, a period
said to be 482 years. However, he goes on to say that "the first seven
weeks must be reckoned from Cyrus to Darius, and the remaining

---

[8]   Josephus has more than one version of the story. In *Ant.* 12.11.2 §434 he
says that Judas held the priesthood three years, while in 13.2.3 §46 he notes that
Jonathan took the office four years after Judas' death. It is generally agreed that
Judas was never high priest. For our purposes, however, the important point is the
seven-year period, in whatever way it is counted.

[9]   Bruce, "Josephus and Daniel," 152.

sixty-two from Darius to Pompey the Roman general."[10] There is some confusion here, since Eusebius himself recognizes that it was some years after Jannaeus' death that Pompey took Jerusalem. Also, it is not completely clear what happens to the last week. The parallel with Josephus may be only coincidental; in fact, Eusebius may simply be offering his own calculations based on data from Josephus. Yet, this seems unlikely because in this section he is commenting on Julius Africanus and does not treat Josephus until later. It is therefore intriguing to ask whether both Josephus and Eusebius are drawing on an earlier Jewish interpretation of the 70 weeks.

QUMRAN

The Qumran scrolls have given us insight into a community which was expecting the onset of the end of the age in the near future. A number of passages indicate that attempts were made to calculate when this would take place; in fact we may have several recalculations which became necessary with the failure of the predicted events to materialize, though the exact scheme is not always clear. One such figure occurs in the Damascus Document:

> In the time of wrath, 390 years after giving them into the hand of Nebuchadnezzar king of Babylon, he visited them and made a plant root sprout out of Israel and Aaron to inherit his land and grow fat in his good earth. They understood their iniquity and knew that they were guilty men; they were like blind men, groping for the way 20 years. Then God regarded their works, because they sought him with a whole heart, and raised up a Teacher of Righteousness to guide them in the way of his heart.

The 390 years of CD 1:5-6 is still taken literally by some scholars, but most see it as symbolic or stereotyped. Quite a few have accepted the suggestion, again by F. F. Bruce,[11] that it forms part of a calculation based on the 490 years of Daniel 9:

---

10   *Dem. Ev.* 8.2 §394b-d, trans. by W. J. Ferrar, *The Proof of the Gospel, Being the Demonstratio Evangelica of Eusebius of Caesarea* (Translations of Christian Literature, Series I Greek Texts; London: SPCK; New York: Macmillan, 1920) 2.129.

11   F. F. Bruce, *The Teacher of Righteousness in the Qumran Texts* (London: Tyndale, 1957) 16-17. Although this interpretation now appears widely in the literature, Bruce seems to have been the originator. About 1983 I asked him if he was the first to think of it; in characteristically modest fashion, he said he thought he was but would not be suprised if someone else had come up with it as well.

Period of wrath	390
Period of groping	20
Stereotyped figure for the Teacher of	
Righteousness (conjectured, not stated)	40
From the death of the Teacher to the end	
(CD 20:13-14)	40
Total	490

This suggestion is convincing primarily because all the data are found in the Damascus Document itself except for the period of the Teacher's activity. The figure of 40 years for the activity of a leader is so well known, though, that even this surmise is not a particularly bold one.[12]

Although Daniel 9 is not explicitly discussed anywhere in the published scrolls, there are other passages which suggest that it was quite important to the exegesis of the sect. The general attempt to calculate history and predict the future is made clear in a variety of statements. For example, "the Book of Periods" is referred to in terms which suggest it was a work which contained such important data. The question of its extent has been much debated,[13] but a relevant passage seems to be found in 4Q181 2:1-4:

> [To Abraha]m [until he bego]t Isaac, [the Generations *vac* 'Azaz'el and the Angels who came to . . . the daughters of] men and they bar[e] unto them

---

[12]   S. Talmon gives a similar set of figures but derives the last two figures of 40 slightly differently:

> 40 years of strife with their adversaries in history (CD 8.26-38);
> 40 years of the final cosmic war (1QM).

See Talmon, "Between the Bible and the Mishnah: Qumran from Within," in Talmon, *Jewish Civilization in the Hellenistic-Roman Period* (JSPSup 10; Sheffield: JSOT Press, 1991) 214-57, esp. 255-56; repr. in Talmon, *The World of Qumran from Within* (Jerusalem: Magnes Press, 1989) 11-52. Since he includes the 20 years of "groping" as part of the Teacher's "40 years" (taken from Ezekiel 4), the figures have to be derived in a slightly different way. See Talmon, "Waiting for the Messiah: The Spiritual Universe of the Qumran Covenanters," in J. Neusner et al. (eds.), *Judaisms and Their Messiahs at the Turn of the Christian Era* (Cambridge: Cambridge University Press, 1987) 111-37, esp. 119; repr. in Talmon, *World of Qumran from Within*, 273-300.

[13]   J. T. Milik (*Books of Enoch* [Oxford: Clarendon Press, 1976] 248-52) has argued that 4Q180 and 4Q181 are two copies of the same work and has restored the text accordingly. This view was opposed by D. Dimant, "The 'Pesher on the Periods' (4Q180) and 4Q181," *IOS* 9 (1979) 77-102. See now R. V. Huggins, "A Canonical 'Book of Periods' at Qumran?" *RevQ* 15 (1991-92) 421-36.

gian[ts . . .] Israel. In the seventy weeks [. . .] and lovers of iniquity and
causing to inherit guilt . . . .[14]

Even more direct is a statement in 11Q Melchizedek which seems
to give the same figure of 490 years as Daniel 9, but in a slightly
different form (2:6-8):

> And [thus will] this event [happe]n in the first week of the jubilee (that
> occurs) after [the n]ine jubilees. Now the *D[ay of Expia]tion* i[s the en]d of
> the tenth [ju]bilee, when expiation (will be made) for all the sons of [light
> and] for the m[e]n of the lot of Mel[chi]zedek . . . .[15]

Unfortunately, the Qumran scroll is problematic to understand at
times because of the lacunae, but the figure of 10 jubilees clearly
given there is the same as the 70 weeks of Daniel, when the jubilee is
taken as 49 years. Further, a little later Dan 9:25 is cited (11QMelch
2:18-19). Milik has also argued that 10 jubilees are mentioned in the
unpublished 4Q390 which he includes among the 4Q pseudo-Ezekiel
fragments (4Q385–386, 391); in his interpretation the reckoning is
likely to begin with the destruction of Jerusalem in 587 BCE.[16] This
is very uncertain,[17] but there are still some indications that the 70-
weeks prophecy was important to the sect.

It is possible that one should also include the *Testament of Levi* 16
here (vv. 1-5):

> Now I have come to know that for seventy weeks you shall wander astray
> and profane the priesthood and defile the sacrificial altars . . . . A man who
> by the power of the Most High renews the Law you name 'Deceiver,' and
> finally you shall plot to kill him, not discerning his eminence; by your

---

14   Trans. by Dimant, "The 'Pesher on the Periods'," 86.

15   Trans. by P. J. Kobelski, *Melchizedek and Melchiresaᶜ* (CBQMS 10;
Washington: Catholic Biblical Association, 1981) 8.

16   Milik, *Books of Enoch*, 254-55.

17   These fragments are being edited by Devorah Dimant; see Dimant, "The
Apocalyptic Interpretation of Ezekiel at Qumran," in I. Gruenwald, S. Shaked, and
G. G. Stroumsa (eds.), *Messiah and Christos: Studies in the Jewish Origins of
Christianity Presented to David Flusser on the Occasion of his Seventy-Fifth
Birthday* (TSAJ 32; Tübingen: Mohr [Siebeck], 1992) 31-51, esp. p. 49 n. 74.
However, she feels only 4Q385–386 and probably 4Q391 belong to Pseudo-
Ezekiel. She excludes 4Q390, putting together 4Q387–390 into a Pseudo-Moses
work; an edition of 4Q390 1-2 is in the press. Some portions of 4Q385 have been
published in J. Strugnell and D. Dimant, "4Q Second Ezekiel (4Q385)," *RevQ* 13
(1988) 45-58; D. Dimant and J. Strugnell, "The Merkabah Vision in Second
Ezekiel (4Q385 4)," *RevQ* 14 (1990) 331-48.

wickedness you take innocent blood on your heads. I tell you, on account
of him your holy places shall be razed to the ground.

Several points in this passage remind one of Dan 9:24-27. The
passage is problematic, however, because in the opinion of many the
present chapters have been thoroughly worked over by Christian
redactors even if they originally had a Jewish origin. On the other
hand, this view has been rejected by some commenators who think
that it is completely Jewish in its present form.[18] The problem has
been that although some fragments of the *Testament of Levi* have
been found at Qumran, until recently no fragments from chaps. 16–
18 seemed to be extant. Now, it has been suggested that some fragments from Cave 4 associated with Aaron (4QAhA and 4QAhAbis)
are in fact a version of portions of *Testament of Levi* 17–18.[19] Thus,
the passage in the Greek text may represent an early Jewish
application of the 70 weeks schema.

MESSIANIC AND REVOLUTIONARY MOVEMENTS

Josephus describes a number of revolutionary leaders who attempted,
without success, to revolt against the Romans. The New Testament
mentions others not to be found in Josephus. There were undoubtedly many others of whom history has preserved no record. Perhaps
the best known are the Zealots who were among the last defenders of
Jerusalem against the forces of Titus.[20] Without attempting to trace
possible links between these various groups we can look briefly at
several references to them:

For several decades after Pompey's conquest of Jerusalem in 63
BCE, attempts were made by Aristobulus II and his sons to reestablish

---

[18]   On *Testament of Levi* 18, see the discussion in A. Hultgård, *L'eschatologie
des Testaments des Douze Patriarches: I Interprétation des textes* (Acta Universitatis
Upsaliensis: Historia Religionum 6; Uppsala: Almqvist & Wiksell, 1977) 268-90.

[19]   É. Puech, "Fragments d'un apocryphe de Lévi et le personnage
eschatologique: 4QTestLévic-d(?) et 4QAJa," in J. Trebolle Berrera and L. Vegas
Montaner (eds.), *The Madrid Qumran Congress: Proceedings of the International
Congress on the Dead Sea Scrolls, Madrid 18–21 March 1991* (STDJ 11; Leiden:
Brill, 1993) 449-501.

[20]   The term "Zealot" has been widely used—and abused—to indicate any of a
range of resistance movements against the Romans throughout the first century.
The Zealots in the narrower sense, however, were only one of several revolutionary
groups at the time of the war with Rome who seemed to have spent as much time
demolishing each other as demolishing the Romans.

their rule over Judah. There is no indication that these unsuccessful revolts and attempted coups were prophetically inspired; they simply wanted back the office and power which they considered theirs by right of inheritence. This form of resistance ended with Herod's taking of Jerusalem in 37 BCE. In the time of Varus, after Herod's death in 4 BCE, there was a general uprising of the Jews, with at least four or five different leaders, three of whom declared themselves king. Again, though, there is no indication of a prophetic motivation (Josephus, *Ant.* 17.10.1–10 §250-298; *J.W.* 2.3.1–2.5.2 §39-75), even if it seems to have had religious overtones.

The pseudo-messiah Theudas, mentioned by both Josephus (*Ant.* 20.5.1 §97-98) and Luke (Acts 5:36), led a group whom he promised to take across the Jordon dryshod. Unfortunately, he did not have the opportunity to demonstrate his river-dividing powers since Fadus (procurator 45–46 CE) send a squadron of cavalry who brought back Theudas' head. Josephus mentions that under Felix (52–60 CE) a number of individuals claimed to be prophets or otherwise acquired followings (*J.W.* 2.13.4–6 §258-65; *Ant.* 20.8.6 §167-172). One of these was an Egyptian Jew who collected a large following (30,000 according to *J.W.*; 4,000 according to Acts 21:37) and intended to overpower the Roman garrison in Jerusalem.

These coups which preceded the war against Rome were all unsuccessful. Many of them were clearly motivated by particular prophetic claims, though we do not know the details of their prophetic understanding and can only speculate that some of them drew on attempts to calculate the time of the end from biblical data such as Daniel 9. Such speculation is not entirely guesswork since we have some brief insights relating to the period of the siege of Jerusalem.

Particularly interesting are certain events which one versed in the book of Daniel could not have failed to see as significant. One of these was the death of the high priest Ananus in late 67 or early 68, whom Josephus describes in encomiastic terms (*J.W.* 4.5.2 §318). Shades of Dan 9:26. Another is the cessation of the daily sacrifices in the very last days of the siege (*J.W.* 6.2.1 §93-94), reminiscient of Dan 9:27. It is hardly surprising, then, to read that even as the Roman armies were breaking through the last defenses, a group of 6,000 went into the Temple court to await God's deliverance (*J.W.* 6.5.2 §283-287). This indicates that prophetic interpretation continued to inspire hope of divine aid up to practically the last minutes of the siege.

EARLY JEWISH ORACLES

Josephus reports on several oracles which circulated among the Jews; these are of special interest in trying to understand the beliefs which inspired the various revolutionary groups as well as his own. When Josephus himself was captured by the Romans, he prophesied the future emperorship of Vespasian, so he tells us, and the claim seems to have substance in view of his subsequent treatment by the Flavian family (*J.W.* 3.8.9 §399-402). His prophecy is actually very similar to that which he gives later, viz., the expectation of a "ruler from the East," which he says also applied to Vespasian (*J.W.* 6.5.4 §312-313):

> But what more than all else incited them to the war was an ambiguous oracle, likewise found in their sacred scriptures, to the effect that at that time one from their country would become ruler of the world. This they understood to mean someone of their own race, and many of their wise men went astray in their interpretation of it. The oracle, however, in reality signified the sovereignty of Vespasian, who was proclaimed Emperor on Jewish soil.

Yet there is an important difference between this oracle just quoted and his own prophecy that Vespasian would be become emperor. To name one, he claims his information came in a dream.[21] The question is the source of this oracle. The Roman historian Tacitus gives a similar story[22]:

> Few interpreted these omens as fearful; the majority firmly believed that their ancient priestly writings contained the prophecy that this was the very time when the East should grow strong and that men starting from Judea should possess the world. This mysterious prophecy had in reality pointed to Vespasian and Titus, but the common people, as is the way of human ambition, interpreted these great destinies in their own favour, and could be not be turned to the truth even by adversity.

Suetonius gives similar information[23]:

> There had spread over all the Orient an old and established belief, that it was

---

[21]   U. Fischer, *Eschatologie und Jenseitserwartung im hellenistischen Diaspora-judentum* (BZNW 44; Berlin and New York: de Gruyter, 1978) 168-74.

[22]   Tacitus, *Histories* 5.13.2; trans. by C. H. Moore (ed.), *Tacitus* (vol. 3; LCL 249; London: Heinemann; Cambridge: Harvard University Press, 1925-37) 199.

[23]   Suetonius, *Vespasian* 4.5 and 5.6; trans. by J. C. Rolfe (ed.), *Suetonius* (vol. 2; LCL 38; London: Heinemann; Cambridge: Harvard University Press, 1913-14) 289 and 293.

fated at that time for men coming from Judaea to rule the world. This prediction, referring to the emperor of Rome, as afterwards appeared from the event, the people of Judaea took to themselves; accordingly they revolted and after killing their governor, they routed the consular ruler of Syria as well, when he came to the rescue, and took one of his eagles.

When he consulted the oracle of the god of Carmel in Judaea, the lots were highly encouraging, promising that whatever he planned or wished, however great it might be, would come to pass; and one of his high-born prisoners, Josephus by name, as he was being put in chains, declared most confidently that he would soon be released by the same man, who would then, however, be emperor.

One might suspect that Tacitus and Suetonius have simply copied from Josephus, but this is not certain; it is possible that they independently followed the same source. A number of scholars have pointed out that Tacitus' oracle has no Jewish features but is completely "pagan."[24] He states that the source of his oracle is "ancient priestly writings," apparently meaning Greco-Roman writings, whereas Josephus mentions "the Holy Scriptures" as the source. Thus, Tacitus could simply be drawing on an oracle current in the Greco-Roman world. Josephus evidently used the same source as Tacitus for part of his account in the *J.W.* 6.5.3–4 §288-312 since the "signs" preceding the fall of the Temple—almost identical in both—fit those well-known in Hellenistic sources.[25] It has been argued that Tacitus and Suetonius both drew on a Hellenistic oracle independent of Josephus' prophecy, but that all ultimately go back to an old Jewish oracle.[26]

The important phrase, though, is "at that time" which all three have. The only passage in the Old Testament likely to have been interpreted as a specific indication of time is Daniel 9. Josephus himself refers to this in *Ant.* 10.11.7 §267 when he states that Daniel

---

[24] A. Schalit, "Die Erhebung Vespasians nach Flavius Josephus, Talmud und Midrasch: Zur Geschichte einer messianischen Prophetie," *ANRW* 2.2 (1975) 208-327, especially 230-34; Fischer, *Eschatologie und Jenseitserwartung*, 161-67.

[25] See O. Weinreich, "Gebet und Wunder: Zwei Abhandlungen zur Religions- und Literaturgeschichte," in *Genethliakon Wilhelm Schmid zum siebzigsten Geburtstag am 24. Februar 1929* (Tübinger Beiträge zur Altertumswissenschaft 5; Stuttgart: Kohlhammer, 1929) 169-460. The relevant part is his second Abhandlung, "Türöffnung im Wunder-, Prodigien- und Zauberglauben der Antike, des Judentums und Christentums," 200-452.

[26] H. Lindner, *Die Geschichtsauffassung des Flavius Josephus im Bellum Judaicum, Gleichzeitig ein Beitrag zur Quellenfrage* (AGJU 12; Leiden: Brill, 1972) 71-72.

"was not only wont to prophesy future things, as did the other prophets, but he also fixed the time at which these would come to pass."
Further in the same context he notes, "In the same manner Daniel
also wrote about the empire of the Romans and that Jerusalem would
be taken by them and the Temple laid waste" (10.11.7 §276). Is
Daniel 9 the ultimate source of this prophecy? Does a common
prophecy lie behind Daniel 9, on the one hand, and a Greco-Roman
prophecy which gave rise to those found in Josephus, Tactius, and
Suetonius, on the other?

The second oracle is in the same context and concerns the action
which made the Temple "foursquare" (*J.W.* 6.5.4 §311-13):

> Thus the Jews, after the demolition of Antonia, reduced the Temple to a
> square, although they had it recorded in their oracles that the city and the
> sanctuary would be taken when the Temple should become four-square
> (τετράγωνον). But what more than all else incited them to the war was an
> ambiguous oracle, likewise found in their sacred scriptures, to the effect that
> at that time one of their country would become ruler of the world. This they
> understood to mean someone of their own race, and many of their wise men
> went astray in their interpretation of it. The oracle, however, in reality
> signified the sovereignty of Vespasian, who was proclaimed Emperor on
> Jewish soil.

It has been argued that the reference is to such passages as Isa
10:34 which speak of "Lebanon" falling through "a mighty one."[27]
"Lebanon" was a symbol for the Temple,[28] while the root לבן means
"four-cornered" in Mishnaic Hebrew. This is interesting but not
certain, it seems to me. Hebrew לְבֵנָה means "brick," but I am not
sure that one can extrapolate from that to the "square" in Josephus.
More likely is that Dan 9:26 is the base of it.[29] Admittedly, רְהוֹב
("wide place," especially the open area in front of the city gate) is a
rather general term and not exactly the "square" sometimes used in
English; nevertheless, it is difficult to find an Old Testament passage
which is more likely to be the basis of this oracle. The LXX text is
even more susceptible to this interpretation.[30]

---

[27]   I. Hahn, "Zwei dunkle Stellen in Josephus (Bellum Judaicum VI, §311 und
II, §142)," *Acta Orientalia* 14 (1962) 131-38, esp. 133-34.

[28]   See G. Vermes, *Scripture and Tradition in Judaism: Haggadic Studies* (SPB
4; Leiden: Brill, 1961) 26-39.

[29]   Bruce, "Josephus and Daniel," 155.

[30]   As already noted by J. A. Montgomery, *A Critical and Exegetical
Commentary on the Book of Daniel* (ICC; Edinburgh: T. & T. Clark, 1927) 380.

A further statement which indicates Josephus' own interpretation is the following (*J.W.* 4.6.3 §388):

> For there was an ancient saying of inspired men that the city would be taken and the sanctuary burnt to the ground by right of war, whensoever it should be visited by sedition and native hands should be the first to defile God's sacred precincts.

An allusion to the same oracle seems to be found in *J.W.* 6.2.1 §109:

> Who knows not the records of the ancient prophets and that oracle which threatens this poor city and is even now coming true? For they foretold that it would then be taken whensoever one should begin to slaughter his own countrymen.[31]

Of necessity many of the points in this section have been speculative. We cannot be certain that the 70-weeks prophecy (or its predecessor) lies behind any of these oracles, but it seems a substantial possibility in at least one case, even if the development of the tradition may have followed a complex path.

JEWISH INTERPRETATIONS IN CHRISTIAN LITERATURE

The expectations of the historical Jesus with regard to the endtime are difficult to determine. He is said to have predicted the fall of Jerusalem. Whether or not this prediction can be traced back to Jesus himself, the "Gospel Apocalypse" (Mark 13 = Matthew 24 = Luke 21) is an important source of data for eschatalogical expectations in the first century. Much of the material in it may be Jewish in origin, more or less worked over by Christian writers. To what extent we have genuine prediction as opposed to reflections in the light of the fall of Jerusalem itself is the occasion for debate among New Testament scholars. There are clearly some allusions to Daniel in the Synoptic Apocalypse. The most obvious is perhaps Mark 13:26 and parallels which quote Dan 7:13-14. Daniel 9:27, among other passages such as 11:31, is probably referred to in Mark 13:14 and

---

31   A similar statement also occurs in *Sib. Or.* 4:115-17: "An evil storm of war will also come upon Jerusalem from Italy, and it will sack the great Temple of God whenever they put their trust in folly and cast off piety and commit repulsive murders in front of the Temple." Fischer (*Eschatologie und Jenseitserwartung*, 176-77) argues that this is based on Dan 9:26-27; however, since this writing probably dates from about 79 CE, almost a decade after the fall of Jerusalem, the actual event of the fall of Jerusalem seems to be the source of this passage.

parallels: "When you see the abomination of desolation standing where it should not . . . ." Lars Hartman has argued that the Apocalypse arose originally as a "Daniel midrash," primarily on Dan 7:7-27; 8:9-26; 9:24-27; and 11:21-12:4.[32]

The later writers Clement of Alexandria (*Stromata* 1.21) and Tertullian (*Versus Iudaeos* 8) see the 70 weeks as ending with the fall of Jerusalem under Vespasian and Titus. Strangely, Tertullian reckons the 62 weeks before the seven weeks, contrary to most other writers, but there is an interesting parallel in Jerome. Jerome in his commentary on Daniel gives a number of computations of the 70 weeks. One of these he ascribes to "the Hebrews"; it computes the 70 weeks from Ezra and Nehemiah to the Bar Kokhba revolt but also puts the seven weeks at the end of the period instead of the beginning. Although Jerome himself refuses to give his own opinion on the prophecy in his Daniel commentary, he does actually do so in his translation of Eusebius' *Chronicle* on the year 433 BCE (86th Olympiad).[33] According his statement here, the 490 years end under Nero with the fall of Jerusalem. It is not clear whether he is simply translating Eusebius' own statement or has added this statement himself. Eusebius' Greek text is not preserved, but the statement is not found in the Armenian nor does Jerome refer to it when he gives Eusebius' own counting of the 70 weeks.

The *Seder Olam Rabba* also reckons the 70 weeks as ending with the fall of Jerusalem in 70. This is a Jewish chronicle ascribed to the second century Yose ben Halafta, though it is probably not that early. Although the figure of 490 years is not referred to explicitly, the dates from the destruction of Jerusalem under Nebuchadnezzar to that under Titus add up to 490:

Exile	70
Persian Period	34
Seleucid Period	180

---

[32] L. Hartman, *Prophecy Interpreted: The Formation of Some Jewish Apocalyptic Texts and of the Eschatological Discourse Mark 13 Par.* (ConBNT 1; Lund: Gleerup, 1966) 235.

[33] See the edition of R. Helm (ed.), *Die Chronik des Hieronymus* (GCS 47; Eusebius Werke, 7ter Band; 2nd ed.; Berlin: Akademie-Verlag, 1956) 114. The Armenian translation of Eusebius' original chronicle is available in the German translation of J. Karst, *Die Chronik* (GCS 20; Eusebius Werke, 5ter Band; Leipzig: Hinrichs, 1911). A comparison often shows the changes made by Jerome in his edition of the *Chronicle*.

Hasmonaean Period	103
Herodian Period	<u>103</u>
Total	490

The question is whether any of these calculations have a common basis. It is very possible that Tertullian and/or Clement drew on a Jewish calculation, perhaps Josephus. A more intriguing question is whether any of these calculations have a pre-70 basis or whether they were worked out only in the aftermath of the Roman destructions.

CONCLUSIONS

The 70-weeks prophecy in its context in Daniel 9 arose during the Maccabean revolt, in 168–165 BCE. It may have made use of an earlier oracle; if so, that earlier oracle may have continued to circulate and be influential. Regardless of this, it seems clear that the 70-weeks prophecy—in whatever form—served as a basis for apocalyptic speculation for two centuries until the fall of the Temple in 70. Whether this use depended on the prophecy as a part of the book of Daniel or whether it (or an earlier version of it) circulated independently is not known. However, whatever form the oracle took, the examples discussed in this essay suggest a relatively widespread use of it.

Following the fall of Jerusalem, the 70-weeks prophecy became a basis for chronographic calculations. This is attested by Jewish sources such as the *Seder Olam Rabba*, as well as by references in Christian literature. By this time, it had ceased to be seen as a prophecy for the future but as one already fulfilled in the destruction of 70. Yet those who believed that God had given the keys to the future in the Bible could not avoid being fascinated by this prophecy with its apparent data for calculation. Thus, Dan 9:24-27 continued to be read and interpreted in various Jewish and, especially, Christian circles up to the present.

It is a pleasure to dedicate this essay to Professor Sanders whose work on early Jewish biblical interpretation has been a stimulus to us all.

DO JEWS READ THE "LETTER"?
REFLECTIONS ON THE SIGN (אוֹת) IN MEDIEVAL JEWISH BIBLICAL EXEGESIS

Michael A. Signer

In celebrating the contributions of James A. Sanders to Christian and Jewish readings of Scripture one could invoke his extraordinary attention to both the minute details of textual criticism, and to the broader questions of signification which the whole canon of Scripture poses to modern readers. He has persuaded his readers that questions of morphology and syntax constitute significant dimensions of biblical study. In addition, he has led both communities of biblical readers to look toward their distinct exegetical traditions to point them toward common strategies for understanding the Scripture. "Comparative Midrash," as Sanders has put it, has encouraged a significant number of scholars to consider how both Jewish and Christian communities in antiquity drew upon common strategies of reading the sacred text in order to recapture its power—renewing and transmitting it from generation to generation.

I hope in these brief reflections to push Jim's project further in the history of Jewish and Christian hermeneutics into the medieval period. Drawing upon an insight from Erich Auerbach about the power of "figural" reading in Christian exegesis, I want to present what appears to be a caricature of rabbinic exegetical techniques by medieval Christians. Then, I shall investigate some Jewish responses to the Christian understanding of Judaism. Finally, I hope to demonstrate how medieval Jewish exegetes in regions as diverse as France, Provençe, and Spain evince a variegated understanding of the word אות or sign in their commentaries on the Pentateuch. I hope that these reflections will demonstrate the value of Sanders' scriptural hermeneutics for understanding the history of exegesis after the closure of the canon(s).

The Bible may have been the book most studied in the Middle Ages. But the commentators who explained it diligently to their students and readers have received less attention in the nineteenth and twentieth centuries than those who composed other types of theological literature. Masters of the Sacred Page have come to our attention through the efforts of historians such as Beryl Smalley or theologians such as Fr. Henri de Lubac.[1] From another perspective, A. J. Minnis has argued that the commentary tradition of the Middle Ages provides a suitable object of study in the history of literary criticism.[2]

If the scriptural teachers in Christian schools have played "background music" to the great scholastic theologians among the historians of medieval intellectual history, the rabbis of France, Germany and Spain have led lives of even greater obscurity. Again, Beryl Smalley called attention to the interaction between Jews and Christians reported in the commentaries by the canons at the Abbey of St. Victor during the twelfth century.[3] Scholars of medieval Judaism have not pursued the history of medieval Jewish biblical exegesis with the same enthusiasm that they have demonstrated for other areas of research such as philosophy, law or mysticism.[4]

This article is dedicated to James A. Sanders—friend and colleague—and grows out of our common love for our late teacher, Rabbi Dr. Jakob J. Petuchowski. An early version of this article was presented at a symposium at California University at Northridge. My thanks to Professor Nancy van Deusen for stimulating my thoughts.

[1]   B. Smalley, *The Study of the Bible in the Middle Ages* (3rd ed., Oxford: Blackwell, 1983); H. de Lubac, *Exégèse Médiévale* (4 vols., Paris: Aubier, 1959).

[2]   A. J. Minnis and A. B. Scott, *Medieval Literary Theory and Criticism: c. 1100–c. 1375: The Commentary Tradition* (Oxford: Clarendon, 1988) 1-11.

[3]   Smalley, *Study of the Bible*, 112-95. H. Hailperin (*Rashi and the Christian Scholars* [Pittsburgh: University of Pittsburgh Press, 1959]) portrays an overly optimistic interaction between Nicholas of Lyra and Rabbi Solomon ben Isaac of Troyes. J. Cohen (*The Friars and the Jews* [Ithaca: Cornell University Press, 1986]) provides a necessary corrective to Hailperin, but his focus is on polemical rather than exegetical literature. My own essays assess the polemical and cooperative dimensions of Victorine and twelfth-century Jewish exegesis: "*Peshat, Sensus Litteralis*, and Sequential Narrative: Jewish Exegesis and the School of St. Victor in the Twelfth Century," in B. Walfish (ed.), *The Frank Talmage Memorial Volume* (2 vols., Hanover: University Press of New England, 1992-93) 1.203-16; and "The Anti-Jewish Polemic in Andrew of St. Victor," in S. Japhet (ed.), *Scripture in the Mirror of its Interpreters: Sara Kamin Memorial Volume* (Jerusalem: Magnes, 1994) 412-20 (Hebrew).

[4]   There is no comprehensive history of Hebrew biblical commentary in English. One can consult the article by W. Bacher, "Biblical Exegesis," in *Jewish*

This paper is an effort to move between two cultures of biblical exegetes in the Middle Ages. Jews and Christian shared a common text, the Hebrew Bible. Jews and Christians, however, diverged in their hermeneutical strategies for reading that text. For the rabbis of late Antiquity the canon of the Bible or "Written Torah" was complemented and augmented by the "Oral Torah." This Oral Torah was transmitted in writing from the third century onward. Demonstrating the continuities between Hebrew Scripture and Oral Law was a consistent intellectual effort of Jewish Sages. Tensions between the text of Scripture and the world of the Rabbis led to the development of rabbinic hermeneutics. in both legal and homiletical genres[5] A number of modern literary critics have found *Midrash* to be rich in polysemic meanings and strategies of interpretation which may foreshadow post-modern or deconstructive literary techniques.[6]

It is this rabbinic emphasis on the flexibility of the written text of Scripture and its harmony with the Oral Law which is denied by Christian Scripture and its later interpreters in the Early Church. In 2 Cor 3:6 Paul declares that the "Letter kills, but the Spirit gives

---

Encyclopedia 3 (1906) 1962-74, or my survey, "How the Bible Has Been Interpreted in the Jewish Tradition," in L. E. Keck, et al. (eds.), *The New Interpreters' Bible* (12 vols., Nashville: Abingdon, 1994) 1.65-82. In Hebrew there is M. Segal and M. Greenberg (eds.), *Chapters in Biblical Interpretation: An Introduction* (Jerusalem: Mosad Bialik, 1983). K. Stow (*Alienated Minority: A History of the Jews in Medieval Latin Europe* [Cambridge: Harvard University Press, 1994]) devotes an entire chapter to the importance of exegesis for understanding Jewish civilization in medieval Europe.

5   On the development of rabbinic biblical hermeneutics the most convenient survey can be found in H. L. Strack and G. Stemberger, *Introduction to the Talmud and Midrash* (Minneapolis: Fortress, 1992) 17-35, on "rabbinical hermeneutics," and part three, "Midrashim," 254-394. For Jacob Neusner's formulation of the problematic of rabbinic biblical exegesis, cf. *Introduction to Rabbinic Literature* (New York: Doubleday, 1994)

6   See the excellent essays and full bibliography in G. Hartman and S. Budick, *Midrash and Literature* (New Haven: Yale University Press, 1986), and S. Handelman, *Slayers of Moses* (Albany: State University of New York Press, 1982). D. Stern ("Midrash and Indeterminacy," *Critical Inquiry* 15 [1988] 132-61) has called for a more cautious approach. He concludes that the concept of Torah in *midrash* can be characterized best by its figurative status. The rabbis conception of Torah as a figurative trope for God—treating Torah simultaneously as identical and not identical expresses both their sense of alienation and their attempt to overcome that alienation intellectually.

life." He assumes that Jews cannot understand their Scripture because they are "hardened." They read their Scripture through a veil, as it were, because their reading lacks "Christ" (2 Cor 3:14). The image of the Jews as reading the Scripture through a veil, or as "blind" (Rom 11:26), is reinforced by the statement in Heb 10:1 that the Law contains only a shadow of the good things to come. While the New Testament privileges a Christocentric hermeneutic for the understanding of the Hebrew Scriptures, the writings of the Church Fathers turn toward a much more severe contrast between the Jewish and Christian readings.[7] Jewish misunderstanding of their own Scriptures is developed into negative rhetorical tropes of Jewish blindness and stubborn refusal to understand truly God's word.[8]

In medieval Europe Jews responded to Christian appropriations of these earlier arguments only in respect to who had the correct interpretation of Scripture and the methods of reaching that interpretation.[9] Joseph Kimḥi of Narbonne (1105–1170) offers the following

---

[7]   The transition from Paul's ambivalence about the "Law" into a full anti-Jewish hermeneutic is the subject of many studies. E. P. Sanders, *Paul and Palestinian Judaism* (Philadelphia: Fortress, 1977), and J. Gager, *The Origins of Antisemitism* (Oxford: Oxford University Press, 1985), are most helpful. More recently Claudia Setzer (*Jewish Responses to Early Christians: History and Polemics, 30–150 C.E.* [Minneapolis: Fortress, 1994]) has surveyed the writings of the Apostolic Fathers.

[8]   B. Blumenkranz (*Die Judenpredigt Augustins* [Basel: Helbing & Lichtenhahn, 1946]) traces negative images of Jewish hermeneutics from the Church Fathers in the Latin west, from Tertullian through St. Augustine. M. Simon (*Verus Israel* [Paris: Éditions E. de Boccard, 1948]) focuses on the developing anti-Jewish themes in patristic preaching in both the Greek-speaking east and Latin west. These books are most helpful in tracing consistent literary themes in writings of the Patristic period.

[9]   A history of Jewish-Christian polemics and biblical hermeneutics in Europe from 1050–1215 remains a desideratum. A. S. Abulafia (*Jews and Christians in the Twelfth Century Renaissance* [London: Routledge & Kegan Paul, 1995]) provides an excellent survey of Latin authors from 1080–1150. For the Jewish side of the argument one should consult H. H. Ben-Sasson, "Disputations and Polemics," in *EncJud* 6.79-103; D. Lasker (*Jewish Philosophical Polemics Against Christianity in the Middle Ages* [New York: Ktav, 1977]) focuses on philosophical arguments within Jewish polemics; and, see D. Berger, *The Jewish-Christian Debate in the High Middle Ages* (Philadelphia: Jewish Publication Society of America, 1979), which provides a survey of the major themes of Jewish polemics, especially for the introduction. Most scholars agree with Jeremy Cohen (*The Friars and the Jews* [Ithaca: Cornell University Press, 1982]) that the entry of the mendicant orders

fictive dialogue in *The Book of the Covenant*:

> The Christian said: "You understand most of the Torah literally while we understand it figuratively. Your whole reading of the Bible is erroneous for you resemble one who gnaws at the bone, while we suck the marrow within. You are like the beast that eats the chaff, while we eat the wheat." The Jew said: "When the Holy One Blessed Be He, gave the Torah to Moses who taught it to Israel, did he understand it figuratively or not? If you say that he did not understand it figuratively but literally and taught it so to Israel, then Israel is not to be held accountable in this matter . . . Know that the Torah is not to be taken altogether literally or altogether figuratively."[10]

The Jew goes on to argue that even the commandments of the Law may at times be understood in a figurative manner. In this fictive dialogue we are presented with the continuation of an argument which began with St. Paul and continued throughout the period of the Church Fathers. In Kimhi's *Book of the Covenant* we have one of the first literary examples of a Jewish response. It is the logic of scriptural language, argues the Jew, and not a hermeneutical lens external to the text that determines whether or not one resorts to figure.

Bartholomew, Bishop of Exeter (d. 1174), expressed the Christian side of the argument in his *Dialogue Against the Jews*.

> The chief cause of our disagreement between ourselves and the Jews seems to be this: they take all the Old Testament literally, wherever they can find a literal sense, unless it give manifest witness to Christ . . . They will never accept allegory except when they have no other way out. We interpret not only the words of Scripture, but the things done, and the deeds themselves in a mystical sense, yet in such a way that the freedom of allegory may in no wise nullify either history in the events or the proper understanding of the words of Scripture.[11]

The Christian claim pushes beyond a stereotype of Jewish hermeneutics as "blind to the truth." Bartholomew acknowledges that Jews do have different approaches to Scripture. However, they

---

provides a significant difference in the frequency and style of Jewish-Christian argument. R. Chazan (*Daggers of Faith* [Berkeley: University of California Press, 1989] and *Barcelona and Beyond* [Berkeley: University of California Press, 1992]) provides a history of Christian missionizing and Jewish response in the thirteenth and fourteenth centuries.

10   F. Talmage (trans.), *The Book of the Covenant of Joseph Kimhi* (Toronto: Pontifical Institute of Mediaeval Studies, 1972) 46-48.

11   Quoted in Smalley, *Study of the Bible*, 170-71.

deliberately limit their exegetical effort to the literal sense. Figure and allegory are a last resort and must always cohere with the logic of the verse. However, any mention of Christ results in the Jews abandoning their resort to allegory.

From these two twelfth-century polemical treatises we can conclude that figural language was well within the scope of Jewish exegetical method. *Figura* in the sense of trope or metaphor is acceptable when the lexical meaning of the biblical text stretches beyond their ability to interpret it according to reason. However, *figura* as phenomenal prophecy of Christ or as the interpretation of events in Hebrew Scriptures within a context of Christian salvation history were rejected.[12]

After this brief description of the argument between Christians and Jews about the nature of Jewish scriptural interpretation, it may be useful to explore the works of two Jewish exegetes as they reflect on their own strategies for interpreting the Torah. Abraham ibn Ezra (1089–1164), who was born in Spain but spent much of his career north of the Pyrenees, describes and critiques four exegetical methods of interpreting the Pentateuch before presenting his own.[13] The first method, developed in areas of Islamic intellectual influence, makes the Torah a textbook of Greek science. It incorporates material alien to Torah as its central message. The second was developed by a heretical sect, Karaites, which rejected the reliable transmission of religion, and advocated that each individual should interpret it according to their own will—even with respect to the divine commandments. The third method, most likely referring to Christians, posits that all teachings and statutes in the Torah are riddles: "They create from their own hearts secret interpretations for every word." He grants that there are passages where the plain and deeper meaning are combined, because words can be used for a variety of purposes. These interpreters, however, abandon their intellectual powers of common sense. Rabbis in Greek and Christian lands developed the fourth approach. They disregard grammar

---

12   On "figura" as phenomenal prophecy of Christ, cf. E. Auerbach, "Figura," in his collected essays, *Scenes from the Drama of European Literature* (New York: Meridian, 1959) 11-76, esp. 57-60 on the idea of figural interpretation and history.

13   On Abraham ibn Ezra's life and works, cf. I. Twersky and J. Harris (eds.), *Abraham Ibn Ezra: Studies in the Writings of a Twelfth Century Jewish Polymath* (Cambridge: Harvard University Press, 1993), and U. Simon, *Four Approaches to the Book of Psalms* (Albany: State University of New York Press, 1991).

completely, and turn only to homiletical interpretations of the sayings of the ancient sages. Ibn Ezra questions why it is necessary to weary the later generation by copying them again? (This question recalls Abelard's critique of Anselm of Laon in the *Historia Calamitatum*.) The fifth method, ibn Ezra's own approach, searches for the grammar of every word. He asserts that he attempts to combine this grammatical approach with the multiple meanings bequeathed to him by the earlier rabbis.[14]

In the next generation and in the geographic region of Provence, Rabbi David Kimḥi of Narbonne (1160–1235) argued that the Torah could be expounded according to thirty-two hermeneutical rules. These rules were composed later than the classical rabbinic period; but were ascribed to rabbis of the second or third century to lend greater weight to their authority. Kimḥi emphasized the role of *mashal*, parable or metaphor, as a method of exegesis. He argued that the commandments or laws were not stated metaphorically. However, other matters were set in metaphoric language, particularly the creation of the world. "Even though the words can be understood in their own context, they also contain a parabolic interpretation which is hidden."[15]

The statements of both ibn Ezra and David Kimḥi echo the formulation in the polemics of Joseph Kimḥi and Bartholomew of Exeter about the place of non-literal interpretation within Jewish scriptural exegesis. They affirm that the ancient rabbis utilized hermeneutical methods which account for non-literal or metaphorical passages in Scripture. Both rabbis reject the idea that divine commandments are to be interpreted only as metaphors. David Kimḥi avers that certain narratives in the Torah do contain a contextual meaning and a hidden meaning. Ibn Ezra asserts that the grammar of the text must be firmly understood, and then a meaning from the ancient rabbis

---

14   Abraham ibn Ezra, *Mavo leferush haTorah* in *Torat Hayyim: Hamisha Humshe Torah* (Jerusalem: Mossad HaRab Kook, 1986), which is the edition of A. Weiser, *Pirushe ha-Torah le-Rabbenu Avraham ibn Ezra* (3 vols., Jerusalem: Mossad HaRab Kook, 1976). For an English translation of the Introduction, cf. H. N. Strickman and A. M. Silver, *Ibn Ezra's Commentary on the Pentateuch: Genesis* (New York: Menorah, 1988) 1-19.

15   Rabbi David Kimḥi, *Mavo leferush hatorah* in *Torat Hayyim: Hamisha Humshe Torah*. On the hermeneutical method of David Kimḥi, cf. F. E. Talmage, *David Kimḥi: The Man and the Commentaries* (Cambridge: Harvard University Press, 1975).

which is most suitable to the context can be found.

The agreement between the polemical statements and the prefaces to the Torah commentaries can be tested further. Do we find evidence of figural language or some aspect of phenomenal prophecy of any sort in the Hebrew commentaries themselves? In the Torah and the prophetic books the Hebrew word אות appears in a number of contexts. This word is often translated as "sign," and refers to something which is yet to occur.[16] We shall observe that a survey of selected medieval Hebrew commentaries from the eleventh through the thirteenth centuries on the uses of אות reveals a variety of explanations. Some of them indicate an affinity with the idea of Christian-oriented *figura* as phenomenal prophecy, as well as the more common use of figurative language.

In Gen 1:14 the lights in the vault of heaven are said to divide day and night, and to be "signs and seasons." Rabbi Samuel ben Meir (1080–1160) explained the word אות as the heavenly bodies providing signs for Hezekiah (2 Kgs 20:10) "for the sun was a sign for him"; and "I will give you signs of blood and fire in the earth and sky" (Joel 3:2); and "from the signs of heaven be not dismayed" (Jer 10:2).[17] In this explanation the heavenly lights are linked to prophetic texts. Each example from the prophets utilizes two of the words from the context in Genesis, "sign" and "heaven." Signs are, therefore, physical or natural events which can be interpreted as bearers of a prophetic message. In each case cited, God's salvation and power are demonstrated.

Divine providence is also the explanation for the rainbow as a sign of the covenant (Gen 9:17). Rabbi Solomon ben Isaac of Troyes, better known as Rashi (1040–1105), asserts that "God showed him the rainbow and said,'This is the sign which I have uttered.'" God's covenantal promise is concretized in the rainbow, and then explained as a sign of that promise.[18]

Rabbi Moses ben Nachman (1194–1274) discourses on the physical properties of the rainbow as a sign. The upper reaches of the rainbow are in heaven and end on the earth so it would appear that they are arrows shooting at the earth (to destroy it). Precisely the opposite is

---

[16]   Cf. M. V. Fox, "The Sign of the Covenant: Circumcision in the Light of the Priestly אות Etiologies," *RB* 81 (1974) 557-96.

[17]   Rabbi Samuel ben Meir, *Peruš ʿal hatorah* to Gen 1:4

[18]   Rabbi Solomon ben Isaac, *Peruš ʿal hatorah* to Gen 9:17.

true. The ends are on the earth rising up toward heaven. This sign-like character of the rainbow may be compared to that of warriors who carry their bow in this manner so that it does not appear that they are shooting when princes approach them.[19] Rabbi Moses uses a pun on the Hebrew word *keshet* which means both a bow which shoots arrows and a rainbow. This is a clever use of a natural sign, a bow for arrows, signifying another natural sign, a rainbow, which in turn signifies a divine covenantal promise. The literal sense is not violated, but the "thing" (rainbow) serves to point beyond itself to a yet-to-be-fulfilled future promise.

The biblical sign may also serve a mnemonic aid for an individual or the community. The אוֹת given to Cain (Gen 4:15) was given, according to Abraham ibn Ezra, so that Cain might believe in God. This is the case, even though the text does not reveal what the sign is.[20] Rabbi Moses ben Nachman elaborated this explanation asserting that "God gave him a fixed sign which would always be with him, showing him the way. Perhaps it implies that as he wandered from place to place he had a sign from God indicating the way in which he should walk, and by that he knew that no misfortune would overtake him on the road."[21]

In the sign (אוֹת) of circumcision (*berit milah*), Rabbi David Kimḥi found a strong correspondence between the physical place of the sign in the human anatomy and its moral implications. God commanded it be placed on the limb which is the source of animal desires, and when a man desires to err sexually that limb will show him the sign and he will restrain from copulating like an animal.[22] Another example of the placement of a sign and its message is to be found in the blood on the doorpost on the Passover night (Exod 12:13). Abraham ibn Ezra explained that the blood was a sign both for the Israelites and for God. The blood was to signal the Israelites not to fear when they heard the cries of the Egyptians over their dead firstborn. For God, acting as the destroyer on that night, the blood was a sign to pass over the houses of the Israelites. Ibn Ezra proposed this double use of the sign over against an ancient midrashic interpretation in Rabbi Solomon ben Isaac's commentary, that

---

19   Rabbi Moses ben Nachman, *Peruš ʿal hatorah* to Gen 9:17.
20   Rabbi Abraham ibn Ezra, *Peruš ʿal hatorah* to Gen 4:15.
21   Rabbi Moses ben Nachman to Gen 4:15.
22   Rabbi David Kimḥi to Gen 17:11.

asserted a univocal significance for the sign as a reminder to Israel. In this earlier explanation the blood functions as a sign only to indicate that Israel fulfilled the divine will.[23]

For Jewish exegetes biblical signs could signify more than one promise. For example, when Moses received his commission to lead the children of Israel out of Egypt, he asked God how he could perform such a mission. The divine response was to assure Moses that "I will be with you," and to provide him with a sign (Exod 3:12). Rabbi Solomon ben Isaac implies that the sign given to Moses is the vision of the burning bush. "As you, Moses, have seen the bush do my bidding and not be consumed, so you shall do my bidding and not be harmed." The same sign indicates another promise, that when Moses brings them out of Egypt he will bring them to the same mountain where he had the vision of the bush. Rabbi Solomon then explains that this verse is a *dugma*, a paradigm of the promise made to Hezekiah. There the same phrase is used to indicate that the fall of the Northern kingdom of Israel will be the sign of another promise that God will restore the decimated land (2 Kgs 19:29 and Isa 37:30).[24] This interpretation of a physical sign as divine promise of future salvation and redemption is a figural interpretation of phenomenal prophecy. Rabbi Solomon ben Isaac utilizes *dugmah* or paradigmatic interpretation as a hermeneutic strategy in his commentary on Song of Songs to indicate the prophetic meaning implicit in that text.[25]

We have observed that David Kimḥi and ibn Ezra both emphasized that metaphor and allegory were not an acceptable strategy for interpreting the divine commandments. Rather, when classical rabbinic interpretation, viz. Oral Torah, understood a particular word or phrase in terms of a ritual prescription, the lexical meaning of the biblical text would be adjusted to fit that prescription. The word אות appears in Exod 13:9 as part of remembering the Israelite Exodus from Egypt, "And it shall be a sign on your hand and a memorial between your eyes so that the Torah of God will be in your mouth because God delivered you from Egypt with an mighty hand." Rabbi

---

23   Rabbi Abraham ibn Ezra to Exod 12:13.

24   Rabbi Solomon ben Isaac to Exod 3:12.

25   S. Kamin ("Dugma beferush Rashi leShir haShirim," *Tarbiz* 52 [1985] 41-58; repr. in S. Kamin, *Jews and Christians Interpret the Bible* [Jerusalem: Magnes Press, 1991] 13-30) argues that Rabbi Solomon utilizes *dugma* as *figura*.

Solomon ben Isaac interprets this passage as commanding the reader to write these portions of the Torah, and fasten them on the head and arm.[26] This explanation comports with the classical rabbinic understanding of the passage as referring to the phylacteries—boxes worn on the left arm and on the head during the morning prayer. Abraham ibn Ezra outlines an argument made by "those who disagree with our sainted ancestors" that the verse refers to the phylacteries. These interpreters understand the sign and memorial as meaning that the words "God brought you out of Egypt" should be fluent on one's tongue, i.e. part of one's daily discourse and thought. Their argument is based on a comparison of the language of this passage with Prov 1:9. Ibn Ezra claims that this interpretation is incorrect, because the book of Proverbs is prefaced with the words "Proverbs or Parables of Solomon," while the Torah is not prefaced with the word "parable." Rather, Torah is to be understood within the context of tradition. Therefore one does not remove the words from their plain meaning when it is in concord with reason.[27] This passage indicates the limits of figural language. The ultimate arbiter of lexical meaning in a legal or ritual passage remained the classical rabbinic tradition.

Medieval Jewish exegetical writings reveal a more profound sensitivity for the figural dimensions of biblical language than Christian exegetes—medieval and modern—have described. The word אוֹת allowed these exegetes to explore dimensions of *figura*. What may be missing in their explanations of figural language is the sense of a post-biblical prophetic signification—a referent beyond the historical dimensions of the Jewish canon of Scripture that ends either with the Books of Chronicles or the books of Ezra-Nehemiah. This prophetic dimension, which many consider to be the essence of Christian *figura*, is not entirely lacking in medieval rabbinic exegesis.[28] The sign on the hand and between the eyes of Exod 13:9 was understood

---

26   Rabbi Solomon ben Isaac on Exod 13:9.

27   Rabbi Abraham ibn Ezra on Exod 13:9.

28   A. Funkenstein ("Nachmanides' Typological Understanding of Jewish History," in J. Dan [ed.], *Studies in Jewish Mysticism* [Boston: Association for Jewish Studies, 1982], and rewritten for his collected essays in, *Perceptions of Jewish History* [Berkeley: University of California Press, 1993] 98-120) offers a detailed explanation of why typological exposition was not favored by Jewish exegetes of the Middle Ages. He focuses on typology that Auerbach would consider the phenomenological prophetic sense.

as a referent to the prayer phylacteries introduced by the Rabbis. Apocalyptic prophecy was discouraged by both ancient and medieval rabbis. To some extent the strong tendency toward apocalyptic interpretation of Hebrew Scriptures by Christians influenced their aversion to *figura* of this type.[29]

Both Christian and Jewish communities searched Scripture for profound meaning during Late Antiquity and the Middle Ages. This paper has, I hope, demonstrated that each group approached that same text with different strategies. Figural language may be derived from Hellenistic concepts of rhetoric, as Auerbach has clearly demonstrated. Its fruitful and productive use is to be found in both rabbinic Judaism and Christianity throughout the Middle Ages.

---

[29] M. Signer ("King/Messiah: Rashi's Exegesis of Psalm 2," *Prooftexts* 3 [1983] 273-84) demonstrates the subtle influence of Christian patterns of exegesis on Jewish explanations of this psalm prior to the twelfth century.

THE BAN AND THE "GOLDEN PLATE":
INTERPRETATION IN *PIRQE D'RABBI ELIEZER* 38[1]

Lewis M. Barth

This essay is dedicated to our colleague, teacher and friend James Sanders, with deep appreciation for his gifts of mind and generosity of heart. He has shared his scholarly insight into *Torah* and *Canon*, and helped us understand the meanings of sacred text in the life of religious communities—his and ours, past and present.

* * *

Pirqe d'Rabbi Eliezer has been an exceedingly popular literary

---

[1]   The text of *Pirqe d'Rabbi Eliezer* referred to in this article is eclectic. It is based primarily on the electronic edition of *Pirqe d'Rabbi Eliezer* used by the Academy of the Hebrew Language in Jerusalem for its *Historical Dictionary of the Hebrew Language*. This electronic edition is based on one manuscript selected for its linguistic properties—New York, JTS Enelow 886 (Yemen, 1654)—and corrected against four other manuscripts. I express my appreciation to the Academy for providing a copy of this text for research purposes.

No printed critical edition of *Pirqe d'Rabbi Eliezer* presently exists. (Dr. Zev Wolf Gottlieb, of Jerusalem, worked many years on the preparation of a critical edition of *Pirqe d'Rabbi Eliezer*. Unfortunately, he died before finishing this work). Nor is there an agreed upon canonical reference system for *Pirqe d'Rabbi Eliezer*. Traditional citation most often utilizes the pagination of the edition with the commentary of RaDaL [= Rabbi David Luria] (Warsaw, 1852), the page division of the edition of M. Higger, "Pirqê Rabbi Eliezer," *Horeb* 8 (1946) 82-119; 9 (1947) 94-166; 10 (1948) 185-294, or occasionally reference to the "critical edition" of C. M. Horowitz, *Pirke De Rabbi Eliezer: A Complete Critical Edition As Prepared By C. M. Horowitz, But Never Published; Facsimile Edition of Editor's Original Ms.* (Jerusalem: Makor, 1972). The Higger text is the basis of the electronic editions found in the Bar Ilan Database and several other CD-ROM diskettes.

The problems of all these texts will be discussed in a separate document "Introduction: the Need for a Critical Edition of *Pirqe d'Rabbi Eliezer*." The only fully developed canonical reference system is found in the electronic text used created by the Academy of the Hebrew Language.

work in Jewish religious circles. It is preserved in over thirty complete and partial manuscripts, dozens of fragments, extensive citations, and numerous printed editions.[2] It was translated into Latin in the seventeenth century; there are modern translations in English and recently French and Spanish.[3] Significant disagreement remains regarding the date and provenance of *Pirqe d'Rabbi Eliezer*; a reasonable consensus of scholarly opinion would place it in the eighth-to-ninth centuries, and probably in the Land of Israel. Regarding its role in the development of rabbinic literature, Joseph Dan and the late Joseph Heinemann described it in somewhat similar literary terms: as a transition work between classical and later Midrash and the retold biblical narrative.[4]

---

[2]   I have prepared a database of all *Pirqe d'Rabbi Eliezer* manuscripts and fragments which are listed in the public domain. Of the total number of over one hundred entries in the database, eighteen are "complete" or nearly complete MSS; these are dated from the fourteenth or fifteenth centuries through the nineteenth century. There are thirty-one partial manuscripts dating from the end of the thirteenth through the nineteenth centuries; the rest are fragments of different lengths.

H. J. Haag's *Magisterarbeit, PIRQE DERABBI ELI'EZER KAP. 43: Aufbau und traditionsgeschichtliche Analyse* (unpublished thesis; Köln, 1978), contains an excellent bibliography of manuscripts and printed editions of *Pirqe d'Rabbi Eliezer*. I am grateful to Professor Peter Schäfer for mentioning this study to me and to Dr. Haag for sharing his work with me. Haag lists forty-three printed editions, beginning with the Constantinople edition of 1514 through a Jerusalem edition of 1973. If printing run numbers were available, we would have further evidence of what we know from citation of the wide popularity of this collection, beginning in the ninth century and continuing to the present.

Finally, Haag lists twenty commentaries to *Pirqe d'Rabbi Eliezer*, of which it is generally acknowledged that the Luria commentary is the most important. See also H. L. Strack and G. Stemberger, *Introduction to the Talmud and Midrash* (Edinburgh: T. & T. Clark, 1991) 358.

[3]   Latin = Konrad Pellikan, trans. (Gagliardi, 1604); English = G. Friedlander (trans.), *Pirkê De Rabbi Eliezer* (London: K. Paul, Trench, Trubner; New York: Bloch, 1916; repr. New York: Sepher-Hermon Press, 1965); French = Marc-Alain Ouaknin, Eric Smilevitch and Pierre-Henri Salfati (trans.), *Pirqé De Rabbi 'Eliezer: Leçons De Rabbi Eliezer* (Paris: Verdier, 1984); and Spanish = M. Pérez Fernàndez (trans.), *Los Capítulos De Rabbí Eliezer* (Valencia: Biblioteca Midrásica, 1984).

[4]   For the literature on dating and literary matters, see L. M. Barth (ed.), "Lection for the Second Day of Rosh Hashanah: A Homily Containing the Legend of the Ten Trials of Abraham [Hebrew texts]" *HUCA* 58 (1987) 4 n. 16 (Hebrew Section), and especially the references to J. Dan, *The Hebrew Story in the Middle*

Pirqe d'Rabbi Eliezer covers biblical material from Genesis through Esther and contains citations from nearly every book of the Hebrew Bible. Yet the historical biblical narrative is often interrupted with chapters dealing with specific topics (charity, resurrection of the dead, acts of loving kindness, etc.), and also includes material on the calendar, passages drawn from *hekhalot* literature, parallels to Islam, and allusions to characters or events found in the Pseudepigrapha, or in *Targum Pseudo-Jonathan*, which are not preserved in main stream midrashic or talmudic texts. Further, already in the nineteenth century, Leopold Zunz pointed to hints of a liturgical midrash on the *Eighteen Benedictions* as part of the underlying structure of this text.[5] All these aspects of *Pirqe d'Rabbi Eliezer* have received considerable scholarly attention.

This paper has a different focus. It is an attempt to deal with the creation of meaning through interpretation.[6] Narrative sections in *Pirqe d'Rabbi Eliezer* re-present biblical stories and appear at first glance to offer a type of reader's digest of the rabbinic reading of these stories. A closer look, however, reveals a very rich and dense narrative structure. The author spins out new conceptualizations of biblical tales which preserve, transform and periodically contradict the biblical text and classical midrashic understandings of stories being retold—all at the same time.

Pirqe d'Rabbi Eliezer 38 represents a typical example of the author's treatment of biblical and rabbinic materials. I will examine the place of the chapter in the context of *Pirqe d'Rabbi Eliezer*, the blocks of material in the chapter, the association between them, and the relation of the material and its detail to previous interpretations of the same biblical material in classical midrashic and talmudic texts.

Ages (Jerusalem: Keter, 1974) 133-41 (Hebrew), and J. Heinemann, *Aggadah and its Development* (Jerusalem: Keter, 1974) 181-99 (Hebrew).

5   L. Zunz, *HaDerashot B'Yisrael* (2nd ed., Jerusalem: Mosad Bialik, 1947) 134-40, and notes on 417-24 (Hebrew).

6   Regarding narrative technique in *Pirqe d'Rabbi Eliezer*, see J. Elbaum, "Rhetoric, Motif and Subject-Matter—Toward an Analysis of Narrative Technique in Pirke de-Rabbi Eliezer," *Jerusalem Studies in Jewish Folklore* 13-14 (1991-1992) 99-126 (Hebrew). The extensive footnotes in Elbaum's article are a mine of bibliographic information on all aspects of *Pirqe d'Rabbi Eliezer*.

* * *

Pirqe d'Rabbi Eliezer 38 is one section of a larger exegetical elaboration of the story of Jacob and his family, covering selected verses drawn from Genesis 25–37 and beyond. This material begins in *Pirqe d'Rabbi Eliezer* 32, is partially contained in chap. 35, continues in chaps. 36–39 and concludes in chap. 48. The author of *Pirqe d'Rabbi Eliezer* imposes a unity on at least part of his Jacob material, chaps. 35–38, through the formal and traditional device of having each of these chapters open with a biblical verse from the Prophets or Writings. The use of these verses has some similarity to that of the classical *ptyḥtʾ* or *proem* verse ("the intersecting verse," in Jacob Neusner's terminology). Here these verses function in an introductory manner; they are applied to the characters, set the theme and shape the meaning of the narrative to follow.[7] Chapters 37 and 38 are strongly linked by sharing the citation of Amos 5:19, which describes—in its biblical context—the terror rather than the false hope of "the day of the Lord":

a. As if a man should run from a lion
    And be attacked by a bear;

b. Or if he got indoors,
    should lean his hand on the wall
    And be bitten by a snake!

In chap. 37, following the order of appearance of characters in the Genesis narrative, the "lion" and the "bear" of the Amos text symbolize Laban and Esau respectively. In chap. 38, Shechem ben Hamor is identified as the third creature, the "snake."[8] In both chapters the verse from Amos is used to suggest the terror Jacob feels in facing one enemy after another. At the beginning of chap.

---

[7]   Eccl 7:8 is cited at the beginning of chap. 35; Prov 4:12 at the beginning of chap. 36.

[8]   Already in *Eccl. Rab.* 1:8 §10 Hamor is identified as a "snake" based on the word tally of *ḥwy*, "the Hivite," and the Aramaic *ḥwy*, "snake" (See futher *y. Qidd.* 65.3). However, nowhere else in rabbinic literature is the "snake" of Amos 5:19 used to describe Shechem. (It is used as a symbol for Edom, Haman and "the Wicked Kingdom," typically referring to Rome). This is the basis of RaDaL's suggestion that Shechem's ethnic designation as *ḥḥwy*, "the Hivite," is related to the Aramaic *ḥwy*, "snake;" but this interpretation is not widespread, neither is it supported by other earlier midrash nor by the translations in *Tg. Onq.* or *Tg. Ps.-J.*, the latter closely related to *Pirqe d'Rabbi Eliezer* in other particulars.

38, Shechem, "the snake," rapes Jacob's daughter and in so doing unleashes a process of revenge which will cause Jacob to flee from local kings and return to his dying father, only to confront his brother Esau again.

Is this, however, what the chapter is about? Part of the difficulty of dealing with *Pirqe d'Rabbi Eliezer* is that a chapter may contain more than one narrative focus or cover several biblical incidents. In addition, the narrative may be shaped to illustrate topics created by the author which flow from his reading of the text. Finally, our own expectations as to content run up against modern labels which have been placed on individual chapters. Thus Friedlander, in his still classic 1916 translation, provides the chapter title for *Pirqe d'Rabbi Eliezer* 38: "Joseph and his Brethren."[9] As will be demonstrated, this is only one of the biblical incidents included here.

Viewed as a whole, *Pirqe d'Rabbi Eliezer* 38 is a two part composition. The first part—composed of five units—is an aggadic narrative covering selected moments in the biblical story: from the rape of Dina (Gen 34:1-2) through Jacob's realization that Joseph is still alive (Gen 45:27). The second part is an extended aggadic essay on the topic of *ḥerem*, the ban. It is introduced by a transition paragraph which functions as explanation of the general meaning of *ḥerem* reflecting on the previous material and introducing the four sections which follow, each of which is an example of *ḥerem*. Of these, the first three examples have the same introductory formula emphasizing the power of *ḥerem*. The fourth example has a significantly different formal structure. In a narrow sense the two parts are connected by both topic and word tally: in paragraph 23 the brothers, having just sold Joseph to the Ishmaelites, now take upon themselves a ban (viz. a vow) not to tell Jacob what they have done.[10]

---

9   Friedlander, *Pirke De Rabbi Éliezer*, 287-302. Heinemann (*Aggadah and its Development*, 192-95) emphasized the "live" issue of the conflict between Jacob and Esau over inheritance of the land of Israel.

10   By listing the verses cited in *Pirqe d'Rabbi Eliezer* 28, it is possible to see the skeleton narrative with which the author is dealing. These verses are usually found at the end of units of meaning—unlike classical Midrash where they appear at the beginning and are the verses to be interpreted. Here they serve as prooftext, as text to be reunderstood by the narrative which leads up to them and introduces them, and—as Elbaum has pointed out ("Rhetoric, Motif and Subject-Matter," 103)—also as elements which further the plot. See Appendix for an outline of the chapter with biblical verses in each paragraph.

Again the question must be raised: what is this chapter about, taken as a whole? The list of *biblical* incidents elaborated in the two parts represents a litany of terrors: rape, revenge, fleeing from fear, a father's death, brothers' conflict over inheritance and tense parting from each other, conflict among children and brotherly betrayal, and later violations of bans leading to execution, or the threat thereof, and to rejection.

It is to these elements in the biblical narrative that the author is responding, but not just to these alone. He is also responding to earlier understandings of this material in rabbinic literature. Most important, I would argue that through narrative elaboration and aggadic essay the author presents us with a composition whose over-all conception and deep theme—symbolized by the word *ḥerem*—is the violation of boundaries, and whose sub-themes encompass the actual or threatened violation of person, of property, of oaths and of the sacred character of the Jewish people.

*   *   *

The root *ḥerem* is first used in paragraph 23. The brothers agree to establish a ban against telling Jacob that they sold Joseph to the Ishmaelites. Judah notes that a ban cannot be established among nine people (i.e. ten are required), so the brothers make God a partner with them. In paragraph 24, Reuben, who has just returned to find Joseph gone, first accuses his brothers of having killed Joseph, then learns of what happened to him and is informed of the ban. In paragraph 25 Reuben capitulates to the ban and is silent—as is God. This act by both Reuben and God explains Jacob's ignorance of the truth, and he exclaims, "Joseph was torn by a wild beast" (Gen 37:33). Paragraph 27 brings it all together: the selling of Joseph causes the famine which requires the brothers to go to Egypt and, finding Joseph there, the ban is annulled. When Jacob hears that Joseph is alive, the patriarch's spirit revives.

This summary of the narrative hardly gives a sense of the richness of the passage or the radically new chain of causation developed by the author of *Pirqe d'Rabbi Eliezer*. There is the obvious irony of subverting a phrase which describes God's relation to Jacob, מַגִּיד דְּבָרָיו לְיַעֲקֹב, "He declareth His word unto Jacob" (Ps 147:19; JPS *Holy Scriptures* [1917]), to indicate what the brothers *will not do*. In addition, the phrase can be understood midrashically as a name of

God.[11] Thus the brothers, by establishing the ban, suggest how unlike God they are. In an act of supreme *chutzpah*, the brothers then make God a partner in deceiving Jacob, thus causing God to violate his own relationship with the patriarch. Regarding storyline, there is a happy ending to this section. In Paragraph 28 we learn that the revival of Jacob's spirit (Gen 45:27) is understood as the return to him of the רוּחַ הַקֹּדֶשׁ, "Holy Spirit," the instrumentality of divine communication, which, as a result of the ban, had departed from the patriarch.

The narrative here is well integrated and, with appropriate prooftexting, presents itself as if it were a summary retelling of the tradition of midrashic understandings of this biblical story. In fact, the entire concluding conception found in *Pirqe d'Rabbi Eliezer* contradicts nearly every element of earlier rabbinic understandings of the scene in which Jacob is presented with Joseph's bloody cloak. So, for example, *Tg. Ps.-J.* Gen 37:33:

> And he recognized it and said: "it is the garment of my son. Neither a wild beast has eaten him nor has he been killed by a human being. But I see through the Holy Spirit that a bad woman stands before him." [12]

This targumic passage contains three notable differences with the material in *Pirqe d'Rabbi Eliezer* summarized above. First, Jacob knew that Joseph was not dead. Second, Jacob understood that the phrase "wild beast" should not be taken literally; it was a predictive metaphor for Potiphar's wife who was to malign Joseph.[13] Third, Jacob received this "prophecy" through the "Holy Spirit."[14]

In *Pirqe d'Rabbi Eliezer*, the author's dramatic use of quasi-halakhic language for aggadic purposes is remarkable. Paragraph 23 contains the statement that "a *herem* is not established with only nine men," [other versions: "is only established with ten"]. It appears here

---

11   Descriptions of God's actions often function as divine names in rabbinic literature. For example, the deity is often described as "The One who Spoke and the World Came in Being."

12   My translation. This passage agrees with and summarizes interpretations of this verse in *Gen. Rab.*, see J. Theodor and C. Albeck (eds.), *Midrasch Bereschit Rabbah* (4 vols., Berlin: Akademie, 1912-1936; repr. Jerusalem: Wahrmann, 1965) 1024. All references to *Gen. Rab.* are to this edition.

13   She is elsewhere likened to a bear. *Gen. Rab.* 84.7 (on Gen 37:2); Theodor and Albeck (eds.), *Midrasch Bereschit*, 1010.

14   See *Gen. Rab.* 84.19 (on Gen 37:29); Theodor and Albeck (eds.), *Midrasch Bereschit*, 1024; and Theodor's note to line 5.

for the first time in rabbinic literature, introduced to justify God's complicity in deceiving Jacob. The brothers force God to become their partner in the ban. God, so to speak, becomes "the tenth man."

In the later development of Jewish legal thinking—from the time of Maimonides through the period of the *Rishonim*—the question of the halakhic authority of this statement provokes extensive debate, but the literary point goes unnoticed.[15] Its ironic use is bound to stimulate unstated but implied questions. Do you really need a *minyan* (ten men) to establish a ban prohibiting those under the ban from telling the truth? Can you establish a ban which violates Torah and subverts the natural relationship between sons and father and the divine relationship between God and Jacob? How could God participate in such a process?

Such questions seem to be of greater moment to the author of *Pirqe d'Rabbi Eliezer* than the selling of Joseph. The gravity of the sin of selling Joseph receives one paragraph (paragraph 26), while the topic of the ban causes the reshaping of the entire Joseph story, provides the topic and themes for the second half of the chapter and stimulates detail after detail in earlier parts of the narrative.

* * *

As previously indicated, the beginning of the second larger section, paragraph 29, attributed to Rabbi Aqiba, serves a dual function. It provides a general statement regarding the meaning of *ḥerem* reflected in the story of the selling of Joseph and also introduces the topic of *ḥerem* to be found in the four examples which follow.

> Rabbi Aqiba says: The *ḥerem* (ban) is the same thing as the *šĕbwᶜâ* (oath) and the *šĕbwᶜâ* is the same as a *ḥerem*. Whoever annuls the *šĕbwᶜâ* is as if he annulled the *ḥerem*, and whoever annuls the *ḥerem* is as if he annulled the *šĕbwᶜâ*. And whoever knows a matter of *ḥerem* and doesn't declare it,

---

15   See the Responsa of the RaSHBA (Solomon b. Adret, 1235-1310, Spain), Attributed to the RaMBaN (Moses b. Nahman, 1194-1270, Spain), §288, *šmᵓ yqšh* and the Responsa of the MaHaRIK (Joseph Colon, 1420-1480, Italy), §37, *mśkyl lkl.* In regard to an earlier period, Marc Bregman has called my attention to the inscription from a synagogue floor in Ein Gedi in which divine wrath is invoked on anyone who would reveal the secrets of the community to "the peoples." See J. Naveh, *On Stone and Mosaic* (Tel Aviv: Maariv, 1978) inscription 70, line 12, p. 170 (Hebrew). Human beings have a natural interest in legal matters, and the exploitation of real or imagined legal rulings in literature is universal. The aggadic use of pseudo-halakhic statements for literary effect needs exploration.

the *ḥerem* is going to come and consume him and his house and all he possesses, "to its last timber and stone", as it is said: "But I have sent it forth—declares the Lord of Hosts—and it shall enter the house of the thief and the house of the one who swears falsely by My name, [and it shall lodge inside their houses and shall consume them to the last timber and stone]" (Zech 5:4).

This passage is a summary statement which both combines and echoes related biblical and rabbinic material on "the oath" and connects this material to the concept of *ḥerem*.

> Lev 5:1(5): The law regarding the *ʾālâ*, "the imprecation or curse/oath" obligating one who knows of a matter to testify about it: "If a person incurs guilt—when he has heard a public imprecation (*ʾālâ*) and—although able to testify as one who has either seen or learned of the matter—he does not give information, so that he is subject to punishment; when he realizes his guilt ... he shall confess that wherein he has sinned" (*TANAKH* [Philadelphia: JPS, 1985].
>
> *Lev. Rab.* 6.5 (on Lev 5:1) opens with a question in which the *ʾālâ* of Lev 5:1 is identified as a *šĕbwʿâ*, an oath obligating testimony: "From whence do we know that the word *ʾālâ* can only mean *šĕbwʿâ*?"
>
> *Lev. Rab.* 6.3 (on Lev 5:1), an extended complex composition on the seriousness of the false oath, introduced with the phrase: "A false oath should not be considered an insignificant thing in your eyes!"

Just as in the *Pirqe d'Rabbi Eliezer* paragraph attributed to Rabbi Aqiba, this earlier composition in *Lev. Rab.* on the false oath also concludes with the citation of Zech 5:4 as threat of punishment for this offense.[16]

As a general statement from which we are to re-reflect on the story of the selling of Joseph, the linking of *ḥerem* with the oath to testify deepens the sense of the brothers' betrayal both of Joseph and their relationship to their father. It places this act in the context of a powerful aggadic symbolization of the biblical and later halakhic requirement to testify to the truth of what one knows and the curse which will come upon one who does not fulfill this obligation.

Following Rabbi Aqiba's statement, the first example of the power of the *ḥerem*, the Joshua-Achan incident, paragraphs 30–37, adds an additional dimension to the aggadic understanding of *ḥerem*. This additional dimension is drawn from a complex of biblical meanings connected with the root *ḥrm* used as a verb in *hiphʿil*. First, the term

---

16   See also CD 9:10-12, in which we find an allusion to Lev 5:1.

can simply mean "to exterminate" (1 Kgs 9:21). More commonly it has the additional nuance reflected in the modern translation "to proscribe." The Israelites exterminate their human enemies and appropriate the booty which is then dedicated to God. Thus, regarding a Canaanite king of Arad who engaged Israel in battle and took some of the people captive:

> Then Israel made a vow to the Lord and said, "If You deliver this people into our hand, we will proscribe their towns" (TANAKH, Num 21:2).[17]

In *Pirqe d'Rabbi Eliezer*'s retelling of the Joshua-Achan incident, the associative chain links the fate of Jericho which has been proscribed, the booty of which is *ḥerem*, and Achan's transgression of the proscription, ". . . Achan son of Carmi son of Zabdi son of Zerah, of the tribe of Judah, took of that which was proscribed . . . (Josh 7:1). with the *Pirqe d'Rabbi Eliezer*'s own emphasis on the violation of the *ḥerem*. Achan violated the public oath obligating him to declare the truth—that he had taken the proscribed booty.

*   *   *

The author of *Pirqe d'Rabbi Eliezer* shares with earlier rabbinic thinking the notion that all events in biblical history—as understood aggadically—are linked by a chain of cause and effect as well as reward and punishment. What is remarkable in his retelling of the material in this chapter is that he adds an associative conceptual chain as well. Here I want to focus on the opening of chap. 38 and its possible thematic relation to the conclusion of the chapter.

Earlier I noted that in *Pirqe d'Rabbi Eliezer* chaps. 37 and 38 are linked by the initial citation of Amos 5:19. *Pirqe d'Rabbi Eliezer* 37 retells the events in Genesis 32–33, Jacob's struggle with the angel and first reunion with Esau. Jacob's enemies, Laban, his father-in-law and especially Esau, his brother, intend to kill him. Jacob escapes from their plots partially through divine intervention. However, he also does so, according to the author of *Pirqe d'Rabbi Eliezer*, by betraying God.

Pirqe d'Rabbi Eliezer 37 contains two examples of this betrayal. First, Jacob bribes Esau with flocks and goods previously designated

---

[17]   The TANAKH-JPS translation adds the following note: "I.e., utterly destroy, reserving no booty except what was deposited in the Sanctuary. See Josh 6:24."

as tithe. Second, Jacob accepts Esau's sovereignty, demonstrating his lack of faith in the biblical blessing. Thus, God accuses Jacob:

> It is not enough that you made *qodeš* into *ḥôl*. But I promised that, "the greater shall serve the younger" [Gen 25:23]. Yet you said [to Esau], "Thus says *your servant* Jacob!" (Gen 32:4; midrashic emphasis).[18]

In regard to our analysis, the first example is revealing. There seems to be a silent conceptual linking of two closely related and biblically based rabbinic concepts: the tithe, viewed as a form of *heqdēš*, property which an owner donates to the Sanctuary, and the term *ḥerem*.

The relevant biblical text is Lev 27:28:

> But of all that anyone owns, be it man or beast or land of his holding, nothing that he has proscribed for the Lord may be sold or redeemed; every proscribed thing (*ḥerem*) is totally consecrated to the Lord.

Though not explicitly stated, the imaginative linking seems to be the idea that even as in *Pirqe d'Rabbi Eliezer* 37 Jacob had betrayed God by using flocks dedicated as *heqdēš*, so his sons and God would betray him by adhering to a *ḥerem* of silence in chap. 38.[19]

This additional association of *ḥerem* and *heqdēš* helps explain, I believe, a remarkable detail in *Pirqe d'Rabbi Eliezer*'s retelling of the story of the rape of Dina, in chap. 38, paragraphs 1–4. *Pirqe d'Rabbi Eliezer*'s reconceptualization of this story is unique. Dina is described here as "dwelling in tents," an expression which is a word tally with the image of Jacob in Gen 25:27b. Regarding Jacob, rabbinic passages are consistent in understanding this phrase as "dwelling in the academy."[20] In addition, the image of women dwelling in tents is a ubiquitous metaphor in biblical and rabbinic literature for ritual and sexual purity.[21] In linking Dina to Jacob

---

18   For a similar use of this verse, see the function of Gen 32:4 as both lection verse and concluding refrain in *Gen. Rab.* 75.1-3 (on Gen 32:4); Theodor and Albeck (eds.), *Midrasch Bereschit*, 877-81.

19   The rabbinic principle of punishment (or reward in kind) is *middâ kneged middâ* ("measure for measure"), the equivalent of "tit for tat."

20   *Gen. Rab.* 63.10 (on Gen 25:27); Theodor and Albeck (eds.), *Midrasch Bereschit*, 693, and *Tg. Onq.* and *Tg. Ps.-J.* Gen 25:27. Note differences with the TANAKH-JPS translation: "a mild man who stayed in camp."

21   For biblical and rabbinic sources linking women in tents with purity, see J. Nacht, *The Symbolism of the Woman: a Study in Folklore* (Tel Aviv: published by disciples and friends of the author, 1959) 35-38 (Hebrew); item: *ʾhl* (tent). My

through this description, the author of *Pirqe d'Rabbi Eliezer* denies what scripture explicitly says about her in Gen 34:1: "Dina went out." This biblical phrase—"Dina went out"—is the basis of the near universal condemnation of Dina in earlier rabbinic sources. Sadly and stereotypically, she is pictured as the cause of her own rape. Earlier images of Dina depict her as a whore, a gadabout, a woman who tried to flaunt her beauty. Since Dina would have had to learn such behavior somewhere, even her mother Leah is drawn into this degrading projection. The view is also expressed that the brothers had to remove Dina forcibly from Shechem, because "it is hard for a woman who has had intercourse with an uncircumcised man to withdraw from him." On the rabbinic hypothesis that bad things don't happen to good people, other traditions make Jacob's own self-righteousness or boasting the proximate cause of Dina's rape. Finally, Dina is viewed as having married Job, an uncircumcised man whom she did not require to convert to Judaism.[22]

The author of *Pirqe d'Rabbi Eliezer* rejects such views, gives Dina a rabbinically positive image, and places the blame for the rape clearly on Shechem who set up a plan to lure her outside and then rape her.

Following up the transformation of the image of Dina, the author of *Pirqe d'Rabbi Eliezer* adds a remarkable detail: as a result of the rape Dina becomes pregnant with Asenath. In so doing, he creates an aggadic genealogy for Asenath which solves the halakhic problem of intermarriage in the biblical story in which Joseph marries Asenath the daughter of Potiphera, Priest of On (Gen 41:45, 50; 46:20). Because of the extensive literature on Asenath and Joseph, from Hellenistic times through the early Muslim period, and because of the perennial problem of intermarriage, the reference in *Pirqe d'Rabbi Eliezer* has attracted significant scholarly interest. The genealogical detail seems to be original with the author of *Pirqe d'Rabbi Eliezer*[23]

---

thanks to Marc Bregman for bringing this book to my attention.

[22]   See *Gen. Rab.* 80.1–12 (on Gen 34:1-30) esp. par. 1–5; Theodor and Albeck (eds.), *Midrasch Bereschit*, 950-56.

[23]   Post-biblical pseudepigraphic tradition is replete with material linking Potiphera, Priest of On, with "Potiphar, a courtier [eunuch] of Pharoah and his chief steward" (Gen 37:46; 39:1) and Joseph and Asenath. This material deals with the question of how a eunuch could have a child and solves the problem in a variety of ways. This includes the notion that Potiphera's wife was barren and that they adopted Asenath. In spite of the detailed attempt of Aptowitzer to trace back to the

Because scholars have emphasized the "intermarriage" aspect of the story, one other detail has not drawn sufficient attention. In paragraph 3, when Jacob realizes that his sons were planning to kill Dina he takes steps to save her:

> What did Jacob do? He wrote on a *ṣiṣ zahab*, the Holy Name and hung it on her neck and sent her away."

Friedlander translated *ṣiṣ zahab* as a "golden plate."[24] At first glance, one might assume that this object was an amulet. As the tetragramaton is inscribed on it, its purpose would be to protect Dina.[25] However, the phrase *ṣiṣ zahab* is not used for amulet in rabbinic Judaism. It is rare in rabbinic literature altogether. The source of this object is biblical. Its physical form and ritual function are described within an extended discussion of the high priest's garments. The biblical context in which *ṣiṣ zahab* appears deals specifically with the connection between *heqdēš* and *ḥerem*:

> You shall make a frontlet of pure gold (*ṣiṣ zahab*) and engrave on it the seal inscription: "Holy to the Lord." Suspend it on a cord of blue, so that it many remain on the headdress . . . It shall be on Aaron's forehead, that Aaron may take away any sin arising from the holy things (*haqodašim*) that the Israelites consecrate, from any of their sacred donations (Exod 28:36-38).

In the biblical context, the *ṣiṣ zahab*, with the holy inscription, placed on the High Priest, gives him the power to remove the sin of the Israelites who commit sacrilege by inappropriately using *heqdēš*. In our story, the *ṣiṣ zahab* thematically consecrates Dina, and thus her daughter Asenath, as holy—thus permitting the later marriage

---

early rabbinic period the tradition that Asenath was Dina's daughter through Shechem, there is little evidence for such an assertion. See V. Aptowitzer, "Asenath, the Wife of Joseph: A Haggadic Literary-Historical Study," *HUCA* 1 (1924) 239-306. For more recent discussions, see C. Burchard, "Joseph and Asenath: A New Translation and Introduction," in J. H. Charlesworth (ed.), *The Old Testament Pseudepigrapha* (2 vols., New York: Doubleday, 1983-85) 2.177-201. To Burchard's "Bibliography" add A. Standhartinger, *Das Frauenbild im Judentum der hellenistischen Zeit: ein Beitrag anhand von Joseph and Aseneth* (AGJU 26; Brill: Leiden, 1995).

24   Friedlander, *Pirke De Rabbi Eliezer*, 288. He notes correctly that the early editions simply read "plate."

25   See the reference to *b. Qidd.* 73b in Friedlander (*Pirke De Rabbi Eliezer*, 288 n. 2) and the comments of Radal referring to Bachya, in the following note.

with Joseph.[26] The purity of Jacob's line is preserved, despite the violation of Dina.

Through a remarkable symmetry of contrasts, this linking of object and concept helps explain why the last incident in our chapter, paragraphs 44–53, refers to a group with whom Jews were forbidden to have contact because they were placed under a *herem*: the Cuthians = Samaritans.[27] Note the detail: these were the people settled in Samaria by the King of Assyria after the destruction of the kingdom of Israel, yet the land would not accept them (paragraph 45). To overcome this they learned Torah and were circumcised—this last detail parallel to the men of Shechem (Paragraph 47). Nevertheless, their descendants were rejected from participating in rebuilding the Temple, and they tried to assassinate Nehemiah. Consequently, Zerubabel and the priests declared a *herem* against them. The manner in which this *herem* is published functions as a reverse mirroring of the plate Jacob made to designate Dina as holy. This *herem* contains a divine name—in this instance—the *šem hamměphoraš* rather than the *šem haqodeš*. It is published in writing, inscribed on tablets, and has effective power because it derives from the authority of the Courts—Supreme and Lower, Celestial and Earthly. The difference is that Jacob's "golden plate" serves to preserve purity despite violation, the purpose of Zerubabel's ban is to render defiled despite purification.

*   *   *

This remarkable chapter centers on the word *herem*, and related notions of *heqdēš* and *šěbwᶜâ*. It is an exploration of the thematic

---

[26]   It is almost as if the author of *Pirqe d'Rabbi Eliezer* removes the sin of Dina as having compliticy in her own rape as the priestly "plate" removes the sin of the Israelites. See R. Bachya, *Commentary on the Torah* (Jerusalem: Mosad HaRav Kook, 1966) 337 (Hebrew), to Gen 41:45 and the reference to Gen 48:9.

[27]   As previously noted, the incident of the Cuthians is also formally different from the three other examples of the power of the *herem*. It is not introduced with the formula "know the power of the ban," and the aggadic development, built on 2 Kgs 17:24, 25, 33, is elaborated by rotating citations with midrashic elaboration from Ezra and Nehemiah.

My thanks to my colleagues Marc Bregman, William Cutter and Tamara Eskenazi for their helpful comments and references. An earlier version of this paper was presented at the first Western Jewish Studies Conference, in San Diego, and I benefited from the discussion and questions raised there.

implications of these terms as they become manifest in the writer's understanding of biblical narratives dealing with Jacob's life and family. This is not a halakhic exploration, but an aggadic musing on boundaries and their violation: of individuals, of property, and of sacredness. It is also a reflection of the mind of a gifted author, with a capacity for association, imagination and creative reconceptualization.

APPENDIX: VERSES EXPLICITLY CITED IN *PIRQE D'RABBI ELIEZER* 38
(Paragraph numbers = AHL e-version.)

The Rape of Dina

1.	Amos 5:19 (Num 35:28)
2.	Gen 34:1-2, 2
3.	Exod 28:36
4.	Gen 41:45

The brother's revenge; fear of Jacob's children;
Jacob and family at Kiryat Arba with Isaac

5.	Gen 34:31
6.	Gen 49:7, 5
7.	Gen 35:5
8.	Ps 128:6

R. Levi: Isaac dies; Esau returns to his land;
Jacob settles in the Land

9.	Eccl 4:8
10.	Gen 28:9
11.	
12.	Gen 36:6
	Gen 36:43
13.	Gen 37:1

R. Ishmael: Joseph is the son of Jacob's old
age; Jacob sends Joseph to his brothers; they
sell him.

14.	Gen 37:3a
15.	Gen 37:4
16.	Gen 37:4
17.	Gen 37:14, 15
	Dan 9:21
18.	Gen 37:16
19.	Gen 37:18
20.	Gen 37:22, 24
21.	Gen 37:27
22.	Gen 37:28
	Amos 2:6
23.	Ps 147:19
24.	Gen 37:30
25.	Gen 37:33

R. Mana: Jacob learns that Joseph is alive

26.	Isa 22:14
27.	Gen 42:3
	Gen 45:27
28.	Gen 45:27

R. Aqiba: "The ban is the same as the oath."

29.	Zech 5:4

Example ("Know the power of the ban").
Joshua's execution of Achan.

30.	Josh 6:24

31.	Josh 7:21
	Josh 7:5
32.	Josh 7:6
	Josh 7:11
33.	Josh 4:3, (8), 9
34.	Josh 7:1
	Josh 7:18
35.	Josh 7:24
36.	Deut 24:16
	(Josh 7:25)
37.	Josh 7:25

Example ("Know the power of the ban").
The war of the Tribes against and punishment
of the Benjaminites.

38.	Judg 18:31
	Judg 20:27
39.	2 Chr 34:30
	Judg 21:5
40.	(Judg 21:9)
	Judg 21:5

Example ("Know the power of the ban").
Saul's near execution of Jonathan.

41.	2 Chr 34:30
	1 Sam 14:24,27
42.	1 Sam 14:41
43.	1 Sam 14:44,45

Example. The rejection of the Cuthians
(Samaritans).

44.	2 Kgs 17:24
	Ezra 4:9, 10
45.	2 Kgs 17:25
	Jer 42:2
46.	
47.	2 Kgs 17:33
48.	Ezra 5:2
49.	Neh 6:2
	Ezra 4:24
50.	
51.	
52.	Ezra 4:3
	Neh 2:20
53.	Ezra 6:12

INDEX OF ANCIENT WRITINGS

INDEX OF MODERN AUTHORS

Schneemelcher, W., 472 n. 15, 473 n. 16
Schneiders, S., 382 n. 10, 388 n. 24
Schnid, H. H., 11 n. 30, 95 n. 81
Schreiner, J., 63 n. 1
Schrey, H. H., 96 n. 85
Schuller, E. M., 168 n. 60
Schürer, E., 137 n. 12, 161 n. 36
Schürmann, H., 449 n. 13
Scott, A. B., 614 n.2
Scott, B. B., 347, 347 n. 12
Scott, J., 272 n. 25
Seeligmann, I. L., 395, 395 n. 4, 399 n. 16
Segal, A. F., 494 n. 43
Segal, M. H., 137-38 n. 12, 614-15 n. 4
Seitz, C., 402 n. 25
Sekine, M., 208 n. 47, 211 n. 55
Seltzer, R., 321 n. 76
Setzer, C., 616 n. 7
Shaked, S., 603 n. 17
Sheppard, G., 296, 296 n. 16, 482 n. 16, 483
    n. 17, 484 n. 19, 489 n. 33
Sigal, P., 436 n. 26
Signer, M. A., 614 n. 3, 614-15 n. 4, 624 n.
    29
Silver, A. M., 619 n. 14
Silver, D. J., 299, 299 n. 21, 311, 312 n. 54,
    322 n. 79
Simian, H., 24, 24 n. 68
Simon, M., 44 n. 6, 45 n. 7, 449 n. 12, 616 n.
    8
Simon, U., 618 n. 13
Simpson-Housley, P., 272 n. 25
Skehan, P. W., 141, 141 n. 21, 145, 183 n.
    28, 194, 195, 333 n. 13, 334 nn. 16, 20;
    341 n. 31
Skinner, J., 397 n. 12
Sloan, R. B., 491 n. 36
Slotki, J. J., 45 n. 7
Smalley, B., 614, 614 nn. 1, 3; 617 n. 11
Smalley, W. A., 195, 335 n. 21
Smilevitch, E., 626 n. 3
Smith, G. A., 54, 54 n. 27
Smith, M. H., 441 n. 34
Sparks, H. F. D., 198 n. 6, 237 n. 46
Speiser, E. A., 6 nn. 13, 15; 8 n. 21
Sperber, A., 428 n. 18, 434 n. 21
Sperber, D., 537 n. 12
Spicq, C., 434 n. 22
Spina, F. A., 482-3 n. 16
Spitta, F., 418 n. 2
Stadelman, H., 133 n. 2
Stamm, J. J., 80 n. 22
Standhartinger, A., 636-7 n. 23
Stegemann, H., 143 n. 27, 176 n. 8, 213 n. 61
Stemberger, G., 615 n. 5, 626 n. 2
Stendahl, K., 345, 345 nn. 6, 7
Stendebach, F. J., 80 n. 17

Stenhouse, P., 553 n. 10, 554 n. 12, 555 n.
    14, 557 n. 17, 564 n. 30
Stenning, J. F., 43 n. 5. 428 n. 18
Stern, D., 615 n. 6
Stern, F., 75 n. 2
Sternberg, M., 384, 384 nn. 15, 16, 17
Stinespring, W. F., 3, 595 n. 3
Stone, M. E., 266 n. 9
Stow, K., 614-15 n. 4
Strack, H. L., 615 n. 5, 626 n. 2
Strawn, B. A., 208 n. 48
Strickman, H. N., 619 n. 14
Stroumsa, G. G., 603 n. 17
Stroup, G., 348, 348 n. 15
Strugnell, J., 151 n. 41, 153 n. 1, 169 n. 62,
    304 n. 30, 603 n. 17
Stuckenbruck, L. T., 197 n. 1
Stuhlmueller, C., 226 n. 5, 229 nn. 18, 19
Suchocki, M. H., 348 n. 14
Sukenik, E. L., 425 n. 12
Sumney, J. L., 473 n. 17
Swete, H. B., 411, 411 n. 18
Syrén, R., 3 n. 2, 5 n. 9, 6 n. 12, 11 n. 31, 12
    n. 36
Sysling, H., 203 n. 30, 587 n. 30

Tabor, J. D., 238 n. 49
Tadmor, H., 399 n. 17
Talmage, F., 617 n. 10, 619 n. 15
Talmon, S., 75 n. 3, 78 n. 13, 90 n. 64, 96 n.
    86, 101 nn. 101, 102; 106 nn. 122, 123;
    107 n. 124, 166 n. 54, 197 n. 2, 206 n. 38,
    217 n. 77, 220 n. 83, 249 n. 17, 304-305
    n. 32, 319 n. 69, 396 n. 7, 397 n. 9, 404 n.
    5, 483 n. 18, 529 n. 16, 550 n. 5, 550-51
    n. 5, 602 n. 12
Teeple, H. M., 231-32 n. 30, 444 n. 1
Teztuz, M., 221 n. 87
Thackeray, H. St. J., 438 n. 30, 440 n. 32,
    574 n. 1
Theissen, G., 46 n. 11, 344 n. 4
Theodor, J., 536 n. 11, 537 nn. 12, 13, 15;
    538 n. 16, 544 n. 25, 631 nn. 12, 13, 14;
    635 nn. 18, 20; 636 n. 22
Thielman, F., 463 n. 44
Thiselton, A. C., 347 n. 12, 348 n. 17
Thompson, T. L., 4 nn. 6-7; 17 n. 53
Tigchelaar, E., 177 n. 17, 178, 178 n. 19, 194
Tiller, P. A., 280 nn. 45, 46
Tov, E., 75 n. 3, 149, 149 n. 33, 242 n. 5,
    319 n. 69, 333 nn. 13, 14; 333-34 n. 14,
    334 nn. 17, 20; 335 n. 22, 336 n. 25, 338,
    338 n. 27, 339, 339 nn. 28, 29; 397 n. 1,
    400 n. 21, 402 n. 27, 403, 403 n. 1, 403-
    404 n. 4, 410 n. 14, 411, 411 nn. 17, 19;
    412 n. 21, 413, 413 n. 22, 529 n. 16, 562-
    63 n. 27

BIBLICAL INTERPRETATION SERIES

ISSN 0928-0731

1. VAN DIJK-HEMMES, F. & A. BRENNER. *On Gendering Texts.* Female and Male Voices in the Hebrew Bible. 1993. ISBN 90 04 09642 6
2. VAN TILBORG, S. *Imaginative Love in John.* 1993. ISBN 90 04 09716 3
3. DANOVE, P.L. *The End of Mark's Story.* A Methodological Study. 1993. ISBN 90 04 09717 1
4. WATSON, D.F. & A.J. HAUSER. *Rhetorical Criticism of the Bible.* A Comprehensive Bibliography with Notes on History and Method. 1994. ISBN 90 04 09903 4
5. SEELEY, D. *Deconstructing the New Testament.* 1994. ISBN 90 04 09880 1
6. VAN WOLDE, E. *Words become Worlds.* Semantic Studies of Genesis 1-11. 1994. ISBN 90 04 098879
7. NEUFELD, D. *Reconceiving Texts as Speech Acts.* An Analysis of I John. 1994. ISBN 90 04 09853 4
8. PORTER, S.E., P. JOYCE & D.E. ORTON (eds.). *Crossing the Boundaries.* Essays in Biblical Interpretation in Honour of Michael D. Goulder. 1994. ISBN 90 04 10131 4
9. YEO, K.-K. *Rhetorical Interaction in 1 Corinthians 8 and 10.* A Formal Analysis with Preliminary Suggestions for a Chinese, Cross-Cultural Hermeneutic. 1995. ISBN 90 04 10115 2
10. LETELLIER, R.I. *Day in Mamre, Night in Sodom.* Abraham and Lot in Genesis 18 and 19. 1995. ISBN 90 04 10250 7
12. TOLMIE, D.F. *Jesus' Farewell to the Disciples.* John 13:1-17:26 in Narratological Perspective. 1995. ISBN 90 04 10270 1
13. RYOU, D.H. *Zephaniah's Oracles against the Nations.* A Synchronic and Diachronic Study of Zephaniah 2:1-3:8. 1995. ISBN 90 04 10311 2
14. SONNET, J.-P. *The Book within the Book.* Writing in Deuteronomy. 1997. ISBN 90 04 10866 1
15. SELAND, T. *Establishment Violence in Philo and Luke.* A Study of Non-Conformity to the Torah and Jewish Vigilante Reactions. 1995. ISBN 90 04 10252 3
16. NOBLE, P.R *The Canonical Approach.* A Critical Reconstruction of the Hermeneutics of Brevard S. Childs. 1995. ISBN 90 04 10151 9
17. SCHOTTROFF, L.R & M.-T. WACKER (Hrsg.). *Von der Wurzel getragen.* Christlich-feministische Exegese in Auseinandersetzung mit Antijudaismus. 1996. ISBN 90 04 10336 8
18. BECKING, B. & M. DIJKSTRA (eds.). *On Reading Prophetic Texts.* Gender-Specific and Related Studies in Memory of Fokkelien van Dijk-Hemmes. 1996. ISBN 90 04 10274 4
19. BRETT, M.G. (ed.). *Ethnicity and the Bible.* 1996. ISBN 90 04 10317 1
20. HENDERSON, I.H. *Jesus, Rhetoric and Law.* 1996. ISBN 90 04 10377 5

21. RUTLEDGE, D. *Reading Marginally*. Feminism, Deconstruction and the Bible. 1996. ISBN 90 04 10564 6
22. CULPEPPER, R.A. (ed.). *Critical Readings of John 6*. (In preparation.)
23. PYPER, H.S. *David as Reader*. 2 Samuel 12:1-15 and the Poetics of Fatherhood. 1996. ISBN 90 04 10581 6
26. BRENNER, A. *The Intercourse of Knowledge*. On Gendering Desire and 'Sexuality' in the Hebrew Bible. 1997. ISBN 90 04 10155 1
27. BECK, D.R. *The Discipleship Paradigm*. Readers and Anonymous Characters in the Fourth Gospel. 1997. ISBN 90 04 10700 2
28. EVANS, C.A. & S. TALMON (eds.). *The Quest for Context and Meaning*. Studies in Biblical Intertextuality in Honor of James A. Sanders. 1997. ISBN 90 04 10835 1

DATE DUE

DEC 11 1998			
			Printed in USA

MITH #45230